Copyright, 1942, by
THE JAQUES CATTELL PRESS

PRINTED IN U.S.A.
THE SCIENCE PRESS PRINTING COMPANY
LANCASTER, PENNSYLVANIA

TO OUR
STUDENTS AND COLLEAGUES

PREFACE

This book had its inception in the conclusion that the time has come for a closer rapport between the physical sciences and the social sciences. In the fact that geographic and geologic phenomena, physical laws and chemical uniformities, heredity, and economic probabilities, as bases for human group behavior have been neglected in most sociology classes we perceived an appropriateness in making available a text which would maintain a balance of attention to (1) relationships within the social structure and (2) relationships of that structure to the non-institutional factors that furnish the matrix for the structure. After a swift anthropological survey of the long past, as a means of establishing an orientation, we investigate the setting in which plural living develops, then proceed to analyze the basic elements of society, and next to show essentials of social organization. After that, illustrative social tensions are examined, and finally we study some of the dynamic factors in social change.

This organization of materials for a sociology text, though developed independently, seems to the editor to be according to the general pattern formulated by L. L. Bernard in the *Journal of Educational Sociology,* Vol. 9, Sept. 1935–May 1936.

The editor asked of the authors that the treatment be restricted to objective analyses, that prescriptions, and judgments concerning goodness or badness of matters reported, be avoided. We claim no uniformity in our ethics. For example, if economic efficiency be inconsistent with freedom, there are some among us who would subtract much more from efficiency for the sake of freedom than would others among us. Some might insist that lack of efficiency could cost us the whole system which permits us any freedom. Others believe that if we yield up the freedom in striving for efficiency, the efficiency has no goal. But our ethics have been mostly left out, not only on this topic but on all others. We present merely the facts—though facts in their sequences and relationships. Let the reader, or the teacher, decide whether a force is to be resisted or fostered; the writers, for the most part, have not reported their opinions. However, writer positions in some cases show through. Be it known that no one of us is committed to a sponsorship of the views of another.

The authors of our text represent colleges large and small, co-ed colleges, women's colleges, state colleges, city colleges, private colleges, teacher colleges, junior colleges. They constitute a cross section of North American sociologists. To as great an extent as was possible the distribution of chapters to writers was based on special interests of the writers, a process which brought more specialized qualifications to bear where they would have most results than would have been possible except for the plurality of authorship and the focusing of attention according to interests.

Another advantage in the multiple authorship is that probably all students who are exposed to the text will be reached by several of the writers. No one paragrapher can appeal to all readers, but in our variety of presentations all students may hope at any page that the next chapter will be more to his style.

The use of type in setting up topics is intended to aid to quick comprehension. Topics in ALL CAPITALS are the major topics. Subordinate to them are the topics in **bold face**; and topics which are a third step down are in *italics*.

Our obligations as authors are many. Insofar as the obligations can be traced to specific printed matter, footnotes and bibliographical references make acknowledgment. For verbatim material we take this occasion to express our thanks to the publishers of the quoted materials, who have kindly granted permission to quote. Several of the writers have reported assistance from their wives, and the editor wishes to express his thanks for their aid, and his thanks to his own wife for library reference work and assistance in indexing.

Helpful suggestions were received from a number of the authors, especially Dr. L. L. Bernard, Dr. M. K. Thomson, and Dr. C. W. Topping. Several of the suggestions have been used, and the editor regrets that the situation prevented the adoption of more of them.

The editor wishes to express appreciation to the members of the staff of The Science Press Printing Company for generously putting at his disposal their expert technical knowledge.

ELMER PENDELL

The Hazleton Undergraduate Center
    of The Pennsylvania State College
Hazleton, Pennsylvania
May 5, 1942

CONTENTS

PART I: PERSPECTIVE

PART II: PERSISTENT INFLUENCES IN SOCIAL LIFE

PART III: THE ELEMENTS OF SOCIETY

PART IV: SOCIAL ORGANIZATION

PART I

PERSPECTIVE

By the long view of the anthropologist we get perspective for understanding the relationships of the details of group life.

CHAPTER 1

ANTHROPOLOGICAL BACKGROUNDS

By PROFESSOR JOHN PHELAN

Carleton College, Northfield, Minnesota

Anthropology is a very comprehensive subject. It is the story of man and his culture as that story is revealed through a study of the physical remains of prehistoric man, and the customs and institutions of contemporary primitive peoples. Though the topics "man and his culture" include the present, by a sort of tacit agreement the field of anthropology has been limited (1) to the period *before the use of writing* and (2) to *contemporary* primitive peoples. The term "primitive" is used to designate existing or very recent cultures *which have been little influenced by Europeans.* The history of these later day primitive peoples is not distinguished; their customs are peculiar; their institutions have strange flavor; nevertheless we must go to them for knowledge of our own customs and institutions, and for understanding of the beginnings of things as they are, because, of practically all of the non-material elements of culture of our actual prehistoric ancestors, there are no records. Long-ago ideas of family life, religion, government, etc., can be known only in general probabilities. Even the material cultures of our own direct but distant antecedents, the tools, weapons and implements made of less durable material than stone, have been destroyed by the ravages of time, for these cultures existed tens of thousands of years ago. Only that part of the record which was made of stone or bone, or, if of softer substance, petrified into fossil form, enables us to reconstruct in part from objects of everyday use a fragmentary account of an age long gone by.

As a subject, anthropology is generally divided into (1) physical anthropology, (2) cultural anthropology, (3) linguistics, and (4) archaeology. *Physical anthropology* is concerned with the bodily structure of man and his forebears, manlike primates that preceded him. *Cultural anthropology* treats of all of the activities of man as they appear in material and non-material forms. Clark Wissler states that there are nine irreducible patterns in the culture of any people: (1) speech; (2) material traits, objects, and the skills per-

3

taining to them; (3) art; (4) mythology; (5) religious practices; (6) the family and the social system; (7) property; (8) government; and (9) war. *Language* or linguistics occupies a peculiar position in that it is a part of culture and a means of transmission of culture. *Archaeology* (the science of antiquities) and *paleontology* (the science of fossil remains) are really separate sciences contributing data and the interpretation of data to anthropology and other sciences. Anthropology makes use of many other sciences, such as biology, anatomy, physiology, geology, geography, etc., in the interpretation of its data.

Anthropology affords a better understanding of modern life as expressed in its social, economic, and political relationships, for it causes us to realize how long man has struggled with these problems and how complicated the solutions are. It should be kept in mind that each element or pattern of culture of the ancient past or of another people must be studied in its time and place setting, showing the relation to other parts of the total culture,—something we are likely to forget to our cost in dealing with modern social problems. The worship of fire, for example, should not be considered as something strange and abnormal, but a normal procedure for those who worshiped fire. The belief of the West Indian Negro in voodoo is logical for his culture.

Through long periods of time a custom may have changed or its significance may have changed, just as the meanings of words change with the passage of time. We wear mourning for the dead as a mark of respect or because we are forced to conform to the custom by public opinion in the community. A change in costume at the time of the death of a relative is a very ancient custom, but in the past the purpose was different. Then a change in costume was a form of disguise worn so that the spirit of the dead in the form of a ghost might not return to trouble the living. Laying flowers on the grave of the dead goes back to "burial with offering," a custom at least 40,000 years old; but the nature of the offering has changed. The ancient offering was a man's tools, weapons, his property, which he might need in another life or from which he should not be separated because private property was a very intimate and personal thing. We must be careful in our definition and interpretation of words. The expression "another life" in the preceding sentence should not be interpreted to mean that preliterate peoples held a belief in immortality. To determine just what is meant by "another life," the concepts of a particular group must be examined.

Anthropology is a useful subject in the development of the art of thinking and in the stimulation of imagination. It provides material that we may consider objectively without having our emotions so aroused that our thinking becomes confused. In the study of modern life our economic, social, religious and political concepts are so hedged in with prejudices that discussion is sometimes not fruitful. Our feelings are hurt, our antagonisms aroused, because we are very sure that we know the answer to many a question to which experts in the field have no answer that satisfies them fully. We can discuss the religion of the Patagonian without heat, and from that discussion we may learn to discuss religion in our times, using intelligence instead of emotion. The record of man and his culture is fragmentary. Parts of that record must be put together; the missing parts must be supplied by the imagination. Social imagination is a great asset for any individual. It keeps him from being dull and boresome to himself and to others. The questions that arise in anthropology stir the imagination. How did man become man? What are the real causes of racial feeling? To what extent does environment determine culture? Does the culture of civilization really pay for the effort expended? There is a story of an old savage who after living the life of civilized peoples for forty years went back to savagery because, he said, "Too much taking pains."

A single question leads to many fields of thought, because it is particularly true of primitive life that the various factors of culture are even more closely interrelated than in our own culture. Religion, for example, though not based on ethical or moral concepts, is a factor in every activity of primitive man. Just why should this be true? If we consider such a question as what changes in man's outlook his erect posture made when he came down from the tree, we find that our social insight is being taxed, for the record is not to be had.

How the History of the Past Is Read

Were we to depend on written history we should know very little about the ancient past. For the record of that history we are dependent on the archaeologist, the spade historian, who in order to learn the story of man, excavates the sites of ancient villages and cities, explores tombs of the dead, prowls into caves once the homes of men, and digs into the refuse heaps of peoples who lived long ago. The archaeologist relies on the geologist for a knowledge of the earth's surface and the age of the earth, on the paleontologist for the interpretation of the meaning of fossils, and the anthropologist for an understanding of culture history. Archaeology is generally divided into prehistoric, that which came before writing, and historic, the record since writing was invented. The history of the past is read from stone and bone, from wood and iron, from shells, clay, skin, hair, feathers or any other material that has lasted through centuries of time in either the natural or an altered state. Archaeological antiquities are usually classified as fixed and movable. Fixed antiquities include refuse heaps, cemeteries and tombs, altars mines and quarries, earthworks, temples, fortifications, and paintings and carvings on objects that cannot be removed. The movable antiquities are the articles of everyday use, whether for work, worship, recreation or family life, such as tools and weapons, utensils, pottery, boats, seeds, food, objects for ceremonial or religious exercises and other material that will interpret the way of life of the past. From these data archaeologists and other scientists endeavor to determine the basic handicrafts, the methods of gaining a livelihood, modes of travel, barter and trade, knowledge of medicine and surgery and the religious and aesthetic ideals of the people.

In the work of excavation great care must be exercised; otherwise a valuable record may be destroyed, for once a site has been excavated it cannot be restored. The question naturally arises, how do things get buried? Some of them were buried intentionally by human beings, such as bodies, treasures of kings, etc.; some were buried, not by human agencies but by forces of nature, such as volcanoes and shifting sands; but more frequently things were buried by refuse. Ancient sites are found deep under heaps of refuse. As refuse was thrown in the street the level of the street was raised so that when a new building was erected it was at a level of a few feet above the old foundation. In some of the countries of the East villages stand on mounds a hundred feet in height above the plains, the result of debris.

An archaeological expedition is a complicated affair. It is generally supported either by private gifts or from the funds of colleges or universities interested in investigation. In a few instances governments have been interested in this type of work. The archaeologist in charge, once the funds have been secured, has to select a staff of specialists who will accompany him to decipher inscriptions, classify fossils, make maps and charts, take photographs of locations and finds, preserve the material by piecing together bits of broken pottery or preventing the desiccation of bones, and interpret the data that are found. The site for an excavation, or a "dig" as it is called, may be located through a study of history, from pictures taken from planes, from logic, such as the natural place for burial of the dead, and not infrequently from pure accident.

Once the site has been determined workmen are secured. In a large dig one or two hundred men may be employed. At first the work goes forward rapidly while the top surface is being removed. The party is usually divided up into small groups consisting of a pick-man, a spade-man, and three or four basket-men. The pick-man is usually an experienced native who uses an army entrenching tool. His is the task of breaking the ground and of discovering any object of interest to the party. The spade-man puts the earth into baskets, watching to see that the pick-man has not missed anything. The basket-men carry the dirt to a light railway by which it will be transported to a spot where it will not be in the way of further digging. The workers are under the direction of a foreman on whose supervision much depends for keeping up morale of the native workers. In order that objects of value be not stolen or broken by careless digging each group that makes a find is rewarded by "baksheesh" in addition to their regular wages. When a pick-man makes a find of anything of possible interest to the archaeologist he reports to his foreman who in turn may report to one of the specialists. Then the specialist takes the place of the laborer if the object has not been fully unearthed. The soil is very carefully removed with a hand tool, dust blown away that a sketch or photograph may be made. If a bit of broken pottery is discovered it must be examined to determine whether it is common or rare, and, if rare, a very careful search is made for every fragment in order that the object may be reconstructed.

The history of the very remote past is not found in sites of villages or cities. The remote past goes back to a time when men did not live in villages but in caves or rock shelters. The fossil remains of man and his work in these early times are scattered all over Europe and Asia and northern Africa. In this work the geologist plays an important part because the record is read not only from fossils in the rocks but from the rocks themselves.

A fossil is not something that is just dug up. The remains of my neighbor's cat that met an untimely fate last year is not a fossil though it might be dug up. A fossil must have sufficient age to be significant. Fossils consist of the actual remains of plants and animals, the altered remains, or the evidences that plants or animals have left behind.

The actual remains, both the hard and soft parts, may have been preserved in ice, frozen soil, oil, or amber. The remains in altered forms are preserved by petrifaction. The flesh of an animal cannot be petrified because it decays too rapidly. Petrifaction is a slow process since other material must take the place of the natural object. So slowly does the process take place that the grain of the wood or the texture of the bone may be discerned under the microscope. Besides the actual remains and the fossilized remains of plants and animals there is the record of their existence from casts and impressions of shells and leaves, tracks and trails of vertebrates and invertebrates, gastroliths (the stomach stones of marine reptiles of the Mesozoic era), coprolites (fossil excrement) and the structures created by the work of animals and men. From these animal and plant remains and from other evidences in the rocks, a fairly complete story of the past may be reconstructed. The time, the climate, the fauna and flora, even the direction of the wind and the weather may be determined. Impression of rain drops in sedimentary sands that became rock may show the direction of the wind; great fissures in the rocks may tell of droughts, and the presence or absence of animals adapted to cold, and plants that withstand hardship, may tell a story of the climate. Even the trees with their rings tell of the passing of the years.

How Old Is the Earth?

The age of the earth is important to the anthropologist because he wishes to know for how long a period of time man has been a dominant force in the control of plant and animal life. The subject has been one that has created heated disagreements between groups of theologians, theologians and scientists, and groups of scientists. The Brahmin says that the earth is eternal. In the middle of the seventeenth century Archbishop Usher gave the date of creation as 4,004 B.C. and even fixed the hour, 9:00 A.M. Many methods have been used to try to determine the extent of geological time: loss of heat from the sun, rate of erosion, sedimentation, and atomic disintegration. The result of the improvement of method and more accurate study has been to extend further and further back into the past the period of the earth's history, a fact which is confusing to the average reader who finds that a hundred thousand years is considered almost negligible in geological time. The age of the earth is now estimated at from three to four billion years.

Assuming the age of the earth to be 3,000,000,000 years and comparing it with one 24-hour day, 86,400 seconds, we should find that the entire period of mammalian dominance was the equivalent of only the last half hour. *Pithecanthropus,* mentioned later in this chapter, came down from the trees only in the last minute of the day, and real man, *Homo sapiens,* appeared in the last half second. So far as we have any record at all of the culture of man it would occupy only the last second of the day, and written history (6,000 years) would be equivalent only to one sixth of the last second of the day. For how long a period will man continue to be a dominant factor? The Dinosaurs of the Mesozoic era controlled the earth for 100,000,000 years, twice as long as the period of mammalian dominance up to the present time. In the mammalians man was a late arrival.

The Origin of Man

Two theories have been advanced to explain the origin of man: special creation and evolution. According to the Mosaic tradition of special creation, as related in the first chapter of the Book of Genesis, God created the heaven and the earth, the land and the waters, the life of the waters and the life of the land, and then, finally, man in the image of God. Theories similar to that set forth by the Mosaic tradition are to be found in Java, North America, East Africa and in other parts of the world. The Mosaic tradition, taking into account the extent of scientific knowledge at the time, is a fairly good statement of the evolutionary theory.

According to the evolutionary theory, sometime, somewhere, in a moist warm spot of the earth life came, microscopic in size, elemental in nature. From that little stirring of life came all other forms of life in the millions or billions of years that have elapsed. The origin of life is still a mystery. The theory of evolution but moves the origin back to a more distant past and to a simpler form. Like any other theory, evolution should be considered only as a good working hypothesis. As a theory it preceded Darwin by centuries. The

Greeks held an evolutionary theory. Darwin is responsible for the method of evolution : life in abundance, struggle and survival of the fittest, though what is meant by the fittest is always an interesting question. One aspect of evolution should commend itself to all. The future of man or of any other form of life has promise of greater development, for evolution is still going on. As a working hypothesis in the study of the cultural development of man the evolutionary theory is useful but has limitations. Development in culture has not always been from the simple to the complex. Language, kinship relationships, and in some instances forms of government seem to have proceeded in the other direction, from the complex to the simple. In languages, for example, Chinese and English are very simple languages but are found in very complex cultures.

Man's Resemblance to the Apes

Despite the fact that no anthropologist believes that man has developed from any existing form of ape, or from any of the man-like primates, *Pithecanthropus, Sinanthropus, Eoanthropus,* and though the "missing link" has not been found and there are many gaps in the history of the development of man-like primates and of man himself, the physical similarities between man and the apes is astounding. Bone for bone, muscle for muscle (man is said to have three more) man and the apes are similar. Recently blood tests seem to show that the blood of a common ancestor flows in the veins of man and the apes. It is a simpler task to point out some of the principal differences.

How Man Differs From the Apes

Man differs from the apes in the following respects :

(1) Man has a chin. The old saying : "Ghosts have no chins," seems to suggest that our ancestors may have been ape-like.

(2) The great toe of man is not opposable to the others. Man has not needed that form of clutch since he came down from the trees.

(3) Man's foot is arched both ways, a fact which has caused modern man no little inconvenience.

(4) Compared to that of the ape, man's body is relatively hairless; however, the hair on the forearm and upper arm of man point in a direction that indicate simian ancestry. The ape sleeps with his arms folded over his head to protect itself from rain, the hairs serving to turn the water aside.

(5) Man has a prominent nose with a high bridge.

(6) Man walks erect, thus having greater freedom of use of the arms and the hands.

(7) The greatest difference between man and the apes is in the size of the brain which in man is from two to three times that of the ape, even of the gorilla which has the largest brain of any ape.

Ancestors of Early Man

In our search for ancestors, since Darwin hypothecated a common progenitor of men and apes, we have tried to find the "missing link." Concerning this creature there has been much controversy ranging from statements that the "missing link" never existed, that if he ever did exist his fossil remains could not be identified, to claims that the "missing link" was the "Taungs" ape, *Australopithecus,* or *Pithecanthropus,* the erect ape-man of Java. Up to date the "missing link" is still missing. Though the evolutionary theory is accepted by anthropologists the chain of descent or ascent has in it many gaps. The evidence is still incomplete.

Since the time of Darwin many fossil remains have been found of ancestors of apes, monkeys and men. These discoveries may be classified roughly as: (1) early, very primitive forms of ancestors of men, monkeys and apes; (2) sub-human forms, manlike primates, not in the direct line of descent but definitely related to men and apes; (3) fossil remains of *Homo sapiens,* ancestors of modern man.

In the first class, the early ancestors of monkeys, apes and men we have:

(1) *Parapithecus,* the fossil remains of an early catharrine monkey, of which only the lower jaw and some teeth were found in the dried-up lake bed of Fayum, Egypt. *Parapithecus* is supposed to be the ancestor of the Old World monkeys; the approximate date of existence is supposed to lie in the Lower Oligocene period, that is 40,000,000 years ago.

(2) *Propliopithecus,* an ancestor of the earliest anthropoid ape, or perhaps the earliest anthropoid ape, found in the same site, the period of time Lower Oligocene. The find consisted of an incomplete lower jaw.

(3) *Pliopithecus,* a fossil ape found in Europe, belonging to the Lower Pliocene, 12,000,000 years ago, probably a descendant of *Propliopithecus.*

(4) *Dryopithecus,* the "oak ape" so called because a fossil oak

leaf was found adhering to a tooth bone; only teeth and jaws found in Germany and Austria; approximate date Middle Miocene, 18,-000,000 years ago.   The best paleontological authority regards man and apes as off-shoots of the *Dryopithecus* species.

These very remote ancestors of monkeys, apes and men are here included to show how fragmentary the evidence is at present.   The dates are at best merely approximations, for in geological time great variations are to be found among authorities in determining the dates of eras and periods.   Thus one may find the beginning of the Pleistocene period given as 500,000, 1,000,000 or 2,000,000 years ago. Anthropologists have placed *Pithecanthropus* in the Miocene, the Pliocene, the beginning of the Pleistocene, the middle of the Pleistocene; that is, in periods ranging from thirty or forty million to five hundred thousand years ago.

The second classification, fossil remains of man-like primates, is still incomplete.   Each year witnesses new discoveries making the record more nearly complete.   Only the most generally known finds are here included.

Australopithecus africanus (the Taungs ape).   The fossil bones of *Australopithecus,* a creature about six years of age, were found at Taungs, in Bechuanaland, Africa.   They are of considerable interest among fossil anthropoids because of the likeness to man.   The facial region, the base of a skull and a cast of the endocrinal cavity were found in deposits dating back to the Lower or Middle Pleistocene.   The skull has the appearance of that of a young chimpanzee; the teeth are more manlike than those of any known ape; the forehead is quite full and reasonably well-developed; the brain is considerably larger than that of the chimpanzee of the same age.   The find is interesting because simian and human characteristics are mixed to such an extent that we might assume he was an anthropoid ancestor, if he had not appeared too late in the history of human descent.

Pithecanthropus erectus, the "ape-man that took a chance on the ground," to quote Hooton, was the earliest and the most startling discovery in the anthropological field.   He was found by Dr. Eugene DuBois, a Dutch surgeon stationed on the island of Java.   The fossil remains were found near the little village of Trinil, on the banks of the Solo or Bengawan river.   They consisted of a low-vaulted skull with a capacity of 900 cc., two-thirds that of the average adult male skull and one-third again as great as the skull of the gorilla; a thigh bone which showed from its conformation that *Pithecanthropus* did not go on all fours but walked erect, and a few teeth. *Pithecanthropus* is supposed by most authorities to have lived at the close of the Pliocene or the beginning of the Pleistocene period, approximately 1,000,000 or 2,000,000 years ago. In stature he was somewhat shorter than the average of modern man. Though no tools were found he must have used some. The brain development indicates that he may have had speech. The teeth were human with some ape-like characteristics. They tell us that the owner did not chew like the ape but in the manner of modern man. The skull cap looks much like that of a great baboon. It has a huge ridge above the eyes. Why *Pithecanthropus* came down from the trees we do not know, but the facts that he had a larger brain than the ape and that he walked erect are indicative of a variation from the ape. *Pithecanthropus* is not ranked in the direct line of descent; that is, he is not supposed to be an ancestor of modern man, but related to man.

Sinanthropus pekinensis, the man of China, was found forty miles from Pekin in cave deposits of the early Pleistocene period, a fact which makes him a contemporary of *Pithecanthropus* and tends to prove that Asia may have been the original home of man, for the island of Java was at the time of *Pithecanthropus* part of the mainland of Asia. The evidence for the existence of *Sinanthropus* is in several finds, at first only teeth, and later several skulls. The fact that only skulls and teeth have been found is a puzzle to anthropologists. It may be possible that these skulls were accumulated by head hunters. Associated with the skulls were found crude stone implements and evidences of fire, the earliest known record of man's use of fire. Up to the discovery of *Sinanthropus* the earliest evidences of fire were in caves of the Mousterian culture epoch, 500,000 years at least later.

Eoanthropus, the Dawn man, the Dawson man, the Piltdown man, as he has been variously called, was discovered by Charles Dawson, an amateur anthropologist in Sussex, England. The remains consist of the skull of a female, a half jaw and some teeth. The skull has a capacity equal to that of the modern European female; the jaw is very much like that of a young chimpanzee. The teeth are intermediate in form between anthropoids and man. This "lady with an ape's jaw" was at first thought to have lived during the late Pleistocene period, but now she has been assigned as a contemporary of *Sinanthropus*. *Pithecanthropus* came first, then a quarter of a million years later *Sinanthropus* and *Eoanthropus*, to be followed another quarter of a million years later by Heidelberg man.

Homo Heidelbergensis was found near Heidelberg, Germany. The only evidence in existence of the Heidelberg man is a massive lower jaw and some teeth. The jaw is larger than any human jaw; the teeth, though human, have primitive characteristics; the chin is completely lacking. *Homo Heidelbergensis* is placed about the middle of the Pleistocene period.

Neanderthal. Neanderthal man is important because we know more about him than about any of the preceding man-like primates. Skeletal remains of Neanderthal man have been found scattered all over Europe and in the countries bordering on the Mediterranean. Though men probably lived in caves long before Neanderthal, we associate Neanderthal man with cave life. Neanderthal man made good stone weapons and tools, hunted big game, and from his manner of burying his dead it is assumed that he lived in family groups and had religion. Doubtless he had clothing, for the weather was cold and changeable during the Wurm glaciation period. He is popularly represented as a gorilla-like creature, but in reality he was very manlike. He was short in stature; his head was massive; his forehead low and sloping. The heavy supraorbital ridge is one of the distinguishing characteristics. He built fires at the mouths of his caves, threw the bones left from his food into heaps and scattered ashes over the heaps that were formed. When for some reason he abandoned a cave it was taken possession of by rodents that formed rodent layers which were later covered by dust, drippings from the rocks and even by the falling of the rocks themselves. When Neanderthal later returned to the cave he had once abandoned, the process of refuse accumulation was repeated. During the latter part of the Wurm glaciation period Neanderthal passed suddenly and unaccountably away, to be superseded by Cro-Magnon, *Homo sapiens,* thinking man.

Cro-Magnon. Cro-Magnon was a fine physical specimen, taller and with a greater brain capacity than man of today. He lived in Europe during the later Cave period of the Old Stone, or Paleolithic, Age. Fluctuations of climate due to the irregular retreat of the ice created conditions to which he had to adjust. His culture may have been very like the culture of the Eskimo of today. Cro-

GEOLOGICAL ERAS, ROCK FORMATIONS, MAIN EVENTS AND APPROXIMATE
DATES OF BEGINNING AND DURATION

Geological Era	Main Events and Forms of Life	Approximate Date of Beginning, Years Ago	Duration
Pre-Cambrian — AZOIC (No life)	Formation of the earth from the sun.	3,200,000,000 (Date merely an estimate)	1,200,000,000 (Duration an estimate)
Pre-Cambrian — ARCHEOZOIC (Primitive life)	Development of mountain ranges which were eroded before the Proterozoic era; primitive one-celled plants and animals but record insufficient.	2,000,000,000	800,000,000
Pre-Cambrian — PROTEROZOIC (First known life)	Earliest known glaciation; great iron-making age due to presence of bacteria; evolution of invertebrates, molluscs, worms, sponges.	1,200,000,000	650,000,000
Primary — PALEOZOIC (Age of Fishes and Amphibians)	Seas sweep over large portions of the earth as continents sink; first forests; widespread glaciation; great coal forming era; world wide continental uplift toward close; invertebrates present; vertebrates appear; amphibians and armored fishes; extinction toward the close of the period of most of the Paleozoic forms; primitive reptiles, sharks.	550,000,000	350,000,000
Secondary — MESOZOIC (Age of Reptiles)	Continents emerging; extensive chalk deposits, sandstones, marl, clay and limestones; reptiles dominant; primitive mammals; large amphibians, early crocodiles and dinosaurs; toothed birds and flying reptiles; extinction of Mesozoic forms toward close of era.	200,000,000	140,000,000
CENOZOIC (Recent life) (Age of Mammals and Man)		60,000,000	To present

Magnon's most important weapon was the spear-thrower and the harpoon, a weapon which is still in use by the Eskimo. During this culture period there was a decided shift from stone to bone tools and weapons. Cro-Magnon had bone knives and skewers, bone whistles and flutes. Shallow stone lamps that have been discovered would seem to indicate that he was no longer dependent for illumination on the light of a fire. Cro-Magnon is best known for his art, paintings, drawings and sculpture. On the walls of caverns are to be found representations of animals and human beings drawn with a remarkable fidelity to detail. Cro-Magnon modeled in clay and knew the use of paints. His art is so perfect that it has excited the admiration of modern painters. The horse and the reindeer were important in the life of Cro-Magnon. In one area the bones of more than one hundred thousand horses have been unearthed. They had evidently been killed by being driven over cliffs and their flesh used as an article of food. The culture of the Cro-Magnon was crude if we measure it by the cultures that followed, but measured by cultures that preceded his, Cro-Magnon shows remarkable advance. Cro-Magnon is accepted as the ancestor of Europeans of the present though Dr. Ales Hrdlicka maintains that present day Europeans are descended from Neanderthal.

Grimaldi. The skeletal remains of a woman of middle age and a boy of fourteen were found in the region near Monaco on the Mediterranean in the caves of Grimaldi. They are important because the bones show some negroid characteristics, though not all anthropologists are agreed on this point. They were found associated with Cro-Magnon skeletons, therefore they are assumed to have belonged to human beings who lived in Europe about the same period of time. The appearance of a Negroid type in Europe has been a subject of much speculation. It is extremely doubtful if these two skeletons are sufficient to warrant the assumption that there was a Negro race in Europe.

SUBDIVISIONS OF THE CENOZOIC ERA INTO PERIODS
Time span—60,000,000 years

	Geological Period	Main Events and Forms of Life	Approximate Date of Beginning, Years Ago	Duration
Tertiary (Age of Mammals)	EOCENE (Dawn of the recent)	Beginning mammalian dominance; earliest lemuroids; marsupials abundant; reptiles few.	60,000,000	20,000,000
	OLIGOCENE (Few of the recent)	First small and primitive anthropoid apes; ancestors of Old World monkeys; early ancestral elephants; forerunners of camels; carnivores; insectivores; *Parapithecus, Propliopithecus.*	40,000,000	10,000,000
	MIOCENE (Minority of the recent)	Cordilleras, Alps and Himalayas formed; Uplift results in cooler climatic condition; generalized anthropoid ancestors of great apes; possibly ancestors of man; marsupials disappear; fossil monkeys; notable advance in horse and elephant families; *Dryopithecus.*	30,000,000	18,000,000
	PLIOCENE (Majority of the recent)	World-wide elevation continues; horses and elephants almost modern; humanoid types; ancestors of apes; *Australopithecus; Pliopithecus.*	12,000,000	10,000,000
	PLEISTOCENE (Most of the recent)	Four great ice advances, separated by interglacial epochs with warmer climate; early forms of modern man; extinct ape-like primates; early stone implements.	2,000,000	To Holocene

The Story of Fire

By ancient legends and from religious ceremonies for the preservation and the renewal of fire we are led to the conclusion that man

SUB–DIVISIONS OF THE PLEISTOCENE AND HOLOCENE PERIOD
Time span—2,000,000 years

Man and Man-like Primates	Glacial Stage (North American nomenclature in parenthesis)	Cultural Stage	Characteristics of Culture Stage
Pithecanthropus erectus (Java man sub-human)	Gunz glaciation (Nebraskan)	Pre-Chellean	Approximate date of appearance 1,000,000. Eolithic (dawn stones) rounded bones of twenty-seven extinct species found in drift with Java man.
Sinanthropus (China man) *Eoanthropus* (Dawson man)	Gunz-Mindel interglacial stage (Aftonian)		
		Chellean	P r i m i t i v e hand-axe, chipped stone, evidences o f f i r e found with *Sinanthropus*.
	Mindel glaciation (Kansan)	No culture	No sub-human form discovered for this period of time.
Homo Heidelbergensis (Sub-human form found in Germany)	Mindel-Riis interglacial (Yarmouth)	Achulean	Paleolithic flints, hand axes, stone chipped on both sides.
		No culture	No data.
	Riis glaciation (Illinoian)	Mousterian	Life in caves, evidences of fire, burial of dead, Paleolithic scrapers and borers.
Neanderthal (Sub-human)	Riis Wurm interglacial (Sangamon)	Aurignacian	Drawings and paintings, awl, piercer.
		Solutrean	Bone needle and dart.
		Magdalenian	Needle with eye, harpoon.
Cro-Magnon (*Homo sapiens*)	Wurm glaciation (Wisconsin)	Azilian	Transitional from the Paleolithic.
Modern man	Present interglacial	Ground stone	Polished stone; domestication of animals and plants; bow and arrow; spears. Period of beginning 25,000 to 18,000 years ago.
		Bronze	Tools and weapons of bronze; the plow, the wheel, writing; political organization. Period of beginning 3,500 years ago.
		Iron	Beginning of modern world of technological a n d social advance. P e r i o d of beginning 1,350 years ago.

Quaternary, Age of Man, the Glacial Age

Pleistocene

Holocene

Eolithic

Paleolithic

Neolithic

used fire long before he had invented the process of making it. Natural fire from volcanoes and lightning must have been familiar to all peoples, but the making of fire was a definite forward step, perhaps the greatest in human history. Before the knowledge of the making of fire it had to be preserved, carried from place to place, borrowed if lost, constantly tended. Fire is made in two ways: friction and concussion. Like many another invention and discovery, fire both extended and limited the scope of man's activities. Fire extended activities through the greater control of the material world. Man was able to provide more comforts, ward off animals, move into areas of greater cold, develop his technology in making tools, shelters and means of transportation. Fire limited activities by increasing the need of taking pains. Fire was a great disciplinarian for the human race. The necessity of watching and caring for fire made it more difficult for women to accompany the men on expeditions. Fire tended to establish forms of division of labor. The making of fire was a man's task; caring for the fire the woman's. Fire established more fully the idea of home. The place to which men returned was the place where the fire was kept by the woman. Fire shortened the period of nursing for mothers in that other foods were made available. The invention of pottery simplified the storage and cooking of foods. Smelting and brick-making paved the way for a new social and economic order. Everywhere man has associated fire with mystical and magical practices. The renewal of fire was a symbol of the renewal of life; the cult of the fireworshiper a recognition of both the beneficent and the destructive aspects of fire. Fire was considered property, and since fire could not be buried in the grave it was allowed to go out that the spirit of the dead might not be separated from that which belonged to it. Fire was the most momentous discovery, the greatest social and economic factor in the history of man.

Art

Anthropological research has demonstrated the truth of the statement that man does not live by bread alone, that before his material needs are adequately provided for he seeks an outlet for the expression of intellectual and esthetic needs in painting and carving, in adorning his body, in singing songs and telling stories, in dancing and religious ceremonials. The original Tasmanian, now extinct, did not provide himself with a shelter; he did not know

how to make fire; but he painted pebbles which represented the
spirits of his departed ancestors and to these pebbles he talked.
Scattered from France to Siberia more than 100,000 objects of art
have been found which because stone, ivory, bone or shells were used
have withstood the ravages of 40,000 years or more of time. These
objects are frequently found associated with the tools, weapons and
human remains of man and with the bones of animals long since
extinct. But it is the art of the cave men which most excites the
admiration of the modern painter. Twenty-five caves have now
been found in France and an equal number in Spain. On the walls
and ceilings of these caves, in the Aurignacian period, men long ago
made pictures which portrayed their interests in life. There has
been much speculation concerning the motives which inspired these
early artists of twenty thousand years ago, but so little is known
about the religious and magical ideals of that time that the conclusions are pure conjecture. One of the earliest expressions of art is
in personal adornment. Flowers and feathers are used for decoration; the face, the limbs, the body are painted, tattoed, mutilated,
scarified; necklaces, earrings, anklets are worn. These are not practices of modern primitive people only. These practices go back as
far as a record exists. Religion has always had a very close connection with art. Man has portrayed his gods. He has tried to show
his respect by artistic expression. Religious ceremonials afforded
an outlet for artistic ability in many forms—clothing, masks, symbols, tokens, processions, dances—all of which were executed with the
most painstaking care of detail. Two kinds of art are recognized
as having had early development among primitive peoples: realistic
and geometric or representative art. The geometric or representative art accompanied the development of technology. Articles of
utility were decorated that they might be beautiful as well as useful.
Besides the decorative art, there was also art for art's sake, making
a beautiful object. There is still much dispute as to the order of
appearance. The logical conclusion would seem to be that they appeared simultaneously. Men would attempt to make pictures of
animals and they would also make use of lines and circles to represent symbols which had meaning to them. The comparison that is
sometimes made of primitive art to the art of children gives a
totally false impression. Primitive art is the work of adults and
not children. The only real comparison that might be useful would
be one of the art of children of civilized and primitive groups. It

should be remembered also that the art of the Cave Men has been rated as of excellent quality by modern artists and that art is coextensive with man.

Music and the Dance

Music is a universal, conscious human achievement expressive of many forms of human emotions. It is associated not only with social pleasures and periods of rejoicing, but also with the crises of birth, puberty, marriage, and death, peace and war. It serves to ward off evil spirits, warn the unwary of the existence of taboos, arouse to a high pitch the enthusiasm of those who are to participate in battle, and mourn the dead. In religious and mystical ceremonies and festivals the gods of fertility and war are propitiated.

In musical achievement, as measured by the invention of musical instruments and ability to use them, the African Negro easily takes the lead. So great has been their progress that the kings of Uganda have orchestras. The American Indian holds second place, while the Australians are poorly supplied. There seems to be evidence that not all of the instruments used by the African Negroes and the American Indians were invented by them. Some of them may have been borrowed from the cultures of other peoples. Stringed instruments used by the American Indian probably came from Europe.

Closely related to music but possessing even greater power and influence over the people is the dance. Like music it serves many purposes in peace and in war. The pattern of the dance varies according to the nature of the ceremony. Generally speaking, dances are group affairs, though an individual may be assigned a special part or execute for the pleasure of others his own performance. In some dances, though it is not a general custom, both men and women perform. In the dance they rarely touch each other. For days before the dance takes place the dancers may be seen practicing in private their part of the ceremony or preparing their costumes. The costume has its own symbolical significance not understood by the uninitiated.

The music for the dance may be furnished by the performers or by a special group of singers. The dance itself is an intricate affair, a strange mixture in many instances of deep religious feeling and tribal buffoonery. In the Pueblo Indian corn dance, for example, the tribal gods of fertility and the Christian god are now both symbolically present and are propitiated with gifts. The music is furnished by a group of singers and a drummer. Each male dancer in the group executes with painstaking exactness his part of the performance. Back of him a woman shuffles with little grace. Weaving in and out among the dancers are figures representative of fertility; gray shadows, the spirits of the dead, hover about while the seriousness of the ceremony is interrupted by the rude gestures of the buffoon. The dance continues for many hours. The performers may drop out to rest and then resume their places. So important are the festival dances that the calendar is based on them.

The Tribe and the State

The tribe is a social organization; the state is a political organization. The functions of the tribe and of the state differ. A tribe is governed by folkways and mores, a state by laws or the will of the ruler. Laws have a rational and a practical character which may be lacking in the mores. Laws are more rigid, definite and inflexible. A tribe comes into being and exists through a feeling of unity; a state through coercion and force. A tribe is a closed group. The form of government in a tribe may be quite definite and complete as in a well-managed family; it may be loose, or it may be entirely missing and yet the tribal character be maintained and common action secured in time of danger. No state, however, can exist without government, some form of central control.

The definitions that have been proposed for a tribe indicate characteristics which may serve to explain the nature of a tribe. The characteristics are: (1) a name, (2) a common language, (3) occupation in a nomadic or settled state of a more or less definite area, (4) intermarriage and inbreeding, (5) capacity for uniting in common action, (6) generally a rude form of government.

The forms of tribal government, where they exist, vary. Generally the tribe is ruled over by a chief chosen because of popularity or prestige. In many tribal organizations the chief enjoys no particular advantages. If young, he takes part in the hunt or any other form of economic activity; if old, his food is furnished him by his friends. He rules with the advice of a council of elders.

The presence of common danger may give rise to a confederacy, one way in which a state may be created. The League of the Five Nations is an outstanding example of a confederacy in American Indian life. The control of the Five Nations was vested in a council of fifty members chosen by the participating tribes. The Five Nations, however, did not constitute a state.

Political government was most fully developed in Africa where military despots ruled by maintaining standing armies. The principal characteristics of these military despotic states are: (1) centralization of power and authority; (2) ownership of land and property by the ruler or his representatives; (3) loss of the rights and privileges of the people, and (4) restriction of the right to rule to members of a limited group.

The government of the Incas is an example of a somewhat different type of political control. The supreme power and authority was hereditary in a single family group. The state was highly socialistic in character. The unit of local organization was a family group, the head man of the family was the representative in a community group; the head men of community groups in regional groups. Over these regional groups the central government ruled. In the event that a neighboring people were conquered an effort was made to integrate them into the general organization and not hold them in subjection. The Inca government fell when the ruler was treacherously murdered by the Spaniards, because too much authority for action was vested in one man.

Law and Government

The origin of law and government is to be found in the folkways and mores, the customs of a people which have been followed for a long period of time. The difference between folkways and mores is not always easy to determine. The mores are that part of the folkways which is considered vital to the existence of the culture of a people. The mores have moral sanction. In our own society raising one's hat to a woman is a folkway, but marriage is a mos.

New conditions of life give rise to new forms of behavior, which, in time, become rules of conduct supported, in many instances, by the religious ideas of a people. These rules of life, since they have grown out of experience or been handed down by traditions, are expressions of the will of the group. They are not imposed on the people by an outside agency or institution until the state comes into existence. Government, therefore, consists of the customs of the peoples and the simple forms of social organization by which conformity to these customs is secured. In the family the authority of the father or the mother is government; in the community the will of the elders, or headman, constitutes government, supported by the action of special officers such as buffalo police; in the tribe, the tribal council gives expression to public will. Crude forms of court are found among several peoples, and depending on the stage to which culture has been developed, agents of the court to carry out the will of the people. In trials in the primitive courts magico-religious exercises are often performed. Evidence of guilt or innocence is demanded from supernatural powers.

Public opinion, the desire for recognized status, the fear of ridicule or social ostracism are powerful factors in control. Many offenses which in our laws would be considered crimes, offenses against the public good, are classed as private wrongs (torts) by primitive societies. The individuals concerned make whatever settlement is made in righting private wrongs. Torts may lead to feuds between families.

Primitives recognize more than we do collective responsibility. If, for example, a member of tribe A kills a member of tribe B, it is not necessary in taking revenge that the guilty party be found and punished. In this instance the killing constitutes a crime because it was done by the member of another tribe. The tribe is responsible. Someone in tribe A must be killed even though it may not be the killer but a helpless old man. Had the victim belonged to another family within the same community the families would have settled the affair, probably by payment of goods.

The Effect of Civilization on Primitive People

Contact of civilization with the social systems of more primitive peoples is inevitable. Even if the white man had not coveted the lands and possessions of native peoples in the Americas and Africa the result would have been the same, for trade and the missionary spirit would have brought them together. The settlement of North and South America may be taken as an illustration. The explorer and the soldier were followed by the trader, the missionary, the settler, and the political leader, the representative of a great power in another land. They brought with them overwhelming evidence of superiority in power, knowledge and resource. Not only were the tools and weapons, the institutions of the white man better, but also the white man's god was superior. Even if the white man had been well-intentioned, which in the past with the exception of the missionary, he was not, generally speaking, the result would have been the same; for in the resulting clash of cultures the white man must have his way and that way is inevitably his own culture, his customs, ideals and traditions. The native peoples must pay the price of the supposed benefits of civilization to them,—the loss of their own culture, helplessness, confusion and degradation. The peoples who came to the New World from England, France and Spain came to exploit not only new lands but new peoples. The settlement of the New World would have been a far different story if they had not been inhabited, for the newcomers would not have been able to profit from trade and from the achievements of the native peoples. The lands and possessions were seized; the people were exploited and massacred; but it was not the loss of property or life that proved to be the major calamity for the native populations. In the face of the great power and prestige of the white people the chiefs and medicine men could not retain the respect of their own people. The moral standards of the native populations, no longer controlled by the discipline of their own culture, disintegrated. Gradually their incentives, their ambitions, their goals, their zest for living were destroyed. Even the missionaries played an unconscious part in this destruction. The ways of the primitive were "heathen" ways; new ways of life must be taught; a more powerful god must take the place of native deities. In recent years the attitude and methods of missionaries have altered since they have come to the realization that a sudden change is harmful for primitive peoples. They show more respect for native institutions and endeavor to help the people live better within their own culture in the hope that in time native populations may accept Christianity as a better way of life. It should be added that conditions at any time in the past would have been worse without the presence of the missionaries. They exerted a restraining force on the rapaciousness of the other incoming groups, and made a greater effort to help the native peoples. But in spite of missionary efforts the native population fell victims to the white man's vices and the white man's diseases. The culture introduced by the missionaries was a culture in which the native people could not share on terms of equality.

In the clash of peoples representing different culture levels, one far superior in material resource to the other, the result is generally entire subjugation or extermination. Amalgamation is not possible, for racial pride on the part of the superior culture group sets up barriers to intermarriage without which class and caste are sure to arise. The provision that is made for the subjugated people must be separate and different. They may not live in the same parts of the settlements; they must be paid lower wages; they must show respect and deference to the white man. Efforts on the part of well-meaning people to improve the condition of subject peoples through education and training makes them, not infrequently, only more keenly aware of their inferior status in life. These racial antipathies have become more pronounced since the discovery and settlement of the Americas.

Our Dependence on Primitive Man

Early man was a wanderer. Nearly all the habitable portions of the world were explored or settled by him in his wanderings. He lived in many of the places which are now the great centers of population. He discovered for us the routes by land and water which are now our great trade routes. He used most of the animal, vegetable and mineral resources. His greatest invention or discovery was fire which, with the possible exception of language, is the greatest socializing force in the world. He domesticated most of the animals and cultivated most of the plants now used by civilized man. He was clever in handicrafts. He knew weaving, sewing, plaiting. He worked in clay, wood, bone and iron. All of our basic handicrafts were first developed by early man. He made tools and weapons. He developed trade systems and markets, some form of exchange to supplement barter, and forms of money. In medicine he had an extensive knowledge of herbs and plants. He used water and steam for cleansing wounds. His practices show that he understood the relation of mind to body in the treatment of disease. He made a beginning in surgery. There are evidences that he operated on the skull and made use of anesthetics. He made some practical application of astronomy and mathematics to the affairs of his life such as agriculture, the calendar, navigation and the construction of buildings. He invented a calendar. His pioneer work in agriculture included cultivation, fertilization, irrigation, storage and preservation.

SELECTED REFERENCES

Benedict, Ruth, *Patterns of Culture*, Boston: Houghton Mifflin Company, 1934.
Boas, Franz, *General Anthropology*, Boston: D. C. Heath and Company, 1938.
Cole, Fay-Cooper, *The Long Road: From Savagery to Civilization*, Baltimore: Williams and Wilkins Company, 1933.

Cole, Mabel Cook, and Cole, Fay-Cooper, *The Story of Man*, Chicago: University of Knowledge, Incorporated, 1938.

Croneis, Carey, and Krumbein, William C., *Down to Earth*, The University of Chicago Press, 1936.

Encyclopedia of the Social Sciences, New York: The Macmillan Company, 1931.

Fairchild, Mildred, and Hart, Hornell, ''A Million Years of Evolution in Tools,'' *Scientific Monthly*, vol. 28, pp. 71–79, Jan., 1929.

Frazer, James, *The Golden Bough*, New York: The Macmillan Company, 1922.

Goldenweiser, Alexander, *Anthropology*, New York: F. S. Crofts & Co., 1937.

Hankins, Frank H., *An Introduction to the Study of Society*, New York: The Macmillan Company, 1927.

Hooton, Earnest A., *Up from the Ape*, New York: The Macmillan Company, 1931.

Hooton, Earnest A., *Apes, Men and Morons*, New York: G. P. Putnam's Sons, 1937.

Hough, Walter, ''Fire as an Agent in Human Culture,'' United States National Museum *Bulletin*, no. 129, 1926.

Keller, Albert G., *Man's Rough Road*, New Haven, Conn: Yale University Press, 1930.

Kroeber, A. L., *Anthropology*, New York: Harcourt, Brace and Company, 1923.

Kroeber, A. L., and Waterman, T. T., *Source Book in Anthropology*, New York: Harcourt, Brace and Company, 1931.

Leakey, S. B., *Adam's Ancestors*, London: Methuen and Company, Ltd., 1934.

Linton, Ralph, *The Study of Man*, New York: D. Appleton-Century Company, Inc., 1936.

Lowie, Robert H., *The Origin of the State*, New York: Harcourt, Brace and Company, 1927.

Lowie, Robert H., *An Introduction to Cultural Anthropology*, New York: Farrar and Rinehart, 1934.

Lowie, Robert H., *Are We Civilized?*, New York: Harcourt, Brace and Company, 1929.

Morris, Ann Axtell, *Digging in the Southwest*, Garden City, N. Y.: Doubleday, Doran and Company, 1934.

Murdock, George P., *Our Primitive Contemporaries*, New York: The Macmillan Company, 1934.

Read, Carveth, *The Origin of Man*, Cambridge: Cambridge University Press, 1925.

Sumner, William G., *Folkways*, Boston: Ginn and Company, 1906.

Sumner, William G., and Keller, Albert G., *The Science of Society*, New Haven, Conn.: Yale University Press, 1927.

Thomas, William I., *Primitive Behavior*, New York: McGraw-Hill Book Company, Inc., 1937.

Wallis, Wilson D., *An Introduction to Anthropology*, New York: Harper and Brothers, 1926.

Wilder, H. H., *The Pedigree of the Human Race*, New York: Henry Holt and Company, 1926.

Yerkes, R. M., and Ada W., *The Great Apes*, New Haven, Conn.: Yale University Press, 1929.

PART II

PERSISTENT INFLUENCES IN SOCIAL LIFE

In this subdivision of our text we examine the conditions in necessary conformity with which any social order develops. We see that society is limited and controlled in the directions of its development by laws that are inexorable, laws that are violated only at risk of the violators' annihilation; that any major tendency toward a change in group ways is subject to the veto power of the physical environment. Not only are human beings guided by chemical and physical laws, and by geographic and geologic inducements, but men's comings and goings are conditioned by the presence and the activity of living things of microscopic size, by the larger animals, and by plants. In human beings, color blindness, nerve sensitivity, pitch of voice, temperament, speed of perception, and comprehension capacity, at least partly hereditary, have occupational significance, and in a variety of other ways have a part in defining the roles of individuals in society. Associated with the physical and chemical and biological laws there are economic laws, and even the mental processes conform to laws.

As we study the earthy facts in the seven chapters of this PART II, we come to know that changes attempted by men harmonize with the rules of the universe, or else men suffer.

CHAPTER 2

PHYSICAL REGULARITIES

By Dr. R. F. Bellamy
Florida State College for Women, Tallahassee, Florida

BASIC NATURE OF PHYSICAL FACTS

Whoever would build a house or construct a theory should look well to the foundation upon which it is to stand. We have all seen cases where imposing structures or beautiful theories have been constructed on shifting, unstable sand. In every case great was the fall thereof.

The application is obvious when we realize that fundamental to every department of human knowledge is a body of laws and principles which has to do with the properties and behavior of physical matter. With finality and inevitability our every action, the very breath we draw, is dependent upon and conditioned by the physical universe in which we live. Our lives and natures and our perceptions are built into the physical universe as a component part of it.

A little change in our powers of perception would make the world appear startlingly different. If the vibrating fibers in our ears were slightly longer or shorter we would hear many sounds which are inaudible now and we would be unable to hear some which are quite familiar. For all we know such a change would enable us to hear snakes as plainly as we now hear dogs barking. We might hear the passage of an electric current through a wire, the passage of light through the air, or the radiation of warmth from a stove. Of course, these are wild conjectures, and in all probability are not at all in accord with the facts. But we would be able to hear many things which we do not hear now, and some of these things would surprise us.

Equally surprising changes would be noted if some physical change were to take place in the retina of the eye. There are probably more colors which we cannot see than there are which we can. A different type of eye might be as superior to ours as the normal eye today is superior to the eye which is color blind. If we were enabled to perceive some of the infra red rays we could see through dense clouds or heavy fog. If our eyes were constructed like those of a bird we would be able to see as far and as well as we can now with a powerful telescope. A nose built like that of a dog would enable one to recognize the odor where a friend or enemy had walked along the road, touched a wall or sat in a chair hours before. Thus even minute changes in the physical structure of our bodies would transform the face of nature. Conversely, as we shall see more plainly later, a different set of physical laws would necessitate such complete changes in our behavior and characteristics that life as we now know it would be impossible. Sir Oliver Lodge has pointed out that even our size determines the working of these laws. Were man a millimeter high on a dewy cabbage leaf, it would appear to him that water stands in spherical balls. Should he touch one of these balls, he would immediately find himself inside and would probably drown before he could get out! This may show how intimately our lives and the laws of nature are interlocked and built together.

Figuratively or literally, as we may choose to believe, we are made of the dust of the earth but in either case we are of the earth, earthy.

Sociological Literature Recognizes Physical Factors

To all who stop and think, the basic nature of physical facts is so self evident that scholars of all ages have recognized it and have sought to incorporate it in their systems of thought. Thales, who so far as we know was the first philosopher, by which we mean the first who attempted an organized explanation of natural phenomena, was primarily concerned with the nature of physical things. We may truthfully say that every philosopher since that day, no matter how prone he may have been to speculate on such abstruse matters as the nature of truth or the freedom of the will, has found it necessary to include in his system some explanation or discussion of physical laws.

Pioneer Sociologists. It need not surprise us to learn that sociologists have followed the same practice. In fact, sociology had its very birth in a cradle of physical sciences. Auguste Comte, who is usually credited with being the father of sociology, became so impressed with the exact working of physical laws that he concluded there must be similarly exact laws in the field of human behavior.[1]

[1] Auguste Comte, *The Positive Philosophy of Auguste Comte*, translated by Harriet Martineau, London: G. Bell and Sons, 1913.

Could we but learn these laws and submit them to exact measurement, he reasoned, we would be able to foresee social happenings and would also have a means by which we could control the course of human events. He even called the study of these laws *"Social Physics,"* giving as an alternative the very inexact and poorly constructed word *"sociology."*

The position taken by Comte has been essentially the one held by every sociologist since that day. To be sure, there has been considerable quarreling as to just how far we might hope to approximate exactness in the measurement of social phenomena, but the basic attitude has been the same.

Since our earlier students of society were philosophically inclined and since they attempted to give an all comprehensive explanation of human society as a whole, they spent much time and energy discussing the bed rock upon which they conceived the social fabric to rest. The present-day student of sociology can well afford to spend some time in studying the works of these earlier sociologists. The writings of Herbert Spencer are especially illuminating. The most pretentious product of his pen was his *Synthetic Philosophy,* a set of ten volumes, containing six thousand pages. It is interesting to follow Spencer's line of thought in the production of this colossal work.

According to his own words, Spencer was interested only in presenting a practical and accurate system of ethics, or an intelligent answer to the question, "What is Justice?"[2] He reasoned quite accurately that this question could not be answered until human society itself was understood,—hence he must write the *Principles of Sociology* before attacking the questions of ethics proper. Similarly, sociology could not be comprehended until the psychology upon which it rested was mastered, and psychology in turn was impossible until built on a sound biology. But here again, biology had no meaning until certain *First Principles* which constituted its underlying foundation were examined.

The upshot of it all was that Spencer wrote his *First Principles, Principles of Biology, Principles of Psychology* and *Principles of Sociology* before actually producing his work in ethics which was what he first set out to do. If we examine the contents of his *First Principles,* we find it contains chapters on "Space, Time, Matter,

[2] Alfred W. Tillett, *Spencer's Synthetic Philosophy,* London: P. S. King and Son, 1914.

Motion, and Force," "The Indestructibility of Matter," "The Continuity of Motion," "The Persistence of Force," "The Persistence of Relations among Forces," "The Transformation and Equivalence of Forces," "The Direction of Motion," and "The Rhythm of Motion."[3] In a word, Spencer realized that there could be no answer to such a seemingly abstract question as "What Is Justice?" until one understood thoroughly the laws and principles of the physical universe. No matter how widely separated the two fields might seem to be, they were nevertheless inseparably related.

Spencer's position cannot be intelligently disputed. However badly mistaken he may have been in some of his pronouncements— and any man who attempts to cover such a large field must make many mistakes—he was correct in what he was attempting to do. His position is just as sound today. There can be no mastery or understanding of human problems until one has at least an "intelligent ignorance" of physical laws and principles. Time spent in this field is valuable on two counts: there are certain facts which are directly important in their relation to social organization and human welfare; aside from this factual knowledge, if one works with physical and chemical phenomena for a time he acquires a certain "feel" which is probably not to be secured in any other way. His appreciation of cause and effect, mathematical accuracy, and the inevitability of natural law gives him an indefinable something which colors his entire attitude toward his own field.

Our earlier sociologists appreciated the value of this training. So fully did Ward realize this that he advised all would-be students of sociology to become conversant with the other sciences before embarking on the study of sociology itself. He thought sociology should not be taken before the senior year at least, and probably not below the graduate level. While we might be more inclined to agree with Gillette that sociology should be started in the first year of the primary school, we must acknowledge that Ward was essentially correct in his belief that no real comprehension of social phenomena could be achieved by one who had no training in the more fundamental sciences. To-day, alas, full many students of some specialized narrow field of sociology, and particularly many workers in various branches of social welfare work have not seen the necessity for securing this background. By their fruits shall we know them.

[3] Herbert Spencer, *First Principles*, New York: D. Appleton and Co., 1916.

Modern Writers. However, there is still general appreciation of the fact that the foundation for the social sciences lies in the field of physical phenomena—in which, of course, we include chemical phenomena. Perhaps as large a percentage of the students see this to-day as ever before. Social philosophers eagerly await the latest pronouncements of the physicists and chemists. As an illustration of this, we may note the interest taken in the modern investigation of the atom. There are those who think this is exceedingly important for arriving at a true explanation of human and social phenomena.. There is some evidence that the path of the electron in its dazzlingly swift and changing flight is truly fortuitous and erratic and is not "caused" by anything or any power within the atom or without. This, some scholars insist, may shed a great light on the age-old question of determinism in human and therefore in social behavior.

Aside from such abstruse questions as this, the sociologist to-day realizes as never before how important the work of the physical scientist is for human society. Dr. Ogburn has pointed out that some seemingly unimportant invention in the field of physical phenomena often proves to have far greater effect upon human society than all the religious and philosophical teachings combined.[4] Others have been similarly impressed. Professor Bossard in his study of *Man and His Universe* has found fit to include a section on "Law and Order in the Universe,"[5] and in like emphasis is Kelsey's *Physical Basis of Society.*[6]

Physical scientists are also beginning to see the way in which the two fields are related. Harold Richards put it this way:

> Science can not evade responsibility for many of our social and economic problems. Behind the electric power, behind mass production in industry and the multiplied bounty of the fields lie physics and chemistry and biology. Science enables massed populations to live in highly restricted areas. Difficulties of social adjustment arise. Thanks to scientific nutrition, sanitation, and bacteriology, plagues no longer cut the

[4] Wm. F. Ogburn, "The Influence of Inventions on American Social Institutions in the Future," *American Journal of Sociology*, Vol. XLIII, No. 3, November, 1937, pp. 365–376; "Technology and Sociology," *Social Forces*, Vol. XVII, No. 1, October, 1938, pp. 1–8.

[5] J. H. S. Bossard (Ed.), *Man and His World*, New York: Harper and Bros., 1932.

[6] Carl Kelsey, *The Physical Basis of Society*, New York: D. Appleton and Co., 1925.

Gordian knot by wiping out vast sections of humanity. The swift transportation and communication made possible by physics and chemistry have revolutionized internal economy and added international complications. In a word, science has come bringing long life, leisure, plenty, kaleidoscopic possibilities of full living—sweet words, but the handling of this bounty is difficult.[7]

In a word, since man began to think in terms of understanding the universe as a whole or in furnishing an explanation for human or social phenomena, he has realized, sometimes dimly, occasionally more clearly, that fundamental to everything else is a comprehension of physical and chemical laws and principles. We cannot neglect this field and acquire an adequate understanding of sociology or, in fact, any of the social sciences.

Significance of Physical Factors Analyzed

The Place of Physical Phenomena in the Scheme of Life and Science Generally. When one attempts to discuss the role of physical phenomena in human society there immediately arises the difficulty of properly limiting the field. It is a modern truism that boundaries between the sciences no longer exist. The best we can do is to indicate broad zones of transition. Even the distinction between chemistry and physics is inexact. In an earlier day, we said that chemistry had to do with those activities or processes which fundamentally changed the nature of the substance, such as electrolysis of water into oxygen and hydrogen, while physics dealt with changes which were external only, such as the freezing of water into ice or heating it until it became steam, but in either case leaving it still water. In other words we were in the field of physics until the structure of the molecule was changed and at that point we entered the domain of chemistry. This distinction has very little significance to-day. As a broad general rule it is still serviceable, but it breaks down at many points.

Chemistry and physics taken together furnish the very bones and meat of such sociologically significant sciences as geography, geology, and climatology. No sociologist to-day would think of neglecting the influences of these factors on the location of cities and factories, the congregation of peoples, the lines of migration, the types of occupation and even the characteristics of religion, government and family life.

[7] Harold Richards, *The Universe Surveyed*, New York: D. Van Nostrand Company, Inc., 1937, p. 3.

On the other hand, the physical and chemical merge just as imperceptibly into the biological, physiological, and psychological. If there are any real race distinctions they must be resolved ultimately into matters of chemical and physical differences. Traits of personality, the significance of heredity, the characteristics of the insane and feebleminded, the influence of different foods and drugs, and many other sociologically significant questions must find their ultimate answers in the chemist's test-tube or on the physicists's scales.

Obviously, it would be impossible to discuss the role of the physical in human society without trespassing on these other fields. Yet there are certain phases of this question which should be discussed apart from the other disciplines.

Significance of Physical Phenomena for Sociology Specifically. (a) In Social Theory and Philosophy.—In general it may be said that an understanding of physical phenomena contributes to the social sciences in two ways. First, their general principles throw light on the theory and philosophy of sociology as we have noted above. This type of contribution has no immediately practical value. It has only academic value, but like all things which have been so classed, it may have ultimate practical value far beyond what one might suppose.

(b) In Social Work and Human Welfare.—Such an understanding may have quite a direct bearing on the practices of social work and all efforts to increase human welfare. As a simple example of the latter, it is possible to foretell which part of a new city will develop into the more expensive residential sections if one knows the direction of the prevailing winds and certain other contributing local factors. Most certainly, this section will not be where the industrial smoke will be blown. This simple fact should have a great deal of value in any scientific attempt at city planning. Ignorance or neglect of such facts may result in undesirable sequences. The Frenchman who planned the city of Washington made quite a mistake and faced the capitol the wrong way.

CULTURE AS MAN'S ADAPTATION TO PHYSICAL LAWS

Early Adaptation to Physical Laws

Automatic and Necessary Adaptations. The distinguishing characteristic of human life is that mankind possesses a *culture*.

Contrasted with animal life which is based on instinctive or auto-matic reactions, and changes only in the process of biological adap-tation over many generations, human beings *learn* from their par-ents and fellows and order their lives accordingly. This learned or artificial behavior we call *culture*, including in the term, perhaps, the artifacts which have been fabricated in the cultural process. Looked at from our present viewpoint, the sum total of human cul-ture is merely mankind's adaptation to the inherent properties of the physical world.

It must not be concluded that physical laws and principles had no significance before the dawn of culture. On the contrary, they were fully as important then as they are now. In fact, they exerted their all-important control over animal life for millions of years before the appearance of man. When a squirrel or woodpecker caught at rough bark with sharp claws, this was as much an adapta-tion to physical law as it is to-day when a linesman straps on his steel climbers before ascending a telephone pole.

In some ways the lower animals utilize the physical forces which challenge man's best efforts to-day. Man's finest glider has never come anywhere near equalling the way a hawk or vulture can take advantage of air currents to be lifted to enormous heights on sta-tionary wings. One would think that the orioles had a thorough understanding of the law of gravity and the danger of a fall when they suspended their nests from tiny twigs over water. No maraud-ing mammal or serpent dare climb out there to get the eggs or young! Even social or group adjustment to physical laws is common among animals. The communal dams and lodges built by the beavers would tempt one to believe that they understood the laws of hy-draulic pressure and had training in engineering.

The behavior of animals is not always marked by such seeming acumen. Sometimes they make fatal mistakes—many times, in fact. The often told story of the eagle who allowed the feathers of his legs to freeze to a cake of ice and was carried over Niagara is merely a spectacular illustration of the kind of thing which happens in multitudinous repetition every day. During a dry season, quail will make their nests in little ditches or gullies, serenely unaware of the fact that water runs down hill and that the first rain will destroy their nests. Perhaps the most spectacular example of wholesale fly-ing in the face of immutable laws—at least outside of the human race—is the way vast hordes of lemmings will migrate downhill and when they reach the sea, plunge in and swim ahead in a straight line until they drown.

There is no difference before natural laws between animals and man. Nature is not only no respecter of persons, but is no respecter of anything else. Animal or man must order his life in harmony with physical facts or perish.

Rudimentary Choice and Utilization. (a) Paleolithic and Neolithic Practices.—It has been pointed out that the physical environment changes the animal, but man changes the environment. This is saying that man alone has been able to grasp the workings of physical laws and take advantage of them in ways that no animal could. While it is true that even to-day man often makes purely automatic adjustments to physical laws as the animals do, still primitive man must have begun making rudimentary planned adjustments at a very early date. It would be fascinating to know who the first man was to discover the highly important fact that flint stone breaks with a conchoidal fracture and therefore leaves a cutting edge. We may not think of this as a highly important discovery of physical law, but nevertheless it ushered in a hundred thousand years of Stone Age culture during which hairy mammoths and sabre-toothed tigers as well as many other beasts were hunted or frantically fought with chipped stone weapons. Early men, alas, also used these weapons on each other, and therefore human society would never again be what it had been for so long. It is probable that the use of chipped stone tools made so much more game available for food that populations increased to the point of something remotely resembling our crowded cities to-day. Then, no doubt, men turned on each other, using their newly discovered weapons with telling effect. There is every reason to believe that man has been essentially the same emotionally throughout all ages, and that the same types of social situations have arisen again and again. It was a little thing—the characteristic method of flint cracking—but it probably had greater social reverberations than the invention of the airplane or the radio. Hardly less important was the much later discovery that stone would not only chip but could be ground smooth or polished. This made available a great many more types of stone and ushered in the Neolithic Age, tolling the knell for the Paleolithic which had centered around the chipped stone for so long. Relatively near to this time, man made two other discoveries or adjustments to the physical world. Without becoming aware of the mathematical formula for buoyancy or in fact any of the exact laws of hydraulics, Neolithic man did learn that a hollowed out log would not only float but would support a number of men. Some one else, probably by accident, discovered that properly worked clay if moulded into a hollow shape and baked or dried would hold liquids and stand heat.

Once again, human society became transformed. Seemingly two of the simplest of physical facts had been recognized—two out of so many thousands—and yet man had become able to cross rivers and lakes and even take extended voyages along the sea coast. He had been enabled to add boiling to his meagre methods of cooking and now a whole new group of substances could be softened and made edible. The effect on the existing group life of the day must have been enormous.

Another similarly revolutionary discovery was the bow and arrow. It is highly probable that no other invention since has had such highly revolutionary effects as the bow and arrow—unless it be the wheel. For the first time man could stand at a distance, even up a tree, and launch deadly missiles at his enemy, whether human or animal. Yet nothing new had been created. The elasticity of wood and the laws of inertia and momentum had existed before in exactly the same way. It was merely a case of utilizing an existing situation.

It would be fascinating if we could know the story behind all these inventions and adaptations. Of one thing we can be sure :— for perhaps a hundred thousand years the discoveries were the result of accident or chance. Moreover, there must have been many foolish and irrelevant practices which grew up in connection with the various adjustments.

Such a thing is not at all unknown in our own day. Some decades ago a building in which there was a safe containing a quantity of gold leaf was burned to the ground. The books in which the gold leaf had been kept were charred and black, while the gold had run together and united. This caused great excitement as it was realized that gold heated in the presence of charcoal could be hammered into a homogeneous mass. Utilizing this discovery, dentists equipped themselves with little charcoal burners and for years heated their gold over the charcoal and hammered it into hollow teeth. This was all very nice until some one discovered that the charcoal had nothing to do with it and the gold could be worked just as satisfactorily if no charcoal were around. Undoubtedly, we do many things of this kind to-day. We have done more in the past.

Not only did early man engage in many such irrelevant practices, but he mixed many queer and superstitious beliefs with his more practical activities. When we think of how common this is to-day, we can conclude that it must have been enormous during the earlier ages. Our own society is shot full of such beliefs and practices. The typical Russian peasant would not think of planting a crop before the fields had been sprinkled with holy water—until the godless revolutionists came along and instituted a different set of beliefs and practices. This is no different from the behavior of a man who refuses to walk under a ladder, or from the way in which a really competent aviator took a Bible and a rabbit's foot across the Atlantic.

Just as the lower animals made some amazing adaptations, so early man utilized the forces of nature in some almost incomprehensible ways. It is thought that the "dew ponds" on the upland downs of England go back to a very ancient day. Yet they are a most astonishing utilization of the principles of the vacuum which is a discovery of just yesterday. If they are constructed on the very tops of hills they fill to the brim, but if rain water runs into them they dry up. How did man discover this? It would task our best scientists of to-day to conceive such a structure without advance information. First a depression on the hill top was lined with hay and this was plastered over with clay. The clay was sealed down all around the edge and if it was a good job the pond would fill up. The explanation is that the layer of hay is an insulation and the clay remains cool. Dew collects on the cool clay and the pond actually becomes full. But if any rain water runs into the pond, the clay around the edges will be washed away, water will get under the clay, the hay will cease to insulate, and the pond will dry up.

How could such a complicated thing have been constructed before the modern understanding of the vacuum, or rather the insulation of containers? Yet, strange as it may seem, hundreds of thousands of such adjustments have been made to unknown physical laws. A great many of them are being practiced to-day. They must have been unusually common during the morning hours of mankind's era.

(b) Practices of Modern Races Outside of European Culture.—

It is possible to get some idea of the way in which Palaeolithic man lived by observing those races who lived under a simpler culture than our modern European civilization. We must not assume too great a similarity between early man and these peoples, but they at least have this in common that iron or steel is not found associated with either and neither has adopted our modern deliberate search for new discoveries.

In the comparatively simple life of these marginal races, it is easier to recognize the role of physical factors than it is in our more complicated civilization. Like the animals on one hand, and like the most enlightened human beings on the other, these men of nature make multitudinous adaptations to the physical forces around them. Sometimes they utilize these forces in ways which would not be expected of peoples without the most advanced scientific information. We meet the principle of insulation again in the clothing of North Siberian tribes. They make coats of two layers of animals' skins and pack dried blood vessels between them. This mesh of blood vessels contains so much dead air that it forms the warmest garment known. It matches in efficiency the other extreme of the Mexican sombrero which keeps the deadly ultra-violet rays of the tropical sun away from the head and at the same time allows a high space for freely circulating air.

Perhaps the Eskimos have shown the most amazing ability to utilize the physical factors around them of any peoples on earth. It may prove surprising to learn that anthropologists consider them the greatest inventors, not even excepting the Americans and Scandinavians. They are the only race which has exhausted its environment. The arctic explorer, Stefansson, reports that they constantly make new applications of these forces and principles. For example, an Eskimo man who needed a sled but had no wood from which to make it calmly folded a walrus skin, poured water on it, and then chopped his sled runners out of the frozen mass. In the face of a seemingly impossible situation the Eskimo have succeeded in constructing a house which has an average temperature of seventy-five or eighty degrees *with the door open* when it is forty or fifty degrees below zero outside. Yet so simple is its construction that it can be erected in a short time after a day's march is over. This shows in a startling way what remarkable results may be obtained by giving attention to ordinary physical laws. The Eskimo alone would furnish all the material needed to give an understanding of the mutual relations between man, his group life, and the physical universe in which he lives. His skin kayak in which he can turn over and over in the water and come up dry is a study in buoyancy; his throwing stick utilizes the laws of levers and the laws of velocity and momentum; and his transparent windows, made from thin ice or the stomach of a walrus, involve several departments of physical science.

Other extremes of climate have called forth similar attention to the physical processes and accompanying adjustments to them. The Blackfellows of Australia and the Bushmen of the Kalahari Desert have succeeded in surviving only by the most painstaking expedients. The ways in which they conserve their meagre supply of water, filtering it through sand, guarding it from evaporation, and supplementing it by ingenious methods of collecting dew and vegetable juices might serve as admirable laboratory experiments for a class in physics.

The world over, primitive men have made characteristic adjustments to nature's inflexible laws. Sometimes these adjustments have appeared small and insignificant and yet had far reaching effects. When the American Indian bevelled his arrow-heads and bound the feathers on his arrow shaft slightly askew he did not seem to be doing anything important. Yet this resulted in the rapid rotation of his arrow and prevented it from "slicing" off at an angle. He was working with the same principle which is employed by the baseball pitcher when he throws a curve, the golfer who intentionally or otherwise gets a hook or a slice, and the manufacturer of our modern firearms who put rifling in the barrels of their guns. Just this slight modification of the arrowhead and shaft feathers made it possible for hundreds of thousands of Indians to live who would otherwise have starved to death had they depended on unmodified arrows.

Like animals and enlightened men, the child of nature sometimes made mistakes. When he did he died. Those mistakes are not found frequently. The reason is that nearly all possible mistakes were made generations ago. It is only when some new invention— like firearms or whiskey—is encountered that new mistakes are made. By mistakes we mean merely incorrect interpretation of physical law which infinitely more relentlessly than the laws of the Medes and Persians altereth not.

Early Historic and Middle Ages Reactions to Physical Laws

We speak somewhat glibly of the dawn of the historic era and have a tendency to think of it as breaking suddenly on a waiting world. Of course, nothing of the kind happened. Had some one been able to live for several centuries covering this period he would have noticed no revolutionary changes—at least no more revolutionary changes than are always occurring. But gradually a new spirit became manifest and man began to seek deliberately for new ways in which to utilize the physical forces. Not yet had he attained the involved laboratory research which is the keynote of to-day, but some progress had been made over the rather effortless adjustments made by less civilized man. Changes came much more quickly now than they had in the earlier days and inventions began to pile up.

Man had been working the soil and planting crops since the Neolithic Age, but now crude ploughs came into use and displaced the digging stick. Slowly man learned to pulverize the soil and keep it from packing during the growing season. Jethro Tull is said to have been the first man to utilize this phase of cultivation. It is fairly safe to assume that he knew nothing about the laws of capillarity and evaporation, but he had stumbled on a way to utilize them. The modern involved soil analysis and minute study of cultivation in agricultural laboratories is but a continuation of the early work with a digging stick.

The wheel is merely a moving lever and follows the established laws of levers. When its use became established it started the long process of improving travelling conveyances and, in fact, all other machinery. The dugout boats of Neolithic man became Roman galleys, Viking ships and modern ocean liners. Little by little, new realizations of the action of physical forces piled up. Some one observing the way a boat was blown by the wind conceived the idea of a sail. The sail had little value until exactly the same forces were harnessed in the water below and a rudder added. Back in Asia the principle of the arch was discovered and no longer were the multitudinous columns of Greece necessary. A whole new universe of architectural possibilities was opened, not the least of which was the fact that now great assembly halls could be constructed for mass meetings indoors, whereas formerly all great gatherings had been of necessity held out of doors.

Quite as remarkable as were the adjustments to natural law were the failures to adjust. Even in the days of Sir Francis Drake, no one would believe that an iron ship would float, although they saw iron pots floating before their eyes. And up until the time of the Russian Revolution the Lapps had never achieved the use of a rudder. Mark Twain (Samuel L. Clemens) has pictured the consternation of a modern man back in the days of King Arthur when he observed the blindness of the people toward the physical world in which they lived.[8]

Modern Industrial and Scientific Practices

Quickened Tempo of Life. Finally what we know as the modern era appeared. This was made possible by a greater degree of understanding physical laws and in turn stimulated a more intensive study of them. Not until improved agriculture, manufacture, and transportation came into existence was it possible for large numbers of people to live together. When this became possible it immediately stimulated a more exhaustive investigation of natural forces and a search for further possible ways in which they could be utilized.

Deliberate Laboratory Research. Finally the stage arrived at which great laboratories were equipped for deliberate, painstaking research. Private business houses vied with public institutions in equipping such centers of investigation. The entire social fabric became colored with the idea of such study. The spirit of to-day is as greatly in contrast with that of primitive man as the gigantic atom-smashing cyclotron is with the unworked stone which the caveman frantically threw at the cave bear.

Sociological Survey of the Adaptations to Physical Forces

We have taken a mere fleeting glimpse at the way in which for a hundred thousand years man has lived in the midst of multitudinous physical forces and has done what he could to adjust to them and utilize them. Every item of the long process has had far-reaching effects on the nature of human groups. It should be noted that all these adjustments were made in harmony with well-known sociological principles. It was man's intense desire for security—for food and shelter and comfort—and his longing for love and social responses which prompted him to put forth these efforts. Man's own nature caused him to make adjustments to physical nature, while physical nature determined the limits within which he could act.

[8] Samuel L. Clemens (Mark Twain), *A Connecticut Yankee in King Arthur's Court.*

POSSIBILITIES AND LIMITATIONS

Primary Characteristics of the Physical Base

Its Static Nature. In the long period of adjustment and experiment, the physical universe has presented two characteristics to mankind.

In the first place, it was static. The physical laws were there to be observed or discovered, but there was no guarantee that man would discover them. Physical nature might suggest, and would certainly limit, but would never *compel* man to accept any particular line of behavior. No one was forced to attach a sail to his boat or guide it with a rudder. Tribe after tribe and people after people have been found who lacked the knowledge of simple physical laws which were utilized by their neighbors. Altogether, mankind has been exceedingly slow in solving the open secrets of the physical universe. There is no knowing how many of them remain undiscovered to-day. Mankind has not been compelled to learn anything.

Its Absolute Nature. The second characteristic which the physical world has presented to man is that it is *absolute*. There are no exceptions. Physical nature is as it is and there is no way on earth that any one or even any group working together can change it one iota.

This is so contrary to human reactions that man has never quite been able to accept it. He has always had a little reserve when confronted with this situation. He has always felt that there must be *some* way by which he could escape the despotism of physical things. Thus throughout human history there has grown up a multitude of fairy stories and accounts of gnomes, witches, genii, or some kinds of deities who controlled physical matter directly without regard to law and order. These creatures were imagined to have the power of doing all sorts of things which were not in harmony with natural law—such as changing pumpkins into coaches, or men into fish. Man's wishful thinking combined with a real and honest ignorance of physical laws has caused him to develop beliefs about magical lamps which could be rubbed and power over matter thereby acquired. These beliefs have taken the form of faith in all kinds of charms and talismans and in intricate formulas and ceremonies. Instead of studying physical nature itself and attempting to discover its laws, man has characteristically spent his energy in attempting to circumvent the laws.

Rich offerings have been made to the gods or other powers in the hope of securing their favor and thereby persuading them to order certain desired results. So desperate have people become that they have made offerings of their richest possessions, even of their own blood, slashing themselves or cutting off fingers and even gouging out eyes. They have sacrificed tens of thousands of human beings at one time, and the number so sacrificed throughout human history must mount into the millions. Zealous and desperate fanatics have even sacrificed their own children or themselves. Probably far more human energy has been expended in this way than has been put forth in intelligent study of these laws which they tried so strenuously to overcome.

Such practices are not limited to savage races. Early christianity was full of such behavior. Holy men and women refused to bathe, slept on stone floors, wore prickly, coarse camel's hair robes next to their bodies, even refused to pick lice and other vermin from their hair and beards. Some lashed themselves with whips until they were streaked with blood. Such things, as a rule in a more moderate form, still continue to be practiced to-day. And in the face of it all physical nature presents the same unchanging, immutable, absolute set of properties and laws. Nature is static and does not compel but is absolute and allows no exceptions.

A Rich and Varied Field. Though static and absolute in its characteristics, physical nature is rich and varied. When man consents to accept it as it is and turns his attention toward utilizing it, the field before him is unlimited and dazzling.

Central in his observed universe is the sun upon which his existence depends in so many ways. Should the sun recede from the earth or approach it by an appreciable distance, life would be a thing of the past. Directly or indirectly, all of our energy may be traced back to the sun.

The very quality of the sun's light is a major factor in human life. Should the ultra violet rays which are so plentiful in the upper strathosphere succeed in getting through to the earth, human life would be snuffed out. Enough of them do get through in the vertical light of the tropics to make life there difficult and perhaps even impossible as a permanent thing for the white race. Professor Ross thinks this tropical light makes monogamous life utterly impossible in that region. He believes one effect of tropical light is to overstimulate the sex drive beyond the point where it can be controlled. Woodruff has argued that the white race cannot even live in the tropics for more than two or three generations at most.[9] He points out the fact that the few white men who live near the equator do not spend their lives in the open sunshine but do office work and live indoors. Other writers have differed from Woodruff, but his arguments are difficult to overcome. At least we can all agree that tropical light is hard on the constitution of a race which has no protective layer of pigment in the skin.

Rains, winds, hurricanes, droughts, and every phase of our weather flow directly from the action of the sun. Destructive though some of these activities may be, they become rich sources of utilizable energy when we contrive means of harnessing them.

Strangely enough we have never yet learned how to utilize the direct energy of the sun to any extent, though we use it in so many indirect forms. When the energy of the sun produces vegetation, we use the plants for food or fuel. When used as fuel we may generate steam or electricity. Vegetation produced millions of years ago is stored up in the form of coal or mineral oils and we use vast quantities of them to do our work for us. Yet we make almost no use of the almost inconceivable amount of energy shed upon the earth by the sun every day. It has been estimated that this energy would be sufficient to stop the rotation of the earth if there was any way of applying it—and provided anybody really wished to do it! Sometimes we arrange a few mirrors in such a way that some quantity of sunlight is reflected on to a tank of water and soon we have generated steam. If this solar engine were ever perfected and made truly practicable it might have a revolutionary effect upon the world. The centers of business and industry would probably be shifted to the desert regions or at least to places where a maximum amount of sunshine could be depended upon. The great coal mining industry, with its multiplied thousands of workers throughout the world would come to a standstill. Gas and oil wells would go begging and filling stations might still exist but they would deal in sunlight-generated batteries rather than in oils and gases. Such cities as Birmingham, Pittsburgh, and Liverpool would practically cease to exist. Foggy places such as London in particular would be hard hit. All major lines of transportation, both ocean lines and railroads would be relocated. In fact, the entire face of the world would be made over.

[9] Charles E. Woodruff, *Expansion of Races,* New York: Rebman Company, 1909.

Even some of the indirect forms of the sun's energy have never been used to the extent that one would think possible. The wind has been used for sailing and to turn windmills for centuries, yet a lot of wind energy goes to waste. It would seem to be a simple thing to store up the energy created by multitudinous windmills in electric storage batteries and then to use it when it is needed. But our engineers have never succeeded in making this practice very satisfactory. For all the use we get of the sun, there are undreamed of possibilities which yet remain for us to tap.

As the sun occupies a central place among physical objects, so the law of gravitation is central among physical forces, at least if combined with the law of inertia. Without gravitation, the very universe, or at least the solar system and many other such systems would not hold together. Rain would not fall, water would not stay in lakes and rivers, houses and other objects would not remain stationary and even man himself would not be able to stay on the face of the earth.

Gravitation, like the sun's energy, has yet to be utilized in many ways. The most obvious waste of gravitational energy is the force of the tides. Man has never discovered a way of using the tides to practical advantage. Perhaps where there is some unusual formation, such as that at Passamaquoddy, some power may be generated. But many of our best scientists are very skeptical whether we shall ever be able to secure much help from the tides.

It would seem that the energy of the waves could be harnessed more easily. Certainly the waves bring to our shores an almost unlimited supply of energy and we stand helplessly and watch them while we burn up our rapidly diminishing supplies of oil and easily accessible coal.

In addition to these more centrally spectacular phases of physical nature, there are multitudinous properties of different substances which may be turned to account. Some materials such as steel and copper are *ductile,* i.e., can be drawn out into wires, sometimes of extreme thinness. If all materials were like granite or chalk, this would be impossible and no wire fences, wire wrapped electrical appliances, no telephone or telegraphs would be possible. Not even a radio could be constructed without wire in our present state of knowledge.

These substances and some others are *malleable* or can be beaten out into thin plates. Without this property we could have no sauce pans, pails, metal cups, roofing, or thin metal tops and bodies for cars and airplanes. The property of *hardness* and the fact that some substances are harder than others makes possible many activities which would otherwise be out of our reach. Our friend, Jethro Tull, would never have been able to cultivate his crops had not iron or even some kinds of wood been harder than the soil. The farm boy could not make a pawpaw or willow whistle and the woodsman could not cut down a tree were iron and steel not harder than wood. Concrete, brick, and steel would make poor walls or foundation for a house if they were no harder than dough or molasses.

The fact that some substances are *elastic* and tend to regain their shape when temporarily distorted makes possible another group of activities. It was the elasticity of seasoned wood which enabled Stone Age man to construct and use his bow and arrow. The elasticity of steel, rubber, and other substances allows for the construction of springs, shock-absorbers, and other such devices. The importance of elasticity may be realized from the fact that the Wright brothers discovered quite early in their experiments that a hollow crank shaft soon cracked in an airplane and a solid shaft had to be employed because of its greater flexibility. Were it not for a certain degree of elasticity an airplane would shake itself to pieces in a few minutes. Any of our modern machines would.

If we may invade the field of biology for a minute we may call attention to the fact that without the elastic cartilages in the joints between our bones we would soon jar ourselves to death.

Most substances possess the property of *cohesion* or the tendency to stick together, though some, such as copper or aluminum, possess a much greater degree than others such as clay or water. If nothing were more cohesive than mercury or air, this would be a most unstable world indeed. On the other hand, life would be impossible if all substances clung together with the tenacity of metal or leather. Other properties of different forms of matter that we need not stop to discuss here have equally important roles to play in the human drama.

Corollary to these properties or growing out of them are certain specified ways in which aggregations of matter act under standard conditions. We may mention *friction* which makes it possible for nails and screws to hold, trains and autos to travel on land, ships to travel in water, and airplanes in air. Friction also allows us to equip our vehicles with brakes or to produce heat. When the Indian strikes one piece of flint against another, a Philippino rubs two bamboo sticks together, or a modern smoker strikes a match, friction is used in each case.

The fact that raising the temperature will cause expansion and lowering it will cause contraction plays its part. It may be such a homely thing as the way a blacksmith heats an iron tire and slips it on a wheel and then pours water on it and causes it to shrink and become tight. It may be the more spectacular application in the expansion of gases in explosives and internal combustion engines, though here chemical action is also involved. When this principle becomes combined with the expansion of crystallization in the freezing of ice, the results are far more important. If it worked in a different way, our streams and rivers would freeze solid to the bottom during the winters and would not thaw out except on top during the summers.

It is unnecessary to more than call attention to the profound influence of electricity and magnetism on human society. What would the world be to-day if all telephones, all telegraphs, all radios, all electric batteries, electromagnets, electrically driven machines and electric therapy were to go out of existence? The Battle of New Orleans was fought several days after the war was over and this was because electrical communication had not been established. We take these things so for granted that we never think of them until some crisis appears. Then we suddenly realize how dependent we are on electrical appliances. When the elevator was out of commission during the Ohio River flood at Pittsburgh the radio artists had to climb stairs to the dizzy height of the broadcasting room. For once they realized the value of electricity! A modern city would soon starve to death were its electrical current completely cut off and if its inhabitants had no way of migration.

The domain of physical matter and the laws which govern it spread out before man in a truly inexhaustible panorama. It is man's adaptation to and utilization of these laws which constitute culture or civilization.

Cumulative Effects of Discoveries and Inventions

It soon becomes apparent that inventions or ways in which the physical forces are utilized have a cumulative effect. Man makes some simple adjustment to the forces around him and this ushers in a whole train of similar new practices. When the internal combustion engine became practicable and autos found their way onto our roads, this was just the beginning. New developments in rubber were called for as well as a whole flock of improvements in the refining of fuel oils and lubricants. New electrical devices found their way under the hoods of cars. Perhaps as difficult a thing to perfect as any was a machine to smash thin such broad sheets of metal that they could be used for car tops. Aside from the hundreds of things which were happening to the cars themselves, there were similarly numerous new features in construction of roads, in garages, filling stations, roadside lunch stands, picnic grounds, tourist camps and many other such features of our modern life.

Booth Tarkington, the gifted fiction writer, matured at just the proper time to see the transformation which the automobile has wrought on American society. He saw the way in which it drove out of existence the picturesque old livery stables, country stores, and thousands of country churches. He was able to appreciate the changes which it brought to the American home, changes so profound that they are beyond the comprehension of our modern young people. He saw also the way it had deeply influenced our educational system, our political structure, and our economic organization. Even our moral and religious beliefs were made over almost in their entirety, simply because the automobile became a practical thing of every day usage. The significant title which he chose for the book in which he discussed this was, *The World Does Move*.[10]

Such a group of practices clustered around some one central element is called a "culture complex" by the anthropologists. In the history of humanity there have been great numbers of such culture complexes. Some that are often mentioned are the "hoe complex" which was followed by the "plough complex." After the white man introduced the horse into America, the Indians of the Plains developed a "horse complex." The horse made over their manner of life in much the same way that the automobile has made over ours.

Sometimes the culture of an entire region centers around some one particular substance or element of the physical environment which because of its special properties lends itself to certain kinds of uses. When this is the case we refer to such a region as a "culture area." Over the Northeastern part of North America the birch

[10] Booth Tarkington, *The World Does Move*, Garden City, N. Y.: Doubleday, Doran and Co., 1929.

tree grew in such abundance that its bark became primary in the culture of those Indians who lived in this region. They made boats of it, the famous birch-bark canoes which aside from the Eskimo kayak are about the best boats which the world has ever known. They made houses of it, and quite satisfactory houses they were. They made baskets of a kind out of this bark and even used it for clothing to a limited degree.

On the Northwest Coast, comprising the seacoast region of Alaska and British Columbia, there grew great quantities of red cedar which could be split into planks and polished. The Indians of this region made plank houses, plank boats, plank boxes, and used planks in many other ways. In the Great Plains region, the Indians lived on Buffalo meat, and made almost everything imaginable out of the skins. They used them for houses, boats, clothing, bedding, shields in warfare, and even for cooking utensils.

All these examples show how one simple utilization of some physical force or property may become the center of a great number of others. In addition to the automobile we can see many such examples in our own civilization. The airplane has developed its own set of accompanying features, such as airports, electric beams, weather reporting stations, etc. It has necessitated great changes in passport laws and practices and has created new and grave problems for immigration and tariff officials. It is hardly necessary to call attention to its revolutionary effect on warfare, but some of its peace-time problems are not so well known. For example, it appears that a dormant type of yellow fever is endemic in South America, but if it were introduced into our country it might become as virulent as it ever was in the days of the dreaded "Yellow Jack." This country has literally billions of the aedes mosquito which carries yellow fever and just one infected mosquito from South America could scatter it abroad all over our country. Is it any wonder that the quite evident possibility of bringing in such a mosquito in a plane from South America gives our various officials a nightmare or that they have developed an elaborate system of spraying and disinfecting these planes?

The telephone and telegraph called out their own groups of accessories and the radio has had more pronounced effects on our lives than an invading army.

The Industrial Revolution was but a series of such inventions or adjustments which followed one another in logical order.

We may expect the same type of thing to happen in the future. Some seemingly unimportant discovery or invention to-day may be destined to make over our civilization as completely as the advent of the bow and arrow did the Stone Age or the introduction of gunpowder did the days of chivalry.

Penalties and Possibilities

We have noted above that animals and primitive men sometimes made mistakes in their adjustments to physical matter and its laws and these occasions were disastrous and even fatal. Civilized man is not exempt from these blunders. Probably he makes more than the animals or savages. He would be expected to since he has so many complicated machines and is always trying out some new thing. Certainly his mistakes are many and terrible. Thousands of boilers have exploded because they were overheated and the pressure became too great. Dams by the hundreds have given way and wiped out whole villages and towns. Ships have proven defective and sunk, airplanes have crashed, parachutes have failed to open, bridges have collapsed, roofs and walls have given way, electric "shorts" have caused fires and wrecked shops, railroad tracks have spread, trains have jumped their tracks, and in thousands of other ways, man has misread the writings of physical nature.

It is always the miscalculations of men which are at fault. Natural laws never behave in irregular or unusual ways.

Some of the mistakes man has made are illuminating in the way they show up human shortcomings. The Iroquois Theatre in Chicago was pronounced absolutely fireproof, and because of its perfect safety it was packed with school children. It might have been fireproof all right if everything had worked according to plan, but the asbestos curtain failed to fall and the interior became an inferno of flame in which more than four hundred perished. When the Titanic was launched she was pronounced unsinkable because of the separate air compartments. But on her maiden voyage an iceberg ripped through her steel skin like so much paper and another tragedy became a monument to man's lack of understanding. The St. Francis Dam in California was supposed to be perfect in construction, and indeed it was. But the engineers failed to test the bed rock on which it was built and the massive concrete walls and huge steel reinforcing rods were crumbled and cut like so much chalk and broom-wire. Although we are learning all the time, we have not yet arrived at the place where we are safe while manipulating the forces of physical nature.

Of late years we have begun to recognize another danger growing out of unwise methods of utilization of nature in addition to such things as explosions and shipwrecks. Our extensive agriculture has resulted in wholly unlooked for and highly alarming conditions. Erosion has increased so gradually that we hardly noticed it until we were rudely awakened to the fact that millions of acres were already destroyed. This eroded soil not only makes farming impossible, but it fills our streams with mud and silt, destroying the fish life and finally silting the river beds until navigation is a thing of the past and destructive floods are the order of the day. A still later development is seen in the dust storms which result from overcropping. The magnitude of these storms may be dimly imagined when we realize that as much as three hundred million tons of top soil have been blown away in one day. The situation is so serious that we are finally realizing that destruction itself is just around the corner if something drastic is not done and done in a hurry. We have played with nature's forces and have released them in ways of which we had not dreamed.

Every one of these disastrous happenings is in harmony with simple physical laws and could have been prevented rather easily had attention been given to the causes. It is within the power of man to halt this destructive action and even repair a part of the damages already done, but to do so we must work in harmony with physical laws and not against them. While we listlessly wait and do nothing the aroused forces of nature quietly carry on their destructive work. Compared to the way in which we dawdle and twiddle our thumbs in the face of national and even human disaster, Nero was a mere piker when he fiddled as Rome burned. If we utilize natural laws properly they will insure our salvation. Neglected or outraged, they will destroy us.

A Look Ahead

It is fascinating to look ahead and speculate on what may lie before us. It is never wise to prophesy except in the most general terms, but there are some things which are so self-evident that we may almost take them for granted.

For one thing, electricity will be used far more widely and probably in many more ways than we have been accustomed to. Already we are seeing just the beginnings of a profound revolution in our manner of living and this revolution will be based in part on electricity.

Another fact which seems certain is that chemistry and physics will come still more closely together and together will bring out some revolutionary discoveries about the nature of sunlight. Already they have found that polarized light has many and peculiar effects. Even the partially polarized light of the "dark of the moon" seems to have an effect on growing vegetation, and it may turn out that the folklore about planting crops in the light or dark of the moon is founded on partial fact. Our strathospheric flights are also resulting in new information concerning light. We may confidently look for new developments in this field which may well be of primary importance to human society.

It is hardly necessary to say that we may look for great developments in the radio, especially television.

Perhaps the most fascinating of all fields which lie just before us is the work of the internal structure of the atom. An atom is an exceedingly small particle, but within its depths a vast store of energy is locked up. It has been said that a single atom contains enough energy to dig the Panama Canal six times over! Our scientists have not yet learned how to control the liberation of this energy on a large scale, and until a few other discoveries are made it is probably just as well that this is so. Should this much energy be liberated suddenly in one explosion, the destruction wrought could hardly be imagined.

Although great strides have been made in the disintegration of the atom, there is far more to do before we can consider ourselves masters of the situation. It requires either millions of volts of electricity or the equivalent in some other form of energy to break up the atoms on which the work has been done to date and some of the more stable elements are still unconquered. But greater condensers are being used and more powerful cyclotrons are being constructed.

Even at the present writing there is in use a cyclotron so big that the magnet alone weighs close to a hundred tons. To protect themselves against the very penetrating radiations which may accompany the process of atomic disintegration, the men who operate this machine are protected by a five-foot-thick lead wall. When we realize that a cyclotron twenty times this size is in process of construction, it seems safe to say that we can expect still more startling discoveries concerning the release of subatomic energy.

Already the products of the cyclotron are finding practical utilization in the sciences, the industries, and above all medicine. Strangely enough the lighter elements become temporarily radioactive after bombardment by the cyclotron and can be used in place of radium for treatment of cancer. It does not yet appear what the future holds for humanity.

While the outlook is so beset with revolutionary possibilities that it is fairly dazzling, it must not be forgotten that there are dangers lurking ahead of us also. We have made many costly blunders in the past and there is every reason to believe that we shall make more in the future. The situation has not changed since the first animals peered forth and began investigating the world. In physical law there abides abundant life or inexorable death.

CONCLUSION

In conclusion we need only recapitulate what we have been saying. Man is a creature of the physical earth, inescapably bound to it, and subject to physical laws. Man is actually a product of physical nature and is so adjusted and constructed that life under any other conditions would be impossible. Should the temperature vary just a few degrees from what it is man would perish. If sunlight contained just a little more or a little less ultra violet light our doom would be sealed. Should the laws of physics be slightly different— as for example if ice would sink—if gravitation did not exist, if friction did not work, if inertia were non-existent, life would be utterly impossible.

Mankind has his existence on an exceedingly thin knife edge, so thin in fact that it is startling and even alarming to contemplate it. Yet, narrow as the edge is which physical nature gives us for our habitation, there is plenty of room thereon for abundant and sparkling life, provided only that the laws of nature are understood and utilized and we order our manner of living in harmony with them.

SELECTED LIST OF REFERENCES

Bossard, J. H. S. (Editor), *Man and His World*, New York: Harpers, 1932, 755 p.—A general introduction to social science with some emphasis on physical factors.

Clemens, Samuel L. (Mark Twain), *A Connecticut Yankee in King Arthur's Court* (Published by various publishing houses in different editions).—This is popularly supposed to be merely a humorous book but in reality is a searching criticism of many existing social customs and a fine picture of social life before our present knowledge of physical laws.

Comte, Auguste, *The Positive Philosphy of Auguste Comte*, Translated by Harriet Martineau, London: G. Bell and Sons, 1913.—Comte's positivism and the way in which he based social phenomena on physical laws can be secured from many other sources, such as encyclopedias and books on social theory.

Kelsey, Carl, *The Physical Basis of Society*, New York: D. Appleton and Co., 1925, 406 p.—The first chapter deals with physical properties and laws.

Ogburn, William F., ''The Influence of Inventions on American Social Institutions in the Future,'' *American Journal of Sociology*, Vol. XLIII, No. 3, November, 1937, pp. 365–376; ''Technology and Sociology,'' *Social Forces*, Vol. XVII, No. 1, October, 1938, pp. 1–8.—Ogburn shows in these two papers how the utilization of certain physical laws and principles determines the characteristics of any society.

Richards, Harold, *The Universe Surveyed*, New York: Van Nostrand, 1937, 722 p. —In the preface the author discusses the relationship between physical science and social conditions.

Spencer, Herbert, *First Principles*, New York: D. Appleton and Co., 1916, 550 p.

Tarkington, Booth, *The World Does Move*, Garden City, N. Y.: Doubleday Doran and Co., 1929, 294 p.—This is an autobiography, the central theme of which is the part played by the automobile in changing the social life of the country.

Tillett, Alfred W., *Spencer's Synthetic Philosophy*, London: P. S. King and Son, 1914, 177 p.—This is a brief, easy, and unusually clear interpretation of Spencer's philosophy.

Webb, W. P., *The Great Plains*, New York: Ginn and Company, 1931, 525 p.— This is an account of the development of the Great Plains. The author explains the development by the invention of three things—barbed wire, the six-shooter, and the windmill.

Woodruff, Charles E., *Expansion of Races*, New York: Rebman Company, 1909, 495 p.—Woodruff discusses the influence of tropical light and claims that it makes it impossible for a pure white race to live permanently in the tropics.

Chapter 3

CHEMICAL REGULARITIES

By Dr. R. F. Bellamy

Florida State College for Women, Tallahassee, Florida

In the introduction to the preceding chapter, attention was called to the fact that man is inseparably bound to the physical earth and helpless to change its laws by ever so infinitesimal a bit. A full share of these laws are chemical laws. For our own convenience we limit the term "chemical" to mean any action which changes the structure of the molecule. Modern laboratory practices are making this distinction archaic, but for ordinary practical purposes it serves very well. Physics has to do with levers and pulleys and machines, with the properties of different substances, with inertia and momentum and all forms of what we call physical work. Chemistry is the field of acids and alkalies, of the compounding of drugs, perfumes, medicines, condiments, paints and fuel oils.

CHEMICAL PROCESSES IN BIOLOGY

Chemistry plays an important role in every phase of nature. All biological processes are chemical. The late Dr. Slosson once said, "Every kitchen is a chemical laboratory, and so is the cook." What he meant was that in the cook's body a multitude of chemical processes were taking place all the time. The distinction between plant and animal life is chemical, and the bridge between them, or the method by which they are linked together and made dependent upon each other is a chemical link. There could be no animal life, and hence no human life or human society were it not for these chemical processes which take place in the bodies of plants.

Chemical Action and Food Supply

Henry Buckle noticed that every race which has ever become numerous and significant in world affairs has had some starch food as its main source of nourishment. The Japanese, Chinese, and other oriental peoples live largely on rice; European peoples center their eating around wheat, rye, barley, or oats; the Irish people sprang into prominence only after the potato had been introduced into their island; the American Indians lived on corn, and the Arabians have dates which give them starch in the modified form of sugar. Starch is a cheap food wherever it occurs, and while it is not a sufficient food in itself, it furnishes heat and energy in large quantities.

If human life in dense masses is dependent upon starch, starch is dependent upon the chemical process known as photosynthesis—the process by which sunlight uses the green chlorophyll in plant tissue to make starch out of air and water.

If starch is a cheap food, proteids are generally expensive. Meats, butter, milk, beans and peas are the more costly portions of our foods. Proteids as well as starch go back to the chemical processes of plant life. Strangely enough it would seem, only one group of plants, the legumes, have the power to take nitrogen directly from the air—even though some three-fourths of this air is nitrogen—and make it available for animals and for other plants. It is this process of nitrogen fixation which the legumes possess which causes the farmer to plant clover, peas, and other legumes to enrich his soil.

This one chemical fact has figured largely in the social affairs of the world during late years. Japan took over control of Manchuria partly for the purpose of trade. But the main thing which they wished to trade for was the Manchurian "bean-cake," the residue left after the oil had been pressed out of Manchurian soy beans. This cake is a marvelous fertilizer for Japanese soil and is a practical necessity if Japan is to raise crops.

Recently man has partially solved this problem of nitrogen fixation, and now by the use of sufficient power he can extract nitrogen directly from the air. Just this partial solution has had far reaching social significance. It has had disastrous economic effects on Chile since the Chilean deposits of nitrates are no longer so necessary for the world. It precipitated a political storm in the United States during the years immediately following the World War. A great governmental project was started at Muscle Shoals on the Tennessee River for the purpose of extracting nitrogen from the air and using it to make explosives. As by-products, electricity and nitrogenous fertilizer were to be made. As we got farther from the war, we heard less about the manufacture of explosives, but the political disputes grew even hotter. After years of bitter congressional and editorial controversies, it eventuated in the T.V.A.

Perhaps we shall some day discover how to endow this artificially extracted nitrogen with vitamins and make palatable food out of it. If we ever do, the whole face of the social world will be changed.

Other chemical processes in the bodies of plants are similarly significant for human life and social organization. In the process of photosynthesis, oxygen is liberated and thus the carbon dioxide produced by animals is kept in balance. Plants and animals in the highly organized forms in which we know them could not live without each other.

Chemicals and Soil Exhaustion

If we want to take a sufficiently long view, the end of all life, both plant and animal, may result from the exhaustion of certain chemical compounds. Potash and phosphate are necessary for plant life, hence for animal life, and man has never yet learned how to make them artificially. They are both quite soluble and are gradually being dissolved and washed away into the sea. By strenuous efforts, man can get some of these substances back but not in sufficient quantities to be of any great significance. Perhaps at some far distant time, all the potash and phosphate will have been dissolved away and plants and animals will inhabit the earth no more.

Animal Life

Chemical processes play an important role in the bodies of animals as well as in plants. Our very life is chemical. Every breath we breathe is a chemical process. The air which enters our lungs and the blood which reaches through a thin membrane to shake hands with it are neither the same chemically after the greeting. Waking or sleeping, night and day, throughout all our lives, this chemical process must be kept continuous. Stop it for a few brief minutes and life is a thing of the past.

Racial Differences

Pronounced racial and therefore social differences have arisen out of this one process. In the hot air of the tropics, the nasal passages are broad and short and we have the flat nose and large nostrils of the Negro, while in more northern regions the nose is narrow and long. Circumpolar air breathed through broad short nostrils strikes the lungs unheated and may result in congestion and hence colds, pneumonia, and tuberculosis. It may very well be that the Negro races will never be able to establish themselves in a region that is very distant from the tropics, at least in those regions where germs of these diseases live.

Less direct social phenomena can be traced back to the variations of this same chemical reaction. Since we are accustomed to seeing long thin noses, we think they are beautiful and our art is full of them. The Negro, on the other hand, considers them hideous until he has lived in a white civilization and has been compelled to accept white standards. There is no way in which we can prove that a long nose is more artistic than a broad one. When we stand enraptured before a Grecian statue or exclaim over the lines of a Burne-Jones painting, we are reacting that way simply because the chemical process of respiration has dictated that the noses of our geographical region must be long and spindly.

Digestion, reproduction, growth, decay, life, disease, and death are chemical. There is always a certain amount of wasting away and dissolution in the different parts of the body, but the moment death occurs a general decay sets in. So long as the organism as a whole is living, this does not occur, though our best chemists are not able to tell us exactly why.

A good many of our racial differences are based on the assimilation of different foods. The African and Asiatic are offensive because of their odor to the European. On the other hand, a white man, even one freshly out of a bath, has a pronounced odor which is distasteful to an oriental. Some considerable part of our prejudices are based on these mutually disagreeable odors. Yet the differences disappear if the two races live under the same conditions and eat the same foods.

Chemical Action and Mental Activity

Even our thought is chemically exerted. Psychological researches have caused some to deny this and to say that there is no indication that any kind of energy is expended during the process of thought. But certainly the brain must be supplied with blood and there are definite chemical changes which take place in nerve tissue. When the central nerve cells send out an impulse along a nerve fiber, it is accompanied by chemical reactions and the reactions and the response of the muscles and glands involve chemical changes.

Glandular Secretions

The most spectacular phase of chemical action in animal and especially human life is that connected with the ductless glands.[1] It appears that all our traits of character as well as our physical appearances can be traced back to these glands. (This does not nullify or lessen the importance of training or education. It merely means that the training works upon the potentialities which are based on glandular structure. The training may even modify the glands themselves on occasion, as in the inculcation of healthful habits which would cause normal glandular development.) Certainly many physical characteristics, such as height, weight, shape of face and body, and at least in some instances color of the skin can be traced back directly to glandular action. The differences between the pygmies and giants is ultimately a difference in the chemical secretions of such glands as the thyroid, the thymus, the pituitary, and the entire system functioning together. Perhaps we could in the course of a generation change the entire race of Negritos into a race as tall as the Scotch by a simple process of glandular surgery! At least we can make such changes in individual cases. However, in our present state of knowledge the changes would not be inherited.

When we mention the chemical action of glands, we enter the field of psychology. We have already noted that the processes of thought are accompanied by chemical action. Evidences are not lacking that the differences in chemical action account for profound mental and emotional differences. It is all very well for us to become irritated with an excessively nervous child or even adult and say, "Oh, quit being so nervous." But it is utterly impossible for one to escape excessive nervousness when the tiny parathyroid glands are out of order. Extreme depression may result from no external cause, but merely accompany a disorganized condition of the thyroid or some other gland. In such a case, all the preaching, exhortation, and "cheering up" in the world will be of little avail, but a shot of glandular secretion may transform our morose individual into one who is happy and optimistic.

General mental ability is conditioned by glandular differences. (For that matter it is well to remember that the brain itself is a gland.)[2] An improperly developed thyroid results in cretinism,

[1] George A. Dorsey, *Why We Behave Like Human Beings*, New York: Harper and Bros., 1925.

[2] The brain does not "secrete thought" but a specific fluid which acts as a lubricant.

which is marked by pronounced physical characteristics as well as mental deficiency. It is more than probable that many if not all forms of feeblemindedness will eventually be found to rest upon glandular deficiencies or diseases. Insanities also may have the same base, at least in some cases.

If mental and emotional differences are based on glandular chemistry, most certainly sex differences are. The controversy which rages over the presence, absence, or amount of difference in the mental and emotional natures of male and female will be answered eventually by appeal to the glands. We know that the removal of the sex glands in either sex results in pronounced mental changes, especially if it is done in early life. Strangely enough a woman will lose here "feminine" characteristics if the cortex of her suprarenal gland is destroyed by a tumor or from some other cause. In such a case, her muscles grow hard, her voice coarsens somewhat, she grows a thin and scraggly but nevertheless quite unfeminine beard, and—most interesting of all—she loses interest in her personal appearance.

So pronounced an effect does glandular action have on our mental reactions that it even affects our physical powers. Under certain emotional stresses, the suprarenal glands become unusually active and throw quantities of adrenaline into the blood. On such occasions, one performs acts which are far and away beyond the possibilities under normal conditions. Heavy loads will be lifted, great speed attained, and fatigue will not appear. During the excitement of a fire or in the heat of battle this phenomenon is most apt to make its appearance.

Influence of Drugs

The influence of chemistry in psychological action is not limited to action through glandular secretions. Drugs produced external to the human body have their characteristic effects, reaching, of course, to death itself. Drugs may stupefy, deaden, or stimulate. They may affect our morals as well as our mental life. Following a dose of Spanish fly, it is useless to expect the victim to remain chaste or virtuous. On the other hand if one drinks from a gypsum spring or takes potassium nitrate the sex appetite is weakened or even destroyed. Marijuana destroys all sense of values, while alcohol, opium, hashish, heroin, and other such drugs have their characteristic effects. Chemicals even have been given to criminals to make them tell the truth.

Another way in which chemical action may have a psychological effect is through light, especially those rays which lie beyond the violet end of the spectrum. In the last chapter we referred to Ross's statement that tropical light makes monogamy impossible.

Chemistry and Social Processes

When chemical action plays such an important role in these different departments of life, it is to be expected that it is of paramount importance to the sociologist. We have already noted various social reactions which go back to the production of starch and proteids, to variations in respiration and to a few other forms of chemical action. These are mere driblets compared to the great stream of chemical influences which flows through human society.

Widespread social disturbances can be traced back to a chemical base. Specialists in the study of the family say that many cases of incompatibility and divorces go back to a lack of sex adjustment. The chemical and hence mental reactions are often so utterly different that there can be no harmony. And the prevalence of cretinism, and those forms of disorganized growth and health, feeble-mindedness, and insanity which we have mentioned constitute a profound social problem and affect society to its core.

Could we analyze it to its depth, we would find that much crime goes back to glandular chemistry, particularly sex crimes.[3] The more horrible and revolting such a crime is, the greater the probability that it flows from the compulsion of disorganized glands. Should we attain complete understanding of the chemical background of crime, that would not in itself eliminate the crime. There would still be the problem of what to do with the individual who was so affected. However, this knowledge should help us anticipate the overt criminal actions and enable us to take steps to prevent at least a good many of them.

At present chemistry functions not only in the causation of crime, but in the solution of it.[4] The Sherlock Holmes of today who is working on some difficult case is apt to be a mild-mannered scholarly fellow who peers into a microscope and boils various substances over a Bunsen burner. It is a matter of commonplace knowledge that human blood can be detected easily and accurately today. No

[3] Max G. Schlapp and Edward H. Smith, *The New Criminology*, New York: Boni, 1925.

[4] Henry M. Robinson, *Science Versus Crime*, Indianapolis: Bobbs-Merrill, 1935.

longer can a murderer escape by claiming that the blood on his over-
alls is rabbit blood. But this is child's play to the type of chemical
work which is done in the solution of some crimes.

One case may be noted as an illustration of the methods employed.
In a New York basement two poorly and raggedly dressed men were
found dead. Each had a twenty-dollar bill in his pocket and no
other money. The circumstances were so peculiar that it was hailed
as the great and baffling mystery of the time. A chemist was put on
the task and he heated the lungs of one of these men in a retort, dis-
tilling out just two drops of liquid. In these two drops he found a
trace of lead. This indicated to him that death had probably occurred from inhalation of gasoline which had lead tetra ethyl in it.
A further investigation disclosed the fact that in another part of
the basement there was a pile of excelsior and other trash which also
showed traces of lead.

From this much to go on, the crime was reconstructed. It was
reasoned that these two nameless men had been hired to set fire
to the building and given twenty dollars each. They had poured
gasoline on the excelsior, but just at that time some one had come
along and they had waited to set fire to it. While waiting the fumes
had killed them and later the gasoline had evaporated. With this
much to go on, the guilty party was apprehended and finally induced to make a full confession. But the essential evidence was
the trace of lead in the two drops of liquid distilled from the man's
lungs.

In the history of human society, chemical drugs have played a
major part. Alcohol seems to occupy the center of this stage. All
races have some form of alcoholic drink—except the Eskimo who
has nothing from which to make it. Apparently alcohol has done
its share in bringing about social intercourse and inter-tribal relations in the past. Plato had noticed the characteristic effects of
alcohol when he said that legislative bodies should *discuss* proposed
measures in the evening but not *vote* on them until the next morning.
His idea was that they would speak more freely when a little "lit
up," but that they would vote more intelligently in the morning
after they had become sober.

Aside from its direct effect upon the consumer, alcohol has had
a profound influence in human society. Those of us who have a
vivid memory of political campaigns when this century was very
young will recall that they seemed to be concerned largely with

acrimonious discussions over what to do about the trade in alcohol. Not only politicians but every one else spent his energy on this question. The W.C.T.U. held thousands of oratorical contests for which they gave bronze, silver, gold and diamond-studded medals. Preachers and Sunday school workers made this question central. Then came our "noble experiment" which could not possibly be responsible for everything blamed on it but which certainly did have a profound effect. The chemical action of fermentation has certainly done its share in agitating human society.

Lest anyone should conclude that fermentation is the demon in the scheme of things, we may point out that its significance for human society is not limited to its effects in alcohol. It is fermentation which makes vinegar and other acids and thus furnishes preservatives. It is the beginning of this process which makes bread rise.

Other drugs with their characteristic chemical action have powerfully influenced human society. The habit effects of tobacco and the social organization based on tobacco cultivation and on the manufacture and distribution of cigarettes and cigars are well known. Betel-nut, coco, and recently marijuana as a consequence of their chemical action have widespread social results.

Other chemical actions, aside from those of drugs, have played their parts. The fact that food decays, i.e., breaks up and recombines into other chemical products, has been important. Early migration routes and trade routes were often determined by the quest for salt. Salt is a fair preservative and was eagerly sought by early humanity. The "salt tax" figured largely in the troubles which preceded the French Revolution. Even such a modern agitator as Gandhi, when he wanted to show defiance to the British government, did not break a window or strike a soldier. He merely went down to the sea-coast, dipped up a little sea water and allowed it to evaporate.

In whatever direction we look, society is influenced, conditioned, stimulated, or otherwise affected by chemical reactions which go steadily on in nature's laboratory. From the first breath a baby draws until the final dissolution of his body, his life has been chemical. These reactions take place independently of human guidance and would continue just the same were there no men on earth. It remains for us now to observe the way man has used the chemical forces for his own ends.

CHEMISTRY AND HUMAN CULTURE

It would be a mistake to believe that some man or some group of men suddenly realized that they could manipulate chemical processes for their own good and began at once to conduct experiments and achieve results. On the contrary, earliest man and even the animals ordered their lives along the lines of chemical principles long, long before the dawn of what we might call the scientific spirit.

Instinctive Adjustments to Chemical Actions

It is amazing to see how much chemical knowledge—or instinct, call it what you will—the lower animals employ. In the selection of their food, no trained dietitian could do as well. They seem to have known all about vitamins millions of years ago. Only recently have we come to realize that liver is such a rich and valuable food. Less than a generation ago it was considered hardly fit for human consumption and was generally given to cats and dogs. Yet the British eagles feed their young exclusively on grouse liver. If squirrels or other animals eat a mushroom or other plant, it is fairly safe for human beings to eat it. The squirrels know the edible mushrooms better than the best botanists do. However, it is not entirely safe for man to follow the food habits of the lower animals, as some of them, especially the birds, can eat foods which are poisonous to man.

It would be fascinating to know how these animals have attained such detailed chemical knowledge. It must be the result of many thousands of years of trial and error, of elimination and survival. Another feature of their behavior which is mystifying is that when taken out of their own environment it is impossible for them to make such intelligent choices. H. L. Stoddard reports that Mexican quail imported into Florida will eat the Coffee Berry and die, but native Florida quail cannot be induced to eat it. Domestic cattle and horses on our western plains sometimes eat the loco-weed and become seriously affected or "locoed" as the local expression is. But there is no mention that this ever happened to the buffalo.

Early Man's Chemical Adaptations

One of the first and undoubtedly one of the most important of man's discoveries was how to make and use fire. The process of making fire is physical, but once made, its action is chemical.

Fire plays such an important role in our lives that it is difficult for us to imagine human beings existing without it, though a few simple groups have done so, notably the Tasmanians. When fire came into use, the chemical background of human society was greatly changed. The first and most significant use—and this is still true to-day—was the cooking of food. Many substances which had been too tough for general consumption now became important articles of food.

Fire worked quite as great a change in the non-material phases of group life, due to the fact that the chemical action of combustion releases heat and produces light. Outside there were coldness and darkness and all kinds of dangers. But within the cave or even within the tribal circle there were warmth and light and safety. Wild animals would not venture near the fire. Expressions of satisfaction and pleasure were seen on the faces around and it was impossible not to develop a group feeling. When a tired, hungry, cold, and badly frightened early man neared his camp a great transformation came over him, and it was natural that he should develop associations of safety and pleasure with fire and the group. Probably the two perfumes which have caused the greatest amount of pleasure and have had the deepest emotions associated with them have been the odor of wood smoke and roasting meat. They still have an exhilarating effect on us when we go camping or on picnics.

Another field of chemical developments was opened when it was discovered how to smelt iron and other metals. In all probability it was discovered accidentally. When iron became available life was never more the same. Slowly the use of iron became more general and more and more different uses were found for it. Chipped stone was a matter of physical forces only, but the production of iron required chemical action. Human society as it is today could not exist without smelting. Everything from pins and safety razors to ocean liners and structural steel go back to the discovery of smelting.

Fire and smelting were not the only chemical discoveries made in this prescientific period. Fermentation was practiced or at least recognized and its products utilized. Various combinations were made in the preparation of food, and quite an elaborate variety of paints were in use. Altogether, even the Stone Age man made quite a respectable number of uses of somewhat complicated chemical actions.

Beginnings of Deliberate Investigations

The Middle Ages alchemist was the forerunner of our modern chemist. To be sure, he had never achieved the appreciation of precise physical laws and he mixed up his chemical knowledge with much magic and superstition. He still marked his pot with a cross to keep the devil out of it so it would not explode, and thus started the name "crucible" which the chemist's pot retains to this day. He performed many mystic rites and incantations and cast numerous spells over his laboratory. But he did a lot of experimenting and his discoveries affected society greatly. It was out of the mystified searchings of these men that gunpowder and many other things still in use had their birth.

Strangely enough, some of the alchemist's wildest ideas seem to be coming back into respectable company. What the alchemist attempted more strenuously than anything else was to make gold out of a "baser" metal. During modern times, this has been the standard joke of all "reasonable" and "scientific" people. Now we realize their quest was not so wild after all. The bombardment of the giant cyclotron has changed sodium to magnesium, aluminum to phosphorus, and nitrogen to boron. Our chemists may yet create gold in quantity.

MODERN SCIENTIFIC CHEMISTRY

Like everything else, alchemy had to pass, and scientific chemistry was born. It was not a case of instantaneous birth, but rather a slow growth or metamorphosis by which our modern chemistry arrived. The end is not yet, but in the modern laboratory greater things are accomplished than the ancient myth-maker could imagine for his genii or wizards.

Significance of Minute Particles

One of the facts which chemists have discovered is the tremendous force which some of their reagents have. When they succeeded in combining nitrogen and glycerine and soaking gelatin full of it, they had produced something which would resolve itself into new chemical compounds in a practically instantaneous way and expand so greatly that its disruptive force was greater than anything previously known. They searched literature for a name which would express this force and finally named it from the Greek word for spirit, "dynamos," and called it dynamite. But dynamite is weak and impotent compared to some chemicals.

Dorsey reports that if one ounce of adrenin were mixed with enough water to fill a procession of street sprinklers twenty miles long it would be strong enough to cause a uterus suspended in it to contract.[5] But even adrenin is weak by comparison with a pituitary hormone which would have the same effect if mixed with enough water to fill five thousand miles of street sprinklers! This mixture would be equivalent to one part of pituitary hormone and 18,750,000,000 parts of water.

Actual practical use is made of reactions produced in this way. Oyster fishermen were disturbed because the oysters would not stick to their bases but would be washed away. They appealed to the chemists to discover what was the matter and the chemists reported that they needed copper in the water. Copper brushes were fastened to a boat and dragged through the water just once, yet that was all that was needed to make oysters attach themselves firmly. When we realize that the tidal currents run back and forth every day, it seems impossible that *any* copper could remain in the water. Yet the single exposure of copper to the water was all that was needed.

Almost equally small quantities of copper have been added to the soil to cure certain plant diseases.

The chemist must work with such exceedingly small portions of matter that at times it taxes our imagination to conceive of them. Certain diseases, such as goiter, may be cured by minute quantities of some unknown substance in food or water. It has been supposed that a diet rich in iodine would prevent goiter and the almost total lack of it along the South Carolina coast has been cited as proof. Certain it is that a rich iodine diet will build up a goiter patient greatly *for a short time*. Yet goiter is unusually plentiful around Puget Sound where the kelp beds dot the ocean, the air fairly reeks with iodine, and the fish which are eaten in such quantities are full of it. It is probably not the iodine but minute quantities of some other substance which is the real factor in the case.

The observed facts often go far beyond the skill of the chemist to analyze, at least up to this time, though the technique is being constantly refined and he may be able to master this problem any day. But the fact that he cannot find the substance which causes

[5] George A. Dorsey, *Why We Behave Like Human Beings*, New York: Harper and Bros., 1925.

the characteristic reactions is evidence that it must exist in almost infinitesimal quantities. Perfumes made from flowers which grow in southern France may be analyzed and synthetic perfumes made with exactly the same formulas, but they will not produce the same odor. The chemist cannot tell what the difference is, but it may be detected.

There are times when these minute differences have great and far-reaching social effects. The medicinal plants which grow in the region of southern Virginia may be grown elsewhere and appear to be identical, but they will not have quite the same medicinal qualities.

Hydrangeas are usually blue in Florida but pink in California. The color may be modified somewhat by putting proper chemicals in the soil, but it is evident that these are not exactly the cause of the difference. Finally, there is the difference in the taste of our food. An expert can tell whether the lamb he is eating was fed on clover or alfalfa—which the chemist cannot do. Differences in the taste of milk, meat, butter, and eggs may be noted fairly easily. In general the farther north anything will grow the better flavor it has. Scientists suspect that this is due to the difference in light, but this has not been established definitely. Tomatoes raised in northern Montana have a fresh fruity flavor and are good eaten with cream and sugar as one might eat fresh peaches or berries or figs. It is devastating to imagine what would happen if one tried to eat tomatoes grown in the southern part of the country with cream and sugar! Maine sweet corn has a taste all its own which distinguishes it from that grown in the middle tier of states, while the sweet corn grown on the Gulf can hardly be distinguished from ordinary field corn.

All these differences are due to minute quantities of some chemical substances which the chemist can sometimes find but which he more often cannot. Profound social effects flow from these differences. The location of wineries and the grape-growing industry, the manufacture of perfumes, the raising of flowers, vegetables, and even meat animals is greatly affected. The last principle mentioned —that of the better flavored fruit growing further north—has quite a noticeable effect. Horticulturists will always be found growing fruits where there is danger of a freeze. California and Florida are both too far north for oranges to be grown safely. The orange raisers must spend great sums of money for smudge pots, brushwood fires and other ways of preventing the destruction of their crops and even their trees. In spite of all these precautions they periodically lose great sums of money by the freezing of their crops. They are too far north to raise oranges—and that is why they will always raise them. The fact that they are so far north secures the better flavor. A little farther north, peach growers and apple men will be found fighting the climate and losing out to it frequently. Like the orange growers, they raise their fruit just as far north as possible.

Equipped with his knowledge of chemical laws and principles and supplied with modern laboratory devices, the chemist turns out new developments, one after the other, and there seems to be no limit to the possibilities. With a frequency which makes us blasé, we read of discoveries, any one of which a few years ago would have caused intense world-wide excitement.

Fertilizers and Insecticides

One of the fields in which much work is being done is that of agriculture. We have already mentioned the way in which nitrogen is taken directly from the air to serve as fertilizer. This is merely the beginning of the work in fertilizers. There are chemical laboratories which raise many thousands of plants for experimental purposes. They have developed and are still developing chemical substances which will greatly accelerate the growth of roots. They have others which will hold back root growth or retard other vegetative processes. It might seem that this last would be a useless discovery, but such is not the case. By retarding growth during the early months of the year, plants may be kept from budding until danger from frost is over. This alone may result in the saving of millions of dollars.

All sorts of questions arise which the chemist is called upon to solve. Pecan trees "rosette" or grow their leaves in dense bunches and refuse to produce nuts. Corn stalks show a red stain at the joints and ears refuse to set on. Wheat straw is too brittle and the wheat falls over before it is ready to harvest. Dozens of such problems arise to vex the farmer, and the chemist must furnish the solution. In some cases the solution is easy and simple, while in others it takes years of expensive research to arrive at even a partial solution. In most cases, it is eventually found that a certain chemical, sometimes in minute quantities, needs to be applied to the soil either to supply a needed deficiency or to neutralize some destructive element which is present.

Chemistry comes to the aid in the fight against organic foes as well as against inorganic deficiencies. New pests, insects or fungus growths, are constantly appearing and often it is quite a problem to devise a scheme of combating them. One of the first problems was to compound a poison for insects which would be harmless to man. This was easy compared with some of the other tasks which have appeared. This can be illustrated by any one of a great number of cases, but the caterpillar which attacked the peach crop a few years ago will do very well. This caterpillar attacked only the ripe or nearly ripe fruit and hence corrosive substances could not be used as a spray. If a poison was applied, the caterpillar calmly bit off a mouthful and spit it out and then proceeded to eat out the pulp without ever again touching the skin of the peach. It is problems of this kind which give the chemist a headache.

This same chemical warfare includes the combat against house pests such as roaches, flies, and vermin of all kinds. Of late years the termites have proved to be so destructive that much attention has been given to their control, and the chemist has actually succeeded in devising practicable means of preventing their destructive work. And when a project like digging the Panama Canal is attempted, it takes a veritable army of chemists to work out a successful method of controlling the mosquitoes.

Crop Selection According to Chemical Content

Not only in the development of fertilizers and plant foods and insecticides, but in the content of the agricultural product itself, the chemist has had a part to play. Two ears of corn may be the same size and similar in appearance, but on chemical analysis turn out to be greatly different. If one is richer in oil than the other, this difference will mean tons of oil in a few acres of corn. By continuous selection based on the chemist's findings, great changes have been made in many agricultural products. A notable example is the sugar beet which has been improved in sugar content until it runs a higher percentage of sugar than the best Louisiana sugar cane.

Recently chemists have gone so far as to make it possible to raise crops without soil. Plants are kept in vessels of water and fed just the combination of chemicals which they need. They achieve better results than the more conventional farmers, sometimes even amazing results. As much as seven bushels of tomatoes have been raised on one tomato plant.

This is not such a pure gain as one might suppose since the chemicals which they use have their ultimate source in the soil. It has not made man independent of the earth. But it already has practical applications and will almost certainly have many more. Some of the Pacific Islands on which we are establishing air fields and radio stations are totally unfit for raising any kind of vegetation. This soilless agriculture is being established there so that the attendants and their families can have fresh fruits and vegetables.

Secondary Processes

Chemistry plays a role equally as great in industry as in agriculture. Few of our foods at present are brought to the table in their original form. Even cooking is a chemical process, but cooking does not exhaust the chemical actions which take place. The ripening of cheese is bacteriological, but it is the chemical change which gives it its flavor. The same is true of butter and buttermilk. Highly involved chemical action has taken place in the preparation of some commercial foods such as syrups, pickles, such desserts as Jello and other gelatins, and even fermented foods such as sauerkraut. It is the chemical action of rennet which curdles milk and makes cheese possible; it is chemical action which changes fruit juices to vinegar. It is chemical action of the acid in sour milk mixing with soda which releases carbon dioxide and makes biscuits rise. It is the blending of chemicals which determines the aroma of coffee and tea.

The chemist has produced many foods which were originally considered substitutes but which we would not think of labelling "ersatz" to-day. It was only a few years ago that vegetable cooking oils were openly advertised as substitutes for lard. It was difficult to get them accepted, too, but now they are generally considered the proper shortening and lard is not desired. When the chemist secured a usable oil from cottonseed, corn and other such grains and seeds, his work was partially done. By running hydrogen through these clear liquids, they were changed into a white, creamy, half-hard substance closely resembling lard. This raised the boiling point and made it a better cooking substance. It also made it look like the lard to which housewives had been accustomed and it was much more readily accepted.

Syrups and sugars were secured from the same sources which supplied the oils and like them were not at all popular at first. Corn syrup would be marketed under some such trade name as "Angel Food Syrup" and if any one said, "Why that is nothing but corn syrup" it would have a disastrous effect on the sales. Now the manufacturers seem to take great pride in labelling their products by their proper names. Many of our breakfast foods have been changed by chemical action until they are no longer recognizable.

Still greater events may be expected. Authorities are now prophesying that within a few years we shall raise cotton primarily for a *proteid* food which will be made from the seed. Next in importance will be the oil, and last of all will be the lint. At present European countries, notably Germany, are experimenting almost frantically with substitute foods. They have, for example, made edible oils out of mineral products. It remains to be seen what actual food values these ersatz materials have.

In this country manufacturers have at times deliberately attempted to make substitute foods for special purposes, such as producing foods which would resemble meat and have most of the food values of meat but which would be acceptable to the vegetarians. Substitute or denatured coffees, teas, and even beverages which resembled beers and wines have been made. In cases like this, the list of substitute foods has greatly widened.

Clothing materials seem to lend themselves to the chemist's ends even more readily than foods. Years ago a passable leather was being made out of paper—and, of course, paper was made from wood or even straw. Much silk was made of tin, or rather other substances were tin treated to form a silk-like material. Our chemists today have gone far beyond this. We thought it was a big step when they made "fiber silk" or Rayon out of wood, but today they make a much finer textile out of air, coal, and water and label it "Nylon." They even make an artificial wool out of skimmed milk.

The utilization of skimmed milk in the industries forms a most interesting chapter in the social significance of chemical work. When our centralized creameries were developed, the cream alone was used and the remainder of the milk was thrown away. Thousands of tons of milk were thus wasted every day. This shocked the chemists and they began hunting for ways in which it could be used. So successful were they that some one has said they now make everything from fish hooks to silk dresses out of milk. This may be a slight exaggeration, but they do make many unexpected things, including an especially fine glue which has been used widely in the making of airplaines.

In building materials, the chemist rules supreme. Primitive man built houses of many different materials—wood, earth, skins, stone, bark, snow, etc., but he used the materials as he found them. Modern man uses practically nothing except wood without changing its chemical structure. Even when he uses stone he fastens it together with artificially constructed cement or mortar. More and more the entire wall is being made of some such product. The great structures of to-day, such as Norris Dam or Boulder Dam, or even our skyscrapers could not be constructed at all without these products of chemical transformation. Structural steel is not only smelted but goes through many processes of annealing or tempering and is alloyed with several other metals.

As important as these heavier and more ponderous substances are in our civilization it is probable that they are not so essential as lighter and more perishable matter. Lester F. Ward was impressed with the fact that our houses, books, etc., tend to become less heavy and solid. He said that the age of concrete and steel had really passed its prime and that we are now living in an age of paper and rubber. Certainly the lighter materials are finding new uses constantly. Cardboard cartons have almost displaced wooden boxes. Various forms of fiber board, pressed wood pulp or such products of sugar cane pulp as celotex are taking the place of plaster, stone, and wood for walls. Linoleum and similar substances are doing the same for floors. Rubber in particular is used in hundreds of ways. It is the most versatile substance known and varies all the way from soft rubber sponges to pipe stems. We are so used to rubber that we still think of bakelite and similar synthetic substances as substitutes for it.

The last development, at this writing, which swept the country so thoroughly was the introduction of cellophane. It has been on the market only a few years, but we now accept it as a matter of course and expect everything from candy to axes to come wrapped in it. We have probably gone somewhat to excess in its use, as it hardly seems necessary to wrap such things as axes in it, but there can be no doubt that it has had great social significance in the way it protects against dangerous disease germs and prevents deterioration.

Not least among the industrial works of the chemist is the research on fuel oils and lubricants. The fuels which we use in our cars to-day bear little resemblance to the crude oil which flows from the wells. Even laymen now talk with some understanding of octane gases, paraffin bases, and cracking temperatures. Cars and other engines are modified to use most effectively the newest type of fuel, thus illustrating how so many phases of our lives are interrelated. Not only engines, but living organisms are so changed and modified. When vegetable cooking oil became practicable, it changed the style for pigs! Formerly Poland China hogs were popular because they made so much lard. But when lard was no longer wanted Poland Chinas became almost extinct and such breeds as Chester Whites, Durocs, Jerseys, and Berkshires took their place. After some years Poland Chinas began making their appearance again, but now it was a changed and improved breed which no longer went all to grease.

Industrial needs, especially in time of war or other crises, often put heavy responsibilities on the chemist. It may be worth our while to give the history of one such case, including a bit of the not-too-technical processes which were involved. During the first World War, Great Britain found that she needed imperatively thousands of barrels of acetone for use as a solvent in the manufacture of guncotton and other explosives. Canada was appealed to to furnish this material. It looked very much like a request for the moon, but the Canadian government appealed to the United States Chemical Warfare Service for a solution of the problem. A base was established at Shawinigan Falls where there was a plentiful supply of limestone, and coal was accessible.

The first step was to heat the limestone ($CaCO_3$) and drive off carbon dioxide, leaving quicklime (CaO). The quicklime was then combined with coal (C) which formed calcium carbide (CaC_2) with a by-product of carbon dioxide (CO_2). The calcium carbide was combined with water (H_2O) which made acetylene, C_2H_2, releasing quicklime or calcium carbonate as a waste product. Acetylene combined with water and the oxygen from the air gave acetic acid (CH_3CO_2H). Acetic acid combined with more of the original limestone gave calcium acetate [$(CH_3CO_2)_2CA$]. When calcium acetate is distilled dry it gives acetone (CH_3COCH_3), which was what they started out to get. When the date arrived on which the British said they must have the huge amount of acetone, it was ready and was shipped to them. This was not the only occasion on which the chemist stepped into prominence as a consequence of war. In fact, modern warfare is predominantly chemical. The Germans had been experimenting with deadly gases for some six years and thought they had perfected something which was so far and away ahead of what any other country could make that they could not be overtaken. But the American chemists went to work and in a few months developed a method of making these gases so much more efficiently than the Germans could that it took the heart out of the Germans when they discovered it.

Chemistry and Medicine[6]

As in agriculture and industry, the chemist has always been important in the field of medicine and will always continue to be so. As a direct cure or specific for a disease, chemical drugs fill a much smaller place than one might imagine. There are only a few chemical compounds, some six or eight, which are specific cures for special diseases. Quinine will actually cure malaria, salvarsan will cure syphilis and some other diseases such as yaws. Chalmoogra oil will sometimes cure leprosy if injected deep into the muscles, and we have recently discovered the curative powers of sulfanilamide and a few other such revolutionary substances. Outside of these few, the action of drugs is indirect. A laxative will put the system in better condition to fight disease germs, or a tonic may have the same effect. Potassium bromide or other sedatives will quiet the nerves and thus give other tissues opportunity to build up. Pepsin will help digest food, but will not directly cure the indigestion. Even such drugs as insulin merely do the work for defective glands but do not cure the glands of their deficiency. However, when it is said that drugs do most of their work indirectly, this does not minimize their importance in the least. As already noted, when the chemist works with some of his drugs he is handling substances which concentrate surprisingly great power in small space. Perhaps as remarkable is the fine selective power which some of them have. There are two sets of muscles which control the size of the pupil of the eye and they cross and overlie each other in the most intimate way. These are the sphincters or circular fibers which encircle the pupil and the radial muscle fibers which radiate out from it in all

[6] Julius Oscar Stieglitz (Ed.), *Chemistry in Medicine*, New York: Chemical Foundation, Inc., 1928.

directions. Atropine will paralyze the circular muscles and also the ciliary muscles which control the lens, but has no effect on the radial fibers. Cocaine stimulates the radial fibers but has no effect on the ciliary muscles. On the other hand eserine stimulates the circular fibers and ciliary muscles, but has no effect on the radial fibers. With these three highly specialized actions, the physician can secure any action he desires for examining the eye. There are other cases of such fine distinctions in the selective action of various drugs on the body.

The chemist can supply substances which will prevent bleeding, deaden pain, induce sickness or vomiting, quicken or slow up the heartbeat, paralyze the tongue, destroy our sense of time, or do almost anything else imaginable. If a physician can discover in the highly complex human organism with which he has to deal just what reaction is needed, it is almost certain that the chemist will have a substance which will produce the desired result. They can even revive life and action in a heart which has ceased to beat.

When we include the substances secreted by our various glands or their synthetic equivalents, the possibilities are greatly widened. Glandular secretions if given in youth will accelerate growth or permanently retard it. They will make one angry or frightened. They will stimulate growth of hair, especially on the face. They will determine the shape of the head, face, and body. They will cause obesity or prevent it. They will make the voice permanently childish or cause it to become coarse and masculine in youth. They will cause a boy to develop feminine characteristics and a girl to develop masculinity. They will destroy the power of childbirth entirely. Even if given in later life they will do many of these things and some others. The glandular chemist even has a substance which will prevent baldness, but it is almost prohibitively expensive.

The use of chemical analysis has invaded some fields which are surprising indeed. At some universities they now take a young aspirant for athletic honors out and let him run a hundred yards. Then they test his blood for the amount of lactic acid in it and they claim this one test will show whether or not he will ever be able to become a strenuous athlete.

A term which we hear much of late is the word "allergy." Allergies are merely the chemical reactions which certain organisms have to specific chemical substances. These are highly individualized and seem to occur without rhyme or reason. One may be allergic to almost anything on earth. Strangely enough three of the most common substances are milk, eggs, and wheat. Although these constitute the staff of life, there are some people who cannot eat them without distress. Probably the most common form of allergy is that to ragweed, the great producer of hay fever. And poison ivy is so nearly universal in its effects that we do not ordinarily classify it among the allergies at all.

The highly individualized ways in which these allergies occur remind one of the selective action of atropine and eserine on the muscle fibers of the eye. It is not an easy task for the physician-chemist to discover why his patient sneezes, coughs, gets a headache, or in some other way indicates that he has an allergy against something or other. He has the entire list of known substances from which to choose and any one of them may be the source of the trouble. Once discovered, however, it is usually possible to take this substance and prepare a solution of it in such a form that it is suitable for injection into the system, thus building up a resistance or an immunization. Not always does he make a complete cure, but frequently he does and nearly always he helps at least to some extent.

The field of serums and immunization is not the least among those in which the chemist is active. We do not think of vaccination for smallpox as being chemical but it is. To be sure, the vaccine is a bacteriological preparation, but it secures its effect through the chemicals which it stimulates the body to produce. The social effects of this one process cannot easily be overestimated. Smallpox formerly killed its millions, and twenty-five or thirty per cent of the population had disfigured faces from pock marks. Both Washington and Jefferson were so disfigured. It is said that many a man refused to marry a girl until she had had smallpox. He wanted to see what she would look like after the disease left her! Now smallpox can be said to be conquered. The process of immunization has spread out to include scarlet fever, diphtheria, typhoid, and any number of other such diseases.

Thus in many ways, the chemist works his wonders in medicine through his knowledge of natural, immutable laws. Each day sees something new and there seems to be no end. Just now it appears that there is a great possibility in the field opened up by the cyclotron and other atom-splitting devices which were described in the last chapter. It is now possible to impregnate diseased tissue with boron or some other such substance and then explode it in these cells by action of the rays from the cyclotron.   This sounds like a highly destructive force, but properly controlled it destroys the disease germs without damaging the human tissues.   It is said that the possibilities may be wonderful.

CONCLUSION

It would be easy to show that chemical action is indispensable for human society.   So easy would it be to show this that we might conclude that nothing else has any special significance.   This would be a great mistake.   It would be just as easy to show the indispensability of the physical factors, the educational, the geographical, or the biological.   Each one of these factors is absolute in so far as human life and human society are concerned.   Any comparison as to their relative importance would be like the old fashioned debate on the question, "Resolved that the liver is more important than the lungs."   The ordinary man would be in a bad way without either. But at present we are interested in the place of chemistry.

If any one of ten thousand chemical reactions or conditions changed but a small bit, the human race would perish.   The tiniest bit of para-thyroid secretion added to the human system would quickly prove fatal.   A little less oxygen in the air and we would smother, a little more and we would quickly burn out.   A little shift in the chemical balance and everything would go to pieces.   Our bodies, our glands and blood, our respiration, our assimilation and all our being must stay as nicely balanced as the chemist's neutral solution which will turn litmus paper neither blue nor pink.

The fertility of the soil, the availability of the air, the vegetation of the earth, the life of animals, the activities of industry, agriculture, medicine, and life itself are based on precise, unvarying chemical laws and principles.   We can take yeast and make whiskey or make bread.   We can use phenol as a deadly poison or can use it to make bakelite and formica.   We can use our chemistry to create an abundant life or we can destroy civilization.   The potentialities for both are furnished us.   The outcome is in our hands.

SELECTED LIST OF REFERENCES

Arrhenius, Svante August, *Chemistry in Modern Life*, Translated from the Swedish by Clifford Shattuck Leonard, New York: D. Van Nostrand, 1926, 286 p.—Interestingly written with many references to social life.

Dorsey, George A., *Why We Behave Like Human Beings*, New York: Harper and Bros., 1925, 512 p.—This has been called the ''jazz of science.'' Somewhat spectacular, but contains a world of information. Chapter four deals with the ductless glands.

Huxley, Julian, *Science and Social Needs*, New York: Harper and Bros., 1935, 287 p.

Robinson, Henry M., *Science versus Crime*, Indianapolis: Bobbs-Merrill, 1935, 303 p.—A good popular discussion of the way science is used in the detection of crime.

Schlapp, Max G., and Smith, Edward H., *The New Criminology*, New York: Boni, 1925.—This book champions the theory that crime is usually the result of disordered glands.

Slosson, Edwin E., *Snapshots of Science*, New York: Century Co., 1928, 299 p.— Short items of interest in chemistry.

Slosson, Edwin E., *Creative Chemistry*, New York: Century Co., 1923, 311 p.— This is deliberate attempt of an authority in chemistry to make the subject popular and to show its practical value.

Stieglitz, Julius Oscar (Editor), *Chemistry in Medicine*, New York: Chemical Foundation Incorporated, 1928, 757 p.

Thornton, Jesse E. (Editor), *Science and Social Change*, Washington: Brookings Institute, 1939, 577 p.

CHAPTER 4

GEOGRAPHIC AND GEOLOGIC REGULARITIES

By G. G. Cole, M.S., Litt.D.,
Wheaton College, Wheaton, Illinois

INFLUENCES FROM THE EARTH'S SURFACE

The geographical environment generally permits a variation of the behavior related to it.[1] Different social conditions may be associated with a like kind of environment; and similar customs may be found in unlike environments. For instance, the Indians of America prior to white settlement had the same natural geographical conditions as the white population has at present—the same climate, plants, animals, minerals, soil and natural scenery. But the cultures are entirely different. Side by side two races or classes of people might migrate to the same region, and the societies of the two react in different directions. Features of coast stimulating to commerce and maritime activity for one group might have no such influence upon others.

However, though the behavior patterns of the two groups might differ, those patterns would in each case be affected by the new environment, would be an attempted adaptation. Changes in geographic conditions produce changes in the ways of people or in their numbers. We may say that man is social; nevertheless, he can survive only if nature supplies him with food, and his social development thus depends on his geographic surroundings. Even when a like social background has made a common culture base, different areas have differences in general culture patterns.

Examples of Geographic Areas

1. *The Fall Line.* This line is distinctly followed down the eastern portion of the country. The areas adjacent to the Atlantic coast below New York consist of the Atlantic Coastal Plain. Tidewater for long distances up the streams, a generally level contour, moderate elevation, and soils adapted to special kinds of cultivation, are some of the characteristics. The social and occupational

[1] See E. T. Hiller, *Principles of Sociology*, New York: Harper and Bros., 1933, p. 233.

82

interests are peculiar to the area. The Fall Line area is in contrast with a more rolling and hilly area geographically designated as the Piedmont (foothills) region. Along this line, at the head of the tide navigation, are found waterfalls. As a result many important cities have sprung up. Among these are Trenton, Philadelphia, Richmond, Petersburg, Raleigh, Camden, Columbia and Augusta. They enjoy special manufacturing facilities as a result of the water power from the falls.[2]

The region below the Fall Line is the region of much of the conservative social attitudes as contrasted with the Piedmont region where migrations are more frequent and the social effects more elastic and changeable. But the Piedmont region is more conservative than the regions beyond, except where the plateau regions have been left aside from the surging developments of commercial, mining and industrial interests; a region sometimes designated as the Cumberland plateau.

2. Geographically, our country as a unit is divided into three large and diverse areas: The eastern forested and agricultural area, the mid-continental and prairie areas, and the western mountain and basin region. The social and population factors differ to a large degree because of this geographical variation.

The Eastern area was the first to be colonized extensively, and here the background cultures were largely a transference of the social conditions of the countries from which the people came. The main source of supply being England, the social dominance of the English language, governmental attitudes, love of freedom, and occupational primacy survived for long periods and still distinguish the social life. The area is roughly bounded by the water-shed separating the Eastern streams flowing into the Atlantic ocean and the affluents of the Mississippi river, although in some respects the more eastern portion of the valley has come into close relationship to the culture of the mountains.

The Mid-continental area comprises the greater part of the valley of the Mississippi, although as stated above, its eastern rim is much like the Eastern area. In like manner the western rim impinges upon the Basin areas of the west so far as occupational and cultural practices are concerned. Here in this middle land has developed the great Corn and Wheat belts of the country. Aside

[2] See W. M. Davis, *Elementary Physical Geography,* Ginn and Co., 1902, pp. 157, 158.

from the effect of the basin upon our country as a whole, Shaler calls attention to the effects elsewhere. He shows that a bad harvest in the plains of the upper Mississippi valley means dear bread in England, fewer marriages, and shorter lives: in other words it produces an effect on the whole social status of that country.[3] The pioneer practices of this region have largely been replaced by a later culture which has resulted from the rapid increase in the means of forming public sentiment. But the pioneer days clustering around the log-cabin society of the eastern part, and the sod-house and dug-out society of the western part are still fresh in the minds of many older people of the present.[4]

The Mountain and Basin region was the last to be populated from migrations from the Mississippi valley and the Eastern areas. However, an earlier Spanish foothold had been gained in some parts of it, and the Spanish customs and culture affected the waves of migration from the east.

3. *Cave and Pile Dwellings.* In the early distribution of mankind into Europe, the natural geographical conditions were factors in establishing the so-called Cave culture and a modification of the Pile dwelling customs. The roaming migrants from the East on reaching Europe found that the numerous caves provided ready-made places for dwellings, but there is ample proof that along with dependence upon such conveniences, there were village and structural homes as well.

Pile dwellings, fitting into the primary needs as protection from enemies and from frequent inundations, have had a wide modern distribution, especially in the tropics. They were formerly numerous in the lakes of Switzerland and northern Italy down to the first century of our era, and existed later in modified form in Ireland, England and southern Wales.[5] In Ireland they were erected on artificial islands, raised in shallow spots by means of bundles of poles weighted down with gravel and clay and fastened to the bottom by stakes driven through the mass. Such dwellings were called Crannogs. Similar structures were found near the Hellespont, built by the ancient Thracians, the floor having a trap door for entrance and exit. In South America, the Warraus, till quite recently, built their dwellings on platforms over water. An alien

[3] See N. S. Shaler, *Nature and Man in America,* p. 149.

[4] See E. N. Dick, *The Sod House Frontier.*

[5] See Semple, *Influences of Geographical Environment,* pp. 319–323.

colony in Burma have added to their pile village floating raft gardens with soil in which are raised food plants. In the headstreams of the Congo similar huts are found supposedly erected as a refuge from the slavers. Structures of like nature are common in the Sulu archipelago, Borneo, New Guinea and parts of India.

Geographical Influence on Location of Cities

It is evident that geographic factors are involved in determining the sites of cities and the congestion of population groups. Cities rarely arise by chance. Among the outstanding natural factors are the following:

1. *Accessibility to Water.* Water is so essential that one of the first requisites for a city is available water. Quite too often the city expands for other reasons and the water supply becomes a very serious problem and requires expensive means to meet the need, as is the case in Los Angeles where water is obtained 250 miles away and in New York which obtains much of its supply from the Catskills 125 miles away. But a city in the beginning will usually develop upon a large stream or where springs are abundant. London probably owed its location to this factor and that many of its suburbs such as Wimbledon, Blackheath, etc., grew up in areas in which gravel patches on the clay produced an outflow in the form of springs. Paris, partly within and partly astride a meander of the Seine, indicates a similar origin.[6]

2. *Accessibility of Location.* Most American cities took their rise before the present development of artificial roads and highways as well as railroads. So locations on navigable waters provided the easiest means of access. Along with this was the advantage secured by being at a ford, an easily bridged spot, or a network of confluences.

3. *Ease of Defense.* Water isolation was one factor in the location of the old Chicago on islands in a swamp. Gibraltar and Copenhagen were protected by water configuration. Innsbruck, Milan, Turin are examples of cities located in walled-in mountain protection.

4. *Favorable Delta Configuration.* This had the double advantage of accessibility and presence of a fertile soil. The location of Alexandria, Astrakhan, Calcutta, Canton, and New Orleans illustrate such conditions.

[6] See Dr. E. G. Skeat Woods, *The Principles of Geography*, pp. 354–358.

5. *Convergence of Commercial Routes.* Where several routes converge, rendering the position a central one, cities arise. Vienna is a good example, for here important routes approach in four directions through gates or passes in the mountains. St. Louis was indirectly a site where early migration routes centered.

6. *Transfer Points.* Wherever one form of transportation changes to another so that goods must be made available for a different means of carriage, a city will arise. Port Arthur and Duluth are good examples, for here transportation of grain coming overland by train is transferred to ships. New York is of this nature for here the immense exports are loaded on ships and imports of goods by water are transferred to railroads and trucks. Liverpool has imports of cotton coming by ship transferred to trains to reach the cotton towns. Damascus and Timbuktu are cities where goods brought across deserts are collected for re-shipment by regular road or river.

7. Presence of desired commodities and facilities for using them in industry. Pittsburgh grew up through the once available local supplies of iron ore, limestone and coal, contributing to ease in iron-smelting. Omaha was stimulated through its grain and stock environment; Galveston, its cotton; Duluth, its iron ore; Butte, its copper; Bedford, Indiana, its oolitic limestone; Berea, Ohio, its fine-grained sandstone.

Climatic Factors

1. *Effect of Cold Climates.* It is at once evident that the distribution of population is sparse in the cold zones. Man has not found it possible to live comfortably in large numbers there. To be sure, temperatures frequently far below zero seem to have small adverse effect on the peoples of Finland, northern Russia and Siberia. But there is little migration to those areas. The occupations, interests, recreations, and clothing are distinct for the inhabitants of such rigorous regions. The difficulties in making a living take so much of their time and energy that they can give little to other interests. Their diet is different for it needs to have a preponderance of the heat-yielding foods.

2. At the other extreme are those regions in which there is *a very hot climate.* Some ancient authorities assumed a variety of social differences due to the variations in results from cold and hot climates. Hippocrites insisted that to develop vigor and bravery a

climate is needed which would excite the mind, ruffle the temper and demand fortitude and exertion. Aristotle insisted that people who live in the cold climates of northern Europe are conspicuous for their spirit, but their lack of intelligence unfits them for political organization and dominion. Asiatic peoples, on the other hand, are described as preeminent for intelligence and inventiveness, but are lacking in spirit and are consequently content to remain in subjection and slavery.[7] He used this as a basis to exalt the merits of his own people. He assumed that the Greeks being intermediate in position, combined the advantages of both extremes without their shortcomings, and were, therefore, the best governed people in the world and by nature fitted to rule the earth. The fact that the later Greek people have not held this preeminence would indicate that his reasoning was defective. Still there was some slight truth in his assumptions.

3. *The Effect of Temperate Conditions.* Between the enervating influences of extreme cold and heat, the temperate zones of the earth would be free from the extreme physical, mental and social handicaps. This is found to be the case. That the greater part of the outstanding culture and civilization has arisen in temperate climes is fully attested by history. To a large extent it has been claimed that the parallel of forty degrees north latitude has been the line axis on which such social developments have largely swung. Here there is less effort required to live than in the cold regions, and the enervating influences of hot climates being absent, there is left a condition conducive to physical, mental and spiritual progress and advancement.

The environmental condition has much to do with play and recreation. Geographic location largely determines games and sports of the people. In cold climates the emphasis is on strenuous sports. Where the conditions are favorable, skating, tobogganing, the snow shoes and skis afford favorite exercises. In temperate regions, running, jumping, tennis, base-ball, foot-ball, cricket, and the like are favorites. In warm countries these are too severe for mere exercise and neither demanded nor pleasant. Here, recreation and games are such as to require small exertion of mind or muscle. Forms of card games, and a recreation of inactivity, resting, sleeping, and avoidance of effort, are most common. Contact with the practices of Europe and America, however, has brought about a

[7] See Franklin Thomas, *The Environmental Basis of Society*, p. 33.

change in this respect. Some games requiring physical exertion have spread despite the climate handicap.

Occupational conditions also vary. In cold climates the entire occupational interest is confined to strenuous efforts at securing food supplies through hunting and fishing. In the hot climates, occupations requiring a small outlay of physical exertion are still further encouraged by the prolific supplies of nature in providing food without intensive agricultural effort.

4. From the various authorities who have attempted to explain variations of voice some interesting assumptions arise. People in cold climates being adverse to opening their mouths wide, have languages which abound in consonants, while those in warm countries are glad to open their mouths wide, and have languages with abundance of vowels. Another version is that the heavy voices of the men of the north are a result of the cold and damp air, and that the voices of the southern people are shrill as a result of warm, dry air.[8]

5. Not only can much of favorable social adjustment be traced to climate but also likewise can unadjustments. According to some authorities, suicides, insanity and crimes of violence, rise in the spring, reach their full height in the early summer, then steadily fall for the rest of the year.[9] After all, is this conclusive? Might it not be from another reason? If so, the season instead of causing the increase due to climate, might be an environmental change which brings more people into contact with each other, thus making more opportunities for crime. However, Dexter[10] found that errors of bank clerks seemed to be more numerous during the warm months, periods of high temperatures, or moderate barometric pressure under conditions of humidity, during calms, and on cloudy wet days, while students show a quicker comprehension when other conditions prevail. It is probable that the weather acts upon the reserve energy rather than the emotional nature.

6. From another standpoint, there is evidently a relation of climate to slavery. In the areas of the earth where the climate is hot and depressing those in control would save themselves as much exertion as possible. They would seek in forced work on the part of others, a solution to their needs. Thus slavery would arise. That such a relation does exist is shown by the experience in our own

[8] See Thomas, *The Environmental Basis of Society*, p. 62.

[9] *Idem*, pp. 100, 101.

[10] See E. G. Dexter, *Weather Influences*, pp. 245, 246.

country. Slavery was a successful solution for such conditions in the South, while climatic conditions of a different nature in the North made slavery unpopular. Slavery has had a great degree of tenacity in hot regions.

Occupations Affected by Geographical Factors

The first advanced occupations were of a pastoral nature. Geographic conditions contributed to these. It would be only where soils and climate were adapted to domestication and keeping of sheep and cattle that population would become permanent. Back of the cluster tendency of population concentration are the natural situation for animal and plant multiplication, the mineral constituents of rock and soil, the humidity and temperature.[11] No race has ever been known to develop a civilization without agriculture. Hence it appears that land favorable to agriculture is basic to social development.

An industrial community is based largely upon resources. Society adjusts its interests to correspond to the natural supplies and products available. The occupations connected with the iron industry develop in regions where coal and iron ore are found. Just as the agricultural and horticultural interest can develop only where climate and soil make such things important, so industrial woodworking must have accessible supplies of forests to provide the material. This is shown by the great drift of furniture factories from Michigan, with depleted forests, to the Carolinas with vast woodlands.

Commerce exists because of the diversity which gives various parts of the earth distinct advantages in the production of certain commodities. Retzel calls attention to some incidental factors of this aspect. He states that the Trade Winds were of special importance in the development of commerce in the era of sailing vessels.[12] This was the time of great enlargement of commercial activity, and gave the initial impetus to modern-day trade.

In government, the geographic factors are at work. Montesquieu enlarged upon the theory that the spirit of liberty, the character of peoples, the forms of government, even the happiness of women, were traceable to geographic influences.[13] Rousseau interpreted the particular form of government as an outgrowth from such influences.

[11] See G. G. Cole, *Geological Factors Influencing Human Society*, Bulletin, Illinois Academy of Science.

[12] See Thomas, *The Environmental Basis of Society*, p. 79.

[13] *Idem*, p. 62.

Geographic Isolation Factors

Isolation, in the large sense, is due to geographic barriers.

The social effects of islands are important. These greatest of all isolating influences have both advantages and disadvantages. Iceland illustrates. When energetic men of Norway at the end of the ninth century found a haven in Iceland, they built up and maintained until 1262 the only absolutely free republic in the world. Residents of the new land made brilliant achievements, particularly in literature. But when colonial importance waned, it was left aside and the blight of extreme isolation settled upon it.[14] Elsewhere, the Ceylonese Aryans, like the Iceland Norse, followed the same effects of isolation. The bearers of this culture were also picked men, as were the early maritime colonists the world over. The sea selects and then protects its island folks.

It is on islands of harsh climatic conditions that the stamp of the primitive and antiquated is strongest. Such are Sakhalin, Sardinia, and Cape Breton. Corsica and Sardinia lying off the main routes of travel are two of the most primitive isolated spots in Europe, or were until late military developments. Here the old Roman plow was still in common use, as it was in the island of Crete; and feudal institutions of the Middle Ages still prevailed to a large extent. The little Isle of Man, almost in sight of the English coast, retained up to the present an old Norse form of government. Here survived the primitive custom of orally proclaiming every new law from the Tynwald Hill before it could take effect, and the other ancient usage of holding the court of justice on the same hill under the open sky. The Faroe islands as well as Iceland are museums of Norse antiquities. Hand-querns for grinding grain, stone hammers for pounding fish and roots, the wooden weighing-beam of the ancient Northmen, and quaint marriage customs give the final touch of aloofness.[15]

The concomitant of isolation is protection. Through this protection, the stages of civilization remained untouched, either tending to survive and adapt or deteriorate and disappear. When learning and Christianity were almost wiped out of the Continent by the ravages of the Barbarian invaders between the fifth and ninth centuries, A.D., they grew and flourished in Ireland. In the seventh and eighth centuries, the high scholarship of the Irish Monks drew to their schools students of the noblest rank from both England and

14 See Semple, *Influences of Geographical Environment*, pp. 435, 436.
15 *Idem*, pp. 442–443.

France. It was from Irish teachers that the Picts of Scotland and the Angles of Northern England received their first lessons in Christianity. These fixed their mission stations again on the islands, on Iona off southwestern Scotland and on Lindisfarne, or Holy Isle, near the east coast of Northumbria.

Many of the restrictive practices diffused into human society have their origin in islands and remote isolated areas, where increase in population would produce disaster. Castration, the custom of late marriage, the exaltation of virginity and celibacy, and the like arise here. The isolated Budumas of Lake Chad allow only the chiefs and head men to have wives, and even the sons of the chief are restricted, only one being permitted to marry. A brass crescent inserted in the ear of this boy indicates that he is the favored one and destined to carry on his race. The other men are eunuchs, becoming big, dull, timid creatures, contributing by their fishing to the support of the thinly populated villages. Infanticide and abortion are widespread in Oceania. In some families children are killed and substitutes purchased at will. In the island of Vanua-Levu infanticide reaches two-thirds of the children. Similar practices are widespread in the Polynesian islands, and a laxity of morals and family stability results. Cannibalism appears to have arisen sometimes as the social solution to over-population.

Mountains have always offered barriers to the diffusion of culture. In fact, culture may surround them, but rarely penetrates them. The Basques of southwestern France are set forth by anthropologists as being outstanding examples of ''cultural islands.'' Here, the society, language, social customs and psychological attitudes have remained unchanged for a period going back into a lost history. The barrier nature of mountains has been the explanation of many political segregations of people and the rise of numerous states which depend upon them for their natural boundary lines.

The world's densest populations are located in regions of gentle relief, short of mountain topography. Yet as exceptions, Japan is a mountainous country, and also densely populated, as is also Java. Our own Kentucky mountains are often described as being rugged, yet the rural population there amounts to over forty per square mile, which is as much as in the level state of Iowa.

That mountains produce a distinct social attitude in the mountaineers has been generally accepted for a long time. The residents of the Cumberland plateau region and the Ozarks have been cited

as groups thus influenced by geographic conditions, although any
careful student must likewise recognize other factors as well, such
as inheritance, traditions, cultural origins, etc. But that there are
these other influences does not minimize the importance of the geographic ones. F. Thomas, in his book on *The Environmental Basis
of Society,* quoted Montesquieu as saying that "mountaineers are
liberty loving, because liberty is about all they possess worth defending, and their natural position makes defense comparatively
easy."[16] It is quite evident that whether this is the cause or not,
mountain dwellers throughout all history have been noted for their
love of liberty and their resistance to encroachments on their rights
from outside.

Forests are isolating factors when they are extensive. The en-
compassing forest of medieval Europe retarded the organization
of people into large states and the building up of a diversity of
society.[17] In our own Midwest, pioneering was held in check by
the vast forest areas. To the family trekking westward in search of
a farm home, the miles of unbroken forests were a fearful ogre. It
was something to be both dreaded and subdued. In it lurked the
wild beast, and the stealthy red man. It hemmed the settlers in,
and made social contacts difficult. They were thrown back upon
themselves for everything they needed. Before they could plant
the crops which meant release from hunger, they must remove the
trees, the brush, and the stumps which stood in their way.[18] While
it seems a waste of valuable timber to us of this age, the only way
for maintaining a foothold lay in the direction of destroying and
burning acres of trees. The ascent of smoke registered the battle
between the pioneers and the forest enemy.

Waste regions have been another type of geographic handicap
to social diffusion. Deserts were barriers to migration in the ancient
world, just as they have proved to be problems difficult of solution
in our American attempts to settle the Great Basin and to construct
highways for many miles through lands devoid of human habitation. Fertile oases and habitable spots, even in such forbidding
surroundings, have enabled man to migrate to these areas and by
his wit and ingenuity overcome some of the bans and boundaries
fixed by geographic features. Swamps were another obstacle to

16 Thomas, p. 158.
17 See R. Peattie, *New College Geography,* pp. 170–173.
18 Peattie, p. 176.

man's distribution. Many areas in Indiana and Illinois a century ago were impossible sites for residence, and were barriers to social acculturation and the spread of human contacts. Over them man gradually gained control by bridging the inlets, and draining and filling the morasses, but he is still limited by the western deserts.

GEOLOGIC INFLUENCES IN SOCIAL LIFE

The Earth as a Home for Man

Geologists see, in the sun, moon and stars, basal relations which affect the social practices of mankind. In their analyses they go back to the causes of climate. They find the inclination of the earth's axis as that is related to the annual swing around the sun, its precessions, its nodal variations, its shifting of distance and other phenomena related to climate. They also find the isostasy or rising and sinking of the earth's surface in relation to the snow-line an important factor in climate. They find the shape of the continents and their positions, as factors influencing the flow of ocean waters and the shifting of the air currents. James Croll has shown that the Gulf Stream brings to the part of Europe within the Arctic circle more heat than comes to that region directly from the sun.[19] Without going into particulars, it is a general principle, quite well established, that the mathematical and constant fluctuations as controlled by the heavenly bodies are important influences upon the customs of men.

Even slight geological changes may produce extensive effects upon the earth conditions. The geological aspect of the Gulf Stream is in accord with this. In a very recent geological time, probably since the coming of man upon the earth, the peninsula of Florida was depressed below its present level, so that the water constituting the Gulf Stream flowed further north over the surface of the depressed peninsula, the current having its northern border considerably above the present site of Tampa. When in this position the waters of the Gulf Stream moved more slowly than at present, reaching the north of Europe with slower momentum and much diminished heat. If its speed were to be diminished in mid-ocean as much as half a mile per hour, the effect would be to lower the temperature of the North Atlantic by several degrees of Fahrenheit —a change not only great enough to affect the distribution of marine life, but also to decrease the temperature of northern

[19] See N. S. Shaler, *Nature and Man in America*, p. 20.

Europe. Were man in Europe at that time, we can judge of the effect upon him.[20]

In the Wake of the Glaciers

From a study of some topographical features found widely distributed, the geologist concludes that Northern Asia and Europe and much of North America were, in comparatively recent times, the location of moving fields of ice of tremendous thickness and possessed of great dynamic power. The lower limits of the distribution in America begins with Long Island which was entirely formed from rock, gravel and sand brought down from the far north by this great vehicle of ice, and dumped into the Atlantic Ocean. From here the limit is traced across northern New Jersey, into the areas along the boundary of New York and Pennsylvania, thence across the northwest corner of Pennsylvania, down into Ohio, crossing the upper courses of the rivers tributary to the upper Ohio, then, with a sharp angle, extending to the southwest and across the Ohio River above Cincinnati, into what is termed the "Knob Country" of Kentucky. From here, it extends in a northwesterly direction across Indiana, central Illinois, and to the Rocky Mountains by way of Kansas.

North of this limit, the ice sheet stood at great height, in its movement from centers determined in Labrador and Keewatin. Its immense weight broke off the granite and other volcanic rock of those areas, and carried this detached material as a load, distributing it over the land areas further south. The evidence of this gigantic transportation is found in the nature of the scattered rock, identified as to the very spot where broken off, and scattered over a landscape which has no native rock of the same kind. Beneath this area thus made the recipient of this "drift," the geological structure is mostly sandstone and limestone, except in eastern New York and the New England states where the native granites are found mixed with the granitic rocks brought down from the north. Prior to the ice sheet the area was deeply eroded and had a rough topography, with river valleys and hills carved out of the sandstone and limestone rocks. To this rock was added the great mass of superincumbent Canadian granites, brought down by the glaciers, scattered thinly on the original hill tops, and deposited in great depths in many of the valleys. Prior rivers were dammed up, with a result

[20] See Shaler, *Nature and Man in America*, pp. 21, 22.

that lakes and marshes were formed and new river courses were formed. The upper Ohio rivers flowed northward prior to the glacial changes, but the glaciers deposited high water-sheds which diverted the streams to their present direction.

Great riches of phosphorus compounds contained in the material brought down by the ice has been added to a soil which without it would be deficient in this essential mineral for plant growth. By additions of lime, the insoluble phosphate contents are rendered soluble and capable of use by plants in their growth. Other elements essential to fertile soils were added in a similar fashion. An expert has said that the farms within the glaciated region produce five bushels of grain more per acre by the same treatments than unglaciated soils.

Similar glacial sheets covered portions of the Old World. The Lake regions of Scotland, England and Ireland show geological configuration similar to those of New York and other American glaciated areas.

Another result of the glaciers was the present distribution of the water supply. With few exceptions, the water-table of this area is within the gravel and sand deposited by the glacier. Almost anywhere that a well is dug down through the earth in the glacier lands, the water-table is reached, and an abundant supply of water is available. In the mid-west the ubiquitous tank raised on high supports, indicates that an abundant water supply is available. The well, sunk down through the glacial drift, easily reaches the water-table, and the pumping station is able to contribute the essential element in human life, copious quantities of pure water—pure, because the glacial deposit is one of the best filtering mediums.

The prevalence of numerous springs in the glaciated areas is largely due to factors related to the nature of the glaciated deposit. Where the glacial gravels overlay the original bed rock, or firm layers of glacial deposited clay, that portion of the rain water which does not run off sinks into the soil. It finds its way to this impervious layer on its way down to the water-table, and follows a path of least resistance by running along the top of the layer, to emerge finally on a hillside, or in a low place, as a spring. The great number and almost universal distribution of such springs has had a great value in making the region the site of prosperous farms and dairies.

The unglaciated areas have a more serious water problem. Here the water-table is found in the joints and crevices of the bed rock. The well must reach the water-table at one of these joints, or a supply of water cannot be obtained. Sometimes numerous wells must be sunk before a chance tapping of water is possible. And when it is, there is a danger that the water in derived from surface sources without the safety of passing through a filtering substance. The advantages to the human family due to the widespread glaciation of ancient times are legion.

Soils

The clays of Flanders, when it rains, hold the water, instead of permitting it to run off or seep away as it does in the soils of the uplands. The housewife has difficulty in keeping her house clean, although the people remove their wooden sabots before entering the house. The floors being low, boards have to be placed on the doorsill to keep out the waters of the field. In the cities, it is a continual fight for cleanliness with the housewife the loser. Roads are poor, and in consequence the life centers in the farm. Each is essentially a village with its own smith, wheelwright, and storekeeper. The establishment is practically an island in a sea of mud. The people are hoe people, hard workers. From the bounty of this rich land came the remarkable culture of the seventeenth century and the intellectual development of Bruges, Antwerp and Louvain.

With attention now to the humus composition of soils, it is evident that humus derived from prairie grass would differ from that coming from evergreen tree leaves. This difference is quite apparent from the recognized superiority of swamp muck, in the direction of fertility of the soil. While the glacial soils contain large percentages of sand and siliceous pebbles, much of it comes from the disintegration of composite rocks like granite, which is composed of feldspar, hornblende, which gives traces of phosphorus, sodium, potassium and lime. All of these are essential to fertile soils. Thus the glacial soils have the advantage of mechanical gravel and fertile ingredients. Along with the more common essential plant minerals are those containing iron, sulphur, manganese, zinc, copper and boron, taken up in solution through the root hairs. In most parts of the United States the soils are supplied with these essential substances, although through their depletion or lack there is the continuous problem in agriculture to add the ones needed. Occasionally, the humus content ferments, giving rise to what are called "acid soils." Most crops do not do well in such soils. Lime is valuable as a corrective. Soils need coarse particles for a mechanical reason, for the rain which sinks into the soil is transformed into soil-water solution on the surface of such grains or pebbles. Soil-water solution is the particular status of water in which it can best be taken up by the growing root hairs.

Our civilization has been instrumental in exhausting the soil of its essentials, especially of nitrogen, potassium and phosphorus, which are constituents of plant tissue used for foods. Some years ago, the late Professor Bailey warned us that the city as a center of human population was sending the vast riches of the potassium content from our soils down into the sea in sewerage. In recent years sewerage treatment plants are saving much of this waste, and making it possible to return it to the soils in fertilizers which they produce. Only a beginning has been made in such conservation.[21]

As an example of how the nature of soils has a bearing upon social attitudes, it is said that if Kentucky had an entire distribution of limestone instead of a partial one, it would have cast in its lot with the South. The limestone soils were the location of slavery, in contrast with the mountain regions. The limestone regions were the homes of the aristocratic wealthy, whose social attitudes differed very much from those of the mountaineers.[22] Another example: In the prairie regions where the soil greatly abounded in the elements fitted for the production of grain the result was a rapid economic development.

Tobacco has changed the habits of men throughout a large part of the world. Soils adapted to tobacco have become especially valuable, for not every soil contains the elements in soluble form essential to tobacco growth. In all probability there is no other plant so exhausting to soils as tobacco. It rapidly uses up the elements it needs and unless this loss is compensated by artificial fertilizer the soil is rapidly deteriorated in tobacco productivity, until it has to be abandoned, producing what is called in the South, "Old Fields." Once these areas were a tragic memento of the destruction from tobacco raising. In recent years with an increased knowledge of soil conservation, many of these areas are being put back into cultivation after years of rest.

The species of cinchona whence comes quinine and other medical

[21] See Peattie, *College Geography*, pp. 244, 245.
[22] See Gustafson, *Conservation in the United States*, pp. 71–77.

derivatives and a score of other American species such as the tomato have come to play a more or less important part in the field or garden. Because there were soils adapted to valuable American plant species, there was a more complex development among the American Indians in the Southwest than that found by the first Europeans. It is thought that the decline in their status was largely due to the deterioration of soil along with the shifting in climate.

The attractions of the sea have been for a century replaced by those of the prairies, where men have found the opportunity to win their way to fortune which their ancestors were compelled to seek by visiting foreign shores. Although there may have been other influences at work in diverting our people from maritime interests, it seems that the more important cause is the open road to the central fields of the continent. After that great domain is possessed, we may fairly expect that the Atlantic coast population as well as those crowded out of the great basin will again turn to a maritime life and rewards.

Petroleum

Two extremely valuable products which geologic transformations in our earth have produced, are oil and coal. Oil has had a strong influence on our recent ways of living, and if production were to cease civilization would necessarily be vastly changed. The length of a list of substances derived from petroleum is surprising. In such a list would be enumerated not only benzine, naphtha, kerosene, gasoline, vaseline, lubricating oils, but dozens of other useful derivatives. When it was found possible to substitute in lamps and lanterns a clear oil derived from distillation of petroleum in place of fish and whale oil an enormous new industry was soon under way.

The light distillate obtained in securing the kerosene was mostly discarded at first. It was a waste product until the discovery that it was exceptionally valuable for cleansing purposes, and for fuel. With the development of internal combustion engines, this lighter product became the most important, for already other means of lighting were superseding kerosene.

It is not in the province of geology to follow up the many ways in which rapid transit has taken place, but the fact is outstanding that petroleum has made it possible.

The use of oil in war has increased war's intensity. The mechanization of war equipments demands that there shall be motive power and lubrication for the gigantic leviathans and juggernauts so characteristic of present day conflicts. Attempts to control the oil supply as a means of gaining victory reveals how very important oil is in modern warfare.

In industry the increasing use of oil would make a long story. In itself, it has produced one of the world's greatest industries. This is important, not alone in its occupational phases but because from it grows many of the social problems of the lands and people who produce petroleum. The drilling for oil, and the discovery of valuable reservoirs beneath the earth's surface, has a greater influence on migratory labor than the discovery of a vast gold field. Families from distant places flock into the oil fields, building and renting homes, camping in tents and portable cabins, or dwelling in trailers. This stimulates trade. The society of such communities has its own social practices and customs. The agricultural interests in oil communities are rapidly eclipsed by the great wealth obtained beneath the soil, which in a short time converts the owner of oil land from a plodding hard-working farmer into a man of leisure.

It is also significant that when these reservoirs have been pumped dry the entire region, once so prosperous and populous, sinks rapidly into economic and social decline. The oil-soaked soil has lost much of its agricultural value. In consequence, such areas become to a large extent bleak and deserted; bustling cities become "ghost towns."

Along with petroleum these reservoirs supply natural gas, chemically like that obtained from the distillation of coal, and, near the source of supply, much cheaper. The industry which especially profits from the use of natural gas is the glass industry. Much of the development in glassmaking in recent years has been made possible by this supply of natural gas. Heating of homes, and cooking, are other uses.

The problem of gas conservation has recently received much attention. The fact that oil and gas areas do fail implies that they will eventually be entirely exhausted. Practical efforts directed to the avoidance of waste of such natural resources is called conservation. Geologists point out that while a few new sources of supply are being discovered, oil is not coming into existence now. Conservation requires that more effective use shall be made of the quantities used or that substitutes and additional material tending to increase the bulk shall be employed.[23] Experiments are being made in combining alcohol and other organic substances with gasoline in order to save the geological supply. Alcohol, being distilled from plant tissue, can be obtained in almost inexhaustible amounts, as contrasted with the fixed quantity of gasoline.

Coal

Another non-metal substance of great social influence is coal. Though the vast amount of coal has existed for untold ages, and laid unused and unknown, its wide utilization has occurred in only the last two centuries. In Europe its value as fuel preceded by several years its use on this side of the Atlantic. In America it appeared at first to be of so little use that sometimes it was used to fill swampy places and mend roads. Now, directly and as coke, it constitutes our major fuel. Its gas, too, furnishes fuel. A liquid part contains light substances from which we obtain ammonia and other products, and from the heavy substance, coal tar, are obtained, through chemical transformations, hundreds of products including medicines and dyes. The industrialists have produced eighteen hundred different dyes and tints for fabrics from this one source.

The Ores

From early days man has valued the metals largely in inverse proportion to their geologic quantities. Gold, at a very early date, because it was scarcer than some other metals, became greatly desired, was ranked as a "precious" metal.

The geological dynamism which scattered gold dust and nuggets through the alluvial gravels of the Pacific slope is an interesting story to the geologist; and is important to students of sociology because of the relation of this metal to the social development of man. A chance discovery of such riches in a mill-race being constructed to aid a few scattered settlers in their occupational existence, was a flame which struck hope and cupidity into the hearts of myriads of struggling and adventurous men all over the world. From the east and the south, even from across the seas, hunters were attracted to this *el dorado*. The great rush in 1849 and the years following acquired social meaning, and its participants came to be designated in history as the "Forty-Niners." It is difficult to trace the extent

[23] See Gustafson, *Conservation in the United States,* pp. 392–407.

to which this gift of the geological background changed destinies and flowed out into the experiences of mankind. One aspect, from a social standpoint, was the change produced in the morals, the attitudes and the social relationships of the men directly involved. Cut off from the influences of home they found themselves out of touch with the old. They developed a carelessness of conduct which was often a complete compliance with the impulses of the moment. While not all of the Forty-Niners followed in this reckless path, many of them did, and the few who stood for law and order were compelled to take matters into their own hands and maintain "Vigilance Committees" until governmental and judicial influences came in to meet the need.

Silver, copper, and tin, as well as gold, were known to the ages. The fact that the ores containing these metals could be smelted at low temperatures and the pure metal obtained, likely made them the first metals to be used. Alloys made by mixing various metals became widely known, and so general was the practice of alloying copper and tin that cultures in many human groups have been designated as the Bronze Age.

Iron might have been known as early as the more easily smelted metals, but since it was worked with more difficulty, requiring higher temperatures and greater skill, its extensive use appears to have been later. The term "Iron Age" reflects the fact that it became central in various cultures. It is a serious question as to whether or not we are justified in arranging the chronological social development of peoples on the basis of their use of metals, but the very attempt men have made to do so points to the influence of one or another metal on ways of living.

The Forests

Plants are a factor in rock disintegration and also in holding the earth's soil firm. This leads into a consideration of deforestation in relation to floods. Because of the extensive removal of trees, the erosive forces have increased in their destructive work on soils and landscapes. To some extent a forest-covering serves as a sponge to hold and absorb rain water. The water held by the network of roots may be slowly given off in surface drainage, but it is much more likely to sink further into the ground and through the crevices of rock to finally reach the water table. In the reduced speed and volume of surface drainage, forest-covered areas are saved from rapid erosion. By arresting the flow of water into the streams the forests also tend to prevent disastrous floods, with their ramified social effects.[24]

Erosion

The erosion of rock is called weathering. The principal agents of such erosion are heat from the sun and action of the water in the forms of rain and ice. After the rock material is broken off, a number of agencies take up the process of reducing the fragments to smaller particles until some are so small as to be carried in suspension in the moving water, the main force for transportation. In this diminutive state it is ready for a final entry into solution. But the main product of erosion and weathering is soil, a mid-way stage between the original bed-rock and the final solution and sediment in the rivers or the sea.

The waters' action in washing away soil is also called erosion. While the isostasy of the continents is continually lifting the land, there is a contrary action of erosion that decreases the height of the lands lifted up. Forests and vegetation, by means of their interlacing roots, act as preventives of erosion, but when they are removed, the washing is rapid. This action is not a new discovery. George Washington is said to have tried various methods to avoid soil washing as early as 1769. Thomas Jefferson also spoke of the devastation of his fields at Monticello. Patrick Henry engaged the same enemy at his farm at Red Hill. These men were familiar with the soil most easily yielding to erosion: the red clay soil of Virginia.[25]

Erosion has been classified thus:

1. Sheet erosion, large areas of uniform slope or level having the surface removed;
2. Rill washing, the beginning of lines of erosion due to uneven surface;
3. Gully erosion, the development of deep furrows;
4. Wind erosion, the moving of dry soil by force of the wind.

The last of these is responsible for the removal of great quantities of fine soil and sand from large areas, the so-called "Dust Bowls."[26]

The loss of soil through erosion is primarily a serious matter.

24 See James, *Outline of Geography,* p. 407.

25 Gustafson, cf. p. 17.

26 *Idem,* p. 87.

Besides, the material thus removed is likely to be deposited in streams, and interfere with navigation. In flood time these streams are unable to carry off the water, and the result is the outspread of devastating floods. Occasionally the erosion results in the deposit of rich alluvial material eroded from the upper valley and deposited in a sheet over the lower valley, enriching the soil, as the Nile has done in Egypt.

Erosion takes place along the sea coast. Its action is evident along the New Jersey coast where, according to estimates, 2200 acres have been carried away in eighty years.[27]

Drainage

Drainage is essential to any area that supports a population. Standing water stagnates and becomes a menace to health. Though most of the earth's surface is drained at least sufficiently for man's purposes, there are some areas where drainage is sluggish, and extensive swamps and marshes have developed. Stagnant waters permit the growth of organic species and a rapid multiplication of such bacteria and plant forms as render the water unfit for human use. In addition, it provides a medium in which organic disease germs can multiply rapidly and endanger the health of man. Moving water, in contrast, exposing the entire mass in time to the effects of the air and sunlight, is purified of organic matter, and the floating mineral matter has opportunity to be washed aside or allowed to settle. The drainage process, then, over most of the earth works in the direction of human safety.

SELECTED REFERENCES

Dick, E. N., *The Sod House Frontier*, D. Appleton & Co., 1937.

Edward, Stewart, *The Forty-Niners*, in *Chronicles of America*, 1920, v. 25.

Fairgrieve, James, *Geography and World Power*, E. P. Dutton & Co.

Gustafson, Ries, Guise, Hamilton, *Conservation in the United States*, Comstock Publishing Company, Ithaca, N. Y., 1939.

Huntington, Ellsworth, *Civilization and Climate*, 3rd Ed., Yale University Press, 1924.

Huntington, Ellsworth, *Principles of Human Geography*, 4th Rev. Ed., J. Wiley and Sons, 1934.

Huntington and Visher, *Climatic Changes*, Yale University Press, 1922.

Huntington and Williams, *Economic and Social Geography*, J. Wiley and Sons, 1933.

James, Preston E., *An Outline of Geography*, Ginn & Co., 1935.

[27] *Idem*, p. 99.

Peattie, Roderick, *New College Geography*, Ginn & Co., 1932.

Pomfret, John E., *The Geographic Pattern of Mankind*, D. Appleton-Century, 1935.

Salisbury, Rollin D., *Physiography*, Henry Holt and Company.

Semple, Ellen Churchill, *Influence of Geographic Environment*, Henry Holt and Company.

Shaler, N. S., *Nature and Man in America*, Scribner.

Spinden, H. J., "The Origin and Distribution of Agriculture in America" in Kroeber and Waterman, *Source Book of Anthropology*, Harcourt Brace & Co., Rev. Ed., 1931, pp. 227–233.

Thomas, Franklin, *The Environmental Basis of Society*, Century Company.

Chapter 5

BIOLOGICAL REGULARITIES

I. Influence of Non-Human Biological Organisms on Social Life

By Dr. Mehran K. Thomson
Professor of Sociology, Michigan State Normal College

VITAL RELATIONSHIP OF HUMAN LIFE WITH ALL LIFE AND LIVING MATTER

Origin of Life

Life, so far as we can judge, exists only on our planet, the Earth. It is further restricted to spotted portions of the surface of the earth from the highest mountain to the deepest ocean, approximately a span of only twelve miles out of the incomprehensibly vast expanse of the whole universe. Where life came from, when it came and in what forms, remain matters of conjecture. It is, however, generally agreed among the authorities that there was a very very long period of time when the earth was barren of life because the environment was not favorable to its existence. Eventually, as the earth passed through many geological revolutions, the favorable conditions of heat, light, atmosphere, moisture, and other essentials came about which made it possible for life to exist.[1] Although life appeared relatively late in the development of our world, it was a good many million years ago. There are several theories attempting to account for the origin of life.[2] But there is no conclusive evidence for any of these theories.

All Living Things Are Kin

No matter what view we take of the origin of life, we are confronted with the fact that all life and living matter are definitely and vitally related to each other. We must go even further and note that living matter contains elements which in themselves are

[1] See Chapter 1 in this text.

[2] That life came from another planet or somewhere beyond our earth, that it always existed, special creation, spontaneous generation, organic evolution, meteoritic and bacterial origin have been advocated by different scientists.

inorganic. In the last analysis living matter is not unlike non-living matter. Life is composed of at least fourteen out of the ninety-two accepted elements which make up our physical world. Traces of additional elements in living matter have been detected to equal the number of letters in the alphabet (C, H, N, S, P, K, Na, Ca, Mg, Cl, Fe, Cu, Al, Cr, Co, Pl, Mn, Ni, Si, Ag, Sn, T, Zn). No one, however, has succeeded in creating life according to this or any formula. There is some ingredient, or process or condition or "spark," that is unknown. "Protoplasm eludes exact chemical analysis."

A species of matter known as bacteria may be said to constitute the link between plant and animal even though the link between living and non-living is still missing. "The living things are not all plants or animals. Nature has been more resourceful, more thorough in trying out the possibilities. Another kingdom, that of the bacteria, using the word in an exact sense, is likewise world-wide in distribution, probably more numerous in individuals and *very important in human* relations."[3]

Thus the extremely vital interdependence of elements, bacteria, plants and animals is indisputable and essential to an understanding of the utter dependence of even the so-called higher forms of life on the basic principles of relationship of all the factors. The foregoing simple nitrogen cycle will serve to illustrate this point.[4]

Prejudice against Humble Origin

We are accustomed to regarding ourselves as so greatly superior to the "lower" forms of life that we are likely to overlook the close

[3] E. B. Copeland, *Science,* LXV, p. 390. (Italics are present author's.)

[4] After H. W. Conn. Compare "If parts of an organism may be non-living, as undoubtedly they may, there is no reason for denying the possibility that part of a cell may be non-living." Reprinted by permission from *Elementary Course in General Physiology* by Scarth and Lloyd published by John Wiley & Sons, Inc., 1930; p. 14. Also "It is a general law that plants live on inorganic, animals on organic substances. And since animals, owing to their incapacity to synthesize protoplasm from simple inorganic bodies, are necessarily dependent for their existence on the food supplied to them by plants, and since plants are unable to obtain the elements required except in the form of inorganic bodies, it follows that the continuance of life on the globe is ultimately dependent on the free supply of carbon dioxide, nitrates, phosphates, sulphates and water. It is thus possible to trace cycles for each of the important elements, following it through its various phases of elaboration into organic, and its degradation into inorganic matter." Topley and Wilson, *The Principles of Bacteriology and Immunity,* London: Edward Arnold & Son, 1929, pp. 1276–77.

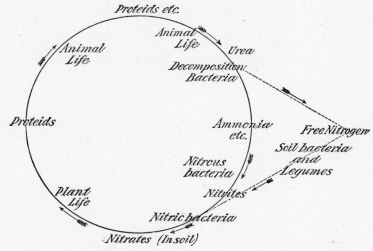

FIG. 1. The nitrogen cycle. (Courtesy of The Blakiston Company.)

vital relationship and interdependence. And yet according to the official summary for the Council of the American Anthropological Association "Man is part of the animal world. In all respects his anatomical structure conforms to that of the rest of the animal world. His prenatal life closely parallels that of the higher mammals. The same influences that control their development after birth control him and he responds in a like manner to the environment in which he is placed." We may accept this truth without being ashamed of the dependence and relationship, for, in the first place origin does not determine value. Very humble beginnings can lead to very great ends. And, in the second place, life in any form is not so lowly after all. It represents an unbroken chain of succession from the very beginning of life. It signifies potentialities beyond our comprehension but well within the scope of our respect and even admiration.

Take the fertilized ovum: it is the most marvelous piece of mechanism in the universe so far as we can judge. Aside from having descended from the very beginning of life, it is endowed with power to procreate and perpetuate itself indefinitely. It is potentially immortal. Although almost microscopic, it is so infinitely complex that it contains all the hereditary factors of countless generations preceding and anteceding itself—the color of eye

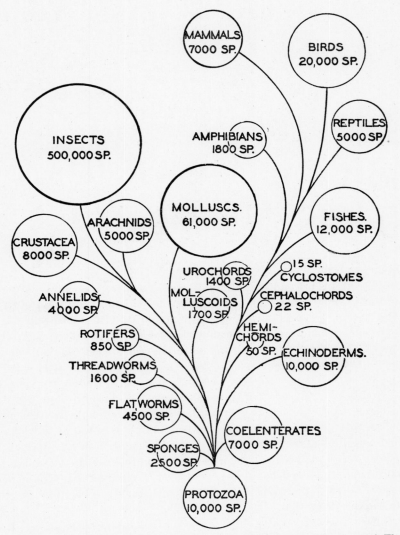

FIG. 2.   A phylogenetic tree of the animal kingdom.[5]   (Courtesy of The Blakiston Company.)

and hair, musical ability or whatever special aptitude it possesses which may be genius or near genius.   In addition it has capacity

[5] The tree of life illustrating the relative number of each species.   Neal and Rand, *Comparative Anatomy*, p. 665.

for growth, development, repairment of injured tissue, in short, all the possibilities of an intelligent human being, not to say a Shakespeare or an Edison.

In a lesser degree, from our point of view, all living matter has certain peculiar characteristics and properties which defy the scientist's ability to duplicate in the laboratory without the aid of living substance. Therefore, life, in every form, deserves our respect and consideration, especially since we ourselves are so intimately concerned with it as will be pointed out presently.

MOTHER NATURE

Nature Holds the Stakes

The name mother is quite appropriate in that she is the original source of all life and being. In addition she is, like a true mother, impartial. In any argument with physical nature or between human nature and non-human factors Mother Nature holds the stakes. She can't lose. To understand physical nature we must understand biological nature and vice versa. To understand or explain human nature we must know something about all nature and vice versa. We are a part of the universe just as the universe is a part of us. We are subject to the laws of gravitation and the rest of the laws of physics and chemistry and all the other commandments of nature.

The Total Environment

While Sociology specializes in the problems of human relationships, these relationships are dependent upon the total environment. In the adjustments and maladjustments of human beings the total environment is ever present and constantly operative. It is only for the sake of convenience and lack of space that we pass over some phases of the total environment in a sketchy manner in order to emphasize the particular area we have set out to explore and expound.

STRUGGLE TO SURVIVE

Survival of the Most Fit

Not only is Mother Nature impartial, but she is also neutral in the gigantic struggle that goes on for survival. The interplay of the forces of nature creates stress and tension causing dislocations which can be balanced only through struggle and conflict. All life must take part in the struggle to survive, to gain a foothold, to perpetuate its kind. The virility of life has been strikingly demonstrated by planting grain after it had lain dormant in the tombs of the Pharaohs for many centuries, and having it germinate and grow. Conflict, however, implies defeat for some and success for some. Those who perish are the misfits; those who survive are the fit. This need not imply anything about the worth of the survivor except ability to survive which may be due to favorable circumstances even more than to individual merit or ability. It means adaptability, accommodation, adjustment. This adjustment to environment is essential to survival and indispensable to supremacy among the survivors.

The actual struggle consists of a conflict between the particular species of plant and animal against a hostile physical environment, such as lack of moisture, too much moisture, unfavorable climate, extremes of heat or cold and the like. The conflict may exist between unlike forms competing for the same thing at the same time, for the same food and the same living space. This type of conflict is known as *interspecific* struggle in contrast with the third type of conflict which is *intraspecific* because it occurs among creatures of the same species, a sort of civil war. The intraspecific conflict is usually regarded as the most vicious and deadly.[6]

The Prodigality of Nature

In this three-cornered titanic struggle many individuals go down. But the species survives as a rule. Apparently nature is more interested in the species than she is in the individual. Among certain insects, the mayfly, lakefly, shadflies, and many moths, the parent dies the moment the offspring is born or its future is assured. The name *Ephemerida* attached to this group literally means lasting but a day. In other instances the wife devours the husband immediately after the honeymoon. Notorious in this group is the widow spider. In fact this practice is the rule rather than the exception among all spiders. The terrific toll taken of the indi-

---

[6] The opposing view is presented by the Russian geographer and naturalist, Prince Peter Kropotkin, on the basis of wide travel and observation in which he points out that the law of mutual aid among creatures of the same species operates sufficiently strongly under adverse environmental conditions to mitigate the intraspecific struggle and render it not nearly so deadly as the conflict against a ruthless hostile nature in the form of extremes of heat and cold, floods and droughts and the like, what Darwin called the natural check to over-population.

viduals to insure the survival of the species is illustrated by some of the best known fish, like the cod, herring and others, whose chances of survival from the egg is one in fourteen million. Thus nature provides a great deal of "cannon fodder" by her extreme prodigality with seeds and eggs.[7]

It is commonly observed that the seeds of apples, grapes, cucumber, watermelon and all vegetables and fruits are far beyond what could possibly be planted and grown. The elm tree will shed bushels of seeds. If all of these managed to grow into full-sized trees, elm trees would soon cover the earth. What is true of plants is equally true of animals. Even the slowest breeders would in a very short time take up all the seats and standing room in the theater of life if given free reign. The elephant, for example, is a very slow breeder, having about the same period of infancy and a bit longer life span than a human being. And yet if all the progeny could survive and reproduce, even this, the slowest breeder among the mammals, would produce nineteen million elephants in seven hundred and fifty years from a single couple bearing only six immediate progeny during a period of seventy years.

Life tends to multiply in geometric ratio while the available space and food supply remain stationary or at best increase only slowly. The tremendous import of this is startling when you consider the possibilities among the faster breeders—rabbits, pigeons and the like. The common oyster lays about sixty million eggs. It has been pointed out that if all the eggs from one oyster survived and grew up to be mamma oysters and continued in like manner for four generations, they would make a pile of oysters eight times the bulk of the earth. And when you get into the realm of microscopic creatures the possibilities stagger the imagination. The prize story is based on Professor Woodrill's experiments with *Paramecium*, a single-celled organism which multiplies by division every day or two. If all the progeny could go on unmolested for nine thousand generations, covering the period of a college course of four years, there would be enough of these creatures extant to fill the known confines of the universe. And by that time mass production of *Paramecium* would attain the incredible speed of light, 186,320 miles per second.

[7] It has been reported that the marine gastropod, ironically called the seahorse, may lay as many as half a billion eggs during one spawning season of only four months, necessitating the amazing production efficiency of forty-one thousand eggs per minute.

This extreme prodigality is necessary for the survival of the species. It also serves to maintain balance among the species despite the havoc it creates among the individuals.

Nature's Balance

In a dynamic order the cycle of conflict, balance, unbalance, more conflict and further equilibrium goes on unceasingly. It is seldom a fight to the death. The same is true of conflict in human society. While labor and capital, for example, are almost in perpetual conflict they also cooperate. Neither wants to destroy the other completely, but merely to gain superior or at least equal power. Neither could exist without the other, hence frequent compromise and balance.

Feet, Teeth, Brains

In the struggle to survive the advantage is with those individuals and species which happen to be the best endowed to meet the conditions of adaptation and survival. The greatest assets in the animal world are feet, teeth and brains. Many ancient forms were lacking in all three aspects, others possessed only one or two. Man alone is supreme in all three essentials and has therefore, risen to the supreme position in the animal kingdom by a tremendous margin. He is practically in a class by himself.

Feet, representing locomotion and the ability to get around, enable the animal to survive because they increase his cruising range in the search of food. During periods of drought or a complete change in the climate or topography of the earth or some section of it, those animals which cannot move on to "greener pastures" are forced to starve. The archaic ungulates who gave way to modern-hoofed animals come under this category.

Teeth are important in determining the type of food that may be eaten. Biologists often classify animals by this token. Herbivores are herb eaters, carnivores are meat eaters and omnivores are eaters of almost anything. Among the herbivores there are the browsing and grazing types. These are obviously highly specialized forms, seriously limiting the range of adaptability. It means that if the right kind of food is not available in the natural habitat or anywhere the animal might go in quest of it, he is in danger of starvation and extinction. Many species of dinosaurs became extinct for this reason. In the interests of efficiency animals and men specialize and then find their adaptability seriously threatened and their chances of survival reduced in a changing environment.

Again, human beings have the advantage in being omnivores. If any doubt existed it has disappeared since the recent contest among college students who have devoured gold fish, mice, phonograph records and sundry other objects. Not long ago a man ate a dollar bill to disprove the statement that "you can't eat it."

Brains, representing intelligence, are the most valuable assets in survival. And here is where human beings stand out conspicuously among the "lower" forms. In sheer bulk, the brain of a human being is larger and heavier than is that of any other animal with the exception of the whale and the elephant.[8] But these monsters are so much larger than a man that another standard must be introduced, brain weight relative to body weight. According to this standard man is supreme with the exception of the field mouse and the humming bird which should be discounted because both of these creatures were once much larger. While their bodies have shrunk, perhaps through lack of sufficient nourishment, their brains have remained the same size and gives them this strange disparity.

It is interesting to note that when you apply the first law of sheer brain weight the advantage is with men over women. A

[8] The following table of ratios between brain-weight and body-weight of a few well known animals (including man) will serve to indicate, in part, the difference in their relative intelligence. Recent studies by Dr. George Crile and Dr. Daniel P. Quiring emphasizing the importance of glands in relation to brain and body weights, indicate the special significance of the relative size of the Thyroid and Adrenals. The size of the brain, according to their theory, is determined by the degree of energy necessary to carry on the life functions of a given animal. On the purely animal rating a man could get along on a brain one-tenth the size of the one he actually possesses. Thus man's tremendous mental activity over and above other animals is apparently due to his super brain,—many times over-sized.

	Brain-weight in Grams	Body-weight in Grams	Ratio between Brain & Body-wt.	Percent of Brain-wt. to Body-wt.
Whale	7,000	70,000,000	10,000	.01%
Kangaroo	65	45,000	692	.14%
Lion	220	120,000	545	.18%
Elephant	5,000	2,500,000	500	.2 %
Dog	120	46,000	383	.26%
Gorilla	400	90,000	225	.44%
Cat	30	3,500	116	.85%
Man	1,400	70,000	50	2.00%

man's brain weighs 1350 grams; a woman's brain weighs 1250 grams. But when you apply the second standard of relative brain weight to body weight, woman has the last word, as usual.

Man's Superior Position

Thus man, possessing *all* the necessary factors for survival, adaptation and supremacy has risen to the top. And the greatest of these is brains plus the development of articulate speech. This constitutes the margin of difference between us and our simian cousins, the various anthropoid (man-like) apes. In each and every other sensory capacity man is decidedly inferior to other forms of life. The ox, the horse, the elephant and many others surpass man in physical strength, in ability to pull a load. The "fastest human" travels a hundred yards in nine and four-tenths seconds, or twenty-one plus miles per hour. The gazelle has been clocked close to ninety miles an hour. An albatross can cover the distance between New York and San Francisco in twelve hours. Birds in flight cross ocean and mountain barriers without stopping. The common house-swallow attains the incredible speed of better than a hundred and fifty miles per hour. Solomon might have sent not merely the slug-gard to the ant, but the holder of the Olympic record in sprinting, for a lesson in speed. If the ant could keep up the same relative speed which he now possesses while his size increased to the propor-tions of a man, he would travel four hundred times as fast as a man. Under similar circumstances Achilles would have had a tough time in his mythological attempt to overtake a tortoise.

Again, the eagle and kindred birds surpass man in the keenness of vision with their ability to spot a fish or turtle from several thou-sand feet in the air and swoop down on him with uncanny accuracy —a lesson in dive bombing. The mongrel dog surpasses his master in the senses of smell and hearing.

And yet, man, through superior intelligence, completely outdis-tances the whole animal kingdom. By adding brains to his more or less feeble physical endowments he multiplies his abilities a mil-lionfold. His hand plus his brains sends out a messenger of death that overtakes his prey or enemy at the rate of over two thousand miles an hour from the muzzle of a gun. His fist plus brains hurls a projectile weighing a thousand pounds a distance of some thirty miles to pierce an armored target which he can't see. His feeble eyesight plus brains creates a two hundred-inch telescope that magnifies the human eye one million times.[9]   Or he uses a microscope which magnifies four thousand times and peeps into the private life of microbes so tiny that a million of them could dance on the point of a needle at the same time.   His feeble voice plus brains enables him to project his music around the world or to can his vocal efforts and preserve them for posterity.   Man has no wings, no feathers, not even patagium, but he has brains with which he constructs a mechanical bird that carries him through space at several hundred miles an hour.   And ere long he will ride with the sun, a thousand miles an hour.   And this is only the beginning.   No one knows what the future will bring by way of man's conquest of nature and mastery over other forms of life.

Our Interdependence with Physical-Biological Environment

Our association, our dependence and interdependence on the total environment is thus apparent.   Elsewhere in this text various phases of this relationship with the outside world, with other species of animals and with our own species are pointed out and treated fully.   It is our privilege and responsibility in this connection to lay special emphasis on the close relationship between man and his non-human biological environment without losing sight for a moment of the fact that a human being functions not only in a world of other human beings, nor only with climate, or any other single factor apart, but with all of them at the same time and all the time. It is only for the sake of convenience that we divide our work and emphasis.

Our method of approach is to point out the very close relationship in the whole biological kingdom including man by cataloging the various ways in which we influence other forms and what they do to us and for us.   Any system or method is as good as the results that it attains.   We believe that this rehearsal of the manifold contacts with this type of environment will serve our purpose best.   The accumulative effect is overwhelming.   Moreover, there should appear many commonplace yet interesting facts that are or should be matters of common knowledge.

[9] The 200-inch telescope on top of Mount Palomer (90 miles from Los Angeles) sees twice as far as the next best telescope.   It can discern stars one billion light years distant.   (A light year is about 6,000,000,000,000 miles.)   It increases the observable volume of space eight times and brings the moon within twenty-five miles of the earth.

WHAT MAN DOES TO AND FOR NON–HUMAN FORMS OF LIFE

Exterminates

We look upon many forms of plants and animals as our natural enemies and seek to exterminate them. A popular radio announcer keeps reminding us during the dull moments of a baseball game "never give a bug a break, give him . . . ," the commercial name of a particular insecticide. There are hundreds of these products as germicides, insecticides, fumigators, insect sprays, deodorants, etc., plus many processes such as freezing, boiling, pasteurizing, sterilizing, electrocuting, immunizing, vaccinating, cremating, to accomplish the downfall of undesirable bugs and germs. Some of the more common chemicals used are formaldehyde, corrosive sublimate, zinc chloride, copper sulphate, calcium hydrozide and chlorine as a poison gas.

Aids

"He gave to friend and foe more than he received," is descriptive of our attitude towards non-human as well as human forms of life. Not only do we try to exterminate some undesirable and deadly forms of plants and animals, but we proffer valuable aid to the desirable and friendly ones. We have a selfish interest in increasing their numbers, in helping them to survive, cultivating and improving the stock and even creating new and better types.

By working with nature and taking advantage of the sublaws of evolution, man performs miracles with plants and animals. These laws are (1) heredity, the conservative element in evolution which transmits unchanged the peculiar characteristics of the parent to the offspring from generation to generation; (2) the law of variation, which is the progressive element in evolution, introducing changes and freak individuals known as sports or mutants; (3) regression, which is the force that keeps variation in check to prevent it from running away with itself.

Out of a field of lilies covering many acres, Luther Burbank (1849–1926) selected a few unusual kinds and by replanting these he developed many new color combinations. By similar methods he "created" ten varieties of berries, new varieties of plums and prunes, many varieties of apples, cherries, peaches, quince and nectarines, many varieties of flowers besides the lilies, the new Burbank potato, new varieties of tomato, sweet and field corn, squash, asparagus, peas, and spineless cacti so useful as animal fodder.

Grafting plants and trees and cross-breeding animals should be mentioned as the most common methods of improving the original stock and introducing new creations. We owe to these processes some of the most highly prized flowers, fruits, berries, all the fancy birds and livestock. Nectarine is a cross between a peach and a plum. Lemons now grow mostly on orange trees. To get the "blue" of the blue spruce it must be grafted. The best grade of cattle, sheep, hogs, dogs, cats, chickens, race horses is all "culti-

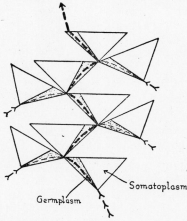

Somatoplasm

Germplasm

Fig. 3.—Diagram to illustrate the continuity of the germ-plasm. Each triangle represents an individual made up of germ-plasm (dotted) and somatoplasm (undotted). The beginning of the life cycle of each individual is represented at the apex of the triangle where germ-plasm and somatoplasm are both present. As the individual develops, each of these component parts increases. In sexual reproduction the germ-plasms of two individuals unite into a common stream, to which the somatoplasm makes no contribution. The continuity of the germ-plasm is shown by the heavy broken line into which run collateral contributions from successive sexual reproductions. From H. E. Walter, *Genetics*, 4th Edition, p. 11. By permission of The Macmillan Company, publishers.

vated" stock. The razorback hog is a sorry critter compared with the Poland China, Yorkshire, Berkshire, Hampshire, Duroc-Jersey, Chester White, and Farnsworth.

Another important law is that acquired characteristics cannot be inherited. This means that no matter what happens to the body or mind of the individual plant or animal during his lifetime he cannot transmit this change to his offspring. Experiments on mice and rats by cutting off the tails of several hundred generations proved that it had no effect on succeeding generations. The last rat had as long a tail as the first. This law is almost universally accepted since Weismann pointed out that there are two types of plasm or cell, the somatoplasm (body cell) and the germ plasm, the germinating life cell. Weismann claimed that these two are independent of each other, hence what affects the somatoplasm cannot affect the germ plasm.

Nevertheless, within these evolutionary limitations, man has succeeded in changing plants and animals both in quantity and quality to suit his own designs.

Protects

One of the methods in securing "bigger and better" plants and animals, or at least *different* ones, has been man's ability to make the environment more favorable by various forms of protection from physical dangers such as heat and cold, famine and disease, providing more and better food, protection from their natural enemies plus restorative and curative means for their survival and improvement. Man is extending the benefits of all his vast learning and scientific techniques to plants and animals as well as to his own kind, just as he uses destructive weapons on his own kind as well as on other forms of life.

There are hospitals and doctors and scientific laboratories which specialize in the care and treatment of plants and animals. Medical and surgical treatment is constantly given pets, farm animals, and other creatures at the Zoo and elsewhere. Not only do we have specially prepared foods for dogs, cats, canaries and other pets and all farm animals, but in certain large centers there is fresh delivery service of special perishable foods, even as we get our daily bottle of milk from the side porch.

Animals and plants are also protected by legal action from the ravages of man himself. Witness laws and licenses covering hunting and fishing. Further aid and protection are offered through fisheries, hatcheries, nurseries, bird sanctuaries, feeding and watering places both for domestic and wild life.

We are often sentimental over certain forms of non-human life. There are many people who endow institutions and laboratories for the advancement of the lower forms of life. It is not uncommon for people to pass on their inheritance to their pets or at least to remember them generously in their wills. There are many dog and cat heirs and heiresses. Recently a woman left a considerable sum of money to her pet goldfish—perhaps in desperate horror of what some ambitious freshman might do to them. One lucky dog got a real human funeral service, and was buried in a bronze casket costing five thousand dollars.

The story is told for a fact that a certain woman who had a husband and two pet dogs was persuaded with difficulty to leave her dogs at home and accompany her husband in his quest for health when he was taken critically ill and advised to go to France for special treatment. Before they reached the other side of the ocean a radiogram broke the sad news of the death of one of the dogs. The woman took the first boat back to the United States, leaving her husband to the tender mercies of a French nurse. And when she returned to France with her surviving "precious" her devoted husband had passed away.

It is also a fact that humane societies for the protection of dumb animals were organized and legalized before similar organizations were formed for the protection of children.[10] Farmers and breeders of horses often turn them out to pasture when they are too old to work. The general's horse takes part in the funeral procession of his master and is afterwards turned out to pasture.

Thus, it cannot be said that human beings are not kind and considerate to non-human life. In contrast "man's inhumanity to man" is all the more striking.

Transplants and Transports

Still another way of increasing the quantity and quality of plants and animals is by removing them to more congenial soil and habitat. When we find that they will thrive in some other locality we ship them around and make up nature's deficiency in teeth, feet and brains so far as these species are concerned. It is claimed that of the sixty basic human foods, more than half were donated to the civilized world by the American Indian.[11] Among the contributions

[10] American Society for the Prevention of Cruelty to Animals was founded in 1866; New York Society for the Prevention of Cruelty to Children, 1875.

[11] The following list enumerates the most important plants originally cultivated by the several Indian tribes before the discovery of the New World in 1492: Agave or aloe, alligator pear, arrowroot, barnyard grass, kidney bean, lima bean, coca or cocaine, cherimoya, cashew nut, chili pepper, cacao, corn, cotton, guava, gourd, Jerusalem artichoke, maize, manoc, maté or Paraguay tea, madia, potato, pumpkin, prickly pear or Indian fig, pineapple, peanut, papaw, oca, quinine, quinoa, sweet potato, star apple squash, tobacco, tomato.

are potatoes, tomatoes, corn, not to mention tobacco which is hardly a food, but a giant industry. In the United States alone the value of the growing crop was estimated at $237,479,000 for 1935, an ordinary year.

Moreover, when certain species are threatened with extinction, man comes to the rescue by affording legal and scientific protection as in game laws, restocking lakes and streams with fish and in the protection of buffalo and reindeer once so abundant and now almost extinct.

Domesticates, Trains, Educates

Domestication of animals was the first step in man's rise to supremacy and ultimately to civilization. So early did this take place in man's long precivilized and perhaps prehuman existence that we have no idea when it actually took place nor how long it took to do it. No animal of significance has been domesticated since early savage man. The earliest paleontological finds show domesticated forms pretty much as we find them today. The authorities usually give woman credit for domesticating all the animals, including man.

Domestication involves a great deal of training and education which is treated under "what plants and animals do for us."

Affords Companionship

It is doubtful if any plants appreciate man's company. But there are at least some animals who appear to do so while other animals apparently have not made up their minds, and still others, judging from their action, do not think much of it. In addition to the long list of ordinary pets and common farm animals who hobnob with *Homo sapiens*, there are a number of unusual ones such as fleas, white mice, giant pandas, seals, skunks, opossums, penguins, gold fish and other types of fish, alligators, kangaroos, monkeys, turtles, frogs, squirrels, and practically all forms of birds and many species of snakes.

Uses Some of Them Against Others of Them

By introducing new parasites he is a veritable warmonger.[12]

[12] Commercial companies in Japan and many other countries have catalogues of these parasites that they send out and have the creatures ready to fill orders. However, it is illegal to import animals or parasites without federal authority because any one of them could easily upset nature's balance as in the case of the English sparrow, the gypsy moth, the Japanese beetle, the Canadian thistle, the Australian mongoose.

The Australian mongoose, for example, was introduced into the United States to prey upon rats. Bird life is encouraged chiefly because the work of most birds relieves us of many common bugs, vermin, grubs and all manner of pests. One lone chickadee devours in the course of a single day thirty cankerworm moths and 5,550 eggs of the same species. Fifth column activities are encouraged among the fungi, bacteria, microbes, as well as among superior forms. The Judas ram at the Chicago stock yards who daily leads hundreds of sheep to the slaughter is another example of our Trojan horse methods in dealing with dumb animals.

WHAT PLANTS AND ANIMALS DO TO US

Some things plants and animals do *to* us; some things they do *for* us. The former are not to our taste or advantage and we list them as unfriendly.

Plants and Animals as Enemies

Poison snakes and savage beasts still claim a total of some sixty thousand human lives annually in certain parts of the world, mostly in Asia and Africa. And the number of these creatures put out of action by human effort amounts to just about the same number, so that the score is about even. The more than unfriendly attitude of some plants and animals is demonstrated by poisoning, killing, causing insanity, transmitting diseases peculiar to themselves, and as ''carriers'' of human diseases.

1. *Poison.* The poison or toxic effect of non-human on human life is both direct and indirect—on the skin, in the internal organs, and in the blood stream. The direct effect on the skin is illustrated by poison ivy, poison oak, eczema, dandruff, hives, seven-year itch, barber's itch and the like. The types which get under the skin are illustrated by mosquitoes, snakes, scorpions, spiders, spoiled food, tetanus (the germs that cause lock-jaw), rabies and the whole tribe of disease germs.

2. *Kill.* Some of the attacks by plants and animals go beyond poisoning and causing slow death by destroying our life immediately. This is demonstrated by animals who might naturally prey on human beings and by others who will fight to kill only when they are cornered or defending their young. At the Chicago Field Museum there is a man-eating tiger who is reputed to have devoured over a hundred human beings. There are numerous cases in which

a man has been gored by a bull or kicked to death by a mule or horse. Insects, despite their diminutive size, can cause instant death to a human being, especially when they attack in great numbers as occasionally happens by swarms of bees, mosquitoes, ants and wasps.

3. *Cause Insanity.* Aside from the fears and phobias due to non-human life there are direct attacks on the brain and nervous system which cause such mental diseases as paresis, which is caused by the spiral organism, *Treponema pallidum* of syphilis.

4. *Contagious Animal Diseases.* Non-human life is heir to many diseases which it does not communicate to human beings and which are of importance only because the injury of the plants and animals by these diseases may be of value to us. Some of the diseases which do not ordinarily attack human beings are anthrax, symptomatic anthrax, malignant oedema, glanders, infectious abortion, hog cholera, foot-and-mouth disease (sometimes, though rarely attacks human beings), chicken cholera, fowl diphtheria and numerous other diseases of the barnyard and many diseases of insects such as those which attack silk worms and bees.

In addition to the diseases which are peculiar to non-human forms of life there are many which are common to both. Among these are bubonic plague, malaria, yellow fever, sleeping sickness, rabies, typhus fever, infectious jaundice, trench fever. The microbes which cause these diseases attack animals, including man, and both may infect each other. In addition there are germ diseases that attack man without intermediate hosts. Among these are tuberculosis, tetanus or lock-jaw, gangrene, and certain forms of food-poisoning.

The strictly human diseases which lower forms almost never get are nevertheless due to microbes. These are among the most serious: smallpox, leprosy, scarlet fever, gonorrhea, syphilis, pneumonia, diphtheria, measles, whooping cough, meningitis, influenza, infantile paralysis.

5. *As Carriers of Many Common Diseases.* A carrier is one who may or may not suffer from a communicable disease, but is a menace to others who may catch the disease by contact with the carrier. Typhoid Mary, a cook, is a notorious example of several generations ago. But our concern here is with animals as carriers and a few examples will suffice. The dread African sleeping sickness is carried by the tsetse fly. Lice carry typhus and trench fever.

Rocky mountain spotted fever is carried by the wood tick. Oysters are often responsible for typhoid. Dysentery and cholera are also filth diseases just as typhoid. And, of course, the mosquito is one of the worst carriers, causing malaria, yellow fever and other diseases. Bubonic plague claimed twenty-four thousand lives in the city of Amsterdam in 1664 out of a population of two hundred thousand. Millions have been slain by this disease in China and India for centuries. It is carried by the rat.

Plants and Animals as Parasites

Like poisons, parasites attack the skin, the vital organs, or get into the blood stream. Examples of skin parasites are fleas, ticks, chiggers, itch mites, lice (cooties). Those which take a lifetime lease on the internal organs are tape worms, hook worms and the like, while those which get into the blood are the disease germs listed above. They are real poachers because they settle down and raise their families. The chills and fevers accompanying most germ diseases are due to the incubating period of the particular baby germs. Each chill means a new batch just hatched and ready to go to work.

Plants and Animals as Pests

Less dangerous and not so fatal are the pests of which there are altogether too many. The house fly and ordinary mosquito are the best known. But there are many other forms which cause a great deal of discomfort and spoil our vacations. The pollen of certain plants is supposed to cause hay fever and other respiratory disorders in some people that are allergic to them. The stinging insects such as bees, wasps, ants, hornets, etc., are called hymenoptera. Other pests are cockroaches, bedbugs, water bugs, lice, fleas, spiders, etc. Both literally and figuratively they get into our hair and sometimes in eyes, ears, and mouth as well. The nuisance value of some insects consists in falling into the "ointment" and other foods and drinks and splattering on the windshield of the automobile and sifting through the radiator. There are other forms whose bad manners of eating and general conduct are offensive to most people. Many people are annoyed and disgusted by cold, clammy, slimy, wriggly, crawling creatures. In fact they offend all our senses of sight, touch, taste and smell.

Speaking of smell, some plants and animals make a specialty of it. The best known offenders, to take only one representative of plant and one of animal, are the stinkweed and the skunk. However, all animals, including man, have an odor that is more or less unpleasant.

Plants and Animals as Thieves and Robbers

The depredations of plants and animals mount rapidly when you add up the untold varieties of fungi, bacteria, molds, worms and moths which attack and destroy our food in the growing stages. The blight of red rust will cut the crop to half, with damage running into the millions of dollars. It takes the labor of a million men to make up the annual loss in this country due to insects alone. Grasshoppers are so devastating that they constitute a class by themselves. They march on the vegetation of a whole section of the country with the speed and thoroughness of an army blitzkrieg. A single county in Utah paid out five thousand dollars in a single day as bounty for dead grasshoppers, at sixty cents a bushel. There was a total of two hundred seventy-four tons of grasshoppers for the day's catch. It took eight million grasshoppers to weigh a ton.

In addition to attacking and destroying growing crops, many plants and animals cause enormous damage to stored food and other supplies. Again, the rodent family along with fungi, molds and moths are among the advance mechanized units of destruction. These marauders attack not only our food and clothing, but everything in sight. The moths which eat woolen clothes and rugs and mohair davenports are the bane of the housewife. And the rats which destroy our grains and our diplomas are not too popular with any of us. The ants and termites do a land office business with the main rafters of our dwellings.

Plants and Animals Cause Accidents, Fear, Terror and Phobias

If we deny will and malicious intent to plants and animals we must list these unfriendly acts as accidents.[13] There are, however, numerous instances of injury done human beings by non-human forms in the ordinary sense of the word, such as accidents caused by leaves on the rail and on the road causing them to become slippery and hazardous. Grasshoppers and other insects spattered on the highways by the millions cause accidents as do stray cattle, pigs, dogs, cows, by getting in front of a car or train. Many farm animals cause accidents to themselves and their owners.

[13] There was a time when pigs and cows and dogs and other animals were brought to trial and condemned to death.

There are a lot of people mortally afraid of insects, dogs and other animals and even of certain plants. They live in constant fear and terror of these creatures. This condition may reach pathological proportions and can be definitely classed as a psychosis. Zoophobia is the name given the excessive and unreasoning fear which grips its victim and causes insanity. Even imaginary animals as the snakes and pink elephants in delirium tremens cause stark terror and indicate how animals may strike fear in the heart of man.

WHAT PLANTS AND ANIMALS DO FOR US

So much for the debit side of the ledger. But there is also a credit column which we shall now consider. And before we get through balancing the books we shall find a neat profit in our favor. Our association with plants and animals has paid enormous dividends in the past and will continue to do so with increasing returns. It has been a most prosperous business association. They do very much more for us[14] than to us, and immeasurably more for us than we do for them. And here is how:

Food

In the three great essentials of life, food, shelter and clothing, we owe so much to the non-human sources that we could not possibly exist without them.

1. *Green Chlorophyll.* This is the vital substance ($C_{55}H_{72}O_5N_4N_g$) without which no life can exist. It is bottled sunlight in usable form. We appropriate it directly from plants and/or indirectly through eating animal flesh.

2. *Bacteria.* Not all bacteria are harmful or dangerous to human beings. In fact most of them are our best friends. They make certain elements available to us besides making a great number of foods digestible and palatable. They ripen cheese and vinegar and leaven the yeast and curdle the milk which makes it digestible. Bacteria are found in millions in the digestive tract aiding the digestive process all along the line.

3. *Flesh of Plants, Fish, Fowl, Beef, Pork, Lamb, etc.* This direct personal attack on the flesh of plants and animals furnishes

[14] ''Of about 600,000 species of insects known to science, not more than 200 can fairly be called enemies of man, and not more than one-half of one per cent of all kinds in the United States are seriously injurious.''—Robert C. Murphy, *The Scientific Monthly.*

us the bulk of our food and energy, especially when we add grains, vegetables, fruits, nuts, berries, etc. It is a somewhat gruesome and tragic fact but nevertheless true that life must be sacrificed to sustain life. We must eat living matter to survive. In a very real sense all living matter is "both a guest and a dish at the feast of life."

4. *Eggs and Egg Products.* The United States output of eggs amounts to 2,600,000,000 dozen eggs annually. Eggs are used in many kinds of foods and commercial products. They constitute one of the staple foods of the teeming millions of this earth, for hens and eggs are to be found in all parts of the world, except in a Greek monastery where centuries ago the pious monks ruled out females in every form. Other creatures besides the placid hen give up their bodies and the fruits of their bodies for the glory of man. Among those who should receive honorable mention are bees who yield us their winter store of honey which supplies us with sweetness to the extent of four million pounds annually. We also rob and exploit plants as well as animals to "make us bread." We squeeze the juices of fruits and vegetables and grains and berries to make us jams and jellies and wine and beer. We tap the life fluid of trees to furnish maple sugar for our pancakes and we take the juice of the pine to make turpentine to adorn our homes and furniture and we grow the rubber to ease our auto rides on this too, too solid earth.

5. *Milk and Dairy Products.* These stand in the same category as eggs and egg products except that they play even a greater role in our diet and health. The average person consumes a great deal of raw milk besides great quantities of cheese, butter, cream, ice cream and many foods in which milk is used. The per capita daily consumption of raw milk is as follows: Switzerland, 1.83 pints; Sweden, 1.48 pints; United States, 1.00 pints; France, .33 pints; Berlin, .30 pints.

> If you were served at a single meal all the average person eats in a lifetime, you would sit down to a beefsteak weighing as much as six dressed steers, confront a giant potato too big for a two-ton truck to haul, cut slices from a loaf of bread higher than your head, and pour milk from a bottle as tall as a bungalow!
>
> In the fifty-six years that the average American lives, recent statistics compiled by the U. S. Department of Commerce show, he consumes 106,400 pounds of food—enough to load to capacity several freight cars.

On other dishes at this colossal feast there would be a half-ton block of butter and a 224-pound slice of cheese. The sugar bowl would be six feet high and the salt shaker would weigh 800 pounds. There would be an egg 12,000 times the average size, an apple seven feet in diameter, an orange weighing 1,100 pounds. Around your table would be piled 1,120 tins of canned fruit, 124 cans of salmon, 600 tins of sardines, 336 pounds of dried fruit, 888 cartons of breakfast food, and, more surprising still, 280 pounds of rice. To top off your meal, you would find a 672-pound box of candy and nearly 6,000 sticks of chewing gum, not to mention fifty-six pounds of walnuts and 1,176 pounds of grapes.[15]

Flavoring Substances and Other Commercial Extracts

Vanilla, spices, peppermint, cocoa, chocolate, the juice of fruits and berries are the more familiar flavoring extracts. Commercially the list includes spices, mustard, nutmeg, ginger, cloves, red pepper, and savory substances such as parsley, anise, sage, etc. In addition to these direct flavors which tickle our palate there is a host of bacteria which ripen cheese to the king's taste and sour the kraut to the Dutchman's taste, and the corned beef to go with the cabbage. Among the commercial animal extracts are adrenalin, beeswax, cod liver oil, gelatin, honey, insulin, lanolin, pituitary extract, testicular extract, ovarian extract, pancreatic extract and ox-gall.

Beverage

Perhaps we would be better off without the use of tea, coffee, alcohol, tequila, and perhaps they should have been listed among the things that plants and animals do to us instead of for us. Nevertheless, many people consider that without these beverages life is bereft of its *raison d'être*. The so-called soft drinks are also derived in some measure from fruits, vegetables and berries. Even the humble dandelion is made to yield up a drink. Men's insatiable appetite for food and drink makes one appreciate the observation that "their god is their belly."

Ornaments and Clothing

The first thing that attracts our attention to the savage is his ornaments of beads, feathers, paints, powders, furs, skins, and all sorts of objects such as sharks' teeth, shells, horns of animals, and

[15] From *Popular Science Monthly*, v. 121, p. 62. By permission.

even human heads and scalps. Clothing was originally mostly ornament and worn around the neck and arms and ankles. Gradually
the severity of climate and the development of a sense of modesty
compelled man to turn his ornaments into clothes. Apparently the
tendency today is to reverse the process once more. It is more effective to tell a woman that her dress is unbecoming than to tell her
that it is immodest. As savage man put away his powders and
paints, civilized woman picked them up.

Ornaments and clothes have increased and multiplied in proportion to man's conquest over nature. A mere cataloging of the materials out of which he fashions his clothes and his ornaments gives
some idea of this phenomenon: cotton and cotton products, wool and
woolen products, silk and silk products (more recently rayon, nylon
and other synthetic materials such as silk from glass), hides and
leather goods, furs, fur for trimming and ornament as well as for
warmth, etc.

Shelter

The bulk of the tribute levied on plants and animals goes towards
man's three essentials of food, shelter and clothing. We have already considered food and clothing. Turning to shelter we find
that man's nest-building activities occupy a major portion of his
energies—especially if we include not only his domiciles but also his
many mighty works of engineering in the construction of roads,
bridges, railroads, manufacturing and commercial establishments,
ships and automobiles, public buildings, museums and palaces. The
commercial use of non-human life is here carried to great extremes.
Henry Ford raises soy beans out of which he extracts oil for use in
the manufacture of car finishes. The meat left is ground and chemically processed to make a durable plastic material for use in the
manufacture of gear shift knobs, horn buttons and distributor parts.
Nearly fifty per cent of soy beans is protein which, when extracted,
is used in the manufacture of water paint and artificial fiber.[16] In
the more primitive stages of his development, man relied more directly on the raw materials of nature, such as weeds, grass, trees,

16 Dr. George Washington Carver of Tuskegee Institute, Alabama, from the
common ordinary peanut has made 285 useful products including milk, butter,
cheese, candies, instant coffee, pickles, sauces, oils, shaving lotions, wood stains,
dyes, lard, linoleum, flour, breakfast foods, soap, face powder, shampoo, printers'
ink and even axle grease.

logs and branches of trees. According to the evolutionary hypothesis man actually lived in the trees even as the apes do today.[17]

Fuel and Lighting

Again we rely upon plants and animals to supply heat for the body and fuel for our homes and factories from whale oil to hard coal. The list includes wood, peat, chips, coal, charcoal, coke, artificial and natural gas, crude oil, kerosene, gasoline and scores of oils. In the more primitive stages animals furnished heat from their bodies by sharing sleeping quarters. The lowly Nazarene was born in a stable. Tallow candles were and still are a fairly standard form of lighting.

Bathing, Washing, Cleaning

The soap and cleaning industries would be hard put without the aid of plants and animals, chiefly the fat of animals, in the manufacture of their products.

Transportation

There seems to be no activity or necessity of a human being which plants and animals do not serve. Aside from his own powers of locomotion in walking and running, which are rather inferior and require great exertion, man has utilized the stronger and better equipped animals for his transportation. Among these the horse has been the star performer along with the camels, the elephants, llama and others. The mule and the donkey are dubbed the beasts of burden. It should be noted that our various means of extremely rapid transit via automobiles,[18] railroad trains, ocean liners and air clippers are extremely modern. Up until only a hundred years ago man relied for land transportation on the patient backs and legs of animals. And even today while animals have been superseded, they have not been completely eliminated as beasts of burden and means of transportation. Only thirty years ago horses furnished power for the trolleys in parts of New York City.

[17] While most animals live in one medium and a few are amphibians, man is capable of living in all the media, and has actually lived in water, land, trees and now air.

[18] Automobiles and steam engines are still powered by non-human life by furnishing gasoline and coal and oil which are plant and animal products. In a very real sense they still carry us around.

Communication

Similarly, man has used animals to carry his message. The most commonly used are carrier pigeons, trained dogs and almost any homing creature. It has pleased his fancy to train crows and parrots to talk his own language, at least in part, the more colorful part usually.

Power, Work

It is a well-deserved tribute to the horse family that modern mechanized burden bearers are classified in terms of "horsepower." The ox, buffalo, donkey, mule, camel, elephant, dog and other forms have shared the chores with the human slave and voluntary worker. Agriculture and, more recently manufacture have absorbed the bulk of animal labor together with numerous construction projects.

Weapons, Utensils, Implements, Furniture, Trophies

Here again plants and animals come to the rescue. Modern man as well as his savage ancestor would shrink immeasurably in his own estimation if he were deprived of his trophies of the hunt and the chase and other tokens of his conquest over plants and animals.

Companionship

Here is another instance in which lower forms of life return the compliment many fold. Undoubtedly animals as pets are more essential to the happiness and welfare of human beings than vice versa. A middle-aged couple recently excused themselves at a social functions, hours before the party was due to break up, on the ground that their pet dog "was so lonesome" when they were away. We wonder which was the more lonesome when apart, man or beast. We are pleased to call ourselves *master* in all human animal relationships. That is significant for the psychological effect on the master. The implicit obedience of the animal and the unquestioning attitude of the horse and other animals raises man in his own estimation and makes him feel superior and important, a real master. Psychiatrists often recommend adoption of pets for people suffering from inferiority complex. It is a matter of common observation that human beings become so definitely attached to their pets that in case of injury or death the human counterpart is laid low by genuine grief and sorrow not far removed, if any, from the emotions we feel when a member of the family passes away. This is a genuine tribute to a great comradeship.

Protection

The dog deserves the title of man's best friend largely because he does not hesitate to risk his life to protect his master from thieves, from fire, from drowning or any other danger which may threaten. There is no end to stories of heroism on the part of the dog, the horse and other animals in this respect. The romantic illustration is the seeing-eye dog and her motherly care and protection for the blind master. Other illustrations of the risks taken by animals to protect man, while not altogether voluntary are nevertheless useful and effective. Canaries are used in mines and wells to determine the presence of deadly gases. Pigs were used in Europe to explode "duds" left over on battlefields when it came time to clear the ground and prepare it for farming. Recently in an experiment with high explosives dropped from the sky, a score of goats tethered in various parts of the field were used to measure the effectiveness of the new weapon. We derive so much comfort from shade trees that honorable mention should be made here to their protective propensities to man's comfort and woman's complexion.

Entertainment

Not content to exploit plants and animals for the necessities of life, to satisfy our backs and our bellies, we train them to amuse and entertain us. The more common animals thus trained include the dog, horse, seal, elephant, the wild beasts of the jungle as lions, tigers, leopards, etc., bears, monkeys, bulls, and in the more lowly forms of leaping frogs, fighting cocks, turtles, lice, fleas and hosts of others including snakes. In addition, many of these animals are given the leading role in combination with man's stage performances in the movies, vaudeville and circus. Some of the more celebrated animals stars are Jumbo, the elephant which made Barnum and Bailey famous; Joe Mendi at the Detroit Zoo, who paid an income tax on twenty thousand dollars he earned annually by his performances; Hi-Yo Silver!, who is known to almost every child in America, and the movie fans are not likely to forget Rin-Tin-Tin, the police dog. Mention should also be made of menageries, zoological and botanical gardens, aquariums, etc.

Sports and Games

In chariot races, ancient tournaments, modern horse and dog racing, polo and numerous other games and sports, animal and man play as a team. In other instances it is a contest between them calculated to end in the capture or death of the animal although man is not always successful. But what makes it a sport is that the animal is given a "fighting chance." This is especially true in hunting and fishing which are regulated by definite rules even as in the contests between man and man—boxing, wrestling, baseball, football and all other games. In Michigan during the deer season an army of hunters equal in number to the regular standing army of the United States make their annual attack on the deer in the north woods and bag almost an average of one for every two hunters. There are at least a score of men killed and many other casualties among the hunters themselves.

Hobbies

Plants and animals constitute a sizable portion of our hobbies as distinguished from pets and sports. The raising of plants and animals, the cultivation or creation of special types, or sheer gardening and landscaping afford exciting diversion to many people. There are eighty-two different varieties of fancy chickens throughout the world, no less than twenty-eight fancy pigeons and so on down the line of highly cultivated plants and animals. Fanciers of special breeds are willing to pay fabulous prices for the champion prize winner at the fairs and shows.

Aesthetic Appreciation

Plants and animals possess rare charm in beauty which contributes immeasurably to man's aesthetic nature. Man is pleased to shower these upon his better half in the form of perfumes, dyes, cut flowers, gardens, landscaping. The classical example is the Hanging Gardens of Babylon. Many forms of plants, flowers, shrubs, and even of animals are cultivated for their "looks" and color. Many forms are used to adorn the person or domicile of human beings—witness, corsage bouquets, feathers worn in men's hats as well as by women who once wore the whole bird on the hat.

Aid in War, and Crime Detection

Man does not hesitate to conscript animals in his battle against his enemies. He uses them in his fight against criminals and wars of conquest or defense. Again he calls upon his best friend, the dog, to stand by him and render valuable service in running down escaped convicts, carry messages across no-man's land and rescue his wounded comrades. But until the very recent development of mechanized armies, the cavalry played a leading role in most of the important battles. Horses have been the mainstay in these regiments, but elephants, camels and other animals have been available.

Objects of Study

At every level of his activity man utilizes plants and animals to his advantage—physical, mental, aesthetic and spiritual. Man has added immeasurably to the knowledge of his own nature by a comparative study of human and non-human life. All the biological and social sciences have contributed to this end—botany, bacteriology, zoology, plant culture, animal husbandry, paleontology, and many others including animal psychology. In our study of instincts and reflexes as well as many diseases and other activities and functions of human beings we have learned a great deal from zoology and comparative studies of all kinds. We often conclude that certain traits are native to human beings because we find them universally distributed in the animal world, such as reflexes, instincts, glandular secretions and the like. Moreover, in the social sciences, and this is our justification for discussing these matters for the moment, there is much to be gained by a comparative study. The monogamic form of marriage is taken by anthropologists to be the rule and all others the exception largely because they find this to be the case in the animal kingdom, with the exception of domesticated animals to whom reference has previously been made.

Objects of Art

As distinguished from the contribution of animals and plants to our aesthetic appreciation, they also furnish many objects of art in painting, sculpture, architecture, landscaping, monuments, etc. The non-human life *motif* runs all through the world of art.

Objects of Worship

What greater example of man's vital connection with non-living forms could we have than the fact that he has used them as objects of worship, the highest expression of his spiritual nature. Religion is in part man's effort to control the environment in the satisfaction of his needs and wants. Propitiation through worship is one form of this indirect control. That he should include animals as the object of worship is a tacit recognition of the possibility of the powerful influence animals were suspected of possessing over man. The superior strength and skill of some forms were greatly admired and emulated by early man. Some peoples still worship the sacred bull, the golden calf, the totem animal. In a less serious mood we have our animal mascots and state flowers. Historically, the notions of *mana,* and reincarnation are rather significant. The goat has played a leading role in many ancient religious ceremonies. "Riding the goat" is a significant statement in our various fraternal initiations. Even in the worship of superior and spiritual deities, animals have played a significant part requiring the sacrifice of the blood of rams and goats and many other animals. The traditional Hebrew religion included and required such sacrifices. Another type of animal sacrifice was the heaping of the sins of the people through elaborate rites and ceremonies on the head of an innocent and unsuspecting goat who was dubbed the "scape goat" and banished from their midst, thus relieving themselves of their bad conscience.

Experimentation

In modern times the blood of animals is offered to the god of science in the form of experiments which we dare not perform upon human beings. Thus, in a very real sense we use animals as scape goats and as substitutes for human sacrifice. Vivisection and experiments on guinea pigs, mice, rats, rabbits, dogs and many other animals are now common practice and almost universally approved.

Medicine and Surgery

Many of these experimentations are for commercial enterprises, but most of them are for humanitarian purposes, to discover the effect of new drugs or surgical methods, inoculations and the like. This brings to mind the celebrated experiments of Pasteur to prevent anthrax in sheep and the more recent experiments of Dr. Myers of the University of Michigan who caused some rats to go crazy by increasing their responsibilities and thus confirming the conjecture that the increase in insanity among human beings is due largely to our complicated and fast pace of living.

Therapeutics

Preventive medicine makes use of vaccination, anti-toxins, and the injection of a mild form of the disease to develop resistance, or the introduction of another disease as in the case of inducing malaria to cure paresis. Vaccination for smallpox really gives the patient a mild case of cow pox or horse pox and thus develops in the blood the fighting forces necessary to ward off the more severe form of actual smallpox. A knowledge of parasites is used commercially to fight dangerous germs and fungi, and to utilize the friendly ones in the production and manufacture of many useful products. Industrial bacteriology is a major science. It covers such processes as the manufacture of yeast, retting of flax, brewing and wine making, production of glycerin, lactic acid, butyric acid, citric acid, and in the decomposition of nitrogen compounds.

Health and Sanitation

Among plants and animals there are certain "natural" preventives and cures that are highly beneficial to human beings. We have called attention to the effect of bacteria in milk and yeast and vinegar and sour kraut to make them palatable and digestible. But these and other bacteria also serve to make us healthy and to guard against disease germs. The knowledge we have gained helps us to provide proper sewage, pure water supply, inspection of raw foods, cold storage foods and packed or canned foods. The larger creatures of the buzzard family are effective scavengers who destroy carrion and keep down the spread of disease. There are also millions of microbe scavengers. The direct action of bacteria in septic tanks is an example of this beneficial effect. Plant life is the medium through which the inorganic substances of the soil and air are made available to the uses of the human organism. It is in the interests of sanitation and health to return the elements contained in dead organic matter to begin the life cycle over again. And this service is rendered effectively for us by plants and animals constantly.

Employment

If we needed any further proof of our utter dependence on plants and animals we get an overwhelming dose of it when we contemplate the great number of occupations and the millions of people employed in these occupations which are directly and indirectly dependent upon non-human existence. Among these is farming, the greatest industry in the world. It is an eight billion dollar industry in the United States, topping all others. Companion industries are dairying, cattle and sheep raising, commercial fishing, canning, packing, soap and fertilizer by-product industries running into the millions of dollars, orcharding, taxidermy, milling, textile industries, tanning and leather goods, landscaping, and hundreds of other industries which provide employment to millions of people and supply the bulk of our national income and wealth.

As Teachers

Many of our vaunted scientific methods are directly copied from non-human biology. Defensive armor and offensive weapons, for example, are copied from the hide and horns of the rhino and similar armored animals.

The poison darts of the pygmies and the mustard gas of the giant militaristic nations are duplicates of tactics borrowed from low-down snakes and insects. Camouflage is as old as the science of protective coloration so apparent in the plant and animal world. This is why the zebra and the tiger have stripes, while the leopard and giraffe have spots. Each in his respective habitat of plains and jungle is best protected from his enemies by these markings to make him less conspicuous. They blend so well with the background that if they remain still you may look right at them without seeing them. One species of gazelle introduces a strategic variation by raising his tail high while in flight. This acts as a signal and the pursuer keeps looking at it because it is so highly colored on the under side conspicuously offered to view. But when the animal suddenly stops and clamps down his tail he is practically invisible among the trees and shrubs. There are worms that look like twigs and until they move you cannot distinguish them as animals because of their shape and color.

In the hoarding of food, building a shelter, evading an enemy or capturing a prey, men have learned much from lower forms. And more remarkable still is our imitation or parallel development in our social life. White ants and termites had a communal life fifty million years before men were men. There are some very interesting similarities. They antedate our system of farming, capturing and enslaving the enemy, milking, building apartment houses, cities, division of labor and professional classes, rulers, workers, a very rigid caste system, etc. In fact, they have carried their social specialization so far as to develop the workers, rulers, and soldiers into separate and distinct classes far beyond what Plato suggested in his *Republic*. We would have an analagous situation if our soldiers were born with a total equipment of fighting accouterments, and our sailors were born with fins and gills, while our rulers possessed the wisdom of the ages.

In their communal life, the social activities, our non-human counterpart display cooperative efforts in building, protection, mutual aid in escaping from an enemy or in capturing the prey. They also communicate through sounds and odors and mechanically poking with nose or paw. They might also be said to have certain folkways which have merged into instinctive activity. Most interesting and enlightening by way of comparison with human society is their family life. We find here the bi-parental type as in ducks, geese and even some fishes. There is the maternal type as the hen in which the mother takes sole charge. And the opposite type, though rare, in which the father takes full charge. The fish illustrates this most effectively. Moreover, the animals have anticipated our youth movement in the so-called "children family" in which the young of the species get together and "raise" each other very much as the children of a family of ten or a dozen often did in the good old days. The reindeer, some pythons and a few caterpillars are examples of this type.

Nor need we stop with the animals. The plants also live in communities and have a social life. There is a definite science known as synecology[19] which deals with the social life of plants. In any given area such as the prairies, forests, valleys and plains, there are large and small groupings of plant life with many subgroups into a community presenting certain definite *dominants* even as in the animal kingdom. Plants have sex, succession, competition, parasites, and depend on wind and animals and water for pollination and colonization. Plants, such as the Venus fly trap, have properties of irritability approaching animal life. Plants, like animals, are alive and made up of living substance. They grow and

[19] The late Doctor McKenzie of Michigan University was the first to write on Human Ecology, borrowing the term from biology where it is still an important approach to botany. Ecology is the branch of biology which deals with the mutual relations between organisms and their environment (bionomics). This term is now more widely used in botany than in zoology and includes physiological ecology, which deals with the study of the reactions to environment and physiographic ecology which deals with edaphic plant societies.

develop. They die. They live out their allotted span, or are preyed upon as food, or die of accident or disease. The plant diseases are classified as due to deficiencies in make-up or lack of nourishment (physical disease), as due to bacteria such as the wilt and blight diseases of fruit trees, as due to virus (analagous to infection

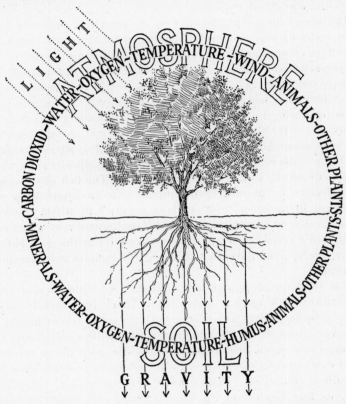

FIG. 4. Diagram showing the principal factors in the environment of land plants. From E. N. Transeau *General Botany*. Copyright 1923 by World Book Company, Yonkers-on-Hudson, New York. Reproduced by written permission.

and contagion), and as due to higher plant action, a good example being the romantic mistletoe.

The contrast between the human and non-human social life is of course obvious and striking, but the comparison is also remarkable when you consider the advantages that human beings have over the other forms. If one were inclined to philosophize he might conclude that nature has been experimenting with plants and animals in developing social life, that human beings are merely another chapter in nature's book. And when one looks at the mess we are making of our opportunity we are not too sure that nature is satisfied and will not make another venture with some other species more worthy of the trust.

CONCLUSION

It is difficult to escape the impression that we owe not only our physical existence to the non-human forms of life, but our whole civilization and culture as well. Apparently there is no area of human interest and activity and well-being in which plants and animals do not play some vital rôle either directly or indirectly. It was to impress this fact through accumulative evidence that we have cataloged the non-human biological factors in social life. There should remain no doubt concerning the tremendous importance of our utter dependence and interdependence on non-human life while we concentrate on the relatively more human factors in sociology.

We call attention once more to the necessity of going even further than merely being aware of the non-human elements in our social life. We must keep in mind the contributing factors of the TOTAL ENVIRONMENT in our appreciation of the problems of human adjustment.

SELECTED REFERENCES

Beaver, William C., *Fundamentals of Biology*, The C. V. Mosby Co., 1939.—Substantial text in Biology. Recommend Chapters XX, ''Economic Importance of Animals''; Chapter XXX, ''Economic Importance of Plants''; Chapter XXXVI, ''Living Organisms,'' and Chapter XXXIX, ''Applied Biology.''

Buchanan, R. E., *Agricultural and Industrial Bacteriology*, Appleton-Century Co., 1921.—Stresses value of bacteria as a human asset.

Haskins, Carly P., *Of Ants and Men*, Prentice-Hall, 1939.—An interesting story well told. An impressive comparison of social life between ants and men.

Jordan, Edwin O., *Bacteriology*, W. B. Saunders Co., 1936.—A thoroughgoing systematic discussion of bacteria in great detail.

Lull, Richard Swann, *Organic Evolution*, Macmillan, 1920.—A standard textbook by an outstanding paleontologist.

McDougall, W. B., *Plant Ecology*, Lea and Febiger, 1931.—A fascinating little book unusually well written. Chapter XVI, *Plant Communities* is of special significance in Sociology.

Neal, Herbert V., and Rand, Herbert W., *Comparative Anatomy*, P. Blakiston's Son and Co., 1936, 540 illustrations.—An excellent representative book for fundamental background materials.

Potter, George Edwin, *Zoology*, The C. V. Mosby Co., 1938.—A thorough, systematic, able treatment of the subject with 440 interesting and useful illustrations and 15 beautiful color plates. Pp. 696 ff. on "Social Relations of Animals," is of special interest to the sociologist as another indication of the unity of all knowledge and the effect of the total environment. While the sociologist is attempting to point out the non-human factors in social life, the biologist is discussing social relations of animals to themselves and to human beings both as values and disvalues to the latter.

Walcott, Robert H., *Animal Biology*, 2nd edition, McGraw-Hill, 1940.—The author stresses life and activity rather than structure which makes it all the more useful for students of sociology.

Walter, Herbert Eugene, *Biology of the Vertebrates*, 2nd edition, Macmillan, 1939.—A bit more highly specialized since it treats the higher forms of animal life. The subtitle, *A Comparative Study of Man and His Animal Allies*, indicates and reflects the attitude of the author.

Whitefield and Wood, *An Introduction to Comparative Zoology*, P. Blakiston's Son and Co., 1935.—Recommended for advanced students.

CHAPTER 6

BIOLOGICAL REGULARITIES

II. INFLUENCE OF MAN'S BIOLOGICAL HERITAGE IN SOCIAL BEHAVIOR

BY EDWIN E. JACOBS, PH.D.

Ashland College, Ashland, Ohio

All trustworthy evidence points to the fact that man first made his appearance on this planet either in the late Pliocene or the early Pleistocene and is, therefore, contemporaneous with the present-day Quarternary mammal group, the last and highest life-type to appear.

While it is true that early man differed somewhat in his physical make-up from the present-day species and that he lived under somewhat different physical surroundings, yet modern man shares with him by far the greater part of his physical and anatomical features. Burdened as he was, and as he still is, with many useless and outgrown organs, man has nevertheless more or less successfully met all adverse conditions and must be regarded as the dominant form of life on earth today. Subject to all the modifying forces which affect all other mammals, man has undergone certain organic and physical changes which have produced types of variants known to the anthropologist as races. The basis for the classification of these variants is usually their skin color and the color and texture of their hair. However, in not a few instances, the differences between these so-called races are so slight that it is difficult to tell where one begins and the other leaves off. This is to say that as yet no race has departed so far from the common parent stock as to be regarded as more than a racial variant, not as a separate species.

Now if the races of mankind are so closely related as really to be members of a single genus and species (*Homo sapiens*), then this fact would at once furnish a unifying basis for a more or less common human culture. For if the races of mankind differed among themselves as much as most separate species of other mammals do, a common religion, common education, common social institutions, and a common culture generally would be most unlikely if not altogether impossible. But as it is, all races being fertile with each other (partial proof of their lack of speciation), not only is it possi-

141

ble to blend their cultures, but their physical types as well. That is precisely what has happened in the past, so that pure races and cultures are becoming more rare. Moreover, the hope of the foreign missionary is based on just this, i.e., that all races are sufficiently alike biologically as to be capable of accepting and profiting by, a common religion, a common form of education, and a common culture. It is the hope also of not a few of the less advanced races, that intermarriage will take place, thus lifting them not only to a more desirable social status but also to a more acceptable physical type.

If the races were separated so widely as to be infertile with each other, certain present-day social problems would disappear. For instance, there could be no such problem as miscegenation, with the corresponding race hybrids, and this would profoundly affect other social problems, among which are inter-race sex morality, race friction, race slavery and subjugation; and it might conceivably affect the right of suffrage where the various races live side by side. But as it is, the races differ so little from each other that they all are moved by common ambitions, common hopes, and common desires. In almost every case where the races or even the so-called sub-races are thrown into close relationship by industry or otherwise, those of the less complex culture vigorously object to anything that looks like segregation and say that they "want to be treated like human beings." Next to the promulgation of the theory of organic evolution nearly a century ago, it is doubtful whether there has been a greater movement of the human mind than that which may be summed up in the expression, "the awakening of the social consciousness" of mankind.

One may expect, then, that the members of a common species would react in much the same way when influenced by common environmental factors; and the human species offers no exception to this rule. For instance, there seem to be insufficient grounds for believing that the very advanced culture of the Incas and Mayas of South and Central America was in any way related to that of Egypt or that the mounds of North America should be related to the dolmans of Europe except that a common idea found expression in common materials and common forms. Moreover, other ideas took common shape as witness the bow and arrow, implements of stone, the use of fire in cooking, and certain elements common to all religions, as the belief in supernatural beings and forces. To be added to the list of common culture traits are: food-getting and laying in store, reckoning at least close relationships, some personal property, artifacts of similar design, the dance, play, personal adornment, magic, language and some form of marriage or sex control. Most students of society also find three primary social groupings to be universal, viz., the play group, the family and the community. All of the above culture forms are so well-nigh universal among the races of mankind as to be regarded as the expressions of a common nature, which is to say, that all men, no matter how they may be classified as to races, are fundamentally alike.

MAN COMPARED WITH OTHER HIGHER MAMMALS

Not only do the various races of mankind share certain biological and, therefore, certain cultural traits with each other, but man shows his similarity to other mammals in many biological features. His cellular structure, his constant need of food and oxygen, his general metabolic processes, his susceptibility to disease, his reactions to poisons and drugs, even the details of his embryology, differ but slightly from those of other mammals, especially the higher apes, the anthropoids.

The following data relative to the anthropoids, when compared with those of man reveal certain similarities: the female gorilla becomes adolescent at about eight years of age and is sterile in later life, her functional periodicity is twenty-eight days, the period of gestation nine months, the young weigh at birth about three pounds, the life-span is about fifty years, twinning is uncommon. The male gorilla weighs about 175 pounds and is four times as strong as a fit young man. The orangutan has twelve pairs of ribs, the other great apes have thirteen pairs. All of the anthropoids are vegetarian in diet. They also lack the median furrow on the upper lip. Spotting is unknown (rare in man).[1]

Man's brain, while showing many primitive structures of the animal brain, also exhibits many fundamental advances. In size it varies around 1450 cubic centimeters; the upper limit of the great apes is about 600 cubic centimeters. Furthermore, the animal brain and nervous system are practically finished at birth, while those of man are not complete until about eighteen years of age. With this advance in the brain, man's receptors or special sense organs also show greater development. These improved special senses afford him contacts with his environment impossible to any other animal.

[1] E. A. Hooton, *Up from the Ape*, Appleton, 1931, Part III.

Many mental traits in man, such as anger or reaction for self-defense, the food- and sex-quest, escape reactions, need of sleep and rest, play and others have their counterparts not only in the anthropoids but in other members of the higher vertebrates. In the light of these considerations, it is evident that man's cultural and social reactions cannot be adequately understood apart from his biological inheritances, for every cultural form and institution is based on man's original nature. If, for instance, one could conceive of man as lacking any one of the important biological traits which he now possesses, the story of his culture would be far different from what it is. When one stops to consider the perfectly incalculable amount of effort put forth by mankind because every individual alive gets hungry, one can then see how one simple primary want may affect a whole nation, even the whole world. In the light of such primary wants, one may also find adequate bases for many wars and conquests, the so-called economic interpretation of history and many other human problems. Not only does the primary want of hunger have a profound influence on human behavior, but other primary needs have far-reaching results. Such is the matter of sex. It staggers the imagination to attempt to estimate the influence of sex in human affairs. It touches every language in the gender of nouns and pronouns. It is present in all religions. It has affected law and custom, mores and folkways, art and dress. Many other examples of how man's biological nature affects his social institutions, come quickly to mind. The student of society must keep constantly in mind that he is dealing with a type of life that is strongly under the influence of certain zoological traits.

Man's Erect Posture

Unlike any other animal, man is erect in posture. Much of his physical structure and many of his habits indicate, however, that he is not perfectly adapted to this type of life.[2] His foot, the muscles of his back and the tissues supporting his viscera are among the structures showing poor adaptation, the latter being the cause of many surgical operations.

The time and effort devoted by children in learning to balance themselves on two feet, and then walking in that position, also indicate that the erect posture has to be learned. Every drillmaster knows the fatigue, even pain, endured by the soldiers while their

[2] George A. Dorsey, *Why We Behave Like Human Beings*, Harper & Brothers, 1925, Chaps. I and II.

ranks are being inspected. Anthropology gives evidence of early man's slouching posture, his ambling gait and his general desire to sit down or lie down even at his meals. The Neanderthal man is pictured with stooped posture, round shoulders and with back and knees bent.

The erect posture which man has maintained throughout all his history, although fraught with certain inconveniences, has, nevertheless, had a profound effect upon his culture. This posture leaves his hands free, thus enabling him to acquire skills impossible to any other animal. It also affords him a horizontal line of sight so that the outlines of his field of vision are extended. Nevertheless his method of locomotion is tiresome and slow and he has had to supply with cunning what he lacks in physical prowess. This early showed itself in the invention of lethal weapons, such as the dart, bow and arrow, traps and snares. Moreover, many of the animals used as food by early man could outrun him, being more fleet of foot than he was himself, so he domesticated animals which were used not only for the chase but also for travel and as beasts of burden. The substitution of animals for human power, fleetness, and endurance must be regarded as one of the most important inventions of early man which has, moreover, continued up to the present day.

Animal Associations

So far as animals associating themselves with other members of their own species is concerned, they may be divided into three classes: solitary, gregarious, and social. Some animals live more or less alone and are associated with other members of their species almost solely for sex purposes. Some birds are solitary as are many reptiles. These types are designated as solitary because their reliance upon the help of others is almost nil. There are other types, however, which are associated in smaller or larger groups, these assemblages being known as herds, flocks, droves, schools or swarms. Many of the ungulates (hoofed animals), and some fish and birds belong to this class. Some advantage seems to accrue to the individuals from such association. Prince Kropotkin[3] spoke of this as "mutual aid," but it is only another phase of the struggle for existence, for no single individual joins such a group except for its own advantage, that is, so it can better meet adverse conditions; and while it is difficult to separate the beneficial influence of the indi-

[3] Prince Kropotkin, *Mutual Aid; a Factor in Evolution*, Knopf, 1917.

vidual from the reciprocal influence of the group, yet the advantage springs from no sense of "mutual aid." It is rather an entirely selfish reaction aiding individual survival. The same general principle holds in the care which the mother exercises in behalf of her young. The biologist well knows that this care springs from impulses primarily concerned with survival of the species. Moreover, this mutual aid is rather remote, for in almost every case where the young is separated from the adult after it has become self-sustaining, the individual lives and develops quite normally alone. For instance, a kitten does not need to learn to catch mice from its association with other and older cats; this reaction is born with it. A calf, if separated from its kind at birth, will when adult, show every bovine reaction. It does not need to learn by association to stand knee-deep in quiet water, to use its horns in defense, to employ quiet tones when near its young, or to recognize its own kind, including the opposite sex. All of these reactions are a part of its inheritances but, as we shall see later, the case is substantially different with man.

As is well known, certain other types of animals live in much closer associations than those just described, notably the Hymenoptera (bees and ants). In such groups the individual can neither survive nor develop alone. In the case of bees, the queen lacks so many of the food-getting reactions that she would starve if not fed by other members of the colony. On the other hand, in other castes of the swarm, the reproductive organs are so atrophied that, were it not for the fertile queen, reproduction within the swarm would be impossible. This type of life is genuinely social. It is exemplified by other members of the Hymenoptera. According to Maeterlinck[4] and other students of bees and ants, division of labor has been carried to a very high degree of efficiency.

Man is Social

In precisely this sense man is social. Recognizing his social nature, Aristotle long ago spoke of him as a "social animal," however, his social nature was not fully recognized until within comparatively recent times, but is now being made the basis of much of our education, religion and government. We know little about solitary man, for as far back as we can trace him, there is evidence to show that he lived in some type of associated groups. The structure and the close proximity of the rock shelters of the ancient cliff dwellers in south-

[4] Maurice Maeterlinck, *The Life of the Ant*, Day Company, 1934.

western United States seem to indicate that these people not only had a family form of life but that they lived in associated communities, likely for protection. In such groups, of course, the gregarious nature of man played an important rôle, for man likes to be with members of his own kind. Giddings[5] called this "consciousness of kind" but associated with this gregariousness was doubtless the idea of aid for survival. Thus a sharp distinction should be made between man's being *social* and his being *sociable,* the latter referring to his desire to be in company with congenial persons, while the former indicates membership in an interrelated group. Indeed, the most unfriendly and uncongenial person, is none the less a genuinely social being.

Take the case of hermits; their language, their ideas of food and its preparation and many of their skills were learned from others before they withdrew to solitary life. The account below illustrates this point. A man is said to have gone out to the river-side and dug up an earthworm with a shell, made a hook out of flint, fastened it to the end of a pole with a strip of bark, baited the hook, and after catching a fish, struck out fire with a flint and cooked the fish! Now if one were to attempt to enumerate all the social elements in this incident, he would be amazed at the number. First of all, there is the fact that a fish is edible, a matter already tried out by others as was every other step in the incident. So instead of this illustrating what solitary man can do, it rather indicates that man is always and everywhere social.

Now this brings us to what has been called the "social paradox,"[6] viz., that both society and the individual were prior in point of time, which, of course, could not be. It is true that man forms and shapes society while at the same time society forms and shapes man, for the personality of any individual reflects the environmental influences under which he lives. MacIver,[7] is doubtless right in saying that the personality is the result of two interacting factors, viz., the biological basis and the social forces which react on this basis. Abraham Lincoln is quoted as having said that the nation cannot live half slave and half free. Others seems to think that it cannot endure if one half is extremely poor while the other half lives in affluence and wealth. Still others point out that crime, divorce, and other social

[5] Franklin H. Giddings, *Principles of Sociology,* Macmillan, 1902, Chap. I.

[6] Carey E. Hayes, *Introduction to the Study of Society,* Appleton, 1926, Chap. XXIV.

[7] R. M. MacIver, *Society,* Farrar and Rhinehart, 1937, Chap. III.

ills affect all of us.   All of these statements contain very large elements of truth and tend to show that man is in large part the result
of societal influence.   The truth as to the so-called paradox seems to
be that society and the individual evolved together.

Man's Long Infancy

According to figures quoted by Panunzio[8] the expectation of life
in 1939 was 55.33 years for men and 57.52 years for women.   Assuming that the human being does not fully mature until about the
twentieth year, it is evident that man spends almost one-third of
his entire life span in a degree of immaturity.   John Fiske,[9] some
years ago, pointed out as the significance of this fact that it affords
an unexcelled opportunity to fit the young for social life through
schooling and other essential training.   To put it in other words,
man is long immature so he can learn, rather than learning because
he is young.   During these years his nervous system is "wax to
receive and marble to retain."

To be associated with man's long infancy, is his relatively limited
reproduction.   Mammals may be roughly divided into two classes,
those which reproduce by single births and those by multiple births.
Man belongs to the former class.   This is in accordance with the
"principle of individuation" of Spencer.[10]   According to this principle, effort in reproduction is centered upon economy rather than
on wasteful numbers.   This has been of great value to man's culture
for it not only tends to keep down the number of offspring but at
the same time enables the female to advance her own individuality;
thus she can reserve her energy for herself rather than squandering
it on a numerous offspring.   It is often pointed out that the shad
lays thousands of eggs but only a few shad ever reach maturity.
With man, the case is different because at best the human family is
relatively small.

Thus, long infancy, limited reproduction, and an early and definite time for female sterility, tend to keep human reproduction
within bounds.   This general situation contributes very considerably
to parents' ability to care properly for their young.   It may be true
that, biologically considered, woman's chief function is reproduc-

[8] Constantine Panunzio, *Major Social Institutions*, Macmillan, 1939, Chap.
IV.

[9] John Fiske, *The Meaning of Infancy*, Houghton-Mifflin, 1906.

[10] Herbert Spencer, *Principles of Biology*, Appleton, 1898, Vol. II, Chap.
XII–XIII.

tion, but, with the declining birthrate, the family is growing smaller, leaving women free to devote their energy to other things. Hence one may confidently expect women to enlarge their sphere as the birth of children and their rearing will less and less interrupt the attempts of modern women at a career.

Subjugation of Women

Another biological principle which has far-reaching results is that of sexual dimorphism, or the disparity of the sexes. According to Havelock Ellis,[11] considerable difference exists not only in outward form and proportions between man and woman, but in many of the vital processes as well, most of which operate to man's advantage. Panunzio,[12] says that the rate of woman's anabolism (constructive metabolism as opposed to katabolism), is twice that of man and under certain conditions may be three times as great. Thus man is the waster of energy while woman is its conservator. Hence the male is more aggressive while the female is more passive. All of this is doubtless related to the genetic sex formulae.

Genetic Sex Formulae

In all mammals (not all vertebrates) the genetic formula for sex is XY for the male and XX for the female. Every cell in the animal body contains a specific number of thread-like bodies known as chromosomes located in the nucleus. In man this number is forty-eight, or twenty-four pairs for both male and female with the differences noted above, viz., a pair known as the sex chromosomes designated as XY in man and XX in woman. This means that man and woman differ in every cell of their bodies. This is true with all other mammals, but the qualities conferred by the Y chromosome in the case of man are very highly differentiated, perhaps as much as, or even more so than in any other mammal, thus affording a genuinely biological basis for both the mental and physical differences between sexes.

EFFECT OF MAN'S BIOLOGICAL NATURE ON CERTAIN SOCIAL INSTITUTIONS

Recreation and Play

Any adequate theory of play must take into account man's animal nature. So fundamental is play that Schiller is quoted as say-

[11] Havelock Ellis, *Man and Woman*, London: Black, 1926, Chap. III.
[12] *Op. cit.*

ing that "man is man only when he plays," for then restraint is cast aside and he reveals himself as he, by nature, really is. Several theories have been advanced attempting to find the underlying basis of play. The four following are among the best known :[13, 14] The first is that proposed by Professor Lazarus, that play is for recreation ; the second, the theory of surplus energy, by Spencer ; the third, the practice theory of Carl Groos ; and, fourth the theory of recapitulation by G. Stanley Hall. All doubtless contain elements of truth but that by Hall is, perhaps, the most acceptable. Lazarus argues that men play for recreation, to get a change of activity and thus relieve fatigue. It is, of course, true that play calls into action muscles not used in certain types of work, so the tired business man takes himself off to the ball game, or, if not too tired, may try a round of golf. There is too, an exhilaration in play not found in work, but while this theory may in part account for play in adults, it is wholly inadequate to explain play in children.

It is also true, as Spencer points out, that play releases energy, for the strenuousness of play steadily advances with the age and strength of the child, ending finally with such games as football and hockey. But it is also true that sick and crippled children play, it often being desirable to put toys and playthings on the bed beside the sick child. Moreover, that energy can be accumulated as a surplus, is not apparent.

Carl Groos,[15] a German writer, some years ago advanced a theory of play for man and animals, often called the practice theory. "The kitten pounces upon the rolling ball or leaf apparently for amusement but she is really training herself to catch mice. Puppies romp and chase each other and make-believe bite as sport, but they are really being educated to attack and defend. It is pointed out that the animal which plays most and best is the one that develops the needed strength and adaptation to the highest point. Likewise, the play of children seems to be naturally directed along lines where development is most needed in later years. The girl's doll and playhouse are direct preparation for the duties of housekeeping and motherhood. The boy's hide-and-seek, free-and-easy scuffle, team

13 W. R. Smith, *An Introduction to Educational Sociology*, Houghton-Mifflin, 1929, Chap. V.

14 Henry C. Lehman and Paul A. Witty, *The Psychology of Play Activities*, Barnes, 1927.

15 Carl Groos, *Play of Man; Play of Animals*, Appleton, 1928.

games and gang organizations are the physical and mental counterparts of his later industrial and business organization struggle.''[16] In fact, Groos goes so far as to say that perhaps the very existence of youth is due in part to the necessity for play; the child does not play because it is young, it has a long period of youth because it must play.

This theory seems fantastic and far-fetched. The recapitulation theory of Hall, a part of his general theory of recapitulation of man's growth and development, probably contains a larger element of truth than any of the other three. He holds that the child comes into the world from a long line of ancestors from which it inherits a great number of motor impulses which seek spontaneous escape. The child is something like an alarm clock already wound up and the mechanism must be released and set going; play is the result. Everyone is aware that probably the worst punishment possible to inflict upon a child is to compel it to sit quietly for a period of time. The fact is, it cannot sit quietly. Schools are beginning to take advantage of this very important fact and so relate learning to the child's spontaneous activity. As Groos pointed out, some animals do play (but not all animals) but their play is neither as strenuous or as prolonged as that of man. The lamb gambols for a short time and then lies down. The kitten chases the rolling ball but soon tires and curls up to sleep, but children play practically every waking minute. Every mother knows that reluctance to taking a bath or to eating certain necessary foods, can be overcome if she ''makes a game of it.'' It is often said that children ''have a right to play,'' but it is more than a right, it is an inborn drive which may be partially thwarted but not wholly eradicated. Perhaps it is well to teach a child *how* to play, but it is unnecessary to teach it *to* play. That is a part of its inheritances.

Recapitulation Explains Other Behavior Patterns

The theory of recapitulation also explains other behavior patterns, for it seems to be true that the human being feels better when in motion than when at rest. This is, doubtless, the reason why adults as well as children like to go on merry-go-rounds, ride in automobiles, use rocking-chairs and go horseback riding. This love of motion also enters into the pleasures of the dance, a custom age-old and worldwide, which has entered into religion, war, feasting and

[16] Smith, *op. cit.*

certain other types of celebration. All of these activities seem to counteract the fatigue arising from quietude.

Biological Basis of the Family

There are many theories concerning the origin of the family, but whatever its origin, the biological factors cannot be overlooked. These biological factors are at least two, viz., man's insistent sex urge and the prolonged infancy of human offspring. It is true, of course, that the sex drive in man does not differ essentially from that of other animals but in no other case does it eventuate in a true family. It is also true that man tends to be polygamous where the sex ratio is unequal and this doubtless contributed to large families among primitive peoples, but, as time went on, the monogamous family emerged, bringing with it many new factors. As a result of this, the mother's place was enlarged and children came to be more highly regarded, and along with these changes came other sentimental values so that at the present time, the biological factors tend to be obscured, but they are none the less real.

There are, moreover, many other differences of detail between the reproductive habits of man and those of other higher mammals, not the least important of which is that the latter have, for the most part, a distinct breeding season while man does not. The breeding season seems to accord roughly with climate and food supply. This seasonal breeding habit together with the fact that most animals mature rather quickly, tend to operate against the establishment of true family life, while man's persistent sex activity, which knows neither seasonal nor climatic barriers, and his prolonged infancy, make for family life. The evidence afforded by the kitchen middens[17] found along many coasts does not seem adequate to prove that early man gathered together for seasonal sex purposes. A better explanation is that these gatherings were in response to the gregarious impulses for hunting, feasting and play.

Family life, and the necessity of the mother's care for the helpless young, contributed to an early division of labor, a feature very prominent in modern family organization. The mother, with the young dependent upon her, was compelled to stay near the hut and fireside and thus domestic duties devolved upon her until she became the indoor member of the sexual union. Meanwhile, the father betook himself away to the chase, in quest of food, and to war. As a

[17] *Shell Mounds*, Encyclopedia Britannica, Vol. XX.

result of this, and in accordance with her inherent smaller size and less vigorous body, woman more and more gave herself over to household work and child-raising.

Biology and Vice

Many forms of vice have a basis in biology, vice here being used to denote sex vice and the use of alcohol and drugs. Sex vice especially represents a deep-seated animal impulse which has always defied societal control. Prostitution was known among the early Jews, it was sanctified by the Greeks and Romans and was known as "holy prostitution," being a religious rite practiced at certain times by female attendants at the temples. There is also evidence in the ruins of Pompeii that a red-light district flourished there. It has been spoken of as "woman's oldest profession" and has at times been legalized by modern governments. Where there is a law against it, if rooted out in one place by the vigilance of the officers, it flees to another, there to flourish clandestinely. As might be expected, the impulse back of all this is stronger and less controlled in men than in women and represents one of the most primitive and persistent animal reactions. It is by no means confined to any one stratum of society, although when carried on in the more refined groups, it is with a considerable amount of stealth. The reformers, to be realistic, have to recognize the persistence and strength as well as the naturalness of the thing they are trying to curb. While useful in itself, this sex drive, if unrestrained, undermines the foundations of culture and saps the vitality of any people.

The use of alcohol also has an animal basis. The underlying reason why people use it is that they like it or its effects, which is the same thing. It has been the experience of foreign missionaries and explorers that the races of the world naturally like strong drink. Much the same may be said about the use of tobacco, opiates and other drugs. Inasmuch as their use is widespread among men, it seems reasonable to infer that the liking for them has a strong biological basis.

HEREDITY

Up to the time of the discovery of Mendel's paper on inheritances in plants, 1901, little was known about heredity. Since that time a vast amount of work has been done in this field by biologists throughout the world. Only some of the most fundamental principles can be given here. These are as follows:

Principles of Heredity

1. The general mechanism of heredity is the same for plants and animals, including man. Therefore, conclusions drawn from experiments on plants and animals seem valid for human heredity.

2. Traits are not lost through the loss of a gene, except where a portion of the chromosome carrying it is lost. Genes may be altered through mutation; this, however, is relatively rare.[18]

3. In general, traits are either dominant or recessive. In the former case, the individual carrying the trait sooner or later shows it, in the latter case an individual may carry a trait and not show it.

4. Parents cannot transmit what they do not carry, nor can offspring inherit what is not transmitted; one must transmit what is carried if offspring are produced in sufficient number.

5. Offspring from the same parents may vary among themselves due to the fact that not all have received the same complex of genes.

6. Both parents may share equally in the transmission of traits.

7. Traits are transmitted on definite ratios.

Inheritance of Mental Traits

Now it is generally conceded that physical traits such as eye and hair color and other easily visible effects are inherited, but many balk at the idea of mental traits being inherited in the same way and on the same ratios as physical traits. If they are not thus inherited, then one must assume a line, on one side of which traits follow given ratios, while on the other they follow different ones òr none at all. Such a belief seems to assume that mental traits are created *de nova*.

This notion may be due to three factors:

1. It is hard to analyze mental traits and follow them through generations of ancestors.

2. It is also doubtlessly true that mental traits are modified more by education and environment than are physical traits.

3. Moral and even religious values are attached to mental reactions and the idea of strict inheritance conflicts with some ideas of the freedom of the personality.

More than this, the geneticists themselves are by no means agreed whether mental traits are dominant or recessive, whether they are the result of a specific gene or the interaction of a complex of genes, or whether mental traits are more plastic than physical ones. Some hold that the much debated I. Q. can be altered by education, i.e.,

---

[18] Laurence H. Snyder, *The Principles of Heredity*, Heath, 1940, pp. 218, ''A mutation is a change in a gene, not the loss of a gene.''

that one can by taking thought add a psychological cubit to his mental stature. Until the geneticists come to some agreement among themselves upon these fundamental concepts, there will doubtless be disagreement over the inheritance of mental traits. However, it would seem, reasoning by analogy, and believing that nature is governed by law and not by caprice, that mental inheritances are on the same basis as physical traits and must follow the principles listed above.

Importance of Inheritance of Mental Traits

If mental traits are passed on from generation to generation, then the matter of directing the development of the race stock at once assumes a new and scientific aspect, and what is more, the subject of eugenics may reasonably be regarded as of supreme importance. The first objective set forth by the National Educational Association at a recent meeting is, that "every child has a right to be well born." To put the thought in other words, one would say that a "dysgenic person has no right to become a parent." This statement is fraught with the utmost significance, for it strikes at the very heart of a large portion of our American population. The offspring of the dysgenic part of the population clogs our schools and costs the tax-payer hundreds of thousands of dollars every year.

The Dysgenic Group and Education

Our public school men have, within recent years, developed a great concern for the "backward" child and have been compelled to set up programs especially designed to help such children through school. These programs consist, for the most part, of reducing the scholastic requirements and substituting therefor some sort of manual training and the setting up of the so-called "opportunity school." In many systems the slow-minded students are run through the usual curricula, necessitating a relaxation of standards. Institutions of higher learning have for a number of years felt the effects of this practice, until now, in order to protect themselves from those who could not possibly profit from a college course, they are accepting as entrants only those from the upper percentiles of the graduating classes of preparatory schools. Even at that, it is evident to every observer that the colleges themselves have had to adapt their courses to meet the mental standards of students of doubtful ability.

Birth Rate of the Dysgenic

The birthrate of the dull-witted part of our population is extraordinarily high in comparison with the birthrate of persons of mental superiority. Resulting from the high birthrate of the less competent, there comes about a rapid decrease in the average intelligence of our population. This "brain-power" decline is strikingly illustrated in a table presented by Lorimer and Osborn in *Dynamics of Population:*[19]

INFLUENCE OF DIFFERENTIAL REPRODUCTION, BY OCCUPATIONAL CLASS, ON
EXPECTED DISTRIBUTION OF INTELLIGENCE QUOTIENTS OF UNITED
STATES SCHOOL CHILDREN IN TWO SUCCESSIVE
GENERATIONS

Haggerty I. Q. classes	First generation	Second generation	Change
	Per cent of total	*Per cent of total*	*Per cent*
140 & up	1.71	1.50	− 12.3
130–139	3.25	2.88	− 11.4
120–129	7.17	6.46	− 9.9
110–119	11.91	11.44	− 3.9
100–109	17.24	16.93	− 1.8
90–99	21.28	21.64	+ 1.6
80–89	18.67	19.31	+ 3.4
70–79	12.01	12.65	+ 5.4
60–69	5.30	5.61	+ 5.8
50–59	1.46	1.59	+ 8.8
All classes	100.00	100.00	....
	I. Q. points	*I. Q. points*	*I. Q. points*
Median	95.90	95.01	− 0.89

It takes only an operation in elementary mathematics to determine the date at which, at such a rate of decline, the majority of our population will be thoroughly dysgenic, socially inept and personally inefficient.

Dysgenesis and Employment

It is evident that man is not increasing his native intelligence, and yet the struggle for existence is becoming more strenuous with each passing year. The day of the unskilled laborer is passing, for industry more and more demands workers with intelligence sufficient to operate a machine. There is thus a steady decreasing demand for

[19] Frank Lorimer and Frederick Osborn, *Dynamics of Population*, The Macmillan Company, 1934, p. 190. The table is quoted by permission of the publisher.

the mentally dull. One of the outstanding medical schools in America recently refused over 700 applications for admission, accepted 75, some 15 of whom must fail. This is more or less representative of other professions, and can mean but one thing, viz., an increasing number of men and women for whom employment cannot be found.

Significance of Human Genetics

Man alone of all the animals whose breeding comes within his scope, constantly and consistently breeds from his culls. Every biologist knows what has been done by selective breeding to improve plants and animals and he also knows that the same general principles of heredity apply to man, yet man fails to put them into practice in application to man. No chicken-raiser or dog-fancier breeds from his culls; he does not even let them run with his sound stock, for he knows that if he does in a short time he will have no sound stock left. Not only do the dysgenic persons burden our schools and tax system, but they add nothing to our national defense and may actually endanger it. Democracy doubtless makes larger demands on the integrity and intelligence of its citizenry than any other form of government. There is no charm in the word democracy. Scores of governments based more or less on democratic principles have risen only to decay. Parents producing offspring with an I. Q. of 80 or less are unwittingly public enemies. The surest safeguard against national decline is a thoroughly eugenic population.

Man can claim no immunity from the general laws of the universe, much less from those in the narrower field of genetics. Genes show an amazing stability, and outside of a few minor mutations in plants and some lower animals, induced by controlled stimulation of heat, chemicals, or electricity, gene mutation is exceedingly rare. This gives point to the general rule that the only way not to continue defective germplasm, is not to breed from strains carrying it.

Notwithstanding the many spiritual values which have been evolved all through man's long history, nevertheless, he still is, and will continue to be, under the control of certain inescapable biological influences.

OUTLINE SUMMARY

I. Culture is adaptation to man's biological traits.
    A. Man arrived late; has changed little.
    B. That men are of a single species is basis for
        1. Common desires,
        2. Common culture traits.

    C. Various universal culture traits are evidence of a common heredity.

II. We have examined various phases of man's biological nature:

    A. Man shows striking similarities with higher apes, as to

        1. Height and weight,

        2. Age of adolescence,

        3. Life span,

        4. Reactions for self defense,

        5. Food and sex quests,

        6. Needs for play and sleep.

    B. Man's erect position

        1. Is not one to which he is perfectly adjusted physically.

            a. Slowness encouraged domestication of faster animals.

            b. Slowness stimulated inventions

                1. Of early weapons,

                2. Of means of transportation.

        2. Causes diseases.

    C. Associations for mutual aid help the individual as well as the species.

    D. Man is social.

        1. Even hermits get from their fellowmen:

            a. Language,

            b. Ideas of food and clothing,

            c. Religion.

        2. The social forces react on a biological basis.

    E. Man's long infancy affords time for adaptation.

    F. Limited reproduction keeps numbers within bounds.

    G. Subjugation of women results from their lesser physical strength.

III. Man's biological nature registers in effects on social institutions.

    A. Recreation and play have biological bases.

    B. Biological bases of the family are

        1. Sex urge,

        2. Prolonged infancy.

        3. Care of children made for division of labor.

    C. Vice has a biologic basis, both as to

        1. Sex vice,

        2. Alcohol consumption.

IV. Principles of heredity.
  A. Give importance to
    1. The presence of dysgenic persons in society,
    2. The decline of average intelligence quotients.
  B. Human beings are now bred largely from culls.

SELECTED REFERENCES

Baitsell, George A., *Human Biology*, McGraw Hill Book Co., 1940.

Bauer, E., Fischer, E., and Lenz, F., *Human Heredity*, The Macmillan Co., 1931 (English translation).

Hankins, F. H., *Introduction to the Study of Society*, The Macmillan Co., (Either edition).

Holmes, S. J., *The Trend of the Race*, Harcourt, Brace, 1921.

Hooton, E. A., *Up from the Ape*, Appleton, 1931.

Huntington, Ellsworth, *Seasons of Birth*, Wiley, 1938.

Lorimer, Frank, and Osborn, Frederick, *Dynamics of Population*, The Macmillan Co., 1934.

Natural Resources Board, *The Problems of a Changing Population* (prepared under direction of Frank Lorimer), U. S. Government Printing Office, 1938.

Panunzio, Constantine, *Major Social Institutions*, The Macmillan Co., 1939.

Popenoe, P., and Johnson, R., *Applied Eugenics*, The Macmillan Co.

Scheinfeld, Amram, *You and Heredity*, Frederick A. Stokes Co., 1939.

Snyder, Lawrence, *The Principles of Heredity*, Heath, 1940.

Spengler, J. J., "Seed Beds of America," *The Journal of Heredity*, Vol. 29, No. 12, Dec., 1938.

CHAPTER 7

ECONOMIC REGULARITIES

BY ELMER PENDELL, PH.D.

Pennsylvania State College

As we have seen in the foregoing chapters, social patterns of living either harmonize with the surrounding facts, or the absence of harmony results in human distress. Of the practices with which various social groups experiment, those practices which lead to distress are in some cases weeded out, but since the experimentation and the weeding out are a continuous process some measure of distress is usual. Besides, the relationships are sometimes so complicated that the web of cause leading to the distress is not readily untangled. The relationships are especially complicated in the *economic* processes, and consequently most social attempts to overcome economic distress are blunderings. The observations are too superficial, the programs too shallow, to do more than shift the distress to other persons or delay it.

In a single chapter on economics we cannot expect to give to the student a thorough comprehension of the forces and limitations among which persons and nations make a living. We cannot have space to analyze specific instances of distress as mal-adaptations to those forces and limitations. But we can enumerate a few fundamental generalizations which men and groups of men cannot afford to ignore, and we can give sketchy explanations of those generalizations. The fact that the explanations must be sketchy may necessitate an unusual degree of concentration on the part of the student.

That which is "economic" is involved in the getting of goods or using them; pertains to the game for gains. Economic *motivation* is the wish, the impulse, the mental leaning, which prompts one to try to get goods.

COMPARATIVE ADVANTAGE

Economic motivation is basically biological. The struggle for survival is both biological and economic. Said Charles Darwin in Chapter III of the *Origin of the Species:*

As more individuals are produced than can possibly survive, there must in every case be a struggle for existence, either one individual with another of the same species, or with the individuals of distinct species, or with the physical conditions of life. It is the doctrine of Malthus applied with manifold force to the whole animal and vegetable kingdoms; for in this case there can be no artificial increase of food, and no prudential restraint from marriage. . . . There is no exception to the rule that every organic being naturally increases at so high a rate, that, if not destroyed, the earth would soon be covered by the progeny of a single pair.

At the end of his chapter XV, Darwin interpreted the results of the struggle in their biological aspects:

Thus, from the war of nature, from famine and death, the most exalted object which we are capable of conceiving, namely, the production of the higher animals, directly follows.

More individuals are produced than can possibly survive, said Darwin; there is a lavishness, a prodigality, a wastefulness of life— but for an individual of any species including man, wastefulness of the means of living is risky. For the individual the struggle is economic; it is the game for gains; it constitutes the wealth-getting activities. Centrally, our economic activities have a momentum as old as life itself. They are the relentless expression of hunger, and of the mental patterns built up in the acts of acquiring goods.

Evolution wastes many individuals of a species, and that very fact makes it necessary for an individual, in order to avoid being himself wasted, to struggle to attain those means which aid in survival. Individuals in any species who use their energy in getting control over the means of sustaining life have usually been most likely to survive. One's advantage is fostered by economizing energy, that is, by *managing* energy.

Of course not all activity is calculated activity. A large proportion of behavior is habitual—and many of the habit patterns are derived from other emotions than a desire to get goods. There are, too, various limitations on choice-making, such as the pressure of custom, and the range of geographic opportunity. Nevertheless, frequently, the brain is used as a balancing machine to measure prospective results of contrasted courses of action. Though the managing process is not constant, and is limited in its application, yet in a proportion of cases sufficient to establish a rule, *a man will take that course which for a given expenditure of energy seems to him likely to yield greatest abundance of the things he wants.*   This economic principle number 1 is the principle of comparative advantage, the principle of economical use of energy, the principle which gives to "economics" its name, which means *management*.   One can think of philanthropic and other exceptions to the principle, in the acts of individuals, where other objectives have temporarily superseded this blanket condition of life, but the rule as such applies on a world-wide range.

Notice that the question in one's mind is not, "Can I do this work better than someone else can do it?"   The important question is, "Can I do this work with more advantage than I can do anything else?"

Comparative advantage must be processed in the mind of an individual; often the decision as to where the advantage lies is short-sighted.   Action must rest with judgments depending on perception of the advantage.

Most fundamental of all economic principles is this principle of comparative advantage.   It is the individual aspect of the struggle which in many ages has been a struggle for survival.   Its influence is sketched in broad strokes by a multitude of writers.   You may have heard of the "economic interpretation of history."   With a great deal of evidence writers such as Karl Marx and E. R. A. Seligman have presented the thesis that major happenings of the past and present are ordinarily brought about in the efforts of people to get control of goods.[1]   Charles A. Beard constructs a case to the effect that politics is essentially a method of getting and keeping economic powers.[2]   Gloria and Bakeless point out the economic basis for war.[3]   Frederick Jackson Turner in his *Rise of the New West* presents American History as mainly a record of men's efforts to get control of goods.[4]   And F. C. Grant has even searched forth an *Economic Background of the Gospels*.[5]   In this chapter we have not followed the principle of comparative advantage to such

[1] E. R. A. Seligman, *The Economic Interpretation of History*, Columbia University Press.

[2] Charles A. Beard, *The Economic Basis of Politics*, Alfred A. Knopf, 1934. See also his *An Economic Interpretation of the Constitution of the United States*, The Macmillan Company.

[3] A. Gloria, *Economic Causes of War*, Kerr Pub. Co.; John Edwin Bakeless, *The Origin of the Next War*, The Viking Press, New York, 1926.

[4] Harper & Brothers, 1906.   See also his other books.

[5] Oxford University Press, London, 1926.

sweeping generalizations; but we do here emphasize that among economic principles the principle of comparative advantage is central.

A principle is a statement of a general relationship upon which other relationships are founded. Of course there are many derivatives from this one we have been discussing, some of which are themselves principles.

Buying for Final Consumption

Some consuming will be done by every person; a different sort under some social situations than under others. Where population is dense, more medicine must ordinarily be consumed than in a sparse population, because disease germs have more bases from which to attack. If custom requires costly caskets for the deceased, those who remain may themselves go to earlier graves from privation in order to "decently" inter the dear departed. If habit requires a pack of cigarettes a day, one may neglect buying the shoes for the children, shoes which would prevent exposure. Consumption depends on biological requirements, on custom, on habit; and in conjunction with them on psychological conditioning of responses. The *processes* of conditioning are subject to psychological rules, but the *directions* of conditioning are largely socially determined. A keen analysis by Thorstein Veblen in *The Theory of the Leisure Class*[6] is richly suggestive of possible directions of conditioning. Men waste goods as a means of demonstrating, or pretending to, a superiority of economic power. This rule, which Veblen crystallized, the rule of conspicuous consumption, is widely applying. The social pliability of desires explains fad and fashion, in types of food and kinds of housing as well as in clothing.

Advertising is an important means by which profit-seekers remake whole segments of the population. By carefully following the rules for conditioning of responses the tobacco companies in the period of a decade made cigarettes indispensable to millions of women. Liquor manufacturers are now using the lesson they learned from the tobacco companies.

Conspicuous consumption is usually competitive consumption. It is sometimes called conspicuous waste, and is popularly referred to as keeping up with the Joneses. Men try to keep status by trying to spend as conspicuously as others in their class.

[6] The Viking Press, 18 East 48th Street, New York.

Difficulty in attaining goods has much influence in leading people to *substitutes,* particularly in matters where waste is futile as a pretense of economic superiority because conspicuousness is not great. Thus, when pork is high in price, there is easy substitution of beef or lamb. After all, the purchasing power has limits, and expenditures in one direction necessitate conservation in other directions. Assuming any given set of social pressures for consuming, one makes comparisons, and judgments on the basis of the comparisons, trying to economize; that is, to manage, to get the most utility for a given amount of effort.

Summarizing our observations concerning purchasing for consumption we present the major points of the following group as our economic principles 2 and 3:

(2) The directions of demands for goods are socially determined through the processes of psychological conditioning.

(a) Men tend to waste goods as a means of showing a superiority of economic power.

(3) Limitations of energy or of purchasing power impose the necessity of judging (making choices) with a view to economizing.

(a) Scarcity necessitates substitution.

It will be perceived that these major rules are paired in a reverse way. The more application one of them has in a given instance, the less truth is there in the other, in connection with that instance. Also, the major rules have wider applicability than their subordinates. (2) (a) would not apply in the First World War in homes displaying thrift stamps and food-saving posters.

Producers, as advertisers, often direct the social pressure that determines the type of consumption. In simpler times, demands developed by biological need or by social pressures exterior to producer influence. Producers merely met demands. Now the producers *create* much of the demand.

Competition, Isolation, Monopoly, Cooperation, and War

There has been, in men's consuming, the building of social patterns which in some phases are inconsistent with actual survival values for the group, yet even here the principle of comparative advantage is in evidence. Given the social standards, whatever they are, and tracing one's wants to these standards one acts to get the most of what he wants for a given outlay of energy. In the acquisition of goods, as an individual seeks his advantage he comes in contact with others who are after the same goods. That is where the struggle comes in; what one individual gets another must do without. In the efforts of individuals to get things which they desire when others are likewise trying to get those same things, we have economic *competition*. When competition is the dominant element in a social situation it serves as a sort of regulator of social relations. Adam Smith had the conviction that each man, striving for his own comparative advantage, works for the benefit of all. Adam Smith is considered the "Father of Economics" because he was first to draw together a large number of observations concerning men's activities in getting goods. His *Wealth of Nations* was published in 1776. The idea that social benefit coincides with private benefit runs throughout his volumes; is set forth directly in his Book I, Chapter 2; and is derived from his assumption that competition leads competitors to socially beneficial behavior. Competition, when it is controlling, has been assumed to *keep prices down* to something near costs, because any variation to higher prices would draw other producers into the making of the product, and the resultant greater amount of product would cause a decline of prices. Competition, when it is controlling, has been thought to *keep prices up* to a level which will meet costs of most producers because, the theory runs, if one cannot meet his costs he gets out, and then the fact that there is a lesser amount of product on the market pushes price up a little. Competition has been supposed to *get the kinds of goods produced that people want*, because those are what they will pay for; and to get *just enough but not too much produced*. It induces just enough men but not too many into each line of production, some writers have thought; and rewards the workers according to their productivity.

But men have long been aware that Adam Smith was over optimistic. The chief trouble is that competition is not a constant—is not a regularly applying fact. Consequently it is only sometimes true that a man working for his own advantage works for the benefit of all. One's comparative advantage leads him to smash competitors if he can; leads him to restrict the opportunities of buyers; leads him sometimes to isolate himself from competitors by going to new frontiers, or, in another situation, to lobby for a tariff to prevent foreign competition. His comparative advantage leads him to advertise in order to sell at high prices, or to condition prospective buyers to pay for goods that harm them. Sometimes comparative advantage leads men to cooperate, thus enlarging the unit of competition; gives the cooperators promise of most returns; and sometimes comparative advantage leads a group, when competition is intense, to go to war against a competing group in the hope of decreasing or eliminating the competition. These developments, competition, isolation, monopoly, cooperation, and war, are derived from comparative advantage in various circumstances.

Specialization and Sale of Surpluses

Comparative advantage is reason for *specialization*, which, with a different emphasis is also called *division of labor*. "Specialization" is the name applied when attention is on the individual's activity; "division of labor" is the term which Adam Smith used with a view to the variety of products which made up the wealth of nations. *One can be more efficient in producing one kind of goods than in producing all the kinds of goods he would like to have.* We present that as our fourth economic principle. In specializing, one makes a surplus, or contributes to the making of a surplus, of that product in which one spends his energy. He barters his product, or, after barter has developed into a money economy, he sells his service or his product.

When a large proportion of persons in a given region specialize in the making of a single kind of product, the fact is described in the term *territorial specialization*. Usually the comparative advantage of the persons directs this specialization to the working up of the resources of the area. If, for a time, the specialization of individuals in a territory is the working up of raw materials from other areas, that particular territorial specialization will eventually be reduced as a consequence of competition with the specialists in more adapted areas. For example, New England cotton mill owners and workers have had difficulties when confronted with competition of southern mills.

We have noted that specialization is a direct result of comparative advantage. It is that activity which will come about from the trials and elimination of less effective trials of individuals.

Social organization of production, of transportation, and of marketing is likely to be merely the development of agencies to implement individual desires. Usually social organization fosters specialization, but occasionally social organization runs counter to specialization, as when Gandhi instituted a primitive production program in India, and when European governments have striven for economic self-sufficiency of their countries.

There is no assurance that advantage to individuals will work to the welfare of all, even under competition. There may be, for example, the exploitation of an oil field; and then a decline. Getting the oil out speedily, before the owners of nearby lots drill offset wells, is the form the game takes. The competitive drilling is costly in the process and too stimulating to the use of the product for long-lasting benefits. However, the alternative to competition is not a smooth-running impersonal social program designed with omniscient wisdom. Perhaps now, as in Adam Smith's day, competition may be as safe a regulator as legislation sponsored by groups as a means of building walls around their vested interests.[7]

RELATIONS OF POPULATION TO LAND

An early bit of research in the social sciences was a study of population. Thomas Robert Malthus was the research man. His father, an advocate of equality of wealth, in discussions of the subject with Thomas Robert, served as a stimulus for an essay by the younger Malthus on *The Principles of Population*, published in 1798.

Population, said Malthus, actually increases to the limits of the food supply; population *tends to* increase geometrically, as 2, 4, 8, 16, 32, etc.—whereas food supply actually increases not more than arithmetically, as 2, 4, 6, 8, 10. Consequently population is always pressing on food supply, and large proportions of the citizenry are struggling along on the verge of subsistence. Population will be kept down to the limits of the food supply, thought Malthus, by wars, in the struggle for land; by disease, which is fostered by malnutrition; by prostitution, which has sometimes grown out of the sex urge when babies were undesired; by actual starvation; and by the lateness of marriages, through which foresight and custom sometimes bring about adaptation of individuals to limited economic opportunities.

These population checks, usually considered evils, are forced into existence or into greater severity, thought Malthus, when population increase makes for scantiness of food per person.

Perhaps the definiteness of the number series with which Malthus formulated his population theory reflected the fact that he had been

[7] See for example, ''Codes, Collusion and Housing Costs,'' by Karl Detzer, in *American Mercury*, July 1940, condensed in *Reader's Digest*, July 1940.

trained at Cambridge University as a mathematician. But whether or not investigator Malthus presented generalizations at the end of the 18th century which apply with exactness nearly a century and a half later, the subject matter with which he dealt may profitably be given careful scrutiny.

Salvage from Malthusian Theory

1. a. Men tend to increase.
   b. Men require, for their living, animals and plants.
2. a. Animals tend to increase.
   b. Animals require, for their living, plants.
3. a. Plants tend to increase.
   b. Plants require soil.
4. Soil does not increase (except in insignificant proportion per annum or per decade).
3. c. The scarcity of soil limits the number of plants.
2. c. The scarcity of plants limits the number of animals.
1. c. The limitation on the number of plants and animals limits the number of men.

Those statements can be summarized in the economic principle to which we give the number 5: *Scarcity of soil limits the number of men.*

The limitation of men's numbers, which depends on the fact that soil does not tend to increase, seems to apply in particular territories, and to particular classes in a community. Robert Scott Moffat expresses the thought:

> The means of subsistence of any trade or profession in any community depends upon the demand for the services of that trade or profession in that community, and the trade or profession that increases beyond the demand for its services violates the law of population as much as if it overpeopled the world.[8]

Whether or not Malthus intended to do so, there is importance in pinning his theory to the here and now and to particular situations rather than to think of it only in connection with a hypothetical future. Do you happen to know a family in which the population is pressing on the food supply?

The Law of Diminishing Returns

Of course it is evident that the earth's area is, within narrow

---

[8] *Henry George the Orthodox*, 1885, p. 17.

bounds, limited. There has been some expansion, as in the reclaiming of shallow sea floors by the Dutch, the building of levees to imprison the Mississippi River, the filling in of shallow water along the lake shore in Chicago and along the Potomac River at Washington, D. C. Such efforts are extremely costly, however, and they emphasize land limitations, rather than freeing us from those limitations. Though hallucinations of omnipotence may be engendered by the dizzying inventions of recent decades, men are still earthborn, and earthbound.

The significance of the land limitation lies in the law of diminishing returns. Incidentally, this law is necessary to and implied in the Malthusian population doctrine, and in our salvage from Malthus' doctrine. On any one part of the earth's surface, units of energy, applied for the purpose of production, will not yield products in direct proportion to the number of applied units of energy. Large applications of energy will ordinarily yield less per unit of energy than lesser applications. Coming to the statement of our economic principle number 6, with a given piece of land, if differing amounts of labor are conceived of as optionally available for production in conjunction with the land, *some one amount of labor will be most productive per man; labor in excess of that amount will yield less per man.* If we have a number of like pieces of land, and apply a different amount of labor on each than on any other, we will find that some one amount of labor yields most product per unit of labor; more labor yields less product per unit of labor. The reason is simply that there is less aid from land to each unit of labor.

For illustration, one man working an eight-acre plot may be able to produce 1600 bushels of potatoes. If two men rather than one were working those eight acres, they might be able to produce 2400 bushels of potatoes. That would be an average of 1200 bushels per man, to compare with the 1600 bushels which the one man could produce.

The lesser per capita return is resultant from (1) the shortage of space for more growing potatoes to spread out in—and so the cause is physical; (2) the shortage of area in which the potato vines can spread their leaves to the sun—and so the cause is physical; (3) the scarcity in the soil of the chemical elements necessary to potato growth—and so the cause is physical. The law of diminishing returns is an economic principle which has physical foundations, and social results.

Dense Populations and Interdependence

Coincident with increased density of population there is more dependence of a people on the products of other lands; or, as an alternative, there is a relatively scanty standard of living. Except as standard of living is scanty, many people will be specializing and selling their surpluses, and buying the surpluses of other specializers. Pennsylvanians part with much of coal and coke and steel; import much of food stuffs. Where there are many disconnected political jurisdictions, as Europe has had, there is likely to be occasional political tampering with the conditions of purchase and sale by means of tariff changes, for example. Such tampering obstructs some people's access to a living, and irritations result. A loss of control of markets and of sources of raw materials means much in terms of incomes. If there should be a change of English relations to the rest of the world; if English exports and imports were substantially reduced, English incomes would likewise be reduced.

But the point that where population is dense, standard of living is essentially dependent on outside trade, is rather direct and obvious. There are more subtle implications, equally compelling.

The acquisition of raw materials from outside, for use in a manufacturing country is approximately the same *in its effect on the absorption of the raw materials* as would be the removal of part of the population of the importing country to the sources of the raw materials. It prevents anyone else from using those particular materials. Japan, for example, if the Japanese continue to reproduce at the rate of 700,000 a year, and if Japan takes care of its people at existing standards, must either export part of her population or import raw materials. And the getting of raw materials from Manchukuo, for example, is not essentially different, as to the amount of raw materials used, from sending to continental Asia part of the Japanese population.

It may have seemed strange to many that England with less land area than the State of Florida supports 37,000,000 people. The fact is that England does not support those millions in the sense of furnishing food and raw materials. England's citizens draw on Canada, Australia, New Zealand and India; and on Italy, Chile, and China. The colonial status of some of these places distinguishes them from the others only in that trade with them may be more readily controlled and stabilized. But whether they are colonies or sovereign countries, the English draw their subsistence mainly from outside lands. *The geographical specialization in this situation merely cloaks over the fact that those outlying areas could not be more densely populated without the probability of imposing on England's people the inconvenience of decreasing their own numbers or working for lower incomes.*

That italicized statement may be startling, and yet the principle on which it depends, our number 7, is simple: namely, *use of earth products in one country prevents their use in another country.* Obvious as is that truth, in our land of plenty it is rarely taken into account—use of resources by one people precludes their use by others; and, as a corollary, *increase of people in a new area is accompanied by withholding of raw materials.*

A few writers have made mention of new uses of raw materials nearer their sources: Moffat,[9] and J. M. Keynes[10] for example; but neither of these has done better than Malthus:[11]

> In the wildness of speculation it has been suggested (of course more in jest than in earnest) that Europe ought to grow its corn in America, and devote itself solely to manufactures and commerce, as the best sort of division of the labor of the globe. But even on the extravagant supposition that the natural course of things might lead to such a division of labor for a time, and that by such means Europe could raise a population greater than its lands could possibly support, the consequences ought justly to be dreaded. It is an unquestionable truth that it must answer to every territorial state, in its natural progress to wealth, to manufacture for itself, unless the countries from which it had purchased its manufactures possess some advantages peculiar to them besides capital and skill. But when upon this principle America began to withdraw its corn from Europe and the agricultural exertions of Europe were inadequate to make up the deficiency, it would certainly be felt that the temporary advantages of a greater degree of wealth and population (supposing them to have been really attained) had been very dearly purchased by a long period of retrograde movements and misery.

But why would the increasing number of people in the new countries not continue to specialize on the old crops and extraction of

[9] *Op. Cit.,* p. 50.

[10] J. M. Keynes, *The Economic Consequences of the Peace,* Harcourt, Brace and Howe, 1920, pp. 23–25.

[11] Thomas Robert Malthus, *Additions to the Fourth and Former Editions of An Essay on The Principle of Population,* Book III, Chapter XII; 1817, pp. 187–188.

raw materials rather than to diversify their energies and reach into occupations that once were England's exclusively? Why would "every territorial state" tend "to manufacture for itself"? W. Stanley Jevons, brilliant English economist of a half century later than Malthus, was first to give the answer, the substance of which follows.[12]

The Transfer of Influence of Diminishing Returns

Comparative advantage of individuals leads to specialization, as we have shown, but when, in the specialty, increasing product is procured with greater effort, rather than go far in production under diminishing returns some members of the increasing population will shift to other occupations. Here is the economic principle, our number 8 : *Increasing population, to avoid the full effect of diminishing returns in agriculture, diversify in their occupations.* Comparative advantage, then, in one situation leads to specialization; in another situation, distinct and predictable, comparative advantage leads away from specialization.

In a wheat producing area, as the population increases, for those who produce on the less fertile land there is less of an advantage in the production of wheat than there was when a person could have more of the land to work with. So it may be just as profitable to some of the individuals to mine iron ore, and as more and more people need work the best mines will bring more gain than the worst wheat land. As the population continues to grow, the best mines will in time be occupied, and men will turn to still other occupations, finally including manufacturing.

Increase in population is not the only condition which would lead to diversification of energy. There might be an increasing diversification in a new country as an adjustment to a situation judged wrongly at first. Industries which were not known about or which were thought not adapted might in time be found to thrive in the raw material country, and energy might be diverted in part from earlier industries and divided with some newer kind of production or other process of acquisition. Accumulation of funds and a new availability of capital goods would be an additional cause for a development of some manufacturing. A tariff against imports might work in the same direction also. A further important reason

[12] W. Stanley Jevons, *The Coal Question,* Third edition, revised in 1906 by A. W. Flux, Macmillan and Co., pp. 420–430.

for diversification in the new country is this: Larger production of a given kind of goods, of which the people of an area produce a surplus, makes a larger surplus, and a poorer market results, stimulating a reaching out to new occupations.

Part of the population, of course, will continue to grow wheat, and part will continue to work the mines, but as to those who might work on the poorer lands or in the poorer mines, they have no advantage in so doing. Their advantage is in manufacturing.

If we have seen that when population is increasing the effect of diminishing returns in agriculture is diversification, we have probably also sensed the fact that in attempting to keep up their own standard of living, the people of the new area tend to bring down the standard of living in an older manufacturing region. The principle, number 9, is: *Diversification in the new area tends to decrease exports of raw materials and to decrease imports of manufactured goods.* As manufacturing increases in Canada, its citizens will use some of the raw materials that would otherwise have gone to England, even for the goods which are dissimilar to the goods of England, because the same kinds of metals and of wood, etc., may be used in the making of many different products. And as diversification in Canada increases, Canadian demand for English finished products decreases, forcing down the prices of English made goods. The same old costs are thereby high in relation to prices obtainable for the products.

Those English manufacturers who cannot meet the growing competition with Canadian firms in manufactured goods quit, and the additions thereby made to the ranks of the unemployed put pressure on wages. In the adverse conditions, some inhabitants of England who previously received only enough income to keep alive, are likely to become victims of undernourishment, subject to the ravages of disease.

We arrive at a series of closely related economic principles: Even though the increase in population takes place in the new countries, the resultant checks to increase of population register in the old countries. Population pressure in old countries is traceable to population growth in new countries. Population pressure is experienced in an old manufacturing country even though there be no increase in its own population, because of the high cost of raw materials and food, and the increased competition for markets. And here is the summary, to which we give our number 10: *Diminishing returns, though they may take place in a new area, work their hardship in old areas.*

Reproduction, the source of population replacement and increase, is biological, is practically universal except as interfered with, and is to be expected. The economic principles which we have been discussing, on the relation of population to land, depend directly on reproduction on one side, on soil limitation on the other, and not on social structure. They are not institutional. Thèse principles apply under state operated industry or under a regime of private property. Folkways, such as late marriages, birth control, sterilization of persons who are social burdens, may be founded on the principles, may constitute adjustments to them. In other words there may be institutional developments which are adaptations to the economic principles just as airplanes and parachutes are adaptations to the law of gravity; but the principles themselves are persistent relationships profoundly influencing human behavior, if not through adaptation, then directly.

PRODUCTION

Courses in Physics, Chemistry, Engineering, Political Science, and Forestry, may each, with its different emphasis, deal with some of the same subject matter; for example an interstate bridge. Likewise, within a subject, say Economics, the same subject matter may be properly discussed under the separate emphases of a number of subdivisions. Our topics are not mutually exclusive; they are emphases. Thus comparative advantage is present in our study of relations of population to land; land relations as well as comparative advantage are part of the conditions of production. All three are necessary to an understanding of sales, and of income; and as a matter of fact, items given emphasis in income would be helpful in understanding monopoly, for example, which is primarily a subtopic of production. For an understanding of economic influences it is well to "study every part after every other part"; in other words to go over the parts more than once, the repetitions, for most effect, being in more extended writings.

Production is a process of change, change in the form of materials or of the place or the time of their availability with the effect of increasing their desiredness. Some writers have defined the concept more abstractly as creation of utilities; and H. J. Davenport has defined it as any change appropriate to command a price.[13]

[13] *Economics of Enterprise*, Macmillan, 1923, p. 121.

There are important economic principles connected with production, some of which we have already discussed. Comparative advantage leads to specialization, as we saw; and the rule applies both in agriculture and in other types of producing. In agriculture, comparative advantage in connection with diminishing returns leads to diversification of occupations with results as shown. Inasmuch as many types of raw materials are agricultural in their sources (principle number 11), *the productivity of manufacturing enterprises is reduced for such enterprises and areas as experience the costliness, by the difficulty of attainment of raw materials.*

In manufacturing, specialization, followed further and further, leads to large-scale production. The fact that in manufacturing there is no early limit to the advantage of specialization has been expressed by some writers as a law of increasing returns, or of decreasing costs, from increasing scale of production. It is intended as a contrast with diminishing returns in agriculture which we have already discussed. Actually, however, there seems to be no law or principle additional to that already stated—comparative advantage leads to specialization.

Production facts include *cost* facts. Costs are resistances to production. They are payments, outlays, expenditures, required to overcome the rarity of factors of production for the purpose at hand. The money expressions symbolize the degrees of rarity in relation to demand.

In dealing with costs, of course the old rule of comparative advantage applies, the rule of economic motivation: one will get a task done with as little energy as is necessary. In money terms, one will get the job done with as little cost as possible.

The factors of production, that is to say, the elements "entering into" production, roughly classified as land, labor and capital goods, have to be paid for, else they will go to other producers, to other production. How much payment is required? That depends on scarcity of the factors of production which are available for the job. Consider the factors of production which are capital goods. Payments for capital goods are largely "over-head costs." Some of the costs for other factors are overhead costs too. Overhead costs are payments which are involved in carrying on production but *which are not regularly proportional to the amount of production.* The costs for the electrically operated lathes and planes in the furniture factory have to be somehow imputed to the tables which are produced with the use of those lathes and planes. The cost for the workmen, particularly if they are on "piece rates," so much per table, or per table leg, will have a regular proportion with the number of tables produced: 1 table, labor cost $1; 100 tables, labor cost $100; 1000 tables, labor cost $1000. The wood cost is likewise regularly proportional to the amount of production. Not so the cost of lathes and planes. The *total* for them is the same, whether the production be 1 table or 1000 tables; and so the *average* is vastly different with different amounts of production; and, at any stage except the beginning and an expansion stage, the *added* cost for lathes and planes when production is increased, is nil. The plane and lathe costs are not regularly proportional to the amount of production; they are consequently classifiable as overhead costs.

Overhead costs make business and industry a gamble the outcome of which depends on demand for the goods. What accounts for the tremendous volume of advertising of recent years? The answer is that with increasing use of machines, increased sales reduce the average costs. Assuming that the machines are on hand, added costs for added production are not much. There is advantage in advertising if it increases income from sales in excess of direct costs plus advertising costs.

The influences of overhead costs are many. We shall here mention, and merely mention, only a few of the most obvious results. Principle number 12: Overhead costs take away reliability from rules for attaching prices to goods. Of course the all embracing rule is, and always has been, "charge as much as the market will bear"; but the puzzle is, how much will it bear? Prices are likely to be very irregular in competition, and, where there is little competition, prices are likely to be extortionate. Principle number 13: Overhead costs lead to more and more centralized control over product, and centralized control over production processes. In order that the advantages of large-scale production may be had by those persons who are in control, they tend to unite with erstwhile competitors and thus to reduce the number of competitors. These two principles come out of the fact that costs for machines and some other types of capital goods are "overhead"; they are not directly (regularly) proportional with amount of production.[14]

The word "costs" ordinarily refers to the unpleasant aspects of a producer's or a merchant's business, as for example his payments for raw materials, labor, etc., and the word "prices" applies to what

[14] See J. M. Clark, *Overhead Costs.*

he charges for his finished products. The use is not very uniform however, and also the same payment is cost to the buyer, price to the seller.

Having surveyed some fundamental truths about production, particularly about production costs, we now go to some closely related concepts classified under the head of "sale," where we look at the pricing processes. That there are connections between costs and prices should be clear; and also we should be aware that the relationships are not regular—are not regular because of the overhead nature of some of the costs.

SALE

Where there is specialization there will usually be production of a surplus—more than the specialist will consume of the product on which he specializes. He will wish to use it as payment for something he wants more. In a primitive situation this leads to barter, an exchange of goods for goods. As an individual produces more surplus of his specialty, and fewer of the kinds of goods he wants, the barter becomes more systematized. It is more advantageous that way; conforms more closely with economic motivation. Some goods being more durable than others, and easier to transport, come to be acceptable, even if one has no use for them himself; they will last until he finds someone who will want them. Thus bone fishhooks became a common item of payment in Ancient Egypt; cattle were "money" among early Romans, so that from their word "pecus," meaning cattle, we get our word, "pecuniary." Decorative bands of shells, called wampum, served as payment among the Indians.[15]

As to particular money systems, we will leave those for your study of economic *institutions;* it serves our purpose here to point out that *money of some sort develops as social contacts become numerous.* That much is an economic principle, our number 14, a fundamental truth concerning the processes of getting goods. Money arises because of comparative advantage, requiring only a little intelligence—enough for an individual to perceive the advantage; to perceive, for example, that the berries of which he has a surplus will rot, whereas the arrow point will last until he finds somebody who has use for it.

After a money system has developed, another automatic prin-

[15] For report of curious commodities which have served as money see chapter I of Tippets and Froman, *White's Money and Banking,* Ginn and Co., 1936.

ciple comes into play, our number 15: namely, increase of money in circulation tends to decrease the purchasing power of each unit of money and credit, make prices higher; decrease of money in circulation tends to take away somebody's purchasing power, make for depression, make prices lower.   White men decreased the value of wampum when they substituted abundant beads in place of scarce shells.   England made more value in a pound sterling when she "went back on gold" at the pre-war weight to the pound after the first world war because there was necessarily a decrease in the number of pounds in circulation.

The *quantity theory of money,* of which the foregoing is a very simple statement, explains why paper money, increasing in quantity, is accompanied by rising prices; each unit of the stuff is worth less as the quantity increases, because more people have some on hand ready to use for things they want; so more units are necessary.

One other economic principle concerning sale should be mentioned.   We give it number 16.   With a given condition of money and credit, how much will one charge for what he has to sell?   Always the general fact has been (and it stems directly from comparative advantage) : *the price is as much as the market will bear.*   How much will the market bear?   Demand and supply will determine that.   The influences affecting demand, as was pointed out in discussing consumption, are largely social.   Supply influences are chiefly the resistances to supply of goods, which resistances are made up by the production costs.   So an analysis of *costs* and an analysis of *consumption* give us some understanding of the price that the market will bear.

INCOME

The same payments which we have just labeled "costs" are, from the standpoint of the receivers, *income.*   As usual, those on the buying side get as much as they can for their purchasing power. The persons selling the factors of production have shares of income distributed to them: interest and dividends go to persons who control capital goods; rent goes to land owners; wages go to laborers. A search for economic principles in *interest* and *dividends,* since it would have to be brief in a course like this, would not be very fruitful; we pass on to *rent.*

Rent is payment for use of economic goods, usually land, and like payment for apples or calico, the amount of the payment depends on supply in relation to demand.   Inasmuch as the *supply* of land is not readily modifiable, the dynamic influence working on rent is *demand* for land. As Henry George pointed out in his *Progress and Poverty,* in a given stage of production technique a dense population turns a larger proportion of total income to land holders than if population is sparse. Even in a socialist state the land would be economized according to the degree of density of the population. Putting these rent facts in one sentence we get this principle (our number 17): *Importance of a given piece of land is in direct relation with the density of population demanding the products of that land.*

Wages are paid for the factor *labor,* dependent as to amount of wages on the bargaining power of the laborers. In a new country, labor is likely to be scarce, and wages, in terms of purchasing power, high compared with the purchasing power of rent. As population increases in comparison with resources purchasing power of wages is likely to fall. If population continues to increase, wages are likely to continue to decline, because there will be a demand for laborers sufficient to use all of the laborers only if wages are low. Bottom limit will probably be subsistence. When the western hemisphere was opened up it drained away the superabundance of laborers from Europe, and supplied more raw materials for European workers to work on. That golden age in Europe lasted until the Americas offered a fading welcome, tightened immigration laws.

David Ricardo, an English financier and economist contemporary with Thomas Robert Malthus, based a wage law on the showing that Malthus had made of population increase. Ricardo's "iron law of wages" is simply that *population tends to increase; that workers, in competition with each other, run the wages down so far that most workers can buy only enough goods to keep them alive.* Ricardo's iron law, which we adopt as our principle number 18, may be looked upon as a principle because, being based on a persistent factor, the generalization itself is persistent. The factor on which it is based is sex urge, the force behind reproduction. The theme is the same as that of Malthus, and Ricardo's formulation differs mainly in that it is put in a terminology of wages. If wages were equal, as they might be in a socialist state, the iron law would mean that the sex urge would tend to send the whole population to a subsistence level.

Has the iron law been in operation since Columbus discovered the Western Hemisphere? The question is about the same as, Has the sex urge been operative since 1492? The answer is yes, but its effects in America have not been adversely noticeable in America —because (a) taking up the slack in resources takes time. If one steps off a cliff the force of gravity continues in operation though it may not have a serious effect until one stops. (b) Institutional controls of population have increased—unplanned adjustments to the iron law. To the earlier celibacy of the clergy and delayed marriages and some abstinence in marriage have been added, it seems, among some Catholic families, timing of the sex act; among some families of the general population, mechanical birth control, more delay of marriage, and more abstinence in marriage; and as state measures, some segregation of persons who are public burdens, and some sterilization. However, a transferred or a retarded result of a law, or as we have previously pointed out, an institutional adjustment to it, can hardly be said to refute the existence of the law.

Now we array the foregoing generalizations in close order.

I. The search for comparative advantage, which is the basis for economizing, is biological.

    A. Evolution wastes individuals. Individuals, to avoid being wasted, have had to struggle to get means of subsistence.

        1. *Prin. 1:* A man will take that course which, for a given expenditure of energy, seems to him likely to yield greatest abundance of the things he wants.

            a. Since much of what men want is goods, on the principle of comparative advantage is based the Economic Interpretation of History.

    B. Though buying for final consumption is partly directioned by social conditioning (*Prin. 2*), even so, in following one's comparative advantage, choices have to be made (*Prin. 3*).

    C. In a variety of circumstances comparative advantage leads to

        1. Competition,

        2. Isolation,

        3. Monopoly,

        4. Cooperation,

        5. War.

    D. Comparative advantage leads to specialization and sale of surpluses.

      1. *Prin. 4:* One can be more efficient in producing one kind of goods than in producing all the kinds of goods one would like to have.

        a. When a large proportion of persons in a region specialize in making a single kind of product, the fact is described in the term "territorial specialization."

          (1) This usually involves working up the raw material of the region.

II. In the relations of population to land,

    A. *Prin. 5:* Scarcity of soil limits number of men.

    B. *Prin. 6:* Labor in excess of an optimum amount will yield a diminishing return.

    C. Interdependence is increased by density of population.

      1. *Prin. 7:* Use of earth products in one country prevents their use in another country.

      2. *Prin. 8:* Increasing population, to avoid full effect of diminishing returns in agriculture, diversify in their occupations.

        a. *Prin. 9:* Diversification in the new area tends to decrease exports of raw materials and to decrease imports of manufactured goods.

          (1) Since increase of people in a maturing area is accompanied by a withholding of raw materials from a country older in manufacturing, *Prin. 10:* the effect of diminishing returns is transferred from a maturing land to an old land.

III. In *production,*

    A. Comparative advantage in agriculture, in conjunction with diminishing returns, leads to diversification.

    B. *Prin. 11:* Diminishing returns in agriculture are transferred, in their effect, to manufacturing, through costliness of raw materials and contraction of markets.

    C. Specialization, followed far, leads to large scale production.

          1. If circumstances permit sale of surpluses.

  D. In the matter of costs,

          1. *Prin 12:* Overhead costs prevent regular relation of costs to prices.

          2. *Prin. 13:* Overhead costs lead to centralized control over products.

IV. Sale:

  A. *Prin. 14:* Sale replaces barter as social contacts become numerous, comparative advantage leading to a development of money.

  B. *Prin. 15:* The more money there is in circulation the less each unit of it is worth, and the higher are the prices; the less money there is in circulation the more each unit is worth and the lower are the prices.

  C. *Prin. 16:* Prices are as much as the market will bear.

V. *Income* in our discussion is limited to rent and wages.

  A. Income receivers take what the market will bear.

  B. *Prin. 17:* Importance of a given piece of land is in direct relation with the density of population demanding the products of that land.

  C. *Prin. 18:* Wages tend to move in reverse direction from land value; and in reverse direction from population numbers.

SELECTED REFERENCES

On the struggle for existence: Charles Darwin, *Origin of the Species.*

Illustrative books which generalize on the search for comparative advantage are Charles A. Beard, *The Economic Basis of Politics,* Alfred A. Knopf, 1934, and E. R. A. Seligman, *The Economic Interpretation of History,* Columbia University Press.

On the relation of population to land, there is still no book more thought-provoking than the *Essay on Population,* by Thomas Robert Malthus: Everyman's Library, E. P. Dutton & Co.

Concerning transfer from a raw materials area to a manufacturing area of the results of diminishing returns in agriculture and exhaustion of resources, the one and only brilliant treatment is that by W. Stanley Jevons, in *The Coal Question.* A third edition, revised in 1906 by A. W. Flux, was published by Macmillan and Co.

For influences of overhead costs see J. M. Clark, *Economics of Overhead Costs,* University of Chicago Press, 1923.

CHAPTER 8

PSYCHOLOGICAL REGULARITIES

By MEHRAN K. THOMSON, PH.D.

Michigan State Normal College

Historically, psychology has quite a past. Some wag has reported the subject in the following sequence. Psychology began as the science of the soul. Then it lost its soul and acquired a mind. Mind in turn gave way to consciousness and consciousness to behavior of a sort. Thus in the course of evolution psychology has lost its soul, its mind, its consciousness.

A partial list of the kinds and methods and points of view in psychology would include the introspective, faculty, functional, structural, physiological, biological, genetic, behavioristic, Gestalt and Freudian.[1]

The types or divisions of psychology make up an impressive list,—general, dynamic, biological, psychological, genetic, child, animal, differential, abnormal, employment, educational, industrial, legal, religious, social, medical, recreational, ethnic, and the psychology of advertising, salesmanship, administration. To this list might be added any number of psychologies in almost any field of human activity in which conduct or behavior is involved.

Concentrating on the irreducible minimum elementary concepts in psychology significant for social life we present the physical factors, intellectual or psychic factors, individual factors and social factors.

PHYSICAL FACTORS: PHYSIOLOGICAL PSYCHOLOGY

Central Nervous System

Psychology is usually defined as the science of mental life or of human behavior. What is the physiological basis of this behavior? It is assumed that even mental processes do not take place in a

[1] For a full account of these types of psychology the reader is referred to the literature on the history of psychology. Cf. W. B. Pillsbury, *The History of Psychology*, W. W. Norton Co., *Psychologies of 1930* edited by Carl Murchison, Clark Univ. Press, G. D. Higginson, *Fields of Psychology*, Henry Holt and Co.

vacuum. The modern psychologist is wary of the term mind because it suggests a contradiction, an abstract entity. He prefers to keep his feet on the ground and begin with something tangible.

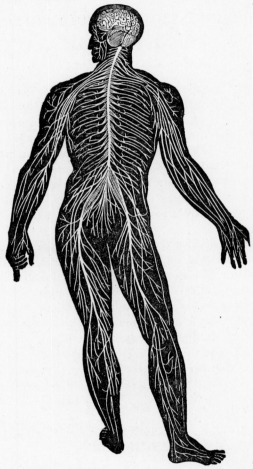

FIG. 1. (From Martin's *Human Body.*) General view of the nervous system, showing brain, cord, and nerves. By permission of Henry Holt and Company, publishers.

Mental processes require the functioning of living mechanism, more specifically, the total organism itself. Therefore instead of saying that we think with the mind or in the mind, it is truer to say that we think with the whole body. The nervous system appears to be more deeply and directly involved in all forms of mental activity. Figure 1, on page 184, makes this evident.

Structurally the nervous system is extremely complex and reaches every part of the body. There are three parts, the brain proper with the two hemispheres weighing approximately fifty ounces, the mid brain, and the spinal cord. The large bundle of nerves leading out of one hemisphere crosses the corresponding bundle leading out of the other hemisphere. Thus when a lesion occurs in the cerebrum, as the large brain is called, and the right

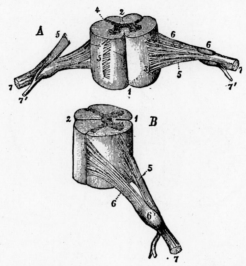

FIG. 2. *A*, ventral, and *B*, lateral, view of a portion of the cord from the cervical region. ×2. (Schwalbe.) 1, ventral median, and 2, dorsal median, fissures. At 3 is the ventral-lateral impression, over which spread the ventral roots (5). The dorsal roots (6), with their ganglion (6′), arise from the dorso-lateral groove, and uniting with the ventral roots form the compound nerve (7). From Ladd and Woodworth, *Elements of Physiological Psychology*. By permission of Charles Scribner's Sons, publishers.

side of the person is paralyzed, it is an indication that the injury is in the left hemisphere and vice versa. The brain is sometimes called the cortex, meaning bark or outside which is also referred to as the gray matter because in the brain the cell bodies, which are grayish in color are on the outside. In the spinal cord the situation is reversed and the cord appears white which is the color of the medullary sheath covering the axon.

The function of the central nervous system is to unify the actions of the individual, to receive impressions from the outside world through the gateway of the sense organs, and to command the muscles to act. There are also many connecting neurones which serve to associate and spread the impulse. Not all the messages go to the main desk as it were,—the large brain. The reflexes, for example, are handled by the spinal cord and the lower brain centers and the individual need not be conscious of the transaction. When a person is taking a nap and a fly lights on his face or someone playfully tickles his ear with a feather, he is likely to raise his hand and brush away the intruder without waking. However, should the

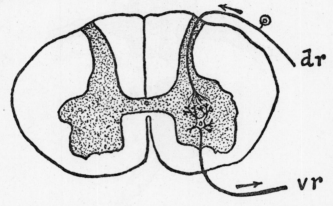

Fig. 3. Diagram of a synapse in the cord. *dr*, fibre of the dorsal root, passing into the ventral horn, and connecting, at the synapse, with a motor cell from which arises the fibre of the ventral root, *vr*. Stimulating *dr* arouses *vr* to activity, but stimulation of *vr* does not arouse *dr*. From Ladd and Woodworth, *op. cit.;* reproduced by permission.

stimulation be increased, the "message" is relayed to the higher centers and the person may be awakened. And upon perceiving the source of the annoyance he may become angry. This in turn affects his glands of internal secretion. Harsh words may follow and blows may be struck and received. Thus what started as a purely reflex act more or less localized in the spinal cord, may reach consciousness and spread to the autonomic nervous system affecting the adrenal gland rousing emotion and ending in violent words and muscular action.

The structure of the various parts of the nervous system is usually determined by the function although there are many identical structural parts which carry on different functions. The division of labor in the main brain centers is called localization of function. Some very unusual circumstances have been utilized in the establishment of these localizations. One of the best known is the celebrated crow-bar case in which a workman received an injury to the head resulting in the loss of considerable gray matter. He managed to survive but was unable to perform certain functions. Other cases, many of them war victims, have served to locate the areas of the brain responsible for certain acts and functions. However, there is considerable spread. One portion of the brain may take over the

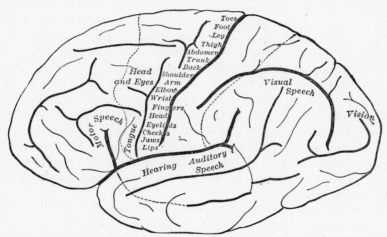

Fig. 4. The human cerebral hemisphere as seen from the left side, showing the localization of cortical functions. From M. Allen Starr, *Nervous Diseases*, 4th Edition; reproduced by permission of Lea & Febiger, publishers.

functions of another part just as a blind man develops a keener sense of touch to compensate for his blindness with the important difference that the function of seeing is not taken over.

One of the chief functions of the central nervous system is consciousness and the thinking process described later. A blow on the head or injury to the brain may cause unconsciousness. Greatly reduced activity, as in drowsiness and sleep, will produce the same result. Thus the brain with all its appendages serves as the mechanism for the functioning of the mental processes. At one time however, no less a personage than Aristotle, the father of all the sciences except mathematics, and something of a physician, believed that the main function of the brain was to secrete tears.   There are also cases on record in which autopsies showed that instead of brains the head contained a large tumor almost completely replacing the gray matter.   And yet the individual in life had been able to carry on a fairly normal existence.

The Autonomic Nervous System

Historically the autonomic nervous system is older than the central nervous system and is still the only system available to many forms of life.   It is made up of sporadic ganglia near the spinal column.   These are connected up in a chain of nerve fibers.   As in the case of the central system there are three major parts in the autonomic system and a fairly well defined division of labor corresponding to the localization of function in the cortex.   The older name for the autonomic system was the sympathetic system.   More strictly the term sympathetic is now confined to the central portion and the two extremes are called the parasympathetic, further subdivided into the cranial and sacral.   As indicated in the diagram Fig. 5, the chief function of the autonomic system is to regulate and control the more or less autonomic processes of the organism,—the glands, digestion, smooth muscles, circulation of the blood, and the like.   Its activity is therefore essentially motor and wholly devoid of sensory duties.

One would hardly guess that any mechanism so definitely physical and chemical as the autonomic system could have any significance for social life.   And yet the functioning of this system is vital in conjugal love, romance, marriage, divorce, anger, hate and countless other social situations.   Take anger as an example.   When a person is threatened or insulted he is aware subjectively of the feeling of fear or anger.   Objectively very important physical and chemical bodily changes are taking place.   The adrenal gland stimulates the liver to liberate the stored up sugar into the blood stream which in turn energizes the muscles and enables the individual to give and receive blows.   In case he is wounded the blood will congeal rapidly. It is a call to mobilize for vigorous action.   While some glands and organs and muscles are stimulated others are slowed down or put completely out of action.   The stomach is one of the latter.   The digestive processes are greatly retarded if not completely inhibited in severe anger.   The mechanism is analogous to the relationship between the brake and the accelerator of an automobile.   Perhaps

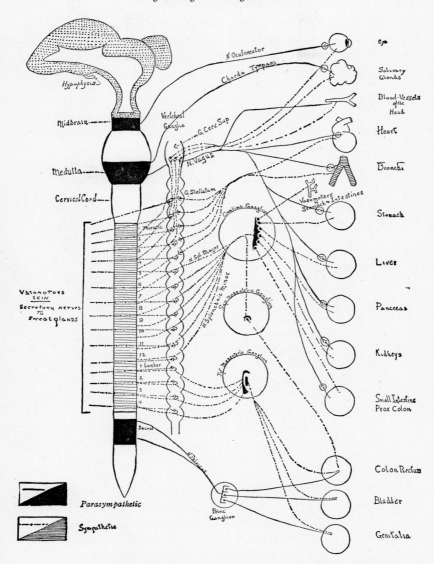

FIG. 5.   Diagram of the autonomic nervous system and the bodily organs excited and inhibited by it.   Sympathetic fibers are indicated by dotted lines; parasympathetic by unbroken lines.   From Martin, *Human Body*, acknowledging Kraus, modified from Meyer and Gottleib.   By permission of Henry Holt and Company, and of The Journal of Nervous and Mental Disease.

this will explain why it is that in polite society people avoid unpleasant topics of conversation during meals and will serve to illustrate the far-reaching significance of physical and chemical reactions of the organism in social life. The ancients were not far wrong in assigning an important role in love affairs to the heart, the stomach and the spleen. During a murder trial one of the jurymen asked to be excused from duty because he was suffering from an attack of indigestion. Said he, "Your Honor, feeling as I do I believe that not only the defendant but the whole court should hang."

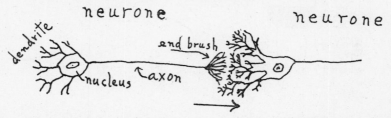

Fig. 6. The synapse between the two neurones lies just above the arrow. Diagram from R. S. Woodward, *Psychology, A Study in Mental Life.* By permission of Henry Holt and Company, publishers.

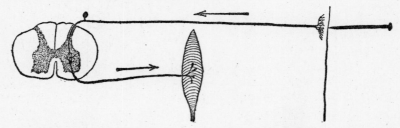

Fig 7. Diagram of a reflex arc. From R. S. Woodward, *op. cit.;* reproduced by permission.

The Synapse and the Synaptic Connections

The unit of mental life or, more specifically, of the nervous system, is the neurone (the nerve cell). And the simplest unit of action is the reflex arc. The neurone is made up of a nucleus, the axon with its end brush, and the dendrites or tree-like branches of the cell proper at the opposite end of the cell from the axon. These nerve cells are shaped differently in different parts of the body. The length of the axon depends on the function and location. Some of the axons are long enough to reach from the spinal cord to the tip of the toe. The impulse travels from the end brush of one axon to the dendrites of another cell, never the other way. The place of meeting is called the synapse. These synaptic connections are not organic unities. They represent a functional rather than an organic juncture. They dovetail into each other. The oftener the act is repeated the closer the connections and the path (of the impulse) is said to be open. This is the theory most widely accepted for explaining skilled acts, skill in learning, memorizing, the perfection of motor acts, and the force of all habits.

Stimulus-Response-Bonds, Stimulation-Integration-Reaction, Habits, Autonomic Reactions

According to the stimulus-response theory of action, the stimulus is the cause, that which stimulates the act; and the response is the effect or the result of the stimulation. The nature of the response or reaction is determined by the part affected. Thus a muscle that is stimulated can react only by contracting, the gland by secreting its peculiar chemical substance, and the nerve by passing the impulse along as described above. The stimulus can take various forms or combinations of forms. It might be mechanical as a blow, chemical as in the effect of drugs, thermal as in the effect of sunlight or a hot water bottle, electrical as in any treatment by electrical appliance or even loose electricity in the atmosphere or from a thunderbolt, and disturbances of the ether as in sound and light waves.

Professor Thorndike, in his experiments on the process of learning, pointed out that this often repeated stimulus-response produces what he called the stimulus-response-bond, a sort of closed circuit. And with each repetition the act becomes more and more automatic. Some of these habitual and automatic acts have the force of an instinct, a succession of integrated activities or chains of reflexes. Sneezing, coughing, yawning, voiding are reflex acts as are the patellar tendon reflex, and the pupillary reflex. Grabbing for your hat when the wind blows it off is not a reflex. It is a learned reaction that has the force of a reflex. "Stimulation-integration-reaction" is another way of expressing the same idea. In this combination emphasis is placed on integration or the central activity. It represents what happens to the individual and the part he plays in the act. In addition to the purely mechanical reactions in the nervous system the individual may be aware of the reaction in consciousness giving rise to a certain feeling tone that may ever after accompany the act.

This is why New Year resolutions are so easy to make and so hard to keep. The stimulus-response-bond or the stimulation-integration-reaction once established forms a sort of reaction pattern which "grooves" the path of the given act. And, strangely enough, the harder you try the less likely you are to succeed. By keeping the idea in mind you strengthen the stimulus which has had its way so long that it becomes reenforced by this process and eventually breaks through. There are also likely to be emotional disturbances and considerable spread even to a simple act. The implication of all this for social life is that, negatively regarded, antisocial habits once formed are hard to break. On the positive side it explains the ex-

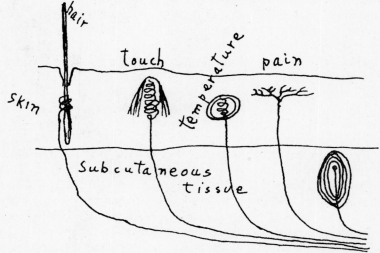

Fig. 8.   Diagram of various sorts of sensory end-organs found in the skin. From R. S. Woodworth, *op. cit.*; reproduced by permission.

pression "to the manor born." Every educator now accepts what the Catholic church has known for many years, namely, that the very early years of a child's life are the most important in the integration of character. It is next to impossible to overcome the personal traits and habits and idiosyncrasies acquired in early life. A gifted and highly educated man who had not learned to read until he was of age and who had spent those early years in an illiterate and uncouth neighborhood, never overcame entirely the mannerisms and grammatical errors of his early youth. And this in turn has had some effect on his social contacts. Another illustration is that of a foreigner learning to speak the native tongue after he has reached maturity and never being able to speak it without an "accent."

Sense Organs

Traditionally everyone had five senses,—hearing, seeing, taste, smell, and touch. Now, thanks to a more scientific analysis, we have eight, nine and possibly more senses. This has come about largely by expanding the sense of touch to include pressure, pain, and temperature sensations as well as the generalized sense of touch. In addition some psychologists add the sense of equilibrium or balance

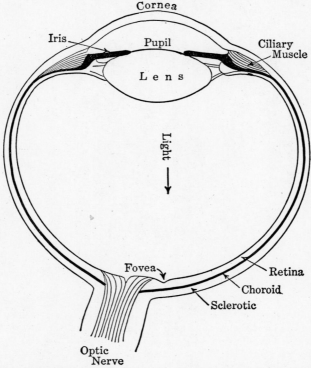

FIG. 9. Horizontal cross section through the right eyeball. From R. S. Woodworth, *op. cit.;* reproduced by permission.

and the kinesthetic sense. The former gives one awareness of motion, position, nausea (seasickness), dizziness and balance. The mechanism is located in the cerebellum and the inner ear. The latter functions through the joints, muscles and tendons. It is a sort of motor or muscle sense by which one judges the relative position of the arms and legs and other organs, and is also made aware of the degree of tenseness of the joints and muscles as in judging the weight of a sack of flour by lifting it.

Every sense organ has definite and distinct sense organs or mechanisms peculiar to itself. The senses of pressure, pain, and temperature were allowed as separate senses because the appropriate mechanism conveying these sensations were identified and are represented in figure 8, page 192, along with the other sense organs.

A person who is deficient or lacking in one or more sense organs is decidedly handicapped in earning his daily bread, in winning a mate,

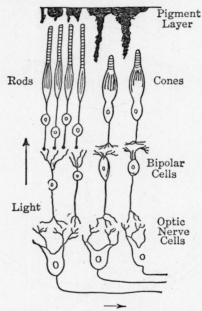

FIG. 10. Sense cells and nerve cells of the retina. Light, reaching the retina from the interior of the eyeball (as shown in Fig. 9), passes through the nearly transparent retina till stopped by the pigment layer, and then and there arouses to activity the tips of the rods and cones. The rods and cones pass the impulse along to the bipolar cells and these in turn to the optic nerve cells, the axons of which extend by way of the optic nerve to the thalamus in the brain. From R. S. Woodworth, *op. cit.;* reproduced by permission.

and in getting on with people in any form of social activity. Conversely, extra keenness in sense perception is a decided asset in human contacts. Sudden loss of eyesight or hearing or other sense organ may necessitate a complete readjustment of one's life, possibly seeking new employment, moving to a new location, the breaking up of family and home ties, and many other readjustments. The reaction on the morale of the individual may be severe enough to cause

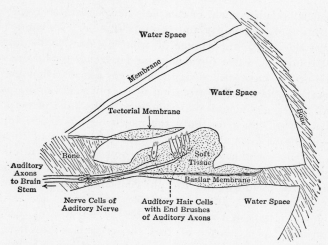

Water Space

Membrane

Water Space

Tectorial Membrane

Bone

Soft Tissue

Bone

Auditory Axons to Brain Stem

Basilar Membrane

Water Space

Nerve Cells of Auditory Nerve

Auditory Hair Cells with End Brushes of Auditory Axons

FIG. 11. A small sample of the sense cells of the cochlea. The hairs of the sense cells are shaken by the vibration of the water, and pass the impulse back to the end-brushes of the auditory axons. The tectorial membrane looks as if it might act as a damper, but may be concerned, as ''accessory apparatus,'' in the stimulation of the hair cells. The basilar membrane consists in part of fibers extending across between the ledges of bone; these fibers are arranged somewhat after the manner of piano strings, and have suggested the ''piano theory'' of hearing. From R. S. Woodworth, *op. cit.;* reproduced by permission.

Surface of Tongue

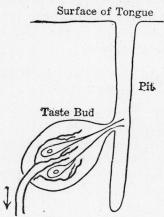

Pit

Taste Bud

FIG. 12. Diagram of the taste end-organ. Within the ''Taste bud'' are seen two sense cells, and around the base of these cells are seen the terminations of two axons of the nerve of taste. From R. S. Woodworth, *op. cit.;* reproduced by permission.

a permanent maladjustment or complete demoralization resulting in disintegration of personality and possibly suicide. We cannot over-emphasize the social importance of what appears to be purely a physical condition. The physiology and psychology of the senses and sense organs have special significance for social pathology.

Thus far we have called attention to the physical factors usually included under physiological psychology. We have attempted to show their significance not only for psychology but also for sociology,—in the broader application and interpretation of these factors for life in a social environment. We now turn to the intellectual and psychic factors in psychology which are important to sociology. It must not be assumed that the physical and psychic factors are distinct and separate. It is not possible to divorce them except as a convenient means of classification for the purpose of discussion and analysis. As a matter of fact the organism functions as a totality, as a person. Every physical factor plays a part in the so-called psychic factor and vice versa. It takes all of it functioning together to produce the actions and reactions of a human being. The nearest we can come to a distinction between the physical and mental is to say that some acts are *relatively* more physical or more psychic as the case may be. Neither would be what it is without the other. Once more we have an important illustration of the complexity and interdependence of the factors that go to make up life, this time within the organism itself as well as with the total environment. It is well to keep this in mind as we proceed to the next section, the whole chapter and the whole book.

INTELLECTUAL OR PSYCHIC FACTORS: FUNCTIONAL PSYCHOLOGY

Elementary Concepts

Among the elementary factors in psychology that are *relatively* more physical and mechanical which we have just discussed are the central nervous system, the autonomic nervous system, glands, muscles, reflexes, neurones, stimulus-response-bonds, stimulation-integration-reaction, habits, synaptic connections, and sense organs. The elementary concepts in psychology that are *relatively* more psychical and which are to be discussed in this section include sensation, perception, ideas, illusion, hallucination, consciousness, the sub-conscious, instincts, feeling, emotion, morale, imagination, dreams and daydreams, somnambulism, learning, memory, recall, association of ideas, reasoning, intelligence, desire, purpose, attitude, drive, motive, volition.

Sensation, Perception, Illusion, Hallucination

Sensation is the simplest experience that a person can have. It is merely awareness that something is happening. It is an immediate on-going experience. The moment that one interprets the experience as due to this or that it becomes a perception. Perception is usually defined as the interpretation of a sensory experience. If the interpretation is a misinterpretation it is called an illusion. And if the interpretation is based on no sensory experience at all, but is manufactured out of broadcloth, it is an hallucination. One illustration may suffice to explain all of these elementary concepts. If one is awakened in the night and is barely aware that something has

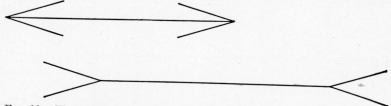

FIG. 13. The Müller-Lyer illusion. The horizontal lines are drawn exactly equal. From J. P. Guilford, *General Psychology*. Courtesy of D. Van Nostrand Company, Inc., publishers.

happened without any notion of what it is, the experience is a sensation. It becomes a perception when he interprets it as footsteps by a prowler in the rooms below. Then if he should muster up enough courage to go below and investigate, finding the sound is not made by a burglar but by the pets playing tag, the experience is something of an illusion. If, on the other hand, investigation proves that there was no sound, that no one else heard any sound and the investigator imagined it, the experience is in the nature of an hallucination. A student reports the following interesting case of hallucination. He says he awoke on a clear moonlight summer night and looking out of his bedroom window saw a three-ringed circus in full sway on the front lawn of the house. He was so impressed that he called the other members of the household to the window and they all saw the circus. There are many illustrations of mass hallucination. English soldiers in the trenches saw the figure of Saint George leading them on in battle. French soldiers often saw Joan of Arc in the

World War. On the high seas someone reports a raft near by with men struggling desperately to save their lives and presently everyone on board sees the same raft. But close inspection proves the experience to be purely hallucinatory.

The social implications of this phenomenon are seen in war hysteria and mob psychology. A powerful leader is able to delude his followers as well as himself. He gets them to see what is not there and to believe the prediction of results that are impossible of attainment.

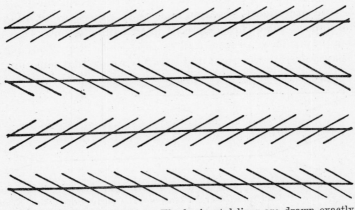

Fig. 14. The angle illusion. The horizontal lines are drawn exactly parallel. From J. P. Guilford, *General Psychology*. Courtesy of D. Van Nostrand Company, Inc., publishers.

Ideas, Concepts

An idea or concept is the unit of the thinking process. As contrasted with perception which is the interpretation of an immediate experience, an idea is a "cold" experience, the external stimulus for which has ceased to function. It is a recalled experience. The stimulus is usually another idea or image. Ordinarily it is easy to distinguish between perception and an idea or concept. Perception being a present experience is more vivid and colorful, more detailed, more intense; whereas the memory of a past experience is less vivid, many details have dropped out, and the whole experience in recall is a bit vague and faded. Thus your memory of the performance of *Lohengrin* you heard a year ago or even a week ago is not so vivid as the performance you are listening to at the moment, assuming you are listening.

However there are exceptions which account for seeing ghosts and pink elephants. Ordinarily the idea of a ghost is not so vivid. But if one is afraid of ghosts this fear intensifies the idea of ghosts until it has the force of a perception or an immediate present experience which accounts for the seeming reality of the image. Lady Macbeth, constantly washing her hands to get rid of blood stains, is a good example. She is so upset by the idea of murder that the emotional disturbance takes the form of guilt represented by bloody hands. There is actually no blood on her hands but the idea of guilt translated in terms of blood is so vivid and intense that it has the force of a perception, of actual blood. Many mental complexes, phobias, hallucinations, obsessions, and the like, are due to this phenomenon of mistaking an idea or concept for a present sensory experience.

Consciousness, the Subconscious

Consciousness is usually defined a bit too simply as awareness, or awareness of the total content of experience which happens to be at the focus. But it remains the deepest mystery in psychology. How it is possible for a human being to "take in" impressions of the outside world and interpret them meaningfully, to carry them in memory and recall them years afterwards, to piece together these experiences and draw accurate and logical conclusions, and the rest of the functions of consciousness have never been satisfactorily explained. The German philosophers rightly insisted that the thing in itself can never be known. All that we have in consciousness is an image, some representation of the reality in the outside world. The reality always and forever remains outside of consciousness. There is therefore no way of knowing, of being certain that this impression or image is accurate. The thing itself is never in consciousness.

However while no one can explain the mystery of consciousness, we may describe the phenomenon and its place in our daily lives. And by applying the pragmatic test we find that our impressions of reality are accurate enough to live by, that they are corroborated by the same or similar reactions in other human beings.

The subconscious is a concept made famous by the Freudians and the psychoanalysts. The theory is that the so-called mental complexes, phobias, obsessions, and other mental derangements are due to some suppressed wish or fear which is pushed beneath the threshold of consciousness by the "censor," the suppressing agent. The

term censor is clearly a personification of a mental process and as
such is highly misleading and unscientific. The whole concept of
the subconscious mind is misleading. Unfortunately the impression
is given that the subconscious is a sort of second mind which acts
more or less independently and usually in opposition to the conscious
mind. An attempt is made to interpret one mystery in terms of
another. If we do not know what consciousness is we certainly are
not any better off to posit a second ''mind,'' the co-conscious or fore-
conscious, and even possibly a third mind, the unconscious. This
theory suggests a layer cake or house diagram of the mental process
as follows:

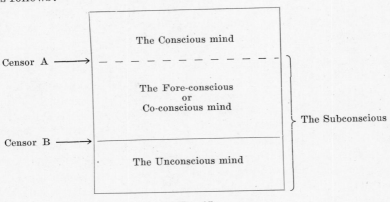

FIG. 15.

Censor A is represented by a broken line because it is supposed to be more
lenient than Censor B in permitting certain ideas in the fore-conscious or co-
conscious to come through to the conscious.
Censor B is represented by a heavy line because it is supposed to be adament,
never permitting any idea to break through to the conscious except in dreams,
automatic writing, etc. This is why dream interpretation is given an important
place in psychoanalysis.

The fact of the matter is that there are no such levels or divisions.
A human being reacts as a unit, a totality, a personality. There is
such a thing as conflict within the individual and even partial or
complete dissociation of personality. But this phenomenon can be
explained on a more logical basis according to orthodox psychology
without positing a second or third mind. It may be illustrated by
figure 16 on page 201.

This is very like the field of vision. If you look right at a definite
person in a large room full of people you see that person more
vividly than the others, and people further removed less and less

vividly as you get away from the person on whom you have concentrated your gaze until, if you get far enough away, you see nothing at all so long as you keep said person at the focus of the field of vision. If the term subconscious is used at all it can be employed meaningfully to represent all past experiences which are not now in consciousness but which may come to the focus by appropriate stimulation and association (potentially conscious) or/and all those relatively more physiological factors of experience which do not ordinarily come to consciousness such as the heart beat, respiration, the flow of blood, the secretion of the glands, and the like. In combining the two we might say that the subconscious represents all

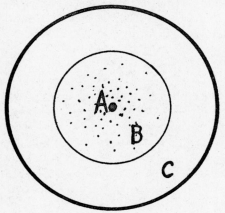

In fig. 16, A is the focus of consciousness, where perception is vivid.

B represents related ideas which are more or less vaguely perceived.

C represents the unconscious or potential conscious (experiences which may come to consciousness by proper stimulation and association) and all past experiences temporarily or permanently beneath the "threshold" of consciousness.

FIG. 16.

those experiences past or present which are not in consciousness at any given moment.

Many impressions are constantly crowding upon the individual and vie for a place at the focus of consciousness. But, since a person can be vividly conscious of only one thing at a time, many stimuli are impressed less vividly and take place below the threshold of consciousness while many more leave no impression at all. The subconscious therefore represents all those experiences which are not sufficiently intense to impress themselves on the conscious self, plus all those past experiences that were once impressed and now lie more or less dormant in the synaptic junctures and which may be brought to consciousness through the appropriate stimulation and association.

The social implications of some of the problems arising from mental complexes, phobias, and neuroses are discussed later under abnormal psychology.

Instincts

The term instinct is another bone of contention among psychologists. Everything from religion to a toothache has been called an instinct. It means so many things that it has ceased to mean anything at all. William McDougall and many older psychologists have given instincts a central place in human behavior. The modern tendency is to minimize their importance and to use more accurate terminology. The behaviorists prefer to speak of chains of reflexes.

In the older usage of the term instinct connotes the unlearned, innate reaction patterns found universally among human beings. Even the older psychologists found it difficult to distinguish between instincts and reflexes. Regardless of whether these innate tendencies are called reflexes, chains of reflexes, instincts, successive reactions, or by some other name, the fact remains that there are apparently a number of such unlearned reaction patterns most clearly demonstrated among the lower animals. The homing and the nest-building instincts of birds and the remarkable activities or successive reactions of the bees are typical examples of instincts. While the human counterpart is not nearly so stereotyped there is nevertheless a number of unlearned, ready-made patterns of action or successive reactions that constitute standard equipment for every normal person at birth, at least in incipient form.

And all of them have great significance for human behavior and social life. All human beings are driven by the appetite for food and sex, they crave to be with their fellows, they fight back, get angry, they are curious, they strive to accumulate, to manipulate, to create, and to do the things that are peculiar to human beings. The Gestalt psychologists claim that all these acts can be explained on the basis of the logic of the situation. Since most people have similar physical and mental make up they react in identical ways in similar situations which gives rise to the supposition of an innate stereotype or instinct. Regardless of what description is given these universal activities the activities remain and concern us more than the explanation. The fact that human beings like to be with their fellows and to find status somewhere is important enough to account for boys' gangs, delinquency and crime. If a boy cannot find a satisfying place in the home and in the school he is likely to seek out a gang or try to organize a gang in which he will feel at home.

Feeling, Pain, Emotion, Morale

Feeling is distinguished from emotion in being more vague and less intense. It is also limited to two tones, pleasant and unpleasant. It differs from pain in that pain is almost always unpleasant and has a definite mechanism for its expression. It is localized, while feeling is a blanket, unlocalized, generalized state too vagrant to find a habitation and a name. Feeling is a sort of miscellaneous column. When we cannot name the experience or state of mind we call it a feeling. Feeling is also used synonymously with hunch which is another indication of its roving nature.

Emotion is more colorful. It is a stirred up state of mind whose activity is limited within the individual whereas instinctive urges lead to series of activities outside the self. It is difficult to say just what are the original emotions. Something of the same difficulties are encountered here as in the case of the instincts. The tendency is to regard them also as successive reactions only more so,—as a "mass of simultaneous pattern reactions." Shand, however, lists fear, anger, joy, sorrow, curiosity, repugnance, and disgust among the primary emotions. Moreover since we may cultivate emotion habits as well as motor habits, many new emotions and configurations of emotions are acquired by all human beings. A previous study of the emotions reveals no less than fifty-four compound emotional states.[2] This same study brought to light the fact that our unpleasant emotions outnumber the pleasant emotions in the ratio of approximately two to one. Hence it would follow that one who lives by his emotions is in for a bad time provided he runs the whole gamut of emotions impartially which need not necessarily be true. One can be choosy and avoid some of the unpleasant ones.

G. Stanley Hall lists 276 morbid fears. Fear as an emotion is probably native and unlearned. What to fear is acquired through experience and constitutes a form of the conditioned reflex. The only native fears according to J. B. Watson are the fear of falling and the fear of harsh unfamiliar sounds.

Emotions play a significant role in human behavior and consequently in social life. If we take the fear emotion as an example we see how it motivates a person's life in social situations. Witness the fear of being an old maid, of losing one's job, one's mate, one's reputation. People often commit suicide when they have lost their reputation and feel disgraced. They fear life more than they fear

[2] Cf. Thomson, *The Springs of Human Action*, pp. 98–104.

death. Then there is the fear of being poor, fear of some dread
disease, and the many fears attending a sense of insecurity. Add
to this the hundreds of morbid fears known as phobias, excessive
fears due to unusually hostile circumstances, and you get some idea
of the tremendous effect of the emotions which fill our insane
asylums, cause demoralization and breakdown of personality, mental complexes and social inadequacy.

Morale has been defined by Hocking as the perpetual ability to
come back. It is a form of efficiency and has emotional tone and
color. It is a "state of self-confidence, contentment, and discipline."
Euphoria is a superb morale. It means supreme integration of personality and the ability to meet the demands of life with certainty,
dignity and poise. It gives a person a sense of adequacy, a sense of
security, and the zest of conquest. In a game, morale means team-
work. In business, it is cooperation and efficiency. In the army,
they call it *esprit de corps*. This is so vital in social life that we rate
the various institutions according to their contribution to the building up of morale in the individual and in the community. Consequently the home, the church, and the school rate high while the
criminal gangs, the underworld, and many "questionable" activities such as gambling, excessive drinking, the bookies, and the like
are rated low. The former are constructive and morale-building
influences while the latter destroy morale and tear down the spiritual
fiber of the individual and the group.

Thinking, Reasoning, Imagination, Dreams, Daydreams, Hypnosis, Somnambulism

These elementary mental processes present no new or mysterious
factors. They are different names for different phases of the thinking and reasoning process itself, of varying degrees of activity in
consciousness. Thinking is done through the association of ideas
originally integrated through sense perception by way of the sense
organs. The synaptic theory provides the most plausible and widely
accepted explanation of the mechanics of this phenomenon. Something you see or hear or touch or taste or smell, or a combination of
these and the other senses acts as a stimulus which sends an impulse
through the neural connections previously established as explained
in the stimulus-response-bond and stimulation-integration-reaction
theory discussed above. The stimulation may come from within as
well as from without. But to get itself into the stream of conscious-

ness it must pass through a set of stimulus-response mechanisms plus a great many connecting or associated systems.

At the risk of oversimplification and yet accurate enough to be worth the risk one might say that thinking, reasoning, dreams, day-dreams, hypnosis, and talking and walking in sleep are all phases of the same process. They represent different aspects of mental activity which is constantly going on day and night throughout life. Sleep reduces the degree of activity. It does not completely inhibit the process. In other words, we are never wholly asleep or wholly awake. We fluctuate between the two extremes without actually reaching either extremity. We speak of some people being wide awake and refer to others as sleepy. The fact is that no one is wholly awake at any time. He is merely more widely awake or less widely awake according to the degree of fatigue, of sleepiness, or threat of danger, etc. We come closest to being wholly awake when we are angry. In anger the adrenal gland liberates the stored up sugar in the liver which when poured into the blood stream energizes the whole system to enable it to clear the deck for action. Anger is associated with fighting and requires that one be alert and strong for self-defense just as fear is associated with running away.

Thus thinking is a mental process in which one attempts to associate all related ideas or associated connections with a view of arriving at a conclusion which is supposed to be true to the facts. In imagination there is a similar procedure except that the conclusions are not necessarily true to the facts. Imagination is more like play, while reasoning is like work. Even imagination cannot employ ideas not previously experienced. It can take old ideas and images and piece them together in new combinations and series of combinations very like surrealism. Witness mermaids, satyrs, unicorns, and centaurs.

The dream represents mental activity at its lowest level. It is more sketchy, disconnected, and "wild." And the deeper the sleep the more disconnected and fanciful the dream. One is likely to believe the dream at the time no matter how absurd because so many of the associated experiences are temporarily out of commission that the dreamer is unable to check on the incongruity of the picture. Thus in sleep-walking, the walking mechanism is still linked up with the thinking processes so that when a person dreams of doing a task he goes ahead and does it, while in normal sleep he takes it out in thinking only because ordinarily the mechanism for walking is "unhitched.'' The same is true of talking in sleep. Both are forms of somnambulism. The speech mechanism is still intact and one may answer questions as in the waking state though many other mental mechanisms are not functioning. The Freudians say we dream to keep from waking up.

Hypnosis is another sleep phenomenon. The subject is anesthetic to all stimuli except the commands and demands of the hypnotist. A person under hypnosis believes what he is told because his critical faculty is temporarily out of commission and he has not the where-withal to contradict the absurd suggestion. He is given a whiff of ammonia and told that it is the essence of rose. He believes it because his memory of ammonia is not functioning.

The daydream is still another type of partial functioning of the mental processes, of spasmatic neural activity. The daydreamer lets his imagination wander at will. Seeing a dog reminds him of his neighbor's dog, then of his neighbor with whom he went fishing, then of the unpleasant experience of falling into the water when the boat capsized. And that reminds him of bigger boats and the English blockade, then the World War, etc., etc. There is another type of daydream in which the dreamer is building castles in the air, planning out his life purpose, or how he is going to get even with a rival. The excessive daydreamer comes to make a pastime of his dreaming. It ultimately resolves itself into a veritable moving picture show in which he is always the star performer. It is so much easier to make a million, to win the fair damsel by manipulating the props of imagination than it is to go out in the actual cold cold world and win fame and fortune against severe competition. The danger of this type of excessive daydreaming is that eventually one is likely to take refuge in a fanciful world, gradually becoming more or less completely detached from the world of reality. And this is exactly what happens in the case of the most common type of insanity known as schizophrenia.

Learning, Retention, Memory, Recall

Learning is the process of retaining in memory through the association of ideas in the appropriate neural connections and other mechanisms with the ability to recall at the proper stimulation. It is a truism in the field of educational psychology that there is no learning without mental activity on the part of the learner and that nothing is ever recalled except through association. What enters the mind together,—is impressed on the mechanism of the learning process together,—is recalled together. You think of B when I say A because you learned the alphabet in that order. We also think in terms of opposites or contrasts as well as comparisons. Thus when I say white you think of black and when I say day you think of night, etc. Memory training consists essentially of methods of improving the learning process primarily through spaced learning, repetition, and the like together with various mnemonic devices which take advantage of the laws of association.

Intelligence

There are numerous intelligence tests on the market and many of them are extremely useful for certain purposes. But no one knows exactly what is being tested because no one can give a satisfactory definition of intelligence. Since most intelligence tests have a time limit it follows that a certain nimbleness of mind is expected from the intelligent. An intelligent person is supposed to solve his problems and to do it in a hurry without too many false moves. Another way of saying it is that intelligence indicates the ability to solve a problem correctly the first time. And problem solving involves finding a solution to a new situation by the process of thinking rather than falling back on memory, habit, or some other stereotyped reaction. In complicated situations and when confronted with a brand new problem these elements are quite obscure if not lacking entirely. The social significance of intelligence is pointed out later under *individual factors*.

Appetite, Desire, Purpose, Attitude, Drive, Motive, Volition

A human being is an active animal. Body and mind he is made for action. He comes into the world with certain needs and wants and acquires a great many more. The appetite of hunger forces him to seek the food necessary to satisfy his craving. The needs for shelter and clothing necessitate other activities. Beginning with these primitive necessities he keeps on adding new wants. He wants not merely to live. He wants to live well. He seeks luxuries. And today's luxuries are tomorrow's necessities. In this insatiable quest for the satisfaction of his growing wants which quickly become needs, he uses his intelligence to develop tools and techniques. The anthropologist classifies tribes and races and peoples according to their use of tools to get what they want. Thus the type and nature of the tools come to designate the type of culture and the degree of complexity,—the stone age, the age of metals, the machine age, the

electrical age, etc. We now speak of the industrial age and industrialized nations and five-year plans for those nations who aspire to
become industrialized. It is claimed by some that there are only
four or five nations in the world capable of waging a modern war
because they are the only ones sufficiently industrialized to stand a
chance in a modern conflict that is so definitely and highly
mechanized.

In addition to the incessant striving to master the forces of
nature in the satisfaction of material wants man is also on the war-
path to dominate and subjugate other races and peoples. The causes
of war are psychological as well as economic. But in either case they
indicate tremendous drive, purpose, initiative, motivation, strong
volition and the will to win. And this is the odyssey of the springs
of human action. It is a long story. We might shorten it by classi-
fying motivation into three major categories. First, there are primitive elementary immediate needs that we call drives to action such
as food, sex, automatic bodily functions like breathing, respiration,
digestion, and the like. These are followed persistently and more or
less blindly. Second, there are other groups of activities such as the
instinctive drives, habits, and emotions of which we are only vaguely
aware as to exactly what is wanted and how the want is to be met.
There is a general state of uneasiness until the desire is met, then
quiescence. Again the same urges arise followed by uneasiness and
quiescence in rhythmic cycles. There is roughly a third group of
needs and wants of which we are definitely conscious and have a
fairly good notion of how to attain them. In building a house, a
bridge, or a boat the skilled mechanics know exactly what is to be
done and how to do it. They work from blueprints. This requires
volition, planning, sustained effort and the overcoming of opposition
and obstacles. Whenever a person is moved by a desire to attain
a certain definite objective he is said to be motivated. A motive is
the active ingredient within a person seeking to reach a goal once
the want is aroused. It is the want itself. The original impulse may
come from without or from within. But once present it stimulates
action which may necessitate the complete mobilization of the total
personality.

Will is not a thing. It is not an entity. It is not a faculty of
the mental life. It is a descriptive term indicating the active self.
When I say I will or I will not I am announcing that I, as a person,
am going to do something or that I am going to refrain from doing
something. Will is the self in action. When there is no action there

is no will any more than there is a lap to a person who is standing. Will power and the freedom of will need not concern us here. There are those who say that a man is a machine and acts when he is acted upon. He responds to his environment as any other physical, albeit extremely complicated, organism or machine. Be that as it may, we know that if we are free to choose at all, that freedom is extremely limited. It is limited by the extent of our desire, by some physical barrier, and by our own physical and mental limitations. A man who desires to break the world's record in the broad jump may not desire it strongly enough to put forth the necessary effort. Or he may be locked up in a cell where it is impossible to leap that far. Or he may lack the necessary physical strength and ability despite the strongest incentive and endless opportunity to practice.

INDIVIDUAL FACTORS: DIFFERENTIAL PSYCHOLOGY

Personality[3]

Personality is the sum total of all one's past experiences plus original nature. It also involves a certain degree of integration. A person must identify himself with his past experiences and be able to recognize himself as the person belonging to these experiences. If the time comes when he cannot do this he will have ceased to be a personality. And such a time does actually exist in everyone's life,—from birth until he achieves a personality. No one is born with a personality. He is born a person and develops, in most cases, a personality. We rightly speak of an infant as it instead of he or she because it has not yet become a personality. Personality develops sooner in some infants than in others just as some cut teeth sooner and walk and talk sooner. But roughly, the average child requires from seven months to a year or more before he has become sufficiently-integrated to be considered a personality.

In some instances a person wants to dissociate himself from some disgraceful act or harrowing experience and gets drunk in order to "forget," at least for the time being. Or he commits suicide and hopes to forget permanently. Or, in case he succeeds in dissociating himself from his experiences, he develops a severe neurosis or complete insanity and becomes blissfully and mercifully ignorant of his personal identity or, more probably, of the disturbing part of his personality. Split and double and multiple personalities though rare do occur now and then. There are some fifty cases on record.

[3] Cf. Chapter 9, "Personality," in this text.

Approximations of split personality occur more frequently and certain forms of it are experienced by all of us. Extreme absent-mindedness is a form of dissociation. Whenever we feel remorse, chagrin, and shame and say we are sorry and are full of regret we are experiencing varying degrees of dissociation of personality. The integration and partial disintegration of personality is represented in the following diagrams:

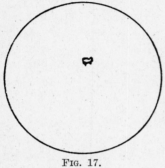

FIG. 17.

Let the circle represent the boundaries in the possible development of a human being at birth. Theoretically it should be possible for him to develop in any direction beginning at the exact center of the circle. But actually this is not strictly true because of hereditary tendencies. Hence we have placed the individual a bit off center at birth in figure 17.

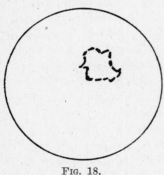

FIG. 18.

Then partly because of this hereditary tendency and the environmental factors which begin to give more or less definite direction to his personality we find him developing as indicated by the ragged outline within the circle. This integration is represented by an irregular configuration because the individual is not very consistent, only approximately so. It is also represented by a broken line because this diagram in figure 18 represents a growing child who is still more or less plastic.

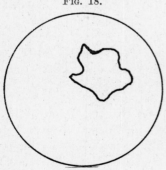

FIG. 19.

Figure 19 represents an adult and hence the outline of his personality development is indicated by a solid line. But the configuration is still askew because no person is wholly consistent. Socrates and Jesus might be represented by circles because they were wholly consistent,—to know what was right was to do what was right. However for the average human being there is a certain degree of consistency so that any act outside of that configuration becomes less and less probable in the progressive integration of personality.

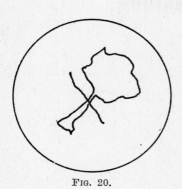

FIG. 20.

And in case a person does go out of his character and do something inconsistent with his personality integration as illustrated in figure 20 there is a split personality with the subjective reactions characteristic of shame, regret, remorse and the like. The man is like a house divided against itself, or like a cat facing a foxterrier, half of the cat deciding to stay and fight and the other half deciding to run away. No animal, man or beast, can be very efficient nor happy under those conditions. This may explain the neurotic who for the most part is a person with one type of personality integration and desperately desiring to acquire a different and perhaps opposite type and not able to make the break. And in case he does kick over the traces he will be worse off than ever because he has literally ripped himself to pieces: Hence the physical break down and the subjective feeling of regret and remorse.

We might indicate how all this ties in with social life by pointing out the tremendous urge to have status. It is a humble mortal who does not belong to a dozen organizations. The psychiatrists have isolated a new psychosis which may be called the joiner's complex. People do not only join many clubs but they go to ridiculous extremes to get into this or that exclusive club. Tragedy is close upon the heels of the loss of money or reputation because they usually involve the loss of status as well. The jails and hospitals are full of people with warped and twisted personalities and some who have completely lost their personality.

Differential Psychology

Types of personality and differences in personality demonstrate the essential factors in differential psychology. This is a phase of psychology which deals with individual differences just as general psychology deals with the likenesses in people. There are many points of likeness and similarity especially when you have classified people into types. But this is far from saying that they are identical. Even so-called identical twins are not really identical. If one of them should read a book or acquire a friend or admire some hero that the other does not, then the identity (if it ever existed) is no more. A similar mistake is made when we assume that two children have the same environment because they were born of the same parents and live in the same house. Apart from the important factor of heredity in which no two people share alike, the different companions of the two children or any experience such as a bad fright or an accident, a vacation trip, or anything which is not shared by the other is sufficient to nullify any semblance of identity.

The nature of the difference, however, is one of degree and not of kind. It is a general truism in psychology that we are all alike in kind and differ only in degree. And yet this difference is serious enough to necessitate a system of psychology known as differential psychology. But it is not serious enough to cancel general psychol-

A   B

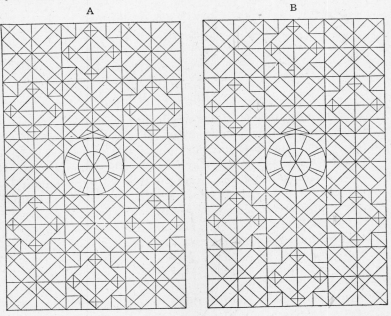

FIG. 21. Mental test specimen. From D. L. Zyve, *Stanford Scientific Aptitude Test*. By permission of Stanford University Press, publishers.

Directions: The two drawings A and B are alike except that in B a certain number of lines are omitted. Fill in all the lines lacking in drawing B so as to make it practically identical with drawing A.

ogy, for if human beings were not alike in kind there could be no science of psychology at all. You would have instead a separate psychology for every person on the face of the earth since there would not be a single statement that you could make of one person that would be true of any other person. In other words, there would be no possibility of generalization and standardization without which there can be no science, no general psychology.

Special Aptitude, Talent

In stressing the importance of the fact that we are all alike in
kind and paving the way for the science of general psychology we

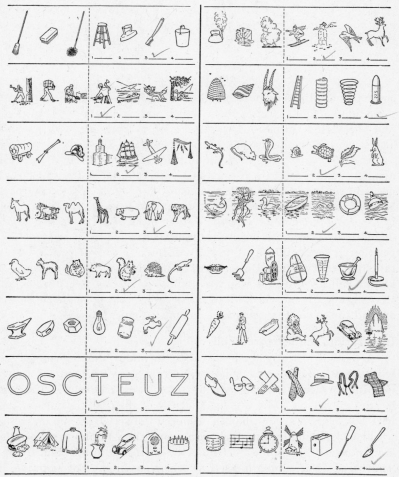

FIG. 22.   A portion of a mental test formulated by E. T. Sullivan, W. W.
Clark and E. W. Tiegs.   By permission of California Test Bureau, 3636 Beverly
Blvd., Los Angeles, Cal., publisher.

Directions: The first three objects in each row are alike in some way.   Find
another object in the same row that belongs with them.   Mark the number of
the drawing which you have decided is correct on the answer sheet.   In the first
row the correct answer is 3.

do not care to minimize the importance of the individual differences. This difference in degree is important in its own right and gives rise to numerous problems of a social nature as well as in personal behavior. Such far-reaching factors as a man's job, his hobby, his religion,—in short, his place in society is determined by his special aptitudes, his talents or the lack of them. "Know thyself" is a wise injunction and worthy of a Socrates.

Employment Psychology

Employment psychology is the science of aiding people to discover their abilities and disabilities, their good points, their strength, their talents, and to direct them along lines calculated to help them find the right occupation to the end of making the best possible adjustment in their vocation. It is an effort to direct their energies in channels best suited to their abilities and talents and temperaments. Many people are constantly striving to be what they are not and never can be. They attempt to do the things that are hardest for them and for which they have the least capacity. This is a sort of unconscious compensation mechanism. On the other hand, many who have achieved distinction in one field sigh for distinction in some other field, usually in the opposite direction. It is said that every famous comedian wants to play a serious role. I knew a college professor who was ambitious to teach every course on the campus. It may be a bit of poetic irony that by the time he got around to the dead languages he committed suicide.

Integration, the Mirrored Self

Attention has already been called to integration in connection with the discussion on personality. From the view point of sociology, integration means adjustment to one's environment. The best integrated person is one who has the least conflict within himself and with his neighbors, one who has mastered the art of getting on in the world, of knowing how to work with people, how to play with people, how to meet "his public." One is aided in this integration by the "mirrored" self, seeing himself as others see him. For example, if one has an idea that he can sing, the first time he sings for his friends he is likely to discover by their reactions whether he is truly a good singer. This holds for any other opinion one may have of himself.

Some people are naturally more sensitive to the reactions of the social group than are some others. These are the ones who accept too readily the judgment of others and are often too timid to do anything that might meet with disapproval or that might put them in a ridiculous light. A child in school asserted that he could do better work if he were not so lazy. How did he get the idea that he was lazy except that he was doubtless told repeatedly by people around him and came to accept their judgment as final.

On the other hand there are social rebels who are reluctant to accept the judgment of the crowd. They follow grudgingly. There are still other rare souls who maintain a self-confidence against any and all opposition, who know they are right and stand by their guns. The great reformers, inventors, prophets, and discoverers are of this stripe. Galileo believed the earth moved around the sun when the rest of the world told him he was wrong. Christopher Columbus was one of a very few men in his day who believed that the earth was round. And yet the rest of the world was wrong.

These and similar cases, however, are exceptions. In the long run and for the most part the opinions and practices of the people around us affect our own personality integration and make social life and cooperation possible.

Disintegration and Demoralization: Abnormal Psychology

The opposite of integration of personality is disintegration. It takes place when the individual feels inadequate to the situation in which he finds himself. His lessons may be too difficult, his tasks beyond his strength and mental capacity, or too many demands are made upon his meager resources. Troubles come in battalions and overwhelm the individual. Or a sudden change of pace will place him beyond his depth. Thus it was with a young man of inferior intelligence. He lived in a rural district and managed to get along working in a saw mill, never suspecting his deficiencies. But when he went to the city to live he got into endless difficulties. He was unable to hold a job. He knew nothing of city life, nor how to spend his time and money. He invariably selected the wrong companions. It was not long before he found himself in the clutches of the law, a bewildered man on his way to demoralization and possible disintegration.

The causes of maladjustment are many. It may be a personal handicap such as physical deformity, mental deficiency, lack of energy and resourcefulness, poverty, lack of training and education, some handicap due to illness or accident, or a combination of these and other misfortunes. On the other hand the cause may be due almost wholly to the environment and a series of untoward circumstances such as unemployment brought on by a financial depression and lack of opportunity to express one's real ability. In defining insanity the superintendent of an asylum applies the following social criteria of adjustability to one's fellows and one's environment. Does he attract attention to himself in a strange and bizarre manner such as measuring the city hall with a match stick (when not a Freshman initiation stunt,—and perhaps when it is)? Does he interfere and quarrel with people, making a general nuisance of himself? Is he able to earn his keep, to make his way in the world?

Social pathology is a branch of sociology which specializes in problems dealing with unadjustments and maladjustments, their causes and extent, and some of the remedial efforts on the part of society to make up its "social deficit." Among the maladjusted groups may be listed the sick, disabled, crippled, blind, deaf, orphans, children who are neglected, dependent, and abused, the aged poor, homeless men and women, tramps, hoboes, bums, prostitutes, the unemployed, the insane, juvenile delinquents, criminals, and all others who constitute a burden or menace to society. It is a question whether the so-called normal or adjusted group will be able to carry the burden much longer or even that they will stay in the majority. A French authority reported some years ago that the human race is going insane at a definite rate and by a certain date not far off, all of us will have gone crazy. An American psychiatrist defines a sane person as one whose commitment papers have not been made out yet. The cold prediction based on statistics is that within the next fifteen years one million of our fellow countrymen will have gained admission to an insane asylum. And insanity is only one of the many forms of maladjustment listed above. Already in Michigan only institutions for the insane and the feeble-minded have had any appropriations from state funds for building purposes during the past ten years. A Detroit municipal judge regards the criminals passing through his court as the wear and tear of society.

SOCIAL FACTORS: SOCIAL PSYCHOLOGY

The Social Impulse, Gregariousness, the Herding Instinct

In our discussion of instincts we called attention to the fact that the term instinct is decidedly in the dog house so far as modern psychologists are concerned. And this goes for the herding instinct as well. Nevertheless human beings do herd. Not all the lower animals exhibit this trait. Lions and tigers are powerful enough to get

along without the aid of their fellows. The cat, a domesticated
tiger, remains a prowler and is not a herder. Apparently the weaker
animals whose young would be an easy prey, herd for mutual protection. It is said that a herd of buffalo in danger of attack by
wolves and other wild animals will form a circle with the males on
the outside of the ring and the females with their young inside the
circle. Thus the enemy is presented a battery of powerful horns
no matter where they attack. It is a matter of common observation
that in a field of grazing cattle or sheep or horses the animals are not
scattered all over the place haphazardly but always in groups,
usually one large group. When an animal discovers that the rest
of the herd are removed by some distance and he is alone, he leaves
the choice morsel he is munching to join up with the group. Apparently he feels uneasy and unsafe by himself.

The most severe form of punishment for a human being is to be
ostracized. Solitary confinement has been abolished from most
prisons as too cruel a form of punishment and is reserved for exceptional cases and for a much shorter period. Many men become
insane under solitary. They attempt to make friends with mice,
rats, lice, plants, or any other living thing that chances to come near
them. William James long ago observed the effect of the social
motive and stated that to be completely ignored is a greater punishment than most people can endure. If no one spoke to you or paid
any attention to you at any time the situation would become intolerable. Far better to be opposed and even maltreated than to be completely ignored and cut dead as though you did not exist.

Suggestion-Imitation

Whether people imitate each other through suggestion as a result
of the herding or social impulse or whether they herd together because they are capable of suggestion-imitation reactions is beside the
point. The fact remains that human beings are highly suggestible
and do imitate each other constantly both consciously and unconsciously. Yawning, clearing one's throat when the speaker is hoarse
illustrate unconscious and mechanical imitation, while the use of the
copybook in penmanship is an example of conscious deliberate imitation. And there are many gradations in between these two extremes.
Tarde regarded suggestion-imitation as so important that he built
his whole system of sociology on his celebrated *laws of imitation*.

The force of suggestion is further demonstrated in advertising
and salesmanship. The objective conditions of suggestibility are

prestige, repetition, positive rather than negative suggestion, and taking advantage of special conditions and situations such as the seasons of the year, etc. The power of prestige is demonstrated by the clever salesman who lets it be known that Mr. So-and-so, the leading citizen in the community, has just made a purchase. The use of testimonials in advertising serve the same purpose despite the fact that everyone knows they have been bought and paid for. Any celebrity can cash in on his prestige by signing testimonials. The greater the celebrity the greater the prestige. The greater the prestige the greater his power of suggestion. A popular athlete who never smoked was asked to recommend a certain brand of cigaret. "What is there in it," he demanded. When told that the honorarium would be two thousand dollars he replied, "For that much money I might even smoke the pesky thing."

Repetition is also effective in suggestion. The first time you are told that a new kind of mouth wash kills germs deader and more permanently than any other brand, you are not impressed. But when you are told the same story from the pages of every magazine you are reading on the train and if perchance you decide to get away from it all and enjoy the scenery and the moment you look out of the window the same horrible story is blazed at you from every billboard you pass, you are overpowered. While no one is really taken in by these highway tactics in the sense of giving intellectual assent, yet all of us are likely to act on the suggestion more or less unconsciously. The next time you purchase a dentifrice you are likely to call for the brand that has been most persistently suggested to you.

The case of positive suggestion is a bit different in that its effectiveness varies with different classes of people. With inferiors, such as servants, employees, and in army life, any suggestion is a command. With equals one does not want to make the suggestion too strong lest he give offense. "Men should be taught as though you taught them not, and things unknown as things forgot." But in the case of superiors, a negative suggestion is more likely to succeed than a positive one. If an office clerk wants to take the afternoon off he is likely to approach the boss with the statement, "I don't suppose I could go to the ball game this afternoon." This is an admission that the boss is the one to decide, he has the power to say no and is likely to do so. The psychology of the situation is to place the boss on the spot so that he might surprise the clerk by showing a streak of generosity and saying yes. Or, in case he does say no, the clerk has lost no great amount of self respect. He merely informed the boss that he did not think he could take the afternoon off and the boss agreed with him.

The timely suggestion is more likely to be effective. During Christmas the shop windows and most advertising carry the Christmas *motif*. People are thinking in terms of the great celebration and any suggestions along these lines have a ready appeal. The same holds for other national holidays and important celebrations and public events.

Mob Psychology

The mob is a very interesting social phenomenon. It is characterized by irresponsibility, violent action, and always extreme suggestibility. A man as a member of a mob will do things he would not think of doing as an individual. He loses layers of civilization quicker than a snake can shed his skin. Apart from mobs of violence such as in the French and Russian revolutions and in lynching mobs, we get approximations of the same feeling in milder form in such mob activities as horseracing, football games, theater rush, and victory celebrations. Individuality wilts and droops. But the feeling of elation and confidence borrowed from the mob is more than adequate compensation. Every man in the mob is strong and fearless. He is the mob. Any opposition is personally resented and fought back. The mob thrives on opposition. In fact one has to be a denouncer to get a mob together. It is a grand and glorious feeling to possess the power to do what you want to do without having to answer for it. A drunk man driving a high-powered car must feel the same way. What is everybody's responsibility is nobody's responsibility. If a student or professor should stand under a tree on the campus and cheer and yell all by his lonesome, every observer would pronounce him insane. The same individual might do this sort of thing at a football game without starting rumors concerning his mental status, for the simple reason that everybody in the bowl is crazy.

Mobs are usually bent on mischief because it is easier to level downward than it is to get everyone to reach a higher level than he ordinarily attains. And emotion which characterizes a mob is very primitive. It was the original language for human beings and is still the only means of communication among the lower forms of life so far as we can judge. This emotional contagion is readily communicated, often resulting in panic and stampede. Anger unites the mob for violent action. Fear separates and disintegrates the mob in disorderly retreat. All herding animals exhibit this trait. Stampede among cattle is illustrated in every cowboy show. When one animal in the herd is badly frightened he communicates this deathly fear to the others and they all run. In the economy of nature under primitive conditions it was apparently an advantage to run first and investigate afterwards. The logic of the situation goes like this: if one member of the group could be so badly frightened there must be imminent danger, hence the thing to do is to run, and run they do. Those who failed to seek safety in flight were destroyed and did not live to reproduce their kind. The modern survivors of all herding animals are descended from those who ran from danger and lived to run again.

As a form of lawlessness, mobs and mob violence have played an important role in social and legal institutions of our country. Mob rule is likely to prevail before the establishment of law and order in pioneer times, and again when the law is inadequate or too slow or the crime committed cuts across deep-seated local prejudices as in the case of certain crimes by negroes.

Leadership

The psychology of leadership is baffling. That it should be possible for one man to dominate thousands and even millions of his fellows seems beyond comprehension. And yet no one can deny the tremendous power of the leader in every walk of life, more especially in the political and military world. Who can estimate the influence of an Alcibiades, a Plato, an Alexander, a Caesar, a Genghis Khan, a Mohammed, a Napoleon, a Hitler? What is there about a leader that sets him apart from his fellows, at whose word thousands gladly face danger and death? Many traits are listed as essential to a leader such as a commanding personality, great physical size, intelligence, loyalty, inscrutability, etc. And yet there are many famous leaders in history who have lacked one or more of these traits. Napoleon with his five-feet-two was no physical giant, yet many men of giant stature quaked in his presence. Moreover there are leaders among animals and children and some of the so-called essential traits surely do not apply to these. What then is the irreducible trait or traits which every leader must have?

Apparently self-confidence, energy, initiative, and willingness to assume responsibility constitute the first group of traits necessary to the leader, for no leader is without such traits. On the other hand, something more is required because many people possessing these traits are not leaders. It is a poor insane asylum that does not boast of at least a dozen Napoleons who strut and give orders. In one asylum there is a man who considered himself the Christ and another who goes him one better and is obsessed with the idea that he is the First Person of the Trinity, God Almighty. There is no lack of self-confidence on the part of some people who, nevertheless, are not leaders.

In addition to self-confidence and initiative a leader must possess superiority in the field where it counts most. Among animals it is mostly physical strength and cunning. In the spring of the year the leader of the herd or pack is challenged by new aspirants and the winner is the undisputed leader until the next main bout. The lead Eskimo dog must be able to lick every other dog. A megalomaniac, one who has unlimited confidence in his ability, ends up in an asylum, the gallows, or on a throne. Everything depends on how much real ability he possesses to back up his superiority complex with just a pinch of luck. There may be other qualities in a leader, but self-reliance and genuine ability are the minimum essentials. Leadership is obviously important in all social relationships. In marriage, for example, regardless of the status of women, the woman will lead if she has qualities of leadership in greater measure than her husband. It is not a matter of legal status, or religious beliefs, nor yet of customs and prearrangements. It is a psychological fact with serious sociological implications.

Propaganda

Here is another important psychological factor in social life. Propaganda is the art of making up the other fellow's mind for him. It traffics in ulterior motives. The propagandist is careful to hide his true motives. He has an ax to grind, a project to put over, something to sell. He has a definite objective which may be jeopardized if he is too apparent with his motives. The lobbyist is a good example of a propagandist. He is employed to prevent the passage of legislation that is detrimental to his employer, but never once does he mention this fact. On the contrary, he gives the impression of being terribly worried over the evils that will befall the public should the proposed legislation become enacted into law. Similarly, the salesman does not come to you and say frankly, "Please buy this car, for I need the money to pay bills, to buy the wife a new coat," etc. He is more likely to say nothing at all about his commission and boost the car, to get you to feel that you must have it to be envied by your friends, in short, that without it life would not be worth living.

All advertising as well as salesmanship comes under this category. We have heard so much about propaganda in war and about false statements deliberately promulgated, that many have come to regard propaganda as essentially evil and fabricated from lies and prevarications. This is not always the case. Propaganda could be strictly true and still be only a portion of the truth. The propagandist is interested only in presenting his side of the case. This is illustrated in the courtroom when the witness takes an oath to tell the truth, the *whole* truth, and nothing but the truth. Immediately he is prevented by the opposition lawyer from telling that phase of the truth which may be damaging to the opposition and his own lawyer watches him like a hawk to keep him from telling that portion of the truth which may embarrass his case.

Education differs from propaganda in that it seeks to tell the whole truth and leave the decision with the student. This is not always the case, for in many phases of education the teacher is expected to prejudice the mind of the pupil in favor of the established code, say the Ten Commandments and other phases of the moral code approved by the community. It is impossible to overemphasize the importance of propaganda in social life, in the daily life of every citizen. Propaganda is doubtless the strongest weapon in human relationships. We are propagandized so persistently and from so many unsuspected sources that it is almost impossible to be sure when you see a movie, read an article, or scan the news that you are not being propagandized.

Public Opinion

Public opinion is conceived and nurtured by propaganda. Together they constitute a power greater than any armed force. Even ruthless war lords who stop at no inhuman act of atrocity, go out of their way to woo the public opinion of the world in justification of their acts by placing the blame on the enemy. This is a great tribute to the force of public opinion. And in a democracy public opinion is the ruling force, even more potent than the written laws in the statute books, because every law becomes a dead letter the moment public opinion is withdrawn from its support. Witness the old blue laws of New England and the Eighteenth Amendment in the larger cities when that experiment was theoretically in force.

The agencies of public opinion are many and exert varying

degrees of influence upon it. The best known are the press, the radio, the pulpit, the lecture platform, and every agency of education and propaganda. In recent elections the newspapers discovered that they are not as potent forces in moulding public opinion as they supposed. The candidate having almost the solid support of the newspapers has consistently lost out in the elections. The Gallup poll and other agencies take soundings of public opinion on various important issues of the day. Not the least value of their findings is the check on changes that occur from time to time in public opinion on such issues as the popularity of candidates for political office, America's attitude on preparedness, aid to Britain, active participation in the war, taxes, limits of national debt, etc. It is significant that public opinion does change and may even reverse itself as it did in the case of the Eighteenth Amendment, the neutrality act, and many other issues. Events abroad, some "incident" such as the sinking of the Maine and the Lusitania, the attack on Pearl Harbor, change or crystallize public opinion over night.

Social Pressure and Social Control

Social pressure is the force that society exerts on the individual to make him toe the mark. It is the power of the many over the few. The agencies of this force are numerous and exceedingly powerful. They include rewards and punishments, folkways, mores, customs and conventions, ritual, fads and fashions, institutions, laws, and the full armed might of the local police, the state militia, and the regular army and navy. Social pressure and social control constitute the might of society against the egoism and self-assertion of the individual. This force has to be strong enough to hold in check the self-regarding motives which are essentially egoistic, self-centered and for the most part anti-social. These impulses have been with the race for countless generations. The veneer of civilization is a recent acquisition or imposition and easily flakes off as we saw in the discussion on mob psychology.

We are born individuals and acquire our culture and a social point of view along with our language and education. It is a long and tedious process making a social animal out of a rank egoist. Nor is the attempt a hundred per cent efficient. Many fail entirely and some become anti-social instead. And the great majority of us are only partly tamed, just enough to get by, to avoid being a menace or a burden. We get along. But the power that keeps us in leash is never relaxed. Rewards and punishments are an old standby.

From the earliest beginnings the child is rewarded for doing the approved acts and punished for the opposite. He soon learns what is expected of him, more accurately, what is good for him. These rewards and punishments take the form of praise or blame, giving or withholding desirable goods, and corporal punishment. They have extrinsic as well as intrinsic value. They may be spiritual as well as material. The people who are obedient to the social code are given medals, elected to office, handed lucrative positions, etc. The anti-social individuals are punished by ostracism, disgrace, imprisonment, and in extreme cases by death.

The social codes as expressed through folkways, mores, fads and fashions, customs and conventions are highly effective in checking the individual. The folkways are the customs and conventions of the group that a person accepts blindly. The folkways are especially powerful among primitive peoples who never question the right or truth of the existing code. Mores are more advanced. They represent the reasoned customs and come close to morality, constituting the moral code. Once the individual accepts the moral code of his group, to violate any significant part of it becomes an immoral act. This is why civilized man is more likely to be immoral than is the savage. Savage man is a-moral, neither moral nor immoral because he accepts his code blindly and without reason.

Customs and conventions lend uniformity to social conduct, and ritual adds dignity and aesthetic value. Fashions differ from customs in that they are more transitory while fads are even more short-lived. It is a custom to wear a hat on certain occasions and to remove the hat on other occasions, but the kind of hat that one wears is determined by fashion. Fads and fashions introduce the element of novelty and change. Ordinarily society does not tolerate change and displays great antipathy towards innovators. It is notorious for killing its reformers and stoning its prophets. But society makes an exception in the case of fads and fashions because everybody is being an innovator at the same time and in matters of no real consequence. It can do no vital harm to society whether a woman wears her hat on the left ear or on the crown of the head. But to introduce any radical change in the major social institutions of religion, marriage, and the form of government is a matter of vital concern and is treated accordingly.

Social control through social pressure is the democratic way of regulating the life of the individual and holding him in check.

Social pressure may be likened to atmospheric pressure which is approximately fifteen pounds to the square inch at sea level, but decreases as one climbs a mountain and increases as one descends beneath the level of the sea. This increase of pressure is at the rate of a ton per square inch for every thousand fathoms. The analogy may be carried still further by pointing out that ordinarily one is not aware of atmospheric pressure because there is an equal amount of pressure from within. Similarly, a person who is well adjusted socially is not aware of social pressure because he is doing not only what society demands of him but also what he himself demands of himself. In other words, he is in accord with the social code. Unfortunately there are individuals who get too high or too low from sea level so to speak and begin to feel the pressure. There are always social rebels who chafe at all restraint. The law-abiding citizen is scarcely aware of the law because he willingly does the accepted thing.

In an ideal society and in a perfectly integrated personality, the social pressure is never felt because it is only as strong as the pressure from within. Should social pressure be unduly relaxed or intensified the balance is upset and the individual or society or both suffer. If individuals are permitted too much freedom the result is lawlessness, crime, and the breaking down of social life. On the other hand, should social pressure become too powerful, individual initiative and personal freedom are jeopardized and men are cowed and unhappy.

TOPICAL OUTLINE AND SUMMARY

In a bird's eye view our topics appear in the following array:
  I. Kinds of psychology
 II. Physical factors: physiological psychology
    1. The central nervous system
    2. The autonomic nervous system
    3. The synapse and synaptic connections
    4. Stimulus-response-bonds, habits, autonomic reactions
    5. Sense organs
III. Intellectual or psychic factors: functional psychology
    1. Elementary concepts
    2. Sensation, perception, illusion, hallucination
    3. Ideas, concepts
    4. Consciousness, the subconscious

    5 Instincts

    6. Feeling, pain, emotion, morale

    7. Thinking, reasoning, imagination, dreams, hypnosis, somnambulism

    8. Learning, retention, memory, recall

    9. Intelligence

    10. Appetite, desire, purpose, attitude, drive, motive, volition

IV. Individual factors: differential psychology

    1. Personality (cf. Chapter 9)

    2. Differential psychology

    3. Special aptitudes, talent

    4. Employment psychology

    5. Integration, the mirrored self

    6. Disintegration and demoralization; abnormal psychology

V. Social factors: social psychology

    1. The social impulse, gregariousness, the herding instinct

    2. Suggestion-imitation

    3. Mob psychology

    4. Leadership

    5. Propaganda

    6. Public opinion

    7. Social pressure and social control

We have called attention to the fact that the physical and structural factors cannot be divorced from the mental and psychic factors any more than a single phase of life can be separated from the rest, except as a theoretical abstraction for the purpose of analysis and study. Just as one needs to take the total personality into account in the simplest psychological reaction, so the import of the total environment must be appreciated in evaluating the significance of any social factor. Accordingly, the mechanics of mental life such as the nervous systems, neurones, synaptic connections, stimulus-response-bonds, habits, autonomic reactions, and the sense organs were described as well as the relatively more psychic elementary concepts such as sensation, perception, illusion, hallucination, ideas, concepts, consciousness, the subconscious, instincts, feeling, pain, emotion, morale, thinking, reasoning, imagination, dreams, daydreams, hypnosis, somnambulism, learning, retention, memory, recall, intelligence, appetite, desire, purpose, attitude, drive, motive, and volition.

Attention was also called to the fact that all human beings are alike in kind and differ in degree. This necessitated the study of differential psychology as well as general psychology. Hence such factors as talent, special aptitudes, employment psychology, and the integration and disintegration of personality were presented as well as factors in social psychology such as gregariousness, suggestion-imitation, mob psychology, leadership, propaganda, public opinion, social pressure and social control.

SELECTED REFERENCES

History of Psychology:
Heidbreder, Edna, *Seven Psychologies,* D. Appleton-Century Co., 1933.
Higginson, Glenn D., *Fields of Psychology,* Henry Holt & Co., 1931.
Murchison, Carl (Editor), *Psychologies of 1930,* Clark University Press.
Pillsbury, W. B., *The History of Psychology,* W. W. Norton and Co., 1929.

Physiological Psychology and Neurology:
Cannon, W. B., *Bodily Changes in Pain, Hunger, Fear, and Rage,* Second Edition, D. Appleton-Century Co., 1929.
Herrick, C. Judson, *Neurological Foundations of Animal Behavior,* Henry Holt and Co., 1924.
Langley, N. N., *The Autonomic Nervous System,* Harvard University Press, 1921.
Troland, L. T., *The Principles of Psychophysiology,* D. Van Nostrand Co., 1930.

Differential Psychology:
Anastasi, A., *Differential Psychology,* Macmillan Co., 1937.
Freeman, F. S., *Individual Differences,* Henry Holt and Co., 1934.

General Psychology:
Dashiell, John F., *Fundamentals of General Psychology,* Houghton Mifflin Co., 1937.
Guilford, J. P., *General Psychology,* D. Van Nostrand Co., 1939.
Skinner, C. E. (Editor), *Readings in Psychology,* Farrar and Rinehart, Inc., 1935.
Valentine, W. L. (Editor), *Readings in Experimental Psychology,* Harper and Brothers, 1931.
Vaughan, Wayland F., *General Psychology,* The Odyssey Press, 1936.

Motivation:
Skinner, Charles E. (Editor), *Educational Psychology,* Prentice-Hall, 1936. Chapter VI.
Thomson, Mehran K., *The Springs of Human Action.* A Psychological Study of the Sources, Mechanisms, and Principles of Motivation in Human Behavior, D. Appleton-Century Co., 1927.
Thorndike, E. L., *The Psychology of Wants, Interests, and Attitudes,* D. Appleton-Century Co., 1934.
Tolman, E. C., *Purposive Behavior in Animals and Men,* D. Appleton-Century Co., 1932.

Warden, C. J., *Animal Motivation*, Columbia University Press, 1931.

Young, Paul Thomas, *Motivation of Behavior*, John Wiley & Sons, 1936.

Personality:

Allport, L., *Personality, A Psychological Interpretation*, Henry Holt & Co., 1937.

Berman, L., *The Glands Regulating Personality*, Macmillan Co., 1924.

Dorsey, John M., *What Is Personality?* Longmans Green and Co., 1935.

Stagner, R., *The Psychology of Personality*, McGraw-Hill Book Company, 1937.

Thorpe, L. P., *The Psychological Foundations of Personality*, McGraw-Hill Book Co., 1938.

Young, Kimball, *Personality and Problems of Adjustment*, F. S. Crofts Co., 1940.

Abnormal Psychology and Psychiatry:

Beers, Clifford W., *A Mind That Found Itself*, Doubleday Doran, Revised, 1925.

Guthrie, E. R., *The Psychology of Human Conflict,* Harper & Brothers, 1938.

Malamud, William, *Outlines of General Psychopathology*, W. W. Norton and Co., 1935.

Sadler, William, *Theory and Practice in Psychiatry*, The C. V. Mosby Co., 1936.

White, William A., *Outlines of Psychiatry*, Nervous and Mental Diseases Publishing Co., 1932.

Social Psychology:

Allport, F. H., *Social Psychology*, Houghton Mifflin Co., 1924.

Bird, Charles, *Social Psychology*, D. Appleton-Century Co., 1940.

Gurnee, H., *Elements of Social Psychology*, Farrar and Rinehart, 1936.

Katz, D. and Schanch, R. I., *Social Psychology*, John Wiley and Sons, 1938.

Shaffer, Lawrence Frederick, *The Psychology of Adjustment*, Houghton Mifflin Co., 1936.

PART III

THE ELEMENTS OF SOCIETY

As we examined, in PART II, the persistent influences that affect social life, we saw not only the foundations on which culture rests but also the aspects of culture which are in immediate contact with the foundations. However, our investigation, in those chapters, was in terms of the foundations rather than of the culture structure. Now we survey the elements of the structure itself.

CHAPTER 9

PERSONALITY

By A. J. Bahm, Ph.D.

Texas Technological College, Lubbock, Texas

Personality, comprehensively conceived, consists of the sum-total of one's characteristics. Some of these characteristics are temporary, passing; some are permanent, enduring. Some of them are constantly obvious; some are hidden, obscure, largely potential. Some have to do with physical construction: size, shape, weight; some with reaction patterns: habits, attitudes, motives; some with social rôles: friendliness, leadership, patriotism. These suggest the complexity of personality factors—the complexity of you and me.

How do we become so complex? By being in a complex world, a world which provides our complex constituents, complex stimuli, and complex problems to adjust to. Survival has depended, continues to depend, upon adequate adjustment to all persistent influences which sort behavior. In a sense, *sociology* is a study of *personality,* especially of the social influences determining it. Of course, conversely, sociology is a study of groups and of the kinds of groups which different kinds of personalities make. Human nature is group nature; personalities are social products. Also, group nature is human nature; groups are personality products. Thus personality is a key concept in sociology.

Personalities are not separate entities, as human bodies sometimes seem to be. They are parts of an integrated universe, and have their nature constantly modified by their physical environment and their social milieu. The whole world works together to produce each personality. Each is unique in some respects. Each is like others insofar as it is produced by like conditions. As students of sociology, we are interested in understanding effects of like and different social conditions upon personalities as social products.

Personality is produced by two sets of factors, internal and external to the body. The distinction is somewhat arbitrary, but we shall find it useful. Originally, all causes of a person were external to him, for before he existed, he had no internal causes. Once an ovum is fertilized, it becomes a potential person and contains inter-

231

nal conditions which determine the kind of person it can become. What it becomes depends also upon whether external conditions are favorable to its development and whether its internal conditions are such as to adjust to the external conditions which confront it.

PERSONAL FACTORS NORMALLY INFLUENCING PERSONALITY

All persons normally develop desires. No normal person is desireless. So important are desires in understanding personality that one distinguished philosopher has gone so far as to define the self as consisting of a bundle of desires.

Although many desires of different people differ, there are some desires, or rather some types of desires, which seem fundamental to personality and which all normal people develop. W. I. Thomas has become famous for his classification of all human desires or wishes into four fundamental types, which may be named (1) desire for security, (2) desire for esteem or social recognition, (3) desire for friendship, love or interested response, (4) desire for new experiences, novelty, adventure. To fail to have some desires of each of these types is to be abnormal.

Desire for Security

Persons desire to secure, conserve, increase whatever is of value to them. The desire to live, to secure life, seems the most basic desire, and fear of death the most basic fear. We desire breath, fear suffocation. We desire food, fear starvation. We desire shelter, clothing, warmth, fear freezing or fatal exposure. We desire health, fear disease. We desire protection, fear enemies. We desire "salvation," fear unknown dangers. These desires determine what we shall do in our association with others. They are internal determinants of behavior. Persons differ in the strength or imperativeness of different desires and have different conceptions of how to satisfy them. Thus personalities differ. Yet persons are similar in that all normal persons have them. Groups differ in their ways of provoking these desires and in ways of providing for their satisfaction. Thus groups differ. Yet groups are similar in that all groups must somehow take account of them. The nature of any personality is always conditioned by the nature of its desires for security.

Desire for Esteem

Persons desire to rate, to "belong," to be recognized as having status. Next in importance to the desire to secure life is the desire to secure status. Next to fear of death is fear of being despised, unrecognized, ignored. Ways of getting recognition are legion. But always they are conditioned, as we shall see, by the groups we participate in, by what is considered worth while in the eyes of those whose judgment we trust.

Alliteratively, we may say there are three types of esteem, namely those we get from possessions, position and personality. (1) *Possession.* We want better clothes, a better house, a newer or more expensive car, a bigger bank account, more property, not merely to be more secure, but to be more esteemed. "Keeping up with the Joneses" means trying to rate as they do. (2) *Position.* Whatever social position our group admires, we would like to occupy. We join clubs, seek office, play to win. We want to be president, governor, captain, star, deacon, editor, chairman, superintendent, manager. We work for grades, degrees, honors. We choose to enter honored occupations, try to keep morally respectable, seek publicity and fame. All this we do because we want to rate, because we desire recognition. (3) *Personality.* Whatever qualities or traits are currently admired in our group, we strive to attain. Beauty, wit, brilliance, honesty, friendliness, strength, skill—if these be approved, we strive to possess them. It is normal to desire to be esteemed.

We normally believe that the greater one's recognition, the happier he is. But—and here is one of the greatest contributions this chapter can make to your understanding of (your own) personality—this belief involves much truth but often leads to an illusion. Actually, though esteem gives happiness, the love of esteem is the root of much unhappiness.

Fritz Künkel, in *Let's Be Normal*, has pointed out that people are normally egocentric, that is, interested in the esteem that others hold for them. Furthermore, people are ambitious, i.e., seek to amplify the esteem that others hold for them. Furthermore, people are credulous, i.e., believe they are or ought to be esteemed more highly than they actually are esteemed. In this latter lies the illusion and the cause of unhappiness. To believe oneself deserving of what in the judgment of others one does not deserve, to believe oneself worthy of what in the judgment of others one is not worthy, to believe oneself valued for what one is not actually valued, is to be in danger. For whenever one's believed rating gets measured by one's real rating, whenever one's self-esteem gets measured by group estimation, whenever one's imagined status gets compared with objective status, if it is too high it must inevitably in the long run get lowered. Recognized lowering of status not only is frustration of desire, but oftentimes is utter defeat. Men are emotional extremists regarding esteem. They tend to press toward a pinnacle of pride, and failing this they fall to a devastating defeat. Künkel conceives pride and mortification in terms of a vertical scale running from a peak of plus 100 feeling of superiority, down through 0 to minus 100 or complete inferiority. "Pride goeth before the fall." One whose recognized social position warrants a plus 20 rating and whose self-rating regarding such position is plus 40, falls, when social circumstances cause correction, not merely to the justified plus 20, nor merely to 0, but to a minus 40, roughly speaking. The emotional plunge is terrible. Embarrassment knows no accurate measure, but everyone's personal experience testifies to some warrant for Künkel's attempt.

Equanimity is more likely for him who is "objective," i.e., by accepting one's social status for what it is, by rating oneself as one is rated by others, by judging one's worth exactly as it is judged by others. To be unsatisfied with one's lot is to be unhappy. To "accept the world" and one's status in it is necessary to happiness. This does not mean one should not strive to "improve" his lot, but only that for tranquility he should not deceive himself that his rating is better than it actually is.

But how can one know what his rating really is? What determines one's value? It is determined somewhat like the value of money. It depends upon how many others are interested in it and how strongly. It may fluctuate from day to day, group to group, situation to situation, depending upon a multitude of varying factors. The value of a person is what he can get himself passed off for in the groups which pass judgment upon him.

Since, as with monetary currency, people try to get the most they can out of their money, people will seek to participate in those groups which set the highest value upon them. In a stable society, one's value tends to become stabilized and more or less unchanging, with exceptions now and then. Just as money often rests on a gold backing and confidence in the integrity of government, so the esteem in which one is held tends to be dependent upon one's actual abilities or usefulness as a member of the group in which he participates, and confidence of the group in his reliability in "coming through" with what is expected of him. Highly inflated personality values, like highly inflated money, are due normally for painful, sometimes disastrous, deflation.

The practical importance of this interest in esteem can hardly be over-estimated. We choose to enter the occupation engaged in by those we admire, oftentimes disregarding our own abilities or fitness. We major under the professor who gives us the best grades, i.e., rates us the highest. We marry persons for love, i.e., self-love, when we marry those in whose eyes we are most esteemed. We are patriotically loyal partly because we cannot bear being despised as slackers. We succeed as salesmen as much by adequately esteeming our patrons as by serving their other needs. We flee from persecution to the land of the free, which means also freedom from being despised.

Dale Carnegie's *How to Win Friends and Influence People* has been popular partly because it has struck a critical keynote in esteem. To "become genuinely interested in other people" makes them feel they are worthy of our interest. To "make the other person feel important," if you can do it sincerely and if the other person trusts your judgment as genuine, is to offer an objective raise in rating. Honest appreciation is the most wholesome spiritual service one man can render another. Honest self-appraisal is the best service a man can render himself.

Pride applies to nations as well as to men. Those nations which take pride in their plus 100 superiority over all other nations and which despise all others as in some measure inferior, are some day, if they are not actually judged so superior by the other nations, doomed to fail and fall. Even for nations, a fight to death often seems better than dishonorable peace.

Religious personalities are prompted in part by what they believe to be the regard of God. If one believes that God approves, all is well. Society is often well-served by the conviction that an all-seeing God condemns anti-social acts. In many people, propriety of conduct seems proportionate to faith in the power of God to rate them for positions in eternity.

Desire for Friendship

Persons desire to be loved, not merely esteemed, though the distinction is hard to draw. Persons fear to be lonely as well as despised. Friendship is of many sorts and degrees, ranging from intimate conjugal love to remote acquaintance. Family life forms fastest friendships. ''Brotherly love'' best exemplifies the family ideal. Lovers, pals, playmates associate in ways that everyone wants. Society can be understood completely only through understanding the contribution that the desire for friendship makes in determining the ways people associate and the kinds of groups they make. Intimate responses provide primary groups. Even mere acquaintance on a friendly basis aids most social activity, oils most social machinery.

Desire for Adventure

Persons desire adventure, not only through travel, but through all varieties of new experiences. Somehow the new is more interesting. Our seemingly boundless curiosity of childhood continues as a desire for interesting books, interesting friends, interesting hobbies, interesting occupations, interesting vacations, and even interesting perplexities of problems from logical paradoxes to crossword puzzles. The opposite of novelty is boredom, and while we may not actually fear it, we constantly seek relief from it. Adventure motivation complicates society. Most recreational groups are, in this broad sense, adventure groups. Many non-recreational groups are conditioned by, must adjust to, recreational groups.

SOCIAL FACTORS NORMALLY INFLUENCING

In the previous section, emphasis has been upon demands internal to the developing personality. In this section the stress will be on the social stimulation originating outside the personality and normally influencing personality development. In the final section we shall weave the concepts together into a synthesis and a summary.

Social psychologists are much concerned about ''social stimuli.'' Persons are stimulated to react not merely to lights, sounds, tastes, odors, pressures, pains, but also to other persons, their movements, gestures, posture, expressions, attitudes, fears. Personalities are in part products of the numbers and kinds of social stimuli affecting them. Differences between person and person are due partly to differences in their social stimuli. Provincial and cosmopolitan personalities differ not so much in biological make-up as in social and cultural make-up. Isolated peoples are comparatively simple in their social reactions. Personalities produced by crowded city conditions tend to be comparatively complex, though often superficial, in their reactions. Sociologists have traced somewhat proportionate relations between increase in the efficiency[1] of communicative techniques and the "social size" of personalities. Minds are large or small, broad or narrow, as they are influenced by many or few group contacts. Primitive tribes tend toward smallness of mind. Modern city dwellers, living in comparative communicative luxury, prompted by press, radio and movies, tend toward world-wide breadth of interests. Socially stimulated contacts provide the "life-blood of society." Numbers, kinds and effectiveness of contacts are keys to understanding both kinds of personalities and kinds of groups.

Simplest among the means of social stimulation is "suggestion." "Suggestion exists when any relatively uncritical and immediate response occurs to a stimulus by means of behavior mechanisms which have already been prepared."[2] In social suggestion the response is to stimuli from other persons. What others do suggests to us what we can do. In the absence of opposing stimuli, we tend to do what others do. We learn to speak English, not French, with local accents, not accents of other regions, because some stimuli are present, others absent. Through suggestion we conform "without thinking," without deliberately imitating the ways of others.

When we willingly copy the conduct of others our conduct is called "imitation"[3] or "emulation."[4] Motives for imitation are many: to secure as others secure, to be esteemed as others are, to fit into friendships which at least in anticipation are more satisfying, to enter interesting adventure. Values of imitation are various: to promote social unity, to economize energy, to stimulate effort, to develop and integrate personality. Each of these values deserves a moment of attention.

Like-mindedness and like behavior promotes spiritual harmony called social unity. The more alike we are the better we understand each other, the more we trust each other, and the more we feel as one. "We-feelings" arise and can be maintained only when recognized likenesses are involved. Imitation is a common source of likenesses.

Energy is economized by conformity. Problems confronting people who must adjust to each other, who must accommodate conflicting interests, sooner or later find a solution through some form

---

[1] "Efficiency" includes speed, diffusion, expressiveness, permanence. See Cooley, Angell and Carr, *Introductory Sociology*, Scribners, 1933, Chap. XII.

[2] L. L. Bernard, *An Introduction to Social Psychology*, Henry Holt and Company, 1926, p. 282.

[3] Bernard, *op. cit.*, Chaps. XXI–XXIV.

[4] Cooley, Angell and Carr, *op. cit.*, Chap. X.

of generally accepted behavior pattern. Manners of greetings, for example, gradually resolve themselves to a relatively small number. Folkways, mores, conventions, customs, institutions, laws—all these are names of socially stabilized behavior patterns which assist in social adjustment. Conformity to them ordinarily aids people to get along better with one another. Effort is saved, energy is economized, by not having to experiment by trial and error each time adjustment needs to be made. Conformity is voluntary imitation to prevalent modes of action. Non-conformity, opposition to social standards, requires a rebellious spirit. Sometimes this is anti-social, sometimes merely conformity to some more remote standard. Change in standards comes only from non-conforming deviation. Radicals who fail to get a following are soon defeated; radicals who have a following are hailed as heroes. Halos hang about those whose deviations succeed in causing conformities adjudged to be better suited to social needs.

Productive effort is sometimes stimulated by rivalry. Rivalry involves a desire to win in some socially approved contest. We must imitate others somewhat if we are to excel them, for if we are entirely unalike how can we compare relative excellence? William James suggests that rivalry does nine-tenths of the world's work.

Personality is developed, sometimes integrated, through imitation. Bernard presents a treatment worth summarizing. He first traces personality development through "direct imitation of persons." The mother model, the father model, transition from mother to father models, incompleteness of father models, outside adult models such as the mail man, delivery man, policeman, fireman, truck driver, tractor driver, railroad engineer, nurses, teachers, playmates and pals all form a part of the picture of life to imitate. Imaginary persons portrayed through stories and tales also allow imitation: from fairies and elfs, fables and "funnypapers" to fiction and idealized biography. Each life and each fable, each hero and each religious character, may add its bit to draw out new elements in each developing personality. And for those whose genius for self-integration is lacking, models may serve as a source of vicarious integration. According to the type of heroes will the worshipers be patterned. Groups are guided by their leaders, and we can better understand groups if we understand what kinds of heroes they have to emulate.

Integration of personality is a central problem, both in psychological theory and in the life of each person. Psychologists are analyzing personality into smaller and finer parts or into more multifarious factors, and, for each, an explanation ultimately must be given as to how it fits into personality as a whole. Each personality, like the universe itself, is both one and many, is both an integer and a galaxy. The life of each person is a constant tension between plurality and unity; each is torn apart through increasing complexity, yet strains to retain its oneness; each expands in response to each new stimulus, yet tends to respond freely only to those to which it can respond unchaotically. The attention-span is limited, and unapprehendable stimuli are soon barred from consciousness. And, when wearied from constant stimulation, a body falls asleep or becomes relatively unconscious.

Keys to personality organization are interests and attitudes. Each interest is, in a sense, a part of a personality. The more interests one has, the more parts he has. The more distinct these parts are from one another, the more split apart he is. All normal personalities have many interests which split them apart in many ways and in many degrees. Yet ''split personalities,'' a term usually reserved for those having some interests completely split from others, are abnormal. Most personalities retain some degree of unity, through having some major interests to which all others are subordinated. The process of constantly unifying constantly multiplying interests is aided by the fact that most new interests are grafted on to interests which we already have. Normally, new desires are new, not entirely, but only in some respect.

Some personalities disintegrate because they do not acquire or retain a dominating purpose. Some acquire their integration vicariously, by imitating some integrated person or personality type. Some few plan their lives according to a rationally integrated pattern, figuring out the nature and purpose of universe, of life, or their own life, and charting the necessary steps toward the goal, and living diligently according to their plan. A complete philosophy of life would account for, and integrate, all possible interests. A completely integrated life would include some feeling of unity with one's fellows and unity with the universe—for one normally has interests in these. Religion, important in many ways, is important especially for its personality-integrating functions. Unity of the personality through unity with some cosmic cause may suffice when other causes fail. One must have ''something to live for,'' self, family, nation, or God, or life won't be "worth living." He who finds something "most supremely worth while" and devotes himself completely to it is likely to retain his integration through every diversity.

Culture, defined in detail elsewhere, fixes limitations upon personality as well as offers frames for unfolding. Three culturally conditioned characteristics of persons may be considered as typical factors influencing personality. They are selfishness, conscience, stereotypes.

Selfishness is commonly conceived as doing what one wants without regard for the welfare of others. Such a conception is incomplete. Cultural considerations condition the degree of regard one has for another. The degree of regard depends upon prior decisions determining social standards. What is considered selfish in one group may not be so considered in another. When a candy plate is passed at a party, with ten pieces for ten people, it's a selfish cad who takes more than one piece. When the party plays a game of gambling for goods with the goal of "winner-take-all," it is not selfish to win. Selfishness depends upon the rules of the game. Whether or not a person is considered selfish depends upon the standards for selfishness set by his group. As people pass from group to group the standards governing selfishness may change. The week-day business bargainer who corners every coin is the same Sabbath-giver who tithes in his brotherhood. Some religious groups require sharing and he who does not is selfish, whereas some business groups require no sharing and he who shares is considered a fool unless he does so for greater gains. Selfishness involves obnoxious self-assertion, but how much self-assertion is obnoxious depends upon culturally conditioned attitudes of each group. Personality development depends upon standards set by one's society. Knowledge of group standards should give insight into personality types.

Conscience is sometimes considered a "still small voice of God" speaking to uncertain souls. Granting such guiding power, perhaps, sociologists still seek the means through which this power becomes implanted. Noting that different groups are guided by different conscience principles, sociologists seek social sources of these differences. Psychologists speculate that conscience is an experience caused by an inhibited response accompanied by a feeling of fear of evil consequences likely to follow from fulfilling the response. Sociologists speculate that differences in group experiences differently determine which tendencies to respond will be inhibited and which not. Customs created by cruel trial-and-error methods carry valuable lessons learned in the past to give guidance in the present. Learning from custom not to fight each other saves the trouble and torture of learning not to fight by fighting. Creating conscience by instruction in customs is a convenient societal device of service in making social as well as physical adjustment easier. Primitive peoples having isolated experiences tend toward uniformity of conscience. Modern men mix their mores through migration, mingling experiences of many lands and times. Students of migration speak of the ''marginal man'' bearing the brunt of cultural conflict on the borderline between two cultures. His conscience, molded in the mores of his homeland, becomes undone under newer mores of his new land. His older inhibitions conflict with newer inhibitions imposed by the new customs. Such sufferings are part of the pains of change.

Stereotypes, like selfishness and conscience, are socially established. Stereotypes are fixed ways of seeing things, just as customs are fixed ways of doing things. Customs save us from learning by doing, so stereotypes save us from learning by thinking. Customs help develop habitual conduct, so stereotypes help develop habitual attitudes. Stereotypically, ''schoolmarms'' have long faces, communists have long whiskers, fat capitalists have long fat cigars. Habits of thinking become unthinking habits. Persons are sometimes subject to social disapproval because they are conceived as conforming to a disapproved stereotyped pattern. Likewise some persons are permitted incongruent preeminence because they can clothe themselves in the symbols of stereotyped admiration. A physician's stethoscope symbolizes wisdom, does not contain it. A lawyer's terminology, ''whereas and whereas,'' conveys knowledge or conceals it. A professor's library boasts of learning, may hide the lack of common sense. A pastor's prayer resounds with reverence which may vanish in vanity not long later. Most nationalistic cultures contain stereotypes of contempt: traveller take care, for he who cries ''Greaser'' in turn is called ''Gringo.''

THE SELF AS A SOCIAL PRODUCT

Personality consists of a number of characteristics among which are one's ideas of himself. What is one's self? At times we identify it with the total personality. At others, it means much less. Apparently the core of self is not a substance, as once was thought. The self, though seemingly permanent, expands and contracts with change in circumstances.

"I" am what I am, but what am I? When my body is ill, "I am ill." When my marble hits yours, "I hit you." When day-dreaming, "I am lost in thought." When you curse me, "I am in-sulted." Thus "I" am a body, a marble, a dream object, and that which is insulted by you. Dubious as it may seem to common sense, the self seems nothing more than one's self-ideas of oneself. I am what I think I am. But, of course, what I think I am depends upon all those things which cause me to think the way I do. My body's limitations are such that I cannot fly like a bird. If for a moment I think I can, I soon learn to think differently. Of course, in dreams, almost anything is possible. What I think I am depends not only on my bodily limitations, my physical surrounding, but also upon what others think of me. If they judge me to be stupid, and if I trust their judgment—as I learn to do much in the same way as I learn to trust the soil beneath my feet—I feel stupid. If they judge me to be a hero, then I am a hero. These judgments may be tempo-rary or they may be lasting, and my self has its momentary varia-tions as well as its enduring nature.

Charles Horton Cooley has contributed to sociology a convenient and significant term—"the looking-glass self." "As we see our face, figure, and dress in the glass, . . . and are pleased or otherwise with them according as they do or do not answer to what we should like them to be; so in our imagination we perceive in another's mind some thought of our appearance, manners, aims, deeds, character, friends, and so on, and are variously affected by it. . . . The thing that moves us to pride or shame is not the mere mechanical reflection of ourself, but an imputed sentiment, the imagined effect of this reflection upon another's mind. This is evident from the fact that the character and weight of that other, in whose mind we see our-selves, makes all the difference with our feeling. We are shamed to seem evasive in the presence of a straightforward man, cowardly in the presence of a brave one, gross in the eyes of a refined one, and so on. We always imagine, and in imagining share, the judgments of the other mind. A man will boast to one person of an action—say some sharp transaction in trade—which he would be ashamed to own to another. The looking-glass self is related to character very much as credit is related to the gold and other securities upon which it rests. It easily and willingly expands, in most of us, and is liable to sudden, irrational, and grievous collapses. We live on, cheerful, self-confident, conscious of helping make the world go round, until in some rude hour we learn that we do not stand so well as we thought we did, that the image of us is tarnished. Perhaps we do something, quite naturally, that we find the social order set against, or perhaps it is the ordinary course of our life that is not so well regarded as we supposed. At any rate, we find with a chill of terror that the world is cold and strange, and that our self-esteem, self-confidence, and hope, being chiefly founded upon opinions attributed to others, go down in the crash. Our reason may tell us that we are no less worthy than we were before, but dread and doubt do not permit us to believe it. The sensitive mind will certainly suffer, because of the instability of opinion. As social beings we live with our eyes upon our reflection, but have no assurance of the waters in which we see it."[6]

Not only one's rating, as Künkel points out, but one's whole social nature is largely a product of the judgments of others. The fortunes of a self are intertwined with those of his groups. He who is born in a lower caste is condemned already; for whoever knows of his caste has already judged his nature and found it lacking. He who is born of nobility or wealth is known or valued for his birthright. And one's attitudes on the great array of human relations and human problems are reflections of attitudes held by others in his groups.

Child training success corresponds definitely to the wisdom of mothers and teachers—wisdom about social rôles. Convince a child that a certain social rôle is admirable, and within the range of his achievement, the job of achieving is already half-done. Teaching methodology is largely a matter of motivation. Subtlety in social approval of students is a great secret of success, provided, of course, the approval is genuine and there are tightly-kept tethers upon the temptation to overrating.

Even when strangers meet, where there is total absence of prejudice or prejudgment about relative ratings, normally there is jockeying for position—quite unconscious for the most part, but effective and constant nevertheless. "I've been to the World's Fair," says one 'teen age youth. "Oh, how interesting, I wish I could have gone," says another, but changing the subject, but not the interest

[6] Cooley, Angell and Carr, *op. cit.*, p. 120–1. By permission of Charles Scribner's Sons, publishers.

in rating, "I've had my name in print." Each displays for the other's information the most "interesting" facts about his life. Each seeks to impress the other with his greatness, as a traveller, author, sportsman, actor, businessman, lover, inventor, or what-not. If real life stories fail, many turn into Major Hooples to fill the gap. Of course, at times it is impolite to talk too much about oneself. At such times, politeness itself becomes a rating factor and some strive to say nothing about themselves and simply listen. To prevent being rated as a bore or as impolite, one seeks to remain silent yet intensely interested. Such behavior is common to strangers and friends, to executives and workmen, to teachers and students, because it is common to all mankind.

Men must see themselves, reflected in other's eyes as "somebody." Happiness and hell revolve about desires to rate and success in rating. Happiness depends not so much upon greater recognition as upon satisfaction with such recognition as one has. But since such satisfaction normally is rare, normally one will seek to improve his status. The man who expects little and gets a lot is happy. Both what we want and what we get is determined in large measure for us by our culture. We can be taught to expect much or to expect little. We can be taught to be humble or to be proud. We are what we are in part because we tend to see ourselves as others see us. Societies make personalities and personalities in turn make societies.

SELECTED REFERENCES

Bernard, L. L., *An Introduction to Social Psychology,* New York: Henry Holt, 1926.

Cooley, Charles Horton, *Human Nature and the Social Order,* New York: Scribners, 1902; *Social Organization,* New York: Scribners, 1909.

Cooley, C. H., Angell, R. C., and Carr, L. J., *Introductory Sociology,* New York: Scribners, 1933.

Folsom, Joseph K., *Social Psychology,* New York: Harpers, 1931.

Künkel, Fritz, *Let's Be Normal,* New York: Washburn, 1930.

Künkel, Fritz, *What It Means to Grow Up,* New York: Scribners, 1937.

MacIver, R. M., *Society,* Chapters II, XXII, New York: Farrar and Rinehart, 1937.

CHAPTER 10

HUMAN GROUPS

By SANDOR BODONSKY KOVACS, PH.D.

Baylor University, Waco, Texas

Group life is an inevitable condition in the continued existence of the human personality and it is also an essential for the development, continuity and survival of culture and civilization.[1] Group life furnishes the natural environment for the development of the human personality. It furnishes the ingredients and the elements and determines their comparative importance in the making of the personality. Without group life there cannot be any human personality, for human life, as we know it, is impossible outside of group association. The hermit and the socially isolated person are human beings only because they have grown up in the society of human beings. What they are at present is the result or the effect of some disorganizing factor in their individual lives coming after they have lived for years in the company of human beings. Human nature in itself is a result of group life as well as a characteristic of human association. In group life original nature is molded to conform to the behavior pattern of the group. Here the characteristic culture of the group is instilled into the life of the individual by the process of socialization. The individual grows into the group through a process so gradual that he is quite unaware of what is actually taking place. To a great extent the individual personality is like many others in a particular culture. The individual personifies his own group and is, therefore, a stereotype. That is, he is one of the majority of the people who make up that particular group. A shift from the prevalent type to another type may be occasioned by war, revolution, the appearance of new inventions and other major social changes. These may be followed by social disorganization which in turn is reflected in personal disorganization. A characteristic culture is reflected in the personality of the individual member of the group.

Group life is not a device on man's part to avoid extinction. Group life is an inevitable condition for the existence of man. It is

---

[1] Some sociologists use ''culture'' in place of non-material culture and ''civilization'' in place of material culture.

a prerequisite for human nature or culture and culture is the social element necessary for the development of the personality of a human being. "Culture is the function of the group's existence, and culture exists at least in an elementary form in all groups . . . on the other hand, culture does not exist outside of a group formulation."[2] The individual human being responds to the social environment furnished by his particular group, otherwise he may be considered by the other members of the group to be in-human or anti-social. The individual member learns to recognize those needs which can be satisfied only in his particular group. The process of socialization not only emphasizes the needs to be satisfied in that particular group life but it also modifies the needs and their satisfaction according to the means available. Even the most basic needs are modified by the means of satisfaction available in a particular group life. For example, all people must eat some food in order to keep alive but not all peoples eat the same kind of food. Some eat vegetables while others, as in the case of the Eskimos, live entirely on meat. The individual builds up food habits and taste for some particular ways of preparing food. These habits and taste are characteristic, in a general way, of the whole group. In about the same manner the individual, reflects in his own life the beliefs, attitudes, ideas, and customs of his group. Customs are reproduced in the habits of the individual and the group mores have their counterpart in his attitudes as well as in his conscience. It is to be kept in mind from the outset that the human personality is not only a product of a particular culture but that it is also a replica in small of that culture.

The essence of group life is social interaction. Group life without social interaction is an impossibility. Social interaction cannot take place outside of group life. The individual is socialized through the medium of social interaction as he is growing up within the group and learns to participate in the group life to a continuously greater extent. The group generates social pressure compelling the individual, in case there is any need for such, to be socialized to the particular norms and customs characteristic of the group. However, as the individual is being socialized, as he is growing up, he makes a place for himself in the group life which in turn gives him a feeling of oneness with the other members, a feeling of security within his own group, and a feeling of importance.

---

[2] George A. Lundberg and others, *Trends in American Sociology*, New York: Harper and Brothers, 1929, page 150.

Ever since man has existed as a human being he has lived in groups. To ask which was first, man as a human being or the human group, is like asking which came first, the egg or the hen. Some students of man's antiquity hold to the view of human groups growing out of the herds, aggregations of people, that were the results of man's instinctive gregariousness. This view is in accord with the idea of cultural development from the simple to the complex, from the so-called instinctive to the culturally acquired. Others hold to the view that the family, the monogamous, the patriarchal family, was the first human group and was the source or the genesis of all the various human groups of today. Whatever may have been the origin of human groups, there are no human beings today without some form of group life, nor is there any record testifying to the fact that human beings lived outside of groups in the past. The number of groups, their variety and their extent, grows progressively with the accumulation and the complexity of culture and the growing number of people participating in that particular culture. A simple culture shared by a small number of people will have only a few groups while a highly developed culture shared by millions of people will have a great number of various groups.

Sociology, to a great extent, is a study of human beings in their group relations.[3] All human associations take on some sort of group form. All human associations depend on social interaction for their continuity. All social interaction, on the other hand, depends on group life. The human group is said to be a human association reduced to some sort of classification on the basis of a tangible form which is to a smaller or greater degree organized around an interest or interests held in common by all its members. And now, with these general remarks in mind, we are going to examine the human groups and some of the most common classifications of them, keeping in mind, however, that the scope of the present chapter does not allow a thorough study of all human groups.

CLASSIFICATION OF GROUPS

Human associations may be classified into several types. In most cases they are classified as either Primary and Secondary groups, or

[3] Sociology may be said to be primarily interested in human associations and the resultant social interaction. But group life represents, and is in fact, the total life of many individuals as members of the group. To arrive at a satisfactory understanding of group life it is important to study the members individually as well as collectively.

as one of these: the In- and Out-groups, the Vertical and Horizontal groups, Temporary and Permanent groups, or some other less used type. In practically all cases of attempts at classification a dichotomous, a two-fold classification, is used. Within such a two-fold classification, however, further grouping is possible. Such a classification may lead the student into thinking that a study of group life is very simple. It needs to be kept in mind that in real life no social situation is simple.[4]

Primary and Secondary Groups[5]

Perhaps the most useful classification of groups is that of primary and secondary groups. Practically all human associations can be classified under these two headings. The primary groups are the most important, the most permanent, and the most fundamental of human associations. A primary group is characterized by an almost continuous association of its members through many years, by a relatively small number of members, by an intimate face-to-face relationship between its members, and by the largest possible number and variety of common interests. Within the primary group the individual spends his most impressionable years and here, under the guidance and compulsion of the other members of the group either individually or collectively, he formulates the most fundamental and the primary habits, attitudes, and a behavior pattern that is a reflection of the culture of the group in the life of the individual. This growth into the pattern of behavior on the part of the individual is, in most part, an unconscious and practically an effortless process. This pattern remains the framework of his personality for a life time. The individual neither can divest himself of this pattern nor is it advisable for him to do so. The common saying, "Like father like son," is a recognition of the process of socialization by which the uniformity of patterns, attitudes, and interests of the primary group are permanently engraved upon the personality of the individual member. It is also a recognition of the permanency of these personality traits superimposed upon the original nature of the indi-

---

4 Sutherland and Woodward, *Introductory Sociology*, Philadelphia: J. B. Lippincott and Company, 1937, page 285.

5 The concept of primary groups is the invention of Professor Charles H. Cooley. In his book *Social Organization* (New York, 1922), he states on page 23: "By primary groups I mean those characterized by intimate face-to-face association and cooperation. They are primary in several senses, but chiefly in that they are fundamental."

vidual. The individual lives within the primary groups practically all his life. In most cases, for example, he never outgrows the family as a social institution. He is born into the family and spends about the first third of his life there, the most important years from the standpoint of personality development. But it would be wrong to think that when he leaves this family he stops developing his personality. When he establishes his own family and with the growth of his own children he is continuously undergoing important changes in the process of socialization. What was said of the family may also be said of the play group. The individual changes playmates from year to year as he moves from one age group to another. When he leaves the neighborhood play group he may join a gang, a fraternity, a secret organization, and the like, which are, in some respect, but overgrown play groups modified to fit the needs of changed interests, responsibilities, and desires of the individual.

The primary groups are the cradle of human nature. They are the most efficient forms of a socializing agency. Within the primary group the members share each others minds, secrets, hopes, aspirations, and ambitions. Sympathy, cooperation, and consciousness of kind are developed in the primary group.[6] The meaning in our culture acquired by such terms as brother, friend, neighbor clearly indicates the influence the family, the neighborhood, and the play group have in the life of the individual. This important and abiding influence upon the individual is due to the fact that he is a vital part of the primary group. He is, in most cases, one of the few people who make up the group. The family, for example, is usually only of some four or five members and seldom more than ten. Hence, the individual is important in the life of the group, for it is to the advantage of the group if he is happy and well. In his welfare are vitally concerned all the other members just as he is, on the whole, greatly interested in their individual as well as collective welfare. In the family he is in contact with the other members at practically all points of his life. Face-to-face relation, intimacy, sympathy, and sharing of interests mutually cannot be maintained with any degree of effectiveness in a large group. The principle seems to be well established that primary relations of this nature are to be found in relatively small groups and as groups grow in size the intimacy

[6] Professor Franklin H. Giddings based most of his sociological system on the concept of ''consciousness of kind'' and ''like-mindedness.'' See his *Principles of Sociology*, New York: The Macmillan Company, 1896.

of contact between their members is inevitably lessened. Consequently, they also lose the deeper sympathy, the more personal association, the more permanent fellowship, and the sense of mutual oneness, which are the fundamental characteristics of primary groups.

For obvious reasons, an individual cannot be a member in many primary groups. He cannot fully participate with his whole personality in many groups. While he is usually a member of the three primary groups, the family, the neighborhood, and the play group, he is also a member of several secondary groups where he is participating only with a segment of his personality. His loyalty to the primary group is much stronger than to the secondary group.

The Family.   The family is the most outstanding of the primary groups. Within the family the individual member lives in a more intimate relationship with the other members than in any other group. It is here, within the family circle, that cooperation for the welfare of the individual by the group and for the welfare of the group by the individual attains its highest level. It is here that sympathy becomes a part of the human personality. Sympathy for the family and for the individual members of the family is the outgrowth of the mutual identification possible because of the many years of intimate association of the members with each other under the most favorable conditions. The family is the primary institution that concerns itself with the development in the individual personality of the fundamental ideas and attitudes which are the basic elements in the behavior pattern of the individual. The first years in the life of the human being have long been recognized as the most important in the formation of life habits and in the establishment of characteristic modes of behavior. In the process of socialization the individual must make constant adjustments. There may be, besides the parents, an older brother, an older sister, perhaps several brothers and sisters, grandparents, and other relatives with whom the individual must learn to live and with whom he learns to cooperate for his individual as well as for the mutual aims and purposes of the family. It is of importance to note that great leaders are usually from families of several brothers and sisters. The family is also the transfer station for the traditions not alone of the family but also of the larger groups, the community and the nation. Within the family the individual member is initiated into and saturated with the ideology of the larger group of which his family is but a part. The pattern of behavior, the basic sentiments, the most fundamental attitudes, the likes and dislikes acquired in the family usually persist throughout the life of the individual.

The Neighborhood. Another of the primary groups is the neighborhood. The most distinctive characteristics of a neighborhood are its relation with a local area sufficiently compact to permit frequent and intimate association and the emergence out of such association of sufficient homogeneity and unity to permit a primary. or a face-to-face social grouping endowed with a strong sense of self-consciousness and capable of influencing the behavior of its several constituents.[7] In Europe the small agricultural village often may be called a neighborhood. Such a village may be peopled, in large part, by the descendents of common parents. When this is the case, the village represents a large family. The inhabitants know each other intimately and usually can trace blood relation between themselves for generations back. Those living in the village but not related to the village people by blood are mostly those who came into the village through marriage. The neighborhood in the case of the agricultural village may center around a church, the village hall, and the tavern or village inn. There is, in many cases, only one religion, one political party, and one social class for the whole village. Here the people may meet each other daily; they know each other intimately; they are vitally interested in each other's affairs and in each other's welfare. They respect each other and look upon each other as equals. The older people command respect. Children are taught to show proper respect for the older people. Such a neighborhood is a relatively permanent group with common interests, abiding sentiments, customs and mores pertaining equally to every member of the group. The traditions of the village are the history of the large family. There is a measure of identification of one member with the others bordering on clannishness.[8]

In the United States the neighborhood is not easily defined. The

[7] From notes taken in class under Dr. Floyd N. House, School of Sociology, University of Virginia.

[8] The European village is a social unit permeated with a religious good-will. It is characterized by industry, orderliness, neatness, sociability, self-respect, friendliness, and polite hospitality. "Such orderly villages usually are found to preserve the effectiveness of primary group controls over the individual conduct, to envelop a relatively homogeneous population, to present a united front of moral and social standards to their members, and to embrace changes from the outside world at an undisrupting pace or in an orderly way." Walter C. Reckless, *Criminal Behavior*, New York: McGraw-Hill Book Company, 1940, page 31.

continuous change accompanying the rapid growth of the cities and the de-centralized social life of the characteristically American open-country neighborhood were not influential in the building up of a stable and well-integrated neighborhood. The agricultural village type of community did not have sufficient time to develop in the United States except in some parts of New England. The heterogeneous character of the population and the available free land for new settlements hindered the development of agricultural villages while the industrial revolution, in part at least, is responsible for the development of large cities where social life is impersonal and where sections or neighborhoods do not have sufficient time to develop. The nearest approach to an agricultural village being a neighborhood is found in the New England town. Another type of neighborhood may be in the process of development out of the suburb on the outskirts of the large city. However, the suburb is economically dependent on the city and is very definitely influenced by the city in education, entertainment, politics and religion. The various districts, natural areas, of the city may also be called neighborhoods. Especially is this true in the case of the immigrant colonies which compare favorably with the village of the country from which the immigrants originated, modified to meet the needs presented by the peculiar situation brought about by being a part of a larger community, the city. This type of neighborhood as well as the developing city neighborhood are due to disappear from our towns and cities because of the increasingly more complex civilization and the decreasing stability of the family. It is being replaced by the secret organizations, the fraternal organizations, and the service clubs in the case of the adults, the Boy Scouts, Campfire Girls, and other similar organizations in the case of the young people. These organizations have some of the characteristics of the neighborhood but they are more restricted in respect to membership and limited as to the number of common interests.

The neighborhood is not alone a geographical location but also a pleasant consciousness of living together with the neighbors and sympathetically sharing their joys and sorrows. The neighborhood is in some respect an extension of the family group and the same sentiments and attitudes prevail in it as in the families making up the neighborhood. Like the family, the neighborhood is actually a part in the thoughts, feelings, and sentiments of the people living there.

The Play Group. The play group is one of the three primary groups and is the third in importance. The family and the neighborhood are groups that can be classified also as vertical groups while the play group can be classified as a horizontal group. The children of a neighborhood group themselves into play groups according to age and sex. It is a selective group as well as exclusive in reference to membership. It is usually of shorter duration than is the family or the neighborhood. The play group is a primary group because it plays an important part in the formation of social habits and the development of social ideas and sentiments in the behavior pattern of the child. Here the child is among equals, for children have a strong tendency to play and associate only with children of their own age and sex. The importance of the influence of the play group upon the development of the personality of the child has not been fully realized. Only recently has there been an effort on the part of communities to provide in the American towns and cities playgrounds where children of a neighborhood can give free expression to their play tendencies under effective social control and under socially conscious constructive leadership.

While the family and the neighborhood are comparatively stable groups the play group is not. It may continue for some time, even for a number of years, without much change, but since the members of the group are developing physically and mentally the group will have to shift to different interests from time to time in order to satisfy the changing needs of its members. Otherwise, the play group will find no reason for its existence. The play group may develop into a gang, the members of which may value their gang connections and gang secrets above those of the family, especially if the members come from poorly integrated families.

In the play group social contact between members is primarily at one point. The individuals making up the group may have other interests in common besides the play tendencies, but such interests are neither incident nor essential for the existence and the continuity of the play group itself.

The play group is being replaced by the clubs fostered in the public schools and by the fraternity in the colleges in a similar manner as the neighborhood is being replaced by the luncheon clubs and the various service clubs. The fraternity takes the young people from various backgrounds and attempts to mold them into one pattern of behavior though the time available for this important work is short, usually less than four years. The fraternity, the luncheon club, and the service club, and other similar organizations may be classified as border-line or marginal primary groups, or as intermediate groups.

The Secondary Groups. The classification of secondary groups includes all the other human associations not included in the primary groups. There are many human groups besides the family, the neighborhood, and the play group which play important part in our culture. So we find among the secondary groups such organizations as the Democratic Party and the Republican Party, each with a very large membership, the various professional associations, the labor unions, the many civic clubs and other groups which serve to satisfy some needs and which give an expression to various interests held in common by their members. The individual obviously cannot belong to many more primary groups than three, but he can belong to a score or more of the secondary groups. For example, an American citizen may be a member of a political party, a church, a professional association or two, one or more luncheon clubs, a literary club, a golf club, a fishing club and other sport clubs, various committees, the Parent-Teacher Association, some honorary societies, and several other groups. It is evident that he cannot be a member of each of these organizations with the whole of his personality. To each he belongs only with a segment of his personality and participates in the group activities only to the extent of his interests in a particular group. He may or may not be personally acquainted with the other members of the group. Some of the members he knows quite well while others he may not know at all. With some of them he has direct, personal, intimate, and social contacts at many different points in his life, and may even be a member in many organizations in which they are members. With the other members he may have only impersonal, formal, and occasional contacts at few points in his life. The nature of the secondary group is suggested in this illustration. The secondary group is characterized by impersonal, indirect, formal, and occasional relations. The members have few common interests and these interests are of such nature that they may be satisfied by one of the secondary groups as well as by another. The Lions Club stands for much the same interests as does the Kiwanis Club. As a matter of fact, people often change membership from one to another of the secondary groups without apparent reason.

In the primitive culture the primary groups are practically the only associations. However, the more complex a culture becomes the greater the number of groups and associations needed to satisfy the various interests and the many possible combinations of interests. In the primitive culture the primary groups are, in most cases, sufficient for the simple needs of the people. But as the number of people in a culture grows the need for more groups grows proportionately. On the other hand, the presence of an ever-growing number of secondary groups in our own culture creates more problems for the individual and brings about a social lag in the wake of which follow personal and social disorganizations.

In the life of the primary group, especially that of the family, the individual participates with the whole of his personality. Here social interaction is most intimate and intense. In the secondary groups membership is large, participation in group life formal, and impersonal. Here the individual participates only with a segment of his personality.

In-groups and Out-groups[9]

Another possible classification of human groups is that of the in-groups and the out-groups. This classification is based primarily on the concept of consciousness of kind. The in-group may be a very small human association or a large group, depending largely on interest or interests shared in common by the members of the particular group. One's own family is an in-group; but so is one's community, tribe, or nation. The spirit of nationalism or ethnocentrism serves as the uniting bond for the people in a nation. It is often consciously fostered by the government in order to unite the interests of the people and to pool its energies for the purposes and aims as expressed by its leaders. The concepts of race-superiority, cultural-superiority, the chosen people of the gods, and other similar concepts are inspired by ethnocentrism and serve as convenient tools in the hands of political leaders in the molding of public opinion for the support of their various policies. Even a dictator cannot wholly disregard public opinion.

Membership in the in-group is based on the we-feeling of the members for each other as against the prejudice and hatred for those designated as foreigners, strangers, outsiders, enemy and aliens. Prejudice furnishes sufficient grounds for the conviction in the case of the individual as well as in the case of groups to feel justified in

[9] William G. Sumner invented the concepts of in-groups and out-groups.

placing one's self above another individual or a group. The member of the in-group holds to the idea that the outsider, member of an out-group, is inferior simply because he is an outsider. This prejudice keeps him from following his curiosity to learn to appreciate the stranger and to understand the outsider. It is very likely that members of the in-group look upon any newcomer with apprehension of conflict or competition in the economic, political, or social life.

The out-group includes all those people who are not included in the in-groups. With persons of the out-group, "we," members of the in-group, do not have anything in common and therefore "we" cannot associate with them in any way. "The out-group, then, is that association of persons toward which we feel a sense of disgust, dislike, opposition, antagonism, fear, or even hatred. It is the group toward which one has no sense of loyalty, mutual aid, co-operation, or sympathy. Rather one is prejudiced against the members of the others-group. The family across the street is inferior to our own. Our neighborhood is better than the one 'on the other side of the tracks.' One's race is much superior to another's. One's antagonisms, one's prejudices, one's hatreds are usually focused around some out-group."[10] In a simple culture it is not difficult to distinguish between the in-group and the out-group; there are only a few in each classification. In our complex society there are many groups in each. An individual may be a member with several others in an in-group as well as to have them as members in several different out-groups. Several individuals may be members of a group, such as fraternity or club, and as such are all within the in-group, while the same individuals may be outsiders to each other as members of various churches and other organizations. The primitive village as a community was relatively small and there were few separate groups within the village. As a matter of fact, the village was, in some respects, the most important group, an in-group. The people in the village knew each other, they were related to each other. Those in the other villages were in the out-groups. The people from these villages were strangers. Strangeness begets fear and fear leads to apprehension. In case the stranger is of a different color and speaks an unknown language, he is looked upon as one to be suspected of bad intentions. It should be kept in mind that while in primitive society groups may conveniently be classified as in-groups and out-

[10] Kimball Young, *Personality and Problems of Adjustment*, New York: F. S. Crofts and Company, 1940, page 128.

groups, in our highly complex culture there are many groups toward which the individual appears to be totally indifferent.

Vertical and Horizontal Groups[11]

The vertical and horizontal groups are a classification of human associations according to social classes, professions, labor unions, and other organizations based on common interests. The vertical groups are inclusive. Membership in them is a natural belonging to the group for the old and young alike. For example, the day-old child as well as the one-hundred-year-old grandfather are members of the community, also the poor and the rich, and all others regardless of creed or faith and social position. The neighborhood, the family, the nation, the church, in a restricted way, and other similar organizations are classified as vertical groups. Whenever a group is composed of people of all ages, of both sexes, of all social classes, and of all political creeds, it may safely be classified as a vertical group, even though the privileges and the responsibilities of the members are not the same.

The horizontal groups include the social classes, the caste, the professional organizations, the various clubs and social organizations whose existence is justified by special interests held in common by only a part of the people in a community, nation, or culture. The horizontal groups are selective in nature. They select and hold only certain strata of the population. A horizontal group, such as a professional association, is often consciously fostered because the members have an interest in common that can best be served by common action though the individual member receives the benefits. Other horizontal groups may be made up of persons who hold together because of class traditions, race and blood relations.

Temporary and Permanent Groups

There are many human groups that are created or brought into being by a need for a definite time and when this need is satisfied the reason for the existence of the group or groups is no more. A group which is brought into being for a definite purpose may disintegrate when the purpose is achieved, or it may be reorganized to serve another purpose. For example, a Good Government League is organized by some people in a community in order to conduct a

[11] The concept of vertical and horizontal groups is the invention of Herbert A. Miller. See his book, *Races, Nations, and Classes*, Philadelphia: J. B. Lippincott Company, 1924.

campaign against the existing local government which is considered
by these people to be too corrupt. An election is held and the party
supporting the old government is defeated. When the new officers
are placed into office the Good Government League is not needed any
more. But the members of the organization learned to cooperate to
some advantage and for this and some sentimental reasons they may
decide to hold the organization together, perhaps under another
name, and may even reorganize and continue as a civic organization suited to satisfy some needs common to all of its members.

Among the permanent human groups are the family, the church,
the community, the nation, and others. The family and the religious organization, giving expression in various ways to the attempt on man's part to understand the supernatural, are probably
the oldest human groups. Those groups which serve to preserve
social values and which play a greater part in the process of the
socialization of the human being are usually the so-called permanent
groups. It should be remembered, however, that every human
group, even the nation, is subject to forces leading to reorganization
or disintegration. "We must remember throughout our study that
groups, even the more stable ones, are not static forms, but are
dynamic and complex relationships of persons whose own interests
are always changing. Any single classification of these relationships
runs the risk of over-simplification. But the different categories are
valuable if we remember that each is a specialized approach, that
each abstracts from a complex situation only a few characteristics
for comparison."[12]

The Crowd, the Mob, and the Audience

The crowd, the mob, and the audience are all temporary groups,
and each, in a significantly different way, is an expression of collective human behavior. They represent the most dynamic, the most
variable, though short-lived, human associations. None of these
remains for long the same. The crowd, for example, may disperse
or it may, when favorable circumstances present themselves, become
either a mob or an audience.

The crowd may be said to be a short-lived aggregation of a large
number of human beings with like, but not common, interests, having a potential unity of sentiments and action. The members of a

[12] Sutherland and Woodward, *Introductory Sociology*, New York: J. B.
Lippincott Company, 1937, page 285.

crowd may have in common an emotional interest of a transitory character. This emotional interest is the outward expression of the seemingly innate curiosity of human beings prompting them to seek an answer to every problem, to investigate every new situation, anything that is strange and unusual. Whether curiosity is an innate tendency in human beings, or to what an extent, remains a debatable question. This curiosity, a peculiar characteristic of all normal human beings, compels the individual to investigate an auto accident, a street fight, a publicity stunt, and other similar social phenomena. The crowd is one of the two lowest expressions of human groups; the other is the mob. They are similar to the packs and herds of animals.[13]

Crowds may be classified into two general groups, the casual and the active crowds.[14] A casual crowd may be a group of individuals waiting for the traffic light to change. The active crowd is well illustrated by the spectators of a game or a contest. Here the individuals are moved by the action on the field and are quick to respond to every change in the action. As soon as the action on the field is over the crowd disintegrates. In either case, the crowd is a human group characterized by the novelty of a situation, by the suggestibility of action of the members, by the anonymity possible for the individual in the group, by a single like interest, and by a short existence.

The mob is usually an emotionally united crowd in concerted action. The dormant emotions of fear colored with prejudice are always present in the individual whether he is alone or in the crowd. When these latent emotions are aroused they unite the individuals into a mob. As members of a mob individuals fail to act as rational human beings. They may be said to be drawn into the field of influence of the psycho-magnetic force generated by the mob.[15] Mob action is usually destructive. The elusive phenomenon, crowd-mind, effects a unity of desire to eliminate a common danger, or supposed

[13] Richard T. LaPiere, and Paul R. Farnsworth, *Social Psychology,* New York: McGraw-Hill Book Company, 1936, page 458.

[14] A more extensive discussion of crowds than is possible within the scope of this Chapter is found in *An Outline of the Principles of Sociology,* edited by R. E. Park, New York: Barnes and Noble, 1939, page 233.

[15] The existence of a ''mob-mind'' is open to question. Both observers of mobs as well as participants in mob action seem to agree, however, that individual members of a mob are swayed by an emotion shared by others and which emotion is the motivating force of the mob.

danger, or administer justice which otherwise may not be administered. At least the members of the mob often justify their action
by the fear of otherwise giving the individual or group a chance to
evade the law. Mob action, though short-lived, is a form of unusually violent and costly social disorganization. In the process of
change that transforms the crowd into a mob feelings are excited,
emotions are intensified, suggestions are followed, inhibitions and
laws are brushed aside, and fear and the sense of insecurity height-
ened. Irritability also becomes one of the primary characteristics
of mob behavior. A classic example of mob behavior is the lynching
mob. "The lynch mob is, as a rule, made up of young men between
their teens and their middle twenties, with a sprinkling of morons
of all ages. Its members are native whites, mostly underprivileged,
the unemployed, the dispossessed, and the unattached."[16] The mob
usually leaves a scene of destruction both of human life and of
property, but no one of the members of the group feels responsible
for the depredation. In most cases the individuals in the mob feel
that they have performed the public some service. Mob behavior is
a kind of a social fermentation, an indication of unsettled social
conditions. Race riots, industrial riots, and other forms of group
clashes are an accompaniment of radical social changes. European
riots since 1848 were mostly political and pre-revolutionary while
those in the East were economic, racial, and religious riots. The
mob may be called an emotional temporary crowd usually "marked
by violent behavior."[17]

The audience may have its origin in a crowd situation. It is
usually a more formal human group than the crowd. The speaker
on the street corner or in the park may attract a crowd which in turn
may become an audience when it remains to listen. The speaker, at
least for the time being, dominates the group, and if it serves his
purpose he may turn the audience into a mob by playing on the
sentiments and emotions of the individuals who respond to the loud-
est voice. The audience may easily be transformed into a crowd and
in turn into a mob. Since the audience is made up of individuals
who are interested not in each other but in the play, the speaker, or
whatever else holds the attention of the group, it breaks up as soon
as the attraction is over, and the individuals go their various ways.

16 Frank Shay, *Judge Lynch*, New York: Ives Washburn, 1938, page 89.
17 Kimball Young, *An Introductory Sociology*, New York: American Book
Company, 1939, page 11.

During the short period of disintegration the audience is in reality a crowd. Another kind of an audience is the group of individuals who come together at a prearranged place and time, without much concern about each other, to hear a program prepared in advance. The attraction may be music, a lecture, a sermon, a play or even a movie.

When an attempt is made to describe and classify some of the short-lived or temporary human groups under the crowd, the mob, and the audience, a serious difficulty arises because they overlap. A crowd may become an audience or a mob, depending on the turn of events and on the direction in which the interest of the crowd is attracted by the leader or leaders who become a part of the situation. The crowd is an incipient mob. It is well to keep in mind that neither the mob nor the crowd is a permanent and static human group. Both of these groups are best understood when they are considered as a social process of becoming something else than what they are. The audience also may become either a crowd or a mob. Its members are in the process of making up their minds individually though the result may seem to be collective action. The members of an audience are the recipients of suggestions that may produce a desire to take part in collective action. The group, in this case, may become a melting-pot of emotion. This pot may boil over and result in social disorganization or it may cool off by the disintegration of the group.

CONTINUITY OF GROUPS

If a number of persons are to spend a certain time in a given location, they will, in all probability, organize into one or several groups, depending on the number of individuals, for play, for gossip, for talking politics, or for some more serious purpose. This organization may be only a kind of drifting together of those who have common interests or it may be directed by some self-appointed leader or leaders in answer to a definite need shared by all of them. It is not uncommon to find fellow commuters on the trains running into large cities forming groups for the duration of the trip for discussions or for play. On these trains daily hundreds of people travel at the same time who get acquainted and who may have no other interest in common than the desire of getting to and from work. Such groups are incidental to life in and around large cities, and their existence depends purely on the fact that people, the same people, are thrown together every day at the same hour on the same train for some time. By two, four, or even more, they group themselves into clubs to play cards or for some other means of amusement. These groups begin and end on the train. Ecological setting serves to bring about human associations by placing people in proximity to each other. The neighborhood, for example, lasts a long time because people are placed, often in spite of themselves, in close proximity for years as neighbors.

Group continuity also depends on the replacement of those members who die or move away or in some other way lose their membership. There is a continuous turn-over in the membership of practically all human groups save in those where replacement is impossible due to the nature of the group. The members of the Spanish War Veterans organization, for example, cannot be replaced by the children of the members or their relatives nor by other people. Hence with the death of the last member the organization comes to a natural end. Most human groups, however, continue to exist by replacing old members by new members through births, conquest, assimilation, or even by immigration. A nation, for example, gains new members and replacements by births, by conquest of other nationalities, and by receiving immigrants. Not a small number of people were added to the number of people in the United States by slave trade and by the continuous stream of immigration. "Between the years 1820 and 1938 there were 38,136,689 persons who came to the United States as immigrants from foreign lands—that is, with the intention of residing here more or less permanently."[18] "Immigration is a peaceful, individualistic aggression upon the land of a certain country by the nationals of other countries. It is peaceful because it is permitted, and it is permitted because the receiving country believes that the newcomers will be profitable to it, or at the worst that they will not be detrimental."[19]

Traditions serve as another factor in the continuity of the group. Every human group that continues to exist for a long time accumulates a body of traditions. Social memory, the container of traditions, is also the medium through which traditions are handed down from generation to generation. "A tradition is a belief held collectively and transmitted from the past, sometimes from the very remote past before written history began. Traditions may undergo

---

[18] Henry Pratt Fairchild, *People: The Quantity and Quality of Population*, New York: Henry Holt and Company, 1939, page 227.

[19] *Ibid.*, page 238.

considerable modification in this process of transmission. . . . Among a preliterate people tradition is the chief method of preserving the accumulated wisdom and beliefs of the people and of handing them on to future generations. But with the advent of literature the vocal recounting of the deeds and thoughts of the past gives way to written records which are much more accurate as to form. However, the early written records are themselves largely traditional, representing merely the transference of vocal traditions to the relatively fixed and permanent form of writing. The written form is no guarantee of the accuracy of the content, but it is a protection against easy modification."[20] Traditions are social values of the group and are often used to support patriotism which may in turn lead to intense nationalism. When social values are endangered by outsiders the members of the group are willing to fight in order to retain these social values. Traditions are fostered by the leaders of the group in order to assure greater unity and provide for a smoother group continuity. It is of great interest to the student of human groups to note that immigrant groups coming to this country give names to their colonies that are familiar and which remind them of their native land. In many of the States one finds cities named after Rome, Prague, London, Berlin, and others. Names of mountains, lakes, rivers, national shrines, and national heroes persist in the traditions of a group even after it has migrated to a new location. Traditions play an important role in group continuity.

Successful and purposive leadership is also important for the continuity of a human group. Leadership occupies an important place in group life. As soon as a number of people are thrown together by necessity or organize for some purpose leaders are appointed either by the group through collective action or by themselves. Leadership is the product of human society, for it arises out of the needs of group life. It is of great interest to the student of social phenomena in its threefold problem in human behavior. First, leadership is a development of the individual personality for outstanding service to suit a singular opportunity to satisfy a need; second, it indicates a certain type of collective behavior, an emotional setting making leadership a possibility as well as creating a need for it; third, leadership rests on social interaction between the leader and the followers.

[20] L. L. Bernard, *An Introduction to Social Psychology*, New York: Henry Holt and Company, 1926, page 572.

UNITY OR INTENSITY OF GROUP LIFE

In general, the unity of a group or human association depends upon the frequency of association, the variety of common interests held in common by the members, and the emotional quality of social interaction. Interests held in common determine in a large measure the frequency of association. Unity of the group in which members have only one or very few interests in common is usually weak. The greater the number of common interests of the members of a group, the greater is the variety of life situations in which they are brought together. This in turn determines the intimacy of the members and the emotional quality of social interaction. For example, in a highly integrated family the members share each other's secrets, hopes, and happiness. They meet during the day at meal time, they talk about financial matters both in reference to the individual members as well as in reference to their collective well-being, they discuss each other's friends, in a frank way, and they criticize one another with a view of helpfulness. They may seem to disagree at times, but they act as one person when the need arises for concerted action. It is very unusual for a boy or a girl to be excommunicated from a highly integrated family. If the individual's offense is considered grievous the whole community may turn against him, except his own family, but the family will share his disgrace willingly and will support him in winning his way back into the community.

Frequency of association leads to greater understanding and to mutual emotional dependency. The more often members of a group meet the more they learn to depend on each other. Frequency of association is partly determined by the number of members within a group. A small group is able to meet more often than a large group. Large groups are faced with the difficulty of retaining the loyalty of their members. Members of a small religious sect, for example, can be influenced to cooperate to the point of fanaticism while the members of a large religious denomination usually lag way behind in cooperation. The smaller the membership of a particular group, the greater is the possibility for a continuous and a highly integrated association.

The moral and emotional quality of social interaction in group life has a direct influence on the unity of the group. This unity, however, resides in the individual members themselves and not outside them. Group life has a conditioning effect upon the individual member's character, interests, and welfare. This conditioning is both negative and positive. The conduct of the individual may be disapproved by the other members either singly or collectively. Those activities that are either in opposition to the wishes of the group or contrary to the interests of the group are considered anti-social. The individual, when he disregards the mores, laws, traditions, and safety of the group may become undesirable and, therefore, excommunicated from the group. A member of a religious organization may be excommunicated, a traitor may be shot to death whenever the group finds it expedient for the other members of the group collectively. However, when the individual member is in harmony with the group and serves the interests of the group, he may be rewarded by special favor or recognition, given special privileges, as the expression of the approval of the group. The greater the control of the group over the life of the individual, the greater is the solidarity of the group. It should be noted, however, that group control operates over the individual mostly when the individual is within the group itself but not so much when he is outside of the group. Moral holidays are usually taken by people who are away from their own communities or at home when they are under some extreme emotional strain which seems, for the time being at least, to place them outside of the influence of the mores of the group. An individual feels free to follow his inclinations and allows himself more liberty when he is outside of the group where there are no people from home to tell on him and where the taboos and the regulations of the group with which he is identified at home have no influence. Vacations, conventions, and various trips away from home have a tendency to bring out of the individual a behavior which at home would bring severe criticism. However, the individual is not always free to do as he pleases when away from his group. Group control operates through the conditioned reflex attitude of the individual which is grounded in his conscience. Conscience is the reflection of the group's mores in the consciousness of the individual member. But, usually, the further from the group he is, the weaker becomes the voice of his conscience.

Every human association, to last, must be based on the consensus of the members arrived at either through consciously directed leadership or by a common desire on the part of the members to work together, to cooperate, in order to satisfy some common needs or to avoid some common danger. This consensus may be called the group conscience. It not only unites the sentiments and feelings of the members but it also centralizes these in some form of group organization. The leadership and the government, even in the case of a dictatorship, direct group life through symbols, creeds, doctrines, in order to bring about a high degree of ethnocentrism. Members of a particular group are told that they are of a pure race while in another group they are told that they are "brothers" because they share the same traditions. In each case an attempt is made to bring about a we-feeling or a consciousness of kind. Regardless of the method used to bring it about, it may be said, in general, group unity depends on collective representation, on consensus, and on some physical or spiritual affinity of the members.

STUDY OUTLINE

I. Collective behavior finds expression in group life which is all important for the:
    A. Existence and the continuation of human culture.
    B. Human nature and its expression in the human personality.
    C. Opportunity for social interaction.
    D. Existence of human beings as human beings.

II. Human groups are classified into various types. Perhaps the most useful classification is that of:
    A. Primary and Secondary groups.
        1. Generally only three human groups are classified as primary: a. The family; b. The neighborhood; c. The play group.
        2. All other groups are classified as secondary. Here we find the church, the political party, the community, the nation, and others.
        3. There are some secondary groups that in some respect have primary group characteristics. "These are organized face-to-face intimate groups, limited in some degree by special purpose and by the fact of organization. . . . They have many of the characteristics of primary groups and may in fact perform many of the functions of primary groups yet organization and the limitations of special purpose give them some of the characteristics of secondary groups."[21]
    B. Other possible classifications are such as the:
        1. In- and Out-groups.
        2. The Vertical and Horizontal groups.
        3. The Temporary and Permanent groups.
    C. The Crowd, The Mob, and the Audience.

[21] Cooley, Angell, and Carr, *Introductory Sociology*, New York: Charles Scribner's Sons, 1933, page 210. Here these human groups are more or less placed between the primary and the secondary groups. It may be, therefore, suitable to call this classification as the "intermediate human groups" which arise in answer to some definite needs out of the total social situation of a highly developed culture.

III. Group continuity depends on:
  A. The ecological setting or the geographical location of the group.
  B. The replacement of members by: 1. Birth; 2. Conquest; 3. Assimilation of immigrants.
  C. Traditions of the group.
  D. Leadership.
IV. Unity of the human group depends on:
  A. Common interests and their: 1. Number; 2. Intensity.
  B. Frequency of association.
  C. Reciprocal influence of the members on each other.
  D. The morale and emotional quality of social interaction.
  E. Consensus arrived at either through consciously directed leadership or through a common desire based on: 1. A sense of brotherhood; 2. Group consciousness reflected in the behavior of the individual member; 3. Collective representation through symbols, creeds, and doctrines.

IN CONCLUSION

The fundamental reasons for the existence of human groups may be said to be two: (1) the community of interests of a group of people can better be protected and can be cultivated to a greater advantage through the cooperation of the members in group life; (2) consciousness of kind based on primary traits, such as physical characteristics, language, and traditions unite into a human group those individuals to whom they are common. These traits serve to identify the individual as the member of a particular group and when these particular characteristics are lacking he is recognized as a member of another group and an outsider. The human groups of our culture are the answer to human desires and needs. They may be said to be the inventions of the people themselves to satisfy their common needs. However, the genesis of human groups may probably be found in the instinctive gregariousness of man.

The individual human being is not a free agent in deciding for himself to which of the most fundamental groups he will belong. He has no voice in choosing his race, nationality, sex, social class, or even his family. His place in these important human groups is determined involuntarily by the accident of birth. He does however have a choice in reference to some of the secondary groups which he may leave at will. The group gives status or social standing to the individual which in turn serves as the basis for security.

Groups vary in size, in composition, in length of existence, and in solidarity. They are subject to the changes within the particular culture of which they are an integral part. Social changes are reflected in the changes within the groups, for they shape themselves to conform to the conditions as they arise and to meet the needs of a changing culture. In a comparatively stable culture, groups remain very much the same over a long period of time. In a rapidly changing society, cultural lag is seen in the attempt on the part of groups to change to new activities, functions, while trying to retain the old structure. Due to the constantly changing pattern of human groups in our highly complex culture the sociologist finds it at times difficult to study human groups. Any of the classifications discussed in this chapter may serve for a discussion on human groups in an introductory textbook in sociology. The attitude is taken here, however, that as yet the most useful classification of human groups is that of the primary and secondary groups. In the primary group the relationship between members is complete and informal while in the secondary group the relationship is partial and formal. The primary group is the most highly integrated human association. Here a small number of people are in a more lasting face-to-face relationship, in a more intimate living together, than in any other group. The family is the most universal, the most typical, of the primary groups. It is also the most important for the continuous existence of the human race. The family is also an in-group, a vertical group, and a relatively permanent group, depending on the type of classification used. Regardless of the type of classification used it is characteristic of classifications that the human groups are sorted out on the basis of a single characteristic or trait. In life, however, groups serve more than one need. Each human group is a dynamic association representing various aspects of social interaction giving an outlet for a number of divergent desires and satisfaction to various needs, often uniting like and unlike human interests.

Culture is the resultant of group life. It is only in group life that traditions accumulate by the passing down of the experiences and the wisdom of one generation to the next, that customs and mores acquire social value, and that human personality develops. Culture is the cumulative result of individual and collective experiences of human beings.

SELECTED REFERENCES

Angell, Carr, Cooley, *Introductory Sociology*, New York: Charles Scribner's Sons, 1933.—This is an attempt to re-emphasize the viewpoint of the late

strength or solidarity of any organization depends on the forces that bind it together.

Unifying Forces. First of all let us look at the *attractive* forces in society. Like giant magnets in the midst of countless steel needles the attractive forces pull human beings into social groups. Without conscious effort and even in spite of effort to the contrary men and women are drawn by the unceasing pulls of attractive forces. Seldom does any one ask why he is drawn, and few indeed care why they are drawn. They only know that they are attracted here or there, and that they follow the pull with little or no effort. From the great mass of society some individuals are attracted to churches and become integral parts of those organizations. Others are attracted to lodges, to clubs, to fraternities, and to almost countless other social groups. Everywhere in human society individuals are drawn together by attractive pulls, tremendous pulls that are fundamental to the stability of social organization.

But unifying forces are not all attractive. Men and women are continuously encountering forces that *push* them into sanctioned groups. For want of a better term these may be called COMPELLANT or COMPULSIVE forces because they drive individuals hither and thither. In blanket title these forces may be summarized as public opinion. Public opinion has held unhappy mates together for years and even decades after attractive forces ceased to hold them in harmonious unity. Public opinion is often crystallized in law and officers of the law appointed to enforce its sanctions, and many of their specific duties consist of forcing individuals to fill their sanctioned places within the social groups.

Although these compulsive forces originate outside the individual who is compelled they stimulate the development within individuals of inward urges that drive them toward unity even after the external forces have been removed. These inward urges, conditioned reflexes, feelings of duty and of responsibility, and personal convictions (perhaps conscience) are the individual's response to this same force. Thus like giant monsters the compellant or compulsive forces engender responding forces within the individual and seem to defy any inclination of the individual to leave his place and his sanctioned responsibility within the group.

Dissociating Forces. Dissociating forces are also of two different types. Within the social organizations are EXPULSIVE forces which might be compared to a charge of high explosives set off in the midst of the steel needles (used to illustrate the attractive force of the magnet) that had been drawn toward the magnet. Sometimes the explosions are so powerful that the needles are hurled beyond the attractive force of the magnet, and are scattered far and wide. At other times the force of the magnet draws them back into their former unit. Few social groups have escaped these inward expulsions. Religious denominations have been divided so often that some of them find difficulty in finding suitable names to differentiate themselves from others. Business enterprises and political organizations are no exceptions. Even nations have been torn by inward

Forces Affecting Social Unity

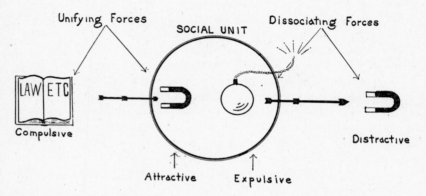

expulsions if not completely destroyed. The simplest form of recreation has its conflict within. A group of boys at their first autumn football practice often argue, then quarrel, and sometimes fight, and the one who happens to own the ball tucks it under his arm and goes home, but they will be back tomorrow, because the attractive forces are indeed strong.

The final group of social forces we shall call DISTRACTIVE because they are continuously drawing individuals from one social group to another. Man finds himself drawn in many different directions at the same time. He is drawn toward opposing social groups, opposing political groups, or opposing religious groups. Children find themselves attracted away from home even while they love and respect their parents. An individual is drawn into one social group by a particular attractive force and later he is attracted from that group to another group by the same attraction. Thus individuals are drawn hither and yon by so many different attractions that they find difficulty in remaining permanently in any social organization.

Social Control. Conscious attempts to strengthen social unities have been, as a rule, limited to efforts to stimulate the unifying forces or to efforts to decrease the dissociating forces. Even though the individuals who put forth the effort may not have been aware of the forces as such they had nothing else with which to work. In many cases reformers have striven only to destroy external attractions or to create public opinion that would force people to stay within and support the sanctioned groups. Distractive forces have been condemned as being wicked, if not "the works of the Devil."

Compulsive and distractive forces are more easily recognized than attractive or even expulsive forces and consequently receive more attention and provoke more discussion. Most of our laws and of our public opinion stress duty to society and oppose any distractive forces. Expulsive and attractive forces are much harder to recognize but they are more vital to social unity. Lasting social unity results from the pull of attractive forces. No social unity can be permanent if accompanied only by external pressure. In fact, forcing individuals into groups produces only masses of individuals, like the thousands within the walls of our penitentiaries, and not social unities in the real sense.

It should be noticed also that those who follow the pull of attractive forces do it gladly and experience happiness in the behavior. They think they are doing it by their own wills, and thus follow gladly. Those who are driven by some compellant force generally resent it and count themselves very unhappy. We like to be attracted. We resent being driven. When the attractive forces are strong and the expulsive forces are weak there is little or no need for compellant forces, and little need to worry about the distractive forces. If churches, family organizations, and governments are to continue, they will do so because they have within them attractive forces which make for social unity.

Thus the four-fold conflict goes on, never completely subsiding. In the midst of it man seeks to find harmony, and hopes to find happiness. Social control, when the forces are understood, attempts to direct individuals into groups where they will encounter the least conflict, or must be able to reduce the expulsive forces and increase the attractive forces so that harmony and social unity may be possible.

Rapid Change and Organization. One of the outstanding results of this century of rapid change in culture is its influence on the forces that affect social unity. With this change has come decreases in attractive forces, decreases in compellant forces, increases in expulsive and tremendous increases in distractive forces. Organizations that have been held together by strong ties for years find themselves with weakening ties, with increasing internal conflicts and ever increasing distractions from other organizations. The family, the church, the community, and the state are in confusion today as a result of these rapid changes and the changing forces that affect their unity.

Some Organizations Affected by Change

The Family. A complete analysis of the forces affecting family unity is not attempted here but it is necessary to look at some of them in order to understand the effect of the changes that have come. A glance at the following chart suggests that man is first of all a physical being and that physical attraction is a very important factor in drawing and holding mates together. This human being, or perhaps we should say physical being, is born into a culture. That culture immediately begins to mould his personality, while at the same time affording common bases for companionship. When the personality traits are pleasing we have still greater attraction. Out of these three come our interests which make still greater attraction in the family. Strange as it may sound when first mentioned, love in the family is nothing more or less than the sum total of the attractive forces that hold mates together. It begins with physical attraction, sex attraction, and is stimulated by sex urge. This is strengthened by cultural attractions and culture controls. Personality traits express this attraction in terms of affection, appreciation, kindness and the like, and the expression increases the pull toward the attracted parties. As the mates live together common interests play an ever increasing part in family unity. Anything that increases the attraction increases the love. Anything that decreases that attraction decreases the love.

The rapid changes that have taken place in the last century have thrown the family organization into a state of chaos. Why? Because those changes have affected the unifying forces of the family.

FORCES AFFECTING FAMILY UNITY

Unifying forces		Disorganization forces	
Compulsive	Attractive	Expulsive	Distractive
PHYSICAL			
Sex urge	Sex attraction, looks, form, health, etc.	Sex incompatibility, homeliness, poor health, etc.	Similar to attractive
CULTURAL AND PHYSICAL ENVIRONMENT			
Public opinion, laws, religion, etc.	Similar cultures, ideals, morals, religion, etc.	Conflicting religion, morals, ideals, etc.	Similar to attractive, often false
PERSONALITY TRAITS			
Fear, sense of duty	Pleasing habits, fidelity, neatness, affection, appreciation, sense of humor, etc.	Noxious habits, rudeness, selfishness, infidelity, lack of appreciation, etc.	Similar to attractive, often false
INTERESTS			
Economic necessity	Common interests in home, religion, children, economy, etc.	Conflicting interests, unsatisfactory standard of living, etc.	Opportunity for independence, careers, personal likes, etc.
LOVE			
Love a sense of duty	Total result of attractive forces	Total expulsive forces and lack of attractive forces	Total attraction to others

ADJUSTMENTS	
(Unifying)	(Disorganizing)
Ability and Willingness: To make adjustments, To forgive, To correct noxious habits, To share responsibility, To plan together, To give and take, To allow for personal likes and interests, etc.	Lack of ability or unwillingness to make such adjustments

Changes in our economic system, the liberation of women, increased opportunity for careers for women, economic independence of women, decrease in the power of church to control marriage, changes in transportation and communication, and countless other changes have affected the forces that held the family together.

First of all, the compulsive forces have been reduced. Religious compulsion which forced many families to live together has decreased, the economic advantage of marriage to women has declined, and public opinion does not condemn separation as it formerly did. Other changes have helped decrease the compellant forces.

At the same time many of the attractive forces have declined. There seems to be no evidence that sex attraction is any weaker than in the past, but there are fewer other attractive forces: fewer common interests, fewer families with children, fewer children in those families who have any, fewer home interests, and fewer couples interested in the same work by which they earn a living. Two-thirds of the families divorced have no children. Most of the other third have one or two children. Few of these separated families own a home or try to own a home. Many times the wife works away from home and they spend little time in the home together. One may be interested in church, the other in movies. They may have affection for each other and appreciate each other but they often fail to express it. Fewer and fewer attractive forces often precede the parade to the divorce court.

The seeming decrease in the attractive forces is largely an increase in the distractive forces. Here is undoubtedly the greatest change. So many new things are distractive to home life. The opportunity for a career among women, the thrill of imagined independence, the seeming higher standard of living among single women, outside entertainments, amusements, and opportunities to become parts of social organizations that take the mates away from each other, the working together of married persons with others than their own mates, the ease in obtaining a divorce, and the physical attractiveness of the opposite sex are only a few of the distractive forces in the present family.

Expulsive forces have always existed and there is little proof that they are stronger today than formerly. Certainly there is no great increase in sex incompatibility, no more sex ignorance, no greater neglect in physical appearance than formerly. There may be more venereal disease, but the greatest change that seems present is a decrease in willingness to make adjustments. Ability and willingness to make adjustments are fundamental attractive forces and lack of ability or unwillingness to make adjustments are strongly expulsive. Individuals who have been divorced and remarried to other mates have sometimes acknowledged that if they had tried as hard to get along with the first mate as with the later one they never would have separated.

In a blind quest for happiness individuals marry, and when they fail to find the expected bliss they seek separation only to try a new venture. In this attempt one thing is pretty clear. Divorce is not the solution to an unhappy marriage when there are children. It neither assures the happiness of the parents nor the welfare of the children. Happy companionship is attained through adjustment, through compromise, through consciously or unconsciously increasing the attractive forces that hold mates together. The happy marriage is today, and will likely be tomorrow, one with undying attractive forces.

The Church. Some folks attend church because of the attractive forces that draw them. Others attend church because of the sense of duty, the fear of public disapproval, or the fear of divine displeasure, or divine punishment. During the last fifty years the compulsive forces have declined. Fewer people go to church to escape hell. Fewer go because of the fear of public criticism. Perhaps there is no less attractiveness in the church services. Probably there has been no great increase in the expulsive forces. Such forces have always existed. Friction between members, conflicts of belief, conflicts between organizations within the church, have been for generations and still are sources of serious difficulty. But the greatest change has been in the outside attractions—the distractive forces. The dance, the movie, the athletic contests, clubs, school functions, and other affairs, with the attitudes surrounding them and existing in the individuals make a continuous pull on the youth of our day away from the church. What a contrast with conditions of thirty to fifty years ago. We went to church every Sunday, and to all mid-week services. There was little else to attend. That is where we found our social contacts, met our future mates, and lined up at the church door after services to escort them home. Most of this has changed and today other attractions make the choices of individuals more difficult and more confusing. Some church organizations have sensed the situation and are making strenuous efforts to increase the attractiveness of the church. These churches seem to be more successful in holding their young people. Some other organizations have spent their energies railing against outside attractions, but mostly with little success. If there is to be a church in the future it will be attractive.

The Community. Community organization has had to change along with the organizations within the community. Every change in the church, every change in the family, every change in the school has affected the community. Strong community organizations generally grow out of strong community interests or strong community leaders. Often they evolve together. As these organizations and their leaders associate and cooperate during a period of years they come to be interwoven, and geared together. They work together with mutual understanding and much cooperation. Families help each other. Schools and churches supplement each other. Other organizations generally try to fit into the whole. Then comes change: change in transportation and communication; change in the church and its membership. The schools centralize and the children are transported to the community center. The social life moves to one center, the business life may move to another center, the school life to still another. The unifying forces that held the community together in the past have been weakened. Fewer persons own their own homes. Many do not stay in any community long enough to become very much interested in it. Many do not expect to make that a permanent place of residence and see no reason why they should be interested. In the larger communities they often do not know the persons who live next door, and do not want to know them. Business men often realize that their trade is going to a larger center and try to organize to keep their business at home. A few community conscious folks have organized amusement groups in an effort to keep the young people in the local community. More and more the problem of law and order is left to officials. The attractive forces decline, the distractive forces expand, the community becomes disorganized, yielding to a larger community down the road.

INTERACTION[2]

Social contacts induce social interactions which take place through the medium of symbols. Through symbols we become aware of each other's ideas, ideals, and conceptions of social values. Man evaluates the relative merits of various possible courses of action to each social stimulus. His evaluation tends to be based on potential satisfactions to himself and his groups, either in the immediate present or some time in the future. Hence, the values attached to any specific culture trait may vary considerably between persons. Since aims and purposes, both general and specific, are variable and changeable, social interactions are correspondingly numerous and dynamic.

Social interactions in such social processes as competition, con-

[2] Dr. Thaden is author of this section.

flict, differentiation, stratification, segregation, and domination-subordination tend to isolate persons and groups, and are generally disintegrating to social organization.   On the other hand, such social interactions as accommodation, compromise, assimilation, and cooperation tend to promote reciprocal, democratic exchange of goods and ideas between persons and groups and thereby engender satisfactory experiences.   These commonly tend to be unifying.

Disunifying Interactions

Sociologists, like Economists, in their descriptions and analyses of social processes, have generally devoted much more space to conflict and competition, and to the other social forces of opposition than to the unifying forces.   This is only natural when the highway of human relationships is so generously strewn with the wreckage of antagonism, strife, and exploitation.   Everywhere there is evidence of the practice of a "dog eat dog" and a "do the other fellow before he does you" philosophy.   In the organic world the struggle pattern is very evident.   In practically all species only a few survive to maturity.   As a rule, the lower down the scale of evolutionary development the more deadly is the "struggle for survival," and the smaller is the percentage that survive.

Competition.   Competition in human society is a more or less impersonal, indirect struggle between persons or groups for the attainment of the same positive value or values.[3]   Competition occurs whenever the desired supply of the factor in question is limited and is inadequate to supply the needs and the wants of those interested.   A small number of college students may vie with others for grades of "A" or "B," if the professor "grades on the curve."   Millions of unemployed are competing with one another for jobs.   Some of those employed are competing with each other for promotions.   More and more women are competing with men in practically all vocations and professions.   Motor busses are competing with street cars and trains, radios with phonographs, newspapers with broadcasting stations, and electricity with gas and gasoline.   Within a community there is competition between stores for customers, between banks for depositors, between churches for communicants, and between auto owners for parking space on main street.

The fourteen thousand sugar beet growers of Michigan are competing with one another in the production of beet sugar.   The sugar

[3] See Leslie D. Zeleny, *Practical Sociology*, Prentice-Hall Inc., 1937, pp. 31, 61, and 438.

beet growers of Michigan are competing with the sugar beet growers of seventeen other states in which sugar beets are grown. The sugar beet growers are competing with the sugar cane growers of Louisiana. The sugar beet and sugar cane growers of United States are competing with similar growers in many other countries. In all of these relationships the social contacts and interactions are quite impersonal, and indirect. In fact free competition in the production of sugar, as in the production of so many things, is circumscribed by governmental regulations. Only about one-third of the sugar consumed in this country, which averages one-hundred pounds per capita, is produced domestically, and two-thirds is imported. From year to year, at least in recent years, the United States Department of Agriculture makes allotments of sugar quotas to the various processing companies. On the basis of these allotments Agricultural Conservation Committees work with the processors in working out allotments between states and counties.

Conflict. A social process that is far more destructive and disunifying than competition is conflict, exemplified by war. Feuds, duels, riots, and lynchings are examples of conflict situations on a smaller scale. Conflict may be defined as a direct, personal struggle between persons or groups for the retention or mastery of certain social values or alleged social values.

Differences and quarrels between persons have been settled by means of *duels* in which deadly weapons are used. The custom became common in France where it is estimated that during the eighteen-year reign of Henry IV four thousand persons were killed in duels. Some kings countenanced the custom on the supposition that it fostered a military spirit. One of the greatest figures in American history, Alexander Hamilton, Secretary of the Treasury under Washington, distinguished soldier, financier, lawyer, legislator, administrator, and author, was mortally wounded in a duel with Aaron Burr. Gradually sentiment and the mores, led to the outlawry of duels. Public opinion changed to the extent that it decreed that personal differences could be settled peacefully. In this country most states have enacted legislation making the sending of a challenge to a duel a felony, and the killing of a man in a duel an act generally punishable by death. Gradually other forms of conflict, even international conflict, may be prohibited by law.

Another form of conflict, namely *feuds*, often for a blood revenge between families, is fought intermittently, which may extend over many generations. The hatreds of the groups are usually centered upon individuals, generally leaders or powerful men. Gangster warfare between rival racketeering gangs, in modern cities, also falls into this category. They have rival candidates for the status of "public enemy number one." Each is a vigilante organization "of the first water."

War. Although the settlement of grievances between persons by means of physical and armed combat has been outlawed the settlement of grievances between countries has not yet evolved that far. Here, differences are still settled by means of armed military forces, through the organized destruction of life and property, until one side surrenders. No longer can war be explained on the basis of a pugnacious instinct, and therefore, that it is inevitable. War is a social phenomenon and has its roots in complex social situations. The economic costs of modern wars are enormous. Elmer Davis figures the direct and measurable cost of World War I to America to be between fifty-two and fifty-seven billion dollars.[4] The immediate cost, mostly paid while the war was going on, was thirty-two billions. Veterans' relief, until it reaches a vanishing point about 1980, may total twenty or twenty-five billions according to Professor Clark.[5] We are told by *Fortune* magazine that "According to the best accountancy figures, it cost about $25,000 to kill a soldier during the World War."[6]

At the moment the United States is engaged in a gigantic National Defense program. Approximately $10,000,000,000 in defense contracts have now been awarded. The figures include $3,300,000,-000 for ships; $1,500,000,000 for construction of factory expansion and for housing; $1,500,000,000 for planes and parts; $600,000,000 for ammunition; $500,000,000 for guns, and $400,000,000 for trucks and tanks.[7]

Unifying Interactions

Many conflict situations are averted by a growing body of men who believe in equality and practice it as much as is reasonably pos-

[4] Elmer Davis, "Our Legacy from the World War," *Current History*, 35: 647, Feb., 1932.

[5] John Maurice Clark, *The Costs of the World War to the American People*, New Haven: Yale University Press, for the Carnegie Endowment for International Peace, Division of Economics and History, 1931, pp. 180–181.

[6] "Arms and the Men," *Fortune*, 9:53, March, 1934.

[7] Defense, Official bulletin of the National Defense Advisory Commission, Washington, D. C., January 7, 1941.

sible; by thinkers who abhor enduring social stratification, whether caused by birth, wealth, race, occupation or religion, inherited or otherwise acquired; and, by people who make sacrifices for the under-privileged and for those preyed upon. Social education, enlightened public opinion, social planning, greater adherence to the Bill of Rights, and social science are among the major factors that tend to weaken dogma, the "cake of custom," predestination, autocracy, suppression, segregation, and other undemocratic and disunifying practices in a dynamic culture. Various forms of mutually satisfactory and beneficial cooperative relationships have been advocated by utopianists, and attempted by social reformers through the ages. Space limits discussion to but a few of the more pragmatic ones and then only to their current manifestations.

Mutual Aid. From very early times men have banded together for mutual protection and self defense. Kropotkin contends that the mutual-aid activities of man are largely responsible for his gradual emergence from his animal-like existence and for his establishment of the great social institutions. He contends that

> new economical and social institutions, in so far as they were a creation of the masses, new ethical systems, and new religions, all have originated from the same source, and the ethical progress of our race, viewed in its broad lines, appears as a gradual extension of the mutual-aid principles, from the tribe to always larger and larger agglomerations, so as to finally embrace one day the whole of mankind, without respect to its divers creeds, languages, and races.[8]

Mutual helpfulness abounded everywhere among the early pioneers in this country. It manifested itself whenever a neighbor was sick, in trouble, or in need of assistance. Corn huskings, house and barn-raisings, and "bees" of various kinds caused neighbors to give their time and energies voluntarily and enthusiastically. Exchange of labor on farms or in house cleaning was not ingrained with thoughts of equating services.

In the more rural areas many evidences of mutual aid may still be observed, especially in times of disaster. On such occasions mutual aid cuts across such barriers as class, creed, or party, and exposes social unity. Out of impulses and practices of mutual aid and a sense of social responsibility grew the Co-operative Movement.

Cooperation. Such slogans as "United we stand, divided we

[8] Peter Kropotkin, *Mutual Aid: A Factor in Evolution*, Alfred A. Knopf, 1902, p. 168.

fall," "Each for all and all for each," "In union there is strength," and "if we don't hang together we'll hang separately" challenge the masses to the effectiveness of cooperative endeavors. Some form of cooperative relationship is essential in order to achieve "the greatest good to the greatest number." Cooperation may be defined as the working together of two or more persons or groups for the attainment of the same social values. This involves a "live and let live" relationship. It nurtures a live and help live formula.

One form of cooperative living has been realized in the voluntary formation of economic organizations functioning under the so-called "Rochdale" principles. The name "Rochdale" comes from the textile center in England where the principles were first evolved. In 1844, a group of 28 poverty-stricken flannel weavers rebelled against the conditions from which they suffered—unemployment, underemployment, exorbitant prices, debts, and adulteration of goods. They pooled their meager savings and formed the Rochdale Society of Equitable Pioneers and began to secure some of their necessities of life co-operatively. Their simple beginning, and the few simple principles under which a Rochdale cooperative functions, has served as a model for many thousands of successful cooperatives throughout the world.

The basic Rochdale principles are: (1) membership open to all; (2) democratic control—each member having one vote regardless of the number of shares he owns, and there is no proxy voting; (3) distribution of net surplus to members in proportion to their patronage; (4) limited rate of interest on members' share capital; (5) business for cash only; (6) business at market prices; (7) promotion of education in cooperation; and (8) political and religious neutrality. Major emphasis is placed upon the first four principles.

It is on the basis of these principles that many rural-electrification companies, oil and gas stations, stores, creameries, cheese factories, credit unions, grain elevators, department stores, livestock shipping associations, laundries, insurance companies, telephone companies, dormitories, boarding clubs, cafeterias, apartment houses, housing associations, hospitals, wholesale organizations, and scores of different types of farmers' buying and selling organizations are now operating in United States.[9]

The Rochdale principles virtually amount to a declaration of economic independence and of economic democracy. Open member-

[9] See "Consumer Cooperatives," *Fortune*, 15: 133–146, March, 1937.

ship means a classless society. Membership cannot be refused because of race, color or creed. Thus class hatred is undermined. It rejects vested interests for itself or for any class in society. Human values are placed above property values by giving the vote to the member rather than to the share of stock. Rewarding patronage rather than investment enables the masses to secure more of the necessities of life than is possible under a system where the profits go to outside stockholders, officers, managers, and advertising. Rochdale cooperatives are self-reliant and ask no subsidies from the government, nor do they demand tariff protection. Non-proxy voting prevents power from being concentrated in a few persons who may be tempted to act dictatorially.

The immediate purpose of cooperatives, especially consumers' cooperatives is economic:

> to make the pennies go farther, to eliminate the extra cost entailed by extravegent advertising and by high pressure salesmanship, to handle only commodities of known good quality, and to fill an increasing number of human wants on a non profit basis. Like the original Pioneers' Society, the present-day movement also has a far-reaching social philosophy. Its final aim is to supply every need of life, social and economic, without profit and by united effort.[10]

Not all cooperatives are Rochdale cooperatives, not even some that may be known by that name. Only those adhering to the basic Rochdale principles are considered in the present discussion. From Great Britain, where the cooperative movement now embraces in its membership seven million people, representing more than one-half of the families of England and Scotland, it "has spread to Sweden to control the national economy; to Denmark to remake the nation; to Finland to give to them something that has become an integral part of the Finnish nation."[11] It is estimated that a few years ago the cooperatives did about 25 per cent of the total retail trade in Finland, 15 per cent in England, and likewise in Denmark, and 10 per cent in Sweden. The percentage of families in each country who are members of cooperatives is considerably higher than that indicated by the above figures as it is the relatively poor lower middle class who tend to belong.

[10] Florence E. Parker, *Consumers' Cooperation in the United States, 1936*, Washington, D. C.: U. S. Dept. of Labor, Bur. of Labor Statistics, Bulletin No. 659, August, 1938, p. 2.

[11] Bertram B. Fowler, "The Masses Go into Big Business," *Scribners*, 99: 195, April, 1936.

In the United States, cooperative marketing of agricultural products is a much better established institution than consumers' cooperatives. Stokdyk states that in the 1937–38 marketing season approximately two and one-half million families sold more than two billion dollars worth of agricultural products through 8,300 cooperative marketing associations.[12] Patronage dividends returned by marketing associations is considerable, although many cooperatives have a policy of rendering services as near cost as possible, and frequently part of the earnings are retained to build up investments. Nevertheless, compilations by Stokdyk indicate that patronage dividends in 1936 by 2639 marketing associations totaled over seventeen million dollars.[13]

The *Credit Union* movement also provides training in cooperation. Credit unions, often referred to as "The Peoples' Banks," may be said to have started in Massachusetts in 1909. Edward A. Filene, a Boston merchant, played a leading role in the development of credit unions in that State. There are now nearly 9,000 chartered unions in the United States, with two and one-half million members, with total deposits of forty-three million, and loans outstanding of thirty-seven million—the average being $92.[14] These figures serve as a sort of index of economic cooperation. The federal government, 42 states and the District of Columbia now have laws governing the formation of credit unions. The federal Credit Union Act was passed in 1934 and since its passage more than 4000 units have been established under federal laws. The so-called "Wall Street Crash" of 1929, the high interest rates per year charged by illegal lenders— 120 to 540 per cent per year on small loans[15]—and relatively high interest rates charged by licensed small loan companies, and credit agencies, have indirectly promoted the phenomenal growth of credit unions in United States.

A credit union is composed of a number of people having some common bond, such as working in the same factory, office, or firm, being members of the same church or association, or living in the same neighborhood. Credit unions are cooperative associations

[12] E. A. Stokdyk, "Cooperative Marketing by Farmers," *1940 Yearbook of Agriculture*, Washington, D. C.: Government Printing Office, 1940, p. 684.

[13] *Ibid.*, p. 688.

[14] Maxwell S. Stewart, *Credit Unions—The Peoples' Banks*, Public Affairs Pamphlet No. 50, New York: Public Affairs Committee, Inc., 1940, pp. 8, 9.

[15] See *Loan Sharks and Their Victims*, Public Affairs Pamphlet, No. 39, 1940.

whose essential function is the supplying of credit. Their primary function is to provide loans to members, when in need, usually at one per cent per month, and secondly, to provide the ordinary person with means of encouraging savings. They are run by their members and are thoroughly democratic, consequently, relatively unifying.

An increasing number of people look upon cooperation as a means of stretching their income on the one hand, and as the true democratic answer to what they consider injustices on the other. James P. Warbasse, who founded the Cooperative League of the United States of America, said that the cooperative movement already includes 71 million members in some 41 countries.

Wisconsin has incorporated the teaching of cooperation in her course of study. In 1935 the Wisconsin legislature passed an amendment to her statutes, requiring the giving of courses in agricultural and consumers' cooperation throughout the public schools of that State from the State University downward. Furthermore, from now on no certificates are to be granted for the teaching of courses in economics, the social studies, or agriculture unless the applicant's course of training has included the subject of cooperation.

Conciliation. An industrial society, such as ours, is continually threatened with strikes, especially during periods of rising prices. The work of conciliation is becoming more and more concerned with the prevention of threatened strikes. The work of the Conciliation Service of the United States Department of Labor was considerably expanded as a result of various developments under the N.R.A. Department of Labor conciliators work on the principle that by bringing the parties in dispute together for a frank discussion of the points at issue satisfactory solution of the problem may be attained without resort to a strike or stoppage of work. During the past three years 996 threatened strikes involving 633,144 workers have been prevented, saving approximately twelve million days of work and wages.[16]

Frequently, the general public is the chief sufferer from industrial strife. This is particularly true when strikes occur in public utilities. Industrial conflicts tend to disrupt equanimity of community life. Racial, national, religious, educational and political "sores" in local communities may be re-opened and friendships shattered. Conciliation and mediation are unifying factors.

[16] *Twenty-eighth Annual Report* of the United States Secretary of Labor, 1940, p. 10.

Mediation. Sometimes no efforts of conciliation are attempted, or if undertaken, they may fail, and conflict of some form, may ensue. In industry it commonly takes the form of a strike. The principal national agency to deal with labor disputes at present is the National Labor Relations Board, created in June, 1934. From time to time special boards are created as the National Steel Labor Relations Board, the Textile Relations Board, the National Longshoremens' Labor Board, and the Petroleum Labor Policy Board.

For the disposition of railroad labor disputes there is the National Mediation Board, created in 1934, which cooperates in the adjustment of disputes with the National Railroad Adjustment Board, also created in 1934. The latter is composed of 18 representatives of the carriers and 18 representatives of employees.

Assimilation. The fusion of two or more persons or groups with dissimilar cultures and values into a we-group constitutes the essence of assimilation. The final stage in the assimilative process is intimate participation and identification. The concept of assimilation is most often employed in connection with the integration of foreigners in our midst. The term is equally applicable to persons or groups moving from one region to another, one community to another, one neighborhood to another within the same community, or from one social stratum to another. All such movements, whether horizontal or vertical, necessitate a realignment of social values, and result in a new form of unification.

There are other forms of interactions that also tend to induce social unity. However, innumerable variables, such as those of heredity, geographic environment, social heritage and conditioning, and group affiliations, place limitations on unity.

We sum up the points of the chapter as follows:

I. Social forces are both unifying and dissociating.
   A. Unifying forces may be either compulsive or attractive.
   B. Dissociating forces may be either expulsive or distractive.
   C. In social control attempts are made usually to strengthen social unity and to weaken social disunity.
   D. Rapid social changes have a tendency to decrease attractive and compulsive forces and to increase the distractive and expulsive forces.

II. Processes of social interactions vary with a group's social values
   A. Some social interactions may be more disunifying than unifying, as
      1. Competition, conflict, differentiation, stratification.

B. Some social interactions may be more unifying than disunifying, as
1. Mutual aid, cooperation, conciliation, mediation,
assimilation.
a. These are vitalized by tolerance, sympathy,
social education, democratic practices.
b. Increasing economic inter-dependence, and
faith in democracy are accelerating the
effectiveness of certain unifying processes.
(1) Rochdale cooperatives are restoring the
primary group relationships that
urbanization has in some measure
destroyed.

SELECTED REFERENCES

The American Institute of Cooperation, *American Cooperation, 1940,* Washington, D. C.: The American Institute of Cooperation, 1940.—A collection of
118 papers comprising the sixteenth summer session of this Institute. An
excellent collection on the practical side of agricultural cooperation, more
particularly the cooperative's use of business principles; also much on the
philosophy of cooperation.
Coady, M. M., *Masters of Their Own Destiny,* New York: Harper, 1939.—A remarkable account of the accomplishments of Fathers Tompkins and Coady
and their colleagues of St. Xavier University at Antigonish in developing
lay leadership and collective action.
Daniels, John, *Cooperation—An American Way,* New York: Covici-Friede, 1938.
—An excellent portrayal of the cooperative unit as a sort of re-birth of the
old-fashioned town-meeting in a new form to meet new conditions. Cooperation is viewed as a first-rate training school in the principles and practices of democracy.
Fowler, Bertram B., *The Lord Helps Those . . .* New York: The Vanguard
Press, 1938.—An interestingly written account of the many easy and democratic ways in which the people of Nova Scotia are solving their problems
through cooperation.
The Inquiry, *Community Conflict,* New York: The Inquiry, 1929.—An interesting collection and analyses of case studies in community conflict situations,
factors that induced them, how they might have been averted, and how steps
of adjustment were made.
May, Mark A., and Leonard W. Doob, *Competition and Cooperation,* New York:
Social Science Research Council, 1937.—This is a scholarly report of the
Sub-Committee on Competitive-Cooperative Habits, of the Committee on
Personality and Culture. Studies in these fields are classified under experi-
mental, sociological, anthropological, and life history approaches and criti-
cally analyzed. Many interesting problems for further study are suggested.
North, Cecil N., *Social Differentiation,* Chapel Hill: The University of North
Carolina Press, 1926.—By far the most exhaustive treatment of the nature

and kinds of social differences and their relations to social welfare, progress and control.

Sanderson, Dwight, *Leadership for Rural Life*, New York: Association Press, 1940.—A timely account of the role of the leader and its evolution in the group and its importance in democratic organization.

Seldes, George, *You Can't Do That*, New York: Modern Age Books, 1938.— Presents a vast array of contemporary examples of ways in which some social forces produce inequalities. It challenges disciples of democracy to action.

Smith, W. C. *Americans in the Making*, New York: D. Appleton-Century Co., 1939.—A recent scholarly work in which social forces and processes are seen in their application in the minds of immigrants. Dr. Smith is author of ''Communication,'' the next chapter in the present book.

Thomas, W. I., and F. Znaniecki, *The Polish Peasant in Europe and America*, New York: Alfred A. Knopf, 1927.—An outstanding book of the problems of culture conflict, accommodation, and assimilation which immigrants encounter in passing from one culture pattern to another.

CHAPTER 12

COMMUNICATION

BY W. C. SMITH, PH.D.

Head of the Department of Sociology, Linfield College,
McMinnville, Oregon

INTRODUCTION

The preceding chapter set forth as social processes several classifications of interaction. As a matter of fact, group life is made up of interaction, for without it a number of men, even though huddled closely together, would be a mere collection or aggregate. According to Park and Burgess, "Society exists wherever several individuals are in reciprocal relationship where they are influencing each other."[1] It is not possible to be a real member of a group unless one participates in a meaningful way in its common activities. These relationships cannot be uni-directional but are based on a two-way movement which involves mutual modification. It is an interplay and interstimulation of personalities upon one another in such a way that they are reciprocally affected. If a child did not interact with his fellows, he would grow to maturity—provided that were possible—without language, ideas, beliefs, or any of the sentiments common to humanity, and he would achieve no personality and accumulate no cultural heritage. Those qualities which have their origin in and derive their meaning from associational life would be entirely lacking. Interaction, then, is the basic social process in the development of human nature, and the medium through which this takes place is communication.

Animal Utterances Are Unreflective Responses

Animals interact and communicate with each other. They respond to touch, to postures or visible movements, to cries, grunts, or other vocal utterances. Ants convey messages to their comrades by the touch of the antennae, dogs by the wagging of their tails, and geese by their calls. While various kinds of sounds may be detected, such as mating calls, cries of distress, and danger alarms, which pro-

[1] Robert E. Park and Ernest W. Burgess, *Introduction to the Science of Sociology*, University of Chicago Press, 1924, p. 348. Cf. pp. 339–434.

duce definite reactions in others of their kind, we may not conclude that any animal decided to emit a particular sound but that it was rather an involuntary expression of emotion rather than a specific communication. The particular utterance was unreflective, denotative behavior, which brought an immediate response in the animals that heard it but it did not convey any connotative meaning. The hen, at the sight of a hawk, utters an excited cry and her brood comes flocking to her. Probably this is not a designed warning at all, but merely a means of giving release to her pent-up fears. She does not describe the hawk or the danger. It is highly improbable that a dog can bark in tones that indicate "cat" or "polecat" as the case may be. According to Mead, animals indicate without signifying.[2] The hen pecks at the angleworm and thus directly, though without characterization, indicates it to her chicks. She is not calling attention to any significant attributes or qualities of the worm.

Animals Have No True Language

Animals have a rudimentary form of communication but it is not language in the true sense. Intent to signify is basic to language. A vocal utterance does not become language until it has a meaning. In a limited measure animals have vocal and gesture habits in their specific cries of distress, of sex desire, or the hen's jubilation at the find of an unusually juicy worm. But animals have not been able to develop a system of sounds as symbols of objects, actions, ideas, emotions by means of which they might communicate with other members of the herd or flock above a rudimentary level. They may announce emotional states and simple wants but they cannot describe objects or present abstract ideas.[3]

Signaling acts are means of communication, but they are not true language. The responses of animals to cries are not answers to connotative symbols. Kittens on a farm soon learn to run ahead of the farmer when he picks up a milk pail and sets out for the dairy barn. They have learned to associate the pail with the stream of warm milk squirted into their mouths in the process of milking.[4]

[2] George Herbert Mead, "The Significant Symbol," *Journal of Philosophy*, XIX (1922), p. 160.

[3] Cf. E. T. Hiller, *Principles of Sociology*, New York: Harper and Brothers, 1933, pp. 92–93.

[4] Cf. John Dewey, *Experience and Nature*, Chicago: Open Court Publishing Co., 1925, pp. 177–78.

COMMUNICATION OF MAN

Man versus Animal

The differential characteristic which distinguishes man from the lower animals is his mental life and its products. He has a superior brain which gives him a decided advantage in his ability to think. But this physical organ alone would give slight advantage over that of the lower animals were it not for the fact of his peculiar ability to communicate with his fellow beings through the instrumentality of language with meanings. Man is the only user of connotative language. He alone has the means with which to transmit ideas and scientific information. It is not uncommon to find animals that have new and useful ideas which are the raw materials for culture building. They display considerable intelligence in the solution of problems, but man is the only creature who can communicate his brilliant insights to his fellow men by means of symbolic description.

According to Köhler, a chimpanzee inserted a stick into the end of a larger hollow one and thus with the elongated double stick was able to pull food into the cage which was beyond the reach of either shorter stick.[5] This was tool-making. But the ape could not write a research article giving a description of his experiments with the bamboo sticks so other apes could get the idea and carry it out without the necessity of going through the same process of trial and error.

Levels of Communication

According to Park and Burgess, communication takes place on three levels: (1) that of the senses; (2) the emotions; and (3) sentiments and ideas.[6]

The Sense Basis. We perceive our fellow men through the medium of the senses and sociologically the eye is the most significant sense organ. Communication is carried on by mutual glances and these penetrate far beyond mere observation. A maiden need not always utter words, for the young swain can read her intentions by looking her in the eye. Furthermore, she may say one thing with her tongue while her eyes tell a different and more truthful story.

As one person endeavors to fathom the thoughts of another, he

---

[5] Wolfgang Köhler, *The Mentality of Apes*, New York: Harcourt, Brace and Co., 1927, p. 127. Cf. pp. 99–172, "The Making of Implements."

[6] Park and Burgess, *op. cit.*, pp. 342, 356–84.

discloses his own inner self through his own eyes. The only way we ever really see other persons is when they see us—the glances are mutual and both are equally revelatory. When we are ashamed we look down to prevent others from seeing us and thus comprehending the full depth of our embarrassment.

Modern life is essentially based on sight, largely to the neglect of the other senses. The sense of smell is used far less and we have comparatively few words to describe odors. Perfumes are used, but few persons can distinguish delicate gradations. In some groups, to be sure, the sense of smell receives more attention. W. H. Hudson[7] tells of the Mosquito Indians in South America who smell each other's cheeks in demonstrations of affection. He also wrote of a boy who, born blind, deaf, and dumb, was dependent on his sense of smell. He could detect the presence of a stranger in a room and would form an estimate of him on the basis of smell.

This suggests, at least, that the sense of smell may be a more important factor than we realize in our contacts with others. To what extent is it responsible for the development of dislikes and prejudices? To what extent do the senses of smell and touch enter into racial antagonisms?

Extra-sensory Perception. It has been customary to state dogmatically that our minds are geared to the sense organs and that nothing enters the mind except through the medium of the five senses. According to Jules Romains, "Experiments place beyond doubt the existence in man of a *paroptic function*, that is, of a function of visual perception of exterior objects (color and form), without the intervention of the ordinary mechanism of vision through the eyes."[8] It is commonly stated that blind people develop keener touch, smell, and hearing. Romains asks if it may not be extraretinal vision. According to Alexis Carrel, some persons endowed with the powers of clairvoyance and telepathy "grasp the secret thoughts of other individuals without using their sense organs."[9] The experiments in extra-sensory perception (called "para-psychol-

[7] *A Hind in Richmond Park,* New York: E. P. Dutton and Co., 1923, pp. 74–91.

[8] Jules Romains, *Eyeless Sight: A Study of Extra-Retinal Vision and the Paroptic Sense,* Translated by C. K. Ogden, New York: G. P. Putnam's Sons, 1924, p. 203.

[9] Alexis Carrel, *Man the Unknown,* New York: Harper and Brothers, 1933, p. 124.

ogy'') at Duke University are, at least, reminding us to be open-minded on the question.[10]

The Emotional Basis. Interaction on the emotional level is important because emotions are aroused when some conflict is going on, when some wish has been frustrated.

Blushing is a peculiarly human mode of expression. It is intimately connected with self-consciousness and indicates confusion, shame, or modesty. If a person spills coffee on the white linen of the banquet table he is likely to blush—he feels uncomfortable and his color indicates to others his predicament. Praise or blame frequently produce blushes. Since small children pay less heed to the reactions of other people, they blush less readily than the sensitive adolescents. The blush is involuntary and because of that is seriously limited as a means of communication. If one could devise a regular code of blushes and could induce them at will, then it would be possible to communicate readily in this way.

The Ideational Level. Interaction on the sensory and emotional levels is confined to the communication of feelings and attitudes. These forms are common both to animals and to man. Interaction on the ideational level is man's great achievement. This makes possible cooperative thinking. If a man goes to London and gets a new idea, he can return to Goose Creek and communicate it to his fellow citizens who may be stimulated to greater efforts by the new notion. A circus animal may be trained to perform feats that seem quite human, but he cannot be turned loose in the jungle to communicate his acquired skill to the other animals of his kind. While the writer had charge of a school in the hills of India, he organized a boy's chorus. When school closed in the spring the boys scattered to their several villages. When the new term opened in the fall, the boys returned and brought new pupils to whom they had already taught the chorus parts suited to their voices.

When ideas are to be transmitted, means other than sensory perceptions and emotional expressions are necessary. Language is the medium for the communication of thoughts and sentiments.

Language Is a System of Symbols

Language is distinctively the human means of communication. It is more than the alarm cry of animals which is a mere general

---

[10] Cf. J. B. Rhine, *New Frontiers of the Mind,* New York: Farrar and Rinehart, 1937; J. G. Pratt, J. B. Rhine and others, *Extra-Sensory Perception After Sixty Years,* New York: Henry Holt and Co., 1940.

proclamation of danger without any specific or discriminating details. Human speech can specify and analyze the situation. Instead of merely shouting "Fire" in the theatre it is possible to announce, "There is a fire on the stage and the side exit is closed."

Language is any conventionalized system of voluntarily produced signs or symbols, be they gestures, sounds, or written characters, for the communication of sentiments and ideas. A language symbol is of such a character that both the recipient and the person using it react to it in the same way. Anything which fits this description becomes language and the precise nature of the symbols is of no consequence, provided that both communicating parties understand them. Intrinsically there is no reason why the concept *horse* should stand for a certain class of objects, except that the English-speaking peoples have adopted that usage. If a child playing with a crayon should by accident scratch the word CAT on the floor, that would not be language because it has no meaning for him and he does not react to it as we do.

Language undoubtedly is man's greatest invention. It enables him to respond to mere symbolic stimuli, or words which have acquired certain meanings, and thus to reproduce the behavior of others without the necessity of seeing them perform. The football coach may read the description of a play and then adopt it for his team without seeing it in action.

Gestures. It is probable that primitive men at first carried on communication by means of gestures or sign language. Gesture language, however, has serious limitations. Watching gestures requires closer attention of the eyes than hearing does of the ears. Furthermore, when one makes gestures, usually his whole body is devoted to that activity. One may use vocal speech, however, while engaged in some other occupation. Articulate speech is so much more flexible than gesture that the latter is rarely used as a sole means of communication.

Vocal Speech. Speech, or oral language, developed early in man's career. If man was actually human when speech came into use, with this acquisition he moved forward more rapidly in his achievement of humanity, for he could then begin to accumulate a social heritage.[11] In the development of vocal language a certain sound was, perhaps by mere accident, associated with a particular

[11] Cf. Charles Horton Cooley, *Social Organization*, New York: Charles Scribner's Sons, 1913, pp. 70–72.

object and after being repeated by others until it was gradually adopted, it came to stand in the place of the object itself and the object was recalled by the verbal sign. The sound, or word, then became the symbol for the object. The word *buffalo* immediately conjures up a mental image of a certain class of animals and it is not necessary to see the object itself. Furthermore, words are subjective equivalents which stimulate appropriate behavior with almost the same effectiveness as the objects themselves. If the words *chocolate bonbon* are spoken, they will have almost the same effect as showing a box containing the real sweets. The symbol, however, cannot be a complete substitute—a real kiss is better than the word, even though it be repeated a hundred times. Mere vocalizations are of no particular importance, but they become significant when they have meanings. When the vocal symbol thus stands for the object itself, it becomes possible to think in concepts rather than in percepts alone, and this is a great advance.

Writing. With the achievement of vocal language, man could communicate with all within hearing distance, in addition to which signalling devices were invented, such as the drum, by means of which sound could be carried farther than the unaided voice and certain contrivances were also developed which could be seen even beyond the range of hearing. But when writing was invented, the amplitude of communication was greatly extended both spatially and temporally. Through writing it became possible to store and preserve language symbols so that they could be transmitted over vast reaches of space and through long periods of time. Written orders from the Secretary of State at the nation's capital direct the movements of consuls in Rangoon, Singapore, and Johannesburg, while the Mosaic code still exerts control over human thought and action after the passage of many centuries.

When the written symbol is stored,[12] it possesses the power of stimulating identical symbolic behavior in another, even though separated widely both in time and space from the original writer.

Any symbol which is sufficiently standardized and effective as a stimulus to release or reinstate certain kinds of behavior may be considered a stored symbol. Various forms of art, musical compositions, photographs, films, or archaeological objects become depositories of stored meaning which can stimulate certain forms of be-

12 Cf. L. L. Bernard, *Social Psychology*, New York: Henry Holt and Co., 1926, pp. 152–55 on the storage of symbols.

havior. A musician sets before himself a sheet with certain marks and that releases for us the compositions of Handel, Bach, or Beethoven.

While primitive man handed on from generation to generation much of his wisdom in the form of folklore by word of mouth and in this way began the accumulation of a social heritage, yet the wise men of that day could not carry in their memories a sufficient fund of information to enable them to progress far in the building of a civilization. The preliterate genius might think big thoughts but at his death there would be a reversion to the original situation for want of a means of preserving his ideas. The secret of civilization rests not so much in the isolated efforts of individuals as in the transmission of these efforts from generation to generation. It was only when it became possible to store symbols so that they could release responses in others that civilization became possible. Through the use of writing no knowledge of use to man need be lost and the accumulations may be stored for use hundreds of years in the future. Without writing no group has advanced beyond the status of barbarism. H. G. Wells has attributed the slow development of Chinese civilization to the complicated system of writing which could be mastered only by a few.[13]

Writing has developed through several stages. At first realistic pictures were used to depict actual objects and events. Such picture-writings, however, are more nearly like monuments for preserving occasions against the flight of time than written messages. Gradually pictures come into use to represent ideas—a bird signifying rapidity; a fox, cunning; three suns under the sky, three days. This was idea-writing or ideography. At first the pictures were similar to those which merely served to recall the pictured objects, but by degrees they became conventionalized so that a few simple lines would represent the object.

The next step, and a very important one, was the representation of sounds rather than ideas by symbols as in the familiar rebus. A tin can, for example, may stand for the verb *can* while several cans may be used for the abbreviation of Kansas, namely *Kans.* In this the pictures do not stand for their meanings but merely for their sounds, and this is true phonetic writing, crude though it may be.

[13] Cf. E. T. Hiller, *Principles of Sociology*, New York: Harper and Brothers, 1933, p. 134. It may be interesting to observe the effect of the simplified system of writing which was recently introduced in an effort to raise standards of literacy among the Chinese.

This is a big step in advance since it shifts the basis of writing from portraiture to phonetics. At first the symbol represented the sound of a whole word, then gradually changed to represent a syllable, and finally the simplest sound, the letter.

Phonetic writing, particularly when it reached the alphabetized stage, was of tremendous importance because of its flexibility and adaptability. Since these symbols may be united in a practically unlimited variety of combinations, it becomes possible to express any idea, no matter how abstract. The significance of alphabetic communication is attested by the fact that coincident with its use came the greatest advance in science, law, literature, and commerce.

Writing and Magic. When one considers the significance of writing, it must impress him as being wonderful. Preliterates have been awed by the civilized man's writing and they have been dumbfounded by his magical marks. D. Crantz reports on the Greenlanders:

> In the beginning of their acquaintance with the Europeans, they were so frightened at the speaking paper that they did not dare to carry a letter from one to another, or to touch a book, because they believed it must be conjuration, that one man could tell the thoughts of another, by a few black scrawls on white paper. They also seriously thought that when a minister read God's commandments to them he surely must have heard the voice first out of the book.[14]

Printing. Printing, particularly with moveable type, gave writing wide diffusion and extended communication. This enabled large numbers of people over a wide area to have access to information which hitherto had been restricted to a few. Printing cheapened the process of recording symbols and thus brought knowledge within reach of the common people. It brought thinkers in all parts of the world into contact with each other and thus promoted the dissemination of existent knowledge and stimulated the search for new truths. The printed page tended to reduce the number of confusing dialects and to standardize national languages which could be used over wider areas. It thus scattered unsettling suggestions far and wide and stimulated a democratic way of life. Political and religious reformers used this new instrumentality to mould public opinion in support of their several causes.

[14] Lucien Levy-Bruhl, *Primitive Mentality,* London: George Allen and Unwin, Ltd., 1923, p. 370.

Language and Thought

Many thinkers have asserted that true thought, in contradistinction to mere perception, becomes possible only when we can attach names to the objects of our thinking. On the basis of his extensive studies of language, Max Müller reached the conclusion that there could be no reason without language and no language could develop without reason. Furthermore, without the capacity to reason, man would be a mere animal. Marett is in close agreement when he states: "If language is a creation of the intellect, yet hardly less fundamentally is the intellect a creation of language."[15] According to Bawden, "Man is *homo sapiens*, the thinking animal because he is the speaking animal; brutes are the dumb animals."[16]

Even the most cursory consideration makes it evident that there is a close relationship between language and thought. We may state with assurance that any new idea remains quite vague in the thinker's mind until he has expressed it in words either uttered or internal.[17] But thought without words is not infrequent. We note the growth of language by the adoption of new words. There must certainly be some thinking before the new words are adopted, but most assuredly it is clearer with them. Without words in which to embody ideas, they would remain embryonic. Words make it possible to bring forth ideas as true thought, which may then be nourished to full status.[18]

The effect of language on thought may be noted in the scientific fields. Although the physicists and other scientists had some 200,000 words available in *Webster's Dictionary*, they developed a special terminology and they have made progress in their fields in direct proportion to their development of suitable concepts. Popular terms were too lacking in preciseness to make for close thinking. Words are more than mere devices for communicating ideas; they are tools which aid in the accumulation of knowledge.[19]

[15] R. R. Marett, *Anthropology*, New York: Henry Holt and Company, 1911, p. 130.

[16] H. H. Bawden, "The Evolution of Behavior," *Psychological Review*, Vol. XXVI, 1919, p. 263.

[17] Cf. Louis H. Gray, *Foundations of Language*, New York: The Macmillan Company, 1939, p. 95.

[18] Cf. Earle Edward Eubank, *The Concepts of Sociology*, Boston: D. C. Heath and Co., 1932, p. 14.

[19] George A. Lundberg, *Foundations of Sociology*, New York: The Macmillan Company, 1939, p. 243.

Language an Economizer of Effort

Language is highly significant in that it shortens the process of coming into possession of the wisdom of past generations. It enables one to use the accumulated ideas of his predecessors, thus rendering it unnecessary to repeat all the experiences of his ancestors. Since he has access to the records of their successes and failures, he need not go through the same long series of trials and errors. If each generation had to start evolving afresh its entire fund of practices, all the energies of the race would be expended in repeating the first faltering steps. By means of writing, each generation may record its own experiences, its inventions, its totality of acquired wisdom and pass it on to succeeding generations so that each may proceed from the point already reached. Every individual in this way falls heir to all the treasure stores of the past ages and may begin to build his career upon that foundation.

A person may through the trial and error process attempt to find the preferable course of action. By means of language, however, he may carry on a conversation with himself and thus make a transfer from overt trial and error to a symbolic trial and error on the basis of words. Gradually the whole problem will be solved internally without the use of gestures or verbalizations. He comes to *think* out his solution. An engineer does not have to test a bridge by the laborious, expensive, and dangerous procedure of loading it with enough locomotives to make it collapse—he can make the test symbolically through the use of mathematical calculations.[20]

Speech, furthermore, is more economical than total overt response. It is both rapid and explicit. On January 15, 1935, the sidewalks of Liberty, Missouri, were ice-covered and slippery. It is possible through words to convey that idea to others now without going out and sprawling oneself full length on the sidewalk.

Both speaking and writing become means of vicarious experience which permits us to acquire ideas at second hand. We may learn from the activities and experiences of others and thus avoid much fumbling around. Words of counsel at a luncheon table did not eliminate all errors nor remove all traces of awkwardness, but through the symbolizations of language the process of trial and error was shortened as the writer was learning to drive an automobile.

[20] Cf. Bernard, *op. cit.*, pp. 144–51.

COMMUNICATION AND SOCIETAL LIFE

Language as a Bond of Unity

A Language Unites Those Using It. "Of all bonds which unite men, none other is so strong as language," wrote D. G. Brinton.[21] Since its roots are so deeply embedded in the emotions, a definite bond of sympathy is created between the users of the same speech. Inasmuch as language is the principal medium of expression through which men convey not only factual information, but feelings, emotions, and sentiments, it becomes apparent that there is nothing else which can so readily establish a community of feeling with others, while the lack of a common speech sets up barriers against close comradeship. During the writer's residence in India where he heard on every hand the babble of strange tongues, and even the English of the Englishman with its different inflection, it was music to his ears to hear some one speak English with the familiar American accent. Immediately on hearing the language of the homeland, rapport was established and it was not necessary to talk about the weather or go through some other verbal sparring in order to find common ground on which to converse. A common speech makes for social solidarity while misunderstanding and strife are concomitants of language divergences.

Latin, the universal language in the Middle Ages, was an important factor in the development and maintenance of the unity of the Catholic Church, but the rise of folk literature in many vernaculars had a disorganizing effect. Scientists and religious leaders have advocated the establishment of a universal or international language, but they have encountered stiff opposition. Volapuk, Esperanto, Ido, Iala, Kosmos, Myrana, Spelm, Universala, Occidental, and Novial are such languages. A chauvinistic nationalism which has increased greatly since the World War has opposed the development of an international language because it would tend to dissolve the antagonisms on which a rabid nationalism nourishes. A universal medium of communication would make for an international mindedness and that does not accord with the provincial outlook of most politicians. Facility of communication permits contacts and fusion of minds and tends to mould all the communicants into a moral whole. It tends to bring mankind together in ever widening circles of understanding and sympathy and to enlarge the

[21] *Basis of Social Relations*, New York: G. P. Putnam's Sons, 1902, p. 164.

outreach of kindly feeling. On the other hand, an international language might become a useful tool for selfish propagandists to stir up strife between nations.[22]

Undoubtedly the most important bond of nationality is that of language. The nationalist movements in Europe since the latter part of the eighteenth century have been tied to language. Invariably a linguistic revival has beeen the prelude to each and every one. This held true in Wales, Norway, Denmark, Ireland, and in most of the minor nationalities of Europe, particularly in case of those which were oppressed. Nationality sentiments have their roots in memories that cling to the common possessions of the people such as the land, religion, and language, but language in particular. A Welsh national song expresses this sentiment thus: "If the enemy has ravished the Land of Wales, the Language of Wales is as living as ever."[23] Patriots have capitalized on this sentiment. When they have sought to revive the national consciousness among their peoples, they have sought to purify the vernacular and purge it of all foreign idioms.[24]

The social history of a group is preserved in its language. Because of the intimate relationship between group experience and language, people tend to cling tenaciously to their vernaculars. Under oppression, and particularly in attempts to denationalize a group, the folk speech has been retained with a tenacity akin to religious fervor.[25] The modern Greeks afford a pointed example of a group that held together through centuries of domination and oppression by the Turks. Even though composed of heterogeneous racial elements to which were added other divisive factors, the group had sufficient coherence to throw off the foreign yoke and re-establish an independent government. Even the intolerable Turkish rule could not destroy the Greek nationality. Two factors—religion and language—formed a nucleus of sympathetic feeling sufficient to preserve the identity of the group.[26] The studies of Leon

[22] Cf. Arthur James Todd, *Theories of Social Progress*, New York: The Macmillan Company, 1918, pp. 407–410.

[23] Daniel J. Williams, *The Welsh of Columbus, Ohio*, Oskosh, Wis., 1913, p. 108.

[24] Cf. Robert E. Park, *The Immigrant Press and Its Control*, Harper and Brothers, New York, 1922, pp. 33–42.

[25] Cf. W. I. Thomas. "The Prussian-Polish Situation: an Experiment in Assimilation," *American Journal of Sociology*, Vol. XIX, 1913–1914, pp. 624–39.

[26] Henry Pratt Fairchild, *General Sociology*, New York: John Wiley and Sons, 1934, p. 39.

Dominian[27] show the difficulties which have arisen because language frontiers have been ignored in drawing political boundaries in Europe.

Language Excludes Outsiders. While language unites a group it also excludes outsiders. To have a feeling of "outside-ness" one needs only travel in a land where he does not understand the speech and where his own is not understood.[28] The reactions of the so-called "heathen" towards missionaries is illuminating. Missionaries who learn the vernaculars well are far better accepted than those who do not. When they say of the foreigner that "he speaks like a native," he has made a place for himself. The one who does not value the language highly enough to master it is given only a grudging entrée into their life.

The expression "universes of discourse" indicate how persons and groups are both united and separated because of media of communication. Not all share equally the current ideas because they do not have equal opportunities to communicate. Language handicaps tend to isolate and restrict participation in the thought life of the day. Darsie's study of Japanese children in California showed a retardation in subjects where the language factor was important.[29] Children of educated parents have larger vocabularies than those of uneducated parents and, other things being equal, can make more rapid progress in school.

Occupational groups such as the cowboy, the criminal,[30] the lumber-jack, the miner, the plumber, the sailor, the soldier, the waitress have their own special vocabularies. Some, like the masons

[27] *The Frontiers of Language and Nationality in Europe,* New York: Henry Holt and Company, 1917.

[28] Some years ago the writer and another American were making a tour in a hill district of northeast India. One evening we stopped at a government rest-house and tried to secure supplies for our party. Five languages were available in our group—English, Swedish, Assamese, Angami, and Ao Naga—but still we could not make the care-taker understand. Finally a Nepali road worker, a foreigner in the area, arrived on the scene and saved the day. The other American, the leader of our party, addressed me in English, I translated that into Ao Naga, then my *syce* (pony boy) translated that into Assamese and the Nepali translated it into Eastern Angami, the language of the care-taker—and we secured our supplies.

[29] M. L. Darsie, "The Mental Capacity of American-Born Japanese Children," *Comparative Psychology Monographs,* Vol. III, No. 15, p. 56.

[30] Cf. E. H. Sutherland, *The Professional Thief,* Chicago: University of Chicago Press, 1937, pp. 235–43.

and tinkers reported by A. T. Sinclair,[31] have secret languages. The American hobo, too, has a rich vocabulary.[32] Families have their own pet words and expressions which are not understood by outsiders. College groups have their slang and their special vocabularies. Marked differences in speech characterize the several social classes in the stratified societies of Europe. In fact, language is quite generally a prime tool of exhibitionism. The carefully chosen words and the distinct enunciation are earmarks of stratification. One of the reasons why the doting father sends his daughter to finishing school is to polish her speech so that she may rise on the social ladder. The slightest indication of billingsgate is a severe handicap in connection with pretensions to superiority.

Communication and Social Organization

Communication Basic to a Common Life. Communication is fundamental in social life. According to Dewey,

> Society not only continues to exist *by* transmission, *by* communication, but it may fairly be said to exist *in* transmission, *in* communication. . . . Men live in a community in virtue of the things which they have in common; and communication is the way in which they come to possess things in common.[33]

Size and Organization of Groups Affected by Communication. Since a group is constituted of interacting individuals, the methods of communication affect both the size and the organization of groups and communities. Men must understand each other, if there is to be any concerted action. In the days of Plato the city state was considered the maximum size for a democracy. It was then necessary for the citizens to assemble in order to discuss issues and arrive at conclusions. It remained for the modern devices of communication to extend to continental proportions the areas in which democratic deliberation is possible.

Groups have enlarged with improvement in the facilities and agencies of communication. Social units dependent upon signs and

[31] "The Secret Language of Masons and Tinkers," *Journal of American Folk-Lore,* Vol. XXII, No. 86, pp. 353 ff.

[32] Cf. Marguerite Arnold, "Communication on the Road," *The World Tomorrow,* Vol. VI, September, 1923, pp. 271–72; Nels Anderson, *The Hobo,* Chicago: University of Chicago Press, 1923.

[33] John Dewey, *Democracy and Education,* New York: The Macmillan Company, 1916, pp. 5–6.

oral forms would of necessity be small and the boundaries of a territory would be coterminous with the circumference of sound or signal. The introduction of writing lengthened the radius while the telephone, telegraph, and radio extended the horizon still further. Changes in modes of transportation used by messengers were important. Foot travel was entirely too slow to enable a central government to keep in touch with activities at distant outposts of an empire. Improved roads and bridges, making possible the use of horses, speeded up communication but even that was too slow to co-ordinate effectively the activities of people living far apart. The railroad and finally the airplane with their greater speed have been important factors in the enlargement of groups.

Through modern means of communication and transportation the region has developed at the expense of the small locality. Tradition still maintains town marshals and county sheriffs but state and federal police are becoming increasingly important. Governmental units are gradually expanding beyond the local areas. Control of public schools is shifting gradually from the local district to the county unit and even beyond. In the Hawaiian Islands all schools are under direct control of the territorial Superintendent of Public Instruction. Relief work has become increasingly a county and state activity. In the Middle West, where counties were laid out on the basis of travel with horse and buggy over dirt roads, proposals are being made to unite groups of counties to make possible a better personnel. With surfaced highways and the automobile this is entirely feasible. Even though regional boundaries usually do not coincide with state or administrative lines, many activities are being organized on this broader basis. Federal Reserve Banks are organized by regions. Governors of groups of states meet to discuss problems of the region and conferences of various kinds are conducted on a regional basis.

The far-flung British empire would soon crack into bits were it not for the highly-organized system of communications. "Three times a day," writes John Saxon Mills, "an official message is scattered upon all the winds of heaven. It is British news, coming direct from the fountainhead, and is not tainted or perverted," as it passes through foreign channels.[34] "These triumphs over space and time have made not only possible, but almost inevitable, the

[34] *The Press and Communications of the Empire,* London: W. Collins' Sons and Company, 1924, p. 2.

cohesion in a single vast political organization of Dominions and Dependencies sundered by half the world's girth and displaying every diversity of race and climate and production.''[35] With three thousand miles of ''salt estranging sea,'' big problems were encountered. Good cable connections with all parts of the empire are of the greatest importance. With the coming of radio an all-British system was developed. The Reuter agency has rendered valuable service by transmitting news to all parts of the empire. To counteract any weaning away from Britain through the influence of American magazines, England gives low postage rates to Canada.[36] Mills suggests that if ''we wish to promote the solidarity of the empire, and the communion of thought and sympathy among its constituent parts,''[37] cheap postage and progressive reduction in cable rates are important.

The whole world is organized into one market-place through rapid communication. World wheat prices were set in Liverpool and now in Chicago. The New York stock market reacts sensitively to events on the battlegrounds of Europe. World-society of today, which, in the words of Park and Burgess,

> depends upon the almost instantaneous communication of events and opinion around the world, rests upon the invention of telegraphy and the laying of the great ocean cables. Wireless telegraphy and radio have only perfected these earlier means and render impossible a monopoly of intercommunication between peoples.[38]

As the various groupings enlarge, an increasing portion of the activities are carried out on the basis of indirect and secondary relationships. The printed page is used more extensively than in the smaller group with voice-to-voice relationships. With greater dependence on the printed page, ideas rather than feelings and sentiments become more important. It may be interesting to speculate on the probable result of the use of television in connection with the radio and telephone. Will they restore more of the face-to-face relationships and increase the sentimental element with a corresponding decrease in the idea base?

Ecological Organization and Communication. Methods of com-

[35] *Ibid.*, p. 3.
[36] Cf. *Ibid.*, pp. 4–174.
[37] *Ibid.*, p. 102.
[38] Park and Burgess, *Introduction to the Science of Sociology*, University of Chicago Press, p. 343. Reprinted by permission.

munication have been important factors in the ecological organization of populations. London became the center of world dominance because she was the point upon which lines of communication focused. New York City is the center of dominance in the United States. By means of modern devices of communication, certain great cities have become the foci for receiving and transmitting information. One of the arguments against daylight saving time in Chicago was the fact that it would interfere with receiving market reports from New York City. In these centers of dominance, many specialized agencies tend to assemble because of the information which is readily available.[39]

Democracy and Communication. Under a democratic form of government it is essential that communication be open and free. It is this which makes possible an intelligent public opinion, the ultimate basis of democracy. The constitution of the United States was aristocratic—not democratic—but open communication has brought change. Interpretations by the courts have been influenced by public opinion. Rapid and efficient communication is essential in the United States. When an important issue arises, it is not necessary for the President to hang a lantern in a church belfry to signal some Paul Revere to ride and spread the alarm, but he turns to the radio and a "fireside chat" gives us "inside information." Many thought the original thirteen colonies could not be held together since there was no adequate means for the transmission of information. Daniel Webster opposed the annexation of Oregon because a congressman would have no means of learning the wishes of his constituents on issues before congress.[40]

The radio has done much to make ideas more nearly universal. It has had a marked influence on political campaigns. In the olden days, a candidate could make a speech to one group and then reverse his position in appealing to another community. When he speaks over the radio, however, that cannot be done since he can be heard by many groups far and wide. In a totalitarian state, however, communication must be controlled.[41]

Language a Social Product. Language is basic in group life of human beings. Through its instrumentality it has become possible to develop a collective life which outstrips that of the lower

[39] Cf. Carl A. Dawson and Warner E. Gettys, *An Introduction to Sociology*, The Ronald Press Company, New York, 1935, pp. 172–225.

[40] *Bell Telephone Quarterly*, Vol. XIX, April, 1940, p. 131.

[41] Cf. Cooley, *op. cit.*, pp. 85–87.

animals. Language makes group life what it is, but, on the other hand, it is a social product and develops only out of association. An individual might devise an elaborate set of symbols, but if he kept them to himself they would not be a language. A person must use the symbols which are current in and understood by a group if he is to communicate with his fellows. A child begins to invent a language for himself but gradually gives it up when he finds there is one already made for him. If his own system of symbols were to be used, his conversations would be restricted to his own family circle. No one person invents a language and has it adopted by the group, but large numbers contribute to the growth of the language—it is truly a group product.

Language and Assimilation

Inability to use the current speech is undoubtedly the most embarrassing and baffling obstacle encountered by the immigrant upon his arrival in America. Full and free interchange of ideas is impossible and he thus remains outside the circumference of influences that would aid in his adjustment. He may, to be sure, accommodate himself to certain externalities by means of conscious copying. He may go through the forms of many everyday activities and actually learn certain routines connected with the food-getting process, but on the basis of such surface contacts he will remain on the periphery of our life. He will have but slight appreciation of the meanings behind the forms that he sees; he can use our institutions only in a limited way. A foreign language tends to weave a cocoon around an immigrant group and to keep it alien. Immigrants from England, since they speak our language, usually assimilate more readily than others, while those who speak Russian, Polish, or Finnish have greater difficulty than those with a Romance or Germanic language. When anyone really learns the language of a country, he thereby takes possession of its culture. If he has only a slight appreciation of the culture, the conclusion is inevitable that he does not understand the language.[42]

Language and Social Control

Language is an important channel through which social influ-

42 Cf. William C. Smith, *Americans in the Making*, New York: D. Appleton-Century Company, 1939, pp. 146–49; William C. Smith, *Americans in Process*, Ann Arbor: Edwards Brothers, 1937, pp. 175–85, 325–29; Park and Burgess, *op. cit.*, pp. 763–69; E. T. Hiller, *op. cit.*, pp. 111–27.

ences operate on the individual to make him an orderly participant in the social scheme. Through it knowledge, tradition, ideals, and other stimuli are transmitted. Undoubtedly it is the most important instrumentality for communicating to individuals the definitions set up by the group and for making manifest the approvals and disapprovals designed to secure conformity. Epithets—words that put a person in an unfavorable light—are hurled at the one who fails to conform. Words of flattery, praise, and blame, likewise, are devices for social control as well as the "don'ts" of the parental ordering and forbidding technique. Preliterate groups depend extensively upon rituals and initiation ceremonies for impressing their novices and for perpetuating the folkways and mores. Nevertheless, they pay considerable attention to the verbal transmission from generation to generation of the folklore which oftentimes bulks large and particular attention is paid to the portions related to the moral order. As a culture becomes more complex, the group can rely less upon ritual and copying of overt behavior but must depend increasingly upon language as a means of communicating its definitions to the members. As the group expands, writing and printing become important media of transmission and without them the present complex social order would be impossible. The modern means of communication make it possible for the constituent members of the group to participate in an orderly collective life. The Old Testament story of the Tower of Babel shows that it was impossible to work together satisfactorily on a project without a common language.[43] While non-verbal gestures are used in communication in some measure, yet language is the foremost medium through which the ideals of the group are impressed upon the individual. Among other things, class distinctions are indicated and in considerable measure maintained by language. In the Assamese and Bengali languages of India, pronouns of address have three forms—inferior, equal, and superior or honorific—each of which demands an appropriate form of conduct.

Language and Culture

Without Language Cultural Accumulations Are Limited. Between culture and language there is such a close relationship that only the most rudimentary social heritage could possibly accumulate without this facile means of communication. One generation or one

[43] *Genesis*, 11: 1–9.

group might learn something from others by imitation, but by this means there would be a great leakage. In attempting to imitate certain forms of overt behavior the results would oftentimes be of slight value because there would be no adequate clue to the meanings behind the behavior. Language makes it possible to convey meanings and thus all the gains can be conserved and handed down from age to age.

In addition to the transmission of culture elements through time, language is an important aid in the diffusion of culture through space. When the Greek language spread throughout the Mediterranean area, Greek culture followed in its wake and took root in several lands. With the adoption of the English language as the medium of instruction in the secondary schools and colleges of India, western influences flowed in more freely. The close tie between the United States and England is no mere accident because through the common speech cultural elements have diffused readily in both directions.

Cultural development is due to a collective learning process. It is not dependent merely upon man's superior brain but upon his superior facilities for intercommunication. It is evident that the development of culture is contingent upon improvements in the transmission of mental products. This enables ideas and inventions to spread widely and thus stimulate others. The interchange of experience through the medium of language in some form is responsible for new ideas and for the elimination of the necessity for all members of the group to pass through the same trial and error process. Since speech was the form of language used before writing came into vogue, we can agree with Case when he says that "Man has literally *talked* his way upward from the lowest savagery to his present comparatively high estate."[44]

Language Reflects the Culture of Which It Is a Part. Vocabularies throw much light on the cultures to which they belong. A study of the vocabulary of the Kachins of Burma provides an excellent introduction to their economic, their social, and their religious life, in fact to their whole culture. Frequently considerable difficulty is met in attempts at translation from one language to another because certain words in one language have no equivalent in the other. A radio announcer would encounter great obstacles in try-

---

[44] Clarence M. Case, *Outlines of Introductory Sociology*, New York: Harcourt, Brace and Company, 1924, p. 254.

ing to report a foot-ball game, play by play, to the Angami Nagas in the hills of India.

The language of a group is so intertwined with its culture that one cannot fully understand the language unless he has an appreciation of the culture. Words are far more than mere vocal sounds. Cooley says that a word is like a boat which becomes freighted with meaning as it floats down the stream of life.[45] Words express group experiences and to understand the words, we must know about these experiences. In the Ao Naga language of northeast India, *motongtaker* means cholera. When analyzed, the word means "that which causes one not to arrive." Cholera is prevalent in the Brahmaputra valley but not in the hills. When some hillmen go to the valley they contract cholera and die before reaching home. Hence, cholera, is that which causes one not to arrive. Our word *sincere* is interesting. In the olden days it was common to have men attest their word by making impressions in wax. When a man was found whose word was accepted without the usual procedure that was *sine cera* (without wax) and the man was honest, dependable, *sincere*.

Gestures, also, reflect cultures. If one compares a Ghetto Jew with his Americanized grandson, the difference will be quite striking. The extravagant shrugging of the shoulders and the unrestrained use of the hands give way to the more moderate gesture language in keeping with the Anglo-Saxon tradition.

Communication and Personality

Language Is the Main Avenue of Participation. Language is the principal medium through which personality is developed since it is the main avenue through which communication passes. It is by this means that an individual acquires information on the basis of which attitudes are constructed. Normally every infant is in a state of isolation and is unable to enter into the life of his fellow-beings until he has acquired some system of communication.

Isolated Individuals Not Really Human. Feral men who grow up in isolation from human contact fail to acquire speech in consequence of which they never really become human but remain in a non-descript state which is neither human nor brutal. No infant can mature without interaction with his fellows. This becomes evident from those who are afflicted with sensory defects or other physical handicaps that restrict their social contacts. Deaf-mutism,

[45] Cooley, *op. cit.*, p. 68.

which prevents individuals from speaking like others because they cannot hear them speak, is an isolating factor. The well-known story of Helen Keller is an illustration to the point. At the age of eighteen months she lost both hearing and sight and lived much like a little animal until the age of seven when her ingenious teacher broke through this hitherto impenetrable wall and was able to spell words into Helen's hand. When she realized that objects had names and that by means of these names she could share experiences with others, a marked change came in her personality.[46]

Language Is the Tool for Making Social Adjustments. Language is used by the child in the process of acquiring a world. He asks about objects and finds they have names and that all behavior as well has meaning which is described by words. Social definitions of objects and of situations which build up the world for the child are conveyed to him very largely through language, through words, and gestures. Human nature grows as the individual meets various situations, and language is the most important tool at his command for making social adjustments. If a person learns the language which is appropriate to one situation he is well adjusted because he then understands and appreciates the meanings, but he may encounter difficulty if he attempts to use that language in another situation where the meanings are different. A boy may grow up on a cattle ranch of west Texas where he learns to rope and brand the calves, but if he moves with his family to Calcutta and decides to rope a wandering "bossy" that eats the family flowers, he may set up international complications, his father appealing to the American consul for protection against the surging mob that has come to avenge the treatment accorded the sacred cow. The words "cow" and "beef" have far different meanings for the devout Hindu than for the Texas rancher. In this new situation the boy will be unadjusted and will not become assimilated until he has learned the language with the meanings the words have in that particular situation.

Language Idiosyncrasies Produce Mental Conflicts. Language idiosyncrasies are frequently serious matters to children of immigrants. A psychiatrist wrote:

Even when the language difficulty is slight, a foreign accent, lack of facility in speaking, imperfect understanding of the full idiom of the new tongue may place a child definitely

[46] Cf. Helen Keller, *The Story of My Life,* New York: Doubleday, Doran and Company, 1921.

outside the pale. He never truly becomes "one of the boys," and frequently adjusts to this situation of essential conflict in a manner that brings him to the attention of the psychiatrists. Especially is variation in accent a source of conflict when the accent derives from an "inferior" culture. The speech idiosyncrasies of the child may then remind his associates at every turn that here is an enemy or a person to be scorned. He functions, not as an individual, but as a representative of a hated race.[47]

The child of immigrant parentage in America often faces trying situations because of the impediments he encounters in his efforts to master English. He hears at least two languages—one at home and another outside—and thus he has no single pattern to follow. In such perplexing situations, personality problems often arise. Language peculiarities make it difficult for some children to acquire status in certain groups and when denied recognition they may turn to misconduct.[48]

EXTENSION OF COMMUNICATION AND ITS SIGNIFICANCE

Extension in Means of Communication

Primitive Means of Communication. Preliterate groups have developed many devices for extending communication beyond the range of the senses. Smoke and fire signals were used for sending messages beyond the reach of the voice. Some American Indians used "fire arrows" for throwing up signal lights at night.

They take off the head of the arrow and dip the shaft in gunpowder, mixed with glue. The gunpowder adheres to the wood, and coats it three or four inches from its end to the depth of one-fourth of an inch. Chewed bark mixed with dry gunpowder is then fastened to the stick, and the arrow is ready for use. When it is to be fired, a warrior places it on his bowstring and draws his bow ready to let it fly; and the point of the arrow is then lowered, another warrior lights the dry bark, and it is shot high in the air. When it has gone up a little distance, it bursts out into flame, and burns brightly until it falls to the ground. Various meanings are attached to these fire-arrow signals. . . . The Indians send their signals very intelligently, and seldom make mistakes in tele-

[47] John Levy, "Conflicts of Cultures and Children's Maladjustment," *Mental Hygiene*, Vol. XVII, January, 1933, p. 44.

[48] Cf. W. C. Smith, *Americans in the Making*, D. Appleton-Century, 1939, p. 284.

graphing each other by these silent monitors. The amount of information they can communicate by fires and burning arrows is perfectly wonderful.[49]

In Africa and North America elaborate drum codes have been developed which make transmission both swift and accurate.[50] Among many savage and barbarous peoples, in addition to gesture language, it is common to use various symbolic devices for conveying meanings, such as a red arrow for war, the pipe of peace, and knotted cords. Among the Kalingas of the Philippines, if the residents of a village wish to be friendly, it is customary to offer visitors bananas. If the visitors wish to accept the proffered friendship, they promptly eat of the fruit, otherwise it is understood that they are looking for trouble.[51] Message sticks have been used in several areas. In Australia notches were cut in sticks as memory aids to the messengers.[52] When a jungle Sinhalese of Ceylon wrapped a knotted creeper in a cloth, it was a summons to the recipient to come to the sender, and the number of knots indicated the urgency of the situation. A lock of hair wrapped around a stick brought tidings of a recent death.[53]

Modern Devices of Communication. Means of communication have developed from a simple interchange of sounds or signals within the range of the unaided senses to an intricate system of channels through which messages may be transmitted to all corners of the earth with the speed of light. Sound and light were used for many centuries. News of the completion of the Erie Canal was relayed to New York City by a series of cannon shots. Herodotus recorded the use of beacon fires by the Greeks. In the siege of

---

[49] Bureau of American Ethnology, *First Annual Report, 1879–80*, pp. 540–41.

[50] Cf. R. T. Clarke, ''Drum Language of the Tumba People,'' *American Journal of Sociology*, Vol. XL, July, 1934, pp. 34–48. It is interesting to compare the drum language with systems of communication developed by prisoners, even when in solitary confinement. Kropotkin tells how communication was carried on by a signal code between prison cells in St. Petersburg in 1874. They had an alphabet and transmitted messages by stamping on the floors or by tapping on the walls. P. Kropotkin, *Memoirs of a Revolutionist*, Boston, 1899, p. 359.

[51] Dean C. Worcester, *The Philippine Islands and Their People*, New York: The Macmillan Company, 1898, p. 342.

[52] A. W. Howitt, *The Native Tribes of South-Eastern Australia*, London: The Macmillan Company, 1904, p. 385.

[53] C. G. Seligman, *The Veddas*, London, 1911.

Syracuse Archimedes used mirrors to signal with beams of light. Napoleon used a semaphore system by means of which he kept in contact with Paris as he moved into Russia. Changes in methods of communication came slowly until, with revolutionary suddenness, electricity brought freedom from the physical limitations of actually carrying messages.

While the electric telegraph had reached the stage of usefulness in ordinary business in England in 1837, it was not until 1844 that Samuel F. B. Morse had built his line from Baltimore to Washington. In 1840 the first submarine cable was laid across the English Channel but it was not before 1851 that it came into regular use. Cable service across the Atlantic was instituted in 1866. So rapid was the spread of the telegraph that in thirty years it had covered the entire civilized world. Gradually out of simple beginnings have come several outstanding developments in recent years. Multiplex transmission has made it possible to send several messages simultaneously over the same wire. Teletyping records a message at the receiving end of the line either through typewriting or typesetting. Teleautography reproduces handwriting so that contracts with signatures can be reproduced in New York thirty minutes after they are signed in London. Newspapers now use the telegraph for transmitting photographic likenesses.

In 1876 the first telephone line was built over a distance of two miles between Boston and Cambridge. In 1884 service was begun between New York and Boston, over a line of two hundred and thirty-five miles. In 1892 Alexander Graham Bell talked from New York to Chicago, spanning nine hundred miles. In 1915 the first transcontinental telephone between New York and San Francisco was opened for public use. In 1927 it became possible to telephone across the Atlantic from New York to London and in 1929 those on land talked with passengers on ships far out on the seas. For more than twenty-five years a private-line teletypewriter service has been available but in 1931 the Bell Telephone System inaugurated a nation-wide teletypewriter exchange similar to telephone service. By this means it is possible to "talk in writing" back and forth on the same connection and have identical typed copies at both ends. Furthermore, through "unattended service," messages may be received and recorded at night when an office is closed.

In 1903 President Theodore Roosevelt and King Edward of England exchanged greetings by means of wireless communication.

From that date the wireless method developed rapidly until it has become one of our most important means of communication. Not only has it added to the safety of travel on sea and in the air but it has materially reduced isolation because radio receiving sets, even in the humblest homes, can reach out and draw from the ether a great variety of programs originating from all parts of the earth.

The progress of inventiveness in the annihilation of time and distance has brought results that make the wildest fairy tales fade into insignificance. On April 25, 1935, the president of the American Telephone and Telegraph Company conversed with his vice-president in an adjoining office—but not directly. His words travelled around the globe—from New York to London by radio-telephone, over underseas cable to Amsterdam, by radio to Java and to San Francisco, and, finally, by wire lines to New York—all in one-fourth of a second.

At present we see the beginnings of what promises to be a great venture in mass communication, one that will take its place beside radio, namely, television. Through this instrumentality immediacy in communication will be attained. It will give no mere report of a past happening, but the snow-bound potato farmer of northern Maine may see the Rose-bowl foot-ball game on New Year's day as well as those who occupy seats on the fifty-yard line in the stadium in Pasadena.

The phonograph and cinematograph also are inventions of comparative recency which play no inconsiderable roles in the field of communication. Through the portrayals of the motion picture, persons in distant localities and in widely divergent social classes may learn to know each other. Newsreels, travel films, and so-called educational films are particularly important from the standpoint of communication.

For many centuries the speed of carrying messages depended largely upon the swiftness of human or animal muscles. When the Greeks won the battle of Marathon in 490 B.C., they dispatched Phidippides to carry the news to Athens. He put forth such effort in racing the twenty-two miles that he fell dead after shouting, "Ours the victory!" The Romans gave the world its first postal system. Yet with good roads it took twenty-six days for Julius Caesar to send a letter from Britain to Rome. Pre-Revolutionary mail service in America was slow, irregular, and costly. When Benjamin Franklin became postmaster of Philadelphia in 1737 it took six weeks for his couriers to deliver letters in Boston. Habitual correspondence in those days was the privilege of only the well-to-do. News often traveled by the most circuitous routes. A news item originating in New England reached North Carolina after it had gone first to France and then to the West Indies.[54] Yet within one and one half centuries the farmer on the wind-swept plains of western Kansas could have parcels delivered to him from Chicago mail-order houses at small cost and in a remarkably short time. The improvement in postal facilities has multiplied social contacts over constantly widening areas. The inauguration of city delivery service in 1863 brought the post office to the door of the urban dweller. Rural free delivery in 1896 brought the farmers in closer touch with the outside world and did much to break down the isolation which had persisted since colonial days.

In considerable measure the acceleration of mail service has been due to improvements in modes of transportation. The interval between posting and delivery began to decrease in 1832 when a courageous postmaster decided to risk the mail on the railway. Since then train service has improved greatly. The new streamlined trains run between Chicago and San Francisco in less than forty hours while the lumbering stagecoaches of the Overland Mail Company made the journey from St. Louis to San Francisco in about twenty-one days. The inauguration of air mail service in 1918 resulted in further reductions in time. The mails have been expedited further through the use of motor vehicles and tube systems in cities.

Significance of Extension in Communication

Historians, anthropologists, and sociologists have been impressed by the revolutionary effects which the extension of communication has had upon social life. The anthropologist sets the invention of writing as the beginning of ancient civilization. To the historian history begins with that event—all prior to that was pre-history. To him the invention of the printing press was the pivotal point in the transition from medieval to modern society. Each advance in the development of artificial means of communication has marked an epoch in the progress of man.

Larger and More Inclusive Worlds Have Become Possible. With the great advancements in the swiftness of communication in recent

54 Cf. *The North Carolina Historical Review,* Vol. VII, October, 1931, p. 382.

decades, social contacts have been extended in space and quickened in time. The control of electricity and the substitution of sound for sight in the transmission process has so extended the radius of inter-action that the whole world has become one large whispering gallery. This has made it possible to escape from a circumscribed environment of the local area and to live in a larger and more congenial one. A person interested in geology or some other specialty may make contacts with like-minded men in all parts of the world and thus through an interchange and cross-fertilization of ideas all may be enriched. Means of communication which lift one out of local confines are instrumental in liberating him from the pressure of particular events that are of no great significance in themselves and enable him to live in a larger and more meaningful world. The broadening contacts stimulate one to make choices from a wider available range of possibilities and thus a dull sameness may be avoided. Ease of communication tends to favor differentiation of a functional and rational sort as over against mere random varia-tions which are fostered by isolation.[55] Extension of communica-tion does not destroy the influence of tradition but it exposes men to a greater amplitude of usages so that they may be more creatively constructive in their choices.

Facile communication gives not only breadth through a wider exposure to contemporaries, but depth as well through contacts with the past which are afforded particularly through writing and printing. It is possible to go back and select from the treasures of the centuries. The whole world turns to ancient Greece for sculpture and philosophy, to the ancient Hebrews for ethical ideas, and to sixteenth-century Italy for painting. Truly, the ideas and experiences of all peoples are placed at our disposal. We have the equipment by means of which we may enrich our culture by myriad traits from every nook and corner of the earth.

The Wider Range of Stimuli Has Liabilities. While greater ease of communication has brought beneficial results it also has its lia-bilities. It makes possible mob-mindedness on a larger scale. As foot-ball games are broadcast over the radio, the whole nation be-comes one great cheering section. More nervous energy is required to participate in the larger world than was needed when one could live in comparative isolation.

The wider range of stimuli has led to a considerable degree of

55 Cooley, *op. cit.*, pp. 91, 95.

superficiality, particularly in our urban life. The constant bombardment through the new devices of communication has resulted in a flitting from one thing to another.

Oftentimes too great dependence is placed on mere mechanical devices. Walter S. Rogers stated at the Institute of Pacific Relations in Honolulu in 1927 that "rapid, reliable, and reasonably cheap international communication is one of the most effective methods of preserving peace among nations." Quite evidently James Bryce would not accept that statement without qualification. He expressed it as his opinion that the World War probably would have been averted were it not for the speed with which the telephone, telegraph, and cable flashed messages between the capitals of Europe in July of 1914. Had the spread of news been more leaden-footed, the slower processes of diplomacy might have worked. As it was, governments had to make decisions quickly and without sufficient deliberation.[56]

CONCLUSION

In any discussion of communication there is a proneness to be carried away by the glamour of the mechanical devices which have been developed in recent decades. The miles of telegraph wire are measured, the tons of books weighed, the number of radio sets counted and then it is confidently assumed that all is well. But a mere thrusting outward into space will not in and of itself result in interaction, mental growth, sharing, integration of life, and the development of a single moral order. Mere mechanical inventions will not unify the world. There are obstacles to communications due to differences in tradition, experience, interest, and language. A telephone is an inert mass of material unless the person at the other end of the line understands the language spoken into the transmitter. Communication from one culture area to another is not a simple matter like the transportation of steel axes. Words, to be sure, may be carried across cultural boundaries but they may be interpreted quite differently in the new setting because of divergences in tradition. An Iowa farmer may speak over the radio and sing the praises of his Poland China hogs, but it will receive a far different interpretation by certain listeners in India. The word "hog" means tasty roast pork to the Iowan but to the devout Moslem it signifies a disgustingly impure animal. When television

[56] Cf. F. S. Chapin, *Cultural Change*, New York: The Century Company, 1928, p. 289.

presents a love-making scene *a la* Hollywood in China or Japan the staid Oriental will be shocked. An appreciation of the other cultures is a pre-requisite to open communication. Prejudices and feelings of antagonism are hindrances. Telephone, telegraph, and postal services have been open between the North and the South for a long time, yet these instruments did not erase all sectional animosities. A southerner stated in 1935 that he was more than twenty years old before he knew that "damn Yankee" was not a single word. Men, to all intents and purposes, have been brought closer together physically but their minds have not been prepared to take advantage of the available facilities in the fullest measure.

Ease of travel and facility in communication, particularly by means of the radio, have tended to wipe out localisms. Peculiarities of speech are disappearing. Local dialects and styles in dress, such as were common in Sweden and other European countries, must gradually disappear. In 1911 there was only one clergyman who could conduct divine service in Wendish and some years before that was recorded the death of the last man to speak the Cornish language.[57]

With the disappearance of local color and picturesque social types, undoubtedly, there will be a tendency to reduce all cultures to a dead level. To a considerable degree, a trend toward a world culture is inevitable. For better or worse, no peoples can now remain unmolested unto themselves and develop the degrees of uniqueness which were possible when they lived in their own little isolated worlds.

It may be a matter of convenience to be able to buy Gillette razor blades in Jubbulpore or Rawalpindi, in Mandalay or Swatow as well as in Boston, but it certainly robs one of some interesting experiences. No Mark Twain of the future will be thrilled with amazement at finding unique and intriguing cultures which may be described for us in a *Following the Equator*. This trend toward world-wide uniformity is exacting a price. The very unprecedented richness of our modern civilization, due to the easy intake of exotic elements may destroy the clarity and harmony of the old culture patterns, and sacrifice the simplicity for mere brilliance and surface lustre.[58]

[57] E. S. Kelley, "A Library of Living Melody," *The Outlook*, Vol. XC, September 30, 1911, p. 286.

[58] Cf. Roland B. Dixon, *The Building of Cultures*, New York: Charles Scribner's Sons, 1928, pp. 265–305.

SELECTED REFERENCES

Babcock, Donald C., *Man and Social Achievement,* New York: Longmans, Green and Co., 1929, pp. 89–111.—A simple account of the place of speech in man's social achievement.

Barnes, Harry Elmer, *Society in Transition,* New York: Prentice-Hall, Inc., 1939, pp. 608–43.—A brief account of the revolution in the means of communication of information and the effects of mass information and mass propaganda.

Bernard, L. L., *An Introduction to Social Psychology,* New York: Henry Holt and Company, 1926, pp. 142–57.—A discussion of the function of language in the adjustment process.

Boas, Franz, *General Anthropology,* Boston: D. C. Heath and Company, 1938, pp. 124–45.—A discussion of the growth of language, language differences, classification, and the relation of language to culture.

Brown, Lawrence Guy, *Social Psychology: The Natural History of Human Nature,* New York: McGraw-Hill Book Company, 1934, pp. 145–89, 487–508, 570–618.—Discusses the place of the senses in social interaction, the relation of language to human nature, and the mechanisms of social interaction—imitation, suggestion, and sympathy.

Burgess, Ernest W., ''Communication,'' *American Journal of Sociology,* Vol. XXXIV, pp. 117–29, 1072–80; Vol. XXXV, pp. 991–1001.—A treatment of the development of communication in recent years and the effects of these changes.

Chapin, F. Stuart, *Cultural Change,* New York: The Century Company, 1928, pp. 279–311.—The significance of cultural changes resulting from the revolution in means of communication.

Chase, Stuart, *The Tyranny of Words,* New York: Harcourt, Brace and Company, 1938.—An entertaining and easily read introduction to the difficult theme of the treachery of words. It may be considered an attempt to tell in simple words what Ogden and Richards meant in *The Meaning of Meaning.*

Clark, G. N., *Unifying the World,* London: The Swarthmore Press, 1920.—A discussion of the inventions which have affected the means of communication.

Cooley, Charles Horton, *Social Organization: A Study of the Larger Mind,* New York: Charles Scribner's Sons, 1913, pp. 61–205.—The classic discussion of communication in relation to the democratic mind.

Dawson, Carl A., and Gettys, Warner E., *An Introduction to Sociology,* New York: The Ronald Press Company, 1929, pp. 251–95.—A treatment of the various mechanisms through which social interaction takes place.

De Laguna, Grace Andrus, *Speech, Its Function and Development,* New Haven: Yale University Press, 1927.—A thorough and scholarly treatment but not easy to read. Part I, ''The Role of Speech in Society,'' is particularly valuable.

De Laguna, Theodore, *The Factors of Social Evolution,* New York: F. S. Crofts and Company, 1926, pp. 277–303.—A good discussion of ''The Improvement of Communication,'' through the development of speech, gesture, writing, printing, and the telegraph.

De Morgan, Jacques, *Prehistoric Man: A General Outline of Prehistory,* New York: Alfred A. Knopf, 1925, pp. 256–68.—A brief sketch of the development of writing.

Dewey, John, *Experience and Nature*, Chicago: Open Court Publishing Company, 1926, pp. 166–207.—A discussion of meaning and communication.

Edman, Irwin, *Human Traits and Their Significance*, Boston: Houghton Mifflin Company, 1920, pp. 214–42.—A popular and interesting account of the development of language. It sets forth the significance of language as a social product as contrasted with the communication of animals.

Eubank, Earle Edward, *The Concepts of Sociology*, Boston: D. C. Heath and Company, 1932, pp. 3–52.—A discussion of concepts and their significance in scientific work with particular emphasis upon the conceptual approach in sociology.

Groves, Ernest R. and Moore, Harry Estill, *An Introduction to Sociology*, New York: Longmans, Green and Company, 1940, pp. 231–56.—A brief, general treatment of communication and social interaction.

Harlow, Alvin F., *Old Wires and New Waves*, New York: D. Appleton-Century Company, 1936.—A readable and thorough historical account of the telegraph, telephone, and wireless.

Hiller, E. T., *Principles of Sociology*, New York: Harper and Brothers, 1933, pp. 81–144.—An excellent general discussion of language and communication in brief compass.

Jesperson, Otto, *Language: Its Nature, Development and Origin*, London: George Allen and Unwin, 1928.—Part I discusses the need for a constructed universal language and the several attempts to meet that need.

Keir, Malcolm, *The March of Commerce*, New Haven: Yale University Press, 1927.—A good, readable, pictorial account of the development of communication in the United States.

Krueger, E. T., and Reckless, Walter C., *Social Psychology*, New York: Longmans, Green and Company, 1931, pp. 34–59.—The significance of language in social life.

Mason, William A., *A History of the Art of Writing*, New York: The Macmillan Company, 1920.—An excellent and readable account of the development of writing.

Mencken, Henry Louis, *American Language: An Inquiry into the Development of English in the United States*, New York: Alfred A. Knopf, 1936.—A study of American speech and consequently of American civilization. A storehouse of interesting and amusing information.

Myerson, Abraham, *Social Psychology*, New York: Prentice-Hall, Inc., 1934, pp. 372–435.—An interesting study of communication and language by a neurologist.

Ogden, C. K., and Richards, I. A., *The Meaning of Meaning*, New York: Harcourt, Brace and Company, 1923.—A study of the science of symbolism and of the influence of language upon thought.

Park, Robert E., and Burgess, Ernest W., *Introduction to the Science of Sociology*, Chicago: University of Chicago Press, 1924, pp. 339–434.—Defines the concept of interaction and presents an important selection of materials.

Reuter, E. B., and Hart, C. W., *Introduction to Sociology*, New York: McGraw-Hill Book Company, 1933, pp. 256–76.—Discusses the concept of interaction, language, and the mechanisms of interaction.

Sapir, Edward, *Language*, New York: Harcourt, Brace and Company, 1921.—

An inquiry into the form and function of the arbitrary system of symbolism that is termed language.

Shenton, Herbert N., *Cosmopolitan Conversation*, New York: Columbia University Press, 1933.—An alluring treatment of International language.

Storck, John, *Man and Civilization*, New York: Harcourt, Brace and Company, 1926, pp. 223–43.—A brief inquiry into language as one of the bases of contemporary life.

Todd, Arthur James, *Theories of Social Progress*, New York: The Macmillan Company, 1918, pp. 407–13.—Language as one of the factors in human advance.

Vendryes, J., *Language*, New York: Alfred A. Knopf, 1925.—An introduction to the history of language which traces speech from its origin to its culmination in the development of grammar.

Wallis, Wilson D., *An Introduction to Anthropology*, New York: Harper and Brothers, 1926, pp. 416–31.—Shows the interrelations of language and culture.

Willey, Malcolm M., and Rice, Stuart A., *Communication Agencies and Social Life*, New York: McGraw-Hill Book Company, 1933.—A study of recent developments in the United States and the influence of these changes on human behavior.

Woodbury, David O., *Communication*, New York: Dodd, Mead and Company, 1931.—A popular and readable account of five great methods of message sending.

Young, Kimball, *Social Psychology*, New York: Alfred Knopf, 1930, pp. 203–32, 399–426.—Discusses language and social interaction and the function of language in thinking.

PART IV

SOCIAL ORGANIZATION

Necessarily our sketching of social organization is not exhaustive. For example, health institutions, though we have not devoted a chapter to them, constitute a very important phase of social organization. They include allopathic, homeopathic, osteopathic and chiropractic physicians; the eye, ear, nose and throat specialists, and the variety of other specialists; their offices and clientele; their various associations; the clinics, the hospitals, the nurses, trained and "practical." They include the county health units and other governmental health agencies, and still other phases important in social organization which we might well have developed—but which we leave as a problem for the students. In other directions we might have dealt at length with the numerous institutions for *transportation,* or with *the institutional machinery for fighting wars,* or with *youth organizations,* or *organizations for research,* or with still other aspects of social organization. But the more topics one covers in a single volume the thinner must be his treatment. The topics which we present are among the fundamentals.

CHAPTER 13

SOCIAL STRUCTURE

BY DR. R. W. ROSKELLEY

Colorado State College, Fort Collins, Colo.

If someone were to come from Mars to visit the different groups now occupying various parts of this earth, what evidence do we have that he would be more interested in the inventions which help us control the physical elements than in those that help people control each other? The philosophy, social techniques, and organizations of modern warfare are hardly less spectacular than the airplanes and guns whose control they determine.

If history or the testimonies of current travelers are to be relied upon, the social controls are no less important than the physical controls. Europeans coming to this country in 1492 were just as interested in the Indians' ideas and organization for war as in any particular weapons that were used. The Europeans were interested in the excellent pottery, basket making, and weaving which were found among the Indians, but they were equally interested in the fact that in a particular tribe, such as the Iroquois, a man's ancestry was traced through his mother's lineage. When an Iroquois married, he took up residence with his wife's household. He acquired no particular rights there; but he still retained membership in his mother's group. It was of interest to the European to learn that the authority in the house of an Iroquois did not rest in the hands of a man, but with an old woman, normally a grandmother or some close relative of other women in the household. This chieftainess supervised the domestic economy in the household and exercised some rather important political functions. She was assisted by a council of the women of child-bearing age. The entire household worshiped a guardian divinity whose cult was taken care of by a special priestess or medicine woman and whose animal fetish or totem was usually painted on the gable of the house.

The Europeans were interested to learn further that among the Iroquois practically all property was communal except that which an individual could carry on his person. The wife's personal property, when given away, was bestowed upon her children or upon the children of her sisters. The husband's property could be given to the children of his sisters but never to his wife or to his own children. Various implements of domestic use, and such items as stored food, war trophies, and medicines, belonged to the adult female members of the household. Food was pooled and distributed by the chief matron to various families in a household. Such communal ownership of food was extended to the village, for all agricultural land was handled in a communistic fashion and no man needed to starve as long as any corn was to be found in the village.[1]

Students of society designate such customs as social structure. Social structure prescribes the role as well as the proper behavior patterns for each individual in almost all situations that may be encountered. It is obvious that the social structure of the Iroquois is not a chaotic assortment of a great variety of patterns but a rather nice integration and balance of functionally related parts. For example, there is consistency in the various roles played by the women, either as heads of households, as members of the council, or in giving away private property. The communal system of distributing food is functionally related to the communal ownership of land and trophies.

Regulative norms or standards that make us behave as other members of the group want us to behave are not the particular possession of any one group but are characteristic of all. Our own society is no exception, and our ways of defining and doing things are just as remarkable to other persons as theirs are to us. Americans are known abroad as organizers of clubs. Whenever a new club is established, one of the first tasks is to outline the ideals of the organization; the constitution and by-laws, written or unwritten, are drawn up prescribing how the ideals of the organization can be achieved. Standards of proper or improper conduct for members of the group are established. Divisions of responsibility are made, duties are assigned, and the necessary approval and authority of the group is given to various individuals.

From such associations there has developed a system of group approvals and procedures that supply standardized modes of conduct for the members. Most of these definitions of right and wrong, plus the approved procedures, may be classified as mores, folkways, customs, laws, or institutions; they give permanence and definiteness

[1] George P. Murdock, *Our Primitive Contemporaries*, New York: Macmillan Co., 1934, pp. 302–303.

to the social structure. Individual conduct is directed and channelized by them, with the result that predicting individual and group
behavior is possible. This predictability of other persons' behavior
makes it possible for each person to plan his own conduct in view of
the probable reactions of other people under prescribed circumstances, thus producing more secure living. Such regulative norms
may be compared to the traffic stop light, the comparison illustrating
the importance of knowing what others will do under certain
circumstances. It is important to note that it is not the stop light
but the social structure that regulates people's behavior at a street
intersection. The stop light merely acts as a stimulus; people proceed when the traffic light flashes green and stop when it shows red
because of certain ideas, attitudes, and behavior patterns which they
have learned as a result of living with other people whose lives are
partially regulated by stop lights.

THE MEANING AND NATURE OF SOCIAL STRUCTURE

When people live together they tend to develop a similarity of
response to stimuli in the processes of human interaction. Thus
each behavior or gesture of a person which is designed to achieve a
desired end is about the same as the behavior of any other person of
the same age and status in that society. Such a similarity of
response of two or more people to a stimulus is called a plurality
pattern. Every act or response is made in terms of the situation
in which it occurs, as well as in terms of the ideals, mores, folkways, and institutions which define the expected behavior. Each
social pattern among the Iroquois, such as authority in the household or communal ownership of property, is an intricate part of
the total social organization or plurality pattern of the society.
The mores, folkways, and the like insure a similarity of response by
members of the tribe to any particular stimulus or combination of
stimuli.

This social organization through which people work together and
achieve certain objectives has been designated by Brown as:
". . . the machinery by which the group maintains its existence and
achieves its purposes."[2] Sumner describes the social structure
found among groups as follows:

> The relations of men to each other, when they are carrying
> on the struggle for existence near each other, consist in mutual

[2] B. Warren Brown, *Social Groups*, Chicago: Faithorn Company, 1926, p. 63.

reactions (antagonisms, rivalries, alliances, coercions, and cooperations), from which result . . . more or less fixed positions of individuals and sub-groups toward each other, and more or less established sequences and methods of inter-action between them, by which the interests of all members of the group are served. . . . Every act of each man fixes an atom in a structure, both fulfilling a duty derived from what preceded and conditioning what is to come afterwards by the authority of traditional customs. The structure thus built up is not physical, but societal and institutional, that is to say, it belongs to a category which must be defined and studied by itself.[3]

This social structure which channelizes human behavior pro-vides a role for each person; it defines what is proper or improper behavior; it is not a matter which can be weighed on scales, measured with a foot ruler, nor analyzed chemically, because these social structures exist in people's minds.[4] A person need not be concerned, however, about the reality of social structure or any factor on the ground that it does not have physical substance. The ghost is just as real to the frightened child as is the mother on whose lap the child may sit. Day-dreaming and other fantasy-thinking may be just as real and may provide just as much satisfaction and enjoy-ment as actual experience. The anticipation of certain events is frequently more joyous than the actual physical participation. We know that man has always been ruled by his own ideas. The organi-zation of these ideas is the social structure of the society, and the ideas are real. To some people the idea of a third term for Presi-dent Roosevelt seemed much more dangerous to democracy than an actual Nazi invasion.

THE DEVELOPMENT OF SOCIAL STRUCTURE

Social structure may be thought of as both a product of gre-garious living and a factor which makes gregarious living possible. Viewed as such, social structure began when man first conceived another biological unit as his neighbor and considered him as some-thing to be reckoned with. It began when the conduct of one person was directed and channelized by the forces of ideals, examples, concepts, and expectations of another.

The social structure of any society has an evolutionary develop-

[3] W. G. Sumner, *Folkways,* Boston: Ginn & Company, 1906, pp. 34–35.

[4] Leopold von Wiese and Howard Becker, *Systematic Sociology,* New York: John Wiley & Sons, Inc., 1932, p. 89.

ment and is subject to constant modification. Because of this, it is not possible to say that the total social structure of any group arose at a specified time. It is possible in any society, however, to show how some development which was of vital concern to all gave rise to a new part of the social structure for the group. The introduction of slavery into the South is such an example. The first white settlers took a social structure with them into the South—certain basic customs, habits, ideals, folkways, concepts, laws, and institutions which prescribed the pattern for individual and group action. The same may be said of the Negroes who were shipped to the South as slaves. There was a clash between the social structure of the white and that of the Negro because each had his idea of right and wrong; each had his idea of how a person should behave. The clash was offensive to each group and necessitated a redefinition of the situation at hand. The redefinition by the white involved a caste system with subjugation and slavery for the Negroes. The institution of slavery introduced new ideals, attitudes, and practices in the South. The Negro could be sold on the market like any other piece of personal property. Among other things he was supposed to work and be loyal to his master. In return the master was supposed to provide food, clothing, and shelter for the slave, even when, because of old age, the slave could no longer work. A number of personal behavior patterns were established involving the slave and the master. It was not proper for the Negro to eat or sleep in the same room as his master; his children could not go to school; he could not ride in the same carriage unless he was tending the child of the master. These very fine points of differentiation illustrate how the social structure prescribes individual conduct in minute detail. Elaborate social organization, such as that reflected in the novel, *Gone with the Wind,* emerged. Some of these relationships developed upon the basis of happenstance situations, while certain customs, folkways, and mores developed on the basis of necessity or convenience.

The Negro did not accept his lot without resistance. Frequently he did not accept his master's definition of what was right or wrong. Behavior patterns of each were sometimes challenged by the other. Each sought his own solution. The race hatred which arose in some instances found expression in various types of resistance by the Negro that from the master's standpoint required suppression. New and varying means of punishment and general treatment arose among the whites to meet the emergencies, new laws were passed, new police powers were granted, and new modes of behavior were accepted and were believed by each group to be absolutely necessary to meet the new situations that arose. These illustrations are sufficient to suggest the new elements that became the basis of the new social structure (the mores, folkways, customs, institutions, laws, and conventions) in the South when slavery was introduced. The significant aspect of the social structure considered so briefly is that in countless ways the Negro cooperated and conflicted with his white master. Their disagreements necessitated adjustments, and in either conflict or cooperation the processes progressed in terms of the particular plurality pattern which prevailed in the minds of either or both at the time. The social structure became the social machinery by which certain objectives were achieved.

A general picture having been presented of what is meant by social structure and of how it develops, the next stage is to analyze some of the more important segments which go to build up social structure. In this more detailed analysis let us remember that social structure is a result of social interaction. Its existence is dependent upon symbols and communication and it does not exist outside the social processes; further, such structure develops around the basic needs and differences of men. The needs involve such things as food, drink, clothing, shelter, sex expression, and the major requirements of social organization and control. Age, sex, and other individual and group differences, as well as divisions of labor and responsibility, constitute a part of the foundation for development of the social structure. This structure of society is passed on from one individual to another by means of education and propaganda. Each member of a group becomes indoctrinated, regardless of whether he joins the group by adoption or is born into it.

ELEMENTS OF SOCIAL STRUCTURE

Folkways

Folkways have been defined as group habits or as customs or usages that, according to Sumner, "have developed out of experience" and are passed from one person or generation to another "without rational reflection or purpose." They are relatively standardized and durable; they are designed to fulfill a need, yet they usually develop without prior intention. The following quotation from Cooley, Angell, and Carr illustrates these attributes of a folkway:

> Let us suppose that a pre-literate band, hard on the track of game, comes to a small stream that is too deep for wading. More or less random exploration of the bank ensues until someone finds a shallow place, which thereupon becomes the crossing place for the band. Note that no one says "Now we must cross here because if we don't we shall have bad luck," or "We must cross here because our ancestors have always crossed here." No one stops to think or to say anything—except perhaps to call to the stragglers that a crossing has been found. As Sumner aptly remarks, "Men begin with acts, not with thoughts."
>
> So presently our primitives are on the other side. Now observe the course of events: If good luck attends the hunting, if all get safely back, if nothing goes wrong, the members of that band will have no cause to remember that ford with anything but approval. On subsequent visits to that locality, those who were there before will direct the party thither, and if there is much crossing back and forth, paths will presently be beaten on the banks, making it easier still to head for that one particular crossing-place instead of any other. Thus the practice will grow up of crossing there. So far the fact that they are crossing there and *not somewhere else* has not been mentioned. . . . Possibly for generations nobody will so far shake himself loose from the routine business of getting a living as to ask questions about so obvious a matter. In other words, while that condition lasts the practice of crossing at that particular place is a folkway. It is one of those taken-for-granted practices that abound in all societies.[5]

Folkways are numerous in any culture. They develop very profusely around such activities as art, dress, sex, birth, death, marriage, and worship. One needs to look at only one or two instances in our society to appreciate the tremendous variety of possible folkways which could develop around a single situation such as serving and eating a dinner. There are a large number of possible ways of setting a table, yet the folkways of setting a table in our society specify the place for each knife, fork, spoon, plate, glass, and dish; the salad plate and coffee cup have their fixed positions. The host and hostess might sit any place were it not for the fact that folkways define their positions. The seating of guests at the table,

[5] Charles H. Cooley, Robert C. Angell, and Lowell J. Carr, *Introductory Sociology*, New York: Charles Scribner's Sons, 1933, pp. 89–90.

the carving of the turkey, the serving of the food, the method of expressing gratitude for being invited as a guest, and the procedure of complimenting the hostess on the quality of the meal are all factors which are determined by the folkways. Many of these folkways are very arbitrary; for example, is there any necessary reason why forks should be placed on the left side of the plate when they are usually used by the right hand? Could it not be just as satisfactory to compliment the hostess by giving a healthy grunt halfway in the middle of the meal, as some peoples do, rather than by making a long complimentary statement which the guest himself frequently does not believe?

Customs

Customs are classified as folkways. Such folkways are characterized by explicitness and positiveness. They are developed in terms of the situation. Behavior which would be proper for a person on a mountain hike would be tabooed on the ballroom floor. Actions that would be acceptable in the sorority or fraternity house might be very improper in a classroom. Custom has been defined by Cole as a "way of acting, common to the members of a country or social group, or at least widely enough diffused among them over a long enough period of time to have become in some degree taken for granted and acted upon in normal circumstances without any conscious exercise of deliberation."[6]

The customs of a group are frequently among its most distinguishing attributes. Such people as the Chinese are known to have accepted and practiced certain customs for many generations. Customs are practiced for long periods because of their compulsive nature. We all follow custom. Straw hats are not worn after Labor Day. Guests at a dinner do not start eating before the hostess does; if they do, their behavior is not approved. Except during leap year, the man is supposed to do the courting and the proposing; girls who act against custom are dubbed by the fellow as too aggressive. The fellow who refuses to follow certain customs when "dating" a girl is told "no" when he calls again.

Fashions

Fashions are also folk patterns which may be classified as folkways. Fashion in society provides an opportunity for the expres-

[6] G. H. D. Cole, *Social Theory*, New York: Frederick A. Stokes Company, 1920, p. 45.

sion of individual variation of dress within the realm of social approval. The co-ed has the opportunity to dress in a great variety of ways, any one of which will fall within the realm of general acceptance. The folkways make it possible for each member of the group to enjoy this variety of response. There are some factors, however, concerning the co-ed's dress about which the group especially concerns itself. They are illustrated by such things as the length of the dress, or the lowness of the neckline. These factors involve items that are considered vital to the welfare of the group. They are not controlled by the folkways but by the mores.

From the foregoing discussion it is obvious that not all modes of behavior by individual members of a group are equally obligatory. At the one extreme there are certain usages the practice of which is optional with an individual; these we call folkways. They are illustrated by such things as men removing their hats in an elevator when women are present or giving their seats to women in a crowded streetcar. From such a point the folkways shade off into those usages which are expected of every individual and are considered indispensable to the welfare of the group. The failure of any person to observe the latter is a shock to others in society who may know of the behavior. When a point is reached where the observance of a practice becomes obligatory to all persons in a society and failure to observe such usages is thought to be inimical to the welfare of the society, the folkways are defined as mores.

Mores

Mores, the plural form of the Latin word mos, which means custom, are the folkways of the group that have moral meaning and by which right and wrong in terms of the welfare of the group are determined.[7] In defining the word mores Sumner said that he meant "the popular usages and traditions, when they include a judgment that they are conducive to societal welfare, and when they exert a coercion on the individual to conform to them, although they are not co-ordinated by any authority."[8]

Mores and folkways are alike in that they both represent folk practices or group usages. They differ in that the observance of the mores is considered indispensable to the welfare of the individual and the group. Mores are thought to have some intrinsic value as to

[7] Kimball Young, *Social Psychology*, New York: F. S. Crofts & Co., 1930, p. 678.

[8] W. G. Sumner, *op. cit.*, p. III.

right and wrong in contrast with the folkways which are the "correct" way to do things in the sense that they represent the expected or current practice of the group. In the preceding discussion dealing with folkways it was shown how they are commonly accepted practices of the people which do not involve moral concepts regarding the welfare of the group. Folkways are convenient modes of behavior and facilitate social intercourse. Any group may have a variety of different ways of accomplishing a task, any one of which would be acceptable if it were understood and established. This is not true with actions which involve public decency or vice where a given pattern is considered either right or wrong. Mores and folkways have some elements in common in that they both are ways of accomplishing tasks as defined by the group. They differ in that the mores regulate practices regarding rightness or wrongness, morality or immorality, while the folkways are devoid of such attributes.

In describing the mores Sumner suggested that they were nonlogical and frequently based upon myths, legends, fictions, or superstitions. People do not analyze them; neither do they examine the premises upon which they are based. The value of a mos is not proved scientifically but is implied by assumption. Mores are based upon sentiment, and people observing them react emotionally to an ethical code.

Neither folkways nor mores are introduced or regulated by such an authority as the church or the state. They need no organized institution to make them effective; their power lies in the moral sanction of the individual and public mind. They need no justification because they exist in their own right.

In commenting on the complusive nature of particularly the mores, Sumner said,

> Groups form standards of orthodoxy as to the "principles" which each member must profess and the ritual which each must practice. Dissent seems to imply a claim of superiority. It evokes hatred and persecution. Dissenters are rebels, traitors, and heretics. We see this in all kinds of subgroups. Noble and patrician classes, merchants, artisans, religious and philosophical sects, political parties, academies and learned societies, punish by social penalties dissent from, or disobedience to, their code of group conduct. The modern trade union, in its treatment of a "scab," only presents another example.[9]

[9] W. G. Sumner, *op. cit.*, pp. 95–96.

Incidents which illustrate society's concern about the relative seriousness of ignoring the mores are numerous. In America foreigners are allowed a considerable amount of personal freedom to follow a number of practices which characterized life in their native land, yet they would be suspected of being "fifth columnists" if they failed to stand while the Star Spangled Banner was being played. Pacifists are allowed to say or print almost anything they desire about the horrors of war or the actions of the government in relation to war during peace time but, because it is against the mores, they must be careful what they say if the country is at war. A person can be a member of one Christian church in America and, without any particular stigma, join another when he moves to another community. Yet the person who becomes a member of one Greek letter sorority or fraternity "just doesn't" change fraternities if he happens to change schools. A person can wear almost any kind of costume in public without serious consequences, but if he were to appear in the nude he would be called an exhibitionist who should be put under police protection and given psychopathic treatment. Each case of trampling the mores illustrated in the foregoing involves the problems of what is right and what is wrong. From all people we expect loyalty to our country and respect for the flag. Improper dress involves problems of immorality and threats to our standards of decency and modesty.

The mores involve positive as well as negative admonitions. In a society where the group is supposed to live according to Christian ideals, every young man is instructed in certain things he should and should not do in the presence of his own sister, mother, or sweetheart; he is also instructed what his duty should be if he is in the company of others whose behavior is not in conformity with the mores. Citizens of each country are instructed in the things they should and should not do. The person who reports acts of spying by someone else becomes a national hero. In schools where the honor system is maintained among the students, it is the student's duty not only to refrain from cheating but to restrain others from doing so.

The power of the mores over the behavior of the individual is a further illustration of their positive admonition. The mores of some groups are of sufficient strength to cause some persons to scar their own flesh and deform different parts of their bodies. The binding of the feet of Chinese girls is an example as is the burning of scars and tattoos on the skins of certain other peoples. Some peoples have been known to bind the heads of their children in such a way as to deform them. Heavy weights are sometimes hung on the ears, noses, or lips of persons in some tribes to develop features which are different than nature would ordinarily provide. The American public would not have been nearly as susceptible to British propaganda during the first World War had it not been for the mores defining patriotism.[10]

The Mores Can Make Anything Right. Sumner, in his writings concerning the strength of the mores, said that they could make anything right.[11] The mores among various types of civilizations have made the offering of human sacrifices an accepted practice. In other groups kidnaping or stealing a wife from another tribe is the approved procedure. Stealing from an enemy is usually defined as a virtue. The killing of a German by an Englishman in both the first and second World Wars, and vice versa, has been a mark of distinction. The mores of the Indians bestow the greatest honor upon the young brave who returns from war with the largest number of scalps. The mores make it right for the cannibal to eat his enemy. The mores of the Russian Revolutionary Communists made the killing of the Russian aristocracy a virtue. Who can predict what the mores may make right in America?

The mores can make an act right at one time and wrong at another. This is due to the fact that culture and circumstances determine the mores. An act which may be approved by a society in war times may be tabooed during a period of peace. At the beginning of the century smoking by women was tabooed; today it is tolerated. Street dresses and bathing suits which are approved for use by women today would have been prohibited not many years ago. Today, Sunday motion pictures and other recreations are approved. One hundred years ago if a person were allowed to take a walk on Sunday it was for the exercise and not for the pleasure; if a person played his violin on Sunday he did so for the practice and not for any psychological rejuvenation.

Law

When the mores and folkways are codified and expressed as enacted rules or regulations whose enforcement is made possible by

---

10 James R. Mock and Cedric Larson, *Words That Won the War*, Princeton, N. J.: Princeton University Press, 1939.

11 W. G. Sumner, *op. cit.*, pp. 521–532.

a politically organized state, we have laws. Laws are more rational and practical than the mores, as well as being more specific, exacting, and inflexible. Sentiment and faith characterize the mores. Laws are positive, while the mores are not rigidly formulated nor defined. Behavior under the laws is conscious, while under the mores it is unconscious and has the sanction of supposed natural necessity. The mores regulate and control great spheres of our lives where the police or the laws do not reach. The enforcement of the law lies in the hands of special agents appointed by the state, such as the public police, highway patrolmen, "G-men," and courts, while enforcement of the mores usually depends upon public opinion. There are conditions, however, such as the arresting of people who will not salute the flag or stand when the Star Spangled Banner is played during war time, when the police power is used to support the behavior expected through the mores.

There is some relationship between the number of laws and the complexity of society. Among primitive people there are but few codified laws, and control of the individuals is made possible through the folkways, mores, or taboos which represent coercive, logically derived restraints upon individual conduct. As interhuman relations have increased in complexity and scope, the laws have increased. A capitalistic economy, such as exists in the United States, with the many new inventions and rapid changes which are taking place in our society, constantly necessitates the writing of new laws. Just as new laws are added every year, many old laws become obsolete. Not only are many laws obsolete in the sense that they are an attempt to control situations which no longer exist, but conditions have been changed to such an extent that the laws no longer provide an adequate control. New laws are frequently related to inventions; for instance, laws governing radio broadcasting. For a period following the introduction of the radio to the public there was relatively little control over any phase of the new activity. Today there are a number of laws regulating a single phase of radio organization, namely broadcasting. The laws controlling broadcasting are an expression of the folkways or usages which developed between the invention of the radio and the enactment of the laws. The laws, rules, and regulations governing automobile production and traffic are examples of folkways which have developed on the heels of the automobile industry.

Europeans have not only been amused at our desire to organize clubs, but they have been astounded at our prolific enactment of laws which express a desire to regulate the minute details of people's lives. European nations, particularly England, have refused to attempt to regulate so many phases of the lives of their citizens with written laws. The English people live more by the common law. This does not mean that the English people necessarily have more freedom than does the average citizen of the United States; neither does it imply that the average Englishman does not know what is expected of him, because the common law of the English is just as explicit as the law which is written in the statute books in America.

Institutions

Another phase of social structure which exists in the minds of people and controls or guides human behavior like mores, folkways, customs, and laws is the institution. The institution has been defined as a "culturalized, more or less standardized, set of habits and associated attitudes and ideas centering around some primary or derived want or need of individuals, such as sustenance, sex, transmission of culture, etc."[12] Expressed otherwise, an institution may be thought of as an organized, standardized, or channelized way of achieving certain objectives. Institutions are established means of satisfying some of man's most basic needs and represent an outgrowth of repeated collective action. As such, they indicate how people should act in a given situation.

In reality, an institution is nothing more nor less than a crystallization and integration of a set of mores and folkways. Marriage as an institution is characterized by a whole series of mores and folkways which regulate the various relationships between husbands, wives, and other relatives. These regulated relations become integrated, that is, they support each other and become functionally related parts of the whole family system. This stability, as well as uniformity of coherence, is achieved with the result that there develops a definable whole that covers a great segment of human interest and life policy. The family life among the Iroquois mentioned in the early part of this chapter illustrates how a variety of actions of people are controlled by the mores and how these actions become ways of meeting the major needs of the people. In our society many of these clusters of mores are given a positive form

[12] Kimball Young, *Social Psychology*, New York: F. S. Crofts & Co., 1938, p. 677.

through legislation, with the result that the privileges and obligations which arise from various series of relationships are given positive definition and adequate guarantees through law. In this way one can readily see how the operation of the folkways and the mores may develop into an institution or prepare the way for a definition of relationships as specified by law.

Our major institutions center around the family, church, state, school, and economic system. Others, however, deal with such things as health, science, welfare of people, communications, recreation, and art. The term "institution" as used in current literature has a wide diversity of meanings. For example, the church and the state are frequently spoken of as institutions. At the same time a charity organization, a brotherhood, or a ladies aid that functions within the church may be referred to as an institution. Easter services are referred to as an institution. The bank as a part of our social structure is designated as an institution. A majority of the institutions do not spring up like mushrooms but represent trial and error experiments usually covering long periods of time in which images, ideas, and attitudes are involved. Most institutions may be thought of as outgrowths of folkways. Some institutions, however, such as modern credit, are partly the result of legislation. In this sense institutions differ from laws. Some laws are enacted that are not based upon the experimental procedure of the group. This is well illustrated by such laws as The National Recovery Act, the Agricultural Adjustment Act, and others. On the other hand the institutions represent a crystallization of common experiences of the group. They have been tried and tested over a period of time. The institutions have some elements in common with laws; both of them are more explicit than the folkways and mores because they are supposed to represent a logical development. Both laws and institutions are characterized by certain regulations with the necessary authority and powers to enable supervision and enforcement of specified measures. The school, the family, and banking each has its authoritative head who is empowered to excommunicate members for actions contrary to the approved modes. Even though many institutions possess coercive physical power, it is seldom used. The father, as well as the school teacher and administrator, now usually handles disciplinary problems with persuasion and attempted consensus. With law the situation is different in that there is usually a great reliance upon physical force to insure observance and enforcement.

One of the significant characteristics of every institution is that every participating member has his role defined and does his part in achieving the objective. The church with its objective of religious education and indoctrination illustrates the regularized procedure and prescribed roles played by different people as a means of achieving a goal. The mores and folkways define the duties and tasks of the clergy and the laymen; the respect and obligations due each other are suggested in detail, as is proper and improper behavior in various social situations. Rituals are carried out according to prescribed rules and regulations; every person knows his functional obligations in relation to the other cooperating persons.

Relation of Institutions to Association. The terms *institution* and *association* are sometimes used interchangeably; there is, however, a distinct difference as used here. An association is a group of people organized to achieve a given purpose or goal, while an institution is the prescribed way or established procedure used to achieve the goal. The associations involve the united action of people, in contrast with the institution which channelizes or specifies how the actions are to proceed in order to achieve the objective. The difference between an association and an institution can be illustrated by the football team or the social unit on the college campus. The group of players is the association, while the different rules of the game and the moves outlined to execute a forward pass or an end run constitute the institution. The social unit, as an organization of students, is an association, but the methods of initiating new members, plus the system of values, divisions of responsibility, and the ideals make up the institution.

Scope of Institutions. The institutions in any society are very numerous. Their numbers are determined by the complexity of the culture and the needs of the people. Our present society in the United States has many more institutions than existed two hundred years ago. An examination of our culture reveals numerous institutions surrounding one basic need. For example, they have grown up around the production systems, be they handcraft or factories; others have been established which are related to our systems of communication, transportation, and distribution; numerous ones are related to various services of credit and banking; there are literally dozens of different ones in the field of agriculture. Each is important and complex. Governmental institutions are as numerous as those dealing with economics. They regulate and control behavior. When a child is born, its birth has to be registered; deaths are recorded. The government has institutions which specify many factors concerning the building of a house, including sanitation, plumbing, lighting, and distance from the street or other buildings. Governmental institutions provide police protection both within and without the community, as well as offering recreational and educational service. Governmental institutions control marriage and divorce; they provide unemployment compensation and old age pensions. Permission from the government is necessary to go abroad. Few days pass when our lives are not affected in numerous ways by such institutions.

This brief summary of the new fields in which numerous institutions function by prescribing usages and channelizing human behavior illustrates the tremendous field of such activity. Because of a combination of factors that will determine the relative weight which institutions will have upon the lives of individuals, it is not possible to suggest how numerous institutions will be in the future. It is significant that institutions vary in the complexity of their structure and the period of their existence. One of the oldest and most complex social institutions now in existence in the western civilization is the Catholic Church. Historically, its existence approximates 1,900 years. As a church it influences more people's lives than any other single institution in western culture. Not only does it reach many people, but it also influences a multitude of spheres of each person's life. Some institutions existing in the Orient antedate the Catholic Church historically, as well as influencing a greater number of people's lives more completely.

Some institutions have a very limited function in comparison with others. The functions of a bank, for instance, are relatively few in comparison with the local church which has a ladies' aid, men's brotherhood, a choir, a young folks' organization, a Boy Scout troop, a gymnasium class, a dramatics club, a missionary society, a social events club, a Sunday school, and a general worship service. There are but few phases in the life of a person who attends church that are not influenced by it in one way or another.

The old town guild represented an institution which functioned in various ways, as illustrated by the following quotation from MacIver:

The original town guilds, for example, were concerned with moral, religious, political, as well as economic, issues. Like all locally bound associations they tended to regulate the life, the customs, and the ideals of their members. Their standards of honesty and honor did not bear solely on the methods of manufacture or trade. They instituted a series of observances which made them part of a system of education, of moral and religious discipline, of philanthropy, of civic administration as well as of good fellowship.[13]

In contrast to the institutions which are very complex are those that are simple, informal, and of short duration. These are illustrated by the honeymoon, the banquet, the auction sale, and the sit-down strike.

Institutions Fix Individual Roles. One noticeable characteristic of the institution has been the presence of regulations, rituals, and fixed roles for each individual that are built around a central concept; an example is the sit-down strike, where the role played by each individual is performed in terms of basic ideas, attitudes, assumptions, desires, concepts of right and wrong, regulations, and rituals. The school is another illustration of how multiple usages find expression in an institutional structure. Everyone begins with the ideals of education and the assumption that every person should learn a minimum of fundamental concepts. The teachers organize the curriculum and outline the plan of procedure which is to be followed. There are tasks, approved procedures, obligations, appropriate roles, and fixed regulations for the students and teachers in practically every situation.

Legends, myths, and superstitions of various kinds can be thought of as constituting a part of social structure. They may be the foundation of an intricate part of the folkways, mores, institutions, or laws.

All people, regardless of race or cultural conditioning, become hungry, thirsty, and sexually aroused by certain stimuli. Their responses, however, as a means of satisfying these stimuli, differ greatly from one group to another and may be said to depend upon the social structure.

SOCIAL STRUCTURE DIRECTS BEHAVIOR

Social structure constitutes the machinery for social control. There is no complete, comprehensive, or detailed statement that

[13] R. M. MacIver, *The Elements of Social Science*, London: Methuen and Co., Ltd., 1921, (New York: E. P. Dutton and Co.) pp. 97–98. Reprinted by permission.

shows to what extent the various physiological activities of the average man in the United States are regulated by the group in which he lives. An examination, however, of a few of the following acts performed by an average individual reveals how extensively our behavior is controlled by the group. The acts which are suggested below are only a partial statement of all those performed, yet there are thousands of folkways, mores, and laws that control various aspects of each.

1. *Eating.* Society regulates the act of eating in various ways; not only are we told what to eat, but when, how, and where we may do so.

2. *Drinking.* Regulated in a similar fashion to eating.

3. *Marrying.* Marriage is controlled by various laws, rituals, and sundry specifications.

4. *Talking.* Each person is taught what constitutes proper or improper speech according to the circumstance and situation. False statements are subject to penalty.

5. *Taking.* Society attempts to control what we are allowed to possess, and any effort to appropriate that which does not belong to us is severely punished.

6. *Mourning.* Rules tend to regulate the behavior of each member who survives another.

7. *Entering.* The buildings into which a person may go are definitely controlled as is the behavior that is tolerated once a person has entered such a structure as a church or a home.

8. *Giving.* There are appropriate rules and behavior patterns that specify what, how, when, and where gifts are presented.

9. *Being Formal.* Various customs demand formality under varying conditions so as to avoid treating others with undue familiarity.

10. *Harming Others or Murdering.* Everyone is protected by the law against any possible harm. Each person who disregards the law "thou shalt not kill" is subject to vengeance and punishment.

11. *Clothing Self.* What, how, and when one wears a given piece of clothing is determined and regulated by society.

12. *Mutilating Self.* Various laws regulate just how extensively each individual may mutilate or allow his own person to be mutilated.

13. *Cleansing Self.* By means of slogans and taboos each indi-

vidual is compelled to adhere to certain standards of personal cleanliness.

14. *Respecting Others.* Each individual in our society is compelled to respect others and refrain from the expression of insults
toward another person.

Many societies allow less personal freedom and activity than our
own, while some tend to be more liberal. This is shown by various
studies that have been made among the cultural groups.[14]

In summary, social structure is the guide and gives direction to
human behavior. Without it community living would be impossible
because each person would do what he wanted to do at will, giving
no regard to other people or to their desires. Social structure is common to all groups of people either in the courts of kings or presidents, in the mansions and offices of industrialists or the slums or
hideouts of criminals, in the laboratory of the scientist or the hovel
of the illiterate. It is the means by which orderliness is established
in either cooperation or conflict between human beings. In the
home, the church, the school, the club, or on the street, every man
knows his role in the cooperative enterprise. The failure of any
person to behave as the group has defined creates confusion. The
competition on the football field is channelized and regulated by
both the written and unwritten rules of the game. Even wars have
usually been waged with some attention to codes of ethics and
folk practices.

From the foregoing discussion it is evident that people do not
respond to stimuli in a willy-nilly fashion. Their responses are
usually channelized and expressed in terms of some ideals, standards, and procedures which they have acquired as a result of living
with other people. In brief, social structure tells each person when
and how he is expected to act in almost every situation.

SELECTED REFERENCES

Cooley, Charles Horton, *Social Organization*, New York: Charles Scribner's and
    Sons, 1924.—A consideration of social structure in terms of organization,
    communication, the democratic mind, social classes and institutions.
Eubank, Earle Edward, *The Concepts of Sociology*, Chicago: D. C. Heath & Co.,
    1931.—Especially pp. 123–130 and 529–531. A brief statement regarding
    the concept of social structure with special emphasis upon definitions, a
    historical statement, and a bibliography.

[14] C. S. Ford, "Society Culture and the Human Organism," *Journal of
General Psychology*, vol. 20–21, 1939, pp. 135–180.

Goldenweiser, Alexander, *Anthropology, An Introduction to Primitive Culture*, New York: F. S. Crofts & Co., 1937.—A treatise on the more material aspects of culture with considerable emphasis upon the social structure.

Linton, Ralph, *The Study of Man*, New York: D. Appleton-Century Co., 1936.— A dynamic interpretation of the various factors that contribute to operational relationships in primitive and contemporary society.

Murdock, George P., *Our Primitive Contemporaries*, New York: The Macmillan Co., 1934.—A brief description of a number of preliterate cultures, illustrative of diverse material cultures and social structure.

Sims, Newell Leroy, *Elements of Rural Sociology*, New York: Thomas Y. Crowell Co., 1935.—A statement of social structure in rural society.

Sumner, William Graham, *Folkways*, Boston: Ginn & Company, 1906.—Probably the best book published on the subject of social structure.

Thrasher, Frederic M., *The Gang*, Chicago: The University of Chicago Press, 1936.—Chapter XVI, entitled ''Structure of the Gang,'' illustrates the social structure of the boys' group in Chicago's slum area.

Ward, Lester F., ''Evolution of Social Structure,'' *American Journal of Sociology*,'' 10: 589–605, March, 1905.—A detailed statement showing how social structure develops.

Wiese, Leopold von, and Becher, Howard, *Systematic Sociology*, New York: John Wiley & Sons, Inc., 1932.—Parts 1 and 3 give a very detailed statement of social structure.

CHAPTER 14

THE FAMILY

By Professor M. L. Jordan

Fenn College, Cleveland

AND DR. ELMER PENDELL

Pennsylvania State College

Various aspects of the family have already been brought to your attention in the chapters on Biological Regularities II, Personality, Human Groups, Social Forces and Processes, and Anthropological Backgrounds. In this chapter the family is analyzed with emphasis on its *functions*.

Groves thinks that a married couple does not constitute a family unless and until a child is added.[1] However, as a part of social organization childless couples make up an important type of organization which can better be considered under the heading The Family than elsewhere. For our purposes the family is a comparatively durable group composed of a man and a woman, together with their children if any, or plural survivors of such a group continuing as a group. The "plural survivors" might be a woman and her children after the death of the husband, or might be the children after the death of both parents, or might be the father and his children after the death of their mother.

FUNCTIONS OF THE FAMILY

A function is a performance, an activity, a working out, a result. We know the family if we know its functions, for with institutions as with appletrees and men, "by their fruits shall ye know them."

We shall list a few items with the hypothesis that they are functions of the family, and then we shall examine them to ascertain if in those particulars the family does work out according to the hypothesis.

A. Functions relating to spouses:
    1. Gratification of wishes:
        a. Sex;

[1] Ernest R. Groves, *Social Problems of the Family*, J. B. Lippincott Company, 1927, p. 90.

  b. Companionship;
  c. Recognition;
  d. New experience;
  e. Security.
 2. Economic production center.
 3. Approved opportunity for having offspring.
 4. Selection of marriage mates for offspring.
B. Functions relating to offspring:
 1. Gratification of wishes;
 2. Education;
 3. Vocational training and vocational guidance;
 4. Psychological co-ordination;
 5. Economic support.
C. Functions relating to society:
 1. Reproduction;
 2. Continuity conservation (passing on traditional ways);
 3. Conduct control.
We proceed now to examine those hypothetical functions.

Functions of the Family Relating to Spouses

In considering the *gratification of wishes* our first item is *sex desire*. The various endocrine glands discharge chemicals called hormones into the blood, and these hormones act as stimulants for various body cells including the other glands. When the various hormones are in just sufficient measure to result in a placid temperament in a placid environment they are maintaining an endocrine balance. Hormones from the sex glands rarely maintain the appropriate flow for placidity. Presumably, in the long eons of human evolution, survival via reproduction has depended on some amount of aggressiveness. The slight upset of the endocrine balance stimulates sex desire and is a prompting toward sex activity. The endocrine balance is temporarily restored by sex expression, and the family relationship is the socially approved opportunity for the repeated restoration, the psychological counterpart of which is the gratification of the sex desire.

However, the opportunity is actually existent only if the husband and wife are in general harmony. If there is a lack of rapport between the mates, the sex function of the family diminishes, even ceases. In part, then, this function depends on and is interwoven with the function of companionship.

The family has had no absolute monopoly in the gratification of sex desire, and in recent decades condemnation of sex relations out of the family has somewhat abated. However, there is little actual approval for extra-marital sex acts; consequently, resultant from any such extra-marital behavior, psychological conflict and tension are likely to be present.

The supplying of *companionship* is still a function relating to spouses, classifiable under gratification of wishes, but in the family there have arisen many barriers to companionship, many obstacles, many competing organizations and situations. When man, wife, and children worked together on a farm the companionship that each received from the others was important. Now 56.5 per cent of the population live in cities of more than 2500 inhabitants; associations of the office or other place of work subtract somewhat from the family's fulfilment of the companionship function. Other relationships compete with the family in furnishing companionship, and in the competition the factors which seem to operate in favor of the family are a happy temperament and similarities or sameness of the spouses as to socio-economic status, occupation, religion, education, mental ability, race, country, community. We shall now briefly survey these factors which help hold families together through gratifying the wish for companionship.

Temperament. A stable, happy temperament possessed by either spouse goes far toward making for companionability. In a person of such temperament there is a generosity, a self-discipline, an habitual yielding to others' wishes. A person of happy temperament is, in popular language, unselfish. If one dominates and the other can remain happy in spite of the domination, the measure of companionship may be large, but if each spouse is willing to hold the ego in control, adjustments are even easier, and companionship has a very strong support.

Socio-economic Status. The story of Cinderella ended with her marriage to the prince. It had to, because, with their contrasted social backgrounds, the sequel would otherwise have been replete with misery. Companionship between persons conditioned in different social strata is likely to be superficial. There are exceptions, no doubt, where both spouses hold intensely a common major interest. In general, however, if husband and wife are in the same income group and in the same social circles their chances of harmony are much greater.

Occupation. Attitudes, ideas, knowledge—these are the stuff of which companionship is made. Roughly 50 per cent of waking time is spent in connection with one's occupation, and mental patterns are molded accordingly. If mates are in the same or closely related occupations they have one good foundation for companionship. If the wife has been in the same occupation but left it at marriage, the rapport is likely to be much greater than if she has no understanding of her husband's routine.

Creed. Though occupation consumes much of a person's time, and therefore goes far in making up personality, yet with most people occupation is merely a means to the end of making a living; to only a few is it a value in itself. Religion, in contrast, consumes relatively little time but strikes deep. It is permeated with concepts that are values in themselves. When a comrade differs, so much the worse for the comradeship; the creed is relatively stable. If creed of man differs from creed of wife, their companionship has at least one weak foundation, though firmness in other supports may prevent its collapse.

Education. Not only are attitudes, ideas, and knowledge, affected by education, but interests, thought processes and habits are likewise influenced. Consequently, a similarity of educational backgrounds seems important to enduring companionship. Among the habits affected by education perhaps most important are the grammar habits. If one who speaks with grammatical precision is paired with one of careless habits there is danger of irritation on both sides.

Companionship without a mutuality of interests is almost a contradiction. Companionship of persons with wide differences of education is unlikely because interests are likely to be diverse. Travel, either locally or at a distance, may offer a common ground of interest to mates of different educational levels, but even it cannot be relied upon to heal the breach that is generally present where educational differences are great.

According to Terman the greatest danger to marital happiness is for the wife to be educationally several years ahead of her husband. This seems to make little difference to the husband, but it makes much difference to the wife.[2]

As pointed out by Dr. Kovacs in our Chapter 10:

[2] Lewis M. Terman, *Psychological Factors in Marital Happiness,* McGraw-Hill Book Company, Inc., 1938, pp. 187–191.

Unity of the group in which members have only one or a very few interests in common is usually weak. The greater the number of common interests of the members of a group, the greater is the variety of life situations in which they are brought together.

Mental Ability. Though education is a series of tests of mental ability, and involves a considerable amount of weeding out, nevertheless there remain wide differences in adaptability even among those who have been exposed to any given level of formal schooling. Similarities in kind and degree of education furnish a reliable basis for companionship, but just as important is likeness in degree of mental ability. Stupidity in one engenders the other's disgust, puts up a barrier to companionship.

For persons of a domineering type, acknowledgment of superiority, inasmuch as it gratifies the wish for recognition, may be as effective as companionship in holding a pair together; nevertheless that relationship is not of the companionship type.

Race, Country, Community. Race probably has little direct bearing on companionship, though it may in a given community have an influence on social status and thus indirectly put a strain on the marital relationship. Background in the same country makes for a mutuality of mental patterns. Upbringing in the same community gives still more assurance of common backgrounds.

From the above considerations it appears that the family does not automatically assure companionship; it does serve to maintain a companionship when the elements of companionship are already present.

The Wish for Recognition. The four wishes of W. I. Thomas have already been brought to your attention by Dr. Bahm. In Thomas' formulation both sex desire and desire for companionship would fall under the wish for response. Another of the persistent approach attitudes toward values is the desire for recognition. Can we classify the gratification of that desire for recognition as a function relating to spouses? Sometimes the family fulfils the function of its gratification; sometimes not. There is opportunity for the husband to discover and recognize such values as his wife possesses and as she holds most worthy; opportunity for the wife to know the husband well. But if the value standards are different the recognition is not likely to be forthcoming. Recognition rests, then, on the same foundations as does companionship.

In Eugene O'Neill's *The Great God Brown,* Margaret loved not the sensitive, esthetic, real Dion, but Man in a mask of strength. The family in that case had no function of gratifying the wish for recognition.

Does the family function in gratifying *the wish for new experience?* Apparently not—except for the brief period while the spouses are learning one another's peculiarities, and perhaps while the first infant is exhibiting the early steps in socialization.

Coming to our last topic under *Gratification of Wishes* as a function of the family relating to spouses, in many families the *wife's wish for security,* in its *economic aspects,* is well served. Less often does a family bring economic security for *man,* although in some jobs married men are preferred on the theory that they are less restless; at least are more definitely anchored. When, as sometimes happens, a woman gives up a steady pay envelope for the gamble of married life there is subtraction from security. When, as sometimes happens, a man is obliged to part with surpluses because of family expenses there is a subtraction from security. The very fact of reduced mobility, too, is for most men a reduction in security inasmuch as one cannot so readily take advantage of distant jobs. Considering the subject from the standpoint of both sexes it is doubtful that *economic* security can be considered a function of the family.

However, there seems to be a security core in the *wish for an organizing center.* There is a wish for a place from which to start out on the activities of the day or week, to which one may return and, if one wishes, relax. One organizes his vacation in terms of a round trip; plans his trip up to the point of return to home base.

Thus the home often serves as an organizing center, a motivation coordinator. However, in many instances it is in competition with the office.

The Home as Economic Production Center. Economic production *in agricultural areas* has been a family function relating to spouses from time immemorial. For centuries, in America as elsewhere, the home was a farm on which sheep were raised and wool was made into yarn, then cloth, then clothing. Grain was sown and reaped and dried and threshed and stored and ground into meal or flour; baked into cakes or bread. Cattle were pastured, sheltered, milked; and butter and cheese were made. Hogs, beef calves, old cows, hens and ducks, furnished an ample meat supply. Horses or oxen supplied the power for drawing farm machinery; also supplied the power for transportation.

The variety of production was broad, and an almost complete family sufficiency was the result. Life was closely integrated, with the family as the unit. Perhaps the most significant fact for us about this agricultural family as a production center is that in early America it involved a very large majority of the population.

Even yet, *in farming,* the family is the main production center, though corporation farming is gaining ground. The production less often now than formerly involves complete processes, however; it is more specialized, and outside economic contacts are more frequent. Also, the persons in the United States not in incorporated places constitute only 36.4 per cent of the population, according to the 1940 census; and according to Landis those actually engaged in farming constitute less than one-fourth of our population.[3]

In discussing the economic production function of the family, then, we have to make separate categories for urban and rural areas.

In the *towns* the shriveling of the economic function has been impressive, and in some classes almost complete. The males are out of family production almost entirely, and it hardly serves as a bond between the members.

The women, in many instances, might be more productive out of the home. No longer do they make candles from bayberries or tallow as they did in an earlier day. They make no cloth, few clothes; rarely do they even bake bread. In some classes they still do the family washing; raise three or four children; sew, cook and bake. In other classes they open up a can, take the paper off the pre-sliced bread, touch a rug with a vacuum sweeper—and with that, except for a little busy work, the day's duties are over.

"From sun-up till three stars shine" is the stint of the man on the farm; and "Woman's work is never done," but in city homes the production duties vary from arduous to obsolete.

Approved Opportunity for Having Offspring. This is our third topic under "functions relating to spouses." In about two-thirds of the instances of pregnancy the family relationship provides economic support for the expectant mother. State and National governments and charity organizations take care of the other third. The third thus provided for are for the most part married, but are in circumstances where the husband is unable to support his family. In the United States illegitimate births constitute approximately 3

[3] Paul H. Landis, *Rural Life in Process,* New York: McGraw-Hill Book Co., 1940, p. 8.

per cent of all births, although of colored births one in seven is illegitimate.

In the countries to the south of us where Puritan influence has been absent the rates for illegitimacy are higher and social disapproval is less. In Mexico, two out of five births are illegitimate; in Panama, according to the Encyclopaedia Britannica, seven out of ten are illegitimate.

In the United States, social sanction accompanies births when parents are married, whether they can support their offspring or not; social sanction is withheld from births when parents are not married; whether they can support their offspring or not. The family relationship is a socially imposed pre-requsite to sanctioned reproduction.

In case of sterility—and sterility occurs in about 12 per cent of couples—the family still provides an opportunity for having children. A frequent means of meeting the situation is to adopt a child, although adoptions are also common where there is no sterility. Recently sterility clinics have been established in many cities, and, according to *Hygeia* for October, 1941, and *Reader's Digest* for the same month, "are reporting success in almost half their cases," restoring fertility to the prospective parents. Artificial insemination is sometimes an aid in such cases. Also, where the sterility of the husband is persistent but the wife is capable of bearing children, if there is to be a child a choice must be made between having a child with the heredity of one of the spouses or acquiring a child by adoption with the heredity of neither. Many families choose the former method. Usually sires are carefully selected; give a heredity result which, if not equal to that of Aristotle or Archimedes, is at any rate more accomplished than the world's average. A study of artificial insemination and its use in the United States by the medical profession has been made by the National Research Foundation for Eugenical Alleviation of Sterility. Questionnaires were sent to 30,000 of the 150,000 doctors of medicine in the United States. Of the thirty thousand, 7,642 replied, 4,049 reporting successful results. Up to June, 1940, there had been 9,238 children born by the artificial method under the supervision of the doctors who reported. The fathers supplied the heredity for 5,728 of them whereas 3,510 were by selected sires. If the 30,000 doctors to whom the questionnaires were sent constitute a representative sample, we may multiply those figures by five to get an approximation of the figures applying to the country as a whole : about 28,000 by fathers, about 17,000 by selected sires; total by artificial insemination about 45,000.

Inasmuch as childless families have been subject to divorce in far greater proportion than have families with children, there seems to be a probability that by adoptions and by artificial insemination the stability of the family will be increased. An important function of the family will be more widely applicable.

Selection of Marriage Mates for Offspring. In many lands the parents take the initiative in arranging matrimonial alliances for their children. In various oriental countries it has been customary for a contract for later marriage to be made while a child is very young; occasionally even before the child is born. In Europe and America, throughout the last century, parental guidance was usually controlling in mate selection, although the youth had a privilege of vetoing a parental choice. The youthful initiative has gradually increased. The parents of the girl hope they retain a veto power in the ''ask father'' tradition, but are not quite sure. The son's parents are resigned to an expression of relative degrees of approval of such girl friends as are brought to their attention. The glorification of romance, and the fact that the wage system gives some degree of economic independence to youngsters, have limited the parental function in the selection of marriage mates of their children to counselling—mostly an expression of ''don'ts''.

Functions of the Family Relating to Offspring

Gratification of Wishes. The yearning for *affection* may be partly made up of the wish for response and partly of the wish for security. Whatever its ingredients, the craving for affection is very real. Various families respond to the wish with feeling or show of feeling ranging in volume from a trace to nausea. The family is the normal source of *companionship* for a child, particularly while he is very young. In families of several children the companionship function is likely to last throughout childhood, particularly in rural surroundings. The wish for *recognition* usually finds a gratification in the family. The parents, and often the other children, are proud of any little accomplishment a child may make. Inasmuch as the family is in a position to get early and frequent information concerning accomplishment, it is in a favorable situation for satisfying this wish. *Security* in the protection of the home is a usual feeling. How often one hears from a seven-year-old, ''My dad can lick your dad!'' Identification of self with a power greater than self prevents a feeling of inferiority.

Education. Leonardo da Vinci, Benjamin Franklin, John Stuart Mill, Benjamin Disraeli, and many other scholarly giants of the past, received a substantial part of their education from their parents. Likewise did many men who never rose to fame, from primitive times until the 20th century. Especially in vocational activity the parents showed ''the young idea how to shoot.'' The cobbler taught his son the art of making shoes; the tailor's sons were tailor's apprentices; the butcher, the baker, the candlestick maker, each took pride in his sons' skill. And Maud Muller, presumably from her mother, learned to rake the hay; probably also to milk the cows, do the churning, the cooking, spinning, weaving, sewing and darning.

As important as training in objective matters was the attitude building, and this too was a function of the family. Folkyarns and religion and morals and economy and loyalty and patriotism and various other attitudes were imparted by the family as part of everyday living.

The schools have taken over almost all of the objective teaching: the training in facts and relationships and in how to do things. Sometimes persons in school systems go so far as to discourage any parental instruction in even the simplest aspects of formal education. The schools' importance is increased if schools have a thoroughgoing monopoly. Except as some rebel parent occasionally calls the schoolman's bluff, the family's participation in objective education is limited almost to teaching the child how to dress himself.

In attitude formation the family function has continued longer; but among many families there is now no assumption of responsibility. Juvenile delinquency, it appears, is often correlated with ignorance and lack of social consciousness on the part of the parents, and because ignorant people specialize on having babies a large proportion of students receive at home little attitude building of a sort calculated to result in social harmony. Frequently there arises the urgement that schools take over the attitude building. As yet attitude building in the schools is supplementary, but as they widen their province the role of the family contracts.

Vocational Guidance as a Function of the Family Relating to Offspring. Until recently this was closely associated with vocational training. The circumstances called for little special attention to vocational guidance. Extra-family contacts were fewer; children by their daily activities became conditioned to their life work. Now such conditioning is accomplished in lesser degree by the parents. Since many of a child's associations are outside the family, his skills and interests are less predictable. The schools are gradually developing testing techniques and are taking over the guidance function. For many children, however, the parents still play the major role in guidance.

Psychological Coordination of a Child by Aid of the Family. The school, the Sunday School, the boys' club or girls' club, are now ministering to large segments of juvenile interests. Nevertheless the home is still home base; is still the integrating factor in the child's life. This fact is brought out in Dr. Topping's chapter on Crime, in Part IV of this book, in which he shows striking correlations between broken homes and juvenile delinquency. Clearly the home conditions are important in unifying the youngsters' personalities.

Economic Support of the Children. Providing for the children remains mainly a function of the family. Ability to provide is not a pre-requisite to having babies, but if parents do chance to have the ability to provide, then providing is a legal responsibility. As previously pointed out, about a third of America's babies are born in families without the ability to support them.

Functions Relating to Society

Functions that relate to the offspring, which we have just been considering, also relate indirectly to society. So do those that relate to the spouses. The functions relating to society which we are about to report are additional to those reported under functions relating to spouses and functions relating to offspring. Most often discussed as a function of the family relating to society is *reproduction.*

Reproduction as a Function of the Family. Except for reproduction, of course, society itself would soon cease to exist.

Each of us is representative of a mighty host of persons connected with us in series of families. The connections are astounding in their multiplicity. Your great-grandmother is one of eight ancestors the third generation removed from you; and from one of her great-grandmothers you derive a 64th part of your heredity. Three hundred years ago, when the founding fathers were swinging axes in Massachusetts forests, your ancestors, ten generations removed, numbered 1,024, unless there had been some intra-marriage among them.

That allows thirty years per generation. The average age of a father at the time of a child's birth is about 32 years; that of a mother is about 28. One ancestor may have been the oldest child in a family, another the youngest in his family; most have been in between. And the average time of their arrival has been about the middle of their mothers' child-bearing periods after marriage: age 28.

Husbands have been somewhat older than their wives. They have usually found it necessary to establish an earning power before getting consent of a prospective father-in-law. The economic prerequisite having delayed them, they have found their field of choice expanded on the one side by the inclusion of younger girls, now developed to the bloom of womanhood, and restricted on the other side by prior selections among girls of their own age and older. The practice of girls marrying older men is thus consistent with economic necessity and it is also consistent with biological survival, inasmuch as it leaves available for actual child-bearing a greater portion of a woman's reproduction period. However, according to Burgess and Cottrell a marriage seems to have a somewhat better chance of durability if the wife is slightly older than the husband.

Each of the thousand and twenty-four ancestors ten steps removed would himself or herself be related, ten generations farther back, with 1,024 forebears, except that from some of them there has come a double heritage; so, in a generation twenty families in the past, each of us would have had 1,048,576 ancestors—except for the converging of lines as when first or tenth cousins mary. And 900 years ago, (30 generations) when Lief Ericson's Norsemen were spinning yarns to their grandchildren about the wonders of the Plymouth Rock region, your ancestors, except for the convergence of lines, would have numbered 1,073,741,824.

One would not have to trace his family tree back the 700 or more generations to Cro-Magnon man's arrival in Europe to find a relationship to his next-door neighbor and to Isaac Newton, Ivan Pavlov, Emil Fischer and Albert Einstein, though the connecting threads might be pretty thin.

Although family organization of some sort has been present for many generations, yet the family as an institution was not planned by anybody as an agency of reproduction.   The family as a specific pairing of John Doe and his wife is only sometimes planned as an agency of reproduction.   Having babies is only incidental to the usual purpose of matrimony—which purpose is the gratification of sex desire camouflaged under the concepts of romantic love.

If there were social planning with regard to offspring—by the state, or by the churches, or by the unions, or by special associations, or even by the pairs of prospective mates—presumably considerations of quantity and of quality would be made effective among the groups doing the planning, inasmuch as reason rather than emotion would be guiding.   Eugenists and some of the protagonists of birth control are inclined to think that if there were more social planning in the matter of reproduction there would be less call for social planning in the fields of housing, care of the poor, unemployment relief, public health, and public playgrounds.

But though children are only incidental by-products of the family institution, yet reproduction lacks social sanction when not under family auspices.

The Family as a Continuity Conservator and a Conduct Guide. Institutions of all sorts are conservative influences, as a rule, passing on the ways of living that have gradually been developed.   Deserving of a thought, in this connection, is the fact that it is the accumulation and conservation of culture which most strikingly differentiates men from other animals.   Emphasis has lately been away from this truth, however, because of the tensions growing out of unequal rates of social change.   Foremost among the institutions as a conservator is the family.

The function of conservator is closely related to the function of reproduction, inasmuch as the conservation of folkways is brought about through guiding the conduct of the children within the family. This *conduct control* is really a process of *socialization,* the children learning to fit into society through the family's instruction in the folkways.

The control is mostly a matter of instilling attitudes and habits into children, training them in ways of living which seem to the parents to have been tested and found workable.   They are not inclined to "try all things," but they do tend to hold fast to that which they think is good.   Thus it is that in their guidance families are conservators.

Now, having analyzed the family's functions, to the extent that space permits, we shall, in section II investigate Motives in Marriage, and after that we shall proceed to III, Relationships between the Family and the State, and IV, Divorce.

MOTIVES IN MARRIAGE

The psychological prompting which results in marriage seems in America to be in only small measure connected with the foregoing functions; seems in fact to be summed up in the word "love"; in other words, sex attraction with a halo: A.1.a. in our listing of functions relating to spouses on page 348. A typical showing is written up in the June, 1940, *Good Housekeeping* by Gretta Palmer. Nearly a hundred couples who had celebrated golden wedding anniversaries had been questionnaired, and nearly all of them had married for love; only about 25 per cent giving also a secondary reason such as companionship, a home, or children.

So ingrained in our American tradition is romantic love that to confess to any other motive predominating over subservience to Cupid is shocking. Apparently, few couples look beyond our A.1.a. For most of them that which leads to the "I do," is a strong emotion, a yearning, a wish to proclaim the magnetism of the object of affection together with a scarcity of words that seem suitable. The popular song writers capitalize on the feeling by supplying a variety of combinations of the words, "you, blue, true; dove, love, above; mine, pine, divine; June, moon, soon."

When, on December 1, 1936, Britain's King Edward VIII abdicated his throne, did he, in connection with his prospective marriage, ponder the functions of the family? Apparently he stopped at A.1.a. (with a halo) though possibly he got as far as A.1.b.

In serious moments, when confronted by a sociologist's questionnaire, college students, though they give little attention to the general array of family functions, do include as desirable qualities in a prospective mate such traits as make for companionship; namely, disposition, honesty, health, education, mutual intellectual interests.[4] Relatively few college students marry; those that marry have relatively few divorces. But for the run of the population, and often for college folk, what gets them is romantic love: sex, with a halo: oomph.

[4] See Wayne C. Neely, "Family Attitudes of Denominational College and University Students, 1929 and 1936," *American Sociological Review*, August, 1940.

RELATIONSHIPS BETWEEN THE FAMILY AND THE STATE

If we were to be complete in our treatment of The Family, in addition to many other topics we would deal with relationships between The Family and various other institutions: the neighborhood, the community, the church, the school, and others. We make no claim to an exhaustive treatment; rather we restrict ourselves to the relationships between the family and a single other institution, the state; and even with regard to those relationships we shall be brief.

Marriage

The State sets the conditions under which the husband-wife relationship is brought into being. If marriage is by consent of a boy's parents, he may be married at age 14 in the states of Colorado, Idaho, Michigan, Missssippi, New Hampshire, New Jersey, Washington; at age 18 in most states. If the girl's parents consent she may be married at age 12 in Colorado, Idaho, Michigan, Mississippi, and New Jersey; at age 16 in most states. Without parental consent men must be 21 years old in most states; women age 21 in 14 states, age 18 in 33 states and District of Columbia; age 16 in North Carolina.

The status of persons may be transformed from single to team by a marriage ceremony performed by any one of various state officials from city aldermen and justices of the peace to state judges, and to governor. For purposes of marriage, clergymen may also serve as state officials; the separation of church and state has not reached to that function. However, little legal responsibility attaches to the clergyman, or to other marrying official as such. Every state requires that a betrothed couple obtain a license. The licensing officer—usually a city alderman or a justice of the peace or a notary public—has whatever responsibility there is in the matter in addition to the tremendous responsibility resting on the marrying persons themselves. However, though a medical certificate is now required in most states, the law makes no requirement for the presentation of a birth certificate, and as to ages the licensing official accepts the oaths of the marrying pair.

Blood Tests

Directly affecting the family are the recent laws requiring medical examination prior to obtaining a license to be married. *Educa-*

tional Health Circular No. 62 published by the Illinois Department
of Public Health contains the law of that state passed in 1937 with
a foreword in an early edition of the circular the first paragraph
of which includes the following:

> Public interest has been aroused in the venereal disease
> situation and in the possibilities of controlling and preventing
> both syphilis and gonorrhea. Indisputable evidence that
> both diseases are widespread, that many people, especially
> women, are innocently infected through marital relations,
> that, about one in each one hundred babies born is congeni-
> tally infected with syphilis, that large numbers are exposed
> at birth to gonorrheal infection of the eyes that may cause
> blindness and that syphilis is responsible for a considerable
> proportion of insanity as well as numerous other ills has led
> to an insistent public demand for a comprehensive, sound
> program of control.

Illinois, New Hampshire, and Rhode Island, at least, have legislated against the marriage of persons affected with gonorrhea, but
for the most part the laws are directed against syphilis. Premarital
blood tests are now required for applicants for a marriage license
in thirty states.[5]

Sterilization

According to literature of the Human Betterment Foundation,[6]
the families from which children are taken to the state homes for the
feeble-minded in California have been multiplying about twice as
rapidly as the rest of the population. Of course this is not to say
that the rate of increase in families from which feeble-minded persons spring is higher in California than in other states, but that in
other states there is less available knowledge on the subject. The
hereditary basis for feeble-mindedness is reasonably well established,
as is also the hereditary basis of some types of insanity. California,
therefore, has undertaken a program of sterilization of such mentally defective and mentally diseased persons as are inmates of state

[5] This information is as of March 1, 1942. Up to the minute data can
be obtained from your own state legislative reference bureau, or from Bascom
Johnson of the American Social Hygiene Association, 50 West 50th Street,
New York, N. Y.

[6] 325 Security Building, Pasadena, California. The Human Betterment
Foundation publishes a brief annual report of sterilization in the various states.

institutions. On a relatively small scale a number of other states are following similar programs.

Sterilization is a surgical operation in which the tubes carrying spermatozoa or ova are severed and closed. The operation, called vasectomy in men and salpingectomy in women, is minor for men, and for women has about the severity of uncomplicated appendectomy. Since the glands themselves are undisturbed, the patient is not "unsexed" but is nevertheless prevented from reproducing by the simple fact that the ova cannot be reached by the sperm cells. Both in purpose and in result sterilization is wholly different from the castration which was practiced by the church in medieval times to provide male soprano voices for cathedral choirs.

The numbers of sterilizations performed under state laws up to January 1, 1941, are as follows:

State	Year first sterilization law was passed	Sterilizations performed		
		Male	Female	Total
California	1909	7,495	7,073	14,568
Virginia	1924	1,636	2,288	3,924
Kansas	1913	1,415	989	2,404
Michigan	1913	513	1,632	2,145
Minnesota	1925	386	1,494	1,880
Oregon	1917	552	898	1,450
Wisconsin	1913	165	991	1,156
Indiana	1907	551	482	1,033
North Carolina	1919	225	792	1,017
Washington	1909	178	489	667
Delaware	1923	322	288	610
South Dakota	1917	212	365	577
North Dakota	1913	185	349	534
Mississippi	1928	149	374	523
Oklahoma	1931	97	373	470
New Hampshire	1917	73	357	430
Connecticut	1909	25	393	418
Nebraska	1915	154	234	388
Iowa	1911	112	224	336
Utah	1925	143	109	252
Alabama	1919	129	95	224
Vermont	1931	66	146	212
Maine	1925	14	176	190
Montana	1923	58	128	186
Georgia	1937	28	99	127
West Virginia	1929	1	45	46
New York	1912	1	41	42
South Carolina	1935	1	34	35
Arizona	1929	10	10	20
Idaho	1925	4	10	14
Totals		14,900	20,978	35,878

According to the Human Betterment Foundation, sterilization as practiced in California saves the state an estimated $2,000,000 per year, and "It enables many handicapped persons to marry and have a life normal in most respects, whose marriage without sterilization would be unwise if not disastrous."

Concerning constitutionality, a state law which provides for sterilization has stood the test of Supreme Court consideration. In the case of Buck v. Bell, the decision, rendered May 2, 1927, upheld the Virginia law.[7]

In summary one may say that through state action sterilization tends to protect society against certain burdensome types of families, while permitting an otherwise normal family life on the part of the individuals involved.

Other Legislative Provisions

Much of health legislation has a bearing on the family, for example the provisions for school doctors, school nurses, vaccination requirements, quarantine for various diseases. So likewise do laws concerning suffrage, property rights, minimum wage laws, ten-hour laws.

DIVORCE

This topic might have been considered under the heading, "Relationships between the family and the state," inasmuch as the state makes the laws under which the family may be broken up. However, the subject reaches beyond the state relationship.

Divorce is a social problem in part because there is a hazard to personality of the divorced persons, but primarily because of its effects on children. The correlation of broken homes and delinquency has already been mentioned. It should be noted, however, that divorces are most frequent in childless families.

Divorces have been increasing throughout most of the country, the rate being fastest for Hollywood, where the practice is a phase of what has been aptly called tandem polygamy. For the United States as a whole approximately sixteen in every hundred marriages end in court; that is, the chances of staying married until death does you part are about five in six. The divorce rate has mounted from 5.9 per cent of marriages in 1890 to 7.9 per cent of marriages in 1900, 8.8 per cent in 1910, 13.4 per cent in 1920, 17.0 per cent in 1930. A slight decline occurred in the 1930's.

[7] 47 Sup. Ct. Rep. 584; 274 U. S. 200.

Various legal grounds under which divorce takes place are cruelty (42.4% in 1931), desertion (27.9%), adultery (7.5%), nonsupport (4.1%), habitual drunkenness (1.5%), and a scattering of other grounds.[8]

The legal reasons for divorce are a framework which sometimes discloses, sometimes hides the real reasons. As an underlying cause of family disintegration, Mowrer gives prominent place to the "Romantic Complex," in which the marriage relation is regarded exclusively as one of response.[9] Romance furnishes the main theme of movie plots and radio singing, and the romantic love theme furnishes the anticipation if not the actual experience of most of our young people.

But of course the alertness of response cannot be forever at a high pitch and the patter of love symbols get boring to some. The wooing cannot be constant—and consequently the romantic conception of the marriage relation "becomes the focal point in marital discord." The dreams crumble, and the lover turns elsewhere for solace, searching, ever searching, for a halo wraith over the prosaic facts of sex.

We get additional light on the phenomenon of divorce by considering it in relation to the functions of the family. In rural areas, where the family retains a large proportion of its former functions, family breakdown is relatively rare. Divorce is a phenomenon of the cities where one lives less as a member of a family and more as a member of many other groups. The less definite role of the family in relation to several of its erstwhile functions—economic production, education, vocational training, economic support, reproduction, continuity conservation,—permits a more pronounced result than formerly from distractions. Since the purpose of organizing a family is usually love, and love is in many cases not only blind but transitory, the stability of the family depends largely on the family's utility. With declining utility in the structure, its stability declines.

SELECTED REFERENCES

Baber, Ray E., *Marriage and The Family*, McGraw-Hill Book Co., Inc., 1939.—
    Because of a demand by student bodies the author has dealt with this sub-

[8] *Marriage and Divorce, 1931*, U. S. Dept. of Commerce, Bureau of the Census, Washington, D. C., 1932, pp. 20–21.

[9] Ernest R. Mowrer, *Family Disorganization*, Univ. of Chicago Press, 1939, p. 158 *et seq.*

ject from a practical point of view. In addition to a bibliography at the end of each chapter there is a list of topics for discussion or reports.

Bernard, Jessie, *American Family Behavior*, Harper and Brothers, 1941.—Special attention is given to the functions of the family.

Burgess, Ernest W., and Cottrell, Leonard S., Jr., *Predicting Success or Failure in Marriage*, Prentice-Hall, Inc., 1939.—The authors have presented much factual material.

Folsom, Joseph Kirk, *The Family*, John Wiley & Sons, Inc., 1934.—''This book aims to integrate the various scientific approaches to the study of family phenomena. It attempts to weave cultural anthropology, individual psychology, history, sociology, economics and psychiatry into a unitary science.''

Goodsell, Willystine, *Problems of The Family*, D. Appleton-Century Co., Inc., 1928.—After six chapters of historical background, there are fourteen chapters dealing with such problems as the instability of the family, mothers working, budgets, birth control, eugenics, illegitimacy, and family relationships.

Groves, Ernest R., *The Family and Its Social Functions*, J. B. Lippincott Co., 1940.—This book is adapted to the use of students who are planning to take advanced work in the field of the family.

Hart, Hornell, *Personality and The Family*, D. C. Heath & Company, 1935.— While this book deals primarily with personality development, yet it is of such a nature that it will be helpful to those who are preparing for certain kinds of social work. Both ''scientific information'' and ''tested wisdom'' have been used in the preparation of this volume.

Himes, Norman E., *Your Marriage*, Farrar & Rinehart, Inc., 1940.—Contains much material on the sexual aspects of married life.

Jung, Moses, *Modern Marriage*, F. S. Crofts & Company, 1940.—The major aspects of marriage with emphasis on the ethical and aesthetic implications of the marriage relationship.

Mowrer, Ernest R., *Family Disorganization*, University of Chicago Press, 1939.— A use of both statistics and case study methods in analyzing divorce and desertion. A selected bibliography.

Terman, Lewis Madison, *Psychological Factors in Marital Happiness*, McGraw-Hill Book Co., Inc., 1938.—This study of 792 married couples yields much insight into the conditions which make for happiness in marriage.

Sait, Una Bernard, *New Horizons for the Family*, The Macmillan Company, 1938.—A careful analysis is made of the interrelationships in, between and among families.

CHAPTER 15

THE COMMUNITY

By Dr. R. R. Martin

Professor of Sociology

Hamline University, Saint Paul, Minnesota

THE CONCEPT COMMUNITY

A Geographic Area

The man on the street responding to the questions of a "curb stone" broadcast would probably define the community in terms of the small world in which he lives. "My community" to him would probably mean a rather definite geographical area designated by some local name. Perhaps he could not define the boundaries of this area by section or township lines; nevertheless, in his own "mind" the area would be quite definite.

This common sense interpretation of community is shared by the scientist. "As originally used in the literature of the Social Sciences community designated a geographical area with definite legal boundaries, occupied by residents engaged in interrelated economic activity and constituting a politically self-governing unit."[1]

However, the man on the street thinks not so much in terms of these interrelated activities as he does the physical area which provides the stage on which the drama of his own communal life takes place. But geographical area alone is not sufficient to constitute a community even in the common sense understanding of the concept. There must be other factors such as people, social relations, institutions, and social organization.

A Psychological Concept

The term community is used some times in a way that almost, if not entirely, disregards the geographical area defined either in terms of the natural physiographic area or the political unit and reduces it to a "state of mind"—to consensus. This viewpoint would leave little to differentiate community from society. One would be a member of a community just to the degree that he became a part of

[1] E. C. Lindeman, *Encyclopedia of the Social Sciences*, Macmillan Co., 1933, Article on Community.

the institutional complex resulting from the crystallization of public opinion. In this sense the community would not differ appreciably from a public.

This viewpoint was quite common a decade ago. Marshall defined the community about that time as "any number of people, whether large or small, who think and talk and act about the same things in much the same way: . . . they have common interests."[2]

In discussing this interpretation of the community, Steiner says, "from this point of view community is not primarily a geographic and economic unity but is thought of as a corporate state of mind or as a mental unity or even as a creative process."[3]

An Area of Social Inter-action

To define the community wholly in terms of geographical location restricts it unduly. To limit it to the social solidarity brought about by unifying ties of a psychological nature is equally unsatisfactory. The community is all of this but it is more. It is a "complex unity which has both physical locus and psychological consensus."[4]

The tendency at the present time is to describe the community more in terms of what it does than what it is. This embraces both of the emphases described above. In keeping with this idea Steiner says, "the minimum essentials for a community are (1) a locality occupied by (2) people who devise some sort of (3) communal organization to further their interests. It is by these three criteria that we are able to identify the community and define its limits."[5] Robinson maintains that:

> the important characteristic of a community is that an individual's life *may* be and commonly is lived within it. . . . The community makes available the goods we want, regulates our sex life, defines the duties and rights of parents and children, arranges the adjustment of children to the local environment, affords opportunities to maintain relations with the supernatural, provides for leisure time, and has machinery for deciding and carrying out group policies.[6]

[2] L. C. Marshall, *The Story of Human Progress,* New York: Macmillan Co., 1925, p. 46.

[3] J. F. Steiner, *Community Organization,* New York: The Century Co., 1930, p. 20.

[4] Frances E. Merrill and Mabel A. Elliott, *Social Disorganization,* New York: Macmillan Co., 1925, p. 788.

[5] J. F. Steiner, *Community Organization,* New York: The Century Co., 1930, p. 20.

[6] Thomas H. Robinson, *Men Groups and the Community,* New York: Harper and Brothers, 1940, pp. 53 and 54.

and Lindeman arrives at this:

> The community thus becomes the area dominated by prevailing systems of social intercourse—an area of social interaction. It is a social grouping in which the fundamental interests of persons find expression; the configuration of interrelated institutions, various phases through which persons express themselves and by which they are controlled. Thus the community process is one of "inter-action giving rise to inter-dependence, cooperation, collaboration, unification."[7]

MacIver holds that the significant identifying criteria of community is "that one's life may be lived wholly within it, that all of one's social relationships may be found within it."[8]

This viewpoint precludes our prescribing definite spatial limitations to the communal area. Under modern conditions of travel the families of a given village may seek the satisfaction of their basic social needs over very extensive areas taking in numerous villages and towns. People living contiguous to each other may go in opposite directions for the satisfaction of the same need. This concept would therefore make the community boundary co-extensive with the movement of its constituent members. While there would be a wide area over which wishes might be satisfied, the major wishes of a majority of the members of the community would in all probability be met within a relatively small area. There seems to be a certain attachment for one's local neighborhood, or his home town. There is a certain centripetal force—a certain cohesion which seems to inhere in the local unit.

As these lines are being written a radio broadcast direct from London brings the information that one of the major problems in this war area is to persuade people to leave the danger zone and seek shelter in districts remote from the danger of incessant bombing. People prefer to go back to their partially wrecked homes rather than to establish themselves even temporarily in new communal situations. One feels more at home in his local "bailiwick" even though he does not hesitate to go beyond its boundaries to satisfy special needs.

For all practical purposes we may define this area in which one's social needs are satisfied, and in which one has a sense of belonging as the social community.

[7] E. C. Lindeman, *Encyclopedia of Social Sciences,* Macmillan Co., 1933, Article on Community, pp. 102–105.

[8] R. M. MacIver, *Society,* New York: Farrar and Rinehart, 1937, p. 8.

Some areas of communal participation, particularly in the rural districts, may be delimited in terms of the "trade area" or the area in which one satisfies the major part of his economic needs such as the purchase of goods, the marketing of produce, and the securing of credit. With the coming of streamlined transportation and communication and modern marketing systems, the territorial boundaries represented by the old village "trade area" have been greatly expanded. Economic needs are satisfied in a number of different sections extending far beyond the boundaries of the local village and its hinterland. This new area of economic interaction may be called the economic community. This new economic community like the social community is not as amorphus as it might seem to be. There are centrifugal forces operating, but they are counterbalanced in part by centripetal forces which tend to give a considerable degree of solidarity and uniformity to the local grouping. The distant market has a certain lure for occasional shopping on a day off or when one is seeking a change of scenery. Frequently it provides a better selection of goods. It may even be that for certain specialties one is forced to market at considerable distance from his neighborhood. What is more significant, shopping at a remote market may reduce the probability of one's neighbor having a dress exactly like hers, or having the neighbor know just what she paid for it. Nevertheless the home town continues to make a strong appeal when one wants to purchase standard brands of goods or to secure credit. While dissenters are to be found, in general man continues to satisfy a large part of his fundamental economic needs near his "door step."[9]

It has long been recognized that this economic community had certain more or less definite geographical limits or boundaries based on certain economic interaction but they were difficult to define until a technique was developed by Galpin. The technique consists in measuring the area within which the major economic functions are carried on from a given center. The measurement was accomplished in the following manner:

> with maps in hand, the surveyor asked the villagers from whom information was desired to point out how far into each section of the contiguous rural territory they or their organization served a majority of the people. This question was put to bankers, merchants, managers of elevators, creameries, co-

[9] Carle C. Zimmerman, *The Changing Community*, New York: Harper and Brothers, 1938, p. 49.

operatives of various kinds, as well as to doctors, lawyers, school principals, editors and officials of social organizations and others. Exceptional services, such as those performed by furniture stores, music stores, and the like limited to a few villages, were excluded. . . .

With this information before him the surveyor drew a line for each service offered by the village and from these lines community lines were then constructed to include the area in which the majority of the people were served by the social economic and religious institutions or organizations of the village.[10]

Galpin believes that this provides a sufficiently exact method for delimiting the economic community. He says,

> it is difficult, if not impossible, to avoid the conclusion that the trade zones about one of these rather complete cultural-civic centers forms the boundary of an actual, if not legal, community within which the apparent entanglement of a human life is resolved to a fairly unitary system of inter-relatedness.[11]

The community as the term is used in this chapter may be defined as the area in which one carries on the major functions of his political, social, and economic existence, and in which he has a sense of belonging.

The Community and the Neighborhood

Community and neighborhood are frequently spoken of as if they were the same thing. While there are social groupings to which either term might be applied with equal descriptive accuracy, some differentiation should be made between the two terms. They do denote certain differences in social grouping. The neighborhood is generally thought of as the small "face to face" group, conscious of its social unity, which lies just beyond the family. It is characterized by primary group control having little if any formal organization. It is a group of "nigh-dwellers."

"The most distinctive characteristics of the neighborhood are its relations with a local area sufficiently compact to permit frequent and intimate association and the emergence out of such association of sufficient homogeneity and unity to permit the primary face to

10 Edmund Brunner and others, *American Agricultural Villages*, 1927, pp. 51–52. Reprinted by permission of Harper & Brothers.

11 C. J. Galpin, *The Social Anatomy of an Agricultural Community*, Madison: Wisconsin Agricultural Experiment Station Bulletin 34, 1915, p. 18.

face social group endowed with a strong sense of self-consciousness capable of influencing the behavior of its constituents."[12]

McKenzie emphasizes the importance of the element of self-consciousness in the neighborhood. This frequently expresses itself in the descriptive names attached to some neighborhood groupings such as "China Town", "Swede Town," etc. . . . Groupings which, because of their size, lose this self-consciousness are no longer neighborhoods but become communities.[13]

Sanderson, on the other hand, would not limit the term neighborhood to a grouping characterized by "self-consciousness" but would include those whose chief characteristic is propinquity. For him the small cluster of houses integrated about some single service or perchance two or three services, but with no formal organization, would constitute a neighborhood regardless of any feeling of self-consciousness that might or might not exist. The fact that the business or service around which this cluster of houses was at one time integrated has disappeared in no way affects the neighborhood nature of the grouping.

Numerous writers have pointed out the tendency for neighborhoods to disappear in our modern communal organization. In fact there are those who would go so far as to insist that the neighborhood rarely, if ever, exists any more in modern western culture. There are, of course, exceptions in isolated territories. However, even in some of these cases the isolation, it is pointed out, may not be as real as it seems on the surface. For example, here and there one finds a ·small cluster of farmhouses constituting a rural hamlet that might seem to be so isolated that a local self-consciousness would be inevitable. Yet, upon closer examination, one might find that each of these families is integrated to a different larger community, with which considerable communal activity is carried on.

The term neighborhood is used sometimes with a slightly different meaning than the one we have been discussing. In the large cities today there are areas more or less homogeneous but too large to possess any considerable degree of "consciousness of kind" that for want of a better term are designated as "city neighborhoods." These have practically none of the elements of the old rural neighborhood.

[12] Niles Carpenter, *Encyclopedia of the Social Sciences*, Article on Neighborhood.

[13] R. D. McKenzie, *The Neighborhood*, Chicago: The University of Chicago Press, 1923, pp. 351–352.

The neighborhood has had an important place in American social life. It has been the most important agency, outside the family, for socialization and acculturation. The rural neighborhood has been called the political and social backbone of frontier America. It promoted interfamily cooperation and exchange of work, provided the basis for visiting back and forth and for spontaneous parties. Neighbors centered their lives in the neighborhood activities.[14]

THE STRUCTURE OF THE COMMUNITY

The structure of the community is a product of the interplay of innumerable complex factors. These factors combine in different ways at different times and in different places to produce varying types of communities. It would not be too much to say that no two are exactly alike structurally. They differ in size, configuration, and complexity. At one extreme is the cross-roads village surrounded by farms; at the other the regional community with its metropolitan city surrounded by a constellation of satellite cities, towns, villages, and open-country communities.

Community structure varies with changes in transportation and marketing systems. In a sense any particular type of structure may be thought of as a stage in an evolutionary process rather than something unique in itself. The principal factor in determining the structure of the community is competition—competition made inevitable by the introduction of new methods of transportation, communication, and marketing organization, and new forms of energy.

There are wide differences in communal structure, yet there is at the same time an underlying sameness. With certain exceptions all communities in this country, large or small, follow a similar structural pattern—an "axiate" pattern the basic elements of which are "centers, routes and rims." The routes radiate from centers like the spokes from the hub of a wheel. Rims appear at the breaks in the routes where land and water meet, where physical barriers change the direction or the mode of movement, or where mere distance makes it impracticable for one to travel farther from the center.[15]

The Rural Community

The rural community in pioneer America was the product of

[14] Harry Elmer Barnes, *Society in Transition*, New York: Prentice-Hall, 1939, p. 648.

[15] R. D. McKenzie, ''Centers, Routes and Rims,'' an unpublished manuscript.

horse and buggy transportation. It is best characterized by the rural village with its hinterland of farm homes. The village was usually located at some break in transportation such as the fork of a river, the head of navigation on some stream, a watering place on an old trail, the junction of two or more major routes of travel, or near the center of a broad prairie. At the center of the village was "main street" lined with the different types of services required to meet the needs of the villagers and the farmers in the hinterland. This street extended out past the village church into the open country. Other roads left the village at different points and meandered through the countryside providing the life lines between the center and the rims of the community. The distance from center to periphery was determined by the "team haul"—the distance one could conveniently go to market and return home the same day. Some of these roads, or routes, extended beyond the communal rims out through "no man's land" to become the connecting link with neighboring communities and the channels for inter-community association.

In a pre-railroad era, the communities were distributed more or less at random. With the coming of the railroad, they became distributed along its lines like beads on a string. In the pre-railroad period the communities were more or less isolated and there was relatively little interdependence among them. In the new arrangement each community had some relation to its neighbors, and the functions of the railroad which was common to all of them related each to the terminal markets to which they became more or less closely tied.

The modern rural community has lost much of its former isolation. It has become more closely associated with its neighbors and particularly with the city. In fact, the rural community, in the sense in which the term was used a few decades ago, is a rare phenomenon in modern American culture. This is even more true of its social and economic life than it is of its structural pattern.

The Urban Community

The urban community differs from the village community more in size and complexity than in any other way. It is a product of the application of mechanical energy to travel and transportation. It is also a product of paved highways, the development of steel structure, improved communication, and the development of other aids to congregate living. The rural village with its single "main street," its one or two story buildings and its simple economy could serve but a very limited trade area. The city with its sky scrapers, its horizontal and vertical transportation (freight and passenger elevators) has piled one city upon another in a relatively small area, has developed a complex social and economic structure, and has brought great sections of the surrounding territory into its trade area. The rural community had a simple undifferentiated structure with main street as the focal point. In the urban center this "single focus differentiates into a number of foci for different activities, a financial center, an administrative center, a fashion center, a recreational center, etc. . . ."[16]

Regardless of the complexity of urban communities they tend to assume something of the same pattern, namely, the highly differentiated center surrounded by a ring of more or less interdependent communities integrated to the center by social and economic ties.[17]

The Urban Community has been referred to as if it were one huge community. It is, to be more exact, a constellation of many communities with certain interests in the larger community which are common to all. Each community has a degree of independence yet each is more or less dependent upon the larger whole. The prophet Ezekiel at one time had a vision of wheels within a wheel. The modern social prophet sees the urban community as a complex phenomenon of communities within a community.[18]

Reference has been made to community structure as a function of transportation, marketing systems, etc. The broader implication of this is revealed by drawing comparisons between cities in western and oriental cultures. In the modern American city with the "axiate" pattern the most sensitive spot in the entire city is found at the city center which frequently coincides roughly with the geographical center. It is here one finds the concentration of business, of brains, of social interaction. Here life is lived more intensely than at any other spot. McKenzie has shown that in the old walled

[16] R. M. MacIver, *Society*, New York: Farrar and Rinehart, 1937, p. 149.

[17] For a more extended discussion of the similarity in city structure see Park, R. E., Burgess, E. W., and McKenzie, R. D., *The City*, Chicago: University of Chicago Press, 1925, Chapter 11.

[18] See President's Research Committee, *Recent Social Trends*, New York: McGraw-Hill Book Co., Inc., 1933, Chapter IX. Also H. B. Woolston, *Metropolis, A Study of Urban Communities*, New York: D. Appleton-Century Co., 1938, pp. 140–6.

cities of the Orient the outer edge of the city is the live or active part. The gates which provide ingress and egress to the city are always the spots of greatest activity. The traffic flow on all streets throughout the city is relatively uniform. The entire city is represented by a symmetrical, undifferentiated pattern of spatial grouping. There are sections of concentrated activity such as the open spaces surrounding temples and shrines where bazaars are usually held but such areas do not constitute segregated areas and semi-independent communal sections as in our American cities.

When modern transportation invades one of these old cities the structure is transformed into that of a western metropolis; spatial reorganization takes place. "The new center of the community gains in relative importance over all other parts. Axiate intramural transportation systems are introduced. Central land values rapidly increase. Hotels, office buildings, banks and department stores rise in or near the center. Population and utilities become redistributed with reference to the new center of dominance and land value levels."[19]

This process is well illustrated in the experience of the city of Tokio.

> The pre-railroad city was a loose federation of villages clustered around the Shogun's castle, now the imperial palace. The villages were connected by narrow winding roads which in course of times became lined with small shops of every description. On the advent of the railroad in 1872, and the construction of the big central depot, a new center of specialized activity commenced to develop. An undeveloped tract of land which lay between the railroad station and the imperial grounds immediately became the site of many important banks and office buildings constructed on western lines and built high above the rest of the city. Wide streets have been opened in all directions from this new region of dominance. Street cars and motor buses have been introduced, affecting a profound reorganization of the spatial pattern of the city.[20]

The Rurban Community

In a pre-automobile period there was little if any competition among rural villages. The slow means of travel made it necessary

[19] R. D. McKenzie, "The Concept Dominance and World Organization," *American Journal of Sociology*, XXXIII, July, 1927, 31.

[20] R. D. McKenzie, *loc. cit.*

for the farmer to trade in the village nearest to his farm and precluded the possibility of his "shopping around" a great deal. This situation gave rise to the general store where one might purchase any and everything needed in the ordinary course of existence. The owner of one of these stores boasted that he carried on hand and ready for delivery everything from "a bottle of castoria to a threshing machine."

This organization, however, could not continue indefinitely. Some communities were "champing at the bit," impatient to expand and take on new responsibilities. In time their opportunity came. The rural telephone and the rural delivery were the first harbingers of change and were soon followed by the automobile. In their train came the farm truck, farm tractor and other power driven farm machinery. The farmer who hitherto had been bound to his locality by the limits of the team haul was released from these ties and was now able to shop around among the different rural villages as freely as the modern homemaker shops among the different stores of her hometown. What was more important the city markets were now available to him. A process of competition was started between the city and its hinterland that finally resulted in a new type of community to which Galpin has given the name "Rurban."

The rurban community can best be grasped if one visualizes a city surrounded by a broad belt in which are located hamlets, villages, and open country farmsteads. The breadth of this belt depends upon the topography of the terrain, the size of the city, type of economic base, transportation facilities, etc. The villages located in this belt retain a few primary services such as grocery stores, gas stations, blacksmith shop, postoffice, and so forth, but for a major part of their needs the people now go to the city. The farmers no longer stop at the local village to trade but follow the improved farm to market roads directly through the local village into the city. Many of those who reside in the villages earn their living in the city.

This rurban belt surrounding the city has developed rapidly during the past decade. In the case of ninety-two of the largest cities of the United States the rurban communities surrounding them increased in population during the period since 1930, more than three times as rapidly as the cities themselves.

The members of this new expanded community—the rurban community—are as closely tied to the urban center as they were formerly to their local village. They are no longer rural dwellers in the old sense of the term. They may live in sparsely settled areas yet they enjoy the same culture as their city brothers; they buy their goods at the same stores, attend the same churches, see the same shows, listen to the same radio programs, read the same newspapers, frequent the same parks and playgrounds, and their children attend the same schools—they are rural dwellers living in the midst of an urban culture. Park has shown the role played by the metropolitan newspaper in carrying the urban culture out into this rurban area; also the method by which the extent of the area may be measured by the circulation of the metropolitan paper.[21]

The Regional Community

Modern improved means of transportation and communication have introduced another new phenomenon in community structure, namely, the regional community, or the region as it is often called. The pioneer community organized on the basis of a horse and buggy economy was of necessity small and usually composed of a single unit which may be represented by a small agricultural village with a cluster of farmers nucleated about it and looking to it for the satisfaction of the major part of their needs. It was necessary for each community to carry on practically a self sufficing economy. Centripetal force was the chief characteristic of such a community. The slow means of transportation, it has been pointed out before, made it necessary for the farmer to trade at the village near his home regardless of the quality of services rendered. It was only when one lived about equal distance from two or more villages that he could exercise any choice.

With the coming of more rapid means of travel and transportation this old village community pattern was broken up. Here and there were villages that, because of some favorable element in their location or in the composition of their constituency, developed more rapidly than others and were able to supply a larger number and a better quality of services. As a result of their unequal growth and the change in "ecological distance" the more favored villages began to exercise a considerable pull upon the constituency of the less favored ones. Many of the small villages soon lost the majority of their services. When people began to find a means of satisfying their economic needs outside the village, it was not long before they

[21] R. E. Park, "Urbanization As Measured by Newspaper Circulation," *The American Journal of Sociology*, XXXV, July, 1929, 60–79.

began to satisfy their social and recreational needs outside the village as well. The large town department store lured them away from the old village general store, and the city houses of entertainment and social life lured them away from their homes and local places of entertainment. Centripetal force began to give way to centrifugal.

As a result of the process just described the boundaries of the old community were expanded to include numerous other communities. Social participation became less intensive and more extensive. The result was an area of participation which included both the urban and the rurban community.

The process of expansion did not end here. Transportation and communication continued to improve and to be made available to an ever increasing proportion of the general population. Revolutions took place in marketing systems and in methods of production. The farm tractor began to replace the horse and the mule in the field in the agricultural areas, and the motor truck replaced the horse drawn wagon on the road. Methods of mass production applied to the various industries tended to reshift the population and the automobile made it more mobile. Business and finance began to be centralized in both function and control. These larger towns began to experience something of the same reshuffling that had taken place among the villages. Those that a short time before had succeeded in drawing the trade from the villages now found themselves caught in the current sweeping toward the cities and the cities in turn began to feel the pull of the metropolitan centers. Business and finance began to concentrate in the metropolitan centers and to extend their influence out into the satellite cities and towns thus expanding communal interests to include a still wider area. Thus the regional community came into existence as an important unit in communal organization. The towns and even small villages continued to have a place in this new communal structure but their relative importance was greatly reduced.

This new community is not a compact city-centered area, as was the urban or the rurban communities. It is multi-centered and may contain several cities, numerous towns, villages, and sparsely settled areas. The old communal patterns both rural and urban were characterized by compact communities many of which were sharply differentiated economically and culturally from their neighbors. The new regional community is composed of numerous territorially and culturally differentiated, yet interdependent units bound together into a functional unity. McKenzie says of this community:

Geographically it extends as far as the city exerts a dominant influence. It is essentially an expanded pattern of local communal life based upon motor transportation. Structurally this new metropolitan regionalism is axiate in form. The basic elements of its pattern are centers, routes, and rims. The metropolitan region represents a constellation of centers, the interrelations of which are characterized by dominance and subordination. Every region is organized around a central city or focal point of dominance in which are located the institutions and services that cater to the region as a whole and integrate it with other regions. The business subcenters are rarely complete in their institutional or service structure. They depend upon the main center for the more specialized and integrating functions.[22]

THE COMMUNITY AND SOCIAL CHANGE

One of the most conspicuous aspects of the community as we have seen thus far is its dynamic nature—its tendency to change. "Change, movement is lord of the universe," and since the community is in reality the universe in miniature it is not surprising that change plays such an important role here. Some one remarked to the editor of a well known national daily one time, "This paper is not what it used to be." The editor made the quick reply, "It never was and never will be!" Something of the same observation may well be made concerning the community. The community (except in pre-literate times) never was the same for very long periods at a time. In fact in many communities change can be observed almost from day to day. Some of the changes may be the result of the natural process of social metabolism which leaves the community unchanged so far as outward appearances are concerned. The changes are more in personnel and in the inner organization of institutions. Other changes are more drastic, affecting structure and internal organization as well as personnel.

Changing Distance

The most obvious changes are the result of the interplay of physical factors or agencies of change, and probably the most important of these has to do with transportation and communication. With these has come a change in distance. The world of our forefathers was measured in terms of rods and miles. Today we express our measurements in terms of the minutes or hours required to span

[22] R. D. McKenzie, *The Metropolitan Community*, New York: McGraw-Hill Book Co., Inc., 1933, p. 70.

the distance from one point to another. We are not so much interested in the number of miles from San Francisco or Seattle to New York as we are in the time required to go from one place to another, and the cost of the transportation. Distance today has come to be largely a "time cost" concept. Not many years ago if one had inquired the distance from New York to one of the Pacific coast communities his information would have been given in terms of the number of miles by railroad, the swiftest means of transportation available at the turn of the present century. The same question would hardly have been asked at the beginning of the previous century because so little was known of the great central plains or the western mountain regions that they could scarcely be thought of as a part of the continent.

The distance across the continent seemed great, and in fact was great, because of the modes of travel at that period. Ellen Semple has emphasized the significance of these distances in her description of the difficulties encountered in following the Oregon Trail from the Mississippi Valley to Western United States early in the second half of the nineteenth century.

> Four months of continuous traveling, over two-thousand miles of weary plodding over plains, mountains, desert, and mountains again, with two-hundred and fifty miles of dangerous navigation on the rapid-swept Columbia; days and weeks of scanty food and scantier drink, of mid-day heat and midnight cold in the plateau desert . . . these were the tests geographical conditions set to the survival of the fittest on the Oregon Trail.[23]

When this statement is contrasted with the following description of the modern means of travel, taken from an advertisement of the United Air Lines we see the significance of some of the changes which are bringing the various parts of the world into closer proximity.

> Far above the twinkling lights of cities and towns, a great United mainliner moves across the starlit sky. In the cool quiet of the air-conditioned cabin twelve passengers sleep undisturbed in their luxurious berths. They left the east this evening . . . will breakfast tomorrow in points as distant as California and the Pacific Northwest.

In the same advertisement this company sets forth as their service "three coast-to-coast sleeper flights nightly and a scenic day-

[23] Ellen Semple, *American History and its Geographical Conditions*, Boston: Houghton, Mifflin Co., 1903, p. 210.

light flight . . . commuter service linking New York—Chicago, and Los Angeles—San Francisco.'' These are the conditions under which one spans the continent in the fifth decade of the twentieth century.

Something of this same thing that took place in transportation is taking place in the area of communication. Near the beginning of the Christian era a letter was sent by Julius Caesar from the barbarian isle of Britain to Rome a distance of approximately one thousand miles. It required twenty-one days for the letter to reach its destination even though there was great urgency for speed in its delivery. A few months ago two American press correspondents, one in Rome and the other in London carried on a casual conversation with each other while all the world listened in after the fashion of neighbors ''rubbering'' on a rural telephone line. This evening people in the most remote parts of America may sit in their homes, turn on the radio, and listen to the voice of news-reporters in London, Rome, Berlin, Moscow, and other world capitols as they discuss the progress of the war during the preceding twenty-four hours. Today the most remote part of the world is as near any other point, so far as communication is concerned, as are neighbors in the next block.

These changes mean much more than mere changing distances and a shrinking world—shrinking so far as the time required to span it is concerned. They mean a change in life conditions, a change in the way of doing things, a change in the way of thinking, a change in all social and communal organization, in short, a change in culture. Distances are so completely broken down that though many miles separate peoples in space, actually they live in close proximity and are neighbors. Under conditions as have been described, community life cannot be the same as when distances were so great that little social intercourse could be had between relatively close neighbors.

In describing the new organization of social structure based upon this changing distance Graham Wallace has coined the term ''The Great Society.'' He shows that our small communities have been expanded to almost national or world proportions. That is, our world has become so compact, the various parts so accessible to each other, that it is actually, for all practical purposes, no larger than one of the old communities. Perhaps the changes in social organization will appear more distinct if we look at them against the background of the community arrangement of preliterate man. His was an atomistic world, that is, one composed of small parts each representing a family, a tribe, a clan, or some other very small group living in relative isolation from each of the other units.[24]

When this situation is compared to the regional community, communal change becomes apparent.

The Control of Social Change

It should not be assumed that these changes are uniform or constant. They differ from time to time in both intensity and direction. McKenzie maintains, however, that even though the changes may be erratic they do follow a rather definite pattern. That is, there is a certain predictability to change. He says:

> The human community tends to develop in a cyclic fashion. Under a given state of natural resources and in a given condition of the arts the community tends to increase in size and structure until it reaches the point of population adjustment to the economic base. . . . The point of maximum development may be termed the point of culmination or climax, to use the term of the plan ecologist. The community tends to remain in this condition of balance between population and resources until some new element enters to disturb the *status quo*, such as the introduction of a new system of communication, a new type of industry, or a different form of utilization of the existing economic base. Whatever the innovation may be that disturbs the equilibrium of the community, there is a tendency toward a new cycle of adjustment. This may act in either a positive or a negative manner. It may serve as a *release* to the community, making for another cycle of growth and differentiation, or it may have a restrictive influence, necessitating emigration and readjustment to a more circumscribed base.[25]

This at once raises the question of the extent to which a degree of control may be extended over these changes. Is change a part of the whole process of cosmic evolution? Spencer was quite certain that it was. There are others who agree; they say that the community is

> curiously resistant to the fiats of man; like the Robot, created by man, it goes on its way indifferent to the will of its creator.

24 L. T. Hobhouse, G. C. Wheeler, and M. Ginsberg, *The Material Culture and Social Institutions of Simpler Peoples*, New York: Chapman and Hall, 1915, p. 46.

25 R. D. McKenzie, ''The Ecological Approach to the Study of the Human Community,'' *American Journal of Sociology*, XXX, November, 1924, p. 292.

Reformers have stormed, the avaricious have speculated, and thoughtful men have planned, but again and again their programs have met with obstacles. Human nature offers some opposition; traditions and institutions offer more; and of especial significance the very configuration . . . is unyielding to change. . . .[26]

Elihu Root once expressed this same idea when he said the community was a growth like that of a crystal responding to forces inherent in the atoms that make it up. There probably remains much to be learned concerning the manner in which these atoms arrange and re-arrange themselves according to social, economic, and cultural forces. It is, however, sufficient for our present purpose to call attention to the fact that a sufficient knowledge of this process has been discovered to make it reasonably certain that the community in its growth goes on developing certain occupational, economic, social, and racial segregations regardless of the efforts exerted on the part of its constituency to obtain homogeneity and uniformity. What is today a desirable residence section tomorrow may be the location of business institutions. The very building that in one generation may house the socially elite in the next may be the home of an immigrant, a factory, or even a house of prostitution.

If the community is to be a living thing decidedly resistant to man's will, moving beyond his control, and responding to certain quite well defined forces within the atoms—if man can only predict and not entirely determine its course, then obviously he must be prepared to meet numerous social problems arising in the course of community changes.

Problems in Community Change

The problems involved in the process of community change are legion. However only a few can be discussed here.

One of the most serious problems arises from the inequality in the rate of change. Ogburn in the report of the President's Committee on Social Trends has shown that some of our most serious problems arise from this lack of uniformity or equality in change— "culture lag." One segment of community organization moves ahead while another lags behind—social stresses and tensions result.

[26] H. W. Zorbaugh, "The Natural Areas of the City" in E. W. Burgess (edt.) *The Urban Community*, Chicago: University of Chicago Press, 1929, p. 219.

Most urban communities have begun their careers as small villages. Institutions were established to meet the requirements of village life. Then the village grew in size and complexity becoming the urban community or city. Even though the social institutions were growing, their growth was mostly in size. In organization, program, and outlook many of them remained village institutions, and as such lost their ability to meet the demands of the new urban culture. This phenomenon can be illustrated by the experience of one of the most important social institutions in the community, namely, the church.

In the growth of the city church from its inception at a time when the city was but a small village, each new unit when organized ministered to an articulate community, equally new and equally conscious of its own identity. The problem of the institution, then, was merely the question of adjustment to its local habitat, a problem which is experienced by any organic or social life in a new situation. There were few symbiotic relationships because each community with its constellation of social institutions lived largely unto itself, experienced little environmental encroachment, and paid little attention to the outside world.

This was true until the web became complex, in fact until the community became city conscious, and a process of centralization set in. Then, the various communities which hitherto had been relatively independent became integrated in terms of the entire city as a unit. But the old parish remained the unit for the church organization, and individualism the church policy.

In the new integrated urban community, the "First Church," which was once the village church, and the original stem from which a number of the community churches sprang, takes the role of a super organization with members spatially distributed throughout the community parishes of the entire city. It assumes certain institutional rights within every parish equal with the parish church, but without having communal responsibility centered in any of them. It maintains a one-sided symbiotic relation with all the other churches of its own faith. It becomes a competitor of every parish church for membership and financial support. It is faced with the alternatives of subsidy, vigorous competition, or extinction. Since the "First Church" is the oldest and therefore probably the strongest, it usually wins in the competition as long as a process of centralization continues to operate in the urban community. This is not so true when the city begins to be decentralized.

In a sense this larger urban institution is urban in size only. In its organization and outlook it is still adjusted to a simple rather than a complex environment. Changes in the organization of the institution frequently have not kept pace with changes in the organization of the environment. Institutional inefficiency and institutional disorganization have been the result.

This maladjustment between institution and habitat is not confined to the church but extends to many of the social institutions. All of this adds its burden to the problem of community disorganization.

Another problem of social change is reflected in the natural history of the community. It has been pointed out elsewhere that the modern community in contrast to the frontier community is a multi-centered, complex organization made up of a constellation of specialized areas. The shift from the simple to the complex has entailed much grating and grinding of the gears of communal machinery. Frequently one area has grown at the expense of another. Certain areas have developed well organized, homogeneous community structures only to find themselves invaded by a type of culture which is inimical to its former solidarity. For example, the business or manufacturing section begins to encroach upon a well organized residential area near the center of the original community. Residents are driven out of the community, leaving only stragglers here and there. Their places are taken by families or individuals of a different culture. Permanent families are replaced by rooming house dwellers who pay no attention to the social institutions which at one time formed the backbone of the community. This area which was once a stable residential community becomes an area of social disorganization.

Perhaps it is an old, well-established, residential area with social institutions to take care of all of its needs that is invaded by apartment houses. The apartment house dwellers may be of the same culture as the older residents but in all probability they are more mobile. Since they do not own their own homes and in many cases not even own their own furniture, and more than likely have no children, they have but a small stake in the community, therefore do not put down any roots. The apartment dweller is the bane of all community improvement clubs and all other social institutions of the community. The first institutions to suffer as a result of this type of invasion are the churches and schools and after them the lodges, community clubs, etc. The invasion of apartment houses into a substantial single family residential area is a signal for the beginning of a process of community disorganization. This disorganization may not be articulate at first and may not be observed by the casual onlooker, nevertheless it is almost certain.

Still another problem is one of obsolescence. This pertains more particularly to areas built up by the groups representing the high income brackets. These people build expensive homes and establish institutions to meet their own cultural needs. In time these homes become old and the question of a new home arises. The tendency is to abandon the old palatial house and move to a new restricted residential district. The house is disposed of either by renting or selling to the highest bidder, irrespective of the ability of the new occupant to fit into the already established cultural pattern. Since this moving out is not done all at once, but is a gradual process, the community loses its original solidarity without being able to effect new community controls in competition with the older ones still remaining. The old institutions are still kept in existence by the few original residents who remain in the community, but they do not serve the new constituents. The new constituency cannot afford to develop its own institutions and as a result loses practically all institutional contact. Those who have moved out of the community may keep their contact with the old institution for a time but sooner or later this contact weakens and ultimately is severed entirely, leaving the old institutions stranded. The matter of institutional adjustment is a complex process by which the old institution must become adapted to the new groups while at the same time the new groups must make some adjustment to the old institutions. Failure of the old institutions to make satisfactory adaptations to the new groups often results in a considerable degree of personal and social demoralization.

One phase of this problem which is frequently overlooked is the effect of change on leadership. The leaders, being the more dynamic, are frequently the first to move out of a community when communal change begins to take place. This robs the community of leadership and leaves it the victim of those whose ambitions for leadership are not matched by training and ability to lead. The communal institutions are thus placed in the hands of inefficient leaders. The results of this are too obvious to dwell upon.

These, of course, are not the only problems involved in social change in the community, but the limits set for this chapter preclude a more extensive enumeration.[27]

INTEGRATION

Reference has been made to the development of the regional community. The solidarity of such a community rests upon the physical agencies of contact and interaction and the marketing systems that are developed to distribute goods and services. In order that a regional community may develop, it must have some channel through which it can be approached and through which the people who populate it can have contact with the outside world. An isolated area cannot for long carry on a self-sufficing economy, but must become associated with its neighbors. Then, too, the various smaller communities that make up the whole must be provided with some means of development. Goods produced within the area must have both inter- and intra-community movement, and the commodities produced elsewhere must have channels through which they can flow to the most remote communities of the constellation. All of this requires an interwoven network of communication and transportation routes. This web becomes vitalized by interdependent economic relationships. These symbiotic relations, together with the agencies and avenues for the distribution of goods and services, lie at the very base of communal integration. They determine the dominant market centers of the territory and their relation to regional and extra-regional markets. These centers cannot function independent of the routes of transportation and communication and the mechanical agencies designed to transport goods and ideas. Therefore, it is not too much to say that the new type of regional community is a resultant of the various agencies of integration.

The importance of the role of integration may become clearer if we think of it in relation to a particular community. Here is a regional community composed of approximately 72,000 square miles of mountainous and semi-mountainous country. The territory is surrounded on three sides by mountain ranges which make approach to it difficult. The larger community is made up of a number of relatively independent areas set apart from each other by physical barriers more or less distinct and some of them difficult to surmount.

[27] For further treatment of the problems of community change see Carle C. Zimmerman, *The Changing Community;* Newell Leroy Sims, *The Problem of Social Change:* W. F. Ogburn, *Social Change;* Harry Elmer Barnes, *Society in Transition.*

One of these areas, for example, is set apart from the neighboring territory by canyons and river valleys with precipitous walls, and is accessible only by roads which have been constructed at great expense. Another area is reached from the table-land surrounding it by tedious and circuitous routes. For many years after the larger community was settled one of the districts—a mining section—was isolated from the rest of the region by mountain ranges crossed only by pack trails and precarious wagon roads. Each of these semi-isolated and semi-independent districts is in turn divided into many sub-districts or communities all of which had to be integrated into some kind of a pattern if this large unorganized area was ever to become a regional community.

The first problem of integration in the community just described was to find some way to connect it with its neighboring communities, both those contiguous to it and those lying in more distant parts of the country from which came certain supplies and to which it looked as a market for some of its goods. Then, each of these semi-independent areas had to be provided with some means of social and economic interaction. During its pioneer period the only means of transportation were the river boats and the wagon trains. Both of these were slow and inadequate. There were few rivers and they were navigable but for short distances. There were few wagon roads and the terrain was rough and difficult to cross—then, too, distances were great. The first integration of any significance came with the building of the main lines of the railroad which spread out with its connecting feeders. This joined the community with its neighbors and welded together the scattered parts or areas into a semblance of unity.

A railroad map of this territory shows that these roads connect practically every sub-district in the area either directly or through a connecting synapse at the city which serves as the dominant center. The railroads were not alone, however, in the process of integration. Complete integration was compelled to await the coming of the automobile, the truck and improved highways. The railroad carried rapid transportation to the larger community and tied the smaller areas together. The automobile carried goods and people out beyond the railroad station to each individual farm and tied the entire area into an integrated whole. Because of the topography of the area, even under the most complete railroad system possible, or at least practicable, numerous districts were left isolated. The automobile and truck have now connected practically the last one of these communities with some terminal market and brought it into the major economic and social web of the regional community.

The experience of the community described above is somewhat typical of the role of integration in communal development. One might conclude from the emphasis upon transportation that there were no other factors important in the process of integration. The agencies for transporting ideas are important as well as those for transporting goods. The radio and the telephone has been of considerable importance in the enlargement of the community boundaries. The telephone has served to lessen the distance from the center to the rims of the community, and for some purposes to eliminate it. No longer do mountains and rivers narrow the fields of social or economic contacts, for with the installation of the teletypewriter, the telephone, or the radio, the small country village on the outer rims of the community is as much aware of all matters of communal interest as are the people in the city at the center. Barriers which for the pioneer were unsurmountable, have been overcome and a new community whose social interaction cannot be measured in terms of spatial distance or physical obstacles, has arisen on the base of the old.[28]

SUMMARY

The term community has been used with little precision in definition. Its usage at times would indicate a geographical area, at others a state of mind, and at still others an area of social interaction. The latter use seems to be the one most generally adhered to. According to this connotation the community becomes an area in which one carries on the major functions of his political, economic, and social existence, and in which he experiences a sense of belonging.

The community assumes numerous structural patterns among which the major ones in contemporary culture are, the village community, the urban community, the rurban community and the regional community, to which the term region is frequently applied. This latter particularly is a recent phenomenon which has developed as the result of improved communication, transportation, and marketing systems.

[28] A substantial portion of the section on integration appeared in modified form in an article by the author ''Integration in the Inland Empire Region of the Pacific Northwest'' published in *Social Forces*, VII, October, 1938, 30–40.

The term community should be differentiated from neighborhood. Neighborhood had best be reserved to describe the small face to face communal groupings in which there is a "consciousness of kind" among the members that make it up—a consensus or solidarity. Community describes the larger complex area of social interaction which has some point of integration and some system of relationships that tie the whole together, yet the relations are, for the most part, impersonal.

The community is in a constant state of flux and change. This change extends to its structure, internal organization, and institutions. The changes are not uniform. Some outrun the others thus creating serious problems of organization. It does not seem possible to control these changes. They appear to be a part of a natural process of community growth. However, community planning is being developed as an attempted control device.

The process of integration illustrated in this region is typical of what is taking place in communal organization throughout the country. The process begins with the small community in the relations between the people and the markets, the church, the school or whatever institutions or services provide the dominant center. From this small unit the process extends out to an ever widening area of communal integration until as McKenzie has said, "the entire settlement pattern of the country is becoming knitted together into an ever finer web of functional interrelationship." It is this process of integration that makes possible the modern community, whether it be rural, urban, rurban, or regional.

SELECTED REFERENCES

Burgess, E. W., "The Determination of Gradients in the Growth of the City," *Publications of The American Sociological Society*, XXI, 1929, 178–84.

Carpenter, Niles, "Urban Growth and 'Transitional Areas,'" *Publications of The American Sociological Society*, XXIV, 1930, 254.

Follett, Mary P., "Community as a Process," *Philosophical Review*, November, 1929, 576–88.

Galpin, C. J., *The Social Anatomy of an Agricultural Community*, Wisconsin Agricultural Experiment Station Research Bulletin 34, Madison, May, 1915.

Gras, N. S. B., *Introduction to Economic History*, New York: Harper and Brothers, 1922.

Hiller, E. T., Corner, Fay E., and East, Wendell L., *Rural Community Types*, "University of Illinois Studies in the Social Sciences," Vol. XVI, No. 4, Urbana, 1928.

Leiffer, Murray H., "A Method for Determining Local Urban Community Boundaries," *Publications of the American Sociological Society*, XXVI, 1932, 137–43.

Martin, Robert R., ''Integration in the Inland Empire Region of the Pacific Northwest,'' *Social Forces*, XVII, October, 1938, 29–40.

McKenzie, R. D., *The Metropolitan Community*, New York: McGraw-Hill Book Co., Inc., 1933.

McKenzie, R. D., ''The Concept Dominance and World Organization,'' *Publications of the American Sociological Society*, XXI, 1927, 138.

McKenzie, R. D., *The Neighborhood*, Chicago: University of Chicago Press, 1923.

McKenzie, R. D., ''The Rise of Metropolitan Communities,'' in President's Research Committee, *Recent Social Trends*, I, 433–96, New York: McGraw-Hill Book Co., Inc.

Park, R. E., Burgess, E. W., and McKenzie, R. D. (Editors), ''Urbanization as Measured by Newspaper Circulation,'' *The American Journal of Sociology*, XXXV, July, 1929, 60–79.

Sanderson, Dwight, *The Rural Community*, New York: Ginn and Company, 1932.

Steiner, Jessie F., *Community Organization*, New York: The Century Company, 1930.

Terpenning, W. A., *Village and Open Country Neighborhoods*, New York: The Century Co., 1931.

Tylor, W. Russell, ''The Process of Change From Neighborhood to Regional Organization and Its Effect upon Rural Life,'' *Social Forces*, XVI, May, 1938, 530–42.

CHAPTER 16.

RELIGION AND THE CHURCHES

BY D. J. BOWDEN, PH.D.

Chairman, Department of Philosophy and Religion,
Elon College, Elon College, N. C.

Introduction: The Religious Experience

In the dawn of human culture, one of the earliest institutions to arise was that of religion. Although modern psychology denies the existence of a "religious instinct" we are forced to recognize in human nature the tendency to hold in high regard those things which manifest potency. For primitive man who had no concept of natural law, all of nature seemed to possess mysterious power; power to harm as well as to help, to destroy as well as to nurture him. He experienced the seasons over which he held no control, the blessings of sunshine and rain, the comforts and destructiveness of fire, the beauty and the mercilessness of lightning, wind, and floods. He experienced pain and disease; he stood in awe before the finality of death. These things he knew, and yet for him they were shrouded in mystery; the mystery of vast uncontrolled and uncontrollable power. No wonder, then, that early man, standing constantly in the clutch of natural forces, should bow down in fear and reverence. These powers gave life and took it away, made skies to burst into fury and to glow with the life-giving warmth of sunshine after rain.

And to these powers man attributed personality. Gods and demons were believed to inhabit and to control everything, and in their presence primitive man was forced to recognize his own impotence. "What shall I do to be saved" was the cry of prehistoric man as much as of his modern brother, and down through the centuries he and his children and his children's children have called upon their gods in time of need and offered thanks to them in time of plenty. Just as every human institution arose to satisfy some need, so the institution of religion became a part of the social structure to meet the need of dealing effectively with these powers. But from primitive hit-or-miss beginnings religion has come to be one of the most potent cultural forces in human society. The Christian Church today symbolizes the major trend of ideals of the American people and exerts an influence which is essential and basic to the current structure of their social organization.

THE HISTORY OF RELIGION

The story of religion is not to be found complete in the history of any one culture or any one civilization. The religious experience is universal, and the roots of religious experience are much the same in every human culture, yet varieties of culture result in varieties of religious expression. Where man is, there religion in some form may be found, but the forms differ as do the cultures in which they exist. Also, as man's knowledge grows, his ideas of God, the world, and of himself evolve. He discovers new characteristics and new relationships; he begins to find increased meaning in life, and to discover order and unity in the processes of nature. The growing consciousness of religious significance in all reality is characteristic of a variety of cultures, and thus religious concepts and practices evolve. Some would call this the process of discovery; others would call it "progressive revelation."

The Search for Security

In the earliest stages of religious experience the recognition of superhuman forces in nature[1] led man to seek ways of controlling these powers and of escaping their undesired effects. And because the powers themselves, though conceived as personal, were thought of chiefly in relation to happenings in the *material* world there was little or no relation between religion and morals. Primitive man sought through religion, not ethical values, but material goods. To obtain good crops, healthy children, good fortune in hunting, or destruction of his enemies, he paid homage in one way or another to his gods.

1. *Taboo, Ancestor Worship, Totem.* Because he feared the power of the gods and because he ascribed to them the calamity which befell his brothers, primitive man gradually worked out a system of prohibitions for himself and his children. Certain objects were not to be touched and certain foods were not to be eaten. To violate these taboos was to bring injury to the individual or to the tribe or both. In some primitive societies it was "forbidden" to

[1] We do not use the term "supernatural" here, for our primitive ancestors knew no supernatural as we conceive it today. To them all forces were aspects of "nature." Having no concept of natural law, early man had no ground for conceiving a "super-nature."

touch a dead body or a woman during several days following child-birth, or boys or girls at puberty. Jews were forbidden to eat "unclean" meats, of which pork is most common today. Hindus were forbidden to eat beef; the cow is for them a sacred animal. Taboos are prohibitions which in primitive society held religious sanction, and the violations of which were severely punished.

Ancestor worship is also characteristic of primitive religion and has survived to the present day, particularly in the Orient. It is reasonable to assume that ancestor worship arose out of the belief that spirits of the dead continued to dwell in the locality which they inhabited while among the living. From this belief which is found to be common to practically all primitive people it is but a short step to the worship of these ancestors who, as spirits, possessed superior age and wisdom combined with great power to effect good or evil.

2. *Magic, Ritual, Ceremony, Sacrifice.* In his search for physical security, primitive man not only sought by taboo and ancestor worship to escape what he thought to be the evil effects of the power of the gods, but he also sought in a positive way to control the gods and to gain a portion of their supposed power for himself. Fetishes (charms, made usually of wood or bone) were worn to bring strength or good luck. Amulets of many kinds were worn to drive off evil spirits of disease and destruction. Elaborate rituals and mysterious incantations were developed as means of obtaining the favor of the gods, and ceremonies including music, dancing, and shouting were believed to be effective in destroying disease or in obtaining the aid of the gods for battle. But magic and ritual were not always effective, and early man sought further favor through sacrifice. Originating as offerings of food and drink for the gods, these sacrificial ceremonies became the most important elements in some religions. In extreme cases human beings were slain or burned as offerings to the deities.

3. *Rise of the Priesthood.* Thus ceremony and ritual may have developed partly as the direct responses of man to his environment, but more directly they arose through the genius of individuals who claimed special powers in dealing with gods and demons. These men gradually constructed elaborate practices in appealing to the gods and found their fellowmen anxious to put their trust in them. Every tribe had its "medicine man" or "shaman" who, as leader of religious practices, magician, and physician, was one of the most powerful men of the tribe. In many cases he came to be revered as

a god himself. From the earliest society to the present day, religious leaders have been revered and set apart because of their supposed unique proximity to the deity.

The Transition from Material to Ethical Goals

The religion of primitive man has been described as a means of assuring his physical security in the face of superhuman natural forces. Magic and ritual were thought to affect the gods. Gradually, however, religion became more than a source of security; it became the chief conserver of mores and customs in society.

1. *Social Origin of Moral Law.* Early man was forced to obtain most of his knowledge from his own experience. He felt the drives of hunger, of sex, of self-preservation, but in satisfying these desires he had no initial guide for conduct. Only through trial and error did he learn that certain foods were poisonous, that incest bred feeble-mindedness, and that protection could best be assured through loyalty to a group. But as he learned these things he passed his knowledge on to his friends and to his children. Many profited by the experience of the one; rules were set down, became tradition, and each younger generation accepted them on the authority of their elders. Thus primitive customs arose.[2]

2. *Divine Sanction.* But as one generation after another accepted customs and folkways from their elders it was not enough simply to say "this is the way our fathers did it." Rather, it was said, "this is the way our fathers and our fathers's fathers would have us do it!" and the assumption of the ghostly presence of these ancestors among the living gave ample force to maintain the tradition. The *customary* way became the *right* way and the only acceptable way. Thus a system of right and wrong appeared and folkways were lifted to the plane of mores. Upon adherence to the mores depended, presumably, the welfare of the individual and of the tribe, but acceptance of the mores was based increasingly upon a social philosophy in which laws regarding property, and the sexes were supposed to have divine sanction, and to be enforced by superhuman powers. As new codes of behavior evolved, the ethical concepts of religion took larger place.

3. *Judaeo-Christianity.* The history of the Jewish faith presents a clear example of the transition from material to ethical goals. Although, in the time of Moses, Hebrew religion had already evolved

[2] See W. G. Sumner, *Folkways*, Ginn & Co., 1906.

far from its primitive beginnings, the god of the Israelites was conceived primarily as a war god; playing the role of a tribal chieftain, and controlling the natural forces of wind, rain, and sun; a jealous god who vented his wrath unmercifully upon his enemies. But as time passed a transition took place: the Jews no longer conceived their god as a mere tribal god, as one among many deities. He became the one *universal* God. He was no longer satisfied with burnt offerings and material sacrifices, but demanded moral attitudes and social conscience on the part of his people; he would not recognize ritual, said the prophets, which was not accompanied by moral living. Social justice and care for the welfare of one's neighbor became more important than sacrifice and taboo. Thus Judaism became an ethical religion and laid the foundation for Christianity, the chief features of which are ethical. Interest in one's own physical well-being which prompted early religious practice has not been eliminated from Christianity, but as the religion has matured, moral values have tended to supersede this interest.

The Great Non-Christian Religions

Although Christianity is the dominant religion in Western culture we must not overlook the existence of other religions, some of them more ancient. The religions of Egypt and Babylonia disappeared with the cultures in which they were nurtured. So also did the pagan religions of Greece and Rome. Others have survived, however, having developed into their modern forms from such primitive beginnings as we have described.

1. *India: Hinduism and Buddhism.* One of the most ancient of present-day religions is Hinduism. At least as early as 1500 B.C. the roots of Hinduism lay in the practices and beliefs of Aryan conquerors in India. In its early form it was essentially a nature religion in which the gods were the personified natural powers of sunshine, rain, and fire. Ritual developed as the priesthood arose, and the priests, because of their claim of magical power, became the dominant caste. Hinduism has, to the present day, retained much of its magic and superstition and dependence upon the priesthood, but within this movement there has also been a vital philosophical development. India today possesses among her 240 million Hindus[3] some of the world's most ignorant and superstitious folk, perhaps, but she also may boast of religious and philosophical insights as deep

[3] All figures for membership in non-Christian religions are taken from J. C. Archer, *Faiths Men Live By*, Thomas Nelson and Sons, 1938.

as the world has ever known. The Hindus were among the first to go beyond polytheism to belief in one universal God who controls all things.

Out of Hinduism came Gautama, later known to his followers as "The Buddha," (The Enlightened One). Buddhism was founded in the sixth century before the Christian Era as a revolt against the superstition and magic of Hinduism. Its founder, Gautama, denied the existence of the gods and the efficacy of material sacrifice and ritual. Religion, he said, is the absence of selfish desire, and must be in the hearts of men. All suffering is caused by desire, and salvation comes only through eliminating this cause. Later Buddhism did not surrender this psychological doctrine, but it did return to faith in the gods, even to the point of making the Buddha himself one of the deities. Buddhism died out in India, but only after it had established itself elsewhere in the Orient. Its adherents today number 140 million, more than half of whom are in China and Japan.

2. *China: Confucianism.* Although Confucianism is said to be losing ground in China today, it may still be ranked with Buddhism as one of the major religions of the Orient. During the 2500 years since the death of Confucius it has done more to mold the culture and customs of the Chinese people than any other factor. Confucius was a moralist and a statesman rather than a religious leader, but those who came after him conceived him as a god and built a religion around his life and teachings. It is a religion which includes much magic and superstitution, but which is more basically ethical than any other non-Christian faith.

3. *Japan: Shinto.* In addition to Confucianism and Buddhism, both of which have been widely adopted in Japan, is the state religion known as Shinto ("the way of the gods.") This movement is primarily a form of religious patriotism based upon the belief that Japan is the "land of the gods," that the Japanese nation is the "chosen" nation of the gods, that their emperor is the "son of Heaven," and that dedication of oneself to the national state is actually dedication to the gods. Shinto practices still include as much magic and superstition as do other oriental religions, but from a sociological standpoint Shinto is most important because of its nationalistic spirit and its military zeal.

4. *Judaism.* Equally nationalistic, but without military interests, is the religion of the Jews who for more than three thousand

years have believed themselves to be God's chosen people. To this prosperous Palestinian kingdom during the tenth century B.C. came division and later destruction and dispersion. Today the Jews are sprinkled over the entire face of the earth, but unshaken is their faith that God will some day bring about his kingdom on earth and that they, his chosen people, will be reunited. The Jews have suffered more persecution, perhaps, than any other religious group in History; Western culture is especially marked by its ever recurring "pogroms" against the sons of Israel. Yet surviving all persecution and all hatreds is the Jewish faith that the God of Jacob will ultimately bring justice for his chosen people who put their trust in him.

5. *Islam.* Out of Judaism, one of the world's greatest religions, have come two other faiths no less great. One of these is Christianity; the other is Islam, sometimes known as Mohammedanism in honor of its founder, Mohammed. The central theme of Islam is its emphasis upon the *oneness* of God, his universal power, and the necessity for man to submit to his will. At the death of its founder in 632 A.D., Islam spread from Arabia into Palestine, Asia Minor, across northern Africa, and into Spain and southern France. Although it has lost its foothold in Europe, Mohammedanism today claims nearly 240 million adherents and is found throughout the continents of Africa and Asia, and elsewhere.

THE CHRISTIAN CHURCH

Nearly every great culture has at its core a great religion; a religion which not only conserves the mores of that culture, but which to a great degree molds the habits and thoughts of the people. The religion of a nation usually determines its world view, and the world view of a nation determines its ideals and its purposes. Just as Hinduism did this for India and Confucianism for China, so Christianity has been a basic cultural force in the entire western world.

History of the Christian Church

1. *Founding and Formative Years.* Christianity is based upon the life and teachings of Jesus of Nazareth, a Jew who in his 29th year was baptized and went about healing the sick and teaching the fatherhood of God and the brotherhood of man. During the four years in which he taught, twelve men became his close associates and disciples, identifying him as the Jewish Messiah. All of these twelve, however, turned against him or fled in fear when he was

accused and tried for the blasphemy of claiming this Messiahship. Crucifixion and burial followed his trial, but to his disciples and to others he is reported to have reappeared, apparently in the flesh. Out of faith in this miraculous resurrection of the Christ the disciples gained new strength and vigor, and the Christian movement gathered strength. Peter, chief among the disciples, and Paul, may well be called the founders of the movement. Paul was largely responsible for carrying the Christian Gospel to the Gentiles and for the systematic character of that Gospel. According to Paul, Jesus was the Christ, the Son of God who had been sent to redeem the world from sin, and who would in time return to claim his own. The message spread from Palestine to Asia Minor, to Greece, and finally to Rome, and churches were established throughout this area. That at Rome soon became the most important church, the Bishop at Rome being acknowledged as settler of disputes among lesser bishops. With the passing of the centuries, surviving persecution, Christianity finally became the only permitted religion in the Roman Empire, and spread throughout all of Europe and northern Africa.

2. *Division.* Seeds of dissension gradually took root within the Church, however, and in the eleventh century the Christian world was torn asunder over matters of organization, authority, doctrine, and practice. Two Christian churches resulted, the Roman Catholic Church retaining its supremacy in Europe, and the Greek Orthodox or Greek Catholic Church taking dominance in the East. Nearly five hundred years later, in the first quarter of the sixteenth century, another division occurred within the Roman Catholic Church. Protestants, so called because they protested against moral and ecclesiastical abuses within this church, became a separate group under the leadership of Luther in Germany and Calvin and Zwingli in Switzerland. They established the Bible as their supreme authority rather than the Pope or the Church Councils as in the Catholic Church. Another break from Papal authority started in England, led by Henry VIII (1509–1547), and was successful, partially because of the growing nationalistic spirit.—The Church of England was established as another Protestant group.

3. *Denominationalism and Church Union.* Unity has constantly been maintained within the Roman Catholic Church, but the Protestant movement has been characterized by division, redivision, and more redivision. Its basic principle of the autonomy of the local church and the right of all men to read and interpret Scripture for

themselves has led to conflicts of judgment, and as a result the United States today contains two hundred or more organized groups of Protestant origin. The membership in organized religion in the United States (as of December, 1937) is summarized as follows:[4]

	Churches	Inclusive membership	13 years and over membership
Protestants	225,032	37,465,655	32,940,965
Roman Catholic	18,428	21,322,688	15,492,016
Eastern Orthodox	654	1,100,043	883,875
Polish National Catholic ...	146	189,620	130,838
Jewish	4,150	4,081,242	2,930,332
Grand totals	248,410	64,159,248	52,378,026

A growing spirit of unity has been in evidence among Protestant groups within the past two decades, however, both in cooperative activities such as the Federal Council of Churches of Christ in America, and in mergers of small Protestant bodies into larger and more efficient units. One of the most significant mergers in Protestant history is that of the Methodist Episcopal, the M. E. South, and the Methodist Protestant groups, effected in 1939. This merger brings together approximately eight million members to form the largest single Protestant body in America today. Smaller mergers of other groups have been completed, and many are now under consideration. Denominational cooperation in the United States is also increasing; there are twenty-one state interdenominational councils with paid executive leadership,[5] and perhaps hundreds of city councils and ministerial associations of an interdenominational character. Protestant churches, after centuries of division, are moving toward unity.

Recent Conflicts and Readjustments

Almost invariably, when a conflict regarding religious beliefs arises it hinges on the question of authority. The beliefs of the Catholic Church are said to be truths "revealed" by God to His Church, and hence infallible. According to this doctrine research and discovery may serve to clarify this revelation but can never abrogate it. The same position regarding "revealed" truth has been generally held by Protestants also, except that the channel of revela-

[4] Condensed from *Yearbook of American Churches*, 1939 edition, edited by Herman C. Weber, p. 5.

[5] *Ibid.*, p. 139.

tion for them is the Bible rather than the institutional church. When newly discovered facts appear to conflict with revelation, therefore, society is faced with the dilemma of the "irresistible force meeting the immovable object."

This conflict of authorities is found in the opposition of "revealed" religion to some recent scientific theories. In many cases scientists have been arrogant in claiming certainty for their theories. In other cases organized religion has opposed, on grounds of divine revelation, theories which are today accepted as warranted facts. The Church, for instance, for many years after Copernicus, continued to insist that the earth was the center of the universe, and that the sun and the stars revolved about it. In more recent years Protestant "Fundamentalists," because their belief in the authority of the Bible seemed to be at stake, fought valiantly against the theory of evolution. But the Catholic Church today accepts the theory that the earth moves, and the Protestant Church does not drastically oppose a modified theory of evolution.

During the past hundred years an equally important struggle has occurred mainly within the Protestant Church, regarding the origin and authorship of the Bible. Scholars in this period have sought the historical setting of Biblical books, the characteristics of their authors, and the forces which caused them to write. This "higher criticism" led to some discoveries and some conclusions which did not accord with traditional beliefs. Consequently the Fundamentalists took arms against the "higher critics" and continued to insist upon a "literal" interpretation of the Bible. The findings of the Biblical scholars, however, are generally accepted today.

Within Protestantism there also arose recently a humanist movement which for some decades gathered momentum, and which reached its peak in the "roaring twenties." Preachers emphasized solely the immanence of God to the extent that some pictured him simply as the personalization of man's ideals; a figment of man's imagination. From this extreme position, involving a glorified confidence in man's ability to achieve his own salvation through social progress, Christian theology is now swinging back to an over-emphasis upon man's depravity and God's judgment upon him. This swing of the pendulum from exaggerated confidence in man to a complete loss of that faith can be measured largely in terms of the alternation of security and crisis in the culture pattern itself.

The theology of crisis is invariably a renewed emphasis on man's impotence and a return to absolute dependence upon God.

The modern Christian, midway between these extremes, recognizes the value of the scientific method for discovery of truth, and does not hesitate to use it and to accept its verified conclusions. His faith is not dependent, however, upon every word that issues out of the mouth of an experimental scientist, nor does he blindly accept tradition. Between these two extremes he takes a position in which science and religion are conceived as two legitimate approaches to truth, but he insists that truth, wherever it is found, is consistent with itself. The Bible for the modern Christian is an accepted guide for faith and practice. He does not take it literally, however, "from cover to cover," but reads each section in the light of the historical period in which it arose. In order to achieve this more reasoned interpretation of religious experience and divine Scripture, therefore, the Protestant Church as a whole is again moving toward higher educational requirements for its ministers. The Catholic Church, on the other hand, has never relaxed its educational standards.

2. *Cultural Change.* "The Church in a Changing World" has been the topic of so many books, lectures, discussions, and conferences in recent years that one cannot fail to realize that the church is truly in a world of flux. It is equally true that this changing social milieu is becoming increasingly secular. Whereas religious agencies once controlled the educational and recreational facilities and activities in American culture the church finds itself today trailing in the wake of state schools and commercial amusements.

Aside from the comparatively few parochial schools of the Catholic church the state has taken full responsibility for primary and secondary education and is increasingly dominating the field of higher education. Church colleges maintain their autonomy only with difficulty, and with increasing taxation of incomes and personal property and investments, the church college will find increasing difficulty in obtaining gifts for building and endowments.

The church has also been forced to surrender its monopoly of the Sabbath. Whereas blue laws once made it a crime to engage in any form of recreation on Sunday we find the Sabbath day becoming little more than a day of freedom from the "job," a day on which commercial amusements, automobile travel, and golf occupy the attention of Mr. Average Citizen. This is less true of rural districts than of urban, although the rural church has also felt pressure in this direction.

The urban church is faced with the recurring problem of ecological variations. A church which is built in the heart of a residential section may within two or three generations, find itself in a business district or in a slum area. As cities grow their populations migrate and although some "downtown" churches are able to retain their membership, others are forced either to surrender their existence or to alter their functions. One becomes a "marriage bureau," another a "community center" for athletics and social contacts, and another a haven for prayer and meditation in a busy street. Its members, in each case, have moved to the suburban or rural areas.

Rural churches, on the other hand, face the problem of unification. The day of the "circuit rider" who served many churches over a wide area is gradually giving way (largely because of facility of transportation) to unification of congregations and development of larger, more effective church organizations. The "larger parish" movement particularly in New England, has shown great benefits in this direction, and points toward progressive development of the rural church under competent, trained leadership which only city churches could heretofore afford.

Christian missions have also undergone a significant transformation within the past generation. Early missionaries went into foreign fields with the view that Christianity had the whole truth and that all other religions were false and worthy only to be destroyed. These men and women were, for the most part, preachers and exhorters. Today, the American Mission Board is sending out relatively fewer preachers and more teachers, doctors, agricultural experts; men and women who are Christian in attitude and outlook, but whose function is that of serving, educating, and aiding adherents of other faiths to discover the more abundant life here and now. The seeds of Christianity are no less sown in these lands, but through education and service as well as through preaching.

3. *Church and State.* Central to all American religious thought is that initial clause from the Bill of Rights which reads: "Congress shall make no law respecting an establishment of religion, or prohibiting the free exercise thereof. . . ." Of equal importance with freedom of speech and freedom of press is the demand for freedom of the individual to worship as he sees fit. This is essential to any

true democracy, and Americans are willing to fight for this tradition of religious freedom. Correlated with the demand for freedom is the equally vital insistence that the state shall not support or subsidize any one religious movement, lest individuals not in sympathy with this movement be forced to support by taxation that to which they are conscientiously opposed. The rise of extreme nationalism, however, is invariably accompanied by the obliteration or at least the reduction to a state of servitude of all independent religions, whether Protestant or Catholic. No such fate appears on the immediate horizon for Christianity in America, perhaps, yet this correlation indicates the close relationship between religious attitudes and the national temper. Any religious movement or sect which refuses to bow to demands of the state is invariably ostracized and often persecuted. The plight of apparently sincere "Jehovah's Witnesses" in the United States is illustrative of this trend.

Whereas Protestantism has seldom united in the seeking of political goals, the political power of Roman Catholicism is undeniable. Recent fervor of Protestant Churches, however, in opposing the appointment of "a personal representative of the President of the United States to the Pope at Rome, with the rank of ambassador," suggests the possibility of joint action of Protestant groups for political purposes. The Catholic church has never accepted, however, the doctrine of separation of church and state, whereas it is the life blood of Protestantism. Some writers, therefore, are predicting a new outburst of conflict on this score, not only between Catholic and Protestant groups but between the Catholic church and the state as well.[6]

THE CHURCH AND THE INDIVIDUAL

Salvation

Man's impotence in the face of cosmic forces is just as apparent today as in the earliest age of the human race. Pain, pestilence, death, and destruction are just as real today as then, and man strives now as then, to escape them. The Christian doctrines of atonement and eternal life have been in the past a source of satisfaction in this regard.

1. *Atonement.* The traditional belief in atonement holds that all men are born sinners, having inherited the sins of their fathers as far back as the original "Adam." But finite man, the theory

[6] See Harold Bosley, "Is a Religious Storm Brewing"; *Christian Century*, Vol. LVII, No. 31, July 31, 1940.

runs, is unable alone to compensate for his sin against an infinite God, and it was therefore necessary for God to send his own son to earth in the form of a man to accomplish this salvation. This, according to Christian tradition, he did, and Jesus Christ, his son, atoned for man's sins by the shedding of his blood. Salvation, therefore, is offered to all who repent of their sins and accept the Christ as their Savior. A more modern interpretation of atonement is the belief that Jesus offers salvation to man, not through his death, but through his life and teachings, and that this salvation is achieved only when man lives in accordance with these teachings. This is said to eliminate the magical element involved in the power of primitive blood sacrifice but is held to be equally meaningful as atonement (bringing man into at-one-ment with the spirit of God).

2. *Eternal Life.* Salvation in the Christian tradition has generally been conceived as the attainment of eternal life, a continued existence either physical or spiritual after death, in which one receives compensation for his sufferings on earth. This "heaven" is variously conceived in different levels of culture, but is generally viewed as a condition of peace and comfort with absence of struggle and pain. Many modern Christians tend to lessen this emphasis upon the future life, and urge the importance of "social immortality" or the "immortality of influence." This view charges man with responsibility for living "the good life" in order to influence individuals and social forces toward achieving the kingdom of God on earth. Thus, when one dies, he is said to become immortal in the effectiveness of his work among men. Some go so far as to claim this as the only form of immortality man may enjoy.

3. *The Abundant Life.* The Christian tradition also includes frequent reference to "The abundant life"; "I came," said Jesus, "that you might have life and have it more abundantly." Superficially this expression is taken as a reference to the "life after death," but the modern Christian applies it also to the life here and now. The Christian faith, he says, gives *meaning* to existence. It offers not only consolation in suffering, but grounds for understanding the complexities of life and for appreciating its beauties; it offers an answer to "the riddle of the universe"; it offers as well an object of religious devotion which is worthy of worship and respect. The Christian faith also serves as a criterion of social and personal values, an ethical yardstick whereby one may measure his deeds. The individual who strives to live the Christlike life has chosen a

guide for his purposive acts, and has thereby eliminated much quibbling within his own mind as to what may be right or wrong. Thus a more stable and more harmonious life is achieved. And in dedication of oneself to a cause, namely the cause of bringing about the kingdom of God, the Christian has found a means toward an integrated personality and mental health. The personality which is wholly dedicated to a cause greater than itself finds most of its inner conflicts and frustrations eliminated. The church is coming increasingly to use the services of psychiatry in dealing with personality difficulties, and psychiatry is using religious faith as a means toward personality integration.

A "Community of Saints"

The Apostle Paul referred to the members of the Christian churches as "saints," not because they were morally and spiritually perfect but because they banded themselves together for a common religious purpose.

1. *Fellowship and Corporate Worship.* The Church today may also be termed a "community of Saints" in that it is composed of men and women joined together for worship and Christian fellowship. The fellowship is not exclusive; it welcomes new members at every opportunity but its uniqueness lies in the object of this social unity. Although some churches have become "clannish" the majority have not made fellowship an end in itself. Christian people gather together at frequent intervals for the purpose of worship, instruction, and exhortation.

2. *The Kingdom of God.* A second function and purpose of the church as a community of Saints is that of striving through joint action to bring about the Kingdom of God on earth. Banded together in this common cause, sincere church members assume the obligation of carrying the Christian gospel to those who have not accepted it. The church is a bulwark of morality, and many of its members are taking to themselves a responsibility for advancing the reign of God throughout the world and within the hearts of men.

THE CHURCH IN SOCIAL CHANGE

In many cultures religion has served the individual as a core for personality integration but it also serves society as a whole. This it has done in two major ways: It has functioned as a means of social control by imparting divine sanction to ideals and standards of action, and it has effected social reform by the unrelenting effort of its "prophets." Thus the church has been both a conserving factor and a radical factor, supporting at one point the *status quo* and at another challenging society to recognize inconsistencies in its culture and to eliminate them before they destroy the social patterns.

Social Control

Paul H. Landis writes: "From a purely sociological viewpoint, religion probably has been of greatest significance in human culture because of its influence in social control."[7] And we might justifiably add that with the family and the government, religion has been one of the most significant if not *the* most significant institution in effecting social control. From the time of early man until the present, in the theory of most religions the divine will has been a vital factor. The concept of the power of Gods or of a God who effectively controls the destinies of men has seldom been questioned, and man throughout the ages has sought the favor of his gods. If man is convinced, therefore, that adherence to the mores will assure him of this favor, conservation of the mores is reciprocally assured. Thus, by giving divine sanction to current ideals and practices, the church not only retains its own significance for man's well being but stabilizes the culture as well.

The means employed by the church for maintaining the mores depends upon the beliefs within the church itself and the authority it exercises over its people. Nearly all Christian thought today is controlled, to some extent at least (consciously or unconsciously), by the belief in a life after this one. This belief includes the promise of future reward for good deeds and punishment for evil ones, and when it is accepted wholeheartedly there is little tendency to question or to oppose the mores. "The church retains the keys to heaven and only the righteous shall enter therein." Implemented with such a weapon as this the Church serves as a major factor in social control.

For those who pay little heed to prospects for future reward and punishment, however, religion offers another strong motive for adhering to the mores, namely that one *profits* by so doing. A popular creed is expressed: "Do business by the Golden Rule; it pays." Such a motto as this, although it is upheld today by civic clubs claiming no organic church connection, nevertheless arose through the teachings of the church. The same attitude is expressed by those who avoid immoral acts because of the ostracism from society which

[7] *Social Control*, J. B. Lippincott Co, p. 237.

might follow, or because of social diseases which might be contracted. Such an attitude is supported by belief in reward and punishment in this world, and the church is not averse to encouraging this belief.

A third means of social control has come through science and education, and is coming increasingly to be adopted by the church. It might be termed the "psychological" doctrine of salvation. Man finds that his greatest happiness, the most abundant life for him, lies in being in harmony with his friends and his surroundings, and that conflict destroys that happiness. But man can remain in harmony with his community most effectively only by adhering to its rules and customs.

Yet in social control also we find religious institutions compromising with forces which destroy the mores. Less than a generation ago the church condemned dancing as immoral, indecent, and obscene. But young people danced, and many churches, rather than lose their youngsters permitted and later encouraged dancing within the church as a healthful activity when "properly supervised." From rank opposition to all "card playing" many churches have evolved to the point of "bridge benefits" for charitable causes; and to dispel the influence of corner pool parlors some churches have installed their own billiard tables, bowling alleys, and skating rinks. Thus the church "keeps abreast of the times" conserving as long as possible the ideals and mores of past generations and taking on new social activities when failure to do so threatens to weaken its influence. Yet with all its compromise the church remains an active force in conserving the moral culture of the past.

Social Reforms

Because it has tended to conserve the mores of the past, oft-times beyond the period of usefulness, the church has often been charged with retarding human progress. Although this charge is not without foundation, it is not the whole truth; all institutions, because they are conservative (and conservation *is* a value) tend to resist change. Law and medicine are equally open to the charge of delaying progress, for in striving to retain adherence to "the best that is known" they examine in a hypercritical light all that appears as new on the professional horizon. Yet the professions of law and medicine have themselves gradually changed and have given support to change in other fields. So it has been with religion; opposing change on the one hand, on the other it has been a driving force for social reform;

stable and conservative, it has always produced its prophets and reformers.

1. *Morals.* No social factor has been more significant in the maintenance of personal morality than has religion. From the time religion began to embrace ethical principles to the present day, the church has been the spearpoint of moral reform appealing to the individual in devious ways to live according to its standards.

But equally availing has been the drive on immoral practices of society as a whole. The minor prophets of Judaism are echoed in the "social gospel" of today, and organized religion is waking to its opportunity. Particularly effective has been the recent activity of the Legion of Decency. Sponsored originally by the Catholic Church, but supported also by individuals of other faiths, this movement within a relatively short period has brought about a drastic reform in the moral tone of moving picture productions. Both subject matter and presentation have been influenced in their moral and educational import. A second movement instituted by the Catholic Church and receiving some support from other socially minded groups is the drive to prevent publication of magazines and periodicals whose obscene pictures and sordid stories are morally disintegrating and culturally destructive. Such a movement will depend for its success, however, upon the unified effort of a large constituency. Other attempts at social reform are numerous, among the most important of which perhaps, were the Anti-Saloon League and the W. C. T. U. of pre-prohibition days. Both of these movements drew their constituency in the large from Protestant churches, and were supported by these churches.

2. *Economic Reform.* Charity is a central teaching of Christianity and members of the Christian Church have ever been admonished to care for the poor. Modern organized charities and agencies for social service took form within the church and drew their early leaders from its members, and although the organized charities have set up independent units, charity is still an important function of the church. But assistance for the poor has come to be regarded in the church as an attempt within a sick society to relieve the suffering, not to destroy the malady, and the church is giving thought to eliminating the disease itself. Among Jewish prophets, many centuries before Jesus, the demand for economic reform rang out most forcibly in the message of Amos. Many of the teachings of Jesus were taken from these prophets, and, with Amos, he did

not hesitate to insist that the rich have an obligation to the poor, and that God's condemnation falls upon any individual or any system operating without concern for the well-being of all classes in society. The spirit of capitalism arose with that of Protestantism and the system based upon free competition, private ownership of means of production, and unlimited profits for the individual developed into a highly complex system with rising industrialism. Business became impersonal, and the system came to involve many relationships which were unforeseen in an earlier day. Investors paid little attention to laboring conditions so long as they obtained their dividends, and managers were forced, because of competition, to practically enslave their workers in order to pay the investors. In many agricultural areas the plight of the "sharecropper" is even less fortunate than that of the industrial worker, his overlord often taking advantage of his ignorance and poverty. Owning no property, heavily in debt, and without education, thousands of "croppers," both colored and white, find themselves helplessly caught in the clutches of near-starvation.

In recent years the church has been developing a conscience in regard to the working man and his conditions of labor, and its members, many of whom are in the investors' and managers' class are finding that vital religion demands attention to the causes of poverty as well as to its temporary relief. The church does not wholly oppose capitalism, nor does it view labor unions as entirely righteous, but the tendency within church groups is toward education in the causes of poverty and the means of eliminating them, bringing to the attention of employers and employees alike the demand for economic readjustment. Most active in this regard are certain denominational committees such as the Council for Social Action of the Congregational Christian Churches, whose educational work is widely recognized and commended.

3. *Racial Appreciations.* Insistence upon the relaxing of discriminations against the Negro in the South, the Japanese in California, the Jew in the metropolitan area, and the Mexican peon in the Southwest has met with varying response from Christian churches. All agree that problems exist but in each case tolerance tends to increase as distance from the problem area increases. Nevertheless, religion has been one of the most active forces in overcoming prejudice and hatred between racial groups, through education of young people in summer conferences, church study groups,

etc. Most movements in America toward cooperation between the races have had their beginning in the Christian churches.

4. *Internationalism.* In a world torn by war little can be said regarding the influence of the Church toward international brotherhood. The church in America (aside from a few numerically small bodies such as the Society of Friends) has almost invariably sanctioned war as a means of protecting democracy and human liberty. Many larger groups now claim the right of individuals as conscientious objectors to refuse to fight, but the Christian church as a whole has not challenged unqualified loyalty to the State. Through all the holocaust of war, however, the faith of Christian nations is in a God of love, mercy, and justice, and Christians everywhere seem to believe that a lasting peace must be based upon these principles.

5. *Social Ideals of the Federal Council of Churches.* The Federal Council of Churches of Christ in America adopted in 1932 a platform of social ideals.[8] Without taking any position concerning the merit or lack of merit of the platform planks, we list them here as reflecting the increased interest of Christian Churches in social reform:

1. Practical application of the Christian principle of social well-being to the acquisition and use of wealth, subordination of speculation and the profit motive to the creative and cooperative spirit.

2. Social planning and control of the credit and monetary systems and the economic processes for the common good.

3. The right of all to the opportunity for self-maintenance; a wider and fairer distribution of wealth; a living wage, as a minimum, and above this a just share for the worker in the product of industry and agriculture.

4. Safeguarding of all workers, urban and rural, against harmful conditions of labor and occupational injury and disease.

5. Social insurance against sickness, accident, want in old age and unemployment.

6. Reduction of hours of labor as the general productivity of industry increases; release from employment at least one day in seven, with a shorter working week in prospect.

7. Such special regulation of the conditions of work of women as shall safeguard their welfare and that of the family and community.

[8] Federal Council of the Churches of Christ in America, *Quadrennial Report* of 1932.

8. The right of employees and employers alike to organize for collective bargaining and social action; protection of both in the exercise of this right; the obligation of both to work for the public good; encouragement of cooperatives and other organizations among farmers and other groups.

9. Abolition of child labor; adequate provision for the protection, education, spiritual nurture and wholesome recreation of every child.

10. Protection of the family by the single standard of purity; educational preparation for marriage, home-making and parenthood.

11. Economic justice for the farmer in legislation, financing, transportation and the price of farm products as compared with the cost of machinery and other commodities which he must buy.

12. Extension of the primary cultural opportunities and social services now enjoyed by urban populations to the farm family.

13. Protection of the individual and society from the social, economic and moral waste of any traffic in intoxicants and habit-forming drugs.

14. Application of the Christian principle of redemption to the treatment of offenders; reform of penal and correctional methods and institutions, and of criminal court procedure.

15. Justice, opportunity and equal rights for all; mutual goodwill and cooperation among racial, economic and religious groups.

16. Repudiation of war, drastic reduction of armaments, participation in international agencies for the peaceable settlement of all controversies; the building of cooperative world order.

17. Recognition and maintenance of the rights and responsibilities of free speech, free assembly, and a free press; the encouragement of free communication of mind with mind as essential to the discovery of truth.

It is apparent from this brief study that the church, as one of the major institutions in modern culture, cannot be separated from other phases of social organization. Its effect is inherent in the family relationship, assuming an official role in the marriage ceremony, a counseling position in dealing with marital harmony or divorce, and a ceremonial duty in time of death. The church is often a social and recreational center for the neighborhood, and sometimes assumes responsibility for the health and education of its people. Although it seeks to maintain its existence independent of government and economic institutions, we find the church frequently taking sides on issues within the fields of government and economics. Thus the influence of religion is felt throughout the entire organization of society.

OUTLINE SUMMARY

I. Primitive man stood in awe before the power and mystery of natural forces, and in this awe arose the religious experience.

    A. Realizing his impotence before the forces of nature, early man sought security by adjusting to these forces, through:

        1. Taboo, and ancestor worship.

        2. Magic, ritual, ceremony, and sacrifice.

        3. The priesthood arose to direct these religious activities.

    B. As social consciousness increased the goals of religion became increasingly ethical rather than material:

        1. Some folkways became mores.

        2. These mores were believed to be sanctioned by the gods and were thus conserved by religion; the ideas of deity, nevertheless, evolved with the mores.

        3. Judaeo-Christianity is a striking example of this development.

    C. The major non-Christian religions of the world today include:

        1. Hinduism, Buddhism.

        2. Confucianism.

        3. Shinto.

        4. Judaism.

        5. Islam.

II. The Christian Church is central in Western Culture.

    A. Its history may be traced from:

        1. Its founding by Peter and Paul upon the teaching and life of Jesus.

        2. To its division into Roman Catholic, Greek Orthodox, Protestant, and Anglican groups.

        3. The Protestant group has further divided into two hundred or more denominations, many of which are now moving toward partial reunion.

    B. There have been many conflicts and readjustments in Christianity, including:

        1. Theoretical conflicts as between science and religion,

higher criticism and fundamentalism, and super-
naturalism and humanism.
2. Adjustments to cultural changes in urban and rural
areas and mission fields.
3. The evolving relation between church and state.
III. The church offers to the individual:
A. Salvation in one or more of the following senses:
1. Atonement in terms of vicarious sacrifice or personal
adjustment.
2. Eternal life as personal or social immortality.
3. The abundant life, in that religion gives meaning to
life, a scale of values, and a growth of integrated
personality.
B. A community of saints for the purpose of fellowship,
corporate worship, and cooperation in bringing about the
kingdom of God.
IV. The church is a vital factor in social control.
A. As a conserver of the mores.
B. As an agency for social reform.
1. It tends to encourage individual adherence to the
mores, and promotes prophetic movements whose
purpose is that of eliminating what are presumed to
be social evils.
2. It seeks to bring about greater understanding and
harmony in economic relations,
3. In racial relations, and
4. In international relations.
5. The Federal Council in its "social ideals" of
churches brings a concise picture of the church's
attitude toward social reforms.

SELECTED REFERENCES

Atkins, Gaius Glenn, *Religion in Our Times,* New York: Round Table Press,
Inc., 1932.—A survey of American religious life between the years 1892
and 1932, showing its historical and social significance.
Douglass, Harlan P., and Brunner, Edmund deS., *The Protestant Church as a
Social Institution,* New York: Harpers, 1935.—A summary of the most
important findings of 48 research projects of the Institute of Social and
Religious Research.
Fry, Luther C., *The U. S. Looks at Its Churches,* New York: Institute of Social
and Religious Research, 1930.—An analysis of the data gathered by the
Federal Census of Religious Bodies of 1926 in terms of membership, distri-

bution, growth, educational activities, and financial status of American churches.

The Hazen Books on Religion, New York: Association Press, 1936–1940, especially:

> Bennett, John C., *Christianity and Our World.*
> Stewart, George, *The Church.*
> Tittle, Ernest F., *Christians in an Unchristian Society.*
> Vlastos, Gregory, *Christian Faith and Democracy.*

Johnson, Frederick Ernest, *The Church and Society,* New York: Abingdon Press, 1935.—A compact discussion of the nature of the Christian church, its relations to the social order, and the problems it faces within that relationship.

Social Action: A pamphlet published monthly (except July and August) by the Council for Social Action of the Congregational and Christian Churches, New York.

Swift, Arthur L., Jr., *New Frontiers of Religion,* New York: Macmillan, 1938.— A study of the church in a changing community, tracing the church's evolution as a social institution, the play of social forces upon it, and its persistent contributions to social change.

Visser T' Hooft, W. A., and Oldham, J. H., *The Church and Its Function in Society,* Chicago: Willett, Clark and Co., 1937.—A summary of the findings of the conference at Oxford, England, on the relation of church, community, and state.

Wickenden, Arthur C., *Youth Looks at Religion,* New York: Harper and Bros., 1939.—An excellent approach to the basic problem of Christian belief in terms which college students can understand.

CHAPTER 17

ORGANIZATION FOR EDUCATION

By Dr. R. F. Bellamy

Florida State College for Women, Tallahassee, Florida

Culture is now recognized as a major concept in the study of society. But culture is merely the sum total of accumulations of education. Hence all inventions, all institutions, folkways, mores, traditions, standards, and similar phenomena become possible through education.

The educational process begins at an exceedingly early age. Sometimes it is said that a child learns more during the first two years of his life than he will during all the remainder of it. When we think of how many primary facts he acquires during this time, this is easy to believe. It is remarkable how much is learned during the first two weeks. If a child is picked up and played with at all sorts of irregular hours, if he is rocked and sung to every time he cries and if no regular program of physiological processes is induced he may always be irregular, irresponsible, and selfish. On the other hand if he learns to eat and sleep at regular hours, and if everything is done for him according to a planned schedule, he may have just the opposite type of character. If a child is well nourished and physically well, it is amazing how regular in his habits he becomes. By the end of two weeks he will probably be waking up for feeding time with as much accuracy as an alarm clock. He has learned the first big lesson about law and order and controlled behavior.

Of course either good or bad training during these early days may be modified later, but never again can anything like as much be accomplished in such a short time. We pay lip service to education as an important factor in human society, but rarely or never do we realize how important it is. Inevitably we think of a baby as being aware of much that it takes him quite a while to learn. The new born child is quite unaware of that most fundamental of all facts— that he himself exists.

The utter emptiness of an infant's mind can be realized if we study carefully the experiences of certain persons who have sus-

418

tained injuries or undergone sicknesses which wiped out all the equipment which they had gained by education.

The case of Mr. Hanna as reported by Sidis and Goodhart is especially illuminating.[1] Mr. Hanna was a young preacher who fell out of his buggy and landed on his head. When he regained consciousness he was mentally a new born babe. Every vestige of his information was gone. He did not know that he existed, or that other beings existed. His first discovery was that he could change the rate of his breathing, and he began to breathe very rapidly. This frightened his attendants who thought he was dying and they began to rub him vigorously. This stimulated him to random, meaningless activity which was disastrous to the attendants as he was a powerful young man. Of course, he could not talk, could not understand anything, and had no sense of time or space. For days, he would reach for a cup on the other side of the room just as he would reach for one within a foot of his head.

The one difference between him and a baby was that he could learn very rapidly. Soon he could use several words. Sometimes his education had ludicrous results. He was given an apple when he was hungry and taught the word "apple." But he associated the word with his feeling of hunger rather than with the external object and hence said "apple" whenever he felt hungry. Naturally they kept bringing him apples, much to his disgust as he did not like apples.

It was a difficult task for him to learn that some things were "living" and others were not. Even then he thought a boy on a bicycle was all one animal, and a horse, buggy, and driver also just one animal. Gradually these points were straightened out and then he learned a still more difficult lesson, namely that some living creatures were "people" and thus different from other living creatures. The most astounding discovery of all was made after he had learned to talk and carry on a conversation. From a chance remark he learned that he, himself, was "people" which surprised him. "Am *I* 'people'?" he asked in amazement.

He had no feeling whatever for his sweetheart and when taken to his church and told to pray he made a simple little child-like prayer, which showed that he had no comprehension of the simplest theological concepts. After weeks of this, his people almost lost all

[1] Boris Sidis and Simon P. Goodhart, *Multiple Personality*, New York: D. Appleton & Co., 1914, Part II—The Hanna Case—pp. 83–228.

hope that he would ever regain his memory. He was eventually cured, and regained his normal self completely. His case is especially valuable since he was able afterward to remember both his former life and his experiences during his abnormal condition.

By studying his case we can get some vague idea of how empty the mind of a child is and how his education is acquired.

Another valuable means of comparison is to study the feral children who have been found from time to time. We need not be surprised that human infants have been raised by wolves, bears, or other animals. Sometimes a mother animal will adopt any helpless infant if it comes to her immediately after her own young are born. Cats have adopted mice or squirrels, dogs have adopted rabbits, and all sorts of such queer foster families have been formed. It would be perfectly natural for a mother wolf to adopt a baby which crawled into her den. A good many such cases have been found.

The most famous case is that of the wild boy of Aveyron, France, who was studied by Itard.[2] This was a most elaborate study, Dr. Itard giving practically his entire time to this boy for several years. When found, the child was not only completely lacking in all human traits but was apparently insensible to cold and heat. He would sleep soundly with snow blowing over his bare legs. After months of effort he was finally softened to the point where he did not like excessively hot or cold bath water and this was about the only way they could get any response out of him. He never did learn to use language, but he finally learned to wear clothes. Experiences with other feral children have been quite similar, unless they were recovered very young, in which case they could be taught human reactions. Without the benefit of education, human offspring do not attain even the amount of intelligence possessed by the lower animals.

In one sense we can quite truthfully say that man is not human until he achieves humanity by education, and it is inconceivable that any society, any institutions, any human reactions, or even human life except in rare cases could exist without the benefit of education.

These unusual and abnormal cases are peculiarly valuable for our purpose, but much may be learned by careful study of normal children from birth until they have attained complete humanity.

2 J. M. G. Itard, *The Wild Boy of Aveyron*, New York: Century, 1932.

Preyer and Millicent Shinn made unusually valuable studies and G. Stanley Hall directed many.[3]

Many seemingly insignificant points which really have deep meaning were discovered through these observations. For example, we may speak of a child as being generous and kindly because he allows others to have bites of his cookie. But actually he does not know that these bites which are being taken diminish his supply of food. When it dawns on him that such is the case, he becomes far less generous. The more light we secure, the more do we realize how important education is in our lives.

A significant feature of education is that it is compulsive in nature and its results are inevitable. There is no escape. Whatever is taught us becomes a part of us. The only possible variation occurs when conflicting education is given. This explains why the lives of uncivilized groups go on unchanged for generations. They are all taught exactly the same beliefs and therefore it never occurs to them that anything could be different. In our complicated civilization we are exposed to widely different beliefs and theories, held by diversified races, nationalities, and classes and hence may vary from what our ancestors have been.

In spite of this diversity there is a multitude of features of our culture which are given to us in such unvarying form that we can not escape them. We can see this by observing some familiar practice such as employing the decimal system in our figuring. We take it so for granted that we think of it as something natural. Actually, it is nothing of the kind, but is purely artificial and merely the way we have been educated. It is just an accident that we think of one and zero as signifying ten—or perhaps it was not entirely an accident since we have ten fingers and began counting on them. We might have considered one and zero as equalling eight or twelve or any other number. The Mayan Indians used a system in which this combination equalled twenty.[4]

[3] G. S. Hall, *Aspects of Child Life and Education,* Boston: Ginn & Company, 1907, 326 p.; G. S. Hall, *Educational Problems,* New York: D. Appleton & Company, 1911, 2 volumes; Millicent W. Shinn, *The Biography of a Baby,* New York: Houghton, Mifflin Company, 1900; William Preyer, *The Mind of the Child,* New York: D. Appleton & Company, 1909.

[4] Cyrus Thomas, *Mayan Calendar Systems,* 19th Annual Report, Bureau of American Ethnology, Part II, pages 693–819; Cyrus Thomas, *Numeral Systems of Mexico and Central America,* 19th Annual Report, Bureau of American Ethnology, Part II, pages 859–955.

It is not difficult to learn to work in some other system rather than our own—as say the duodecimal. Then 10 = twelve, 11 = thirteen, 20 = twenty-four, 30 = thirty-six, 65 = seventy-seven and 100 = one hundred forty-four. A simple sum in addition would be as follows:

$$
\begin{array}{ccc}
379 & & 852 \\
835 & \text{or subtraction would be} & 597 \\
\underline{487} & & \underline{277} \\
1479 & &
\end{array}
$$

This is just as simple, just as natural, just as easy, and just as accurate as our decimal system. But it is utterly impossible for our children to grow up using it. They have been educated otherwise.

It is equally impossible for our children to grow up speaking Tasmanian or Korean languages. It is as impossible for them to use some language which they have not been taught as it is for them to have green blood in their veins, and purple hair on their heads.

The further we explore the inevitability of education's influence, the more important we see it to be. We think of ourselves as being free to make up our own minds, and in a sense this may be true. But in another sense it is far from true. A good Protestant will be so thoroughly convinced of the truthfulness of his convictions that nothing can shake them. He may live in a perfect heaven of calm serenity and tranquil assurance, or his profound certainty may take the expression of loud and vindictive attacks on all those who disagree with him. His positive assurance becomes more detailed than this and he clings to specific sects or denominations. To suggest to him that he might be a Catholic would sound so preposterous that he would be highly amused or violently incensed, depending upon his disposition. Yet a tiny shift in his life would have meant that he would have felt exactly the same way about the Catholic faith. Had he been born across the street, raised in a Catholic family and sent to a Catholic school, he would just as inevitably have been Catholic. The boy who *was* born into this Catholic family became an ardent Catholic and thinks *he* never could have been Protestant.

The two would probably unite and agree that it would be unthinkable for either to have been a Mormon, a Buddhist or a Mohammedan. Neither would consider for a minute that an adherent of one of these faiths *might* be right. Yet had either of them been born and reared under the influence of one of these religions he would have accepted it fully. The only way in which one might possibly change from one religious creed to another would be exposure to varying educational influences.

Not only religious convictions, but our attitudes in all departments of life are similarly determined by educational influences. We may be made to appreciate this fact by listing, somewhat at random, a number of beliefs or attitudes which are held with practical universality in this country. We take the following for granted:

Children take the surname of their fathers.

Married women acquire the surname of their husbands.

A man supports his own children.

A man's property or his debts are inherited by his children.

Polygamous marriage is wrong.

Democracy is the best form of government.

Citizens have the right to vote and thus choose their officials.

One *owns* certain things or has *property*.

A laborer is paid for his work.

The educational system is divided into three parts, (1) elementary (2) high school (3) college.

The government stands the expense of education.

Vacation comes in the summer.

Dogs, cats, horses, snakes, and worms are not to be eaten.

Three meals a day are eaten.

Knives, forks, and spoons are used for eating.

Chairs are used to sit on and beds are used for sleeping.

The list could be extended indefinitely, but it is sufficiently long to include beliefs ranging from the most profound and significant to the rather inconsequential. And everyone of them is the fruit of our education. There is not one of these beliefs but what would be considered absurd and ridiculous in some other countries.

It is the mass of beliefs such as these which make up the essence of our lives and our civilization. They could all so easily have been different! The reason they are not different is that we have been *taught* to accept and believe these.

Aside from these widely held beliefs, there are characteristic attitudes of different classes of society which just as surely flow from their specific training.

A man who has been reared in a laborer's family and constantly subjected to conversations about the "oppression of labor" and "grinding the faces of the poor" will enter into a violent strike with all the religious fervor of a martyr or a patriot. A scion of a wealthy family brought up in an atmosphere of contempt for the "great unwashed masses" and with a feeling of natural superiority and privilege will consider such a strike and especially the violence as base and evil, probably worse than treason or murder. This attitude is wholly the result of training, as the same wealthy heir might be taught to think of the responsibility of wealth and the right of labor to organize and receive a living wage. Many such wealthy young people are being trained in this manner.

Similarly, our attitudes on all other such matters flow from the educational influences to which we have been exposed. Black and white children play together in complete lack of racial antagonism until taught that one race is superior to the other or is dirty, criminal, ignorant, overbearing, cruel, or rapacious. Half a century ago the American child raised in a typical home would believe the Indians were cruel, treacherous, murderous, but perhaps somewhat picturesque and heroic people. Today, the concept of the Indian which is developed is quite different. Sometimes intense racial attitudes can be built up rapidly as may be seen by the wave of anti-semitism which has developed in various regions of the world.

Since education plays such an important role in human society, there can be no understanding of the course of history or the social activities of today without a comprehension of the educational factors which lie at the foundation. Interestingly enough, there are certain fundamental characteristics of all educational systems which are identical or nearly so. And there are educational principles which are demonstrated among all peoples and at every period of time. This fact is so significant that it is quite worth our while to make a rapid survey of some of the high lights of education as it has played its part among earlier and simpler peoples.

THE PART OF EDUCATION IN EARLIER CULTURES

Savages and uncivilized races generally have much more elaborate educational systems than we are wont to suppose. In many instances they are almost comparable to our own in their complexity and organization. Perhaps it is universally true that such races teach the young people how to perform the necessary work of the tribe. African youths are taught very early to care for the cattle, to keep them from straying while they graze, to guide them into safe places and to bring them home at night. Among some African tribes it is a common practice to give a little boy a calf and he will grow up with it, riding it, caring for it and playing with it much as an American boy might grow up with a specially well loved dog. In other tribes, the children are taught to care for goats in the same way. In Palestine, North Africa, and Western Asia the children take care of the sheep or goats and become so attached to them that they would risk their lives to save them. This is an old, old practice and is mirrored in the way David while just a lad cared for his father's flock. Older children rather than parents or adults teach the younger children this practice.

With practical universality, the youths of uncivilized peoples are taught to use the common tools at an early age. When the Ao Naga boy is old enough to walk he is fitted out with a belt that has an ax-carrier attached in the rear. This is done to make his back "hard" and to teach him how to carry this inevitable tool. By the time he is grown the carrying and use of the ax in everything from cutting bushes to building a house or defending himself has become second nature.[5]

Indian boys are fitted out with little bows and arrows and are encouraged to shoot chipmunks, rabbits, and birds. The fruits of their markmanship are cooked and eaten and they are made to feel that they have done something which really counts. Such practices are world wide or nearly so. Everywhere, we find the children of preliterate peoples learning from a tender age how to perform the acts upon which the life of the group depends.

Little girls are trained as carefully as the boys. When a Plains Indian mother staked down a buffalo hide and began flensing it with her stone knife, her little daughter could be found working on a corner with a smaller knife of exactly the same pattern. When weaving, basket making, or pottery was going on the little girls would be around, watching and helping in whatever ways they could. They began very early to help in the cooking and other housework.

The vocational training extended much farther than mere skill in handling tools. Frequently the youths were given elaborate training in the various activities of the tribe. Plains Indian boys would be taken out of the camp by a "medicine man" or other leaders and given long talks about how to creep into an enemy camp

[5] W. C. Smith, *The Ao Naga Tribe of Assam,* London: Macmillan, 1925. (Dr. Smith is author of our Chapter 12: Communication.)

and bring away some of their horses. Then a boy would be selected to go into camp and get a "horse." What he was really expected to do was to steal a piece of meat which the women were drying in the sun. If he succeeded and brought back the meat they would roast it and have a feast.[6]

Charles Eastman, a Sioux Indian, relates how his uncle would send him after a bucket of water at night. It might be bitter cold, but he would be expected to slip out past the guards, crawling through snow and ice perhaps, and to return with the water from the distant spring. It might take him an hour or two to make the trip. Having accomplished the task, his uncle might just pour the water out and tell him to go and get another bucket full.[7]

It would be a mistake to conclude that all the training of preliterate children was industrial or vocational in nature. Much of it was specifically designed to toughen them and develop qualities of bravery, manhood, patience, and perseverance. Little fellows only three or four years old would be yanked out from under the warm skin covers early in the morning and dropped into icy water. They soon learned to make this regular ice bath a voluntary practice. In some tribes a boy would present a switch to an older man and be whipped until the switch was worn away. All sorts of such toughening practices were used, and apparently they succeeded well.

It must be borne in mind that these practices which we have described were not for punishment. They were voluntarily accepted by the youth for constructive purposes. They were quite apart from the disciplinary measures which primitive youngsters as well as civilized children occasionally need. A rich variety of methods were used as punishment. Whippings and scolding were, of course, widespread. Some oriental groups laughed at their children when they were bad and made them feel silly. An African tribe made a practice of rubbing pepper in their eyes. Sometimes they were told frightening stories. But punishment for wrong doing played an exceedingly unimportant role among uncivilized peoples. Life was simple and there were few rules to break. The children were kept busy and active in so many ways that they had little occasion to be "bad." And the traditions and practices of the group were so intense that the children rarely thought of going against them.

Equally important in the education of these people was what

6 Frank B. Lindeman, *American*, New York: John Day Co., 1930.

7 Charles A. Eastman, *Indian Boyhood*, Boston: Little & Brum, 1930.

we might call the cultural and spiritual side of life. Religious beliefs and practices were always inculcated, sometimes informally, at other times by quite formalized methods. Much history and myth was taught by means of stories and songs. The youths were required to learn some of these by heart and if a young man was to become a Shaman or leader he would have to learn a great many. As a rule, these stories were sacred and could not be told lightly or imperfectly. Only specially ordained members of the tribe could tell them, and even they could tell them only under special conditions. The young people rapidly learned to think of these accounts with reverence and awe.

Occasionally special pedagogical devices would be employed in the use of these stories. The Plains Indians constructed "winter counts" which were series of pictures, one being added each winter. Events were grouped around these pictures and the boy might be taught a dozen or more important things which happened the year they had smallpox. It was a simple matter to count the pictures back until the picture of a smallpox victim was reached and this would date the event. Another way of keeping dates was to have a bundle of small sticks for each event and to add a stick every year at some specified time as when the first snow fell.

It is significant that esthetic training was combined with the practical. A crude arrow-head might fly just as well as one artistically chipped, but from the first the boy would be taught to strive for beauty and perfection. Pots, baskets, skin garments, boots, and all such artifacts were not satisfactory if they were merely utilitarian. They must be beautiful.

The high point of the educational process was reached when the youth was initiated into manhood. This occurred at an earlier period than it does with us, usually coming at early adolescence. Their initiation ceremonies were made as elaborate and impressive as possible. Sometimes they were highly painful. They usually lasted several days and might extend over months.

Among some Indian tribes, the boy would first go out by himself and pray and fast for four days and nights. Then he would go through a full day of torture consisting of lacerations, perhaps amputation of a finger joint or two and other severe mutilations. Through it all he would get no food or water. But if he came through it without giving any indication of pain he would be given glad acclamation and welcomed into the brotherhood of adult men.

The initiation of girls was usually not so spectacular but was just as severe, frequently consisting mainly of long isolation and the denial of good foods and other pleasures.

If we examine the educational system of these preliterate peoples closely, we find much food for thought. The elements of their procedure find their counterparts in modern civilization. Some of their practices are generally considered as relatively new principles today while others are still topics of lively discussion. For example, we notice that the uncivilized boy made real arrowheads and used them to kill small game. We now believe that our children should make real things such as doorstops, boxes, tables, and desks rather than just to practice making good joints, polished surfaces and the like. We have the problem of combining cultural and esthetic training with our vocational and industrial education, and we have seen how that was done in preliterate education. The question of "toughening" is surely a live issue today, with many educators pointing to the training of the German youth and vociferously insisting that our own people have been dangerously softened. There is agreement that we should develop vigorous bodies and unflinching dispositions, but there is considerable uncertainty as to just how it should be done.

Teaching group loyalty or what we call patriotism was most successfully done by nearly all uncivilized races. Granting that they had a much simpler task than we have today, it may still be true that they employed some principles which we could use. Even their elaborate and severe initiation rites were quite literally their "commencement" ceremonies. Educators are generally agreed today that ceremony and ritual have a profound effect. It is interesting to note that when schools, courts, churches, and other institutions do away with such formalities they are prone to lose their influence, even the loyalty and esteem of their personnel. Strangely enough, those schools which practice rather severe hazing are characterized by deep "school spirit" and those which lack it seem to have general indifference in their student bodies.[8]

Considering the close parallels between the problems, techniques, methods, and principles involved in the education of primitive peoples and modern civilization, both the student *of* education and

8 The writer has had this under observation for several years. A good many specific instances could be mentioned, but of course it would not be in order to make names of specific institutions public.

about education can profit greatly by a careful and analytic study of simpler tribes.

In somewhat more advanced groups, the same familiar pictures are repeated. The ancient Hebrews furnish us such an example. Unfortunately we do not have an elaborate account of their educational practices preserved, but we catch a few incidental glimpses. For one thing, we know that the mothers played a prominent role in training their children. This crops out in different places in both the Old and New Testaments. Luke repeatedly states of Mary that, "She kept all these things and pondered them in her heart." She must have spent many long hours with the infant Jesus and as a result he was able to converse with the learned scholars and even defeat them when he was only twelve years old. Such instances are not entirely unknown today.

We may be sure that one thing greatly emphasized among these Hebrews was intense devotion to their people or country, illustrated in the case of Jephtha's daughter. When informed that she must die because of her father's rash vow to sacrifice the first thing which came to meet him, she readily acquiesced. Her one request was that she be given a period of time in which to "bewail her virginity"! She had been taught that she should bear children for the good of her country, and the thought of imminent death was not as great a source of grief as the realization that she had failed in this respect.[9]

Another prominent feature of Hebrew education was the extensive use of ritual, particularly ritual mixed with poetry and music. The Hebrew word which we translate "prophet" is literally "poet," and the books of the prophets are written in poetry. Much of this material, especially the psalms, proverbs, and the book of Ecclesiastes, and Song of Solomon is in the form of songs. These songs and others similar to them were used extensively in their services. A most elaborate ritual was used when the yearly pilgrimages brought them all together at Jerusalem.

We cannot be sure why the second commandment was given, namely that no pictures could be drawn or graven images made, but whether by intent or not it did prevent the construction of copies of the temple or its altar. If such copies had been made, the yearly pilgrimages would have fallen off and many people would have wor-

---

[9] The question of historicity is not significant. Whether they be history or myth, these accounts picture typical attitudes.

shipped at other temples. But the continued participation of the Hebrew people in the ceremonies at Mount Zion was a great factor in developing and preserving that intense racial solidification which neither Roman nor Middle Age efforts were able to destroy and which continues and exists today. It would be difficult to find a more pronounced illustration of the educational influence of ceremony and ritual. Such illustrations of the role of education in societies of the past could be given in almost endless number. But this would become a History of Education and would be out of place here.

Our interest is in those sociological principles which we may find demonstrated or illustrated in educational practices. The primitive peoples and the early Hebrews have furnished us valuable material, and the same would be true of any period or any people whom we might study. The Middle Ages and early modern times present some peculiarly clear-cut exemplifications of such apparently general principles.

It has often been observed that human institutions seem destined to be changeable and almost ephemeral. Cooley and Ward both discuss this in detail, Cooley stating that all institutions are "cyclical" in nature and Ward expressing the same idea in the botanical term "sympodial development."[10] Both conclude, as have other students of society, that institutions arise because of definite specific needs and for a while satisfy these needs efficiently. As time passes the institutions specialize, harden, become formalized and lose their usefulness, perhaps even becoming destructive. Eventually there comes a reconstruction and a change of emphasis, or the institution may die out entirely and something new take its place, thus starting a new cycle in which the whole thing will be done over again.

The writers mentioned above speak as if this program of origin, specialization, decay and change were automatic. Probably, they did not intend to give this impression. But a careful study of institutions tempts one to subscribe to such a theory. Perhaps the matter is quite simple after all. Human beings, differing from the lower animals, have the power to initiate cultural inventions and thus they work out something which satisfies their needs. As conditions always change, the institutions change with them. At any

10 L. F. Ward, *Pure Sociology*, New York: Macmillan Company, 1911; C. H. Cooley, R. C. Angell, and L. J. Carr, *Introductory Sociology*, New York: Charles Scribner's Sons, 1933, Chapter 25, "Institutions," pp. 402–415.

rate, it is quite evident that not only true love but all other institutions refuse to run smoothly. If one keeps in mind this cyclical nature of institutions, it will make it much easier to understand certain changes which educational systems have undergone and which they seem destined to continue to undergo.

The onset of the Middle Ages was a point at which a specific type of education arose in response to a definite social situation. Hundreds and thousands of pagans of widely varying creeds were being converted to Christianity without knowing anything about it. Frequently an entire tribe or group would become officially Christian merely because the leader ordained it to be so. The behavior of these untrained—and actually unchanged—hordes shocked many Christian leaders so severely that they ran off into the wilderness to get away from it and thus the practice of becoming hermits arose. But other stayed with the job and attempted to teach these ignorant novitiates what Christianity really meant. Thus began the catechumenal schools which presented a compact, definite mass of information and doctrine as final truth. Education became authoritative, dogmatic, mechanical, and without any opportunity for personal reasoning. As Monroe expressed it, education for a thousand years possessed very little of the intellectual element.[11]

The time finally arrived when this concept crumbled away and something new took its place—something which sufficiently met the demands of the later time. In the fifteenth century the Renaissance made its appearance and the educational system took on new life. It is significant that no entirely new theories or concepts were developed. Merely the old fundamentals which had existed in early Greek and Roman times were re-accepted. Emphasis was now put on classical literature, and interest in poetry, drama, art, and literary style was reborn. Even glimmerings of physical education were in evidence.

This humanism, as the movement was called, was just as prone to become formal and lifeless as its predecessor. During the sixteenth century it degenerated into a slavish copying of mechanized style in writing essays, frequently called "ciceronianism." Little or no attention was paid to the content of what was being written and most especially the student was not to use any originality. His one task was to copy and to treat the topic assigned as nearly exactly like Cicero would have treated it as possible.

11 Paul Monroe, *A Text Book in the History of Education*, New York: Macmillan Company, 1915.

Of course, the situation was not so simple as this sounds.   The old authoritative theory of education retained many adherents and not all humanists succumbed to the narrow worship of unmodified style.   The humanistic movement took on ethical and reformist expressions, especially in germanic countries, but all phases alike became formalized.   This tendency is well illustrated by the change which came over Martin Luther himself.   At first he said, "What there is contrary to reason is certainly much more contrary to God." But towards the end of his life he said, "The more subtle and acute is reason, the more poisonous a beast, with many dragon's heads, it is against God, and all his works."

Again according to the manner of human institutions, the humanistic movement gave way sometime in the seventeenth century and what we call "Realism" came upon the stage.   This did not differ much from early humanism, at least in its early stages. Classical languages were still emphasized, but they were now used for the purpose of learning about human nature and understanding human motives.   This ran into the theory, rather shocking to the older educators, that young people should be trained to live as "men of the world," to lead useful and happy lives.   In the form of "sense realism" emphasis was put on training the senses rather than the memory and what may be called the beginning of the scientific movement was foreshadowed.

The same program of vigorous birth, narrow specialization, formalism and getting out of touch with vital needs could be traced through the disciplinary theory and into the development of naturalistic, psychological and sociological concepts.

These changes which we have noted are not so full of interest as mere historic facts, but because they illustrate universal tendencies and procedures which we probably shall always have with us.   In larger or smaller aspects, educational practices, as well as other types of group activity, are always becoming formalized, getting out of line with current needs, being remodeled and started out anew.

COMPARISONS BETWEEN THE OLD EDUCATIONS AND THE NEW

This hasty glimpse at the educational practices of an earlier day should help us view the modern educational scene with greater insight and understanding.   He who would comprehend our educational procedures does in truth need all such assistance possible. At first glance, it would seem that there could not be anything more complicated, more heterogeneous, and more conflicting within itself. It would be difficult if not impossible to think of any educational theory or practice which is not being advocated or used somewhere today. Apparently we have everything but unity.

A more careful and thorough examination does much to dispel this appearance of limitless contradictions. There is really far more agreement than one would at first suppose. The great mass of dissension is about details of method, most of them rather trivial in nature. The differences in fundamental doctrine are more verbal than actual. A careful analysis of any outstanding theory shows us that its essential features would be accepted almost universally.

Analysis of Similarities

Herbert Spencer was a pronounced individualist, an advocate of rather extreme laissez-faire, a utilitarian and quite a unique person besides. Add to all these characteristics the fact that he formulated his theory nearly a century ago and we would expect to find him advocating something as far from current ideas as the East is from the West. We do find him saying some queer sounding things. He did not believe in public education at all. But his basic principles have a strangely modern sound, or rather a sound as of continuous validity.[12]

Is there an educator today who would deny that the purpose of education is *preparation for complete living?* To be sure a common criticism is that education is not a preparation for living but is living itself. This is mostly just words and no doubt would have been accepted readily by Spencer himself. It is no real criticism of the proposition under discussion. Following Spencer's reasoning farther we find that he considered that knowledge of greatest importance which leads directly to self preservation. This is followed in order by the knowledge which leads indirectly to self-preservation; knowledge of rearing offspring; knowledge of social and political life such as shall make one intelligent as a citizen; and lastly, the knowledge of literature, art, and esthetics generally. This table is commonly criticized harshly and extensively, but the

[12] Herbert Spencer, *Education: Intellectual, Moral, and Physical,* New York: L. S. Burt Company.

objections turn out to be leveled at specific details of wording rather than at the basic features.

Throughout his treatment, Spencer makes statements which sound as if they were pronouncements of leading authorities today. He insists that the essential question is to learn how to live, not in a material sense, but in the widest sense as a useful and well adjusted member of society. Individualist as he was, he yet emphasized the social side of education. His vigorous insistence on the importance of training for rearing children and his indignation and dismay that such training was neglected are quite identical with what we hear and read on every side.

Spencer was chosen for comparison with current educators because in so many ways he was the very antithesis of modern thought. Since it develops that he agreed so closely with us in his fundamental theories of education, we should expect other writers to agree at least as closely. Lester F. Ward was as socialistic in his thinking as Spencer was individualistic, yet they said practically the same thing concerning their tables of values.[13] Ward stated that some things were *essential*, namely self-preservation and race preservation. The aesthetic, the moral, and the intellectual were non-essential, at least for mere existence, but he considered them quite essential for life on a truly human level. An application of Ward's ideas would be that it might be wise to cut appropriations for teaching art and music if necessary to make an appropriation for hog-cholera serum. But the ultimate purpose of the serum would be to make it possible for people to prosper and thus a little later indulge in still more art and music. It would be difficult to find any deep-seated difference between Ward and Spencer or between either of them and the men whose names we see in current educational journals. Dr. William H. Burnham once pointed out that Comenius had said everything which was contained in an up-to-date and widely used book on education. Similarly, we could find noticeable agreement between the educational philosophies of Froebel, Herbert, Pestalozzi, and other well-known authorities of yesterday and today.

This comparison is not made for the purpose of praising these men or extolling their theories. The significant point is that they all faced the same fundamental situations. They all had the same problems to solve. These were old, old problems when Rome and

[13] L. F. Ward, *Pure Sociology*, New York: Macmillan Company, 1911.

Egypt and Nineveh were young. They were grappled with by prehistoric man and uncivilized races of the whole world. And using common ordinary sense, all those people who pondered over them came to conclusions which were similar in their broad outlines.

Differences in Details and in Methods

The logical consequence of such a state of affairs might seem to be a complete agreement and a final solution of educational problems. This would mean a standardization of procedure and the acceptance of a final perfect program which would never need to be changed. But no such eventuation as this can ever be hoped for or expected. On the contrary, we shall always have dissensions, arguments, gropings, and uncertainties. Even if all our questions were finally answered to the satisfaction of every one concerned, they would not stay answered. The world changes, both in its physical and human aspects, and every change brings about new problems. While fundamentals may remain the same, specific *methods* vary immeasurably. There might be perfect agreement between a Sioux Indian, a medieval school man, a pioneer American schoolteacher and a modern educator that young people should be trained in the manner of making a living. But the Sioux would teach his boy to track buffalo and shoot a bow, the medieval scholar would learn to be a squire and polish armor or be apprenticed out in some handicraft, the pioneer lad would be taught how to handle an ax and drive an ox team, and the modern youth might pound on a typewriter or wire armatures for automobiles.

It is this vast difference in external conditions and the corresponding difference in attempts to meet them which accounts for the rich diversity of educational practices of all times and all places. The variation is boundless. First there are the greatly differing climatic situations. The ultimate aim of teaching hygiene is obviously rather uniform, but the specific method would be different among the Eskimos, on a tropical isle which had lepers among its inhabitants, and in a modern city. Another factor would be the cultural and technological differences. Much of primitive man's education was given in the form of stories orally told. Since late medieval days, we have used books, printed and handwritten. Now there is added the possibility of utilizing the radio, the cinema, and the multitudinous devices of laboratory technique, such as microscopes, dictographs, library card catalogues, and the familiar devices which surround us in such rich profusion.

In addition to all these, there enters the personal element. One instructor may devise or employ a method which proves to be highly successful, but someone attempting to copy this method might fail completely. Hence there will always be vast differences in educational procedure and there will always be the possibility of observing, studying, adapting and modifying and learning new and more effective ways of accomplishing our ends. A glimpse of some of the most outstanding such practices should increase our appreciation and comprehension of the role which education plays in social phenomena.

THE GREAT TEACHERS

Occasionally some great educator or some group of educators has been responsible for such far-reaching social phenomena that the examples left us are especially significant. It need not always be some one who exerts his influence directly through the formal medium of the school. The effect may never have been dreamed of by the one responsible. Such a case was that of Burne-Jones who is said to have changed the physical type of the English women. These women consciously tried by diet, dress, and exercises to resemble the figures he painted and therefore the type was changed. Acting on this principle, Mussolini has ordered the Italian artists to paint large matronly looking women in the hope that this type will become more common and hence more children will be born. Rousseau exercised such educational influence through his books that it has been said he caused the French Revolution. The great mass of his countrymen at that time could not read, and only a few Frenchmen read his books, but his ideas were sifted down until they became generally known and talked about. Similarly, *Uncle Tom's Cabin* is known to have been a prominent factor in bringing on the War between the States. In essence, all such world-changing personages as Confucius, Buddha, Jesus, Mahomet and later John Wesley, Martin Luther, John Calvin, Mrs. Eddy, and many others were primarily educators. In fact we frequently hear the expression, "The Great Teacher."

These leaders exercised their influence outside of formal educational circles. Within these circles, other such suggestive events have transpired. A greatly neglected educational leader, especially in English books, was Bishop Gruntvig who transformed Denmark and through the example of Denmark influenced the other

Scandinavian countries and to a lesser degree such far distant peoples as our own Americans of today.[14] When he appeared on the scene, Denmark had collapsed with the fall of Napoleon and the entire country seemed to have lost morale. Bishop Gruntvig conceived the idea of developing folk High Schools in which such subjects as agriculture, dairying, shop work and various phases of technical training were given. Some of these held short term sessions which farm people could attend during slack periods.

Gruntvig's central purpose was a desire to develop a rejuvenated national consciousness and a rich Danish culture. Hence, accompanying these practical courses, there was emphasis on music, physical training and Danish history of an informal type which was planned to develop patriotism and pride in their country. The results were astounding. Denmark rapidly regained national pride and took one progressive step after another. The cooperative dairies, pig clubs, and marketing organizations made themselves felt all over the world. It is reported that they put some big butter, eggs, and bacon trusts out of business *in London,* aside from the way they dominated Danish affairs.

They are still the models for the remainder of the world. The conditions are well described by Professor Bransom who wrote after his survey of European agricultural conditions: "There is nothing rotten in Denmark, not even the fish which the housewife buys alive at the market."[15] In addition to their utilitarian effect, these schools have brought much enlivening interest into Danish life. It is quite customary for an old Danish farmer or shopkeeper to take a six weeks vacation and attend a folk school for training in portrait painting. Or these people may study music, literature, woodcraft, history or anything else which they enjoy.

The influence of Gruntvig survives today in such far distant examples as the short courses for farmer youths at some of our state universities.

Another significant instance was the so-called Turner Movement in Germany a century or so ago. This put emphasis on physical training to the point of achieving everything physically possible of the human body. It may be significant that this was followed by a great outburst of literature, art, music, and scientific scholarship.

[14] Nikolai F. S. Gruntvig, 1783–1872. About all there is about Gruntvig in English is in Educational Encyclopedias.

[15] E. C. Bransom, *Farm Life Abroad,* Chapel Hill: University of North Carolina, 1924.

Such illuminating examples could be given in great numbers, and the more they are studied and understood, the greater becomes our comprehension of the inner workings of human society.

CONTEMPORARY EDUCATION IN AMERICA

When we come to the contemporary scene, we find nothing essentially new except the rich diversity of method as mentioned above. We are still trying to do what the caveman and savage tried to do.

The Shift from Home to School

As with all peoples of antiquity there is still much education given in the home. Little by little the educational importance of the home has been whittled away by the exigencies of modern civilization, but there is yet a great residue remaining. The transfer to the school began generally in the field of industrial, technical, and trade education. Our pioneer schools limited their activities to the three R's and it would have sounded like sheer insanity to those old schoolmasters to suggest that they include housekeeping and agriculture in the curriculum. In those days the girls learned to cook and sew from their mothers and the boys learned to plow and plant and reap from their fathers. This made for strong solidarity in the home and was characterized by a conservative, slowly-changing social life.

As time went on, the agricultural colleges and trade schools were organized and a few ''experts'' were developed. As this type of training became more popular it spread to other colleges and was taken up by the high schools. Now it has reached down in one form or another until it appears in the kindergarden and play school. While they are still little more than babies the children are taught to dress themselves, put up their coats and wraps, take care of their dishes and do rudimentary housekeeping jobs. They are also taught to plant and care for flowers in window-boxes and flower pots. These are the beginnings of a more or less efficiently planned trade or technical training which will reach its peak only when the infant has come to complete adulthood.

Under present conditions it is impossible for very much of this training to be given in the home. In a great many cases, both parents work and do only the lightest of light housekeeping. They work under circumstances which make it impossible to have the children around. If the father is in the building trades he will be working on skyscrapers or at least surrounded by complicated machinery and tools. It is completely out of the question for him to have his children around watching and helping him. Similarly the mother who is a stenographer in a bank or a clerk in a drug store cannot give her daughters the training that the pioneer house-wife could.

This drift of education out of the home has been so great that we rarely realize its extent. Even the function of story telling has been taken over by the schools. Many a perplexed parent has attempted to tell his child a bedtime story only to find out that the child knew more stories and knew them better than he did.

All this has meaning from a sociological standpoint. Every time some phase of education is lost to the home, a corresponding weakening of home ties is effected. Moreover, the element of difference or variability is introduced and the established practices and beliefs of the parents have less chance of being continued in the child. This is merely another way of saying that society becomes more variable, has less respect for old customs, accepts new ideas more readily, and encounters the many' advantages but also faces the dangers attendant upon a more flexible type of life.

However, the educational function of the home is far from being extinct. It is still true that character and characteristics are alike formed primarily in the home. The influence of home training is not lacking in importance. It is only less important than it formerly was.

In the case of practical and technical training, the early man had a comparatively easy job. For one thing, he knew just what his children would be when they grew up. The training they required was relatively simple and limited to a small number of activities. Today, the parents have little idea what training their children will need. Should a young woman consult a vocational guidance counselor, she would find that there are over five thousand ways of making a living which are open to women. Perhaps no one has even been able to list all the ways open to men. It would be of little avail to give a child training in cotton farming and have him grow up to be an aviator. Moreover, a thorough training in some trade or profession may be of little value in the same field in a few years. New inventions and labor saving machinery bring to naught the skills acquired by many years of study and application. Such changes are taking place every day and thereby putting fully trained workers in the position of unskilled laborers.

Furthermore, much of the truly practical training of today is in fields far removed from any kind of physical activity. For example, if preparation for democracy be a goal of educators, a valuable bit of practical training would be a preparation for recognizing disguised propaganda and seeing the fallacy in misleading statistical statements. Our technical education takes widely varying forms. As might be expected, it varies from highly efficient programs to groping, somewhat useless gestures.

"We Learn by Doing"

High schools generally offer a few courses in manual arts, typing and stenography, home economics, and other such occupational subjects. Practically all states have agricultural colleges and engineering schools, although the types vary greatly. Some states have well-developed schools of mines. Others give instruction in fisheries. Special courses in almost any kind of trade or occupation may be found in the catalogues of our schools.

In addition to these schools, there are many other agencies for technical training. Night classes both on high school and college level are scattered profusely through the land. Business colleges and trade schools make their contributions. Many private firms give complicated and carefully worked out courses of training for their employees. Some big electrical concerns have worked out a system of training which extends over years and which is headed by highly paid educational experts.

An interesting fact is that our trade education draws on the primitive man's principle of learning by doing. Usually, the school shop or laboratory furnishes an opportunity for the use of the hands but with increasing frequency the students do actual work in the everyday world of events. High school boys will alternate, spending a given amount of time, probably two weeks, in school and then working in some shop for the same length of time. Usually, in such cases, there are two boys who alternate with each other. Some thirty years ago this was considered a radical educational procedure, but it has become quite matter of fact now. Though we may not always recognize it, this same principle is employed in many other types of work. There are barber "colleges" where incipient barbers work on the hair and beards of customers under the watchful eyes of instructors. Nurses secure their experience "in training" and frequently the only way a graduate nurse may be distinguished from the student nurses is by her uniform. Doctors serve their time as "interns" and even before they achieve that rating they perform much medical service as student practitioners. School teachers are given experience as "student teachers" in demonstration schools or by special arrangement in other schools. And even young men who are preparing for the ministry attend a "homiletics" class and get up and preach impassioned sermons to their fellow students and teachers.

Thus, we follow the method in which the primitive man trained the rising generation in the ways of the clan and tribe. In their totality these training activities function as a powerful and extensive force in molding modern society. Should they go out of existence or even be modified, human life would be vastly different from what it is.

Attention to Aesthetics

Even our aesthetic training has come back to the principles demonstrated by primitive man and practiced in ancient civilizations. We have seen how uncivilized men worked their concepts of beauty into their implements, dwellings, clothing, and other artifacts as a matter of course. They also employed song and poetic expression in their daily lives. This practice persisted among the Hebrews, Persians, Greeks, Romans and early Germanic peoples. At the height of her glory, it is said every third man in Persia was a poet. Homer and countless other wandering bards sang history and tradition to the common people directly and they repeated this poetry and added to it through their own powers of versification. The secret of the architectural charm of the medieval cathedrals of Europe may be that the common laborers were artists in their work and every part represented the workers' creativeness. The same artistic touch has been attributed to the people of our Eastern mountains where we have only recently discovered an aesthetic value in the log houses, the patchwork quilts—candlewick spreads, the basketry, pottery, and pine needle work, and even in the whittled ornaments.[16]

For some reason not clearly understood, the early phases of modern civilization turned away from the artistic and emphasized the utilitarian. So far did this tendency go that offers by artists to

[16] Allen H. Eaton, *Handicrafts of the Southern Highlands*, New York: Russell Sage Foundation, 1937.

decorate business houses free of charge were scornfully refused. The refusal may have been partially caused by the Puritan reaction against foppishness and artificiality. It may have been a part of the exultant pride in the many practical inventions which were appearing so rapidly. Whatever it was, art and music became the concern of a few highly gifted members of the privileged classes only.

In America, it was a case of necessity to allow these matters to fall into neglect. The stern hard pioneer conditions demanded a concentration of time and energy on the most practical and utilitarian knowledge and skill. Now we are rapidly beating back to the long deserted arts of the common folk. As early as the kinder-garten or play school, children are put to work with paints and crayons and colored blocks and fabrics. Primary schools, high schools and colleges continue this work. The models adopted are the handicrafts of the mountaineers, the native Indians, the Negroes and other simpler and more artistic groups. Expensive looms and high priced instructors are secured to teach our young people how to weave a "log cabin" spread such as we used to see only in the humble homes of isolated and quite ignorant mountain people. The display of a class in pottery might well be an exhibit of an Indian tribe—except perhaps that the symbolism in the designs is apt to be something startling if it is ever recognized. And our fine musicians pay tribute to certain types of folk music which would have been scorned a generation ago. Old, old "fiddlers" and singers are encouraged to recall the dimly remembered folk dances and games of their youth and these are taught as precious gems to the younger generation. In Britain a few years ago, it was discovered that just one old man and his daughter knew certain songs and games and great pains were taken to get these recorded before they were lost entirely. These old folk dances have spread like wild fire in some places. Especially in certain church groups where dancing is not approved and these folk dances have been accepted as substitutes—but are called games and *not* dances—one may see otherwise digni-fied preachers, enthusiastic matrons, awkward old bachelors and ecstatic young people all jigging away with great vigor and ear-nestly applying themselves to learning the steps.

The trend is definitely back to a folk art. The Little Theatre Movement is a part of this, and thousands of young and old people are now putting on plays, studying dramatics, and writing their own plays in many cases. The interest with which this type of thing is being received may be judged by the fact that sometimes an auditorium will be packed by farmers who have travelled fifteen or twenty miles over snow-choked roads with the thermometer reading below zero just to take part in singing folk songs or listening to a play put on by local talent.[17]

Of course, the practice of the schools and the attitude of the people generally go along together. In addition to education in the so-called "fine arts" the art departments of our schools now consider it a part of their work to give instruction in dress design and household decoration, in flower arrangement and selection of shrubbery, and even include such homely things as how to set a table attractively.

The phase of our civilization which seems to be just ending— possibly ending in a world-wide catastrophe and collapse—has been marked by a turning away from the aesthetic and by a development of commercial, industrial, and mechanical activities to a degree which is incomprehensible even to us who stand and see it before our eyes. It remains to be seen what type of human society will accompany our present swing back to the natural arts.

Spiritual Emphasis

We have seen how modern educational practice shows a tendency to get back to the primitive man's principles in so far as technical or practical training and also aesthetic training is concerned. It is not so clear just what we may call spiritual and social education. In fact, the one characteristic of this phase of our education is its great uncertainty. No one seems to know what to advocate. Even when we see some highly successful method put into practice, we are not at all sure we want to utilize it. There can be no denying the fact that the Nazi system of education has developed a fanatical loyalty, a superabundant confidence and a truly religious zeal which amounts to extreme readiness to serve and die. Even if we were assured that we could do quite as thorough a job with our own young people, we would probably reject it. To secure this we would have to sacrifice something which we call freedom or perhaps personal integrity and initiative. Dr. William H. Burnham has shown that educational systems since the early days have

[17] M. Patten, *Arts Workshop of Rural America*, Columbia University Press, 1937.

vacillated back and forth over the question whether to sacrifice *freedom* or *efficiency*. He also shows that the sacrifice of freedom does not necessarily result in efficiency for any great period of time.

Perhaps our own American method of teaching social responsibility—which is the equivalent of morality—will prove to have survival value. It must be acknowledged that at present it is merely groping and feeble, but it does appear that a start has been made and it is not at all improbable that it will rapidly crystallize and develop. The sense of impending national danger may be the spurt to such quickened development. Quite commonly now our schools are teaching courses which are called "social science" or even "sociology." Or we may hear our youngsters say in true American fashion that they are taking "Pad" or "P–A–D." This turns out to be a course in *Problems of American Democracy* and may get down to such practical things as disposal of garbage and the methods employed in raising the necessary funds for that purpose.

Back behind this there may have been a lot of incidental training in citizenship beginning in the kindergarten when the children were taught to build a playhouse together. On the other hand, it may be followed by college courses covering much the same field and also more specialized courses in political science, economics, and sociology. If there is any one characteristic of our college education today which stands out with especial clearness it is the fact that there is a greatly increased interest in the social sciences. It is to be supposed that this will be reflected in our social behavior.

Play

As in other phases of our education, the formal school alone is not the only agent for such social and citizenship training. Our social attitudes are formed very largely in our play and recreation. It is only comparatively recently that we have considered the play activities as a legitimate part of education. Our attitudes on this question have changed tremendously. Such changes are even mirrored in our proverbs or pithy sayings. An old familiar saying which used to be quoted frequently was: "Work when you work and play when you play, is a very good rule as any can say." But now we hear: "One should not distinguish too closely between when he is playing and when he is working."

Henry S. Curtis a quarter of a century ago, called attention to the fact that our entire educational system developed the practice of carefully weighing our actions and delaying our responses. And, he pointed out, in all questions of morals, "He who hesitates is lost." As an antidote to this practice of hesitation, he explained that the play activities have a tendency to demand immediate action. They teach one to size up a situation instantaneously, recognize the proper reaction with equal lack of delay, and *act*. It was this idea which caused him to give so much time and energy to the development of organized playgrounds.

The rapid way in which organized recreation for both adults and children has swept the country is astounding. Today we have multitudinous basket ball teams, baseball and soft ball teams, touch-football teams, and other team activities. In addition golf and tennis and other forms of sport have been quickened and swimming has increased by actually thousands of per cent. By comparison we may say that a quarter of a century ago we had *nothing*. The effect of this movement can be seen much more easily if we look at some group other than ourselves. When the United States took over the Philippine Islands, the favorite occupation of the natives was head hunting. All the pressure that the American Army could bring to bear did little to prevent this. But when they introduced baseball, footraces, tugs-of-war, and other such games, head hunting rapidly faded out. When the natives first started to play baseball, they all carried spears and would stick them up in the ground while engaged in specific activities. But if the man at bat hit the ball, he would grab his spear and run for first base. The shortstop would quickly jab his spear in the ground and grab at the batted ball. The first baseman would also jab his spear down and get ready to receive the throw. Naturally, all this took a lot of time and as they became more interested in the game they left their spears at home. Perhaps something not greatly different from this is happening to us as we learn more and more to pour our interest and energy into games and recreations.

There are also many other non-school activities which exert their influence. The influence of the Boy Scout Movement is rarely appreciated. Some of the best minds in the country are administering this work. Not the least significant phase of the Scout work is that approximately as many men are working at it as there are boys in it. The Scout Oath, the Scout Law, the scout traditions and ideals, and the activities of scouts generally exercise an influence which may be greater than that of our national congress and all the laws it passes. Similarly, the Girl Scouts, Camp Fire Girls, and many other organized activities for both sexes play their part.

When one begins to look around, there is a vast amount of education along social and ethical lines which is being exercised. It is not too well crystallized and the ends are not clearly seen, but there is still a force exerted which has most significant effects on human society.

DYNAMIC EVOLUTION IN EDUCATION

Viewing the educational scene as a whole, one gains the impression that it is a dynamic thing, a changing system, and not something static and fixed. Moreover, one gains the impression that it is a process of evolution, a definite trend, a system of change which has order and meaning. With his usual clarity of insight, G. Stanley Hall interpreted the meaning of our educational growth in a way which apparently rings true. He said there have been three different philosophies or theories which dominated our colleges and through them our entire educational system.

First, there was the English system which was embodied in such early schools as Harvard and Yale. These were founded for the purpose of educating ministers. The idea was that a favored few would attend these schools and receive a culture and polish which would lift them far above the common herd. Their education would consist of languages, literature, history, philosophy and theology.

The next was the French idea which was introduced by Jefferson and which took its expression in the University of Virginia and other schools patterned after it. This ideal was a bit more democratic than that of early Harvard and Yale, but was still far from practical for the common man. This movement emphasized training in the humanities as the earlier schools had, but also training in the sciences. However, the emphasis was on general science with a minimum of specialization and little or no application.

The third movement came from Germany and is expressed in our great state universities and technical schools. The idea behind this is specialization, technical training, and practical education.

As a conclusion, Hall decided that the American schools would never really come into their own until a phase was reached which was truly American and not borrowed from any European situations. His belief was that this American theory would be characterized by *social* training, by emphasis on citizenship, service to society, and group participation generally. In the light of our present emphasis on the social sciences, it seems as if we may be entering this American phase now. With this thought in mind it should be interesting to watch our further development.

SUMMARY

In summarizing we may say that education is an all-pervasive presence which accompanies us from the cradle to the grave. Although its formal expression is in the school, it is met in countless other forms—propaganda, the press, the home, the pulpit, the playfellow on the street. It's influence is compulsive and may not be escaped. We *are* what we have been educated to be. From earliest times, primitive peoples have utilized certain principles of education which are just as sound today as they ever were. They employed these principles in imparting practical, aesthetic, and moral or social training. We do essentially the same thing today. Our vastly more complex civilization makes our task far more difficult and we have evolved many varying techniques. The present emphasis of our educational system is on social efficiency or social worth and we well may be entering on a new phase of civilization which will differ as markedly from those gone before as the Coolidge Era differed from the day of ancient Greece or the Medieval Ages.

SELECTED REFERENCES

Amidon, Beulah, *Democracy's Challenge to Education*, New York: Farrar & Rinehart, Inc., 1940.

Andrews, John N., and Marsden, Carl B. (Editors), *Tomorrow in the Making*, New York: Whittlesey House, 1939, Chapters 2–5, pp. 20–81.

Bear, Robert M., *The Social Functions of Education*, New York: Macmillan, 1938.

Beard, Charles A., *Wither Mankind?* New York: Longmans, 1928, Chapter 15, "Education."

Buffalo Child Long Lance, *Long Lance*—An Autobiography, London: Faber & Gwyer, 1926.

Case, Clarence M., *Social Process and Human Progress*, New York: Harcourt, Brace & Co., 1931, 336 p., Chapter XI, "Education as a Social Process," pp. 217–234.

Cooley, C. H., Angell, R. C., and Carr, L. J., *Introductory Sociology*, New York: Charles Scribner's Sons, 1933, Chapter 25, "Institutions," pp. 402–415.

Dewey, John, *Democracy and Education*, New York: Macmillan, 1937.

Dewey, John, *The Way out of Educational Confusion*, Cambridge: Harvard University Press, 1931.

Eastman, Charles A., *Indian Boyhood*, Boston: Little & Brum, 1930.

Giddings, Franklin H., *The Mighty Medicine*, New York: Macmillan Company, 1929.

Harper, Samuel N., *Making Bolsheviks*, University of Chicago Press, 1931, 167 p.

Hart, J. K., *Education for an Age of Power*, New York: Harpers, 1935.

Hart, Joseph K., *A Social Interpretation of Education*, New York: H. Holt & Co., 1929.

Itard, J. M. G., *The Wild Boy of Aveyron*, New York: Century, 1932.

John Dewey Society, The—Yearbooks, New York: Appleton-Century Co.
> First Year Book—1937
>> *The Teacher and Society*, Edited by W. F. Kilpatrick
> Second Year Book—1938
>> *Educational Freedom and Democracy*, Edited by H. B. Alberty and B. H. Bode
> Third Year Book—1939
>> *Democracy and the Curriculum*, Edited by Harold Rugg
> Fourth Year Book—1940
>> *Teachers for Democracy*, Edited by George Axtelle and William Wattenberg

Lindeman, Frank B., *American*, New York: John Day Co., 1930.

Mead, Margaret, *Coming of Age in Samoa*, New York: Morrow, 1928.

Petrie, W. M. F., *Revolutions of Civilization*, New York: Harper & Brothers, 1912.

Robinson, Thomas H., *Men, Groups, and the Community*, New York: Harper & Brothers, 1940, Chapter 12, ''The School,'' pp. 323-348.

Seay, Maurice, *Adult Education in the Tennessee Valley*, Lexington: University of Kentucky Press, 1938.

Sidis, Boris, and Goodhart, Simon P., *Multiple Personality*, New York: D. Appleton & Company, 1914, 462 p., Part II, ''The Hanna Case,'' pp. 83-228.

Snedden, David S., *Sociological Determination of Objectives in Education*, Philadelphia: J. B. Lippincott, 1921.

Spencer, Herbert, *Education: Intellectual, Moral, and Physical*, New York: S. L. Burt Company.

Sutherland, R. L., and Woodward, J. L., *Introduction to Sociology*, Revised Edition, New York: J. B. Lippincott, 1940, Chapter 18, ''Educational Organization,'' pp. 495-524.

Wright, Verne, and Elmer, Manuel C., *General Sociology*, New York: Farrar and Rinehart, Inc., 1938, Chapter 12, ''Educational Organization.''

CHAPTER 18

ORGANIZATION FOR LEISURE

BY DR. SAMUEL GARVIN

Head of the Department of Sociology of the University of Dubuque,
Dubuque, Iowa

THE USE OF LEISURE HISTORICALLY CONSIDERED

The privileged classes in all ages and countries have had time to
play. For the toilers the measure of playtime has been meager.
Yet even they, at least the men among them, had an occasional holiday, granted by their masters—a day of national or religious significance. In Greece the Olympic games were for the aristocracy,
the few free citizens who constituted one tenth of the population.
In Rome, peasants, slaves and gladiators might furnish the sport for
emperor and senators and die to make a Roman holiday, but any
longing for free amusement was unfulfilled. Browning's Pippa had
"one whole day" of leisure in the 365. Women were rarely admitted to the merrymakings. They bore man's burdens but did
not share his pleasures. Games came out of kings' houses. Our
common cards, with which so many hours are beguiled, were invented to relieve the burdensome leisure of a monarch. Knights,
with their ladies' favors upon their arms, broke lance on shield for
a king's entertainment. If it opened the gates of death to some,
on the other hand it opened, also, a door to his majesty's favor.
Hunting was royal sport and none might poach on the king's pre-
serves. The use of weapons—fencing, throwing the spear, archery
—was sport of the nobles, but was taught to the yeomanry for
serious purposes.

Leisure in Pre-Colonial Europe

The Renaissance was a time of popularization of sports. In this
era the humanitarian values were emphasized. An awakening interest was shown in dancing, music, pictorial and plastic arts, and,
more especially, in the drama. The latter, fostered by the church,
took secure hold on the popular imagination. In the Reformation
there was an emancipation of the mind from Middle Ages traditions
and social mores. Luther indorsed and emphasized the moral and

449

creative value of athletic sports and games. But the spectre of
want was always present, the hours of toil long and arduous, and
the wages were scarcely sufficient to keep the wolf from the door.
The fuller emancipation of labor awaited the discovery of new lands
and the advent of the machine and became a reality only with the
unfolding of the Industrial Revolution.

For many hundreds of years all cloth was woven on hand looms.
Water, then steam power, drove the shuttle with ever-increasing
speed. Power-driven machines took up the work in other crafts as
well. A limited market was quickly supplied. When the market
was glutted men and machines were compelled to mark time till
new orders came to the mill or new markets were opened.

Leisure had come, but it was seasonal, a fact which has always
been a problem of employment. The idea of limiting the hours of
work to spread production over the entire year and for the employment of more laborers had not yet been born. Closing the factory
or the mine for a week or a month until consumption would overtake
production brought no satisfaction to the low-wage laborer. In the
best of times he was often hard-pressed to make his earnings meet
his needs. But leisure must be reckoned with, for, welcome or un-
welcome, it had at last arrived.

Relaxation in the American Colonies

In the American colonies strikingly contrasted attitudes prevailed toward play; indeed, toward life in its entirety. Massachusetts and Virginia were not so far apart geographically as they were
in ideals. The planters were of the English gentry, with their in-
dentured servants. The Puritan settlers, whatever had been their
social rank in England, were a colony of workers. Work was moral;
leisure immoral. Life was oriented around the plough, the axe, and
the spade. This attitude was emphasized by their environment. If
one would live, he must toil. The soil was poorer, the climate more
rigorous than in Virginia.

In New England, starvation, which was only a step behind the
settlers, sometimes overtook them. The forest pressed upon them,
and stealthy foes lurked within the shadows of the wood. It was
this that caused the General Court's order that "No person, house-
holder or other, shall spend his time idly or unprofitably under pain
of such punishment as the Courte shall think meet to inflict."[1]

[1] Peter Force, *Tracts and Other Papers*, III: 2.

Even Jamestown felt the pinch of circumstance. Sir Thomas Dale sternly decreed that any tradesman unfaithful and negligent in daily attendance upon his occupation would be "condemned to the galley for three years."

Toil was the price of survival. Even the forest, of such great value to man, was an enemy that had to be overcome. Land had to be cleared to make way for crops. To reclaim a farm from the virgin forest and leave it arable was the work of a lifetime. The conquest of a continent was not a task for the idler or dilettante. It required all the settlers' resources.

To the challenge presented by the difficulties was added the lure of opportunity. Here was the unclaimed wealth of a continent for him who could take it. Industry and frugality marked the earlier times. Waste and prodigality came later. The struggle left little time for leisure. Rest was only for those too old to toil.

Play among the Puritans. Even in those sternest times, however, the impulse to play was not wholly conquered. Among the earliest and most common of all diversions were drinking and dancing. "Worn down by endless work, many of them felt the urge for some release for pent-up emotions."[2] Of these two, drinking was well in the lead. The tavern was the traditional meeting-place for convivial spirits. At first the only drinks were beer, ale, and hard cider. Soon, however, West India rum found its way into the colony. Its potency none can doubt. We read in the complaints of the Fathers that it was debauching many. The tendencies of the times are revealed in the ordinances passed by several of the colonies against dancing, tavern sports, and card playing. But no amount of legislation could destroy the desires for recreation.

Gaiety in the Old South. We think of Virginia as the antithesis of New England, but there was little difference in those early days when making a living was a precarious engagement. When life became easier the contrast was more manifest. Here was the spirit of "Merrie England." Maypole dancing, horse racing, wrestling, cudgelling, chasing the greased pig, singing and fiddling contests, were some of their many diversions. To these were added, only a little later, cockfighting, boat racing, and fox hunting. The planter's life was modelled on that of the English country squires. They were very proud of their fleet saddle horses and packs of hounds.

[2] Foster Rhea Dulles, *Americans Learn to Play*, IV, Appleton-Century Co., 1940.

Whoever has read the life of Washington will know the cultural pattern of Virginia in the period it was now entering.

Merriment beyond the Mountains

But it was the Puritan rather than the Cavalier that was the prototype for the people beyond the Appalachians. The Puritan thrift had left an indelible stamp on the American mind. As the pioneers opened up the great West, even their play leaned to the thrifty side. The life was rural. Husking bees, apple parings, log-rollings were the common diversions. In the first, favors went with finding the red ear. The trees were felled and trimmed, the brush piled. Then the neighbors came and rolled the logs into great heaps for burning. The wives came with their husbands and these women prepared the sumptuous meals for the logrollers. For the young people there was always dancing—sometimes on a barn floor, at other times the dedication of a new home into which the family had not yet moved. In winter there was sled-riding—long sleds with straw to sit on and buffalo robes to shut out the cold, and plenty of sleigh-bells on the farm horses. The young swain's ambition was to take his lady in a swell-bodied sleigh with curving dashboard, a high-stepping horse to draw the steel-shod runners swiftly over the hard-packed snow. With these pleasures was the severe toil of the frontier broken and its sombreness brightened.

Fishing and hunting were also sports with a utilitarian leaning. The forests were full of game, the streams and lakes well-stocked with fish. Often the only fresh meat on the table for months was game—deer, wild turkeys, quail, pheasants, wild pigeons, ducks, geese, and brants. Fish was extensively used on the sea coast and, inland, often relieved the monotony of the frontier fare. The frontiersman was an expert with the rifle. He who could not shoot through the head a squirrel in the top of a tall tree was a mere neophyte. Deer yielded both clothing and meat. Fur-bearing animals furnished a welcome addition to the pioneer's meager wardrobe.

Ranch and Mine

America was not homogeneous, and climate and geography accounted for a wide variation in sports. Another cause of heterogeneity was the different nationalities of which the country was composed. Many and varied customs, sports, mores, habits, came with the immigrants. Geographical and topographical features

are responsible for two components of our American life not soon
to be forgotten: one is the western ranches and the ranch towns;
the other, the mining camps. Millions of acres of unarable land
in the mountain and near-mountain areas were taken by the
cattle barons. The range was open and the cattle, often numbered
by the thousands, were tended by those picturesque figures known
as cowboys. The ranch house was apart from the bunk-house
where the cow-punchers lived. The number on a ranch ranged
from a half-dozen to half a hundred.

They were famous for two things: riding and shooting. In
horsemanship they were the best and, since, in the days of the
wild West, a man's life often depended on "the quickness of his
draw," few could be found who were not expert revolver shots and
little less efficient with the rifle. Far from town or city, their life
was austere in the fullest degree. Only on pay-day were they permitted to respond to the lure of the saloon, the gaming table and
the brothel. Their favorite stunt was to gallop into town discharg-
ing revolvers into the air, then make a mass attack on the nearest
saloon and line up at the bar.

The typical mining town rose, first, as a result of the gold stampede in '49. Mushroom towns sprang up—flimsy frame buildings
with false fronts and sheet-iron roofs. The saloon came first of all
institutions and was the general meeting place for the community.
The gambler in frock-coat, silk hat and diamond stud was always
present to gather men around the poker table. Faro and monte vied
with the artificial charms of lewd women. This life is embalmed in
much racy literature, notably in Bret Harte's tales and Mark
Twain's famous *Roughing It.* Shootings were common. The
code declared you must give a man a chance to draw. If you beat
beat him to it you were not guilty. Only "dry-gulching" was murder. Recklessness and extravagance characterized their recreation.

The Rise of Urban Amusements

We have reported rural amusements for the most part, but, till
after the eighteenth century, the United States was rural. The
first census was taken in 1790. The rural population included the
open country and those living in towns of less than 8000. These
constituted 96% of the population. When the union of states was
consummated there was not one city of 50,000 inhabitants. But
gradually the towns evolved.

The theatre. Nothing has ever rivalled the theatre in its appeal to the city. The drama is older than Greece, where it first became popular. It was loved by Rome and baptized by the church in the Middle Ages. To it Shakespeare had dedicated his immortal genius before 1600. English sailors held theatricals aboard their ships. The first serious invasion of America by the drama was in the early years of the eighteenth century. In 1703–4 the English actor, Anthony Ashton, was staging a series of plays in New York. But it was not until 1750–70 that New York became theater-conscious. In 1752 a famous English troupe toured the South. The most brilliant theatrical season on the continent for the years 1773–4 was in Charleston, South Carolina.[3] The theatre's gradual growth until it reached a climax in 1880–1910 has been well recounted. There was basis for this saying, "The play's the thing"; but concerts, too, received a substantial measure of attention.

Racing. Other attractions were luring the urban pleasure-lovers. The Long Island race-track dates from 1766. However, not alone in the cities but also in rural regions racing was enjoyed.

Cockfighting was popular in the last half of the eighteenth century. One clergyman records in his diary that he hurried from his prayers lest he would be late for "the fighting cocks."[4] In this same period shooting and swimming matches, tennis, cricket, golf and boating were attracting increasing numbers.

THE EXPANSION OF LEISURE

The Machine Age

Leisure is no longer a perquisite of the privileged alone but the prerogative of all classes. The present condition is the result of machine production far beyond all other causes. It began with the Industrial Revolution and broadened with the gradual introduction of new labor-saving machinery. A laborer working alone without a machine made twenty pins a day. When Adam Smith died (1790) one could, with a machine, make 4800 per day. One hundred years later he could make 2,500,000 in the same time. In 1818 a pound of nails cost 37 cents. In 1893 they could be bought for 2 cents. A Hoe printing press does the work of 300 pressmen and requires one man to run it. Including all lines of industry one man can do

---

3 Willis, *The Charleston Stage*, 59–77.

4 Earl, *Colonial Days in Old New York.*

more than twenty men could do in 1800. Everywhere machine craft has been displacing handicraft.

With the speeding up of production the market was more quickly supplied. Not only was a smaller number of laborers needed but fewer hours were required of those who did work. Then machines were driven more rapidly and so were the workers. Efficiency was everywhere emphasized and the inefficient were eliminated to join the increasing ranks of the unemployed. Beyond a certain age men were unfit to stand the strain and were replaced by younger men. Standardization took the place of variation and individualism. Initiative and creative genius were at a discount. Man, the worker, became a part of the machine.

The invention of new labor-saving machinery threw men out of employment faster than new industries could absorb them. This, with the increasing speed in the operation of men and machines, was steadily increasing unemployment. By 1929 we had a normal unemployment of about 3,000,000 people still capable of working and anxious to work. The decreased purchasing power of the American people as a result of the crisis of 1929 and the semi-paralysis of world markets greatly increased the amount of enforced leisure. An acute problem confronted society. The potentialities of much leisure for either activity conforming to the mores or for activity disapproved has long been recognized.

Automobiles. Probably the most change-laden single development of the machine age has been the automobile. On the one hand it has been the main cause of the decline of the rural community, by taking the farmers directly to the larger markets, and on the other hand it has tended to relieve the congestion of crowded city tenements by making the suburbs accessible. It has caused the bankruptcy of trolley car companies, and the disappearance of their tracks. Railroad financial difficulties have resulted from motor competition; and straightened, levelled, hard-surfaced highways have sprung from auto license fees in conjunction with auto owners' political demands. Because the range of easy travel has increased from the four miles of the day of the dobbin-drawn buggy to forty miles in the car, anonymity has developed, and with it petting and robbery and various other types of conduct that were previously restrained by neighborhood opinion.

Among the changes in social organization that the auto has brought about might be mentioned the creation of license bureaus, the organization of state motor police, automobile departments of insurance companies, the laws concerning speeding, parking, inspection, the recent emphasis on National Parks, the American Automobile Association which furnishes legal advice, hauling service, and political pressure to keep the gasoline taxes low.

These facts apply in the United States, where there is one car for every 5.5 persons. In China there is one car for every 16,000 persons.

The automobile is often an instrument for carrying on business, but the evening and holiday accident rates, or a glimpse at Sunday travel, is sufficient evidence that the subject is appropriate to a discussion of Organization for Leisure.

The Radio. Broadcasting began in 1920. In that year the Westinghouse Electric and Manufacturing Company established station KDKA in Pittsburgh and began the transmission of regular programs. Although its practicability had been demonstrated by Marconi in 1895 to the Italian government, twenty-five years went by before its commercial and cultural value became evident. The transmission of messages from city to city by the use of no more substantial medium than the air was like the conjuring of a magician. It has been of inestimable value, especially to navigation. The responses to the SOS calls of floundering ships have robbed the sea of many thousands of victims. The Westinghouse program revealed its possibilities as an educational, cultural and recreational medium in addition to its commercial value. Its uses were multiple.

Whatever other purposes it served, amusement was and is its chief function. One can have, in the morning, setting up exercises or the price of hogs in Omaha; at noon, the Pullman Car Porters Quartet, and in the evening an address by Senator Sorghum. Or one studio will broadcast the crooning of Rudy Vallee, another the blaring noise of a jazz orchestra, and a third the classic strains of grand opera. Mrs. Roosevelt will be sandwiched between a prize fight and the virtues of toasted tobacco in cigarettes.

This new absorbent of leisure is valuable to those who are passively inclined and a boon to the aged, the infirm and all those others who are also shut off from the great outside world because of physical disability. Its appeal was universal. Every cultural level could be satisfied. So the people bought radios, forty-one millions of them. In 1939 the public paid for new sets and the repair of old ones $675,000,000 and the capital investment in broadcasting stations was $405,000,000, while the sale of time by these same stations brought in $140,000,000 of revenue.[5] No other such means has ever been found for propagandism and the control of public opinion. A message over a national hook-up would reach probably 50,000,000 people.

Baseball. With something of a foundation on four-old-cat, rounders, and town-ball, and a contribution from English cricket, real baseball began in New York in 1842. Interclub games were played in the 'fifties. The Civil War seems to have been responsible for a rapid gain in the popularity of the game in the succeeding decades. In the rest camps the soldiers played ball as their favorite recreation. At the first post-war meet of the National Association in 1865, ninety-one clubs were represented. Professionalization of the sport came about when the Cincinnati Red Stockings were hired as a professional team. In 1872 the magazine, *Sports and Games,* hailed it as the national sport.[6] Such it is today. The World Series is considered the outstanding sporting event of the year, the annual gate receipts for this series often amounting to more than a million dollars.

Football. Next in national interest to the major league games of baseball is college football. The game dates as far back as the reign of Edward II of England but was revived in this country at Harvard and Yale about 1872. Some 4000 persons saw the first Princeton-Yale game in 1878. The game made its way slowly but successfully into other American colleges. Now the noted games of the season will often draw 50,000 to more than 90,000 spectators for a single game. The post-season games receive the widest publicity: the Rose Bowl at Pasadena, the Cotton Bowl at Dallas, the Orange Bowl at Miami, the Sun Bowl at El Paso and the Sugar Bowl at New Orleans. The record attendance was the Army-Navy game of 1940, numbering 102,000; the Rose Bowl drew 90,000 in 1939. Each participating team received $100,000.

Golf and Lesser Diversions. Golf dates from the colonial days but suffered an almost total eclipse for an hundred and fifty years. In 1888 it was sponsored and introduced to polite society in New York by the St. Andrews Club—an import from Scotland. It is popular wherever Scots foregather, but not with them only. It is the darling of the country clubs which, strange to say, flourish only

[5] *World Almanac,* 1940.
[6] *Sports and Games,* 1872.

in an atmosphere of urban wealth. These have a capital investment of $850,000,000 and cost their patrons $450,000,000 per year.[7] In the same period with golf, lawn tennis was introduced to the elite of various eastern cities. Its grass courts have been superseded by concrete and no play area is complete without one or more of these courts. Its strenuosity proclaims it a game for the young, leaving to age the milder game of golf. Archery has waves of popularity. In 1939, 1,500,000 people were participating in the use of the bow. Time and space would fail me to tell of cycling, skating (both ice and roller), skiing, hockey, trap shooting, squash, boating, and many another sport. Wealth had come and with it leisure for many. The irrepressible impulse to play had occasion to assert itself.

Commercial Organization for Leisure

Movies. The legitimate theater all the way from Shakespeare to vaudeville began to yield to the motion pictures in the 1890's. The first movies were peep-shows where one put a nickel in a slot and his eye to a hole and saw tiny moving figures against a dark background. Thomas A. Edison had a major part in the series of inventions by which the cinema has become the foremost amusement of our time. In the first decade of the present century the usual showing was of a single 1,000-foot reel in black and white, the story pictures dating from 1903. Explanations and conversations were flashed on the screen in print, interrupting the picture. A pianist at the front of the theater, with an eye on the screen, attempted to keep the music in harmony with the mood which the actors were portraying. In the second decade the feature film of several reels became popular, although there was a brief interruption at the close of each reel for rethreading the projector. When in 1928 Warner Brothers released a new film, *The Jazz Singer*, featuring Al Jolson, another miracle had been performed, the synchronization of sight and sound. The talkie had arrived. In the 30's came the perfection of color pictures. The next step seems to be the commercialization of television.

Inasmuch as box-office receipts are the criterion by which the management and the producers judge their shows there has been a tendency to pander to emotions that were already more active than most people considered harmonious with the social well-being. On Christmas Eve of 1905 Mayor McClellan of New York revoked 550

7 Steiner, *Americans at Play*, p. 75, McGraw-Hill Book Co.

licenses. In 1922, with attention to widespread criticism, the Motion Picture Producers and Exhibitors of America formed an organization with Will Hays as "Tzar," and undertook a measure of cooperative control. However, the tendency has been toward gradually increasing laxity.

Non-Commercial Organization for Leisure

As leisure increased, many persons thought the directly purchased pastimes were inadequate in both amount and variety, and thought also that some types of commercial amusements were of unwholesome influence; and finally, that amusements should be made available even for persons with little purchasing power.[8] As early as 1880 James A. Garfield had declared that the social struggle was divided into two parts: first, the struggle to get leisure; and then the struggle of working out uses of leisure when we get it.[9] In 1885 a notable step was taken when Boston opened the first outdoor play center for children. In the next two years nine more playgrounds were provided in the same city. In 1889 the Charlesbank open-air gymnasium was established. This was the feeble beginning by municipalities of the present-day extensive and varied programs.

Chicago and Los Angeles were pioneers of the twentieth century movement. In 1906 the Playground Association of America was formed to become a clearing-house for ideas on equipment, organization and supervision for recreation in cities as well as rural areas.

Recreational Areas. 1. Municipalities. Through park boards, recreation commissions or school boards or, in some cases, through these bodies acting more or less interdependently, municipalities prepared to meet the growing demand for both outdoor and indoor recreation. If cities already had park areas they were equipped for play, and the baleful signs "Keep off the grass" were removed. Other cities used school playgrounds until parks could be purchased and equipped. These were of two kinds: (1) the larger areas like Lincoln Park, Chicago, Central Park, New York, or the famous Golden Gate Park of San Francisco, which appealed to the whole city, and (2) neighborhood playgrounds, oftentimes of only a single block, to serve the small community. Where space was not otherwise available buildings were demolished to meet the need of some

[8] Folsom, *Culture and Social Progress*, Longmans, Green and Co.

[9] Lecture at Chatauqua, N. Y., 1880.

crowded area. Due to the persistent campaigning of Jacob Riis whole blocks of tenements were pulled down to give breathing space in New York's congested east side. By 1930 so rapid had been the progress of this movement that New York had one acre of park land for every 485 people; Chicago, one acre for every 566 persons; Philadelphia, one to every 248; St. Louis, one to 279; while San Francisco was first in park acreage with one acre to 221 residents.[10] City planning commissions and architects were persuaded to make more liberal provisions for playgrounds. Some cities openly adopted the standard set by the National Recreation Association, setting aside one-tenth of their municipal area for recreation.

The use of school grounds as play centers for the community in the larger municipalities has been the rule rather than the exception. The school building is often open for community purposes. The play supervisors were paid out of the educational budget. In 1930 seventy school properties were operated as community playgrounds by the school board of St. Louis at an expense of $343,000 compared with an expenditure of $1,207,000 from the municipal budget.[11] This proportion is probably normal for cities of this class.

2. Extra-Municipal Areas. Adjacent to many cities lie state or national parks which give greatly increased recreational opportunities. New York has 90,000 acres of such parks; Chicago, 46,000; Cleveland, 10,000; Boston, 11,000; Los Angeles, 12,000. Many of these tracts are on sea or lake shores and contain excellent bathing beaches. In her park areas Los Angeles is fortunate in the possession of twelve miles of sea-bathing beaches.[12] Some have provisions for camping, riding, cycling, picnicking. Many have rifle and archery ranges and dancing pavilions.

It is in such parks and the national forests that have been built the youth hostels.[13] As yet these are confined largely to the New England area but are rapidly spreading westward. They have bedrooms with beds and blankets, cooking facilities, toilet rooms, a dining and a living room. They encourage hikers and cyclers, all those who like simple, rugged living and travel light both in baggage and purse.

[10] Annual Report on Recreation, City of St. Louis, 1936.

[11] *Ibid.*

[12] Annual Recreational Report, 1939.

[13] Studebaker, *Leisure for Living*, Office of Education, Washington, D. C., 1936.

Cities Expand Their Programs. The sources from which funds were obtained to finance the municipal program were three: (1) allocation from the city budget, (2) the public school funds and (3) the beneficence of private citizens. In addition to these are the semi-public institutions such as the Y.M.C.A. and Y.W.C.A. which collect and disburse their own funds and set up their own programs. Municipalities were broadening their programs and increasing their budgets. Meanwhile the number of cities offering recreational facilities was steadily increasing. Steiner reports that in 1910 only 180 cities had programs for the use of leisure. In 1920 the number had increased to 428. In 1930, 695 cities had recreational organizations; in 1933, 1039. The number of recreational leaders had increased in one year from 28,000 to 43,000, while the attendance had grown from 294,000,000 to 375,000,000.[14]

The seriousness with which the new playtime was regarded is shown by the amount allocated from city budgets. The major municipalities were spending from $1,000,000 upward a year. Recreation commissions were formed. Leaders were being trained. One city of one million inhabitants is offering over 100 varieties of athletics, sports, arts, crafts, games, hobbies, with an annual attendance of 25,000,000.[15] Other cities have like programs and directing personnel.

National Parks. A tract of mountainous country lying principally in northwestern Wyoming, but including a small area in eastern Idaho and southern Montana, famous for its streams, lakes, hot springs, mud volcanoes and geysers, was set aside in 1872 by the United States government as Yellowstone National Park. This was the beginning of a movement to create and develop an extensive system of national parks. To these were added allied areas: national historical parks; national monuments, which include such widely varied regions as the Mesa Verde, Colorado, one time home of the Cliff Dwellers, and the Katmai Valley of 10,000 Smokes in Alaska; national military parks, notable among which are Chickamauga and Gettysburg; national battlefield sites, including the Chalmette Monument and grounds near New Orleans and White Plains, New York; these, with our national cemeteries, national historical sites and national parkways, had a total area on June 30, 1939, of 20,817,000 acres.[16] These could not all be classed as recrea-

14 *Ibid.*
15 Annual Report on Recreation, Los Angeles, 1939.
16 *World Almanac*, 1940.

tional. Many of them tend to inspire us with a deeper patriotism; others tell of our historical background; but whether they be patriotic or historical or scenic, they yield ample returns for the use of our leisure.

When automobiles had passed the experimental stage the demand grew for smoother and more dependable roads on which to travel. Dirt roads were not conducive to speed. The federal government and the states, sometimes in co-operation, have now laced the country with 113,000 miles of hard surfaced highways. This further increased the demand for cars and cars of higher speed. In 1938 the people of the U. S. were owners of 25,261,000 passenger automobiles and operated, at the same time, 4,224,000 buses and trucks.[17] America was moving on rubber-tired wheels. The manufacturers were building from two to four million autos each year. There is no means of knowing how many of these are solely for recreation. But America had become travel-minded. The cost of travel in 1938–9 was far beyond the amount spent for all other uses of leisure. Compared with the expenditure for motion pictures the ratio is six and one-half to one. One of the great attractions to motorists was the national parks. In 1939 more than 16,500,000 people visited these playgrounds.

Other Federal Agencies. In addition to the National Parks Service other agencies of the federal government have given serious attention to the matter of providing ways and means for the use of leisure. Much of the work of the C.C.C. camps has been in the national parks and national forests to make them more attractive. In state and local parks 100,000 acres have been made available for public camp grounds and picnic areas with cabins, shelters, fireplaces, parking plots and sanitary conveniences. Of large and small dams, 350 have been constructed to afford facilities for swimming, boating and fishing, and to provide wild-fowl refuges. Almost 8000 miles of foot and horse trails have been made.

W.P.A. Of the W.P.A. budget almost 10 per cent has been allocated for recreational purposes for the W.P.A. personnel and the communities they are serving. These funds were used for four different objectives: (1) to open new areas for recreation, (2) to supplement municipal budgets, (3) to provide recreational leaders in both new and occupied areas and (4) to hold regional conferences for leadership training. By the end of 1935 there had been selected

[17] *Ibid.*

for operation 4,261 projects to extend or improve recreational facilities, such as public parks, playgrounds, athletic fields, stadiums, golf courses, tennis courts, swimming pools and bathing beaches. In a wholly different area of life have been the 836 projects that extend recreational operations to mural painting, theatrical performance, choruses and orchestras and allied arts. These are conducted by the Community Organization for Leisure of the W.P.A.[18]

The Department of Agriculture, using the state colleges of agriculture as a medium, is carrying these ideas into rural areas. The consolidated schools and rural churches are the focal points for such promotion. The Farm Bureau and the 4–H Clubs are the agencies expected to carry out community programs. The possibility of urbanizing the rural areas instead of providing amusements that will be an integral part of the rural culture pattern has received some attention.

The N.Y.A. Still another movement under federal auspices is the National Youth Administration, organized under the Office of Education of which J. W. Studebaker is commissioner. It works in close co-operation with the state W.P.A. administration of recreation. The initial funds for this movement were secured from the General Educational Board. It gives part time employment to needy youth in accordance with their abilities and, so far as possible, adequate recreational facilities which will be open, also, to all the young people of the community.

Other Agencies. The list of agencies concerned with recreation is by no means complete. To these must be added *state* parks and forest areas, beginning with the prohibition of further sale of the Adirondack forest, by the state of New York in 1885. In 1935 the *Social Work Year Book* reported that 43 of the 48 states had established parks and forest areas amounting to 7,000,000 acres. No figures seem to be available as to the number and acreage of county parks. *National Recreation Year Book* for 1940 reports 131 counties with recreational budgets. Steiner reports 72 participating counties with 108,000 acres of parks in 1930. In many instances both states and counties have their own organizations to promote recreation.

Almost every social institution and organization has something to offer to those seeking diversion. For many years a majority of churches have been attempting to promote the social as well as the

[18] Studebaker, *op. cit.*

spiritual life of the community. Dinners, concerts, plays and picnics are sponsored by women's organizations, men's clubs, young
people's societies. In the cities the larger churches had social, educational and recreational rooms either part of or apart from the
building dedicated to worship. Parish houses, club rooms and community buildings housed Boy Scout troops, Girl Reserves and Boys'
Clubs. Some of the more wealthy and liberal provided gymnasiums,
billiard rooms, bowling alleys, basketball courts, even swimming
pools. Hiking and hobby clubs were promoted, and even basketball
and soft-ball leagues. Catering to leisure became a serious part
of the ecclesiastical program.

Service Clubs—Rotary, Kiwanis, Lions, Optimist—were formerly
called luncheon clubs. Some of the leaders in these organizations
saw that to remain luncheon clubs alone was inevitable suicide. A
varied list of beneficent objectives were set up. As the Mystic
Shrine has for its objective the treatment of crippled children, the
Kiwanis International specializes in underprivileged children.
These all have their sports and athletic activities; they also provide
vacation camps, cabins, and sometimes club rooms for Boy Scouts,
boys' club members and other similar groups. They promote high
school and college basketball and football and develop interclub
leagues in softball, volleyball, bowling and kindred sports. Secret
fraternities—Masons, Odd Fellows, Elks, Eagles and others—are
purveyors to the play instincts of their members. No Masonic
temple is complete without its billiard and card rooms, dining facilities, and dancing floor. In a recent investigation of a city of 45,000
conducted by the writer no less than 190 organizations were offering
leisure time activities as an integral part of their programs.

The National Recreation Association lists as the ten most attractive recreational pursuits:

Swimming	Music, vocal and instru-
Soft ball	mental
Baseball	Folk dancing
Skating	Social dancing
Tennis	Hiking
Basketball	

These are only a beginning, and they all belong to one category,
except music. But this list of physical sports could be increased
almost indefinitely: canoeing, boating, cycling, horseshoe pitching
(one club in southern California pitched more than 70 tons of steel

per day), ice hockey, ice and roller skating, skiing and a score of others. In the realm with music are the drama, drawing, painting, sculpture, architecture, decorating, landscape gardening. Gardening is old as civilization, but has never lost its attraction. It offers both physical and emotional satisfactions and admirably combines both recreational and utilitarian values.

Hobby-Riding. The pursuit of hobbies has long been a favorite pastime. It appeals to all classes and conditions. Earnest Elmo Calkins has listed nearly 700, ranging all the way from anagrams to xylographs and from tropical fish to tear bottles. Some pursue a hobby with the spirit of a dilettante, while to others it becomes a primary objective of life. They grow from one's desires, needs and abilities. His desires may be conditioned by mental and financial resources, or by his native ability. An income that is absorbed by domestic demands would not permit him to become a collector of rare rugs, antique jewelry, or Chinese jade. Someone has classified all hobbies under four heads: (1) doing things, (2) making things, (3) acquiring things and (4) learning things.[19] Here are leisure occupations that are always educational and recreational and, often times, creative. King George VI has the most famous stamp collection in the world while President Roosevelt is almost equally noted as a philatelist, a hobby that is shared with more than 2,000,000 other people. Hall discovered aluminum in riding a hobby. Anton van Leeuwenhoek made microscopes. William R. Hook made discoveries of the cell. Mendel worked out his laws of heredity. Tony Sarg fashioned his marionettes. George Eastman became an authority on photography.

RE–SURVEY

Organized Leisure

Deliberate organization for the use of leisure time belongs to the twentieth century; almost overnight it has become a major social interest. The ways one spends the hours in which he is free from labor are not only an index of his character but an opportunity to enrich it. Eight hours out of the twenty-four he is in the shop or factory and does what he must. The remainder of the time he does what he desires to do. What he does with this leisure is important, not to himself alone, but to society. The individual may use this

[19] Earnest Elmo Calkins, *Care and Feeding of Hobby Horses,* Leisure League of America, 1934.

off-time destructively or constructively; toward anabolic or catabolic ends.

Commercial amusements antedated planned provision for leisure by social organizations. (1) The motion picture theatre was the most successful caterer to newly-acquired leisure. The romance and glamour of the silver screen appealed to the masses. It lifted them, for a time, out of the sordidness of their environment and the humdrum of their daily toll. (2) Professional baseball was attracting its many thousands who found vicarious satisfaction in the skill of the players. (3) Race tracks were multiplying with their bookmakers to levy additional toll on the purses of their habitues. (4) Every city had its amusement parks, fully commercialized, the questionable virtues of its varied and sometimes lascivious shows proclaimed by the professional "barker." The most famous of these and the first to be opened is New York's Coney Island, with a peak attendance of 800,000 people daily. (5) The prize fight, which later was euphemistically labelled the boxing match, as early as 1892 was given much publicity by the press and drew crowds that paid fancy prices for ring-side seats. The box office returns from the Tunney-Dempsey match in Chicago were $2,650,000,[20] the largest amount ever received from any single exhibition in the United States. (6) Beer gardens, dance-halls, bowling alleys, billiard rooms and dime museums drew crowds to their glaring gas lights. The old stand-by, the saloon, blossomed out in new regalia. Music was added, and dancing, while none-too-fully dressed waitresses served drinks or, in turn, danced with their patrons.

Those who were interested in personal and social values saw in this increasing leisure a menace and an opportunity: a menace because the people had no preparation to enable them to use it profitably; an opportunity to employ this large amount of time for creative living.

But this unused time was being given to commercial amusements, with little deliberation concerning their values. The first national attention to this new social condition was in 1929 when President Herbert Hoover named a committee to survey social changes in this country in order to throw light on emerging problems. Funds for the researches were given by the Rockefeller Foundation. The work was finished and the report given in 1932.[21] Upon the basis

[20] Foster Rhea Dulles, *Americans Learn to Play*, Appleton-Century Co., 1940.

[21] Jesse F. Steiner, *op. cit.*

of these findings programs were made and some already made were revamped. Commissions were constituted by municipalities, communities and states. They provided parks and other playgrounds, bathing-beaches, swimming pools, amateur baseball diamonds, tennis courts, concrete highways, bridle trails, picnic and camping grounds, even dancing pavilions and orchestras.

The Opportunity for Leadership. The poverty of individual initiative, the pauperism in ideals, the haphazardness of these early attempts, pointed clearly to the opportunity for leadership. Organizations were formed that were first regional, then national in their scope. In all important centers directors of recreation are functioning. In 1938 more than 1204 cities had organized and made appropriations for such activities in their annual budgets.[22]

Leisure has at last received matter-of-fact consideration. The masses, left to themselves, with no adequate mental resources, will either flounder helplessly or fall into the hands of a rather ruthless commercialism. But under leadership one person may discover unknown capacities and another may find a better way to accomplish some cherished objectives. To some, errors may be pointed out that have barred the way to excellence; others may easily be turned from some futile quest that would lead only to disillusionment.

Liberty Essential. These values cannot be secured without organization and direction. But in this new movement there is danger of over-organization and a leadership that assumes too much authority to be consistent with freedom. Without the free play of personal desires and the largest amount of individual liberty consistent with harmony, recreation loses much that is widely valued. In play as well as elsewhere democracy itself has an appeal. The game must be played according to the rules, but it will be the one the participants wish to play. During his working hours the laborer is under authority. He must yield his will to that of his employer; or if in business for himself, to an even more exacting authority, the public. But once he has turned homeward he is under no mandate except his own. He will do now what he pleases to do and that marks the difference between work and play. His activity may be just as strenuous in his play as in his work, or even more exacting, but he is impelled by his own desires.

The leadership that guides with invisible hands does not repress native desires, but leads them into considered channels. A leader,

[22] *Yearbook* of the National Recreation Association, 1940.

having the usual caution against regimentation, will teach new games and develop greater skills in old ones; he will remove difficulties and inhibitions; he will stimulate self-education and direction.

ORGANIZATION OF THE CHAPTER BY TOPICS

Use of leisure historically considered
    Leisure in Pre-Colonial Europe
    Relaxation in the American Colonies
        Play among the Puritans
        Gaiety in the Old South
    Merriment beyond the mountains
    Ranch and Mine
    The rise of urban amusements
        The theater
        Racing
        Concerts
        Dancing
        Cockfighting
The expansion of leisure
    The machine age
        Autos
        Radios
        Baseball
        Football
        Golf, and lesser diversions
    Commercial organization for leisure
        Movies
        Other commercialized amusements
    Non-commercial organization for leisure
        Recreational areas
            Municipalities
                The use of school grounds
            Extra-municipal areas
        Cities expand their programs
        National parks
        Other Federal agencies
            The Department of Agriculture
            The National Youth Administration
        Other agencies
        Hobby riding

Re-survey
    Organized leisure
    The opportunity for leadership
    Attention to liberty

SELECTED REFERENCES

Blumer, H., and Hauser, P. M., *Movies, Delinquency and Crime*, New York: The Macmillan Co., 1933; one of the Payne Fund Studies in Motion Pictures and Youth.

Chase, Stuart, *Men and Machines*, Macmillan, 1937.

Cutlen, G. B., *The Threat of Leisure*, Yale University Press, 1926.

Furnas, *The Next Hundred Years*, Reynal and Hitchcock, 1936.

Jacks, L. P., *Education through Recreation*, New York: Harpers & Brothers, 1932.

Menke, Frank G., *Encyclopedia of Sports*, George G. Renneker Co., 1939.

Neumeyer, M. H. and E. S., *Leisure and Recreation*, A. S. Barnes and Co., 1936.

Park, Arthur Newton, *The Challenge of Leisure*, New York: The Macmillan Company, 1934.

Stieri, *The Book of Indoor Hobbies*, Whittlesey House, 1939.

Thurston, *Delinquency and Spare Time*, Cleveland Recreation Survey, 1918.

CHAPTER 19

ECONOMIC INSTITUTIONS

By J. HAROLD ENNIS, PH.D.

Cornell College, Mount Vernon, Iowa

Human society is basically a set of relationships. The individual, carrying on all the activities necessary for living in the group, is knowingly or unknowingly affecting the behavior of others. He conditions the behavior of the group, and in turn the individual's own thinking and acting are reciprocally influenced. In short, social interaction is a fundamental factor in every human group.

Not only does the individual in a social group find himself in the midst of a continuous process of interaction, but economic (and other social) institutions are likewise subject to the same process. No economic institution is functionally isolated. The institution of private property is affected by, and in turn affects, the prevailing family system. Economic institutions are likewise related closely to educational, political, and religious institutions. This interrelationship and interdependence between different types of social institutions is noticeable in their origin, as well as in their later development. There is, for example, a close relationship between Protestantism and the beginning of capitalism.[1] This factor of interdependence of one economic institution upon another economic institution, of reciprocal relations among all types of social institutions, is quite basic to an understanding of their true nature.

THE FUNCTION OF AN ECONOMY

It is well to raise the question early in this description of economic institutions as to the exact function served by economic organization. What, after all, is an economic system supposed to do? Is there a set of functions common to all economic systems—feudal, communistic, or capitalistic?

An attempt has been made by F. H. Knight to organize in more or less logical sequence a pattern of functions fundamental to any

[1] One writer has on this issue made a study of exceptional merit; see R. H. Tawney, *Religion and the Rise of Capitalism.* Also cf. Max Weber, *The Protestant Ethic and the Spirit of Capitalism,* 1930.

economic system, ancient or modern.[2] Five main functions are identified: first, the function of fixing standards and the notion of efficiency; second, the function of organizing production; third, the function of distribution; fourth, economic maintenance and progress; fifth, adjustment of consumption to production within very short periods.

The first function is that of setting standards. In the simplest form of society this was merely a matter of individual choice. Thus a savage who was thirsty would drink from a near-by stream, or if he were hungry he would directly appropriate wild fruits from the forest. "But when the production of wealth is socialized there has to be a *social* decision as to the relative importance of different uses of productive power, as to which wants are to be satisfied and which left unsatisfied or to what extent any one is to be satisfied at the expense of any other."[3] This point is important with reference to any type of economy. Either a democratic or fascist organization may decide that bread is less important than guns. Again under feudalism a social decision was involved in deciding what goods and services were to be produced.

The decision as to what is to be produced is logically followed by the second function, namely, the function of organizing production. Professor Knight points out two aspects of this process. The first is "the assignment or *allocation* of the available productive forces and materials among the various lines of industry."[4] For example, in a free-pricing capitalistic economy comparative costs would determine whether a certain unit of labor will be utilized in automobiles or in the manufacture of tractors. Similarly the pricing system determines whether wood may be utilized for furniture or paper for text books, whether coal may haul a freight train or be converted into chemicals. The second aspect of organizing production is "the effective coordination of the various means of production in each industry into such groupings as will produce the greatest result."[5] This latter is largely an engineering problem.

The third main function of an economy is distribution. In a primitive or unorganized society this function would be unknown

[2] "Social Economic Organization," by F. H. Knight, Chapter VII, in *Contemporary Society* (Social Science II), ed. by Harry D. Gideonse, Copyrighted by the University of Chicago, 1940. Quotations used by permission.

[3] *Op. cit.*, p. 130.

[4] *Op. cit.*, p. 133.

[5] *Ibid.*

because each individual would satisfy his own needs directly by his own efforts. However, in organized society where production is socialized, the relatively specialized contribution of one producer cannot be isolated from that of another. It becomes obvious that in an assembly line of a modern automobile factory neither the workman who sets the engine block on the auto frame nor the one who fastens the headlights in place can directly eat or wear his own labor. It is said that they trade their labor for money, a "medium of exchange," which in turn may be redeemed in a wide variety of want-satisfying goods and services. When it is realized that in any country a relatively intricate specialization and division of labor has developed, it becomes clear that some social mechanism of distribution is essential.

The fourth function is that of economic maintenance and progress. This refers to those factors of cumulative change, whether "good" or "bad," that develop out of: (1) different rates of population growth and major variations in population composition that influence either the ability to produce goods or the desire for goods; (2) the material factors aiding or hindering production, such as a newly built power dam or an exhausted ore deposit; (3) development of technical processes and changes in the form of business organization. This fourth function, says Professor Knight,

> is a matter of standards or values to decide how much progress society can afford or cares to have at the cost of sacrificing present values, and what forms it shall take; it is a matter of productive organization to utilize the determined share of available productive power to bring about progress in the amount and of the kinds decided upon, and it is a problem of distribution to apportion the burdens and benefits of progress among the members of society.[6]

Society is called upon to face still another type of problem. This fifth task or function to perform is that of adjusting consumption to production within very short periods. It is easily illustrated in agricultural production. The existing supply of corn, for example, must suffice until the next corn crop and it must be apportioned in some fashion among the different consumers and their varied needs.

These five problems have arisen in every society, and various methods have been used in attempts to answer them. Thus through the long period of human history many different types of economic systems have developed; all were concerned with these five tasks and

[6] *Op. cit.*, p. 135.

in one manner or another have offered their solutions. It should be pointed out, too, that the relative magnitude of any of these five problems is conditioned by three factors: the knowledge concerning and the relative abundance of natural resources; the nature of human wants; and third, the achievement in technology, or the so-called "state of the arts." It is obvious that the relative scarcity of mineral deposits and the relative abundance of rich land suitable for agriculture would encourage the development of an economy in which the latter was dominant. This would have a profound effect upon nature of standards set under those conditions. In like manner a reciprocating relationship (both a cause and effect relationship) is noted between any one of these five functions on one hand and the nature of human wants on the other. It is equally clear that the level of economic development, whether it is characterized by the wide-spread use of machinery or is a simpler handicraft stage, modifies the type of answer given to the five problems outlined above and is itself affected by whatever answer is given. The social process of interaction is here definitely present.

THE RISE OF THE ECONOMIC ARTS

The Beginning of Invention

Who the first man was, what he ate, and where he lived probably will always be a matter of conjecture. Fragments of knowledge are constantly being added to the store of information by anthropologists, but any complete picture can never be given of man's earliest economic habits.

It has been pointed out that the very "essence of culture is inventing or achievement."[7] An invention, sociologically speaking, starts as a mental pattern in the mind of some human being. This pattern becomes a physical tool or a social relationship.[8] It is often diffused by communication, and thus becomes a portion of the cultural achievement of a group.

Stone Weapons and Tools

In the far distant past some member of one of the earliest primitive human groups found that he could to great advantage fashion a stone tool. This conclusion may have been reached by chance or

[7] C. A. Ellwood, *Cultural Evolution*, New York, The Century Co., 1927, p. 5.

[8] C. A. Ellwood, *op. cit.*

as the result of reasoning and planning. In either case this first great inventor saw the superiority of his hand-wrought stone or wood instrument over unworked material. It may have been that crudely flaked stone provided a better cutting edge than any stone found at random in a natural state; the better "balance" of a roughly worked stick as a club may have demonstrated its superiority over any fallen branch. But whatever the first crude tools and weapons may have been, their advantages were communicated to other members of the group. From time to time improvements in the construction of these tools were made by individuals of ability, and these superior tool patterns were in their turn diffused among those who were in contact with each other. Thus knowledge accumulated. Stone tools gave way slowly to metal tools and simple metal tools were more and more replaced by more complicated machines.

Other Arts Connected with Food, Clothing, and Shelter

The invention of the first stone ax was an item of significance. In itself it might be called the greatest of all economic revolutions if it were not true that many centuries probably intervened between its first chance use and its later development. The great importance of the ax lies in the fact that it was one of the earliest extensions of man's control over his food supply.

It is probable that one of man's very first attempts to achieve security against starvation was the mere storage of food. This may have been no more than the placing of dried berries and nuts in a cleft in the rocks. With the idea of food storage established as a means of warding off hunger, it was an easy stride to providing better means for keeping food until need was greatest. Storage pits were dug in the ground with wood or stone slab tops, and platforms were erected in trees out of the reach of marauding beasts.

Anthropologists studying the skeletons of ancient man have noted the long arms, the short trunk and legs, and they have reasoned that possibly very early man dropped in ape fashion from low-hanging tree branches to the backs of his prey. This more difficult method of catching his food no longer was necessary when the stone ax, the spear, and later weapons were invented.

The food of very early man was of course eaten without cooking. The use of fire did not appear until the Paleolithic period, and this was a noteworthy revolution in itself. Undoubtedly something of a balanced diet was achieved by consuming wild plants and nuts together with raw meats.

Another social revolution took place with the taming of animals. The early dependence of man upon the chance returns of the hunt undoubtedly kept him close to the margin of starvation. It is not precisely known whether the domestication of animals was the cause or the effect of the beginning of a permanent home. At any rate with his more or less permanent home and development of the art of taming animals, man achieved another control over his food supply.

It is not known when or why man first used clothing. Students of early cultures have developed novel theories in explanation of this cultural trait. Some have said that the need for protection against the wind, sun, or rain necessitated clothing. It is possible that on a return trip from the hunt an early inventor noticed that the slain animal across his shoulder sheltered him from the storm. This may have caused him to fashion the skin of other animals to guard him against cold, moisture, or the burning sun. Others say that early man developed clothing as an expression of his artistic sense. It is possible that the first clothing was mere ornamentation. And still others declare that the growing consciousness of sex accounted for the origin of clothing.

Some of the earliest types of *Homo sapiens* lived in caves or crude shelters along rocky cliffs. Of this we are certain because of the remains found in such well-known caves as those at La Chapelle-aux-Saints in France and elsewhere on the continent of Europe. These rock shelters offered protection against unpleasant weather, wild beasts, and possibly other groups of ancient man. As man continued to experiment with new methods of controlling his environment, he began to construct other houses that more nearly fitted his requirements. Thus early Indian houses in the region that is now north-eastern Nebraska were unusually well planned to meet the weather conditions of that area.[9] Circular houses were built half sunk below the earth's surface, and the frameworks of poles and brush were covered with several inches of dirt. This type of house was both warm in winter and cool in summer. It was a successful early counterpart of our modern air-conditioned homes.

[9] Cf. Earl H. Bell, *Chapters in Nebraska Archaeology*, Vol. I, Lincoln, Nebr., 1936.

THE INSTITUTION OF PROPERTY

The Nature and Origin of Property

If the term property is used in its most general sense it may be defined as the exclusive use, enjoyment, and control of those things which are of value in so far as they serve to satisfy the fundamental personal and social needs.[10] When these things are controlled by the individual they are private property. If they are controlled by a number of individuals who as a group have rights of use and enjoyment against other individuals or groups, they become group or common property. Thus a suit of clothes or a book may be private property when no use claims are recognized against them other than those of a particular person. A church, a club house, or a public-owned electric light plant may be regarded as common property for the members of their special group.

It can be seen from the definition given above that property itself is a right or claim. Walton H. Hamilton has with some drollery defined property as "a euphonious collocation of letters which serves as a general term for the miscellany of equities that persons hold in the commonwealth."[11] From the viewpoint of the economist, property is "the right to income; that is, the right to the benefits or services of wealth or free persons."[12]

The importance of the institution of property to human society can hardly be overestimated. It is basic to an understanding of any culture. Ernest Beaglehole has well said: "In true perspective, the system of ownership in a community is essentially the mechanism which standardizes and gives stability to the relation between the members of the society and the body of material culture and natural resources which they have at their command. It stands therefore at the basis of economic welfare and reacts strongly upon the efficiency of production."[13] The property concept is in truth a focal point about which, for good or for ill, our economic processes operate.

Like all basic social institutions, the economic institution of property is a product of the long process of social evolution. Modern property concepts are probably vastly different from those rudi-

10 See Ernest Beaglehole, *Property; A Study in Social Psychology*, New York: Macmillan, 1932, p. 15.

11 *Encyclopaedia of the Social Sciences*, Vol. 12, New York, 1934, p. 528.

12 Fairchild, Furniss, and Buck, *Elementary Economics*, New York, 1936, p. 16.

13 Beaglehole, *op. cit.*, pp. 131–2.

mentary attitudes developed many thousands of years ago when man first thought of things, and even ideas, as *belonging* to him or his primary group.

It is, of course, probable that the exact nature of the origin of property will never be known. But many anthropologists give prominence to the place of marriage by capture as one of the earliest forms of property. Thorstein Veblen declares that "the earliest form of ownership is an ownership of the women by the able bodied men of the community."[14] This writer definitely discards the idea that seizure of things marks the beginning of ownership. He says, "It is difficult to see how an institution of ownership could have arisen in the early days of predatory life through the seizure of goods, but the case is different with the seizure of persons. . . . Except where there is a slave class of men, the women are more useful, as well as more easily controlled, in the primitive group. . . . After the usage of capture has found its way into the habits of the community, the women so held in constraint and in evidence will commonly fall into a conventionally recognized marriage relation with their captor. . . . This ownership-marriage seems to be the original both of private property and of the patriarchal household. Both of these great institutions are, accordingly, of an emulative origin."[15]

The same author believes that property, originating in the manner above described, developed first in the early stages of barbarism.[16]

Other writers give considerable attention to property values arising out of primitive marriage.[17] "In Fiji, for instance, Wilkes tells us that the women are kept in subjection. . . . Like other property, wives may be sold at pleasure, and the usual price is a musket. Among the Shoshones, the man is the sole proprietor of his wives and daughters and can barter them away or dispose of them in any way he may think proper. . . . In a very definite sense the woman is a form of property, since she may serve as a pawn in a creditor's custody and is inherited by her husband's brothers while herself barred from inheriting any of his possessions."[18]

[14] T. Veblen, "The Theory of the Leisure Class," in *What Veblen Taught*, edited by W. C. Mitchell, New York: Viking Press, 1936, p. 216; also *The Theory of the Leisure Class*, New York: The Modern Library, 1934, pp. 22–23.

[15] From *Essays in Our Changing Order* by Thorstein Veblen, pp. 47–48. Copyright 1934. By permission of The Viking Press, Inc., New York.

[16] *Ibid.*, p. 44.

[17] Cf. Beaglehole, *op. cit.*, Ch. VI.

[18] Beaglehole, *op. cit.*, pp. 158–159.

The Evolution of Property

According to Lewinski[19] the whole evolution of property may be traced back to four fundamentals:

1. The economic principle.
2. The principle of numerical strength.
3. The growth of population.
4. The relation of nature to human wants.

In the first place, the underlying assumption is that man tries to obtain the *greatest possible quantity* of economic goods necessary for the satisfaction of his wants with the least possible effort. In following this procedure man engaged in appropriation of nature's abundance and the accumulations of the efforts of other men.

The second principle developed out of the clash of interests between the "haves" and "have-nots," between those who adhered to the prevailing institution of property and those who wanted a "reshuffle." The numerical strength of its adherents determined to a great extent what policy was followed.

While these first two principles were largely *constant* elements that were not subject to change, the third principle was a varying and dynamic force—namely, the growth of population. "It put an end to the original abundance of land, and by diminishing the area at the disposal of each man forced him to pass from nomadism to the cultivation of soil, and to settled life."[20] Lewinski indicated that the increase in population became so great in some areas that even a more intensive use of the soil could not prevent land scarcity. As a result the class of poor grew more and more numerous. In this country the passing of the frontier with its adverse effect on certain classes was noted in the classic works of Henry George.[21]

The fourth principle relates to the relative abundance or scarcity of natural resources. Variations in the quality of the soil, for example, profoundly influence the formation of property. For one thing, "The greater the amount of labor incorporated in the soil, the sooner and the more strongly does individual ownership establish itself."[22]

19 Jan St. Lewinski, *The Origin of Property and the Formation of the Village Community*, London: Constable & Co., Ltd., 1913.

20 *Ibid.*, p. 60.

21 Cf. Henry George, *Progress and Poverty*, Garden City: Garden City Publishing Co., 1926 (originally published in 1879).

22 Lewinski, *op. cit.*, p. 61.

Corporate Property

The most significant type of business unit at the present time in the United States is the corporation. This form of business organization is no new institution, since it dates from the days of the joint stock trading companies which built up the mammoth merchant empires of England and Holland in the Seventeenth Century.[23] However, its great growth as an instrument through which property rights were exercised starts with the early Nineteenth Century. Today it stands as the dominant type of business organization.

It has been commonly pointed out that a corporation is an artificial being, invisible, intangible, and living only in the eyes of the law. This definition shows rather clearly the legal characteristics of this form of business unit; it is a fictitious person having status in the eyes of the law and having existence quite apart from the individuals who compose it. A charter or certificate of incorporation is the official document giving validity to its creation.

But the modern business corporation is no longer a mere legal "gadget" through which business affairs between individuals are carried on. It is of far greater social significance. As recent writers have said, ''The corporation has, in fact, become both a method of property tenure and a means of organizing economic life. Grown to tremendous proportions, there may be said to have evolved a 'corporate system'—as there was once a feudal system—which has attracted to itself a combination of attributes and powers, and has attained a degree of prominence entitling it to be dealt with as a major social institution.''[24]

The extent of contemporary corporate control over property is little short of amazing. For example, Willard L. Thorp of the Bureau of Foreign and Domestic Commerce has estimated that at the present time corporations do from 60 to 65% of the total volume of business in the United States.[25] Interesting comparisons may be made in an effort to visualize corporate size. Thus, the Metropolitan Life Insurance Company and the American Telephone and Telegraph Company each have assets larger than the total assessed valuation of the State of Missouri, or Texas, or Iowa. The Pennsylvania Railroad Company has greater assets than all the assessed valuation

---

[23] A. A. Berle, Jr., and Gardiner C. Means, *The Modern Corporation and Private Property*, New York: The Macmillan Co., 1933, p. 10.

[24] *Ibid.*, p. 1.

[25] Part 1, *Temporary National Economic Committee Hearings*, p. 96.

of property in Kansas, Maryland, or Kentucky. Either the Standard Oil Company or the U. S. Steel Corporation's assets are larger than the assessed valuation of West Virginia. Many other illustrations of a similar character might be given.[26]

The social situation created by these and multitudes of other instances has several aspects. For one thing, not only has the wealth of many individuals been concentrated into great segments but the essential control has been given over to other individuals or groups. Thus old property relationships are broken. This may be witnessed in the fact that many stockholders (legal owners) of corporations do not bother to fill out and return their voting proxies, through which legally the owners may exercise control and direction. In the second place, the development of a system of economic activity through the corporation has made possible an expansion of the area under coordinated control. The factory system, the basis of the industrial revolution, brought an increasingly large number of workers directly under a single management. So also, the modern business corporation, equally revolutionary, centralized the control of wealth.[27]

Inheritance

Closely attached to the philosophy of private property is the concept of inheritance. Inheritance refers to the exclusive right to use and to control the material goods which a deceased person has left—subject, of course, to the prevailing rules of society.

From a social point of view many writers defend inheritance because, they say, it is quite probable that the right to make family bequests is a strong incentive to industry and thrift. There is much truth in this idea that many families consume less than they produce (in other words, save) and maximize their production through efficiency in order that goods or a command over future goods may be passed along to other members of the family.

There seem to be two important social consequences to inheritance. In the first place, the act of "saving" adds its own special character to the family. It has been well said that "The permanence of the family has a social value which the right of inheritance helps to maintain."[28] In the second place, inheritance encourages

[26] See table in *Final Statement of Senator O'Mahoney, TNEC Report,* March 11, 1941, pp. 17–18.

[27] Berle and Means, *op. cit.,* p. 3.

[28] *Encyclopaedia Britannica,* New York, 1937, Vol. 12, p. 356.

savings, and savings are essential for the expansion of the economic plant. As old capital is exhausted and as new capital is required for additional enterprises, savings must be relied upon to meet this need. Any device through which savings are encouraged is thus of great social concern.

It is generally felt that the right to make free bequests has in British capitalistic society undoubtedly been a factor in favor of maximizing production. An offsetting factor should be mentioned. To the extent that a few individuals keep to themselves a considerable portion of the annual income without making any direct contribution, and to the extent that this situation may discourage others more actively engaged in production, there has been a reduction in productive efficiency.

No one truly knows what the real effect is of a system of inheritance upon the efficiency of production, or the amount of savings and national wealth. This institution has not been the subject of adequate study. It is probable, however, that the British system of primogeniture—in which the bequest is passed along to the eldest son—is responsible in part for the concentrated landed estates in England. For a period Russia abolished the rights of inheritance, but it is difficult to say what the consequences were to the total economic product in that country. However, there is little question that the rules of inheritance under modern capitalism tend to make for the concentration of the ownership of property. With this trend there has developed a salaried managerial class to supervise and operate these aggregates of wealth.

STAGES OF ECONOMIC DEVELOPMENT

At this point it is appropriate to raise a question as to the meaning of a "stage" of economic development.[29] A stage is not a period or segment of time sequence. This is true because it occurs at different times in different countries. Thus feudalism is frequently associated with England in the twelfth and thirteenth centuries. However, important aspects of feudalism were found in North Eastern Europe as late as the beginning of the twentieth century.

It has been held that an economic stage is a condition through which change occurs gradually. Thus "One condition comes in to

[29] A stimulating and critical discussion of economic stages is found in "Stages in Economic History," by N. S. B. Gras, in *Journal of Economic and Business History*, May, 1930, Vol. II, pp. 395–418.

threaten, then to rival, and finally to supplant the old."[30]   In this
sense a discussion of economic stages is useful in pointing out trends
and transitions from one social and economic level to another.   No
stage in itself is to be regarded as either absolute or final.

Primary Stage[31]

The most primitive stage of economic life was that in which man
was not a producer of capital or economic wealth.   This means
essentially that earliest man did not have any great accumulated
stock of goods or tools for aiding production.   Ancient man lived
directly on the generosity of nature.   If wild game and uncultivated
plants were abundant, his hunger was satisfied.   If they were scarce,
he starved.

Division of labor, that important social phenomenon of specialization, was practiced in a crude form.   Men probably assumed most
of the responsibility attendant upon the killing of game and the
physical defense of the family.   Women cared for the infants, collected the wild food plants, and aided in the fabrication of clothing.
A further division of labor occurred when simple trading began.
Some individuals and groups began to exchange crude tools, food
products, skins, and other items common to their culture.   This was
the simple beginning of commercial specialization.   A rapid expansion of this development took place when special skills appeared and
when regional specialization reflected the uneven distribution of
natural resources.

The limitations of this stage are apparent.   The evident lack of
man's control over his environment made his existence perilous.
The absence of economic security in any economy must carry with
it a corresponding dearth of social stability.

Nomadic Economy

The ushering in of this stage was attended by a marked increase
in security.   Chief characteristics were the cultivation of the soil,
domestication of food animals, and more extensive use of the metals.

The difference between any economic stage is largely a matter of
degree, and that point is well illustrated in comparing this economy
with the preceding one.   Man as a barbarian or nomad still did not
have a settled existence.   His knowledge of his world was too inadequate to permit him to supply all of his material wants while living

[30] *Op. cit.*, p. 396.

[31] According to the classification of Lewis H. Morgan in *Ancient Society*
this stage in cultural evolution is that of savagery.

in one spot. The truly significant aspect of this stage was to be found in man's cultivation of the soil. A settled existence now came within the range of actuality. While man continued to move about, his domestication of animals and simple agriculture made him a true economic producer rather than a mere collector.

Economic wealth or capital thus became possible on a rather considerable scale for the first time. Savings now emerged as an economic phenomenon. Rather than merely accumulating berries and roots against a period of possible starvation, man began to consume less than he produced in order that the resulting stock might further production for the future. Producers' goods thereby came into existence and a further division of labor developed. This factor is at the very foundation of modern economic systems.

Village Economy

This stage is best illustrated by a description of the manorial system in England following the Norman invasion in the eleventh century. By this time man in Europe for many centuries had written records, he practiced a more advanced type of agriculture, and he had developed a more or less settled government.

Village life in the Middle Ages was organized under the manorial system. The manor or vill was the estate of a lord occupied by dependent cultivators. Custom determined largely the nature of the relationship between the lord of the manor and his peasants. Usually about half of the manorial lands were farmed by the villagers, while the rest was cultivated directly by the lord for the needs of himself and his household.

The manorial village itself consisted of the crude cottages of those who tended the fields, the village church, the home of a few specialists, such as the priest, the miller, the brewer, and the blacksmith, and finally, the manor house. This latter was the residence of the lord and his retinue. Sometimes the lord, who might be either a nobleman, an ecclesiastic, or the king, owned several manors. In such a case the absent lord had a representative, known as a bailiff, who served as general manager.

There were frequently five distinct economic classes on the manor. Mention has been made of the first class, the lord or princely class. This of course was a very small proportion of the population. The second class was the freeman. He was legally free from most of the feudal obligations due to the lord. The freeman usually paid a fixed rental in money and kind for his right to cultivate land. In addition he performed some labor at irregular intervals on the lord's own lands. This was known as "boon work," but the amount of it was less than for the general class of serfs. It should be noted that the rental paid by the freeman to his lord was regarded as payment not so much for the use of property as for the "protection" of the lord. In turn the lord rendered feudal payments to the crown. Thus a complicated organization of obligations bound by custom held the system together.

The third class was the villein. He customarily tilled about thirty acres of land, while the freeman usually held a larger amount. Both in an economic and a legal sense the villein was inferior to the freeman, although he was not a slave. He was, however, tied to the soil, and could not leave the manor without the lord's permission. The real mark of the villein status was his "week work," which consisted of several days' work from each week that was required on the lord's land. In addition the villein was compelled to give "boon work." The freedom of the villein was further restricted by a list of fines, fees, and other penalties. Marriage of the villein's children, visits to other manors, trespassing, and the like were all subject to close regulation. The villeins constituted the largest and most important class on the manor.

A fourth class included the cottars or bordars. A member of this class was very similar in his general status to that of the villein. The class was recruited from the slaves and from the younger sons of villeins. Since the land holdings of the cottars were usually not more than five acres their status was below that of the villein. In effect this class constituted a sort of reserve labor supply, and it has thus been referred to as the emergence of a wage-earning class.[32]

A small class of slaves constituted the fifth group. They were regarded as the property of the lord, and they were probably used only in his household.

The basic occupation of the three largest groups, the freemen, the villeins, and the cottars, was agricultural labor. Their system of farming was unlike anything in the Western world. The arable land was usually divided into three great open fields, one was planted with wheat or some other winter-sown crop, a second with barley, rye, oats, or beans, and a third was "rested" in an effort to recoup its vitality. The second year the fallow or "rested" field would be planted and one of the other two fields remained idle. For

[32] D. W. Roberts, *An Outline of the Economic History of England*, London: Longmans, Green, and Co., 1933, p. 9.

the third year a further rotation took place, and thus each field had one year of rest in every three. This was known as the "three field system."

A further characteristic in manorial agriculture must be noted. Each one of the fields under cultivation was divided into more or less regular strips, and each strip was usually about forty rods long and four rods wide. These measurements, of course, were very rough, although each strip contained about one acre of land. A villein's thirty acres or strips usually would be divided equally among the three great fields; furthermore the ten strips in each field would be in ten widely scattered places. The partitioning of the land into a multitude of strips, which from a bird's eye view took on the appearance of a patch-work quilt,[33] carried with it a rough equality. Each villein thus had his share of both the good and bad land. Of course the time wasted in moving from one strip to another made for great inefficiency.

The absence of any extensive trading made the medieval manor a comparatively self-sufficient economic unit. The inhabitants of each manor baked their own bread from their own wheat, brewed beer from their own grain, made their own clothing from locally raised flax and wool, and developed their own tools. With the exception of a few commodities, such as salt, tar, and iron, they lived a life quite independent of the rest of the world.

Compared to modern standards this was a highly inefficient system. However, it must be said that not only was human existence possible, but actually the manorial system offered security and stability over any period previously known.

Town Economy

Just as agriculture is identified with the medieval village, the rise of industry and the growth of trade is associated with the town. But before a brief description is given of town economy, it is necessary to point to a few outstanding factors that contributed to the decline of the manorial system.

One of the defects of life on the manor was that no opportunity was given for initiative or enterprise. One's occupation and status were determined by heredity and custom. No opportunity existed on the manor for the villein or cottar who wanted "to get ahead," to improve his lot. Consequently it was inevitable that ambitious

---

[33] See the maps of medieval fields in V. G. Simkhovitch, *Toward the Understanding of Jesus*, Macmillan, 1925, p. 164.

serfs began to violate the tradition that no serf could leave the manor. In the fourteenth century many villeins and cottars in England moved into the towns and cities.

In addition, many lords who found that compulsory work by serfs was both poorly done and reluctantly given entered into contracts with their serfs on a money rent basis. This shift from the customary arrangement to a rental basis resembling our landlord-tenant system was known as commutation.

Also in the late thirteenth and early fourteenth centuries it became desirable both for lords and customary tenants to enclose the more fertile portions of waste lands and to consolidate the strips of land. This practice tended to disturb and destroy the old order.

A final important factor affected both village and town. Between 1349 and 1351 a terrible plague known as the Black Death killed probably between a third and a half of the entire population. The effect on the supply of labor may well be imagined. Land lay idle, crops rotted in the field, food became scarce, and prices rose. Thus laborers tended to find themselves in a favored position. Villeins demanded commutation, and others left the manor for the high wages of the towns.

The chief function of medieval towns was their service as centers of trade. Medieval trading, unlike nineteenth century individualism, was carried on as a monopoly. Thus all trading privileges were supervised and controlled by an organization known as the merchant gild. Any individual who was engaged in buying or selling, wholesale or retail, paid his entrance fees and dues to the gild for this trading privilege. Non-members were fined if they attempted trading activities, and strangers were given trade permission on payment of a fee. The gild not only served as a regulator of the monopoly on trade, but it had a social function as well. Gild members were paid sickness and unemployment benefits, widows and orphans of members were given assistance, and other services were rendered. This organization, the gild, first developed in England at the close of the eleventh century and lasted well into the fourteenth century.

As the towns grew in size and trading expanded normally, the membership of the merchant gilds also increased. Finally this growth reached a point where the management of the organization became difficult. Individual craft members such as the tanners, the fish merchants, the shoemakers, and the bakers, realized that while they had little in common with other trades they did have many interests of their own to protect. Thus each craft formed its own organization, and these new associations were called craft gilds. They were very similar to the old merchant gilds, but were more specialized. Again a complete monopoly of the trade or craft was attempted and enforced. Rules for regulating each craft were laid down, standards of workmanship were set, and new members were trained in the trade. Levels of training for apprentice, journeyman, and master, were developed. Furthermore, prices were fixed, and most forms of competition between members severely regulated. The craft gilds provided a closely supervised framework within which a virtually complete monopoly operated.

In truth it must be said that the craft gilds of the fifteenth and sixteenth centuries gave a certain degree of security and protection to their members. They provided a minimum standard of quality, at least, for the consumer. Judged from modern standards, the regulations were stifling to the most efficient producers because no reward was given to greatest excellence. The standards tended to be set at the level of the least efficient.

National Economy

As the centuries passed in Europe trade continued to expand, first spreading out locally until it covered each principality and state, and then passing in many instances beyond national borders. This development of trading is roughly comparable to the spread of railroads in the United States, although the latter covered a much shorter time. The railroad network reached out usually into those states where the greatest trading possibilities existed. This is not to say that no trade existed before the railroads came. On the contrary, rudimentary trading was to be found before the time of railways in the same manner that considerable international trade was carried on in Europe by such organizations as the Hanse League and Merchant Staplers even before a national economy was well developed.

But before the development of the factory system was well under way, a preliminary or intermediate stage must be noted. This was known as the Domestic System. In this stage of industrial development fabrication of the product or manufacturing still took place at the workman's own home. Capital that had naturally accumulated in trade now found it profitable to shift to industry—to the control of manufacturing operations. In other words, many traders began to serve as middlemen, first, in supplying raw materials to the workers, and second, in taking the finished product, such as cloth, for sale to the consumer. In some cases the merchant begun to buy the looms and other tools used by the craftsman. In any case there was a loss of control over the process of manufacturing and sale of goods that had previously rested with the craftsman. The worker was no longer independent, and the groundwork was being set for the factory system.

While part of the foundation of the factory system in England was laid in the manner just described, several other factors contributed their part. One item was the appearance of several ideas and inventions that made possible the widening of the scope of the known world at that time. The tentative acceptance of the idea that the world was not flat, the invention of the telescope, the mariner's compass, and the astrolabe, were in this category. With the attending development of a new and wider basis of trade, with a new and abundant supply of raw materials, added reason existed for expanding a system in which the process of production should be enlarged to meet new needs.

It is clear that the growth of strong nations into more or less compact economic and political units during the sixteenth and seventeenth centuries is attendant upon the expansion of industry, the widening of the market, and the increasing power of wealthy merchants and manufacturers. The social gain in terms of increased production was tremendous, although this was accompanied by a certain loss of control of production by the craftsmen. The latter no longer worked for themselves.

Nationalism in its flower is well represented by what has frequently been called "The Mercantile System" of the sixteenth and seventeenth centuries. It is something of a misnomer to use the term "system" in this connection. Mercantilism was really a philosophy, an attitude toward the business and political affairs of the day. Typically a mercantilist was a businessman, trader, or politician of that time who believed in bending most economic efforts toward the building of a strong nation. To that end they frequently urged that their country be an exporting nation, sending abroad valuable finshed goods in exchange for raw materials, and thus build up a "favorable balance of trade." This so-called "favorable balance" was usually reckoned in terms of a bountiful supply of gold and silver. They reasoned that the strong nation was one with the greatest control over the precious metals. On the side it may be pointed out that this policy is in some contrast to contemporary monetary policies in the United States with the present effort to "sterilize" gold.

Without attempting an evaluation, it may be said that mercantile policy, with its emphasis on gold, tended to raise prices at home. Higher prices and increased profits were a powerful stimulant to industry and a search abroad for markets. This in turn gradually led to the development of colonies and—so far as the English were concerned—British Imperialism.

World Economy

It is a comparatively short step from economic nationalism to a world economy. It should be clear by implication that the national economy of the eighteenth century carried with it the very roots out of which the modern interdependent economic world has grown. Mercantilism's demand for colonial possessions led to the rise of the great overseas empires of Great Britain, France, Germany, and earlier, Holland and Spain. After the preliminary period of conquest was over, it was found that no country had a monopoly on raw materials. Even powerful countries like the United States and Russia, rich though they were in natural resources, found that their prosperity was inseparably tied to the economic life of other nations. Not only were the United States and other large nations dependent on other areas of the world for certain raw materials, but the interdependence of markets precluded economic isolation on a national scale.

This last generalization may be illustrated in the following manner. The United States does not have enough raw tin and rubber for its needs. The problem is not solved merely by shipping those products into the United States. Tin mine owners and rubber growers must be compensated for their products, and the only way in which that can be done over any considerable time is for certain consumers abroad to accept our goods and services in exchange. Trade, thus, is always a two-way proposition. Unfortunately the public has in too many instances looked at only one side of the exchange.

Coincident with the rise of trading in England, the greatly expanding market, and the growth of empire in the eighteenth century was the application of mechanical ingenuity to improving the productive process. In the middle of that century scores of important inventions were devised. So significant is that brief period that it is frequently referred to as the "age of invention." Many of the inventions were applied to the textiles, as Kay's flying shuttle and Hargreaves' spinning machine. Others related to steam power machinery, to transportation, and to fabrication of metals.

Equally significant in mid-eighteenth century were certain changes taking place in the organization of industrial production. This is popularly referred to as the rise of the factory system. This system was made possible by the great inventions previously mentioned. It displaced in its turn the domestic system that had succeeded that stage in which the craftsman dealt directly with the consumer. Now in the factory system the workman no longer carried on his trade in the home, but he was a completely dependent worker who relied entirely on his employer for the means of his livelihood.

Furthermore, the machines that he worked—ever growing in complexity and cost—were housed in a separate building to which he must go for employment. The conditions under which he worked were now no longer a matter over which he had control, as had been the case in the home industries. Filth, inadequate light and fresh air, long hours, and child labor, in early factory employment were the rule. Literary figures of that day were quick to call attention to the social responsibility, but decades passed before factory acts were effective.[34]

With the factory system was created a new social and economic class of wealthy employers, great industrialists, the so-called ''captains of industry.'' Heretofore the merchant had been the dominant figure in the seventeenth century order. Now the business man was ''coming into his own'' for the first time. He was a specialist in organizing the factories, financing the enterprises, and collecting and training great numbers of workers. It should be emphasized, too, that the business man was drawn from among the most enterprising individuals of all social classes. In this respect the old order based on heredity and custom had passed.

The factory system heralded modern industrialism into the world. The effect was almost without parallel in the world's social history. Every form of human activity underwent change as a result of the factory. The large-scale production of wealth now lowered costs to a point where standards of living could be raised to new levels. A material life was now possible beyond anything pre-

[34] See Thomas Hood's ''The Song of the Shirt'' and Elizabeth Barrett Browning's, ''The Bitter Cry of the Children'' in *Poems of Justice*, ed. by T. C. Clark, New York: Willett, Clark and Colby, 1929.

viously known in man's entire history. While this economic revolution—and the factory system probably warrants that term—carried with it many problems that have not yet been solved, it may be said that the social gain through a higher living standard is truly tremendous.

CHARACTERISTICS OF MODERN ECONOMY

Transition from a Simpler Stage

It should be understood through tracing the different stages of economic development that each succeeding stage is based upon that which has gone before. Furthermore, each stage tends to set up conditions out of which social change occurs. Thus our economy of the second quarter of the twentieth century has its tap-roots in the economic conditions of the nineteenth century. It is well to describe those conditions.

Individualism and the Free-Pricing Economy

The rise of the factory system, creating as it did a dependent labor class, also brought into being the highly independent business man. This latter class found itself in conflict, at least in eighteenth century England, with the remnants of a feudal system based on custom and with some of the ideas of the merchantilists.

It will be remembered that the craft gilds were complete monopolies of trading and production. No goods could be made or sold without sanction of the gild. Prices were regulated and standards were set usually on levels that allowed relatively inefficient producers to work. Such regulations that gave no freedom to initiative were repugnant to the enterpriser or business man, but these restrictions did not disappear until some time after the factory system developed. Furthermore, the mercantilists in their (sometimes misguided) effort to build a strong nation frequently urged their countries to forbid importation of certain commodities and to offer bounties for the importation of still other products.

To all of this interference by the state with the natural flow of trade and development of industry, the business man of the late eighteenth century objected strongly. Adam Smith, writing in his *Wealth of Nations* in 1776, gave classic utterance to this point of view. He demanded that the state "keep its dead hand off industry." At that time the voice of Adam Smith was quite representative of the business man of his day. Thus by the late eighteenth century, *laissez faire,* or non-interference by the state, was the prevailing policy. However, it must not be thought that the struggle for economic freedom from interference and regulation was easily or quickly won. Cultural lag was in evidence. Even after widespread violations of restrictions on importation were in evidence, many forces operated to prevent an honest facing of the issue. It is of historic interest only to note that one of the questions asked of Wesley Methodists was whether they engaged in smuggling.

Not only did Adam Smith and his followers lash out against restrictions on freedom and initiative of their day, but they were quick to point out that if man is allowed to follow his own selfish ends he will thereby contribute to society. That is, man as he competes with others to provide for his material needs will provide socially useful goods and services. Competition, then, serves as a regulator that eliminates the unfit and at the same time rewards and encourages the fit.

Further, Smith indicated that in the absence of artificial price-fixing devices, commodities would be produced in the quantities required. If a shortage in shoes developed, other things being equal, the price of shoes would rise. Enterprisers watching this increase in price with its possibility of profit would turn from less remunerative production to the fabrication of shoes. Conversely an over-production of shoes would lead to a drop in prices and a consequent fall in production. Individualism and competition were thus closely allied to a free-pricing economy.

Nineteenth Century Capitalism

The term capitalism is subject to many interpretations. It may be defined so loosely that it would include any society in which capital, the accumulated wealth of past effort, is used. Rather obviously such a definition could be applied to virtually every stage of economic history. Usually capitalism refers to that type of free-pricing economy in which production is carried on by private capital.

Certain rather distinctive factors were present in the capitalistic structure of the United States during the last century. These are in addition to the English heritage of individualism, competition, and a free-pricing economy. Probably the first point to be noted was the great profusion and variety of natural resources. Vast quantities of most of the metals and coal, rich timber lands, the world's best agricultural lands, and almost unlimited water power resources were found across the country. If raw materials were a requisite to an industrial society, the country's future was assured.

A second factor was the relative scarcity of labor. The frontier in this country disappeared about the close of the nineteenth century. But so long as free and cheap land was available, labor was constantly drained from the industrial labor market. This factor tended to hold wages up in comparison to the price of other commodities.

The next factor was the relative scarcity of capital in this country. The manifestation of this fact is apparent when one reflects upon the amount of foreign investment in the railroads, for example, by British capital. Industries of all sorts were partially owned at least by investors abroad.

A fourth factor was the rapid technical developments that took place. The spread of the railroad net from 1850 to the 1880's is only one illustration.

While the English contribution of individualism has already been discussed, it must be remarked that at no time has it been better exemplified than during the first three quarters of the nineteenth century. It was during this period of unrestrained competition that the great fortunes of Carnegie, Gould, Harriman, and Rockefeller were made.

The reaction to ungoverned competition started during the 1870's in the transportation field. It was inevitable that the practice of many railroads in charging exhorbitant rates and in discriminating between customers should draw protests. The loud cry of the agricultural interests led to the so-called Granger Acts, and finally to the Interstate Commerce Act of 1887. Similarly attempts were made to regulate "combinations in restraint of trade" by the Sherman Anti-Trust Act of 1890.

In common with other producer groups labor began seriously to organize in the later part of the century. First attempts through the old Knights of Labor aroused great interest but did not endure. The American Federation of Labor, beginning in 1886, adequately met the needs of that period for an organization through which labor's voice might be heard.

Twentieth Century Capitalism

The capitalistic structure of this century differs from that of the previous century to a considerable extent in degree. While technical advances were well known in the previous century, they did not approach their wide application until the twentieth century. For one thing, the modern conveyor-belt and assembly line technique so successfully applied to the automobile industry was virtually unknown before 1910.[35]

A further difference in degree between the two centuries may be noted in the size of business corporations. The first billion dollar corporation was not developed until the end of the last century.

On other points there is an even sharper contrast between the two centuries. This century has not been characterized by a scarcity of labor. On the contrary there has been noted for many successive years an unemployed labor force varying from one or two million able-bodied men to probably fifteen millions.

In a similar fashion no scarcity of capital is noted. Instead of being heavily dependent on other countries for our capital needs, as was the case in the nineteenth century, this country now in due turn has been supplying the needs of the world. This century saw the United States become a creditor instead of a debtor nation. The implications of this factor are too involved to be discussed here, but, for one thing, it includes a complete readjustment of the United States' position in world trade.

Along with the increase in savings and the growth of capital has been the development of more complicated organizations through which direction and control of capital is exercised. So powerful have been the banks and other financial institutions in this century that some writers refer to their dominance in this period as "finance capitalism," as distinct from industrial capitalism.[36]

Certain significant strides were made by labor that merit attention. The labor movement in the United States really did not get under way until the latter half of the last century. But little progress was made in the legal recognition of labor's rights until the present century. Almost overnight a change took place of considerable importance. With the passage of the Wagner Act of 1935, company unions were discouraged, and the right of labor to select its own representatives and bargain collectively was made the guiding principle. The machinery for safeguarding this rule was the new National Labor Relations Board. The fundamental significance of new trends in labor's position is not to be found in any single

[35] An interesting account of the consequences of labor-saving devices in a particular industry may be seen in *Changes in Technology and Labor Requirements in Corn Crop Production*, WPA National Research Project, Washington, D. C., 1938, and similar studies.

[36] Cf. H. E. Barnes, *Society in Transition*, New York: Prentice-Hall Co., 1939, pp. 163–176.

piece of federal legislation, however. Probably one of the most important trends has been the development of what might be called a property interest in the job. The right of employers to hire and fire has definitely been limited in recent years and is only one expression of this principle.

Recent Aspects of Social and Economic Control

There is little doubt that there is a definite trend in very recent years toward a controlled economy in this country. Whether or not business and labor leaders and the consumers desire this change, centralization of economic control and central planning is becoming the rule in our economy.

The prolonged and severe depression of the 1930's brought about considerable experimentation. One of the remedies attempted was the passage in 1933 of the National Industrial Recovery Act. This measure contemplated the elimination of wastes and the more efficient organization of production and distribution through a system of national economic planning. While it was declared unconstitutional by the United States Supreme Court in 1935, it did widen and deepen the groove which has been followed since the date of its passage.

With the development of trade associations through which employers were able to organize effectively, with the great growth in size of industrial and financial corporate structure,[37] together with the so-called New Deal legislation, no great industry could be said to be free from regulation. One of the great strongholds of individualism and free-pricing has always been agriculture. But the Agricultural Adjustment Act of 1933, with its national planning of production, contemplated a complete readjustment of the pricing structure of both industry and agriculture. Secretary of Agriculture Wallace had said that the measure was temporary, though necessary to protect the highly individualistic farmer who was buying in a controlled and planned industrial market. But today even the farmer ceases to look upon the national farm program as being temporary.

The passage of the Social Security Act in 1935 was another step toward a controlled economy. The aged, the handicapped, and chil-

[37] Little publicity has been given to the federal government's study of the concentration of economic power in the United States. Over thirty volumes of hearings have been published by the Temporary National Economic Committee of the Seventy-Sixth Congress during 1940–41.

dren, together with others who may be victims of circumstance, are guaranteed a minimum of care and protection.

The growth of governmental control has been rapid. So fast has it extended that it is doubtful if even the responsible boards and commissions realize the inherent force of their new strength. Certainly the implications are not fully understood. Even the Federal Reserve Board, one of the older centralized control groups, has only in recent years realized the tremendous potentialities in the regulation of the rediscount rate and the purchase and sale of securities in the open market. The development of powerful institutions through which economic control is exercised carries no automatic guarantee that a particular policy will be adopted with wisdom. It remains to be seen whether we have that wisdom. But at one point there is certainty, the twentieth century marks the rise of controlled economies not contemplated by nineteenth century capitalism.

SELECTED REFERENCES

Louis M. Hacker, *Triumph of American Capitalism*, Simon & Schuster, 1940.—This volume is a readable, scholarly account of American economic development.

M. J. Herskovits, *The Economic Life of Primitive Peoples*, Knopf, 1940.—An interesting book that well summarizes our knowledge concerning primitive economic life.

E. A. J. Johnson, *An Economic History of Modern England*, Nelson, 1940.—An exceedingly brief but well-executed sketch of English economic history.

A. W. Jones, *Life, Liberty, and Property*, Lippincott, 1941.—This unusual sociological treatment attempts to investigate the attitudes of different classes toward various situations involving property.

E. C. Kirkland, *History of American Economic Life*, Crofts, 1939.—A better than ordinary study of the material growth of this country.

Carl Snyder, *Capitalism the Creator*, Macmillan, 1940.—An able writer here defends capitalism against its critics.

A. J. Toynbee, *A Study of History*, Six Volumes, Oxford, 1940.—A truly monumental study is here included with the hope that a few students will desire a more extended treatment of historical processes.

National Resources Committee, *The Structure of the American Economy*, Two Volumes, U. S. Government Printing Office, 1939, 1940.—These two volumes are an able survey and analysis of the major aspects of our national economy. Volume two gives special attention to the planned use of American resources.

Students can derive great benefit through reading samples from some of the Congressional hearings. Special attention is called to Hearings before the Temporary National Economic Committee: Investigation of Concentration of Economic Power, 1940, 1941, and also Hearings and Reports on Violations of Free Speech and Rights of Labor, 1939–1941.

CHAPTER 20

ORGANIZATION FOR GOVERNMENT

By ELMER PENDELL, PH.D.
Pennsylvania State College

GOVERNMENT IS POWER

Organization for government means, centrally, organization for control. The most distinctive feature of government is force. Government, whether a local unit or a larger unit, is supreme among the institutions in its implementation for compulsion. The word "sovereignty," often used to distinguish government, means, essentially, *power*.[1] The fog of mysticism that usually surrounds the term *sovereignty* seems to result from the fact that the effectiveness of government grows out of the *popular belief* that power exists, rather than directly out of the power. In other words, the effectiveness of government in the control of social behavior depends on an item which is one step removed from the essence of sovereignty, which essence is power.

The State Is a Unit of Power

Power supreme; power above which no other is recognized, applicable over a given area and over the persons in that area—such is the distinctiveness of a State. Other associations besides states have force. Unions can and do put pressure on their members and on employers. Industrial corporations have the power of the purse over employees. Racketeers exercise power over their members and over their victims. Churches exercise a moral force, a force of opinion of associated members. The difference between their power and that of the state is a difference of scope and supremacy.

And what about county government and city government? Those possess derived power, delegated power, subservient, subordinate power, at least as a rule, though sometimes the servant dominates the master: Illinois seems not to have much directioning influence on Chicago; there is evidence that Reno runs Nevada.

[1] See Harold J. Laski, *A Grammar of Politics*, Yale Univ. Press, 1925, p. 45.

Implementation of Power

Laws set the patterns for behavior, sometimes crystallizing practices which a majority already follow, often establishing a rule
which carries a trend somewhat farther than before; rarely they
reverse a trend.   Laws are of two major categories, criminal and
civil.   Criminal laws define what shall be regarded as offenses
against the state; civil laws set forth what shall be regarded as
offenses against one's fellowmen.   Civil laws are in part statutory,
that is, enacted by a legislature, and in part they are judge-made.
In England and the United States a somewhat larger emphasis is
placed on case law, meaning law formulated by judges to fit a particular previous case, than in France, for example, where more
weight is put on the statutory codes.   Even in France, however,
judges, in their interpretation and applications of statutes, are
making law.

The statutes, both criminal and civil, where representative government prevails, are made by a legislature, sometimes so labeled,
sometimes called a congress or a parliament, or a city council.
Where representative government does not exist, then the possessor
of power arranges for the formulation of the statutes.

Administration, the work of putting the laws into effect, is carried on almost entirely by *bureaus*.   "The Administration," so-
called, has little to do with administration except to keep the bureaus
manned; and to the extent that there is a use of a civil service merit
system, even keeping the bureaus manned falls outside the scope of
The Administration's work.   A "bureau," in the broad sense, may
be a "department" or an "office" or a "commission" or a "committee" or even a "bureau"—any staff of people doing government
work.

Often the laws are complicated, their workings somewhat obscure to the legislature.   Representatives of a bureau make recommendations for changes in the laws which they are administering.
On approval of a compliant committee of the legislature, the legislature itself passes the amending laws mechanically.   This process
is what gives rise to the concept of "bureaucracy," the determination of the policies of a government by its bureaus.   Often the
bureaucrats become ambitious, with a wish to extend the scope of
their influence.   Mr. McNutt is widely supposed to have prompted
the 1940 extensions of the Social Security Act.   If he had done so,
we would have had an illustration of bureaucracy.   As a matter of

fact, bureau heads and bureau underlings in bureaus under McNutt had been planning the extension for at least three years before McNutt was appointed to his job. We still have our illustration of bureaucracy.

The building up of personnel is a frequent device by which a bureau chief or sub-chief attempts to improve his own status. If he is boss over forty men and women, he will seem more important and can reasonably ask for more salary than if he is boss of ten. By one pretext after another he adds to his personnel.

The existence of some degree of policy making by bureaus, and the building up of bureau staffs, are little asides intended to give a realistic view of bureaus. Importantly, for a grasp of government organizations, the laws are administered by bureaus.

What, then, is the work of the so-called administration: the president of the United States, the governor of a state, the Canadian premier, the prime minister of England? For each of these, policy determination has come to be his chief work. Where new legislation is necessary for facilitating his decisions, he has the legislation formulated. He is, in plain language, a *manager*. He gets his power to manage, not from any constitution but from the use of patronage, and from the gradually developed expectation of the citizenry. In the United States we may test the expectation of the public in the fact that those presidents who have interpreted their job as that of manager have been accounted "strong" and have usually been re-elected; those who have thought they were to administer the laws but not to participate in the formulation of the laws have been considered weak presidents.

Courts, in determining the directions in which power is to be applied under the laws, constitute an important phase of organization for government. They do not themselves have power, but because they are backed by power they do much to set the patterns of social behavior.

Other than laws, legislatures, bureaus, manager, and courts, as instruments of government, are armies, policemen, sheriffs, detectives, juries, state's attorneys, sergeants at arms, jails, jailors, prisons, wardens, prison guards.

A State of the United States Compared with the National State

Each state, as well as the National Government, conforms to our definition of a state; each is a unit of power above which no other is recognized, applicable over a given area and over the people in that area. There is an overlapping of territory between the National Government and the governments of the smaller states, to be sure; but there has been a sorting and separation of the fields in which power is applicable. Each state in its sphere is supreme. Through interpretation, the sphere left to each of the forty-eight states has become steadily smaller; nevertheless, in its remaining scope a state of the United States is supreme; no higher power is recognized.

AN INDIVIDUAL IS BORN INTO A STATE

A state is an institution which has an association as its body, its immaterial aspect being a set of attitudes. The attitudes are those of the functionaries, and those of the general citizenry. For the functionaries, that is to say, the employees who make the state a working organization, their attitudes are expectation of a pay check, habit of going to work at a given time and place, realization of favors or the lack of them by those higher up, if any are higher up, knowledge of election day and that their security of position may be or will not be affected thereby. These attitudes, and the psychological leanings the functionaries bear toward their routine of duties, help to make up the state. The general citizenry constitute the state, in part, by its feeling of favorable emotion during a patriotic parade, by the ''consciousness of kind'' of one citizen in his relations with others, by pride in the accomplishments of other citizens, by the thought that the state is a protector of ways of living to which one has grown accustomed, by loyalty to other persons who have shared one's experiences, and by respect for the government's power.

As soon as an individual is born, the pre-existing attitudes of his parents and others with whom he is associated begin to take shape in his own thoughts. He becomes conditioned to their ways of thinking; their ways become his ways. He has a favorable leaning toward the political party, the lodges, the church, of which his parents are members, and his feeling toward the state grows out of their feelings. If his associates hold conflicting views, he finds it necessary to search for the views that conform with greatest consistency with his previous attitude pattern. In this matter the state is like the other institutions. The idea that government exists as a result of a social contract between the citizens and the functionaries must yield to the greater realism that the state is an institution into which one is born, to which he is gradually fitted, and which, as a consequence of his conditioning, he comes to support.

KINDS OF GOVERNMENT

"That this government of the people, by the people, and for the people shall not perish from the earth," said Lincoln. The important preposition in that trinity of phrases is *by*. It, and it only, implies **representative government,** government which is popularly described as "democratic." Representative government requires that the general citizenry have frequent opportunity to select the persons who are to represent them. The representative is responsible to those who will have an opportunity to vote for him or for some other of their choice at a subsequent election. Responsibility in government implies that if one's expressions as a representative do not represent the electorate with sufficient accuracy there will be termination of the trust.

In the National Government of the United States, a citizen may be represented by a "representative," by a "senator," and by a "president." The citizen has a chance to pass judgment on his representative at the end of a two-year period, on his senator at the end of a six-year period, on his president at the end of a four-year period.

In England the members of only one house of parliament are elected. The election is for five years, but if the majority of the members of the house of commons disagree with the prime minister on an important issue he is expected to declare a general election by which his policy is tested as to its popularity. To vote against the man who voted against the prime minister's measure is to support the prime minister. The representative status of a member of parliament is often more frequently tested under such a system than is representation in the United States. However, bills rarely come up for action except as they are initiated and sponsored by the cabinet, so there is really more centralized management, less possible initiative on the part of the citizens or their representatives than in the United States.

An **oligarchy,** government by a few, is not always distinguishable from representative government. The problem is likely to be, what is the extent of the suffrage, the right to vote? In the United States we exclude that large group of persons who have not yet reached their 21st birthday. Before 1920, in most states women were excluded.   Before 1870, negroes were not permitted to vote, and most of them are still excluded.   A century ago in many states persons not possessed of real estate were not allowed to vote.   Probably we are safe in saying that, considering all these limitations, in 1800 the United States was governed by an oligarchy.

Farthest from representative government is *one man control.* It appears that more people have lived under that form of government than under any other.   The pattern fits the orientals under Genghis Khan, fits the ancient Assyrians and Egyptians, the Greeks of the days of Pericles, the Romans under and after Julius Caesar, most Europeans in the late Middle Ages, the Russians under the Tsars, and now again most of Europeans under the dictators.   And these are just examples.

Sometimes there are combinations of the basic types.   A limited monarchy combines representative government with one man control, the power being in some cases predominantly with the king, in other cases mostly with the representatives of the people or of some of them.

Limitations on monarchy have sometimes evolved because of difficulties of the monarch in collecting revenues.   To get the money has been easier if those who paid it were given a veto power on the spending.

One man control in recent times seems to evolve from representative government in similar series of steps: (1) the domination of a political party by a single man; (2) party purges by which that domination becomes an internal party dictatorship; (3) violence, or purchase of votes in a general election, or use of the patronage power in winning the election, or a combination of these forms of corruption; (4) licensing of industry, thereby, by giving to an official the right to refuse a license, centralizing control; (5) less emphasis on rules and an increase of personal judgment of a government man in the application of law.

RELATIONS OF GOVERNMENT TO LIFE

Any government involves control over citizens.   Jefferson's view was that that government is best which governs least, thereby leaving the largest possible proportion of decisions to individuals, and subjecting them to the least amount of compulsion.   The times in which he lived were relatively simple.   There still are many who are in agreement with Jefferson's generalization who nevertheless see, in the greater complexity of denser populations, a need for much more government participation in the affairs of the people than earlier conditions required. They consider that that government is best which governs as little as is possible in the maintenance of working adjustments for the most important problems. Other persons for various reasons wish to expand the scope of government.

In a simple relationship, government defines crime, attempts crime prevention, referees private disagreements, deals with foreign affairs, maintains a simple money system, perhaps maintains a small army and navy. A peaceful citizen has little to do with his government except to pay a small tax, and perhaps to vote.

In contrast with a simple situation, initiation of a postal system involves some complication but not much. The fees meet the costs, or almost meet them, and the service is considered by most people a benefit. A school system, if under the same state, may add much to controversy. Public road building, or railroad building, and upkeep, increase the danger of graft.

As the population grows denser and specialization of occupations is carried further, the tasks of government management and the dangers of corruption increase rapidly. Economic activities of private persons require regulation. Banking carries much power over lives, even over those without bank accounts, through inflationary credit or contraction of credit. Regulation or government operation may develop. Overhead costs in machine production lead to limitation of consumers' choices, lead to costs low in comparison with prices, lead to concentration of income, and thereby to unemployment. The state is called on for help, and then the government becomes the "givermint." Whenever individuals in large numbers find the forces about them adverse, find themselves slipping, they are likely to call on their state or national state for help. If the state complies, it thereupon exercises more power, controls lives more fully.

Also, as population expands, land and other geologic resources, becoming relatively scarcer, come into focus as social wealth; conservation is called for; government becomes the agency for conservation, custodian in behalf of future generations. Thus, in various directions, governmental activities become more numerous and more complex. Individuals have their goings and their comings more largely ordered by the state.

Has the increased reliance of individuals on their state any bearing on dictatorship?

Connection between Socialism and One Man Control

As government activities multiply, the overlapping and the inconsistencies of measures which have been instituted by men at cross purposes with each other, become more glaring. Is dictatorship in the making? That seems to depend on (1) the degree of complexity of the problems, (2) the degree of intelligence of the electorate, (3) the amount of education of the electorate, and (4) the machinery for the application of the intelligence and the education to the problems of government.

Representative government can survive without much intelligence or education if the problems are simple. But if the problems are complicated a greater facility in solving them is necessary to the survival of representative government. Is it not enough that the representatives as distinguished from their constituency have the facility in solving the problems? The assumption to this effect is that the electorate needs to know only when it hurts. But a voter must know when a problem is solved reasonably well, else he will continue to be dissatisfied, and will throw out the official who has done a reasonable job, in favor of someone who promises more. Or he will retain an incompetent official and give him more power on his complaint that the reason for his failure is his lack of power.

Definitely on the side of government-by-the-people, and indispensable to it if problems are difficult, is intelligence among the masses. If and when intelligence is inadequate, and "the masses," by something other than typographical error become "them asses," democracy is in danger. Intelligence is a requisite to democracy for the solution of problems of government, not in a fixed measure but in ratio with the complexity of the problems. As the state takes on more and more activities, in other words becomes more socialistic, unless there is a high degree of intelligence and education on the part of the public, there is an increasing probability of dictatorship merely because bureaus will overlap in their supposed authorization if not in their actual authorization. They will make conflicting judgments, will duplicate each other's work in part and leave some work undone. Either widespread intelligence or centralization of control may avoid these results—but if the intelligence is lacking the centralization is to be expected.

Relation of Dictatorship to Freedoms

A dictator inevitably suppresses freedoms. With the coming of a dictatorship, freedom of speech, of press, of radio, of teaching—

individuality—must go, no matter how benevolent the dictator may be. The reason is that except as the thought processes themselves are controlled, the majority of the people are sure to differ with the dictator on many of his decisions. Multiple objectives would make that true, and multiple objectives there would be, except as the purposes of men are made to spring from a single mind. The dictator must, then, in order to remain a dictator, control the purposes of men. Propaganda and suppression of freedoms become routine.

PECULIARITIES OF GOVERNMENT IN THE UNITED STATES

Two Sets of Power

Each person living in the United States is subject to two states, one of them Wyoming, or the comparable state of the United States, the other the National State. The smaller unit of power imposes on him the obligation to commit no damage to the person or property of another, to marry not more than one wife, to support his children if he can, to fulfill such contracts as he enters into, to pay his state and local taxes. The National State requires that he do no counterfeiting of money, that he not use the mails to defraud, that he serve in the army or navy if congress so provides, pay taxes if they are levied. As we pointed out in comparing a state with the United States, the powers are divided.

Important is the fact that the National State gets its power, under our representative government, directly from the people, and not from the separate states. That feature seems to account for the durability of the United States. The city leagues of Ancient Greece were undependable, evidently because the central power was derived from the other governments, each jealous of the central power and afraid of it, and at the same time in a strategic position to withhold necessary finances. The confederation of American States that preceded the United States was not adequate for its problems for the same reason. The recent League of Nations likewise depended for its existence on the sufferance of its member states, and was not in a position to carry on independent action against an offending member state.

If ever an organization of the states of Europe is seriously considered, or a United States of the World, the concept of direct reliance of the central government on persons and not on other states may well be included. In the United States of America it has worked.

Pressure Groups

One casts a critical eye over the list of groups putting pressures on legislators for the sake of gain. Is government in America just a public acquiescence in special privilege? Townsend's followers become powerful again; the American Federation of Labor fights the C.I.O. in congress for legislation intended for the welfare of its members. The National Association of Manufacturers, the National Electric Manufacturers Association, the National Association of Wool Manufacturers, all claim legislative triumphs for their members. In various industries, private committees help mold the nation's laws, cataloguing representatives, steering bills, giving the signal for concerted protest or support of members and their friends. In the automobile industry alone we find ten associations making life miserable for a state legislator who feels inclined to vote for an increased gasoline tax, or for a congressman who supports a measure to further regulate motor carriers. Does government by the pressure groups and for the pressure groups come to be "the right of the stronger"?

Perhaps so, but in spite of that probable truth government appears to be motivated in part by other thoughts than profit seeking. With the steady increase of concentration of industrial control after the Civil War, corporation barons were the remote control steering committees for legislation; political policies were largely dictated by business men's pressures. More recently, though the gain-getting ideals continue in evidence, and more gain-getting groups are in politics, nevertheless, much of organized action springs from non-monetary ideals.

Setting an early example for the new type of representative government was a powerful body of churchmen, the Anti-Saloon League. Their calculated placing of votes, their singleness of purpose, their tenacity, which led to the adoption of the 18th Amendment, are well known. Is it so well known that, though their success was their temporary undoing, they are back in action again, following the tested mobile-vote method? According to the second item of their six point program, "The League will work for the nomination and election of dry councilmen in villages and cities, dry legislators in states, dry senators and representatives in the national Congress for the purpose of securing the most extensive and effective local, state and national prohibition laws."

Incidentally, we notice a difference in manner of enforcement among various types of laws. A soldiers' bonus requires an appropriation bill and some clerical work, and an enlargement of tax bills, postponable through government borrowing, and the burden indistinguishable from other burdens when it is borne. A law prohibiting billboards along the highways requires only infrequent inspection. Violation of the law is expensive and the violator is easily detected. Speed laws, and plant quarantines, require a staff of law enforcers. Prohibition against narcotics has been difficult of enforcement but not impossible, because of the widespread abhorrence of the drug habit and the relatively small number of law violators. Prohibition of traffic in alcoholic beverages presented a tremendous enforcement problem because of the large proportion of the population who aided and abetted the violators.

Thus far the Anti-Saloon League has not given special attention to the conditioning influences which increase the use of liquor: advertising, by radio, magazines, newspapers and billboards, and the showing of drinking in the movies as if it were a commonplace and respectable pastime.

Cooperating with the Anti-Saloon League is the National Women's Christian Temperance Union, for long an educational body, but now in a minor aspect a pressure group in addition. The organization maintains a "legislative director" in Washington, who keeps the members throughout the nation informed when to write to congressmen.

Lobbying appears not to be among the duties of the W.C.T.U. legislative director; but lobbying, though magnified in occasional public discussions, is a relatively superficial aspect of pressure group tactics. Basically the substance of pressure is the gaining of actual representation in the legislative body, and the method is, merely, standing ready to shift one's vote to those candidates who are most in sympathy with an organization's objective, or at any rate least hostile. This use of the mobile vote, most fruitful in primaries but also of significance in general elections, is most effective of course when the members of a pressure group stick together in their voting. A legislator already in office may be willing to represent a group, whether or not it has a lobbyist, if he realizes that thereby he can gain more votes for re-election than he loses.

The National Grange and the International Order of Good Templars, the former having state and national legislative reporters, are other pressure groups with prohibition as one of their planks.

Also, prohibition is one among the objectives of the International Reform Federation, a pressure group, like the Anti-Saloon League itself, organized in the churches.

Pressure group government is a type of representative government. Often, of course, the representation is of a minority. Occasionally, in these days of transition to a greater measure of pressure government, movements develop and get legislation passed without the adversely disposed people ever realizing their own power.

An active and interesting political battle has been waging for several years between two determined pressure groups, both thoroughly familiar with the new political methods. Curiously, both of them are fighting for ideals; the members of neither get any monetary profit from victory. Birth control advocates, under the leadership of Margaret Sanger, operating recently as The National Committee on Federal Legislation for Birth Control, are now organized as the Birth Control Federation of America. Primarily, their objective is to prevent suffering from physical strain and poverty which result from badly timed and too numerous offspring. Their chief method has been to get petitions filled urging the passage of legislation to legalize the mailing of contraceptive information and devices by physicians. They have had the support of the Universalist General Convention, the Unitarian Association, the Central Conference of American Rabbis, the New York East Conference of the Methodist Episcopal Church, the General Council of Congregational and Christian Churches, and the Committee on Marriage and the Home of the Federal Council of the Churches of Christ in America. The General Federation of Women's Clubs, with 2,000,-000 members, has also gone on record in favor of birth control.

In opposition stands the marvelously organized National Catholic Welfare Conference, directed by seven archbishops and bishops, with departments of education, press, social action, legal affairs, executive affairs, and lay organizations. Effective informational organ is the monthly publication *Catholic Action*. The applicable purpose of the Conference is "To participate, through Catholic lay representation, in national and international movements involving moral questions." The Lay Organizations Department supervises the National Council of Catholic Men and the National Council of Catholic Women.

The National Council of Catholic Men and the National Council of Catholic Women "function through some 3,000 affiliated societies'' and constitute the channels through which pressure is applied to congressmen, and to state legislators. ''Both organizations,'' said the Most Reverend Austin Dowling, in *The Ecclesiastical Review* for October 1928, ''are accomplishing work of vast importance—in securing common action when needed, by all men's or women's organizations. . . . One has but to review for a moment the vicious, well-financed anti-Christian propaganda of birth control, or sterilization legislation, or the denial of the sanctity of marriage, or the public temptations of the youth of the day, to realize that both N.C.C.M. and N.C.C.W. are opportune and far-reaching channels of Catholic influence. . . . .''

Said Miss Agnes G. Regan, Executive Secretary of the National Council of Catholic Women, in a letter of February 17, 1936: ''The only time when the National Council of Catholic Women is in touch with governmental agencies is at a time when questions involving fundamental moral principles are involved, such as the passage of laws endorsing birth control, sterilization, the socalled Equal Rights Amendment, etc. It is then our province to protest, through our representatives and through correspondence, against the passage of such measures.''

Another organization working against birth control as part of its political program is the Catholic Daughters of America, with 760 courts or units, 200,000 members.

Recording the score, no national birth control legislation of significance has been enacted, although a supreme court decision now permits birth control information to go through the mails. In a few states the birth control protagonists have managed to get the right to support birth control clinics; and in the Carolinas, legal restrictions having been legislated away, the public health clinics dispense birth control information to persons on relief.

Most thorough technique in pressure politics has been applied by the National Council for the Prevention of War. In its heyday in the 30's it built its plan of action on an analysis of political structure, working in the precincts, the smallest political units. There it established mobile vote peace bodies, making politicians aware of the peace objective, ready to vote for those political candidates most clearly representative of the anti-war attitude. The mobile vote feature applied both in the primaries in the selection of party candidates, and in the general elections between parties. Although the ''Mugwump'' mobile vote principle is basic to any pressure group, it was more than usually definite in the consciousness of the workers of the National Council for the Prevention of War.

Canvassing precinct voters to see where they stood, and securing united action among the favorable ones, was not new. It was the method used by Aaron Burr in New York City in the cause of the Jeffersonians in 1800; the method for which Burr was rewarded with the vice-presidency. It was the method that Tammany Hall brought into disrepute by teaming it with the spoils system and using it for questionable purposes. Organizing members by precincts and keeping members informed just how their congressmen voted on legislation for peace, the National Council for Prevention of War was effective. It was financed by the Carnegie Foundation; was in cooperation with twenty-eight other peace organizations.

In opposition to the detailed legislative measures of these peace groups stood the Daughters of the American Revolution, and the National Society of the Sons of the American Revolution—both political pressure groups. The 144,000 Daughters, variously active, consistently passed resolutions for the guidance of their members and the information of legislators, urging legislation for military training, urging legislation in support of a merchant marine, urging a larger navy and a larger army.

Most of the societies referred to have taken positions on more measures than those mentioned; most of the issues have had more protagonists and more opponents than those named. We have merely sketched, in broad outlines, illustrative pressure groups, to show the part that pressure politics play in American government.

Polls

Informal testings of public opinion may not be something new under the sun, but the polls of the recent decade seem to have attained a degree of accuracy which is new. The *Literary Digest,* a weekly news and editorial reporter, rose to its pinnacle on the popularity of its publication of the results of its sampling of public opinion on timely subjects. But its readers came to expect more than it could deliver. When it predicted erroneously the results of the election of 1932, its subscription list rapidly shrank, and in a startlingly brief while it had gone out of existence. Methods of sampling seem to have been improved since then. Gallup polls and *Fortune* polls have not yet been known to make a serious error. They test opinion not only on popularity of candidates, but on public approval or disapproval of prospective legislative measures, thereby keeping congressmen in close touch with national opinion.

Political Information for Voters

Although a congressman now has the means to know how the general public stands, and through voter letters how part of his constituency stands, most voters are still completely in the dark as to where their prospective representatives stand on any issue. It has been a principle of representative government that the more inclusive the suffrage the more must the public be educated. As Gladstone remarked after the passage of the Reform bill of 1867 which lengthened English voting lists, "We must educate our masters." It was no coincidence that the Forster Education Act was passed in 1870. In spreading general education, America has done much, but in making education available for political purposes America has done almost nothing except by way of the pressure groups. Specifically, we have almost no machinery other than pressure groups by which we may learn the attitudes or other qualifications of candidates in the primaries. Well qualified men hesitate to compete for office because of the prospective shame of being defeated by persons whom they consider to be lesser fry, knowledge of their own merits not being available to the voters. A meagre supply of facts is usually available for the general election, but that is too late, inasmuch as each party has usually nominated candidates of quality generally thought to be less than the best of its membership, and, additionally, custom causes adherence of many voters to their respective parties no matter who may be the candidates.

A few attempts have been made to shed light where light would make a difference. The Civic League of Denver has issued pamphlets of information for voters concerning candidates and measures. It not only reports facts, but it gives recommendations. Possibly this last feature might lend itself to improper use, or at least lead to suspicion. Also, the facts reported about candidates include little concerning candidates' *positions on issues*. The Portland (Oregon) City Club follows the same pattern. There are a few other experiments with the same purpose.

Applicable to a small proportion of voters, but for them a more complete linking up of general education with political judgments, is the Manitowoc Plan,[2] an invention of Dr. R. J. Colbert of the

[2] Reported in *Kiwanis Magazine* for November, 1940, and *Reader's Digest* for November, 1940.

University of Wisconsin. Young people, as they approach their first voting day are assembled to discuss the issues in the impending election, and to dig out information. No recommendations are made. Apparently no systematized way of getting information to other voters has been undertaken. The neophyte voters are organized by volunteers out of the coming-of-age class of the previous year. "Nearly 100 counties in 24 states have followed Manitowoc's example."

OUTLOOK FOR REPRESENTATIVE GOVERNMENT IN THE UNITED STATES

Once upon a Time Abundance of Land Aided Government-by-the-People

Under the feudal regime of the middle ages in Europe, the lords of the manors held sway over their underlings, custom furnishing checks, but not very dependable checks, on arbitrary exercise of power. Kings, there were, and king makers; the latter as well as the former being landholders. The Church, a law unto itself in that day, owed much of its power to its landholdings and the revenues from them. Even as the commercial revolution and the industrial revolution developed, giving power to merchants and to manufacturers, the common laborers and even the craftsmen had very little representation in government. In the English colonies in the new world the same sort of government as that pertaining in England was assumed to be fitting—but its modification was early; pressure for extension of the suffrage was constant. Massachusetts Bay received a charter vesting authority in the governor, deputy governor, assistants, and freemen of the company, but of the 2000 settlers arriving in 1630 only 12 were freemen.[3] The others very soon demanded a voice in government, and, as landholders themselves (and church members) many were admitted as freemen. *America's free land was beginning to have political effect.*

In Connecticut, Fundamental Orders were drawn up by the townsmen—a home-made constitution—the qualifications for voting being left to the separate towns. Thus isolation was leading to decentralization; economic independence was bringing about equality in government.

New Netherlands, governed by the Dutch West India Company,

[3] A. E. Martin, History of the United States, Ginn and Company, vol. 1, p. 57.

gave fewer advantages to settlers than did neighboring English colonies, and when inhabitants asked for representation, despot Peter Stuyvesant was saddled on them instead. However, when English troops arrived, Stuyvesant's minions bent the knee no longer— welcomed the rescue.

Virginians squatted on Carolina lands, and when proprietors with a 1663 grant from the king sent a governor, these self-suffi- cient democrats resented. Planters from British West Indies, under the same proprietors, were similarly inclined to think that govern- ment, superimposed, was not in keeping with their condition. Carolinians broke up the proprietors' government by force; pre- ferred a royal colony with more self-government.

But the sweeping advances in self-government came after large numbers of settlers had crossed the Alleghenies. Little leaven of precedent for aristocracy was there. But more important than that, each family was a separate economic unit, connected by few ties with other families. Clothing was made on the farm from raw material produced on the farm; food was grown almost 100 per cent by those who ate it; even the artificial lights were made from tallow or bay- berries grown on the farm. Why should one take orders from anybody else? For some purposes, to be sure, group action was helpful, but farmer Doe would participate only if it were under- stood that his participation was to be on an equality with that of everybody else. Thus, several years after the Declaration of Inde- pendence, men were born relatively free, and in political rights practically equal. Jefferson's Utopia had become reality; govern- ment was by initiative of the governed. Free men had been earth born of free land.

This may be worth an extra minute: To say that land was free is another way of saying that *men were scarce.* A man needed to truckle to no one as a condition for obtaining his daily breed. Though the character-forming self-sufficiency of men was most pro- nounced in the pioneer regions, even in the eastern factories the workers usually had the possibility, and the consciousness of the possibility of going to the western lands if their local environment was unsatisfactory. And enough of them did go to maintain a scarcity of men in the east. Equal political power was the logical outgrowth of the psychological attitude developed by economic independence.

Throughout the 19th century our abundant land helped to

prevent crises in our national economy by furnishing an outlet for restless and dissatified urban laborers. But the land conditions that brought about America's democracy, and for a time helped to preserve it, are not the land conditions that now prevail. The following changes impose different influences:

1. Land, though cheap, is not free any more. When people move in, they usually have to be subject to a mortgage, payable in money, and with interest payable in money.

2. The very abundance of land and of people on it have increased competition in the sale of products, made farm prices low.

3. Use of farm machinery has increased that competition. Prices of products being low, paying off the mortgage is hard; even paying interest is often a difficulty.

4. Custom has led to specialization to such an extent that even those who have no debts, most of them, have no thought of producing their own living; they think in terms of a cash crop.

5. Taxes re-inforce custom in requiring participation in purchase and sale. And the sale has to be at low prices.

Those are just a few of the newer conditions that prevent our rural areas from simplifying, as they used to, our problems of government. Instead of aiding democracy by solving urban labor problems, as they did in the past, our farms themselves have lately been an added burden to democracy, complicating the difficulties of government.

Complexity Increases

It is unnecessary to write at length on the variety of ways in which industrial production is growing more complicated. Specialization is the rule, and it becomes more and more detailed. A man used to think himself specialized if he were a cart-wright; further subdivision of tasks made his grandson a wheel-wright; and now, making the hub caps alone constitutes several jobs. The division of tasks is accompanied by the allocation of some men to the making of machines, only indirectly related to the making of finished products. This "indirect production" complicates the relationship of men to men; makes the exchange process more important; gives more occasion for tie-ups; makes more headaches for political leaders. Organized labor, occasionally blocking the smooth flow of goods, increases the responsibility of government. The maze of interrelationships seems to stem from inventions, and further puzzles are to be expected.

Economic Problems Put a Strain on Democracy

To regulate human relationships in the complexity of a machine age, centralization of political power is to be expected. The readiness with which that centralization has proceeded, however, seems to imply no very great value placed on the dignity of the individual, or perhaps a lack of knowledge of the prerequisites of that dignity. But at least there must have been some regulatory activity—and cumulative mechanical inventions, making for more complexity of living, are likely to bring even more regulation.

This means that freedom of individuals is likely to grow less. Even if democratic government prevails, and if each individual participates actively in the government that rules him, nevertheless he will presumably be more and more unfree. That a person sanction the speed laws does not make him any the less bound. That he vote for a regulation that only plumbers may adjust pipes, ties his own hands. That he favors a tax on butter substitutes limits his choices as truly as if a dictator had done so. Necessity of coordination of specialized groups drives us to greater subjugation of individuals; more unified controls. One might multiply illustrations indefinitely, but already the point should be clear that though regulations may be processed through one's own judgment or the judgment of one's representatives in government, one may be enslaved in the bonds of his own making. Says MacIver:

> In the large scale association, the average member occupies both a passive and an active role. . . . As in the state he is both citizen and subject, so, in degree, he is in every great association. The passive role bulks more largely the greater the association grows, and thus the members are apt to feel that its elaborate machinery lies wholly outside themselves, beyond the area of their control.[4]

For most people, however, a thralldom in which one participates is less bitter than a thralldom imposed by a despot—even a benevolent despot. May we not expect, then, that government, though centralized, may nevertheless become more democratic, more by the people? It is not the amount of power that a government has that determines its classification as dictatorship or democracy,

---

[4] R. M. MacIver, *Society*, Farrar and Rinehart, 1935, p. 245.

but rather it is whether the exercise of that power involves a responsibility to the people. May we not expect the public to participate in government more fully and more effectively as time goes on? The answer may be put in the form of another question: What amount of intelligence will the average citizen have? If his intelligence is little, he will be bored with attemping to balance arguments; will attribute his joys and his woes to persons rather than to forces; will turn over his powers to some demagog who promises much.

Leaving that problem for your contemplation and investigation we summarize what seem to be the most important sociological phases of organization for government.

SUMMARY

I. Government is power.
  A. A State is a unit of power above which no other is recognized. On the basis of force in reserve, a state keeps the actions of people in large measure coordinated.
    1. For the implementation of power we have, among other agencies,
      a. Laws:
        (1) Criminal, practically all of which are legislated, and
        (2) Civil, which are
          (a) Statutory, and
          (b) Judge made.
      b. The legislature also implements a state's power.
      c. The application of the laws is normally by bureaus.
      d. The so-called *Administration* is a manager.
      e. Courts furnish direction for some of the state's power.
  B. A state of the United States, like the National State itself, is supreme in the phases of power which it wields.
II. An individual is born into a state.
III. Government may be classified as
  A. Representative government,
  B. Oligarchy,
  C. One-man control,
  D. Combinations and transitions.
IV. Government is closely related to industry and to life,
  A. Increasingly so in the evolution from simplicity to comlexity involving
    1. More regulation by government, and
    2. More probability of dictatorship.

B. Socialism implies one-man control,
    1. Which seems to be inconsistent with freedoms.
V. Government in the United States involves
    A. Two sets of power,
    B. Pressure groups,
    C. Polls,
    D. A scarcity of political information for voters.
VI. The outlook for representative government in the United States seems to depend on whether or not mass intelligence can comprehend increasingly complex problems.

SELECTED REFERENCES

On pressure groups the pamphlets put out by the pressure groups constitute the most illuminating literature. Additionally, see:

Kenneth G. Crawford, *The Pressure Boys*, New York: Julian Messner, Inc., 1939.

Peter Odegard, *Pressure Politics, The Story of the Anti-Saloon League*, Columbia University Press, 1928.

E. E. Schattschneider, *Politics, Pressures and the Tariff*, Prentice-Hall, 1935.

Belle Zeller, *Pressure Politics in New York*, Prentice-Hall, 1937.

For information on the activities of bureaus, see for example, *United States Government Manual*, (three editions per year) published by the Office of Government Reports, Washington, D. C.

GENERAL

G. E. G. Catlin, *A Study of the Principles of Politics*, The Macmillan Company, 1930.

Raymond Garfield Gettell, *Political Science*, Ginn & Co., 1933.

Frank R. Kent, *Political Behavior*, New York: Wm. Morrow & Co., 1928.

Harold J. Laski, *A Grammar of Politics*, Yale Univ. Press, 1925.

Harold D. Lasswell, *Politics: Who Gets What, When, How*, Whittlesey House, McGraw-Hill Book Co., Inc., 1936.

R. M. MacIver, *The Modern State*, Oxford Univ. Press, 1926.

PART V

SOCIAL TENSIONS

In the dynamics of complex modern living, situations arise in which the emotions of some people are in disharmony with the emotions of others. For example, a body of taxpayers, helping by means of their tax money to support a group of dependents, may feel that the burden is unwarranted. Their emotion is in opposition to that of the recipients of the benefits. The emotions are social forces, and being in opposition they set up tensions.

A person getting a living by robbing banks arouses an antagonism in bank cashiers and in depositors and in those who sympathize with them. The emotions of the bank robbers and their friends are in opposition to the emotions of the depositors and their friends, and the emotions, as opposed social forces, constitute a social tension.

PART V deals with important areas of tensions.

CHAPTER 21

POVERTY

By VINCENT H. WHITNEY, M.A.

University of Maine, Orono, Maine

WHAT IS POVERTY?

Poverty as a Concept

A difficulty in arriving at any universally acceptable definition of poverty lies in the fact that we are dealing with an abstraction, something non-material, a concept involving the setting up of standards which are themselves not subject to any general agreement. Is the individual who has no employment and no outside income, who must live in a substandard slum dwelling, who is suffering from malnutrition and lack of fresh air and sunlight, living in poverty? There would no doubt be general agreement that he is. But suppose that this same individual falls heir to a small farm in a rural area of his state where he is able to obtain better food, plenty of sunshine and unpolluted air, a reasonably satisfactory though modest home, and an annual cash and produce income of $1,000. Is he still living under conditions of poverty? Or again, suppose a family accustomed to an annual income of $50,000 finds itself limited to an income of $5,000 a year. May this family be represented as having been overtaken by poverty?

The answer, once again, depends upon our concept of the meaning of poverty. We can only emphasize here the extreme relativity of the concept. What may represent riches to one individual or one family may, in the eyes of a second individual or family, constitute a condition of poverty. In general usage, then, poverty is a term without definite boundaries, a term for which boundaries must be assumed by the researcher and ascribed merely for reference purposes, the later reasoning to be scientific only in the sense that it is systematically related to the basing point.[1]

Basically, most of the sociologists' definitions center the problem of poverty around an insufficiency of resources. Since, however, the

[1] Various students have attempted to bring "poverty" to a preciseness of meaning. See, for example, John Lewis Gillin, *Poverty and Dependency*, p. 22; James Ford and Katherine Morrow Ford, *The Abolition of Poverty*, p. 1.

great majority of us, regardless of our position on the economic scale, will tend to feel our resources inadequate at many times to satisfy wants, we must again limit our term. It appears that poverty is a position on the socio-economic scale within which individuals and groups are unable, due to inadequate income or inadequate control of income or both, to attain a level of living of sufficient abundance to allow full and productive participation in the life of community and nation in terms of the standards of those social units. Much more simply, poverty is a condition in which economic inadequacy spells insufficient food, clothing, and shelter.

The Meanings of Poverty

The implications of poverty are almost endless. We must, first of all, keep in mind that its results go far beyond individual hardship and suffering to derived conditions in community and nation. Individual poverty is closely related to unemployment, disease, vice, crime, bad housing, insecurity both physical and mental. The list might be extended indefinitely. One promotes the other and each promotes the all.

It is important, then, not to forget through our discussion that individual poverty and national poverty are closely related. While it is obviously true that a nation may be rich in resources and possessed of a large national income and still have the benefits of these concentrated largely in the hands of a few individuals or families, it must be noted that such a nation may well lack national security. The poverty of either the individual or the nation may spell insecurity for both.

No figures are available which indicate with any exactness how great a proportion of the American people is living in a condition of poverty. Such statistics as are at hand show clearly, however, that at least two-fifths of our population is in the poverty group if we define that to include those who are unable to conform to community standards of physical, mental and social efficiency established by the other three-fifths. In 1935–1936 there were in the United States some 40 million families. Of these nearly one-third (32 per cent) were found to have annual incomes of under $750. Nearly one-half (47 per cent) received less than $1,000 and over two-thirds (69 per cent) received under $1,500. Thirty million of these families numbered two or more persons.[2] At best, life oppor-

[2] National Resources Committee, *Consumer Incomes in the United States,* 1938, pp. 4–5.

tunities for persons in these income groups are limited. Again, however, we must call attention to the necessarily subjective nature of a "poverty line."

Other, but not conflicting, definitions of poverty have been implied by the published reports of government agencies. Federal emergency relief to farmers reached its highest point in the first four months of 1937 when the monthly average numbered 297,000 farmers and $5,013,000. The Federal Surplus Commodities Corporation shipped surplus farm commodities in each month of the fiscal year 1938–1939 to some 3 million families and 11 million people.[3] In February, 1936, the Federal Works Program carried approximately 3,850,000 on its rolls, about 450,000 of whom were enlisted in CCC camps.[4] In one month alone, June, 1935, the direct and work relief expenditures of federal, state, and local governments combined amounted to $204,359,000 and went to 6,404,000 families numbering 22,457,000 people. By June, 1939, approximately the same number of families but with only 19,500,000 persons was receiving $304,523,000.[5]

Those of us who have had but slight access to such statistics as those cited above have been able to catch something of the spread and depth of poverty in the frequency with which, in even a short drive, closed and boarded factories, dilapidated and eroded farms, filthy and decaying tenements, have come into view. Whether we use such indices as these or watch the drop in income tax returns which the depression years of the thirties ushered in, or turn to figures on increasing national debt and taxation, or adopt any of a hundred other measurement approximations, we may be sure that a large proportion of people in the United States, and for that matter, the world over, are living in poverty. The extent may vary with the region of the country, with the racial, cultural, occupational groupings of the people, with the urban and rural divisions of our population. Poverty is both widespread and deep-rooted.

ATTITUDES CONCERNING POVERTY

So long as general human faith supported the maxim *The poor are always with us,* there seemed slight need to expend effort on any determination of the causes of poverty. We usually seek causes in order to produce results through an attack upon underlying causal

[3] Josephine C. Brown, *Public Relief, 1929–1939,* Henry Holt, 1940, p. 335.
[4] *Ibid.,* p. 342.
[5] *Ibid.,* pp. 343–344.

factors. The long-held theory that poverty was inevitable, a theory which is by no means dead today, precluded very much search for causes. Through many centuries the presence of poverty in society was considered as inevitable as that man must eat to live.

It would hardly be correct to leave the impression that no one ever wondered about the factors which produced poverty. Probably increasingly since the first recognized state of poverty men have done so. Their utterances, however, have tended for the most part to place the blame for poverty on a single cause rooted in their own times and to offer little with which to attack the problem beyond the practice of almsgiving which, as the Fords point out, serves chiefly to perpetuate the state of poverty by relieving the most immediate and acute suffering and by creating the illusion of security.[6]

Primitive man considered poverty within a religious framework. Pestilences, calamities, and other natural phenomena were construed to have been sent by the gods as punishment for sin; and gradually individual poverty came to be explained in this same fashion. As society gradually became stratified and the division between poor and rich became more apparent, the theory was ventured that poverty arose from class domination and exploitation. This explanation began to take form under the Hebrew prophets and was again primarily religious in spirit. Hereditary explanations of poverty likewise have existed from early times.[7]

In the eighteenth and nineteenth centuries the question of poverty attracted the attention of a growing number of individuals each of whom attempted to produce proof that some single factor lay at the base of poverty. Such men as Karl Marx, Henry George, Adam Smith, and numbers of their contemporaries, set forth various explanations, describing poverty as an end result of the capitalistic system or of defective methods of taxation or of similar economic factors. Others who pointed to poverty as due to the fault of the individual himself found widespread acceptance. The poverty-stricken individual was poor because he was a drunkard or a drug addict or because he was simply lazy, shiftless, immoral, unworthy. In the light of our present-day body of accumulated knowledge we shall see that such explanations are tenable only in partial measure.

[6] Ford and Ford, *op. cit.*, p. 13.

[7] John Lewis Gillin, *Poverty and Dependency*, New York: D. Appleton-Century, 1937. Ch. 5, discusses in some detail these and other historical explanations of poverty and dependency.

Attitudes Concerning Distribution of Income

Attitudes about poverty are likely to be interlinked with attitudes concerning related economic problems. Certain students of economics deny that any substantial lessening of the tension of want is possible under a system of capitalism. One of the most provocative critics of capitalism writes: ''The fundamental question at issue is the inability of capitalism to produce abundantly and then to distribute its products amply to the whole population.''[8] In partial amplification of this statement he adds:[9]

> The increasing application of power has accentuated the tendency already introduced by the use of machinery to reduce the number of man-hours required to produce a given quantity of commodities. The rational adjustment to this situation is to reduce the hours of labor and to increase leisure time. The capitalist resists this solution because he wishes to keep down his labor cost and to maintain and increase his rate of profit. The inevitable consequence is an increase of unemployment which reduces purchasing power. Decrease of production follows, which leads to economic depression with all its disastrous consequences.

This point of view maintains that poverty cannot be eliminated under capitalism without removing the latter's reason for existence, that is, the making of profits.

Other economists, dwelling on the point that concentration of purchasing power is a cause of chronic unemployment and so a partial cause of poverty, nevertheless consider that purchasing power can be decentralized without destroying the incentives and the voluntary processes that have made capitalistic countries areas of relatively large average incomes.

Thorough treatment of the controversy between opponents and protagonists of capitalism would require a large volume. In a work of this kind we can merely suggest the sweeping importance of the issue.

HOW DOES POVERTY ARISE?

Poverty is the outgrowth of a complex interrelationship of hereditary and environmental factors in the life of the individual, with multiple factors of a social, economic, political, biological, and

[8] Maurice Parmelee, *Farewell to Poverty*, p. 13.

[9] *Ibid.*, p. 59. These quotations are reprinted by permission from *Farewell to Poverty* by Maurice Parmelee published by John Wiley & Sons, Inc., 1935.

geographical nature which are contained in the broader environment which we call society. What is true of the individual is equally true of the group.

Rarely indeed, if at all, will it be possible to state bluntly that an individual case of poverty is due to poor heredity or to unwise expenditure of income or to any single causative factor. Such a factor may appear predominant, but careful inspection will tend to reveal it as at most a nucleus in a cluster of causes. Our poverty-stricken individual will in general require a complex description. He may, for example, be revealed as a person handicapped by (1) the inheritance of a predisposition to tuberculosis; (2) inadequate schooling and vocational training; (3) residence in a stranded industrial community; and (4) the burning of his home and belongings. Such a hypothetical list could easily be extended. But this example should be sufficient to indicate the manner in which single factors relate to one another and contribute individually and collectively to the total poverty.

Some of these factors may be controlled in part at least by the individual or group. Any given person may decide upon a wise or unwise expenditure of such income as he has; he may decide whether to put forth the effort required to receive a particular type of vocational training; he may decide whether it is worth the effort to take certain precautions in his work which may protect him from accident and subsequent loss of earning power. On the other hand over other factors he has no control. He cannot exercise any magic powers to prevent a season without rain ruining his crops; he cannot correct defective heredity with which he may be born; he cannot act to release himself in his generation from pressure of population upon resources which is depressing national income of which his individual income is part. He cannot even undo past acts which have resulted in population pressure in his own family.

Fluctuations in Purchasing Power of the Purchasing Unit

It often happens that even those workers whose jobs continue find themselves plunged to the poverty level as a result of a rise of prices. Wages and prices do not move in unison. As a result a worker who finds 25 dollars a week barely sufficient to pay his costs of living when soup is selling at seven cents a can and a suit of clothes is available at 15 dollars will find his weekly wage entirely inadequate when soup sells at ten cents a can and a suit of clothes at $22.50. Poverty, then, may accompany wages which are high in comparison with previous wages, if prices have increased faster. In fact, whenever prices rise more rapidly than wages, many families are certain to experience new or deepened poverty. The unequal rates of change constitute one of the major strains in our economic system.

Unadaptive Judgments

The mere fact that a given family possesses a seemingly adequate income is, of course, no guarantee in itself that that family will not fall below the poverty line. Speculation, playing the races, extravagant buying—in short, any form of mismanagement of income may prevent a family from obtaining in adequate measure the standard provisions for living. Most of us would find it possible noticeably to increase our real incomes through the application of knowledge to our purchasing and maintenance of goods. Difficulties are chiefly that we lack exactly that information calculated to furnish us with criteria for our purchases; and secondly, that such information as we do possess, we are often too lazy to use to our advantage. We may know, for example, that thousands of miles of wear will be added to our automobile tires through shifting them from wheel to wheel each two or three thousand miles. Yet how many of us will expend the effort necessary to see that such a change is made? Furthermore, it is exactly the poverty-stricken classes who have the least access to information on comparative values. Consumer guides such as *Consumers' Union* and *Consumers' Research* are rarely available to them.

As Gillin has pointed out, family expenditures are affected by traditions, habits, advertising, and installment buying. High-pressure advertising with its creation of new wants and the ability to satisfy these wants through installment buying, which includes, most often, extra fees or carrying charges, is part of the picture. Many times the wants created may be legitimate ones; many times manufacturers of products of dubious value succeed in creating through widespread advertising efforts wants which reduce markedly the portion of consumer income available for the maintenance of healthful living. The purchase of certain articles or certain brands may become habitual even when a more satisfactory article or product is available elsewhere. Similarly habits of saving or of total expenditure may come to dominate the family-ways. Families with small incomes find great difficulty in accumulating any savings at all and may soon give up any attempt to do so. As a result any personal crisis situation which may arise is apt to mean new or increased poverty for them.

Hereditary Factors in Poverty

It seems obvious that poverty may be received by the individual as a social inheritance. The child who is born into a family whose income is not adequate to provide wholesome living inherits manifestly a position-in-life on the poverty level. If he escapes it eventually, it must be in spite of rather than with the help of this social inheritance. He is in especial degree subject to the hazards of malnutrition, lack of education, lack of vocational training, inadequate housing, poor play equipment, disadvantaged companions. In short, he is handicapped by a lack of invigorating contacts with life and by lack of a background of security out of which he may conduct his explorations. Similarly, an individual born in a poverty-stricken nation inherits socially the national handicap under which his country is struggling.

But biological heredity rather than social heredity is the usual connotation of the word "heredity," and we must not ignore biological heredity as a cause of poverty. An individual may inherit some degree of mental defect; he may inherit not tuberculosis but a predisposition to tuberculosis or to some other physical or mental disease. Such defects may be, or under certain conditions of strain may become, such that the individual is incapacitated and rendered unfit to take his place in the world of self-supporting people. Wherever such physical or mental deficiencies limit the ability of the individual to maintain himself, they contribute to his state of poverty.

Factors in heredity are, of course, intertwined with factors in environment. We cannot today measure the relative importance of the neighborhood and the germ plasm, the family attitudes and the endocrine glands; but all contribute either to independence or to poverty.

Geographic Factors in Poverty

Man has not yet learned to control nature except in fragmentary proportions nor are there prospects that he will do so in any immediate future. What he has done is to adjust himself to her ways and, in so doing, to increase the benefits which he may obtain from her and to decrease the hazards with which she surrounds him. Man's lack of control is most obvious where severe drought parches a wide section of farm land and destroys fields of produce; where torrential rainstorms suddenly batter crops to the earth; where subsequent floods sweep away not only farm produce and livestock but barns and houses, manufacturing plants, and sometimes whole villages; where hurricanes and volcanic eruptions and tidal waves or any other nature-born disaster occurs. There we have a circumstance which man can control only imperfectly and not at all if nature exceeds his calculations in the force of her attack. The sweeping away of foodstuffs, property, possessions, is manifestly a reason for poverty. With the aid of the Red Cross, the Disaster Loan Corporation, and other private and governmental agencies, many individuals and families overtaken by natural catastrophes may return to a level above the poverty line. Many others will find themselves permanently reduced to membership in the poverty group.

In the summer of 1940 floods in the state of North Carolina washed so much debris into the mountain coves that agricultural authorities reported that they would never again within our time be tillable. Such a catastrophe means additional poverty in an area already subsisting on an extremely meager standard of living where much of the mountainous hill-country through repeated plowing and sowing and long years of soil exhaustion and soil erosion is marginal land. In all parts of the world wasteful methods of exploitation have gradually produced exhausted physical resources, have left stranded and poverty-stricken populations.

Demographic Aspects of Poverty

Howard W. Odum has listed as one of the major reasons for the widespread existence of poverty the lack of adaptation of the people to the living resources and geography of the nation.[10] This statement is a link between our mention of geographic factors and those of population pressure. Even before the time of Thomas Malthus, but particularly with the publication in 1798 of his famous but since modified theory of population growth, namely that population tends to increase at a rate far beyond that at which subsistence is increasing, questions of population pressure have attracted the attention of students.

Malthus, by the time of the last edition of his famous essay, indicated his belief that:

[10] Howard W. Odum, *American Social Problems*, Henry Holt, 1939, p. 255.

1. Population is necessarily limited by the means of subsistence.

2. Population invariably increases where the means of subsistence increase, unless prevented by some very powerful and obvious checks.

3. These checks, and the checks which repress the superior power of population and keep its effects on a level with the means of subsistence, are all resolvable into moral restraint, vice, and misery.[11]

In short, Malthus believed that there existed and would continue to exist a general tendency for populations to grow even more rapidly than the increase in their food supplies and other necessaries of life would permit. When, in a given population, more persons were born than could be cared for with the existing means of subsistence, then there would of necessity be suffering and death as ways of keeping population within the limits circumscribed by the amount of subsistence. Malthus did not envision a program of control of births which would permit a people to choose between having children up to the limit of subsistence and limiting its births in order to raise its standard of living and, in so doing, supposedly to lessen its misery and suffering. Yet that increasingly is the choice which the people of all westernized nations are finding it possible to make today.

Just as Malthus predicted, population has increased with the tremendous increase in subsistence made possible by the revolutions in industry, agriculture, and transportation and communication which we usually designate by the term Industrial Revolution. His belief that great misery and poverty must accompany such a growth in numbers is, on the contrary, not necessarily true in our westernized world since individual families to whom the addition of a child would mean a burden dragging them down to the poverty level, now are able more widely than ever before to exercise a simple expedient to check their numbers and to maintain their economic standards of living.

We should note two points here. First, obviously there are still many families and many nations which, through failure to exercise a rational control over the number of their members, are living in a condition of poverty. An annual income of $1500 may enable a single individual to live in modest comfort. Spread over a family

[11] Thomas Robert Malthus, *An Essay on Population*, London: Ward, Lock & Co., (reprint from last edition revised by the author), n. d., p. 14.

of six the same income may spell poverty. This leads directly to the second point: we must keep in mind that there is a definite and real connection between human numbers and poverty. A heavy pressure of population upon resources spells poverty today as surely as it did for Malthus in his age. Nations which feel the press will, if no other recourse is opened to them, almost inevitably turn to war.

We may profitably notice too that there is a definite connection between poverty and family size. Various studies of families on our relief rolls have shown them to be larger in number of members than comparable non-relief families. This does not mean that the giving of relief causes families to have a large number of children. Much more likely is the explanation that large families, which are more difficult to support, make it necessary for many low-income individuals to have their names added to the relief rolls. This hints at a problem which has worried some of our students of population, namely, that the groups within our population possessing the smallest incomes, the least education, the poorest diets, in short those least able to care for large families, have been giving birth to the greatest number of children, with a resultant tendency to spread rather than to check poverty.[12] Since information on the limitation of family size is available with little or no trouble to our upper and middle economic groups, the chief opportunity for a lessening of this cause of poverty would seem to be the spread of information on family limitation among the less privileged economic groups. That such a movement is increasingly sanctioned by our *mores* would seem to be indicated by the progress of the spread of birth control information among all classes of our population. Public clinics for relief-level persons have been available as part of the public health programs of North Carolina since 1937 and of South Carolina since 1939. We may undoubtedly look for the spread of such state programs.

Further Causes of Poverty

It might seem that the causes of poverty have been rather thoroughly covered. Actually, our discussion might take us much farther than the limits of a single chapter will permit. Students of the subject have given lengthy discussion to other causes of poverty: to ignorance, miseducation, and a school system which is not fully

---

[12] Cf. Frank Lorimer and Frederick Osborn, *Dynamics of Population*, The Macmillan Company, 1934, Chs. 9 and 10; Warren S. Thompson, *Population Problems*, McGraw-Hill Book Company, 1935 (2nd edition), Ch. 10.

adjusted to twentieth-century living; to war, whose role in the production of poverty must be so obvious to all of us that we simply
call attention to it; to depression; to accidents; to industrial disputes
for which we lack adequate methods of solution; to certain types of
technological improvements which have reduced employment; to
haphazard and unplanned relief methods which have in the past
often neglected rehabilitation as an end.

And so we might continue. One fact, however, is apparent.
Whatever may be the causes of poverty—and they are legion—
poverty, once established, tends to become self-perpetuating. Poverty breeds more poverty. It condemns the children of the poverty-
stricken to slum homes, inadequate diet, limited education, delinquent standards; it means malnutrition, inability to earn a living
wage, general helplessness; it means, in the final analysis, more and
deeper poverty. Poverty is not the phenomenon of one generation.
Where it lives, it also breeds.

HOW DO WE ALLEVIATE POVERTY?

If we assume poverty to be a negative value of importance to
many, the question presents itself, is poverty preventable and if so
at a cost of what other values?

Inasmuch as there is no single cause for poverty, it seems likely
that there is no single solution. Proponents of single-factor solutions seem to have lost sight of the intricate maze of causation which
lies behind poverty and are possibly engaging in ''tabloid thinking,''
that is, over-simplification of a complex situation. On our part we
shall be interested, in this section, then, in whether, if there is no
single solution for poverty, there may be a solution which involves
multiple factors. In short, is poverty preventable?

We can safely say that if poverty is to be prevented or even
lessened, this must be done on the basis of a knowledge of the facts
which cause poverty and of the methods of treatment which are
logical and possible. We must know, for example, not only the
extent of poverty but also what poverty does to the life-history of
an individual.[13] Poverty can never be measurably lessened so long
as we merely generalize its causes. We must have research and
more research in a wide variety of the social sciences and applied
sciences, in sociology and biology and education and social work and

[13] For a penetrating insight into the latter see Caroline Slade, *The Triumph
of Willie Pond*, Vanguard, 1940.

many more. As Gillin tells us, we are, when we fail carefully to diagnose our problem, in the position of the old-fashioned doctor who prescribed a dose of calomel for any and all bodily upsets. With this in mind, let us look at more specific possibilities of lessening the ravages of poverty so widespread in our civilization today.

A Sound Economic Base

A safeguard against extension of poverty seems to be in order, for example, in the matter of our natural resources: our forest land, our mineral wealth, our soil, all of which are today being rapidly exploited.

As regards distribution of incomes, it may be possible to work out a balancing of incomes among workers in various fields without restriction of production, and in that way to provide for larger totals and more goods per capita. If we find ourselves today dumping milk by the roadside, restricting our wheat and cotton acreage, limiting the outflow of industrial production whenever the market contracts, it is not because these products, both agricultural and industrial, are in excess. Recent surveys of the Brookings Institution, the federal government, and individuals indicate that the American people can use all that American labor, both on the farm and in the shop, can possibly produce. The problem is one of distributing these desired goods to this potential market, or, in other terms, of so distributing income that vast segments of our population who today have no income with which to make purchases of these products will obtain the wherewithal. The reduction of poverty probably requires a regularity and a spread of employment such as has not so far characterized our productive system.[14] Programs such as our present Social Security legislation have set in motion are themselves means of redistributing national income intended to mitigate somewhat the force of irregular employment. Stabilization of employment may involve increasing governmental control over and participation in industry and agriculture. Governmental control as a goal intermediate to the reduction of poverty is probably in conflict with the freedoms and the opportunities for individual choices which once characterized America and which are still distinguishing as American culture traits.

However this may be, our government has recently been under-

[14] For a plan to effect such stability see Alvin H. Hansen, *After the War— Full Employment*, National Resources Planning Board, 1942.

taking various types of socio-economic activity, and still more recently has more effectively implemented some of its earlier practices. The blue and orange stamp plan of the Federal Surplus Commodities Corporation is notable. This plan, which its proponents hope to establish on a nationwide basis in the near future, is designed to distribute certain agricultural products, of which there is a surplus on the market, more effectively than was possible under the old system of distribution wherein such surplus commodities as rice, cereals, grapefruit, butter, and so on, were bought by the Federal Surplus Commodities Corporation and distributed in individual communities, to which they had been shipped, to relief clients who came in person to distributing warehouses and received whatever surplus products were on hand. Under the old system an individual with no refrigeration facilities might receive four or five pounds of butter to last two or three weeks; or another who lived on the edge of town and had a number of apple trees behind the house might come home loaded down with a few bushels of apples, for which he had no need, and nothing else except a two-pound package of rice. Obviously such a system of distribution creaked badly at the hinges.

Under the new plan of distribution, the Department of Agriculture simply designates, each month, a list of a dozen or two agricultural products of which there is a national or regional surplus. It does not itself purchase these designated surplus commodities but allows individual merchants in areas where the plan is in operation to make the additional purchases as part of their regular buying. Families with relief incomes are then allowed to purchase from the relief agencies orange stamps, the number ranging between certain minimum and maximum limits, which are good in all stores participating in the plan for cash purchases of any articles carried. With the purchase of the orange food stamps the relief client receives as a bonus without further charge a number of blue stamps equal in value to one-half the amount of the orange stamps which he has purchased. These blue stamps may be used only to purchase articles on the surplus list, but there is a choice among any of these products. In this way it is possible for the individual with a relief income to increase both the amount and the variety of his purchases and to obtain a more adequate diet. Merchants, for their part, have found the plan resulting in a definite increase in their profits. Growers of surplus commodities have found a market for these without the necessity of dumping or selling at a loss. Of course the plan serves rather to alleviate attained poverty than to check the incidence of new poverty.

As yet unanswered is the question which has sometimes been raised concerning the whole relief system, as to what effects it has on the psychology of recipients. However, concerning the relative efficiency of the blue and orange stamp system over the earlier lack of system, there seems to be no doubt.

The Social Security Program

Similar in nature are the various governmental programs which have been enacted under the Social Security legislation. These varying programs, aid to dependent children, old age assistance, unemployment compensation, aid to the needy blind, and so on, are instrumental in reducing economic inadequacy among those groups covered by their provisions. However, they in no way put an end to the continued growth of the fundamental causes of poverty. Nor do they in any sense lessen the amount of national poverty. This latter we could not expect since what we have here is simply a case of taking our money out of one pocket to put in another, or, perhaps more aptly, taking our money out of several pockets to put in several other pockets.

Individual Incapacity

Along another front, what may be done to reduce poverty insofar as it stems from incompetence of the individual? Logically, we might first of all ask what factors are responsible for personal inability to attain independence. In past centuries our question would have found ready answer in the widely held belief that the poor were poor simply as a result of their own shortcomings. They were viewed by the middle and upper economic classes as a group characterized by individual shiftlessness, thriftlessness, and bad habits, a drain upon the workers of the community by choice. While we of today have by no means divorced ourselves completely from this view, we are nevertheless gradually developing a realization that the great majority of our poverty-stricken population have started life with two strikes against them. Large numbers are handicapped by an inferior biological inheritance; many others must struggle against the injurious and vicious influences of rural or urban slums. Practically all suffer from limited educational opportunities. Inadequate diets, the far-reaching effects of which we are only now beginning to realize, are the rule rather than the exception. When we keep in mind such facts as these, it can hardly be construed as strange that many of our poverty-level incompetents become thoroughly imbued with feelings of hopelessness and despair, with an attitude of indifference toward their own futures. Their feelings are readily understandable. It is easy enough for those of us who occupy more privileged positions in society to talk of laziness and careless habits, to insist that those without jobs "try a little harder" in their efforts to find work. Actually large numbers of our poverty-stricken have been born with either or both biological or social heritages which effectively limit their chances ever to exist independently. It has been often said and remains true that they are in large measure the product of circumstances beyond their immediate control.

It must be apparent, then, that any attempts to lessen the incidence of poverty must include broad attacks on diverse fronts. Even clearer will be our understanding of this necessity when we realize that only 14 per cent of our population has completed high school and that nearly 50 per cent has not completed even the elementary grades; that public clinics in large numbers of our hospitals are finding it necessary to treat first of all for dietary deficiency up to 85 per cent of all cases admitted for other causes.

Poor Heredity

To some of us, no doubt, reduction of poverty due to hereditary causes may seem to offer a concrete area of attack. There seems to be little doubt that our knowledge of heredity, while still far from complete, is sufficient as it stands to prevent the major portion of existing poverty which may properly be attributed to hereditary factors. There may be conflicting values involved, however. At any rate we fail to make use of the knowledge which is ours.

Prevention of such poverty as is due to hereditary traits requires, first, special training and the provision of environments suitable to overcome, insofar as this is possible, the limitations imposed by the deficiency; and secondly, the limitation of births. The latter can be achieved by three methods: (1) birth control; (2) segregation; and (3) sterilization. There can be little doubt that the spread of legalized birth control clinics and the incorporation of adequate programs of education on the subject of family limitation as part of our national and state public health programs would mean a lessening of undesired and undesirable births in families where hereditary taints are known to exist. That such a program is coming seems to be borne out by our changing attitude toward the question of family limitation. Even the Catholic Church now places its opposition not against birth control but rather against the artificial methods of birth control which are in general use. Students of population strongly suspect, though the number and scope of the studies so far made is insufficient to be called conclusive, that our educational efficiencies are being constantly cancelled by the fact that a larger and ever-larger proportion of our population is coming from our lower economic groups who, characterized as they are by poverty and its attendant conditions of ill-health, educational limitation, and generally poor environmental circumstances, are possessing gradually less and less capacity for intellectual development.[15] If this is so, the control of births among those groups who are unable to care for large families except under relief conditions which are too often wretched in themselves, may well become a question of public policy. The question is particularly applicable with regard to persons with hereditary deficiencies.

Large numbers of the latter group will not, however, be sufficiently equipped to make use of such information on family limitation as may be made available to them. For them either segregation or sterilization may be necessary.

Segregation, however, has patent shortcomings as a method of weeding out poor heredity in large portions of our population. Most of our idiots and imbeciles are so obviously defective in their ability to care for themselves that their opportunities for procreation, whether under institutional supervision or not, are extremely limited. On the other hand the sizeable group within our population who are either morons or normal individuals carrying hereditary defects, cannot be segregated except at staggering cost and even then only imperfectly. Nor would segregation seem desirable for a large portion of these individuals who, with proper vocational training and limitation on their opportunities to transmit their defects to succeeding generations, may well live as useful if not brilliant members of our communities. Today we cannot accurately say what proportion of our population is characterized by mental defect. It seems likely, however, that the number under care in either public or private institutions at any one time does not consti-

15 Lorimer and Osborn, *op. cit.*, pp. 343–344.

tute over ten per cent of the national total. Segregation of the unfit would undoubtedly reduce the incidence of poverty, but its tremendous cost makes its application dubious.

Similarly, sterilization is not to be thought of as a means of ridding our population of all its mentally deficient members. However, the use of this relatively simple operation which in no way interferes with sexual powers but does effectively prevent procreation would mean that large numbers of our higher-grade mental deficients would be able to continue as members of society and to exist without being forced to the extremes of poverty to which large families would seem almost inevitably to lead them. Sterilization, now legal in over half our states as well as in many foreign countries, is not a panacea or solution for all our social ills. Its further application could, however, be a partial preventive of poverty.

POVERTY INCONSISTENT WITH DEMOCRATIC GOVERNMENT

All that has been possible in this chapter has been to indicate in abbreviated form some of the most important data available with reference to the extent, causes, and prevention of poverty. Our discussion might well have been extended to fill a volume of several hundred pages. It would require such a volume to point up the threat of poverty to democratic forms of government; yet we may hardly close without noting again that totalitarian forms of government breed freely on the fertile soil of a poverty-stricken and disillusioned citizenry, eager to grasp at any program which promises a measure of security greater than is theirs at the moment, however illusory that security may prove in practice. We must note too that measures to prevent poverty may be negated by war.

There is no doubt that enough of the causes of poverty is known to allow the prevention of at least a significant portion of it. The problem is complex. If it is to be solved, the solution will require the activities of multiple government agencies, private agencies, and individuals. It will demand organization and effective unity. And even when consolidated effort has been exercised, there will remain the need for constant vigilance, to see that objectives once attained are not relinquished.

SELECTED REFERENCES

Booth, Charles (ed.), *Life and Labour of the People of London*, London: The Macmillan Company, Ltd., 1902.

Ford, James, and Katherine Morrow Ford, *The Abolition of Poverty*, New York: The Macmillan Company, 1937.

George, Henry, *Progress and Poverty*, New York: D. Appleton Company, 1880.

Gillin, John Lewis, *Poverty and Dependency*, New York: D. Appleton-Century Company, 1937 (3rd edition).

Hobson, John Atkinson, *Poverty in Plenty*, New York: The Macmillan Company, 1931.

Hollander, Jacob H., *The Abolition of Poverty*, Boston: Houghton-Mifflin Company, 1914.

Kelso, Robert W., *Poverty*, New York: Longmans, Green and Company, 1929.

National Resources Committee, *Consumer Expenditures in the United States, 1935–1936*, Washington, 1939.

National Resources Committee, *Consumer Incomes in the United States, 1935–1936*, Washington, 1938.

Parmelee, Maurice F., *Farewell to Poverty*, New York: John Wiley and Sons, 1935.

Parmelee, Maurice F., *Poverty and Social Progress*, New York: The Macmillan Company, 1916.

Rowntree, B. Seebohm, *Poverty, a Study of Town Life*, London: The Macmillan Company, 1901.

CHAPTER 22

CRIME

BY DR. C. W. TOPPING

Associate Professor of Sociology and Economics, University of
British Columbia, Vancouver, Canada

THE STUDY OF CRIME

Crime has been and remains one of the great social problems of
humanity. The study of crime from the scientific viewpoint is
recent. Lombroso died thirty-three years ago (1836–1909). The
American Institute of Criminal Law and Criminology was founded
in the year of his death, with the first issue of the *Journal* appearing
in 1910. Healy, Burt, Gillin, Bates, Patterson, Sutherland, Hughes,
Shaw, the Gluecks, and other outstanding scholars and administrators whose work will be described in this chapter, are our contemporaries.

What is crime? A definition is particularly difficult because of
the necessity of reconciling religious, philosophic, legal, psychological and sociological viewpoints. The cleric tends to identify crime
and sin and to regard a crime as an act displeasing to Deity. No
lawyer would concede such a definition. To him a crime is a violation of law, with treason as the crime of crimes since it endangers
the life of the state itself. At the other extreme is the sociologist
who is likely to define a crime as a violation of any conduct norm
whatever. The best compromise definition is perhaps that of Maurice Parmelee:[1]

> A crime is an act forbidden and punished by the law,
> which is almost always immoral according to the prevailing
> ethical standard, which is usually harmful to society, which
> is ordinarily feasible to repress by penal measures, and whose
> repression is necessary or is supposed to be necessary to the
> preservation of the existing social order.

A definition of crime might be followed by a classification of
crimes. One might then define a criminal, a delinquent and a
juvenile delinquent, with classifications in each case. However, the

[1] Maurice Parmelee, *Criminology*, Macmillan, 1918, p. 32. See Thorsten
Sellin, *Culture Conflict and Crime*, Social Science Research Council, 1938.

treatment of the subject in this chapter proceeds with a definition of a *criminologist* and a tentative classification of criminologists, in the belief that a review of the writings of sincere students of the phenomena associated with crime and criminals will reveal the factual basis of the science more quickly and more convincingly than could any categorical series of definitions or classifications.

A Classification of Criminologists and Their Writings

A criminologist will be defined as a writer who has done serious work of an original nature in the field of crime and delinquency. If the name of a writer appears in more than one category it signifies that he has made a definite contribution in each classification in which he is listed.

1. *The Supernaturalists:* Those who believe that a criminal act results from some force extraneous to both the individual committing the act and to the environment in which the individual finds himself. Biological, psychological, and cultural factors are recognized by this group but the ultimate factor is a supernatural force.

    a. The Religious Group: St. Augustine, St. Thomas, The Thomists, many contemporary church groups, etc.

    b. The Classical Group: Beccaria, Bentham, Feuerbach, Rossi, Garraud, Joly, etc.

    c. The Popular Group: Persons who have made no scientific study of crime but who have definite opinions on the subject which they do not hesitate to express.

2. *The Psychobiologists:* Those who believe that criminal behavior results from some force at work within the individual.

    a. The Anthropological Group: Lombroso, Goring, Goddard, Dugdale, Berman, Ferri, Garofalo, Hooton, etc.

    b. The Psychological Group: Burt, Terman, Adler, Bronner, Gault, etc.

    c. The Psychiatric Group: Healy, B. Glueck, S. and E. Glueck, Drucker, Hexter, Fernald, etc.

    d. The Psycho-analytic Group: White, Alexander, Aichhorn, Kenworthy, Reik, Flugel, etc.

3. *The Sociologists:* Those who believe that criminal behavior results from some force at work within the environment.

    a. The Propagandist Group: Dickens, Hugo, Cooper, Darrow, Kavanagh, Lindsey, Campbell, B. Shaw, etc.

    b. The Historical Group: Lewis, Fosdick, Brockway, Barman, Cass, Lou, etc.

c. The Administrative Group: Lawes, Fishman, Hughes, Ruggles-Brise, Patterson, Bates, Vollmer, MacCormick.

d. The Inmate Group: Black, Withrow, O'Hare, Hobhouse, Brockway, Debs, etc.

e. The Legal Group: Wigmore, Pound, Moley, Archambault, Best, etc.

f. The Situationalist Group: Ferri, Tarde, C. Shaw, Thrasher, Hayner, Tannenbaum, etc.

g. The Survey Group: Burgess, Wickersham, Moley, Eliot, Robison, etc.

h. The Multiple Factor Group: Gillin, Sutherland, Parmelee, B. Shaw, H. Ellis, Cantor, Reckless, Sullenger, Rogers, S. and E. Glueck, Healy, Burt, Gault, etc.

This brief outline has been set down in the interest of clarity. A treatment in greater detail follows:

The Supernaturalists

1. *The Religious Group.* The theories of primitive peoples concerning crime and punishment are interesting and instructive but have had little influence on modern attitudes and control programs. With the coming of the Medieval Period and the fusion of the philosophy of Aristotle, the theories of the Roman jurists, the teachings of the Christian church, and the beliefs of the Jewish Old Testament a body of criminological theories and practices came into existence that are still potent today. It is because of the existence and the power of the traditions which grew up during this period that a Supernatural School of Criminology must be recognized. What were some of the main tenets of the group? They tended to identify crime and sin, to stress free will and personal responsibility, to believe in expiation through punishment and in the individualization of punishment. The followers of St. Thomas were prepared to recognize a determinism of Divine origin. The individual was responsible to God alone; the agents of the State and of the Church acted upon delegated authority.

Church courts adopted a humanitarian attitude, did not inflict capital punishment, and administered their own canon law. They introduced witnesses and torture with a view to establishing guilt by confession both as to deed and as to intent. Responsibility permeated every circumstance of the crime and the extent of responsibility had to be determined in each case as had the extent of punishment. The point of focus in an ecclesiastical court was the criminal himself rather than the crime. Here was a soul that had sinned; here was a human being with possibilities of purification and regeneration through confession, expiation, and punishment. Rebellion against God, an evil will, deliberate choice: these must be overcome. God, not society, was ultimate and to Him the ultimate wrong had been done. Few theories have given greater dignity to the criminal. Yet these theories are held by few, if any, criminologists today.

2. *The Classical Group.* Under Medieval theory responsibility had to be determined specifically in each case, as had the amount of punishment. The details were left to the presiding Justice since the law could not anticipate the attendant circumstances in each particular case. Abuses grew up, judges became venal, class prejudice entered into court decisions, friends brought pressure to bear, the majesty of the law came into disrepute. Cesare Beccaria (1738–1794) cried out in passionate protest against the arbitrary and tyrannical power of the judges of his time. His *Crimes and Punishments* (1764) opens with a statement of the social contract theory and he, as a matter of fact, acknowledged himself to be a disciple of both Rousseau and Montesquieu. Beccaria mentions specifically as worthy of censure secret accusations, the long confinement of accused persons before trial, capital punishment, the subversive influence of the friends of the judge, severity in crimes against property, and the abuse of the pardoning power. He advocated absolute equality before the law, that legislators should make the laws, that judges should determine guilt and pronounce sentence, that punishments should be set down in detail in the laws and that they should vary in severity according to the menace of the crime to society, that punishments should be certain and prompt rather than severe, and that the whole process of law should aim at deterrence and prevention. Punishment should be public, immediate, necessary, the least possible, proportioned to the crime and determined by the laws.

Bentham developed these theories in England and Feuerbach in Germany[2] while the Neo-Classical School (Rossi, Garraud, Joly) modified them so as to bring them more into touch with the realities of life, especially with reference to extenuating circumstances.

[2] Raymond Saleilles, *The Individualization of Punishment*, Little, Brown, 1911, p. 52.

The Classical School influenced directly the French Penal Codes of 1791 and 1810 and indirectly the criminal law of New York State as well as British common law and British penal codes.[3]

3. *The Popular Group.* To this group belong students of crime and others, who, in spite of the writings of scientific criminologists, remain unconvinced that crime is a natural phenomenon to be studied and brought under control by objective methods. They commonly insist that free will, supernatural powers, and the personality of an administrator are more potent than biology, geography, and social conditions in the control of crime. It is probable that the group is numerically larger than all other groups combined. The contribution of the group to the science of criminology has been negligible.

The Psychobiologists

1. *The Anthropological Group.* Cesare Lombroso considered crime to be a natural product growing out of factors that could be observed and measured and that were largely anthropological. His *The Criminal, in Relation to Anthropology, Jurisprudence, and Psychiatry* appearing as a small pamphlet in 1876 had grown to a three volume work by 1900, had firmly established an objective method for the study of the criminal, and had, in the words of Ferri, given rise to a "whole library" of studies in criminal anthropology. The congenital criminal was at first considered a throwback to a primitive type exhibiting the same anatomic, psychologic, and social traits. Later a triple theory was developed in which moral insanity and epilepsy were added to atavism as basic in accounting for criminal types. Lombroso conducted psychological as well as anthropological studies and modified his theories considerably in his later writings. The work of this scholar stands as a pioneering effort by an original mind, and the founder of the Positive (Italian) School of Criminology well merits the title of founder of scientific criminology. Beccaria had made the transition from a religious hypothesis to a philosophic hypothesis, Lombroso based his studies on scientific hypotheses.

Enrico Ferri, the greatest of the Lombrosians, broadened the research base of his master to such an extent that he merits listing with such modern scholars as Gillin and Sutherland in the Multiple Social Factor Group. Ferri repudiated utterly the "free will"

[3] *Idem*, "Introduction to the English Version," by Roscoe Pound.

hypothesis of the Classical Group and argued, "In order to be a criminal it is rather necessary that the individual should find himself permanently or transitorialy in such personal, physical and moral conditions, and live in such an environment, which become for him a chain of cause and effect, externally and internally, that disposes him toward crime."[4] The Classical School had concerned itself with juridical analysis, Ferri focussed attention on the criminal himself and on his environment. He continued the anthropological work of Lombroso and supplemented it with work on natural and social factors in crime causation. The function of penal treatment is stated as the protection of society, a statement with which most modern criminologists would agree. Ferri gave a classification of criminals which included a "born incorrigible" class, and carried his "penal substitutes" to extremes but his *Criminal Sociology*[5] can still be read with profit and his contention that criminal jurisprudence should become criminal sociology merits the most careful consideration of legislators and of the judiciary.

Dr. Charles Goring by the use of control groups demonstrated that the criminal stigmata listed by Lombroso were widely diffused among the general population. His studies have been considered until very recently to have settled the question of a criminal physical type.[6]

Earnest A. Hooton has revived the study of criminal anthropology at Harvard university by accumulating an enormous mass of data from jails, penitentiaries, etc. The material has been subjected to statistical analysis and has been checked against control groups. The Hooton studies focus around the questions: Do criminals of the same racial origin differ in their bodily characteristics according to the type of crime they commit? Do criminals of any given racial or national group differ physically from the law-abiding population of identical ethnic origin? Do the various hereditary physical groups which we call races differ in their criminal propensities? The Hooton laboratories have yielded an affirmative answer in each case. Frank A. Ross in reviewing *The American Criminal: An Anthropological Study, Vol. I: The Native White Criminal of Native Parentage* is stimulated but unconvinced.[7] He thinks that the mate-

[4] Enrico Ferri, *The Positive School of Criminology*, Kerr, 1913, p. 22.

[5] Appleton, 1900.

[6] F. Tannenbaum, *Crime and the Community*, Ginn, 1938, pp. 198–201.

[7] *The American Journal of Sociology*, Vol. XLV, No. 3, November, 1939, pp. 477–480.

rial should be reworked and that particularistic studies should be undertaken to supplement the more general studies. Ross argues that the Hooton statistical procedures do not yield criminal types in the Lombroso meaning of the term.

Robert L. Dugdale's study *The Jukes* which is summarized in Estabrook, *The Jukes in 1915* and which has itself gone through many editions has proved to be one of the most controversial volumes of our time. Clarence Darrow argued in the *American Mercury*[8] that he would prefer Max Juke for a neighbor as against Jonathan Edwards, but F. H. Giddings, in the Preface to the Edition of 1910, holds the book to be an outstanding example of correct and meticulous sociological investigation. Dugdale gathered his own data, did field work to gain first hand impressions, based his generalizations on the facts collected, and regarded his conclusions as tentative. The facts presented concerning the 1,200 descendents of Max Juke over a period of seventy-five years are thought-provoking and can be confirmed by modern studies; but the problem remains, namely, to what extent is the situation affected by heredity. Davenport, Popenoe, and others have continued research in the Dugdale tradition. A comparable study of the Kallikaks was made by Henry H. Goddard in 1912.

A physical examination is routine in a modern prison entailing the collection of masses of material amenable to scientific analysis. Physicians recognize the importance of physical handicaps as related to compensatory behavior in children. It is a truism that tonsils must be removed, limbs straightened, and eyesight improved if humans in need of treatment are to lead normal, satisfying lives. Physicians believe in themselves and in their work and this is particularly true of the endocrinologists as interpreted by Louis Berman who writes, "The life of every individual, in every stage, is dominated largely by his glands of internal secretion."[9] Few criminologists would accept this statement without the most rigorous investigation.

2. *The Psychological Group.* Cyril Burt's *Young Delinquent*[10] entitles this scholar to rank as the outstanding representative of persons conducting research into the psychology of juvenile crime

---

[8] *American Mercury,* Vol. 6, October, 1925, pp. 147–157.

[9] Louis Berman, *The Glands Regulating Personality*, Macmillan, 1928, p. 110. See also M. G. Schlapp, "Behavior and Gland Disease," *Journal of Heredity*, Vol. XV, 1924.

[10] University of London Press, 1925.

and delinquency. The thesis of the book is that delinquency in juveniles is nothing but an outstanding sample of childish naughtiness. The author, after enunciating his thesis, proceeds forthwith to an analysis of the case of a young murderer by the name of Jeremiah Jones who has not yet turned eight. There follows one of the most careful and scientific studies of young delinquents that has ever been produced by a single individual: heredity, the home, the community; physique, intellect, temperament, general instability; sentiments, complexes, and neuroses: each receives meticulous treatment in its bearing on the central problem. Burt has been surprisingly successful in the intergration of highly varied materials into a compact and intelligible whole. He concludes that psychological conditions are a major factor in more than half the cases studied (55% boys, 56% girls) but is prepared to admit that other factors, including biological and cultural conditions, have considerable influence in particular cases especially as secondary factors. The broad experience of this scholar and the large number of cases passing through his hands are likely to win respect for his opinions which have a natural appeal in the first instance on account of the clarity and reasonableness with which they are put forward.

Drucker and Hexter in *Children Astray*[11] present fascinating case materials covering an experiment in mingling delinquent and dependent children in one institution. The cases are written up in non-technical language and the results of treatment are given. The writers both stress and illustrate the unique traits of each ward in contrast with the dull sameness of the delinquencies for which commitments were made. The volume should be read by all persons interested in young delinquents.

The Unadjusted Girl[12] is written with that brilliance and insight which characterizes practically all of the work of W. I. Thomas. The ancient and continuing problem of sex delinquency in young girls is restated from a modern viewpoint that recognizes its complexity. Not all hypotheses are followed through to a logical conclusion nor are all generalizations supported with adequate data but an hypothesis as brilliant as that of the four wishes requires little support. It is clear to Thomas that adolescent girls become delinquent, not for economic reasons: money and the like; but for psychological reasons: the wish for new experience, the wish for

[11] Harvard University Press, 1923.
[12] Little, Brown, 1923.

security, the wish for response, the wish for recognition. And other scholars taking up these four wishes have contended that they act as drives in other behavior situations and may ultimately take the place of instincts, prepotent reflexes, etc., in psychological literature.

3. *The Psychiatric Group.* Dr. William Healy of the Judge Baker Guidance Center, Boston, is the undoubted leader of this group in which the inspiration of his personality and his own industry have induced a productivity matched in few fields of contemporary scientific endeavor. His chief contribution has been the bringing to bear in his clinics, on the delinquents passing through his hands, all the resources of psychiatry and of social case work with a view to the rehabilitation of these maladjusted persons. It is not possible, in the opinion of Healy, to have too much information on a case and he has advocated since 1926 "thoroughly critical studies of what really are the results of its (civilization's) dealings with delinquency and crime."[13]

The most direct method for finding out the sources of the polygenesis of delinquency is through a study of the mental life: emotional attitudes, ideational content, thwartings, dissatisfactions, etc.[14] The main classes of variables that are known to be effective in producing anti-social conduct are as follows:[15]

1. The physical and mental equipment of any given individual as it may exist at any given time.

2. The formative life experiences of the individual.

3. The formed reactive tendencies of the individual— mainly to be thought of as elements of ideational life, emotional tensions, and habit formation.

4. The environmental influences and social pressures which have been active recently, prior to, or at the immediate time of the commission of delinquency and crime.

Healy is convinced that heredity, degeneracy, general physical structure, mental defect, epilepsy, endocrine disorders, and diseased tonsils have been overrated as explanations of causes of delinquent beginnings and careers. Special physical conditions such as over-

---

[13] *Delinquents and Criminals*, p. 3.

[14] "Psychiatry and the Juvenile Delinquent," *American Journal of Psychiatry*, Vol. 91, No. 6, May, 1935, p. 1315.

[15] "Crime and the Individual," *Proceedings of the Association for Research in Nervous and Mental Diseases*, Vol. XIV, December, 1933. See also *Twenty-five Years of Child Guidance*, Illinois Institute for Juvenile Research, n.d.

development in adolescence may be causative but the worst criminal careers upon the records of the clinic are the life histories of persons diagnosed as abnormal, unstable egocentrics. Many criminals and delinquents have also been diagnosed as constitutional inferior personalities and a lesser number as organically driven persons, (restless and unstable but not hypo-manic).

The Judge Baker Foundation Case Studies were valuable as teaching aids especially when issued with the staff comment detached from the manuscript of the case to permit of free discussion by the students. *The Individual Delinquent*[16] published in 1915, in spite of the fact that Healy at this time regarded therapy as of the future and limited himself to considerations of etiology, diagnosis and prognosis, created a revolution in thought concerning delinquency comparable to that created in the field of biological evolution by the publication of Darwin's *Origin of Species*. *Delinquents and Criminals, Their Making and Unmaking*[17] a study of the effectiveness of treatment methods in Chicago and in Boston also broke new ground. *New Light on Delinquency and its Treatment* (1936) records the findings of an experimental project concerned with delinquent and non-delinquent siblings conducted by Healy and Bronner in cooperation with the Institute of Human Relations of Yale University. The delinquents were classified into three groups at the conclusion of the project and a statement was set down concerning modification of behavior trends in each of the three groups. Group I comprised 26 delinquents suffering from "abnormal personality, neuroticism, or severe mental conflict." Fifty-eight per cent of this group were continuing the behavior that had brought them under observation when a check up was made two years or more after the treatment period. The delinquency ceased in one case during the treatment period. Group II comprised 50 delinquents handicapped by adverse home and community conditions (social pathology). Forty-six per cent of this group were still delinquent at the time of the check-up. Sixteen ceased to be delinquent during the treatment period. Group III comprised 67 cases where "factors of personality difficulty and social pathology were not so severe or so piled up that they seemed to offer insuperable obstacles to therapy." Nineteen per cent of this group were still delinquent at the time of the check-up. Fifty-five ceased delin-

[16] Little, Brown, and Co., 1927.
[17] William Healy and A. F. Bronner, Macmillan, 1926.

quency during the period of treatment, of whom seven had lapsed into delinquency two or more years after treatment ceased. Institutional treatment is regarded as the most suitable control for members of Group I, foster home treatment for members of Group II. The failures in the case of members of Group III are considered more significant than the successes.

The three broad practical implications of the project should also be mentioned :[18]

(1) Delinquency should be treated as a "form of rational behavior" dependent on definite causations—as "one mode of self-expression."

(2) Many serious cases of delinquency result from an attempt on the part of the offender to achieve compensatory satisfactions, to bolster up his ego, etc.

(3) The only logical procedure in treatment is first to determine the cause of the symptoms.

Child Guidance Clinics, which did not exist on this continent in 1908, have grown up in great numbers and have spread to England, Holland, France, and Poland.[19] Bernard Glueck's *Studies in Forensic Psychiatry,* appearing in 1916, gave a considerable impetus to mental hygiene while Stevenson and Smith's *Child Guidance Clinics, a Quarter Century of Development* presented a stimulating and encouraging historical statement of the growth of child guidance centers.

Sheldon and Eleanor Glueck continued the work of Healy and his Associates in a series of studies: *500 Criminal Careers, 500 Delinquent Women, 1000 Juvenile Delinquents,*[20] which aimed to present in detail and in rigorously scientific form the results achieved by the contemporary program of treatment for juveniles in the United States. The conclusions reached give small encouragement to those who have devoted their lives to work with juvenile delinquents. The Massachusetts Reformatory, for example, failed in eighty per cent of the cases checked by the Gluecks to make any appreciable difference in the lives of the young persons committed to the care of the officials of this institution.[21] The conclusions of

[18] *Op. cit.,* pp. 200–206.

[19] William Healy, *Twenty-five Years of Child Guidance,* Illinois Institute for Juvenile Research, n.d., pp. 1–2.

[20] *500 Delinquent Women,* Knopf, 1934; *1000 Juvenile Delinquents,* Harvard University, 1934.

[21] S. and E. Glueck, *500 Criminal Careers,* Knopf, 1930, p. ix.

Later Criminal Careers confirm those of the earlier studies. The chief factor inducing change from anti-social to social behavior appears to be maturation, growing up, and the basic problem for educators, psychologists and correctional workers the task of speeding up this benign process of nature.[22] The prolific writings of the Gluecks are packed with facts, analyses, tables, conclusions, summaries and recommendations. They have cleared the ground for a new and more constructive approach to the perennial problem of anti-social behavior on the part of young persons.

4. *The Psycho-Analytic Group.* G. Stanley Hall and William A. White were influential in introducing Freud and Freudian concepts to American scholars. White definitely entered the field of criminology with the publication in 1933 of his *Crime and Criminals.*[23] The concepts of this school and the stimulating effect of these concepts on contemporary thought and research are well stated in Volume XLV of the *American Journal of Sociology.* The Freudian influence on criminology has been indirect rather than direct but Healy has employed psychoanalytic techniques where he considered them helpful, as have others. In *Roots of Crime,* Alexander and Healy present the findings of sessions with confirmed delinquents in which psychoanalytic procedures had been applied to behavior problems. The study demonstrates the importance of repressed factors such as emotional fixations, unwholesome identifications, deeply sensed libidinal thwartings and an unacknowledged wish to return to the infantile state of irresponsible dependency of the prison regime.[24] The thesis is that emotional factors create inner tensions which are relieved by criminal acts. Healy advocates careful analysis as a substitution for incarceration.

Theodor Reik's *The Unknown Murderer*[25] is crammed with case materials drawn from works on psychology, criminal jurisprudence, anthropology, and the author's own experience. Reik is very much disturbed by judicial errors and is convinced that they can be reduced by psychoanalysis. The officials have concentrated on the murder and have ignored clues lying at their feet. A thorough

---

[22] S. and E. Glueck, *Later Criminal Careers,* Commonwealth Fund, 1937, pp. 202–212.

[23] William A. White, *Crime and Criminals,* Farrar and Rinehart, 1933.

[24] Wm. Healy, ''Psychoanalytic Contributions to the Understanding and Treatment of Behavior Problems,'' *American Journal of Sociology,* Vol. XLV, No. 3, November, 1939.

[25] Hogarth Press, 1936.

analysis must be made of the total situation: judge, jury, witnesses, public and the murderer. Analysts should refuse to give testimony in court as experts competent to determine the guilt or innocence of a defendant in a murder trial. He argues that it is not possible to determine psychologically whether an urgent desire to kill has actually resulted in a murder or not. The aim of the Berlin Psycho-Analytical Institute, according to this scholar, "was to train the representatives of criminal law so highly as to be able to dispense with those representatives and eventually with the law itself."[26]

The Sociologists

1. *The Propagandist Group.* It is probable that Courtney Ryley Cooper should rank as the greatest of the contemporary propagandists, with his *Ten Thousand Public Enemies* (1935), *Here's to Crime* (1937), and *Designs in Scarlet* (1939).[27] Some persons may class these three volumes with salacious literature rather than with criminology, nevertheless, they have points in common with the book of Amos. There is the same vividness, the same concrete detail, the same burning passion against what the Jewish prophets made a habit of calling sin. Cooper realizes that the dangerous criminal is the organized criminal and does not hesitate to say so. He pays well deserved tribute to the police officers, prosecutors, jurors, guards, parole board officials, and others who go straight in spite of pressure from the underworld and the paid servants of the underworld.

Bernard Shaw's "Preface" to *English Prisons under Local Government*[28] is a masterpiece. There is probably no more brilliant treatment of crime in the brief compass of one hundred pages in any language; and the essay is competent as well as brilliant. This fact will be clear to any criminologist who reads the Recapitulation.[29] To be classed with Shaw's sparkling tirade is a Chapter in Harry Elmer Barnes's *Society in Transition*,[30] titled "A New Perspective on Crime in Contemporary America." The newest thesis of this versatile scholar is that the real criminals in the United States are the pent house millionaires who organize and direct the lesser fry of the organized crime rings. Since these men are never caught,

26 *Op. cit.*, p. 248.
27 See bibliography.
28 Sidney and Beatrice Webb, Longmans, 1922.
29 *Op. cit.*, pp. lxix–lxxiii.
30 Prentice-Hall, 1939, pp. 675–719.

imprisoned, and studied the science of criminology gives a false perspective on crime and must be reorganized from the foundations up. Thus Barnes supports Campbell, and Marcus Kavanagh[31] supports both of them in urging a reorientation of criminal justice so as to place the racketeer and his accomplices in the center of the police net.

Eugene V. Debs, Ben B. Lindsey, Miriam Van Waters, Frank Tannenbaum, Austin Campbell, O. C. J. Withrow, and Joseph F. Fishman[32] have supported Bernard Shaw in his passionate condemnation of the vindictiveness, stupidity, apathetic cruelty and downright terrorism with which the criminal, in contrast to the insane person, has been treated in our day. Broker Campbell gives to his series of articles[33] the title "House of Hate," Inspector Fishman calls one of his books *Crucibles of Crime*,[34] Presidential Candidate Debs has an article "Wasting Men."[35] Lindsey, and Van Waters have few equals where it is a question of constructive interpretation and defense of neglected and misunderstood adolescents.

2. *The Historical Group.* The list of scholars who have contributed historical studies to criminology is so extensive as to make its inclusion out of the question. A few works have been selected at random for mention and comment. *The Development of American Prisons and Prison Customs, 1776–1845* by Orlando F. Lewis,[36] based as it is on personal contacts and obscure documents, is unlikely to be duplicated and has, therefore, unique value. Barman has written the standard work on the English Borstal System,[37] the Webbs the standard work on English Local Prisons,[38] and Smith on Rural Crime Control.[39] Fosdick has pioneered in the study of police systems,[40] Robinson of penal institutions,[41] and Lou of

[31] Marcus Kavanagh, *The Criminal and His Allies*, Bobbs-Merrill, 1928.
[32] See bibliography.
[33] *Maclean's Magazine*, Vol. 46, Aug. 1 to Dec. 1, 1933.
[34] Cosmopolis Press, 1923.
[35] *The World Tomorrow*, Vol. V, No. 8, August, 1922.
[36] Prison Association of New York, 1922.
[37] S. Barman, *The English Borstal System*, King, 1934.
[38] *Op. cit.*
[39] Bruce Smith, *Rural Crime Control*, Columbia University, 1933.
[40] *American Police Systems*, Century, 1921.
[41] *Penology in the United States*, Winston, 1922.

juvenile courts.[42] The annual *Proceedings*[43] of the American Prison Association and the *Year Books*[44] of the National Probation Association provide excellent source materials for historical research in criminology as do articles in the *Journal of Criminal Law and Criminology*.[45] A very important volume in the history of theory is De Quiros, *Modern Theories of Criminality*.[46]

3. *The Administrative Groups.* Lewis E. Lawes of Sing Sing has written a number of books, an unusual achievement in a warden, since a prison administrator under the traditional policy of most States is commonly advised by his superiors to remain silent. The inmates cannot talk, the wardens dare not. Yet the administrators and the inmates are likely to know more about crime and criminals than all other groups combined. *Invisible Stripes*[47] is an outstanding book for this reason alone: It presents both the inmate and the official points of view in a single volume. Two documents have been interwoven; a diary of an inmate participant observer who is something of a philosopher, and a trenchant analysis of the causes of crime by the author of 20,000 years in Sing Sing. "Only as we recognize crime as a challenge to betrayed democracy can we effectively destroy it."[48] This is the conclusion of the Sing Sing collaborators.

Another administrator who never permitted himself to be snuffed out by a mantle of silence is August Vollmer, formerly Chief of Police of Berkeley, at present Professor of Police Administration at the University of California. The closing sentence of his *The Police and Modern Society*,[49] "Democracy's strongest reliance is the police," dovetails with the thesis of *Invisible Stripes*. The agent of the public is the police. This agent must be both improved and supported if law and order are to prevail on this continent. The body of the book consists of a realistic account of the work and difficulties of the police in America.

Sir Evelyn Ruggles-Brise represents the orthodox English ad-

[42] *Juvenile Courts in the United States,* University of North Carolina, 1927.

[43] The Association, New York.

[44] The Association, New York.

[45] First number 1910. Editor, Professor R. H. Gault of Northwestern University.

[46] C. Bernaldo De Quiros, Little, Brown, 1911.

[47] Farrar and Rinehart, 1938.

[48] *Op. cit.*, p. 314.

[49] University of California Press, 1936, p. 237.

ministrative point of view,[50] William St. Pierre Hughes the orthodox Canadian administrative outlook.[51] The former was President
of the International Prison Commission in 1924 and has summarized the pronouncements of this organization from 1872 to 1910
in his *Prison Reform at Home and Abroad*. Alexander Patterson[52]
represents English Borstal.

Sanford Bates[53] may be selected as representative of the type of
administrator that may be developed in a modern penal system.
Courtney Ryley Cooper, who is none too respectful of officialdom,
recognizes his worth and pays him tribute. Members of the American Prison Association, in which he has long been a leader, characterize him as intelligent, informed, fair-minded, as able, dynamic
and tolerant. Austin H. MacCormick,[54] whom Bates encouraged
to take up administrative work, is carrying the traditions of the
Federal Bureau of Prisons into New York State.

Inspector Joseph F. Fishman's *Crucibles of Crime* is the most
powerful and moving expose of the American county jail that has
appeared in print.

4. *The Inmate Group*. Persons familiar with the relationship of
Clifford W. Beers[55] to the mental hygiene movement will not despise
the writings of former inmates of penal institutions. The most
notable person who has written of his prison experiences is Eugene
V. Debs. Debs adopted the extreme view that less harm would be
done to society if all persons incarcerated in prisons were released
than the harm society will suffer in the long run by keeping these
persons confined.[56] Much praise has been accorded English prisons
in recent years. A study by two conscientious objectors, who were
incarcerated during the war, Stephen Hobhouse and A. Fenner
Brockway, presents concrete evidence to demonstrate that these
prisons were not models for the world in 1922. This elaborate

[50] *The English Prison System*, Macmillan, 1921.

[51] Superintendent of Canadian Penitentiaries, author *Reports of the Superintendent of Penitentiaries*, 1919–1931.

[52] *Across the Bridges*, Arnold, 1928.

[53] At present a member of the Board of Parole of the State of New York;
has been successively Commissioner of Correction for Massachusetts, Director
of the Federal Bureau of Prisons and Executive Director, Boys Clubs of
America.

[54] Commissioner of Correction, New York City, Field Work for *Handbook
of American Prisons*, Putnam, 1925.

[55] *A Mind that Found Itself*, Doubleday, Page, 1927; First edition of 1908.

[56] *World Tomorrow, loc. cit.*

monograph, *English Prisons To-day, being the Report of the Prison Enquiry Committee*,[57] is carefully documented and bears the stamp of sincere scholarship. The Prison Commissioners, who had at first supported the Enquiry, withdrew that support when they discovered that the inmate point of view was to dominate the findings.

Eubank and Clark's, *Lockstep and Corridor*[58] is one of the earlier inmate autobiographies with comment, of which Clifford Shaw's, *The Jack Roller*[59] is perhaps the best example.

The statements in O. C. J. Withrow's, *Shackling the Transgressor*[60] are specific. The author gives one the opportunity to prove or disprove what he records. Such sentences as the following are representative:

> At that period (1927) the food was so bad that many meals could not be eaten and many plates of stew stank to the skies. . . . Hot water was plentiful; soap was fair; brush was vile. . . . Razors were not sterilized and diseased men interchanged with the untainted without comment. . . . Sunday was the worst day in seven. . . . I make the deliberate statement that no one is ever taught a trade in Kingston penitentiary. . . . Dust and dirt everywhere! That was my first impression of the library. . . . Only thirty-five minutes are allowed for school each day. . . . I had some necessary bridge work done by this (the penitentiary) dentist for which my family paid and which had to be replaced on my return home. . . . "We tame lions here," said the warden, "We'll tame you." That was the spirit of the institution. Mentally sick men were not studied or considered. They were brutally punished. . . . The visits of friends are definitely discouraged. . . . We went over the personnel frequently and, though we (the inmates) endeavoured to be entirely fair in our judgment, we could name less than twelve (out of one hundred and fifty) of the officers who were not completely subservient to the system.

The volume closes with a series of recommendations that are surprisingly similar to the recommendations to be found in any *Annual Report of the Superintendent of Canadian Penitentiaries:* A National Society for Penal Reform; higher standards for staff; classification of inmates and individualization of treatment; work

57 Longmans, 1922.

58 Charles L. Clark and Earle Edward Eubank, University of Cincinnati Press, 1927.

59 University of Chicago Press, 1930.

60 Nelson, 1933.

with pay; an enlarged and improved educational, vocational, and religious program; a modernized hospital; good meals; abolition of the Remission Branch and the substitution of a Parole Board. Superintendent W. S. Hughes had been making such recommendations since 1919, the *Report of the Royal Commission to Investigate the Penal System of Canada, 1938,* contained them, the *Report of the Ontario Royal Commission on Public Welfare, 1930,* went beyond them and included recommendations for the reorganization of "the most difficult feature of our social system—the jails."[61]

5. *The Legal Group.* The legal group stems from Beccaria rather than from Lombroso. It stresses philosophy, logic and legal precedent rather than research, science, and experiment. As a result criminal jurisprudence is less coincident with scientific criminology than one might have been led to expect. The most active agent in bridging the gap between the courts and the sciences is, perhaps, the *American Institute of Criminal Law and Criminology*[62] with its official organ the *Journal of Criminal Law and Criminology.* The *American Law Institute*[63] has made a considerable contribution in its Model Code of Criminal Procedure and in its model program for the correctional training and treatment of young offenders worked out by a special committee of lawyers, jurists, sociologists, psychiatrists, criminologists and prison administrators[64] as well as in its continuing research. The *American Bar Association* has also been active in this work of integration.

The *Report on Criminal Procedure* of the *National Commission on Law Observance and Enforcement*[65] lists the essentials of a criminal proceeding as:

(1) To bring the accused before or within the power of the tribunal, (2) a preliminary investigation to insure that the cause is one which should be prosecuted, (3) notice to the accused of the offence charged, (4) opportunity to prepare for trial, procure witnesses, and make needed investigations, (5) a speedy trial, (6) a fair trial before an impartial tribunal, and (7) one review of the case as a whole by a suitable appellate tribunal.

[61] *The Report of the Royal Commission on Public Welfare, 1930,* King's Printer, Toronto, 1930, p. 77.

[62] Initiated in 1909 by Dean John Henry Wigmore.

[63] Organized in Washington, February 23, 1923.

[64] Rockefeller, John D. 3rd, "Salvaging the Young Criminal," *New York Times Magazine,* November 10, 1940, p. 10.

[65] U. S. Government Printing Office, 1931, p. 16.

That the actual procedure is much more complicated and confusing Judge Marcus Kavanagh makes clear. Three chapters[66] of his *The Criminal and His Allies* are taken up with the technicality. He recommends a statute of eighteen words to deal with this particular evil. "All laws and rules of courts concerning forms, practise and procedure shall be directory only, and not mandatory."[67]

Roscoe Pound wrote *An Introduction to the Philosophy of Law*,[68] he also served on the *Wickersham Commission*. "Philosophy," he writes, "has been a powerful instrument in the legal armory and the times are ripe for restoring it to its old place therein." Then, in the very next sentence, "the science of law—that science—in which philosophy may help us."[69] Pound has been eminently successful in integrating philosophy, law, and science in his writings.

Raymond Moley deserves mention for his work on the *Missouri Crime Survey*[70] and for his *Our Criminal Courts;*[71] Mr. Justice Archambault for his Chairmanship of *The Royal Commission to Investigate the Penal System of Canada, 1938,*[72] Judge Ben B. Lindsey for his advocacy of juvenile courts, and Clarence Darrow for his eminence as a criminal lawyer and for his *Crime, Its Cause and Treatment.*[73] Bests, *Crime and the Criminal Law*[74] sketches the social implications of certain legislative enactments.

6. *The Situationalist Group.* Enrico Ferri, almost at the time of the birth of scientific criminology, recognized the importance of environmental factors. He advocated free trade (as related to smuggling), emigration (as related to recidivism), progressive taxation (as related to tax frauds), the use of metallic money (as related to counterfeiting), higher salaries for public officials (as related to the corruption of public servants) and improved roads (as related to rural crime). Such changes he classed as "penal substitutes."[75] Gabriel Tarde may also be classed within the situationalists. He writes, "We have every right, it seems to me, to conclude that

[66] *Op. cit.*, Chaps. XIII, XIV, XV, Bobbs, Merrill, 1928.

[67] Kavanagh, *op. cit.*, p. 199.

[68] Yale, 1922.

[69] *Op. cit.*, pp. 10, 11.

[70] Macmillan, 1926.

[71] Minton Balch, 1930; also *Politics and Criminal Prosecution* and *Tribunes of the People.*

[72] King's Printer, Ottawa, 1938.

[73] Crowell, 1922.

[74] Macmillan, 1930.

[75] *Criminal Sociology.*

criminality . . . implies physiological and even physical conditions, but . . . it is to be accounted for better than in any other way, by the general laws of imitation.''[76] Thrasher's study of 1313 gangs,[77] Beard's study of juvenile probation,[78] the Burgess study (with Bruce and Harno) of the indeterminate sentence and parole,[79] and Queen's study of the county jail[80] have each and all demonstrated the importance of environment in its relation to crime and delinquency. Frank Tannenbaum is aggressively environmentalist.[81]

The most prolific of the situationalists is Clifford Shaw and his work is also the most convincing. Shaw and his associates had studied between 1921 and 1929 more than 100,000 individual offenders (school truants, juvenile delinquents and adult offenders). Their contacts and observations led them to believe that physical, psychological, and psychiatric summations of delinquent behavior did not tell the whole story. The cultural anthropologists gave them a lead but the first monograph coming out of the *Institute for Juvenile Research* under Shaw's editorship and direction was a study in geographic distribution.[82] This new ecological approach to the delinquent and to delinquency has stirred up much controversy but the case for delinquency areas appears to be definitely established by supporting studies. *The Jack Roller* (1930), *The Natural History of a Delinquent Career* (1931), *and Family Backgrounds in Male Juvenile Delinquency*[83] elaborate other supporting aspects of the environmentalist thesis. Shaw and his associates have demonstrated that delinquent behavior becomes more intelligible ''when studied in terms of the social situation in which it has occurred.''

An analysis of ''The Prison as a Community'' by Norman S. Hayner and Ellis Ash[84] deserves mention since it brings out more clearly than any previous research project that basic division of many prisons into an administrative world and an inmate world.

76 *Penal Philosophy*, Little, Brown, 1912, p. 416.

77 *The Gang*, University of Chicago Press, 1927.

78 *Juvenile Probation*, American Book Co., 1934.

79 *Parole and the Indeterminate Sentence*, State of Illinois, 1928.

80 *The Passing of the County Jail*, Banta, 1920.

81 *Crime and the Community*, Ginn, 1938.

82 *Delinquency Areas*, University of Chicago, 1929.

83 See bibliography.

84 *The American Sociological Review*, Vol. 5, No. 4, August, 1940, pp. 577–583.

Status in the one world implies loss of status in the other: thus the two worlds never meet. In such an environmental situation the rehabilitation of inmates is bound to be exceedingly difficult if not impossible. Austin Campbell highlighted the situation in his phrase "House of Hate."[85]

7. *The Survey Group.* The most elaborate modern criminological survey has been the publications of the *National Crime Commission on Law Observance and Enforcement.*[86] Appointed by the President of the United States with very wide powers the Commission issued fourteen monographs each prepared by an outstanding authority or a group of authorities in conjunction with a field staff. Such varied subjects as the causes of crime (Report No. 13), the cost of crime (No. 12), criminal procedure (No. 8), prosecution (No. 4) and criminal statistics (No. 3) are treated. Report No. 11 deals with *Lawlessness in Law Enforcement,* Report No. 9 with *Penal Institutions Probation and Parole,* Report No. 14 with *Police.* Recommendations are specific and to the point.[87]

The *Report of the Royal Commission to Investigate the Penal System of Canada* (1938) is the most important criminological document published in Canada during its entire history. The Commissioners visited one hundred and sixteen penal and reformative institutions on this continent and in Europe, held public and private hearings in all Canadian Provinces, conducted independent researches, and prepared a report covering more than four hundred pages.[88] A centralized prison system embodying the principles of the English penal system and to be administered by the Dominion Government is advocated.

The *Workings of the Indeterminate-Sentence Law and the Parole System of Illinois* (Bruce, Burgess, Harno) is notable because of the controversial nature of the matter at issue and of the objectivity with which the surveyors conducted their investigations and reported their findings. "The Committee recommends that the Parole Board seriously consider the placing of its work on a scientific basis by making use of the method of statistical prediction of the non-viola-

[85] *Maclean's Magazine, loc. cit.*

[86] Superintendent of Documents, Washington.

[87] See No. 9, pp. 170–174, No. 14, p. 140.

[88] See Topping, "The Report of the Royal Commission on the Penal System of Canada," *Canadian Journal of Economics and Political Science,* Vol. 4, No. 4, November, 1938.

tion or violation of parole both in the granting of paroles and in the supervision of paroled men.''[89] This is the first and most important of the two recommendations made concerning factors determining success or failure on parole. The Report is favorable to parole and the indeterminate sentence on the basis of the legislation and administration in Illinois.

The *Report of the New Jersey Prison Inquiry Commission*[90] (1917, Barnes); *The Cleveland Foundation Survey of Criminal Justice in Cleveland*[91] (1921, Adler, Pound, Fosdick, *et al.*); *The Illinois Crime Survey*[92] (1929); *The Report of the Ontario Royal Commission on Public Welfare*[93] (1930); and the *Report of the Massachusetts Special Crime Commission*[94] (1933) are representative of the innumerable studies of crime and criminal justice that have been undertaken on this continent within the past twenty-five years.

8. *The Multiple Factor Group. The Child in America*[95] (1928) and *The Clinical Treatment of the Problem Child*[96] (1939), volumes in which the authors summarize and evaluate current research and control programs, make clear the futility of any single panacea approach to the vast problems which must be faced by anyone aiming to study or to control delinquent behavior. Sullenger's, *Social Determinants in Juvenile Delinquency*[97] illustrates admirably the trend towards a study of the total situation but the book fails to achieve scholastic greatness because of the uncritical attitude of its author, especially in the chapter on the ''Prophylactics of Juvenile Delinquency.'' Such scholars as Ferri, Burt, Healy, Clifford Shaw and the Gluecks, on the other hand, while paying tribute to the total situation hypothesis have conducted their researches on that aspect of the general problem which impressed them as most worthy of emphasis. It is probable that no contemporary scholar is sufficiently well informed to cover the whole field critically and authoritatively. The most likely candidates for authorship of such a mag-

[89] *Op. cit.*, p. 267.
[90] State Library, 1917.
[91] The Cleveland Foundation, 1921.
[92] Illinois Association for Criminal Justice, Chicago, 1929.
[93] King's Printer, Toronto, 1930.
[94] Senate Document, No. 125, 1933.
[95] W. I. and Dorothy S. Thomas, Knopf, 1928.
[96] Carl R. Rogers, Houghton-Mifflin, 1939.
[97] Wiley and Sons, 1936.

num opus are Thorsten Sellin,[98] Robert H. Gault, John Lewis Gillin,[99] and Edwin H. Sutherland.[100]

These three scholars might be classified as belonging to the Summation Group of which other members are: Bernaldo De Quiros,[101] Havelock Ellis,[102] Maurice Parmelee,[103] Nathaniel Cantor,[104] and Walter C. Reckless.[105] De Quiros presents a precise and scholarly summary of the writings of nineteenth century European students of criminological theory, penology, and the scientific investigation of crime. He states that the transition has been from arguments over responsibility and free will to a recognition of the necessity of penal tutelage, with its emphasis on individualization of treatment instead of corrective punishment. Incurables should remain perpetual wards of the State.

In *The Criminal* Havelock Ellis summarizes criminological research between 1875 and 1890. The work was undertaken with considerable trepidation and largely because no one else appeared to be ready to attempt the task. The volume won for its author an international reputation. Parmelee wrote one of the earliest general texts on criminology to appear in the United States, Reckless has written the latest; in between has come the encyclopaedic work of Gillin and the keenly analytical work of Sutherland. Cantor's writings are characterized by a broad tolerance and understanding that is none too common in criminological literature. This is especially true of his treatment of the problems of the public official and of the legal group.

The breadth of outlook and the tolerance of Robert H. Gault is recognized by persons familiar with the *Journal of Criminal Law and Criminology,* since, under his editorship, this publication has accepted articles from all groups, thus becoming a genuine forum for the discussion of all aspects of the science. His *Criminology,* written from the psychologic viewpoint, is factual, concise, suggestive, stimulating, and scholarly. Gault writes:[106]

[98] *Research Memorandum on Crime in the Depression,* Social Science Research Council, 1938; *Culture Conflict* and *Crime, Idem.*

[99] *Criminology and Penology,* Century, 1926, etc.

[100] *Criminology,* Lippincott, 1924. Revised as *Principles of Criminology,* 1934 and 1939.

[101] *Modern Theories of Criminality,* Little, Brown, 1911.

[102] *The Criminal,* Walter Scott, 1890.

[103] *Criminology,* Macmillan, 1918.

[104] *Crime and Society,* Holt, 1939.

[105] *Criminal Behavior,* McGraw-Hill, 1940.

[106] Heath, 1932, p. v.

The acquired attitudes . . . are probably the greatest sources of our behavior whether it be making professional visits upon the sick or robbing banks. These attitudes develop out of infinitely numerous reactions to our environment; reactions that are facilitated or retarded by reason of our native capacities, our prepotent reflexes, etc.

Whatever agencies are set up, therefore, for dealing with the criminal must be examined as to their merits by reference to their suitability for developing appropriate attitudes among criminals and all others who come into contact with these agencies.

This scholar evidently appreciates both the psychological and the sociological viewpoint. He is therefore listed with the Multiple Factor Group as well as with the Psychological Group.

A Select List of Contemporary Criminologists

Professor Harrison A. Dobbs in a review of current literature on difficult behavior and delinquency situations[107] lists, out of a total of eight books, three volumes with which William Healy was associated. Are there other criminologists who are sufficiently notable to be placed in a category with this able and stimulating scholar and administrator? The following volumes are put forward as worthy to rank with Healy's *Individual Delinquent*: Beccaria's *Crimes and Punishments* (1764)[108] integrated philosophy, law and criminal jurisprudence; Lombroso's *The Criminal* (1876) was the first objective study of the criminal and entitles the author to be called the founder of scientific criminology; Ferri's *Criminal Sociolgy* (1893) marked him as the outstanding representative of the Positive School of Criminology and as one who had given the new science a "total situation" base; Ellis's *Criminal* (1890) made the research findings of scientific criminologists widely available and stirred public interest not only in England but throughout the world; Goring's *The English Convict* (1913) introduced the control group and gave the quietus to research in criminal anthropology with a resultant florescence of research in other aspects of the subject; Bernard Shaw's "Preface" to *English Prisons under Local Government* (1921) compressed into one hundred pages the most trenchant and stimulating treatment of crime and criminals that has ever been written; Burt's *Young Delinquent* (1925) revolutionized the thinking on juvenile delinquency in England; Gillin's

[107] *Proceedings National Conference of Social Work*, 1938, pp. 298–312.
[108] See earlier footnotes and bibliography for publishers of these volumes.

Criminology and Penology (1926) did for this continent what the
writings of Havelock Ellis had done for Europe; Shaw's *Delinquency Areas* (1929) established the ecological approach to crime
and criminals on a firm foundation; Kuhlman's *Guide to Material
on Crime and Criminal Justice* (1929) performed the spade work
for the later classified and annotated bibliographies that have appeared; The Glueck's *500 Criminal Careers* (1930) made an end of
all the loose writing about the success of contemporary methods of
penal and reformatory treatment; Shaw's *The Jack Roller* (1930)
demonstrated how the "own story" can become a scientific document of almost unrivalled worth in treatment; The Glueck's *Preventing Crime* (1936) set standards likely to influence for the
better all future annual reports and all future criminological laboratory manuals; Sutherland's *Principles of Criminology* (1939)
illustrates how a ripe scholar can keep abreast of the times in which
he lives; Hooton's *The American Criminal* (1939) the courage and
industry with which a scientific problem, presumably settled, may
be reopened and reoriented.

The following dynamic leaders must rank with research scholars
in any evaluation that aims at completeness: Sanford Bates, E. R.
Cass, Raymond B. Fosdick, Hastings H. Hart, William St. Pierre
Hughes, George W. Kirchwey, Lewis E. Lawes, Ben B. Lindsey,
Thomas Mott Osborne, Alexander Patterson, Roscoe Pound, Sir
Evelyn Ruggles-Brise, August Vollmer.

English Prisons Today (1922), the *Publications of the National
Crime Commission* (1931), and the *Report of the Royal Commission on the Penal System of Canada* (1938) should be set down as
enterprises to which hundreds of persons contributed.

THE CONTROL OF CRIME

The Situation

The Statistical Picture. A general picture of the crime and delinquency situation throughout the world is difficult to present.
The *International Penal and Penitentiary Commission* issued findings on 22 countries in 1935.[109] The general conclusion of this study
was that even prison statistics, the easiest to obtain, are still very
inadequate in many countries and that where they do exist international comparisons are difficult because of differing methods of
presentation.

A *League of Nations Report*[110] (1936) makes comparisons for

[109] *Apercus des Systemes Penitentiaires*, Staempfli, Berne, 1935.

[110] Multigraphed document supplied by the John Howard Society of British
Columbia, Vancouver, B. C.

prisoners per 100,000 of population by countries. No data is given for Albania, Portugal, Spain, Turkey and the U.S.S.R.; other countries showed widely varying rates. Some high rates were: Southern Rhodesia (1935) 234 per 100,000 population, Union of South Africa (1934) 232; Finland (1935) 231. Some low rates were: Nigeria (1934) 2.5 per 100,000; Honduras (1934) 12.9; the Irish Free State (1934) 19.4. The rate for the United States was 158 per 100,000, for Germany 156, for Poland 150, for Italy 126, for Canada 114, for France 56, for England and Wales 30, and for Scotland 26. This means that Canada had approximately the same number of prisoners in her penal institutions[111] as were in the prisons of England and Wales (12,000); the United States almost seventeen times that number (200,000).

The following facts concerning the Canadian situation may be taken as representative of trends on this continent.[112] At the beginning of the century convictions for breaches of traffic regulations were 185; by 1936 they numbered 237,000 which was 63% of all minor offences for that year. The ratio of major to minor offences has increased steadily since 1911 but was still in 1937 but 1 in ten. Persons of the age-group 20–30 were ten times as numerous in prisons as persons of the age group 50–60. The average time spent in jail was 2.5 weeks with a turnover of 1984 per cent in jails as against 61 per cent for penitentiaries.[113]

The Department of Justice of the United States has, since 1929, been publishing a quarterly bulletin on the basis of crimes known to the police. The Bureau of Prisons puts out a number of statistical documents including an annual statement concerning prisoners in State and Federal prisons and reformatories. The Department of Labor has issued a considerable body of factual material through Children's Bureau Publications: *Juvenile-Court Statistics:* 1931 (No. 222), *Juvenile Delinquency in Maine* (No. 201), *Youth and Crime* (No. 196), etc. The Report of the National Commission on Law Observance and Enforcement contains much factual material: *Report on Prosecution,* pp. 186–221; *Report on the Causes of Crime,*

[111] U. S. A., 1933; Canada, 1934; Great Britain, 1935: populations Canada and Great Britain 1931, U. S. A. 1935 (S. Y. B.).

[112] *Canada Year Book, 1938,* Dom. Bureau of Statistics, Ottawa, Canada; also *Statistics of Criminal and Other Offences,* King's Printer, Ottawa, annual.

[113] See article by R. E. Watts, *Journal of the American Statistical Association,* Vol. 26, March 1931, pp. 11–20.

Vol. I, pp. 355–389; etc. There are, in addition, the elaborate and detailed surveys of specific areas, the reports of public officials, and the analyses of research students.

The National Bureau of Criminal Identification contains the records of approximately five million criminals. The Penitentiary of the City of New York was constructed to accommodate 2,200 but the prison population on December 31, 1939, was 3,013.[114] Vollmer estimates that 15,000 homicides, 100,000 robberies, 400,000 burglaries, 950,000 larcenies, and 350,000 auto thefts take place each year in the United States. Homicides for the period 1900–1904 were 2.4 per 100,000 population, for the period 1930–1934 they had increased to 9.1. George W. Kirchwey had demonstrated statistically in 1926 that robbery with violence constituted the crime wave of that period.[115] Robberies declined steadily over the period 1930–1936; burglaries over the period 1934–1936.

30,894 burglars were arrested by the police of the United States in 1934, of whom 11,492 (37.2 per cent) had previous criminal records. The rate per 100,000 on the basis of burglaries known to the police in reporting cities was computed as 334.8. The larceny rate computed on the same basis and for the same year was 771.0. The rate for theft of automobiles was 287.3 (142,823). The percentage of automobiles recovered in 1918 was 79 per cent, by 1933 it had jumped to 91.7 per cent.[116]

These facts and trends are presented as representative of a growing body of materials made available by statisticians for the clarification of the situation concerning crime and criminals in the United States. They must be supplemented by the factual findings of psychologists, of sociologists, and of other scientists if anything approaching a complete picture of the total situation is to be achieved.

Crime and the Individual. The founder of scientific criminology stressed physical factors and established an international reputation by a meticulous analysis and summation of anthropological

[114] Prison Association of New York, *Annual Report*, J. B. Lyon, Albany, 1940, p. 99.

[115] *The Survey*, Vol. LV, No. 11, March 1, 1926.

[116] See U. S. Department of Justice, Bureau of Investigation, *Uniform Crime Reports*, Government Printing Office, Washington, v. d. See also Vollmer, *The Police and Modern Society*, "The conclusion seems inescapable that the trend of the crime rate is upward, although the exact amount of increase has not been ascertained" (p. 16); also Sutherland, *Principles of Criminology*, pp. 29–48.

and morphological materials. The work of Hooton, Berman, and others may reestablish the physical as fundamental in causation, selection, and identification but this is unlikely since the contemporary trend is in the direction of eliminating criminal types altogether.

Age appears to be the most significant physical factor. Young people have always been more criminal than their elders. The Gluecks have worked out their theory of benign maturation on this hypothesis which is supported by the findings of their numerous studies. Healy will admit no significant correlation between delinquent tendencies and physical findings except in the case of over-development in girls.[117] Other physical factors that have been considered significant are: physical handicap as leading to compensatory criminalistic behavior;[118] head injury as leading to instability;[119] endocrine imbalance as leading to a general disturbance personality.[120]

Goring and Goddard[121] were convinced that there is a close relationship between low grade mentality and crime. A study by Miner indicates an incidence of eighty per cent for children appearing before the juvenile courts in Manhattan and the Bronx.[122] Rates of 25 per cent (Terman),[123] 28 per cent (Anderson),[124] and 21 per cent (The Gluecks)[125] establish a basis of probability. Murchison[126] and Adler[127] concluded that feeble-mindedness was no greater in delinquent and criminal groups than in other groups while Wallin[128] found a greater percentage of feeblemindedness in a group of non-delinquent school children than in a group of delinquent children in St. Louis. Sutherland concluded, after going carefully over 350 studies covering 175,000 offenders, that the more recent the investi-

[117] *Delinquents and Criminals*, p. 208.

[118] Burt, *op. cit.*, p. 417.

[119] Healy, *New Light on Delinquency and its Treatment*, p. 40.

[120] E. Kretschmer, *Physique and Character*, Harcourt, Brace, 1925.

[121] *Op. cit.*, p. 9.

[122] J. B. Miner, *Deficiency and Delinquency*, Warwick and York.

[123] Lewis M. Terman, *The Measurement of Intelligence*, Houghton Mifflin, 1916.

[124] *Mental Hygiene*, Vol. 3, p. 177.

[125] *500 Criminal Careers*.

[126] *Criminal Intelligence*, Clark University, 1926.

[127] *Parole and the Indeterminate Sentence*, p. 231.

[128] J. E. W. Wallin, ''Delinquency and Feeble-Mindedness,'' *Mental Hygiene*, Vol. I, pp. 585–590.

gation the lower the percentage of feeble-mindedness in the group.[129] The weight of opinion appears to favor the conclusion that there is a greater incidence of both defectives and psychopaths among the delinquent population than is to be found in the general population.[130]

The factors of the inner mental life are more difficult to isolate and evaluate. Eichhorn, Alexander and others have demonstrated their importance. The criminal personality in Healy and Bronner's *New Light on Delinquency and Its Treatment* appears as a thwarted personality. The blocking of fundamental drives within the family group and the failure to achieve a satisfying status in this group is particularly effective in bringing about a delinquency pattern in the life of a participant member. Why emotional disturbance should exhibit theft, etc., as a symptom is not entirely clear but the facts to the researchers are sufficiently obvious to warrant a conclusion that the two are related.

The importance of habit in the formation of a criminalistic pattern of behavior is coming to be recognized. R. H. Gault has perhaps stated this position the most forcefully and the most succinctly of any contemporary scholar.[131] The criminal personality is a professional personality, the same as that of the physician or the clergyman. It is built up through a long and continuing series of contacts and experiences. Aptitude, opportunity, satisfaction; formal and informal education in criminalistic techniques; theory, practice, experiment: all are combined in the matured and hardened law-breaker.

Crime and the Community. Enrico Ferri stressed the fact that his master, Lombroso, had made psychological as well as anthropological studies of criminals, and he himself came very quickly to a recognition of the importance of sociological factors in criminality. Later scholars have built upon his presuppositions and have supported and broadened his conclusions.

It has been held by a number of legislators that the best way to get a bad law off the statute books is to enforce it. Such a posi-

[129] ''Mental Deficiency and Crime,'' Chapter 15 in *Social Attitudes,* edited by Kimball Young.

[130] John M. Gillette and James M. Reinhardt, *Current Social Problems,* American Book Company, 1937, pp. 658–661.

[131] *Op. cit.,* p. v. See Healy, *The Individual Delinquent,* Footnote p. 160; also Footnote National Commission on Law Observance and Enforcement, Report 13, Vol. 1, p. 6.

tion is a recognition of the importance of public opinion in law making and in law enforcement. Roscoe Pound in his *Criminal Justice in America* has stated the position clearly insofar as it relates to enforcement.[132] The attitude of the police, of the courts, of a particular judge or magistrate, of a jury: these are amenable to scientific observation, and they are related to crime. The organization and functioning of police, courts, community recreation programs, etc., are likewise related to delinquency and crime. These, too, are being studied in detail by scholars who are making clear the fact that the malfunctioning of these agencies causes maladjustments which affect the whole community. Certain studies of the League of Nations indicate[133] that the community is, so far as certain kinds of crime are concerned, an international community.

The most careful sociological researches have concerned themselves with the local community. Some of these have studied the agencies of control, others have dealt with crime causation. Few recent studies have dared to ignore the community with the result that the findings of the psychobiologists concerning environmental factors supplement the materials put forward by the sociologists, and make out a strong case for meticulous research on group phenomena.

Age has been considered a biological fact. It has implications for psychology and for sociology. Habits formed in childhood and continued over a considerable period of time are difficult to change. Criminal gangs organized by children as play groups, if they survive until the children reach adulthood, are likely to be well integrated to run smoothly and to reach the objectives which those in control set for them. "Chronic truancy—was the first step in a criminal career."[134]

The family has come in for its share of analysis. One would expect to find a high positive correlation between family destitution and crime because of the high incidence of theft in criminal behavior. Breckenridge and Abbott (76 per cent for boys, 89 per cent for girls), Lund (66 per cent), Burt (56 per cent) found this high correlation in the families studied by them. Later studies

132 Holt, 1930, p. 120.

133 See *Report on Traffic in Women and Children*, Parts I and II, League of Nations Publications, Geneva, 1927; also Elizabeth P. MacCallum, *Twenty Years of Persian Opium* (1908–1928), Foreign Policy Association, 1928.

134 *New York Crime Commission Report*, Legislative Documents, 1928, p. 444.

have not supported these earlier findings although the matter is far from settled.[135] The correlation between the broken home and delinquency is more clearly established. (Shideler, 50 per cent, Healy and Bronner, 50 per cent, U. S. census report 56 per cent, Cooley 47 per cent, The Gluecks 60 per cent).[136] Slawson, using a control group, found ratios of 45 per cent (delinquent group) to 19 per cent[137] (school children control group). A Shaw and McKay study found ratios of 42 per cent to 36 per cent.[138]

Relationships within the family have been studied by many scholars. The conflict of old-world and new-world cultures as appearing between the first generation and the second generation American is regarded as significant in accounting for the more frequent court appearance of the latter. The importance of the attitude of a parent toward a specific child and of that child towards a specific parent, as coming out in the Healy studies, has been mentioned but an even more significant finding is set down in the same document,[139] namely, that the successful results obtained in the case of 48 delinquents of Group III were due, almost entirely, to the close cooperation of the parents.

Shaw and McKay have summarized the findings of their elaborate studies of *Social Factors in Juvenile Delinquency* for the National Commission on Law Observance and Enforcement under twenty-four headings.[140] These findings may be generalized and abridged as follows:

> a. Juvenile delinquents tend to be concentrated in areas of criminality integration adjacent to the central business district and to heavy industrial areas. Rates vary inversely with distance from the centre of the city and remain constant over long periods of time despite the change in racial elements occupying the areas.
> b. Areas of criminality integration are characterized by specific features such as high land values, low rents, physical deterioration, decreasing population, high rates of depen-

[135] See Chap. IV, Vol. I, Report No. 13, National Commission on Law Observance and Enforcement.

[136] *Loc. cit.*

[137] John Slawson, *The Delinquent Boy*, Gorham Press, 1926.

[138] National Commission on Law Observance and Enforcement, *Report on the Causes of Crime*, Vol. II, p. 283.

[139] *New Light on Delinquency*, p. 182.

[140] *Op. cit.* under footnote 138, pp. 383–393 (Vol. II was written by Shaw and McKay).

dency, high rates of foreign born, and high rates of adult crime.

c. The areas are also marked by the breakdown of the conventional agencies of social control and dominance by criminal elements.

d. Delinquency is group phenomena consisting of traditions transmitted through contact with groups and companions and satisfying fundamental desires of certain age groups. A delinquent career is the product of a natural process of development.

e. The subtler aspects of family situations require detailed study as more important than formal and external aspects of the home or the fact of a "broken home."

Thrasher's, *The Gang*,[141] Zorbaugh's, *Gold Coast and Slum*[142] and many other studies, including additional investigations by Shaw and his Associates, confirm these findings.

The prison as a social force should be mentioned here. It will be treated in detail as an agency of social control.

Agencies of Control

The Police. The impression one receives from reading Raymond B. Fosdick's *American Police Systems*[143] is that European police are superior to American police but that there has been very great improvement over the years in the police of this continent. Sutherland[144] considers the two fundamental problems concerning police to be (1) to understand them and (2) to improve their efficiency.

Bruce Smith in his *Rural Crime Control* has dealt at length with the sheriff, the constable, county constabularies, the state police, the coroner, and the justice of the peace. He traces the rise of each functionary both in England and the United States and contrasts the contemporary situation in the two countries. He writes:[145]

It is not too much to say that the suppression of rural crime has become a task of the first magnitude. . . . The fundamentals of rural life are changing almost from day to day. . . . Yet the rural justice machine has gone on almost unchanged.

Smith contends that the administration of justice in the

[141] University of Chicago Press, 1927.
[142] University of Chicago Press, 1929.
[143] Century, 1920.
[144] *Principles of Criminology*, Third Edition, p. 231.
[145] The Southworth Press, 1933, pp. v–vi. By permission of the Institute of Public Administration, New York, N. Y.

United States is the most severely localized of any in the world and advocates the control and financial support of police forces by the States, State police officers taking over from local police officers through a system of amalgamation or otherwise. He would make the county prosecutor responsible for the coroner's function, detailed arrangements to be worked out with the medical profession.

> The sheriff, the constable and the coroner may have to be discarded[146] entirely and new instrumentalities substituted in their stead.

Few persons are more familiar with city police forces than August Vollmer. His *Police and Modern Society* combines the realism characteristic of a seasoned and competent administrator and the breadth of outlook characteristic of a ripe and erudite scholar. The volume is packed with facts, comparisons, and generalizations. Crime may be controlled ultimately through "concerted, coordinated action by all social agencies" but "The police, with their opportunities for firsthand information, and their primary responsibility for protection of society against crime and criminals, must take the lead in community programs for crime prevention."[147]

What are some of the chief difficulties that retard the carrying out of this program? How can the police be made more efficient? Vollmer approaches the problem from the point of view of the responsibilities of a police force. These are found to be (1) the control of major crimes (murder, robbery, burglary, larceny, automobile theft, racketeering, kidnaping, etc.); (2) the control of vice (prostitution, gambling, liquor, narcotics, etc.); (3) the control of traffic (safety, the prevention of congestion, parking, education, general enforcement, etc.); (4) general service (the enforcement of federal and state laws and municipal ordinances, care of the sick and injured, the location of missing persons, the investigation of suicides, the apprehension and detention of the mentally deranged, emergencies such as disasters, strikes, and riots, the care of juveniles, miscellaneous complaints, etc.); (5) crime prevention.

Merely to state these responsibilities is to reveal many of the difficulties inherent in the situation. Traffic fatalities increased 500 per cent between 1913 and 1932. The burden of reducing these fatalities has been thrown upon the police; so has the duty of tag-

146 *Op. cit.*, p. 278.
147 *Op. cit.*, p. 3.

ging cars for overtime parking. The control of vice has caused municipal police forces so much difficulty and has led to so much corruption and loss of morale that a separate unit to handle this highly specialized problem is recommended by experienced police officials.[148] If the duties of a police force became so narrowed that the main function of the police was in fact, as in theory, the prevention and control of major crime, then, the citizens might with greater confidence expect the apprehension and conviction of perpetrators of serious crimes. This would mean for the whole United States the apprehension of close to 2,000,000 persons in any given year, admittedly a considerable task for even such great police forces as exist. The trend appears, however, to be in the opposite direction with the police taking over such administrative duties as are commonly carried out by police forces in Europe.[149]

The following constructive suggestions for increasing the efficiency of modern police forces have been made by various authorities:[150]

(1) Increased length of tenure for police executives.[151]

(2) Freedom from interference by corrupt political and other pressure groups.

(3) Greater stability in the fundamental organizational set-up.

(4) The adoption of scientific principles of administration and a recognition of the importance of preventive work.

(5) A reduction in the number of unenforceable laws passed by legislatures and in the technicalities of court procedure.

(6) More careful selection, better treatment, and more specialized training for police officers.

(7) The adoption of a consistent policy concerning vice and the continuation of this policy for a sufficient period to test its effectiveness or ineffectiveness.

(8) The installation of modern signal systems, equipment, records, and laboratories.

A careful perusal of the literature of the subject leads to the

[148] *Op. cit.*, p. 2.

[149] Sutherland, *op. cit.*, p. 235.

[150] See *Report on Police*, No. 14, Reports of National Commission on Law Observance and Enforcement, especially Chapter IX; Sutherland, *op. cit.*, pp. 231–258; Cantor, *op. cit.*, pp. 67–76; Tannenbaum, *op. cit.*, pp. 128–173, 223–253.

[151] The average term of office in 10 cities of 500,000 and over was 2.41 years.

conclusion that a statement written twenty years ago is still applicable to the municipal police forces of this continent.[152]

> It cannot be denied that our achievement in respect to policing is sordid and unworthy. Contrasted with other countries in this regard we stand ashamed. With all allowance for the peculiar conditions which make our task so difficult, we have made a poor job of it. Our progress has fallen far behind our needs. Successful in the organization of business and commerce, pre-eminent in many lines of activity, we must confess failure in the elemental responsibility laid on all peoples who call themselves civilized, of preserving order in their communities.

The Courts. The justice of the peace is considered by Smith to be the most dynamic functionary in the control of rural crime. The following trends are noted in this institution: a reduction in total numbers of justices of the peace; the substitution of fixed compensation and part-time or full-time service for the fee system; higher general qualifications; an increase in the number of justices of the peace who are members of the legal profession; continuance in office for longer periods of time; wider territorial jurisdiction; and the appointment of a justice's clerk to take care of routine.[153]

The justices of the peace also function in the urban community but here their duties pertaining to criminals have largely been taken over by police magistrates and justices of muncipal courts. Persons presiding in these courts conduct preliminary hearings in felony cases and have powers of summary jurisdiction, subject to appeal, in minor cases. In the superior courts (county, district), presided over by judges, are tried serious cases, again subject to appeal to appellate or supreme courts. There are, in addition, specialized courts such as traffic courts, juvenile courts, and courts of domestic relations. The system is highly complicated with the office of the prosecutor ranking as the most dominant single institution associated with it. No detailed descriptive account can be attempted here.

How can the system be changed so that it may function more efficiently? The most careful brief analysis of prosecution in the modern city is Pound's *Criminal Justice in America.*[154] Inefficiency

[152] Fosdick, *op. cit.*, pp. 382–383; see also *Report on Lawlessness in Law Enforcement*, Report No. 11, Nat. Comm. on Law Observance and Enforcement.

[153] Smith, *op. cit.*, pp. 286–289.

[154] Holt, 1930, pp. 182 *et seq.*

is found to be related to a failure to utilize the available scientific
knowledge and to a lack of business methods in handling the work
that must be done. Or to quote Kavanagh,[155] ''Thus while science,
commerce and learning ride on through the years on steeds of
flame, the law drags itself along on broken wings.''

The Report on Criminal Procedure (Report No. 8) and *The
Report on Prosecution* (Report No. 4) prepared by the National
Commission on Law Observance and Enforcement contain recommendations that parallel those of other professional and lay groups
including bar associations and the American Law Institute[156] and
are in many instances based upon them. They may be summarized
and abridged as follows:

 a. The development and adoption of principles and concepts concerning the objectives of criminal justice, to which
principles and concepts the whole system, its organization
and procedure, should be adjusted. (No. 4, p. 181)
 b. Such an organization of the legal profession in each
State as shall insure competency, character, and discipline
among those who are engaged in the criminal courts. (No.
4, p. 38)
 c. There should be a fuller and more general public appreciation of the importance of the inferior criminal courts
and of the personnel, tenure, and mode of choice of magistrates and judges of municipal and petty tribunals. (No.
8, p. 46)
 d. Juvenile delinquency is the heart of the problem of
crime prevention. (No. 4, p. 179)
 e. A system of review of a criminal case as a whole in one
appeal. (No. 8, p. 48)
 f. Procedural details should be governed by rules of court
(to be revised as experience dictates), not by rigid legislation drawn by one set of men and interpreted and applied
by another. (No. 8, p. 46)
 g. There should be a modern organization of the inferior
courts . . . and complete elimination of the fee system.
(No. 8, p. 46)
 h. The public must be thoroughly conscious of the need
of removing the administration of justice from politics and of
insisting that appointments be made on the ground of conspicuous fitness alone, so that no appointing power will think
of choosing a judge or magistrate (or Federal district at-
torney or prosecuting officer) on any other basis. (No. 8,
p. 46; No. 4, p. 37)

[155] *Op. cit.*, p. 176; see also the writings of Raymond Moley, Wayne L.
Morse, Alfred Bettman, John H. Wigmore.
[156] See Report No. 8, p. 49: Statement by Monte M. Lemann.

i. Provision for legal interrogation of accused persons under suitable safeguards. (No. 4, p. 38)

j. Careful working methods and administrative practices in nolles, acceptances of plea of lesser offence and other forms of dismissals and dispositions without trial, whereby the responsibility for these dispositions will be definitely located, careful records will be required and the dispositions will be based on thorough inquiry and on definite principles. (No. 4, p. 180)

k. Abolition of requirements of grand jury indictment in every felony case; right of the accused to waive trial by jury; increase of the judge's control over the conduct of the trial. (No. 4, p. 180)

l. Greater recognition of the region, as distinguished from arbitrary units like the city, as the unit in the structural organization of the administration of criminal justice. (No. 4, p. 181)

m. Gradual development of centralized State informational service, including identification of the offender, criminal record of the offender, and the social history and facts concerning the mental and the moral characteristics of the offender, as well as judicial and prosecutional statistics. (No. 4, p. 181)

n. Gradual development of special tribunals for passing upon the disposition issue, with special qualifications in the personnel of such tribunals to pass upon the disposition or treatment problem, and with appropriate procedure and appropriate informational bases for the solution of the disposition problem in the case of each individual offender. (No. 4, pp. 181–182)

Many of these recommendations are based on the findings of surveys and crime commissions. Mr. Bettman, who made the analysis of these surveys, writes:

None of the surveys attempted to set up, for application in practice, a comprehensive integrated and selfconsistent program. . . . Sooner or later each State ought to bring about a statement of such a comprehensive program, which will be the chart or design in accordance with which an improved system of criminal justice in that State can be graually, progressively, and harmoniously developed. (No. 4, p. 184)

Prisons. The term prison is used here to cover any institution used as a place of forcible detention for delinquents or criminals. It may signify a Federal or State prison, a county or city jail, a reformatory, a lock-up. Such institutions belong together as the representative crime and delinquency control devices of our time. No longer are law-breakers drawn and quartered; nor are they transported forcibly to distant lands; nor are they hanged in any considerable numbers; they are instead imprisoned in a highly variegated group of lock-ups, jails, prisons, and reformatories.

A lock-up is frequently attached to a police station as a place of safe keeping for such persons as are likely to do damage to themselves or to others, or who must be forcibly detained for trial.[157] First offenders have had some tormenting experiences in lock-ups. These places have sometimes been operated without standards of cleanliness; and some of them have not been limited to the function of temporary detention.

> From many points of view, the jail is the most important of all our institutions of imprisonment. The enormous number of jails is alone sufficient to arrest the attention of the student of penology and to make him realize that the jail is after all the typical prison in the United States. There are in the United States today (1922) approximately three thou-and jails . . . from two-thirds to three-fourths of all convicted criminals serve out their sentences in jails. . . . The jail is, with small exception, the almost universal detention house for untried prisoners. . . . Whether for good or for evil, nearly every criminal that has been apprehended is subjected to its influence.[158]

The jail has been uniformly and universally condemned by criminologists as a school for crime, as a survival of a medieval English institution that has ceased to exist in the country of its birth.[159] Stuart Alfred Queen wrote a book in 1920 titled *The Passing of the County Jail* but the county jail has not gone, since there remained as many county jails in existence in 1939 as in 1920.[160] The *American Prison Association Committee on Jails* has been active over the years especially in the period when Hastings H. Hart was Chairman.

Richard A. McGee, President of the National Jail Association, and Warden of the Penitentiary of the City of New York made the

[157] There are approximately 11,000 in the United States alone. See Sutherland, *op. cit.*, p. 264.

[158] Louis N. Robinson, *Penology in the United States,* Winston, 1922, p. 32.

[159] Sidney and Beatrice Webb, *English Prisons under Local Government,* Longmans, 1922.

[160] Sutherland, *loc. cit.*

following indictment of the jail system in an address before the American Prison Association Congress of 1939.[161]

The founders of the National Jail Association were convinced that the annual reading of papers in denunciation of the jail nuisance would neither remove nor reform it. A program was necessary. This program is beginning to take definite form. It is a program of action and it begins with an indictment.
The true bill charges of the typical American jail that:
It is needlessly expensive.
There are too many of them.
They are dirty.
They are unhealthful.
They are corruptly operated.
They contain too many persons who do not belong in jail.
They are centers of illicit political activity.
They are breeders—not healers of crime.
They fail in their most elementary function, that of safe detention.

A descriptive statement by the members of the *Ontario Royal Commission on Public Welfare, 1930*,[162] is evidence that the conditions above reported are not confined to any one country or to any one administrative group. Young and old inmates, they stated, first offenders and hardened criminals, drunkards and drug addicts, are herded together. Occupations are not systematically provided; inmates are shut in their cells for 12 hours or more without light. The forty-seven jails of the Province according to the report, are as likely to promote as to prevent offenses.

An article in *The Prison World* entitled "The Menace of the County Jail"[163] and giving the same sort of detail entitles one to assume that the jails have not changed much over the last ten years. Criticism has resulted in better buildings but since it is the basic treatment program that is at fault such action merely touches the fringe of the problem.

In 1923 the Federal Penitentiary at McNeil Island was as unorganized as a county jail.[164] Today its regimen is carefully sys-

161 Quoted in *Ninety-fifth Annual Report*, Prison Association of New York, Lyon, Albany, 1940, p. 97.

162 *Report of the Ontario Royal Commission on Public Welfare*, King's Printer, Toronto, 1930, p. 77.

163 *The Prison World*, Vol. 2, No. 5, September–October, 1940, pp. 79 *et seq.*

164 The writer used to take between 50 and 100 students to this prison for observational purposes each year between 1923 and 1929.

tematized, and its standards are emulated by state institutions. What constructive features should a prison possess? Interested groups ranging from administrators to inmates appear to be in agreement on the following:[165]

a. Modern standards for lighting, heating, sanitation, etc.;

b. Opportunities for constructive labor for which a small remuneration is paid;

c. Proper facilities for medical care;

d. A psychological or psychiatric clinical service;

e. A program of cultural, vocational, and religious education that meets the standards set by accrediting bodies for such services;

f. A library of carefully selected books and magazines;

g. Careful selection and adequate training for both guards and senior officers.

h. Periodic rigorous and thorough inspection by competent officials;

i. Treatment to be based on hard common sense rather than on either sentimentality or brutality.

Thomas Mott Osborne[166] has stressed training in and for citizenship; research scholars such as Gillin the application to the task in hand of the findings of the various sciences;[167] Warden James A. Johnston, of San Quentin and Alcatraz, the importance of an educational program:[168] these are superficial differences. Underneath is general agreement that the function of a modern prison is the protection of society both immediately and ultimately with the ultimate protection implying a broad program of reconditioning prison inmates with a view to returning them to society not only as law-abiding citizens but as active supporters of law and order. Thus appears to be passing that period of lethargy and apathetic cruelty[169] symbolized by the county jail.

Substitutes for Incarceration. Since incarceration in an institution is considered to be the dominant method of treatment on this continent today, the statement on the other methods in spite of

[165] See address of James V. Bennett, President, American Prison Association and Director of the United States Bureau of Prisons, *Congress Proceedings,* 1940.

[166] *Prisons and Common Sense,* Lippincott, 1924, pp. 16–49.

[167] *Op. cit.,* p. 851.

[168] Personal letter and conversations.

[169] See Topping, "Apathetic Cruelty," *Island Lantern,* Vol. III, No. 12, March 1, 1927, U. S. Penitentiary, McNeil Island, Wash.

the fact that these other methods are daily becoming more important, will be brief. The more common substitutes for imprisonment are (a) suspended sentence, (b) probation, (c) extra-mural employment, (d) fines, including fines on instalment, (e) parole, (f) boys' clubs, (g) community organization.

a. Suspended sentence: The suspended sentence has been an effective conditioning influence for first offenders of known good reputation. Such a person may never appear before a court again. The most common use of suspended sentence is not, however, for this purpose, but to persuade an unemployed youth to leave town. When used as a device to control the behavior of habitual offenders it has positive danger.

b. Probation: Probation implies a suspended sentence together with oversight by an official of the court, known as a probation officer. This officer assumes oversight of and responsibility for the good behavior of the accused. All juvenile courts and many adult courts have probation officers attached to them. Foster home placement may be used in conjunction with probation.

c. Extra-mural Employment: This device was used with considerable success in the Province of Ontario. In lieu of a prison sentence the offender went into employment, frequently on a farm, where he received the same wages as other farm laborers undertaking similar work. In contrast to earlier contract systems the prisoner retained his wages which went, largely, to the upkeep of his family.

d. Fines, including fines by instalment: A prison sentence with the option of a fine in lieu of imprisonment is the most common sentence of a court. As many as eighty out of one hundred persons given this option fail to pay the fine, and go to prison. These eighty persons would have gone free if they had been able to raise the money to pay the imposed fine. English courts by permitting fines to be paid by instalments have greatly reduced the prison population of England and Wales.

e. Parole: Parole is similar to probation except that it comes after a prison sentence has been served in part instead of before it. Parole is a method of rehabilitating the law-breaker in the community by oversight and direction on the part of a social worker. or other interested person.

f. Boys' Clubs: These are clubs, under various names, organized and directed with the deliberate purpose of combatting delinquency in a given community.

g. Community Organization: This is a definite control program for a given community based on research and action with a view to achieving certain objectives.

The largest factor operative in the reduction of the prison population in England has been these substitutes for incarceration. It is possible that in the near future they will have an equally powerful effect on penal populations on this continent. For the moment they must be regarded as secondary rather than as primary in the control of crime and delinquency in Canada and the United States.

RECAPITULATION

Crime has been a serious problem of humanity since the days of Cain and Cromagnon. The spectacular proceedings associated with the apprehension and conviction of notorious criminals have tended to induce in the minds of the general public an emotional attitude towards crime which has retarded rather than helped a scientific solution of this ancient and perennial problem. The reticence of prison officials and of former inmates of prisons has resulted in the general public, including newspaper reporters, receiving a false impression of the basic elements in the crime situation. The result has been morbid curiosity and hysterical outbursts rather than those essential elements of effective control: reasoned opinion, sound judgment; steady, concentrated pressure.

During the Middle Ages the church was dominant in criminological theory and practice; later the philosophers and the legalists. With Lombroso science entered the picture. Research criminology has made considerable progress during the past twenty-five years with the findings of research scholars in process of application through administrative controls. Trends may, therefore, be indicated by presenting a statement of the matters on which research criminologists are in agreement.

1. a. Criminal behavior is but one aspect of the total behavior of an individual and is the same in essence as the rest of his behavior. Crimes exhibit a dull sameness while the personalities revealed through close study of delinquents and criminals are found to be unique, interesting, and dynamic.

b. Since criminal behavior is the same in kind as other behavior the findings of all the sciences devoted to the study of man and his environment may be brought to focus upon it.

c. There is little possibility of eliminating crime completely in a free, democratic State. Reduction of the present crime rates, however, seems to be within reasonable expectation.

2. a. Incarceration, the dominant control device, is not particularly effective in reducing the incidence of crime.

b. The jail with its lack of constructive program and with its opportunities for acculturation in the techniques of crime has been adjudged unsuited to crime control.

c. A prison conducted along democratic lines embodying the principles of the kangaroo court[170] is not accepted by many outside the Osborne group.

d. Sincere students of the modern prison are in general agreement on the elements to be embodied in an effective prison: clean modern plant, labor, proper food and medical care, psychological and psychiatric clinical service, sound cultural and vocational education, a carefully selected and carefully trained staff, rigorous inspection, an absence of both brutality and sentimentality.

e. Substitutes for incarceration, such as fines on instalment, probation, parole, and community organization, which have been found very effective in Europe, have not been so widely or so effectively used in the United States and in Canada.

3. a. There is general agreement that a solution of the problem of juvenile delinquency would go a long way towards a solution of the problem of criminal behavior on the part of adults. Adult crime has its roots in youthful misdemeanor.

b. The home, the school, and the community are dominant social forces in the process of the formation of criminal behavior patterns and of criminal gangs.

c. The professional criminal and the receiver of stolen goods are coming to be recognized as the organizing forces behind the crime waves.

d. If the public is to be protected, persons associated with the control program must be selected on the basis of fitness alone and must be freed from interference by pressure groups including machine politicians.

4. a. The trend in research criminology is to stress less than formerly biological and psychological factors with increasing emphasis on psychiatric and sociological factors.

[170] A system of government of local jails by inmate trusties who organize themselves into a court with judge, sheriff, etc. See *The Survey*, October 1, 1923, ''Fish, Fish'' by William Akers, for an account of a session of the Pierce County Jail Kangaroo Court.

b. Habit formation and community organization are seen to have great force both in the growth and in the combatting of criminality.

c. The total situation must be taken into account in an analysis of crime causation.

d. To be effective research must be specialized and must deal with one minor aspect of the total picture.

e. Definitions are difficult and unsatisfactory. The factual basis for control programs is far from complete. Yet, in line with other applied sciences such as medicine, the applied science of criminology is likely to continue to develop on the basis of hard common sense, the available findings of science, and the trial and error of experimentation. It is probable that a majority of criminologists will agree with William Healy when he writes,[171]

Altogether it can be seen that our research into fundamental causes has left us with the conviction that the checking of a delinquent career once started is no easy matter. In any treatment project there is no royal road to success. And, we are afraid, the same must be said about prevention in general. For the sake of relief from our extraordinary national burden of delinquency and crime, much greater interest must be manifested not only in expert work with individual offenders, but also in mass attacks upon the whole problem.

SELECTED REFERENCES

Aichhorn, August, *Wayward Youth*, Viking Press, 1936.

Alexander, Franz and Healy, William, *Roots of Crime*, Knopf, 1935.

American Prison Association, *Annual Proceedings*, The Association, New York.

Annals of the American Academy of Political and Social Science, Vol. 157, September, 1931, ''Prisons of Tomorrow.'' (ed.) Thorsten Sellin.

Barman, S., *The English Borstal System*, King, 1934.

Barnes, Harry E., *The Repression of Crime*, Doran, 1926; *A History of the Penal Reformatory and Correctional Institutions of New Jersey*, MacCrellish and Quigley, 1918; *Society in Transition*, Prentice-Hall, 1939, Chaps. 16, 17.

Bates, Sanford, *Prisons and Beyond*, Macmillan, 1936.

Beccaria, Cesare, *An Essay on Crimes and Punishments*, Milan, 1764.

Berman, Louis, *The Glands Regulating Personality*, Macmillan, 1928.

Black, Jack, *You Can't Win*, Macmillan, 1926.

British Columbia, *Report of the Advisory Committee on Juvenile Delinquency*, King's Printer, Victoria, 1936.

Brockway, Z. R., *Fifty Years of Prison Service*, Charities Pub. Comm., 1912.

Burt, Cyril, *The Young Delinquent*, Appleton, 1925.

[171] *New Light on Delinquency and Its Treatment*, p. 216. Reprinted by permission of Yale University Press.

Canada, *Report of the Royal Commission to Investigate the Penal System of Canada*, King's Printer, Ottawa, 1938; *Reports of the Superintendent of Penitentiaries*, King's Printer, Ottawa, annual; *Statistics of Criminal and Other Offences*, King's Printer, Ottawa, annual.

Cantor, Nathaniel, *Crime and Society*, Holt, 1939.

Cleveland, *Criminal Justice in Cleveland*, 1922.

Cooper, Courtney R., *Here's to Crime*, Little, Brown, 1937; *Designs in Scarlet*, Little, Brown, 1939.

Culver, Dorothy C., *Bibliography of Crime and Criminal Justice*, Wilson, 1939; superseding Kuhlman's (1929), Culver's (1934).

Darrow, Clarence, *Crime, Its Cause and Treatment*, Crowell, 1922.

De Quiros, B., *Modern Theories of Criminality*, Little, Brown, 1911.

Drucker, S., and Hexter, M. B., *Children Astray*, Harvard University, 1923.

Ellis, Havelock, *The Criminal*, Walter Scott, 1890.

Eubank, Earle, and Clark, Charles, *Lockstep and Corridor*, University of Cincinnati, 1927.

Ferri, Enrico, *The Positive School of Criminology*, Kerr, 1913; *Criminal Sociology*, Little, Brown, 1917.

Fishman, Joseph F., *Crucibles of Crime*, Cosmopolis Press, 1923.

Fosdick, Raymond B., *American Police Systems*, Century, 1920.

Gault, Robert H., *Criminology*, Heath, 1932.

Gillin, John L., *Criminology and Penology*, Century, 1935; *Taming the Criminal*, Macmillan, 1931.

Glueck, Bernard, *Studies in Forensic Psychiatry*, Little, Brown, 1916.

Glueck, Sheldon (editor), *Probation and Criminal Justice*, Macmillan, 1933; *Crime and Justice*, Little, Brown, 1936.

Glueck, Sheldon, and Eleanor T., *500 Criminal Careers*, Knopf, 1930; *Preventing Crime* (editors), McGraw-Hill, 1936; *Later Criminal Careers*, Commonwealth Fund, 1937; *Juvenile Delinquents Grown Up*, Commonwealth Fund, 1939.

Goddard, Henry H., *Feeble-Mindedness, Its Causes and Consequences*, Macmillan, 1914.

Goring, Charles, *The English Convict*, H. M. Stationery Office, 1913.

Healy, William, *The Individual Delinquent*, Little, Brown, 1915; *Judge Baker Foundation Case Studies*, The Foundation, 1922–1923.

Healy, William, and Bronner, Augusta, *Delinquents and Criminals, Their Making and Unmaking*, Macmillan, 1926.

Healy, William, and Bronner, Baylor, and Murphy, *Reconstructing Behavior in Youth*, Knopf, 1929.

Healy, William, and Bronner, A. F., *New Light on Delinquency and Its Treatment*, Yale University Press, 1936.

Hobhouse, S., and Brockway, A. F., *English Prisons Today*, Longmans, 1922.

Hooton, Earnest A., *The American Criminal*, Harvard University, 1939.

Illinois, *Committee on the Study of the Workings of the Indeterminate Sentence Law and Parole in the State of Illinois. A Report* by A. W. Bruce, E. W. Burgess, A. J. Harno, and J. Landesco, Illinois Parole Board, 1928.

Kavanagh, Marcus, *The Criminal and His Allies*, Bobbs, Merrill, 1928.

Kretschmer, Ernest, *Physique and Character*, Harcourt, Brace, 1925.

Laune, Ferris F., *Predicting Criminality*, Northwestern University, 1936.

Lavell, A. E., *The Convicted Criminal and His Re-establishment*, Ryerson Press, 1926.

Lawes, Lewis E., *20,000 Years in Sing Sing*, Long and Smith, 1932; *Life and Death in Sing Sing*, Doubleday, Doran, 1928; *Invisible Stripes*, Farrar and Rinehart, 1938.

Lewis, Orlando F., *The Development of American Prisons and Prison Customs, 1776–1845*, Prison Association of New York, 1922.

Lindsey, Ben B., and Evans, Wainwright, *The Revolt of Modern Youth*, New York, 1925.

Lombroso, Cesare, *Crime, Its Causes and Remedies*, Little, Brown, 1911.

Lou, Herbert H., *Juvenile Courts in the United States*, University of North Carolina Press, 1927.

MacCormick, Austin H., *The Education of Adult Prisoners*, National Society of Penal Information, 1931.

Missouri, *Missouri Crime Survey*, Macmillan, 1926.

Moley, Raymond, *Our Criminal Courts*, Minton, Balch, 1920; *Politics and Criminal Prosecution*, Minton, Balch, 1929; *Tribunes of the People*, Yale, 1932.

Murchison, Carl, *Criminal Intelligence*, Clark University, 1926.

National Commission on Law Observance and Enforcement, *Reports Numbers 1 to 14*, Government Printing Office, Washington, 1931.

National Probation Association, *The Year Book*, The Association, annual.

O'Hare, Kate R., *In Prison*, Knopf, 1923.

Ontario, *Report of the Royal Commission on Public Welfare*, King's Printer, Toronto, 1930.

Osborne, Thomas M., *Society and Prisons*, Yale, 1916; *Prisons and Common Sense*, Lippincott, 1924.

Parmelee, Maurice, *Criminology*, Macmillan, 1918.

Patterson, Alexander, *Across the Bridges*, Arnold, 1928.

Pound, Roscoe, *An Introduction to the Philosophy of Law*, Yale, 1922; *Criminal Justice in America*, Holt, 1930.

Prisoners: *Federal Offenders, 1932–33*, Bureau of Prisons, 1934; *Prisoners in State and Federal Prisons and Reformatories*, Government Printing Office, Washington, annual.

Prisons: *Annual Report, 1930*, Bureau of Prisons, 1930.

Queen, Stuart A., *The Passing of the County Jail*, Banta, 1920.

Reckless, Walter C., *Criminal Behavior*, McGraw-Hill, 1940.

Reckless, W. C., and Smith, M., *Juvenile Delinquency*, McGraw-Hill, 1932.

Reik, Theodor, *The Unknown Murderer*, Hogarth Press, 1936.

Robinson, Louis N., *Penology in the United States*, Winston, 1922.

Robison, Sophia M., *Can Delinquency be Measured?* Columbia University, 1936.

Rogers, Carl R., *The Clinical Treatment of the Problem Child*, Houghton, Mifflin, 1939.

Ruggles-Brise, Sir Evelyn, *The English Prison System*, Macmillan, 1921; *Prison Reform at Home and Abroad*, Macmillan, 1924.

Russell Sage Foundation, *Bibliography of Juvenile Delinquency*, The Foundation, 1930.

Saleilles, Raymond, *The Individualization of Punishment*, Little, Brown, 1913.

Schlapp, Max G., and Smith, Edward H., *The New Criminology*, Boni and Liveright, 1928.

Scott, W. L., *Juvenile Court in Law and in Action*, Canadian Welfare Council, Ottawa, 1930.

Seabury, Samuel, *Final Report*, New York, 1932.

Sellin, Thorsten, *Research Monograph on Crime in the Depression*, Social Science Research Council, 1938; *Culture Conflict and Crime*, Social Science Research Council, 1938.

Shaw, Clifford (with Zorbaugh, McKay, and Cottrell), *Delinquency Areas*, University of Chicago Press, 1929; *The Jack Roller*, University of Chicago Press, 1930.

Shaw, Clifford, and Moore, M. E., *The Natural History of a Delinquent Career*, University of Chicago Press, 1931.

Shaw, Clifford, *Family Backgrounds in Male Juvenile Delinquency*, University of Chicago Press, 1934.

Shaw, Clifford, and Myers, Earl D., ''The Juvenile Delinquent'' in the Illinois Crime Survey, 1929.

Shaw, Clifford, and McKay, Henry D., *Social Factors in Juvenile Delinquency*, Report on the Causes of Crime, Vol. II, for the National Commission on Law Observance and Enforcement, Government Printing Office, Washington, 1931.

Slawson, John, *The Delinquent Boy*, Badger, 1926.

Smith, Bruce, *Rural Crime Control*, Columbia University, 1933.

Stevenson, George S., and Smith, Geddes, *Child Guidance Clinics*, Commonwealth Fund, 1934.

Sullenger, Thomas E., *Social Determinants in Juvenile Delinquency*, Wiley, 1936.

Sutherland, Edwin H., *Principles of Criminology*, Lippincott, 1939.

Tannenbaum, Frank, *Osborne of Sing Sing*, University of North Carolina Press, 1933; *Crime and the Community*, Ginn, 1938.

Tarde, Gabriel, *Penal Philosophy*, Little, Brown, 1912.

Thomas, W. I., *The Unadjusted Girl*, Little, Brown, 1923.

Thomas, W. I., and Dorothy S., *The Child in America*, Knopf, 1928.

Thrasher, Frederick M., *The Gang*, University of Chicago Press, 1927.

Topping, C. W., *Canadian Penal Institutions*, University of Chicago Press, 1930.

Trought, T. W., *Probation in Europe*, Blackwell, 1927.

Van Waters, Miriam, *Youth in Conflict*, Republic Pub. Co., 1925.

Vollmer, August, *The Police*, Illinois Crime Survey, Chapter 8, Chicago, 1929.

Vollmer, August, Monroe, David G., and Garrett, Earle W., *Police Conditions in the United States*. Report for the National Commission on Law Observance and Enforcement, Government Printing Office, Washington, 1931.

Vollmer, August, *The Police and Modern Society*, University of California Press, 1936.

Vollmer, August, and Parker, A. E., *Crime, Crooks, and Cops*, Funk, Wagnalls, 1937.

Wallack, Walter M., *The Training of Prison Guards in the State of New York*, Teacher's College, Columbia University, 1938.

Warner, Sam B., and Cabot, Henry B., *The Judge and Law Reform*, Harvard University, 1937.

Webb, Sidney and Beatrice, *English Prisons under Local Government*, with *Preface* by Bernard Shaw, Longmans, 1922.

White House Conference, *The Delinquent Child*, Century, 1932.

White, W. A., *Insanity and the Criminal Law*, Macmillan, 1923; *Crime and Criminals*, Farrar and Rinehart, 1933; *Twentieth Century Psychiatry*, Norton, 1936.

Williamson, Margaretta A., *The Social Workers in the Prevention and Treatment of Delinquency*, Columbia University Press, 1935.

Withrow, O. C. J., *Shackling the Transgressor*, Nelson, 1933.

Zorbaugh, Harvey W., *Gold Coast and Slum*, University of Chicago Press, 1929.

PART VI

SOCIAL CHANGE AND CHANNELS OF CHANGE

A shift in an ocean current, the development of a dust bowl, the spread of an insect pest or of a germ that feeds on human tissue, initiates changes in attitudes and interests of persons. A war, a decision concerning educational procedure, the cumulative effects of birth rate differences, likewise initiate changes in attitudes and interests. No matter what event or agency or group brings about a change in attitudes and interests or persons, the change in attitudes and interests, once made, will in turn have an effect on social organization itself.

Though each part of the network of organization is connected with other parts and with the non-social matrix, nevertheless, some phases of causation are more dynamic than others. We select for treatment a few of these dynamic factors.

CHAPTER 23

POPULATION IN THE UNITED STATES

By ELMER PENDELL, PH.D.

Pennsylvania State College

MAN TOTALS

The 1940 Census

The population of the United States in 1940 was 131,669,275 people, to compare with a 1930 figure of 122,775,046. The increase during the decade, then, was 8,894,229. Those figures are so large as to be difficult of comprehension, even the figure showing the increase. To put meaning into them, let us observe that the *increase* is more than the total 1940 population of 15 of our states, as follows:

Arizona	499,261
Delaware	266,505
Idaho	524,873
Maine	847,226
Montana	559,456
Nevada	110,247
New Hampshire	491,524
New Mexico	531,818
North Dakota	641,935
Rhode Island	713,346
South Dakota	642,961
Utah	550,310
Vermont	359,231
West Virginia	1,901,974
Wyoming	250,742
Total	8,891,399

The *increase* in the United States population during the 1930–1940 decade is more than the population of Canada with the exception of the province of Quebec. In another comparison, the *increase* of our population between the last two census dates was more than twice the population of the whole United States when the Constitution was adopted. Even at the time of our first census in 1790 our population was only 3,929,214.

Population Expansion Since 1700

Concerning European population Dr. Robert R. Kuczynski in the Encyclopedia of Social Sciences tells us that there is no reason to assume that previous to 1700 any increase had occurred for centuries. He reports that from 1700 to 1800 the combined population of Norway, Sweden, Finland, France, Spain, and Italy, rose from 61,000,000 to 69,800,000 or 14.4 per cent. During the next century, however, the population expanded from 185,759,000 for all Europe to 455,367,000, an increase of 145 per cent, a rate of increase ten times that of the preceding century.

In the United States from 1800 to 1900 the increase was terrific— from 5,308,000 to 76,938,000 or 1349 per cent.

Except for a slight decline of numbers in Europe during the decade of the First World War the trend continued to a total of 505,100,000 in 1930; the United States' total rising to 122,775,046 for that year and to 131,669,275 for 1940, and to an estimated 132,-800,000 by April 1, 1941.

What had happened? What were the causes of the rapid rate of increase after 1800? We are looking for the *differentiating* causes, of course. The sex drive was a factor, but it was operative in the Middle Ages when population was at a standstill as persistently as in the prolific 19th Century. If population is socially dynamic, that is to say, active, moving, tending to bring about change as a consequence of power within itself, that power is the sex drive. Throughout the Middle Ages it brought into being hordes of anonymous sufferers who lived for a day or a decade of pain, and who then were crowded to an unrecorded death. The food and clothing were scanty, the housing unhealthful; disease was widespread and almost uncontrolled. It was not through any increase in birth rates that people multiplied in the recent century. There were births in abundance in the previous time. The sex drive continued in its persistence, but the *distinguishing* causes of population increase operated through *reduction of death rates.*

Differentiating Causes of Population Expansion

The Agricultural Revolution. When "Turnip" Townshend initiated the rotation of crops about 1730, he was in the vanguard of a series of changes that made starvation rarer, increased the span of human life. Bakewell bred sheep about 1750, and the Colling Brothers began the breeding of Durham cattle, steadily selecting from what were at first the scrawny 400 pound scrub stock of the times, pointing the way to the 2400 pound pure breds that now win the ribbons at our state fairs. Jethro Tull, who was brought to your attention in the chapter on Physical Regularities as having slowed up evaporation through pulverizing the soil, also invented a drill. These were typical of changing ways that permitted people to live to and through the period of reproduction, and thereby to increase their numbers.

The Industrial Revolution. In 1769 James Watt invented intake and exhaust valves for a steam cylinder; by so-doing opened a door to a new industrial order. Already, in cloth-making, John Kay had made a flying shuttle, and James Hargreaves had invented a spinning contraption by which eight spools were turned on a wheel. And for steel-making Abraham Darby had engineered a forced draft. The marvels of power transportation, power machine shops, power textile factories, have followed in their turn, making the long-stored-up resources of the earth available to keep men from dying.

New Earth. The Americas, in the past two centuries, have been yielding raw materials for European manufacture, and food for Europe's tables. Just as important, the earlier deluge of gold from the treasure troves of the Aztecs and the Incas had replaced barter with a money exchange, stimulating specialization in production, with its relative efficiency—supplying a living for new millions.

Other Social Causes of Population Growth. After William Harvey, in 1628, reported the circulation of the blood, a knowledge of illnesses and how to combat them gathered momentum. Many lives were saved that in earlier centuries would have been snuffed out. The major developments in this field came too late to justify their inclusion as a primary factor in population growth, came, in fact, after the rate of growth was declining. Nevertheless, they were not without significance.

The spread of printing presses, the stabilization of ship routes, and the growth of universities generalized knowledge, aided in survivals. Ownership changes occurring during the decline of feudalism gave incentives for the development of foresight, probably made for survivals.

In America, as in Europe, all these factors applied, but additionally there was the vast expanse of a virgin continent of such fertility that if one "tickled it with a hoe it laughed with a harvest." Coal yielded low cost energy; and iron and timber were plentiful for making homes and implements. Men lived; even babies lived.

The 19th Century Rates of Increase

The population of Europe could not continue indefinitely at the 19th century *rates*. Much less could the *American* rates of the 19th century continue. Up to this topic we have reported population numbers; but notice that the United States *rate* of increase from 1790 to the Civil War was approximately 35 per cent per decade. If that rate had continued to the present time we would now have 319 million citizens—almost two and a half times as many as we have. The year 1940 is 150 years since the first census date. If the increase of 35 per cent per decade continued for another 150 years our population would number over 26 billion people, about 13 times the present population of the whole world. Our negroes alone would number more than ten times the present total population of the United States.

The figures, in their almost incomprehensible immensity, have a resemblance to those applying to the oyster and the paramecium that Dr. Thomson mentioned in Chapter 5. They point to developments alternatively inevitable: either the birth rates had to fall or else the death rates had to rise.

Kuczynski computes the rate of increase of the United States population for the 19th century as a whole to have been 2.58 per cent per year. That means little until we see it in perspective. An illustration or two should help:

Sir Thomas More, born in 1478, eventually aroused the disfavor of Henry the VIIIth and was executed. Meanwhile, for a critical contrast with social institutions in England, he had written and in 1516 published "Utopia" meaning "nowhere," the land of make-believe. Suppose that instead of going into politics and losing his head, and instead of picturing a Never Never Land, he had in 1500 organized a group of a thousand people to preserve among themselves and their descendants by opportunistic methods a rate of increase as high as that which prevailed in the United States during the 19th century.

Possibly he could have induced Copernicus, his mathematical contemporary, to become a member—and, while we are organizing for him, we may as well include another genius of his time, Leonardo da Vinci; and the explorer Columbus. As the years rolled on, Galileo and Johann Kepler might have been invited to join, and from time to time others: Descartes, Shakespeare, Newton, Voltaire, Benjamin Franklin, Priestley, Auguste Comte; still others. La

Grange, grandson of Descartes, would have been a member auto-matically. Only a thousand at the start, the group by 1950 would number over 60 millions. Assuming England as their locale, they would have crowded out all the other Englishmen, Scotchmen, Welshmen, and Irishmen from the British Isles, and would have begun to overflow into Canada and Australia.

If William the Conqueror and his wife if he had one, and the descendants of the two of them, had maintained a two and a half per cent per annum rate of increase for the 880 years from the time of the invasion of England in 1066 to 1946 they would number over 4 billions, twice the population of the whole world. The Chinese would have vanished long ago; they couldn't have stood the standard of living. The Germans and the Japs, the Russians and the Turks and everybody else but the sons of William would have ceased to be.

You say that the rate would not have continued; that wars and famines and changes in folkways would have prevented? That is what I am telling you; in the long view our 19th Century rate is utterly fantastic.

A Declining Rate of Increase

The numbers of human beings in the world continues to increase, but the rates of births have been declining. England and Wales experienced a decline from 31 births per thousand of the total popu-lation in 1840 to 15.8 in 1931. The German rate declined from 37 in 1840 to 16 in 1931; that of France dropped from 28.3 in 1840 to 17.4 in 1931. The United States rate plunged from 48.3 births per thousand people in 1840 to a low of 16.7 in 1936. Our rate has been somewhat higher since, and with the defense boom is substantially higher since 1940. Family size in the United States in 1890 was 4.9 persons; in 1930 there were 4.1 persons per family; in 1940 the aver-age was 3.8 persons.

The decline in the rate at which our population is increasing is striking. The population increases presented as percentages of the population for the specified decades show the decline in the rate of growth. In the following table these rates are set forth as total per-centage increases, and then in other columns are shown the increases by native births and the increases by immigration, the latter two series smoothed by moving averages of a three decade scope. For the moment we invite attention to the column of totals; the others will be referred to following the table.

PER CENT INCREASE IN U. S. POPULATION BY DECADES
(Base: Population at beginning of the applicable decade)

Decade	Totals	By native births		By immigration	
			By moving average covering 3 decades		By moving average covering 3 decades
1790–1800	35.1	35.1	....	....	......
1800–1810	36.4	36.4	35.8	....	......
1810–1820	36.0	36.0	•34.8	....	......
1820–1830	33.5	32.1	32.2	1.3	......
1830–1840	32.7	28.5	29.3	4.2	4.6
1840–1850	35.9	27.5	26.5	8.4	8.2
1850–1860	35.6	23.5	22.1	12.1	9.3
1860–1870	22.6	15.2	20.5	7.3	8.9
1870–1880	30.1	22.8	17.7	7.3	8.3
1880–1890	25.5	15.1	17.6	10.4	7.8
1890–1900	20.7	14.8	13.1	5.8	9.2
1900–1910	21.0	9.5	11.0	11.5	7.8
1910–1920	14.9	8.7	10.1	6.2	7.2
1920–1930	16.1	12.2	9.1	3.9	3.6
1930–1940	7.2	6.4	....	0.8	......

Immigration. The question often arises, did the phenomenal rates of increase in American population in the 19th century depend on immigration? More than thirty-eight million foreigners arrived here between 1820 and 1940, and at first thought one might think the total to be greater than it would have been otherwise by at least that amount; might think that if the immigrants had not come the total would be less by at least thirty-eight millions.

But the evidence seems not to bear out such a conclusion.

The foregoing table setting forth the per cent increases of population by decades also shows in what measure the immigrants of each decade participated in the increase. But it also shows that the birth rates of the native born declined in a rough inverse correlation with the incoming of the aliens. In fact the birth rates declined so much that even supplemented by the immigrants they made a continuously declining rate of growth. Francis A. Walker, who was Superintendent of the United States Census in 1880, observing the seeming connection of decline in native births with growth of immigration, formulated a displacement theory of immigration. The native born, he thought, because of the presence of the immigrants, in a measure equal to the number of immigrants deny themselves the opportunity of having children of their own. He contended, then, that immigrants do not add to the population; that we merely have more neighbors but fewer babies.

Walker's generalization, though shooting in the direction of truth and probably hitting the target, seems not to hit the bullseye. There is probably not a one-for-one substitution of immigrants in place of our own children. The facts appear, rather, as an aspect of a broader generalization; namely, that *as a population gets denser the folk attitudes tend to discourage further increase.* Still broader, population increase by some people tends to prevent reproduction by other people. We discussed this latter point in an international application in our chapter on Economic Regularities. We discuss the italicised rule in further detail in two other connections in this chapter.

The Rate of Increase in the Recent Decade. The 7.2 per cent rate by which the country's population grew between the 1930 census and that of 1940 is itself so large that in the long view it could not be maintained. Again let us refer to the methods of compound interest. Suppose that in 450 B.C., when Pericles was at the height of his power in Athens, he and his celebrated partner Aspasia had undertaken to defend an ideal of a 7.2 per cent increase per decade. Suppose they had converted not all of Athens to the program but only 8 other persons—including, perhaps, Socrates and Thucydides, respectively 20 and 21 years old in 450 B.C. By 1950 A.D., if the ten and their descendants had lived up to their 7.2 per cent per decade ideal, those descendants would number more than 300,000,000. By this time, to keep up that rate, they would have had to invade Sparta and exterminate the Spartans, and to treat similarily the other inhabitants of all of Greece, Germany, and in fact half of Europe.

But the *decline* in the rate of our increase in attracting wide interest. Notice the foregoing table again, particularly the moving average of native births. We have taken a three-decade average and moved it down the chronological scale merely to take out the humps and thus to get a clearer idea of the trend. Statisticians are making guesses based on the trend as to the probable time when our population total will cease to grow, and as to whether or not it may decline thereafter, and if it declines, at what rate. Economists are calling attention to prospective changes in industry resulting from a larger proportion of old people. Legislators are anticipating increasing pressure for old age pensions. School superintendents are considering which grade school buildings to abandon.

Present Ratio of Population to Land

We should like to treat the topic "Present ratio of population to *resources*" but that is so sweeping that in a book of this sort we could only "scratch the surface," so, as our topic shows, we deliberately limit ourselves to the surface.

The sex drive is kept in various degrees and types of control. Folk attitudes develop, influencing birth rates. Other folk attitudes, and conditions of food supply, clothing, housing, and disease, influence migration and death rates. Density of population reflects the births, migrations, deaths.

In general, the industrialized areas of the earth are more densely populated than are non-industrial areas, drawing, as they do, on outside areas for raw materials and markets, and using their own resources in excess of geologic replacements.

There are several agricultural areas, however, in which population density is comparable with that where factories dominate the economic pattern. Barbados, a British possession in the West Indies, has only half an acre per capita. The Nile River Valley and Delta average approximately 0.6 of an acre per capita.

We list a few other densely populated regions for comparison with our own states. The figures relate to the time just before the 2nd World War, except that United States figures are computed from the 1940 census:

	Acres per capita
Average for Europe	4.4
France	3.3
Germany	1.8
Italy	1.8
British Isles	1.3
Japan	1.3

	Acres per capita		Acres per capita
United States	13.7	Oregon	56.6
Nevada	637.4	Nebraska	37.2
Wyoming	246.1	Kansas	29.2
Montana	168.4	Texas	26.3
Arizona	145.5	Washington	24.7
New Mexico	145.4	Maine	23.5
Idaho	101.6	Oklahoma	19.0
Utah	95.5	Florida	18.3
South Dakota	76.2	Minnesota	18.3
North Dakota	69.5	Arkansas	17.3
Colorado	59.2	Vermont	16.5

Iowa	14.8	West Virginia	8.1
California	14.5	Michigan	6.9
Mississippi	13.9	Indiana	6.7
Louisiana	12.2	Delaware	4.7
Georgia	12.1	Illinois	4.5
New Hampshire	11.7	Ohio	3.8
Missouri	11.7	Maryland	3.4
Alabama	11.5	Pennsylvania	3.0
Wisconsin	11.1	New York	2.2
South Carolina	10.3	Connecticut	1.8
Virginia	9.5	New Jersey	1.2
Tennessee	9.2	Massachusetts	1.1
Kentucky	9.0	Rhode Island	.9
North Carolina	8.8		

If we were to place the birth rates for the states beside the acres for the same states we would find that the states with large acreages per capita are more likely to have high birth rates than are states with few acres per capita. For the year 1938 the birth rates of the ten states with most acres per capita averaged 22.3 births per thousand of the population, the comparable birth rates of the ten states with fewest acres per capita averaging 15.3. Again it appears that as population gets denser the folk attitudes tend to discourage further increase.

On this point the figures pertaining to Canada are also applicable. The rate of increase for the Dominion as a whole from 1921 to 1931 was 18 per cent. If we array the eleven provinces in order of acres per capita in 1921, and show the per cent of population increase from all sources during that decade, we get the following:

	Land acres per capita in 1921	Per cent increase or decrease of population 1921 to 1931
Northwest Territories	101,059	21.7
Yukon Territory	31,614	1.7
British Columbia	438	32.3
Alberta	270	24.3
Manitoba	230	14.7
Saskatchewan	201	21.6
Quebec	141	21.7
Ontario	79	10.1
New Brunswick	45	5.2
Nova Scotia	24.8	− 2.1
Prince Edward	15.8	− 0.6

If we lump together the population of the five provinces at the top of the list, we find an increase in population of 23.3 per cent during the decade, whereas the five with fewest acres per capita increased 16.2 per cent. (The rate of increase for the United States as a whole for the comparable decade was 16.1.)

Notice that our method in dealing with the Canadian figures differed slightly from the method with the States. We examined birth rates of the states and related them to the density of population as shown by the census figures nearest in time. For Canada we computed population changes from all sources, using the figures at the beginning of the census period in determining the population density. Results by either method seem to support the generalization that as population gets denser the folk attitudes tend to discourage further increase.

We must not jump to the conclusion, however, that these folk attitudes are dependent entirely on comparative economic opportunities. Spengler points out that some of our states with abundance of acres per capita appear fully as heavily peopled as more populous regions when their true "arable size" is mapped.[1]

Population and War

Population Pressure as a Cause of Aggression. Some groups are less sensitive to the changes in population density than are others, and the numbers in those groups increase until opportunities for making a living are less abundant than previously, and sometimes less abundant than in other lands. When they reach a stage in which there is a substantially greater flow of emigration than of immigration, or where such emigration would occur except for legislation, there exists in that situation a threat of aggression. If the emigration is terminated, the folk attitudes relating to reproduction may change, or the threat of aggression may grow louder.

There are other causes of war than population pressure. Usually the causes occur in a complex development. Usually population pressure is present in the mixture.

Effect of War on Population. Often the story is told that Napoleon, with his repeated conscriptions, took two inches off the average height of subsequent generations of Frenchmen, and perhaps something off their mental stature.

[1] J. J. Spengler, "Seed Beds of America," *Journal of Heredity*, Dec., 1938, p. 483. See also Goodrich, Allin and Hayes, *Migration and Planes of Living*, University of Pennsylvania Press, 1935.

Whether that be true or not, the statement points to the fact that generals, and war departments and parliaments, and kings, in their wish for winning armies do select their men. In fact our own drafted soldiers are now called "selectees." Some of the rejectees have defects which have been caused by environment, but with them are nearly all persons who have hereditary defects. As a result of a large war, a subsequent generation will ordinarily be composed of the offspring of selectees in less than the usual proportion.

DIFFERENCES IN BIRTH RATES

We learned in our chapter on Economic Regularities that *except as men exercise foresight* they increase to the limits of their resources. Obviously, however, the term "men" is very inclusive; in facing actuality one must have a "break-down" of the term. *What* men are exercising foresight? *What* men are increasing to the limits of their resources? Are there any correlations between (1) those who exercise foresight in the matter of reproduction and (2) other social classifications? Is the exercise of foresight related, in the individual, to any other social attributes? And the foresight—is it a canny contemplation concerning food supply for self? or may it include what one considers to be well-being for offspring? or may it include still other values, not immediately related to bread and butter?

"The Race Is Not to the Swiftest, Nor the Battle to the Strong"

The many studies of American birth rates point consistently to this generalization: *The more training an occupation requires, the lower is the birth rate of persons engaged in that occupation; the less training an occupation requires, the higher is the birth rate of persons engaged in that occupation.*

Governmental statistical information on the subject is available in *Birth, Stillbirth, and Infant Mortality Statistics,* Fifteenth Annual Report.[2] Table 10, beginning on page 248, shows the figures for 1929. There follow a few samples, reporting, for mothers between ages 35 and 39 to whom a child was born in 1929, *the total number of living children* classified according to occupation of father. Mothers of ages 35 to 39 are presented rather than mothers of all ages because their families are more nearly complete than would be those of mothers of all ages.

[2] Compiled by the Department of Commerce, Bureau of the Census, published 1929 by the U. S. Government Printing Office, Washington, D. C., available from the Superintendent of Documents.

Coal mine workers	6.4	Porters	4.8
Dairy farm, farm and stock farm laborers	6.2	Plumbers and gas and steam-fitters	4.5
Dairy farmers, farmers and stock raisers	6.0	Foremen and overseers in manu-facturing	4.4
Laborers: Building, general and not specified	5.6	Electricians	4.1
Other specified laborers in manu-facturing and mechanical pur-suits	5.4	Pressmen and plate printers	4.0
		Jewelers, watchmakers, gold-smiths and silversmiths	3.6
Furnacemen, smeltermen, heaters, pourers	5.3	Photographers	3.5
Bootblacks	5.2	Designers, draftsmen and inven-tors	3.4
Blacksmiths, forgemen, hammer-men	5.1	School teachers	3.4
Average for all occupations	5.1	Lawyers, judges and justices	3.1
Laborers in coal and lumber yards, warehouses	5.0	Bankers, brokers and money lenders	3.1
Janitors and sextons	4.9	Physicians and surgeons	3.0
Semi-skilled operatives	4.9	Technical engineers	3.0
Laborers in public service	4.8	Chemists, assayers and metallur-gists	2.9
		Architects	2.7

Inside the Extraction of Minerals group we find that coal miners' wives of the ages given had 6.4 children, their foremen 5.9 children; the operators, officials and managers 4.4 children.

Noticing that farmers have twice as many children as the physicians who help the farmer tots into the world, it is interesting too, to find that total living children of the farmers' wives in the age group reported was 395,021 whereas the total for physicians and surgeons was 2,168.

Contrasts within the foregoing list are impressive, but even more striking is the contrast between the birth rate of persons of special distinction on the one hand and, on the other hand, the birth rates of the various occupational groups. Who's Who in America lists one person in approximately 4200 of the population. Age of entries averages above 50 years at the time of inclusion. Their families, practically all completed, average only 2.1 children. It appears that persons of such accomplishment as is given special value by their fellowmen are participating meagerly in the recruiting of subsequent generations. In the United States the meek, or at any rate the unaccomplished, inherit the earth. We have built up machinery for selection for merit in many lines, but selection for honors and for responsibilities seems to operate as selection away from reproduction.

Data from various sources harmonize in showing that achievement is closely correlated with few or no offspring. The conclusion is inescapable that, as a matter of probability, unless the folk attitudes change, any one of the readers of this chapter, if he is represented at all in the population of America a hundred years hence, will be represented by the offspring of the least accomplished offspring of his own least accomplished offspring. Stated more broadly, *each generation of Americans is engendered predominantly by the unaccomplished of the previous generation.*

The fact that recipients of government relief have more than average number of children does nothing to upset that generalization. We learn from the Federal Emergency Relief Authority that between October, 1929, and October, 1933, 1,612,891 offspring arrived in families on relief. These constituted 12.7 per cent of the total relief roll population, while children of the same age in the general population were only 9.6 per cent of the general population.[3]

A significant study was made by Bernard D. Karpino and Clyde V. Kiser covering data collected in 1935 and 1936 from approximately 2,250,000 persons in 18 cities[4]. The comparative net reproduction rates for various classes as percentages of net total reproduction rate were as follows:

Socio-economic class	Net reproduction rate as percentage of net total rate
Annual family income:	
$3,000 and over	60
$2,000–$2,999	79
$1,500–$1,999	90
$1,000–$1,499	107
Under $1,000:	
Relief and Non-relief	137
Non-relief	113
On relief	164
Educational attainment:	
College	74
High school	97
7th or 8th grade	123
Under 7th grade	139
Total population	100

[3] *N. Y. Times,* Mar. 10, 1935.

[4] Published in *The Milbank Memorial Fund Quarterly,* 40 Wall St., New York, N. Y., October, 1939. The Milbank Memorial Fund has made a number of studies on difference in birth rates.

Another study which further illustrates the prevalent inverse correlation between accomplishment and births appeared in Howard M. Bell's *Youth Tell Their Story*.[5]

MEDIAN NUMBER OF LIVING CHILDREN IN PARENTAL FAMILY

Classification of youth	Median number of living children	Number of youth on which median is based
All youth	4.7	13,466
White relief families	6.0	1,128
White non-relief families	4.4	10,226
Negro relief families	5.8	498
Negro non-relief families	5.8	1,535
Father's occupation:		
Professional-technical	3.6	749
Office-sales	3.6	1,185
Managerial	4.0	2,145
Skilled	4.7	3,071
Semi-skilled	4.9	1,511
Domestic-personal	4.9	382
Unskilled	5.6	1,281
Farm owner-tenant	6.1	2,106
Farm laborer	6.9	500

The prevalence of differences in birth rates is manifest. Many persons agree to the fact of their existence, and agree also that there are inborn structures which make for mental differences, since mental processes are dependent in part on inherited physical brains, and nerve cells and glands. Nevertheless, many of these people believe that the figures are without significance; believe that the tests of mental differences, insofar as they purport to be tests of hereditary capacities, are not valid. Our intelligence quotients, and our occupational attainments, they maintain, relate to nothing but previous training. This problem is big enough to require a separate topic.

Implications of Accomplishment

The subject is difficult. We present the following steps for what they are worth.

1. If there is a goal which not all can attain, then the attainment represents the possession of abilities greater than those of the average of the unsorted members of the same group; and as partial foundation for the abilities, *inherited capacities.*

[5] This was a study of the Conditions and Attitudes of Young People in Maryland between the Ages of 16 and 24, conducted for The American Youth Commission, American Council on Education, Washington, D. C., 1938. The table is from p. 23.

2. That Mr. X tried for the goal and succeeded tells us that he has the inherited capacity required. But here is Mr. Y who never even tried for the goal; perhaps with training he would have been as successful as was Mr. X. Yes, perhaps he would. That Mr. Y did not try for the goal does not tell us that he lacks the required inherited capacity; but since the goal is beyond the reach of some, then to be grouped with those who did not try and are therefore untested is to say that the chances of the possession of the required inherited capacity are fewer than if one is in the group of those who by actual accomplishment have demonstrated the possession of the required inherited capacity. That Mr. Z tried and failed does not tell us that he lacks the required inherited capacity— it may be that he lacks the required training instead—but at any rate his chance of possessing the required inherited capacity is no greater than are the chances of Mr. Y, who did not try the test; his chance of possessing the required inherited capacity is not so great as the chance of Mr. X, who for a surety has the required inherited capacity. Y's chance or Z's chance is less than that of X merely because they are among the untried (or the failed), and the untried (and the failed) include some persons who lack the required inherited capacity. There is some chance that Y and Z are the very individuals who lack the capacity to attain the goal.

3. The reasoning is similar with regard to high school graduation, occupational accomplishment, and intelligence quotient tests. These tests measure inherited capacity in the same way that attainment reports more capacity than no-test, applicable in large numbers; applicable as a probability to an individual. To win an Olympic marathon race demonstrates endurance. There is a sorting out process in it. Perhaps Mr. A., who never thought of racing may have as dependable a heart and lungs and nerves and muscles as the marathon winner; but the chances are that he has not—as a matter of mathematical logic—because he is one of a group the average endurance of which is much lower than the average endurance of marathon winners. He belongs to the unsorted persons who did not run. Similarly, those who score among the highest ten per cent on an I.Q. test have demonstrated inherited capacity (plus training) which capacity is—as a matter of logical necessity—greater than the average inherited capacity of those who do not try the test, or who score a lower I.Q.; although, to be sure, some of the individuals of the groups who do not try the tests or who get low scores may have inherited capacities which, under other circumstances, would have put them in the upper ten per cent.

4. Likewise, to win a livelihood is to meet a test that the environment has imposed. To win, under the rules of the

game, is to demonstrate a capacity greater than the average
of the non-tested folk. Perhaps a certain man on relief has
as much capacity as has the self-reliant person—but the statistical chances are that he has not that much capacity. He
is in a group which includes many who could not meet the
tests under any circumstances. He may be such a one or he
may not be, but he is more likely to be inadequate than is the
man who by actually earning his way demonstrates that he
has the ability to do so.

Let us reconstruct the probable tests to which men were subjected by the wild environment of primordial ages, and compare
those tests with I.Q. tests and incidence of unemployment. Those
random problem boxes of archeological times did weed out the candidates for a long life, yielding the goal to only the fit. To be sure,
the changes in types of men must have been slow, measured by the
standard of one man's life span. But they did make men of the last
20,000 years vastly different from dull-witted pithecanthropus of a
half million years ago; they did bring the human species to a facility
of accomplishment not matched among the other animals. The tests
of environment—rough weather, floods, insect pests, bacteria, attacks of animals—were ill defined, and they must have applied
adversely to both capable and incapable individuals, but the relatively capable ones survived in greater ratio. The capable would
interpret earlier the signs of flood; would be more likely to prepare
for cold weather, would quicker see the applicability of effective
remedy to a disease, would be more successful in evading or combatting animal enemies or human enemies.

Only a slight difference in brain structure or nerve structure, or
gland structure would be necessary to a slightly favorable survival
rate, and only a slightly favorable survival rate would be necessary
to shape the emerging species after the pattern of those members
who had the favorable survival rate.

And so, in eras of devil-take-the-hindermost, slight brain cell
variations which would facilitate adaptation would make for successive generations of increasing brain power. There were biological
implications in success and failure.

There seem still to be biological implications in success and
failure. However, since the devil no longer eliminates the hinder-
most; since society insures the survival of its less fortunate members,
the implication is not that the failures will fail to be represented
among later generations. Inasmuch as the failures reproduce more

abundantly than the successes the implication seems to be that *society, the insurer, jeopardizes its own survival through the survival of its burdens.*

CAUSES OF DECLINE IN AMERICAN BIRTH RATES

It is worth noting that the birth rates have been declining in all classes. If we can figure out the reasons for that fact we shall have knowledge which is not only helpful in itself but which may throw light on the *differences* in birth rates.

Partial explanation for the declining birth rates lies in the fact that separation of the sex drive from reproduction has lately been possible by means of contraception. This development is important because the sex drive now operates less generally as a motive for reproduction. The psychological basis of sex drive is biologically inherited, and is persistent. In contrast, *the psychological bases of reproduction exist mainly in social values.*

Security is a value of great influence, and it seems to apply in a consideration of the prospects for one's children as surely as in the planning for one's own future. Just as a wave of robberies would make one hesitate to wear diamonds or even to buy diamonds, so the uncertainty in these complicated times as to what would happen to a child in the welter of competing stimuli which might tempt him to waywardness is a drawback, a restraining influence to reproduction. Another restraining influence is that in a time of rapid change in world politics the political uncertainty makes for a fear for the future happiness of children. A third item of uncertainty is that pertaining to the prospects for future earnings.

Examining our social values further, we find that the relative value assigned to reproduction has been actually diminishing. There seems to be an application of the widely applying generalization that the more of a thing there is, the less of goods each unit of it is worth. The more oranges there are, the lower is the value per crate. The more money or credit there is, the less each unit of money will buy. Likewise, in a world so crowded with people as this modern world is, the worth of an individual to others is not likely to be much. The social value of a person is further reduced by transportation so efficient that people can and do circulate rapidly. In colonial times neighbors were scarce and neighbors were prized. A person's total emotion registering in friendship probably was no more then than now, but friends were fewer, and a friend was a value worth risking life for. Women were particularly rare, but recently the advice has had more meaning: "Never run after a woman or a bus; there'll be another one along in a minute." The campaign for equal rights is not the only reason for the decline in chivalry; as effective a reason is the number of women. And of course men have lost value too, as men have multiplied. As to babies, they seem to have suffered in value with the rest of us. Bell found that of the 11,707 youths who indicated the number of children they considered ideal (including the 1,057 who desired no children at all), the median number of children desired was 2.7.[6] These are the youths whose parents had a median number of living children of 4.7.

Another point is related to the quantity aspect of value: As the increase in population tends to cause the submergence of the individual in general appraisal, he is stimulated to exert greater effort to remain an individual instead of becoming an indistinguishable member of the masses. The greater effort to accomplish something subtracts from the attention that one can give to a family. Value of children goes down.

Besides the fact that more acquaintances makes for less value for your average acquaintance, and the fact of an increasing rapidity of circulation, which has the same effect on value per person as more people would have; and besides the greater intensity of the struggle to be something more than a grain of sand on the seashore, stands this fact: The concept of prospective children tends to lose value in competition with concepts of non-human objects of various kinds. In the accelerating tempo of living, the items that have values which compete with the value of children are myriad. We want the landlord's goodwill. Landlords often restrict houses and apartments to couples with no children or with no more than one child. Movies, dances, thrilling books, adult classes, bingo; above all else, automobiles, are in the competition with children. Children would interfere with one's established associations and with one's routine of activities, particularly if one marries rather late. Those illustrate the objects of desire which compete with children.

Recapitulating, (1) Prospects for security of children as to character molding influences, as to political surroundings, and as to economic opportunities have been fading as the world's population, and particularly America's population has increased.

[6] Howard M. Bell, *op. cit.*, p. 36.

(2) Children have shared in the general decline in per capita importance which results from many people and from rapid circulation of people.[7] (3) Since the days when one might be a big toad in a little puddle, recognition has been harder to get, costs more energy, and the desire for recognition, thus handicapped, acts as a retardant to reproduction. (4) Children are in an increasingly severe competition with non-human objects.

Other changes have occurred which help to explain the diminished social value of children. Number 5 among the psychological retardants to reproduction is this:

(5) There is a widespread belief, stimulated by behaviorist John B. Watson, and held by many sociologists and their students, that one child is as good as another so far as heredity is concerned. Corollary of that belief is a rule of conduct—let the other people have the babies.

(6) A reverse value established on the basis of any of the foregoing attitude developments is likely to leave its basis and become independently influential. With children' declining in value, having children is no achievement. Nor has reproduction been directly correlated with other distinctive achievement—the social pre-requisites to reproduction are available to almost anybody. The very fact that distinguished persons have relatively few babies puts a value on the *fewness* of babies. Having children becomes "so plebeian," especially if one has more than one or two. Thorstein Veblen's reasoning in *The Theory of the Leisure Class* explains the scanty social value in reproduction in whatever measure it explains the scanty social value in last year's dresses.

(7) Children are no longer an economic asset as they were when most men were in economic production for themselves, using their children as their laborers. Children have lost value in part because they have ceased to yield economic goods in excess of their costs.

(8) A man was once master, if not of all he surveyed, at least of his own household; and particularly of his children. His wife, also, had authority over the children, as second in command. The relationship was recognized by the neighbors, and by the children themselves. The father was expected to shape the youngsters as he saw fit. But in recent years, as schools and boy scouts and musical organizations and radio entertainments and "funny" papers gain

---

[7] This seems to apply to offspring in prospect. When and if they become actualities they, with their uniqueness of personalities, take on monopoly value.

more of a grip on the children the authority of the father and mother declines. In control over children there is little now to warm the ego—because there is little control over the children. This is the converse of the fact, numbered 4 in the foregoing list, that the children are in an intensifying competition with other values. Parents are too! But expressed with a view to parental motivation, there is a declining function of children as a means of gratifying the wish for recognition.

CAUSES OF *DIFFERENCES* IN BIRTH RATES

Even before much was known about birth control it appeared that in men who had many interests or intense interests sex drive constituted a smaller proportion of motivation than in those who lived on a less abstract emotional level. Those with many interests married later. Of course now there is the obvious fact that families whose members are likely to accomplish relatively much have greater facility in getting birth control information than have persons of more limited social contacts. This, perhaps, is a temporary reason for differences in birth rates, lasting until contraceptive knowledge is more general.

But what about the application of the eight motivating stimuli which we have had under consideration as causes of the general falling off in birth rates? We suggested that the causes of the general birth rate decline might throw light on the birth rate differences. Do they? If those causes operate with special force on persons who have accomplished much or on those who have reason in ability to expect to accomplish, then those same causes that bring about the general decline are likewise responsible for the still further decline of births among the accomplished.

Six of the eight do appear to apply in special measure.

1. Delinquency hazards, political hazards, and economic hazards require some amount of analytical ability for their perception. Accomplished persons, being more often trained in analysis, would be more sensitive to the presence of the hazards. Also they are more likely to be alert to world conditions than are the unaccomplished— more alert to the conditions that constitute the hazards. Consequently, this restraint on reproduction would apply with special emphasis to persons of outstanding achievement.

2. The decline in per capita importance would probably be noticed more readily by persons of achievement, especially since they

circulate more, have contact with more people. The response would be a greater curtailment of reproduction.

3. The struggle for recognition would have little effect on those who had given up, or who never had any plans for gratifying that desire. Those with reason in ability to expect to accomplish much would therein have reason to expect recognition; would tend to marry later and when married to have fewer children.

4. Accomplished persons would have wider acquaintance with competing interests, and their stimuli for building up those interests would be more numerous. Children, as a possible objective of such persons, would be more likely to clash with the competing interests. In many instances the children would be sacrificed.

5. Belief in substantial equality in heredity, as a reason for not having babies, would probably be, for the most part, most pronounced among persons who get into the usual sociology classes. They are among the classifications the members of which have been reducing their birth rates most.

6. The disapproval of large families, the setting up of a value for fewness of children, would be more likely on the part of those who have been much affected by the other reproduction retardations; would be a consistent rationalization of their value pattern; would, then, be an additional reason for scanty reproduction of persons of achievement.

That ends our list of motivations which appear to cause the persons with special abilities to limit their reproduction. Numbers 7 and 8 of our list of motivations causing general decline in birth rates probably have no special application. The fact that children are an economic liability, and the fact that children serve less well than formerly in gratification of the desire for recognition probably apply as forcibly among the unaccomplished as among the accomplished.

In the psychological restraints to offspring, which we have set forth in this and the previous sections, we have the reasons for the statistical trends reported earlier in the chapter. They apply most forcibly where population is dense; as we have seen they apply least in the regions where human beings are relatively few. They apply most actively in the large cities, least on the farms; most actively in the densely populated states, least actively in the states with most acres per capita. They operate to keep man-totals within the limits of the food supply; they cushion men's contact with those limits. They tend to keep the human species within bounds, tend to keep a balance in nature, operating with numerical results similar to the results of food shortage and enemy attacks among sub-human species and sometimes among human beings.

SOCIAL PROTESTS

There are many persons who are concerned about the differences in birth rates. They protest that the very foresights which tend to prevent population crowding do so by limiting the children of the foresighted; that men of foresight paradoxically yield their place in the world to men less capable of accomplishment. These protesters develop a social value strongly favorable to reproduction of the accomplished—at least for the other fellow.

Others show no signs of interest until the folk attitudes which reduce birth rates spread to such an extent as to affect the numbers of people available for political units, school systems, football teams.

The man-total aspect, being a matter of gross numbers rather than of refinements and analyses, requires only a casual attention for the stimulation of interest. Consequently, as to the general birth rate decline a larger proportion of people can be expected to develop an opinion—with possible political results.

Recently espoused plans for subsidizing reproduction are based on this man-total interest. In the bonuses-for-reproduction plan there seems to be a focusing of the fact that children are economic liabilities, number 7 in the foregoing lists. It appears that a money subsidy would offset only that one obstacle to offspring, their money costs. If money bonuses for reproduction were to be at all effective the likelihood is that they would stimulate larger families only among people insensitive to new hazards, people with little basis in ability to hope for accomplishment, families with relatively few contacts with other people and few contacts with objects of competing value. Possibly reproduction in families of this type may be stimulated by money bonuses, with, of course, an augmentation of birth rate differences. However, in some foreign lands payments have been made on a basis of size of families, but apparently with very little effect of any sort on birth rates.[8]

[8] See D. V. Glass, *Population Policies and Movements in Europe*, N. Y.: Oxford University Press, 1940; G. F. McCleary, *Population: Today's Question*, George Allen and Unwin, Ltd., 1938; Gunnar Myrdal, *Population, A Problem for Democracy*, Cambridge: Harvard University Press, 1940; W. B. Reddaway, *The Economics of a Declining Population*, New York: The Macmillan Company, 1939.

SELECTED REFERENCES

Carr-Saunders, A. M., *World Population*, Oxford University Press, 1936.—A well balanced treatment by an eminent scholar.

Dublin, L. I., and others, *The American People, Studies in Population*, Annals, American Academy of Political and Social Science, November, 1936.— Essays by leading writers on various phases of population problems.

Goodrich, C., Allin, B. W., and Hayes, M., *Migration and Planes of Living*, with maps by Thornthwaite, C. W., and Slentz, H. I., Univ. of Pennsylvania Press, 1935.—Traces relations of population to economic opportunities.

Lorimer, F., and Osborn, F., *Dynamics of Population*, The Macmillan Co., 1934. —Social and biological problems resulting from present trends in birth rates.

Milbank Memorial Fund *Quarterly*, Milbank Memorial Fund, 40 Wall St., New York, N. Y., particularly Vol. XV, Numbers 2 and 3, wherein Dr. O. E. Baker and Dr. Frank Lorimer discuss the future of American population.— Nearly every issue of the *Quarterly* carries material dealing with population.

Myrdal, Alva, *Nation and Family*, New York: Harper & Brothers, 1942.— Sweden's population policies are reported.

National Resources Committee, *Problems of a Changing Population*, prepared under direction of Lorimer, Frank, United States Government Printing Office, 1938.

Pearl, Raymond, *The Natural History of Population*, New York: Oxford University Press, 1939.—Fertility, contraception, world population; extensive bibliography.

Pitkin, Walter B., *Must We Fight Japan?* The Century Co., 1921.—And after the present war, must we fight Japan again?

Reports of the Bureau of the Census.

Thompson, W. S., *Population Problems*, The McGraw-Hill Book Co., 1935.— Methods of analysis, trends, and problems.

CHAPTER 24

SOCIAL CONTROL

By L. L. BERNARD, PH.D.

Washington University, St. Louis, Missouri

Control and Social Control

Non-living things are controlled mechanically, chemically, or electrically. Lower types of living organisms, especially plants, are controlled in a similar manner. The higher animal organisms are also controlled in these ways for less refined adjustments, as in a pugilistic encounter, when soldiers are bombed, or criminals are gassed or executed in the electric chair. But for most purposes men are controlled through psychological processes. That is, stimuli of some sort are applied to them and the desired responses may be gained thereby. The most important responses are produced for purposes of social control through well selected stimuli applied to sight and hearing, although tactile, pain, heat and cold, olfactory and taste sensations are also frequently used with a close approximation to the desired results. The stimuli most frequently employed at a high level of culture for purposes of control are verbal stimuli. This is because the desired responses can be more adequately represented or described in words, spoken or written, than in any other way. Non-verbal stimuli are likely to be much more simple and less specific and therefore to lead to less adequately controlled responses, except where the responses are relatively simple and automatic. Automatic responses, set in operation by simple and concrete sensory stimuli, present fewer problems in social control and usually operate at a lower level of control.

Social control is to be distinguished from individual control merely by the fact that in the former either (1) the stimuli to controlled responses proceed from a collective situation or (2) the stimuli operate upon a number of persons simultaneously or in succession, thus producing controlled collective behavior. Of course, both processes may operate together, with the result that collective stimuli may produce collective responses. But in all cases the stimuli operate upon individuals and it is they who respond, either singly or in collective situations. Typical examples of the exercise of social control by one or more of these collective processes are to be found in the teacher or preacher or musician, or even in a phonograph or a radio, performing for an audience; in an orchestra, a theatrical company, a pageant, or a military or police squad amusing a group of listeners or regimenting an individual or a group of offenders. Every book or newspaper, every published law or verbal command or traffic signal provides stimuli by means of which desired responses are controlled. Social control is therefore primarily the individual or collective application of effective stimuli to the production of responses in people.

Purposive and Non-Purposive Control

This process of exerting control over others through the application of stimuli adequate to the production of the controlled responses is not necessarily either conscious or purposive. Probably most individual and social control through the application of stimuli is non-purposive so far as any individual is concerned, and much of it is even unconsciously exercised. We are so habituated to certain types of responses connected with the most ordinary functions and processes of our daily living that they occur with little or no attention or forethought on our part. This is the case with the performance of tasks to which we have become used. It is also true of much of our dressing, eating, going and coming, habits of conversation and recreation, reading, and various forms of social intercourse. If we had to think about and plan beforehand everything we did we could not perform more than a fraction of the activities we now engage in and our civilization would be much less advanced than is the case at present. Most of our time and attention would have to be given to what we now regard as the minor and relatively fixed details of life and there would not be sufficient opportunity for planning and executing the more important and advanced forms of behavior that serve to adjust us to our less routinized problems and functions. It is by saving time, energy, and forethought on the everyday adjustments which are taken care of by automatic responses that we are able to meet the new problems that arise and think out the sorts of behavior in ourselves and in others that will produce the responses which are called for.

Purposive control is necessitated in new situations and when the adjustments in old situations are not working well. When new problems arise and call for new adjustments to be made to environment either the individuals who make the new adjustments or other persons who are responsible for their making the right adjustments must analyze the situation and find out what adjustments need to be made and how they can best be put into effect or performed and controlled. If the individual making these adjustments performs these functions for himself we have individual self-control. But if parents, guardians, teachers, foremen, group leaders, army officers, governmental officials, or social planners and administrators must undertake these control functions we have social or collective control. In such cases the controller not only must plan what is to be done but he must determine and apply the stimuli that are necessary to produce the required responses. These two functions of the controller may be and often are separated in practice. If the required responses have already been determined upon by tradition and custom, or by some institution or board of control, all the controller has to do is apply the appropriate stimuli. Thus teachers, preachers, advertising and propaganda experts, policemen and soldiers rarely determine policies or objectives in social control but confine themselves in the main or wholly to the manipulation of control stimuli. That is why these and other similar types of controllers spend most of their time studying methods or the techniques of control in their respective fields and give so little of their energies to the sociological aspects of social control. But the social planners— those who determine the results that education, religion, social work, government, policing, etc., should achieve—reverse this process. They study the end processes of social control for adjustment and leave to the everyday technicians the problem of putting these determined ends or adjustments into effect. The processes of planning are the more difficult aspects of social control and the experts who exercise this function are ordinarily the most honored by society. In the early part of this chapter we shall deal with the techniques used in the application of the required stimuli and in the last part some of the problems of social planning will be passed in review.

The Historic Types of Social Control

The writer has elsewhere classified the major historic types of social control under five chief categories as follows: (1) control through force, (2) control by intimidation, (3) control by means of fraud, (4) control through propaganda or emotional persuasion, and (5) control by means of rational persuasion. These are the types of controls, sociologically considered, as distinguished from the agencies of social control, which will be referred to later.

The most primitive of the social controls is the use of force or violence. This method is employed by the animals as well as by man himself. It is practically the only method available before intellectual language is sufficiently developed to indicate adequately the behavior desired of the persons or organisms controlled, and before the imaginations of the controllers have developed to the extent that they are able to formulate and express in words, gestures or pantomime the thing they desire to have accomplished. Indeed, it is pretty clear that gesture and pantomime must have evolved out of the use of force. For example, shaking one's fist in the face of an enemy is a gesture composed of part of the act of striking and the pantomimic dance which pictures the slaying of the enemy or the seizure of women by a body of warriors are merely methods of saying in very primitive language forms what the controllers intend to do or have already done in concrete cases. Thus language in its early stages as a control mechanism must have developed directly out of the use of force.

Language, when used as a substitute for force, takes on the significance of intimidation. It involves a threat (as in shaking the fist) or an anticipation or promise (as in the ritualistic dance descriptive of an act of violence) of a deed of violence. As a consequence we list intimidation as the second evolutionary or historical form of control. It comes into existence and begins to supplement the actual employment of force when intellectual language develops to the point where it can be used as a substitute control process. Intimidation is used by the higher animals as well as by man, taking the form of gesture and emotional expressions used as threats, or even of emotional vocal language, as in the case of the barking of the dog or the hissing of the serpent. Intimidation becomes verbal only among men. It gradually develops greater volume than the use of force as a means of social control. Although it is most used among savages and the illiterate and relatively ignorant, it has by no means vanished from the world.

The use of fraud as a control begins while force is still the chief method of control and it continues through the dominance of intimidation and in its turn becomes the chief control. Fraud takes on a great many forms. In its early history it was exercised primarily by means of forceful and violent invasion of the peace of others. Later, as the lower forms of language developed, it became chiefly intimidatory fraud; and later still it assumed primarily a positive form in which the desires of individuals for unusual or unwonted advantage were exploited by the controllers. This application of the methods of control by fraud could develop only as the use of intellectual language became sufficiently apt that strong appeals to cupidity, lust, vanity, and hate, as well as to fear, could be made verbally and understood by the intended victim of fraud. The chief forms of fraud at the present time are economic, personal subornation, and political and ecclesiastical deception.

As the practice of using intellectual language for purposes of social control increased and as the language itself was transformed from the category of intimidation to that of persuasion of advantage to be derived from certain types of procedure, fraud merged into propaganda. The dominant type of control at the present time is propagandistic, and propaganda is still mainly fraudulent. This is so largely true that some commentators—Professor Lumley, for example—are inclined to characterize all propaganda as "bad" or fraudulent. The reader will of course understand that by the use of the term fraud here it is not meant to suggest that all the fraud referred to is criminal fraud. Only those forms of fraud that society regards as most reprehensible are made criminal or illegal. Perhaps the largest category of fraud has always been immoral fraud, which is considerable in our time. Condoned fraud, which scarcely receives the characterization of immoral, is also voluminous in modern society, but is perhaps less so than in early times.

The fifth and final historic form of social control is rational persuasion. It, like all the other major forms of social control, grows out of preceding forms. As the masses who are controlled by persuasion become more intelligent and critical of the verbal techniques used upon them they demand increasingly more logical arguments and dependable data from the controllers before they will be persuaded. This demand inevitably results in a growth of rational persuasive methods at the expense of the emotional and fraudulent methods still so strongly emphasized in propaganda. But it would be a mistake to suppose that persuasive control through verbal language—either oral or written—has as yet come to be chiefly rational. It still remains primarily emotional and fraudulent, although not necessarily criminally fraudulent, and it cannot be otherwise until the masses who are controlled by the leaders have made themselves sufficiently intelligent that they are able to detect fraudulent persuasion.

The Oscillation of the Major Controls

On the whole it seems that the use of force, intimidation, and fraud as social controls has been diminishing and that propaganda and rational persuasion have increased in volume within the last few centuries, and especially within the last few decades. But we should beware of supposing that this general movement has been in any sense regular and without oscillations. As a matter of fact the curve of development of the major methods of social control is no smoother than that of any other evolutionary trend. Yet it can scarcely be questioned that there has been such a trend, in fact a perfectly natural trend. The use of force or violence for purposes of control is laborious, exhausting, and dangerous to the controller and the controlled alike. The employment of threats and intimidation is a labor- and time-saving device as well as a conserver of life, limb, and property. But it can be made available only as language develops in its service. Fraud is an even more facile and less exhausting procedure, and when it reaches the form of emotional persuasion or propaganda it may often be mistaken for a beneficent method of control. It has taken on the form of good will, although it lacks the substance. It is also a much more democratic procedure in control than any of the three preceding historic modes of control. Thus we recognize propaganda as not only a higher type of social control but also as being dependent upon the development of a larger employment of more or less abstract language forms and of the attainment of considerable power of self-determination and self-rule on the part of the masses. The effective employment of rational persuasion in social control is possible only to a society in which reflective thinking on the basis of adequately tested evidence has become more or less habitual. Science is the chief aid to such control, not only for the controller but also for the controlled.

Yet, in spite of these general natural trends in the development of forms of social control, there are many reversions to the earlier and lower historic forms. Force and threats may be said to lie back of all the other methods of control when these have failed. . . . Force is applied mainly under present conditions by criminals and dictators and the military-minded for purposes of exploitation of the weak. The resort of the German, Italian, Russian and Japanese dictators and militarists to the use of force on a vast scale for the conquest of the rest of the world is an unparalleled instance in modern times of the return to barbaric and savage methods of social control. If all mankind is not to revert to barbarism such methods of international piracy will have to be eliminated as individual piracy has been suppressed within the last few centuries. . . .

The Passive Controls

Passing now from the general types of historical controls already discussed to the specific techniques of social control, we find it useful to classify them under the two headings: (1) passive controls and (2) active controls. Both of these types of social control techniques may be used for purposes of exploitation or constructively in the interest of the promotion of social and individual welfare. The social or ethical value of a control technique is not inherent in the technique itself, but depends on the use made of it. In this respect a control technique is like a fact or principle of science or any technological process. It is neutral, but the use made of it has decided moral and social implications. Thus a strike may be called for socially bad or good ends; explosives may be employed in mining operations or in that type of wholesale murder known as war.

The passive controls are those in which the controller is as little aggressive as possible. Strategy takes the place of force and threats, and the strategy itself tends to employ or make opportunity for the operation of natural forces and processes rather than to rely upon the use of fraud. The most important of these passive controls are non-resistance, appeasement, non-cooperation, the boycott, the embargo, the lock-out and the various forms of the strike. Non-resistance, properly speaking, operates when the controller allows the other person who seeks to control him or a collectivity to do as the opposition pleases. This is a highly negative control technique, but it may have the advantage of averting a portion of the destructive wrath of the enemy when resistance would be wholly useless and would merely result in inciting the opponent to more active violence. If the more powerful party or group can be relied upon to experience some sense of justice, non-resistance may actually call this to the fore as the emotion of anger dies out as a result of having nothing to exercise itself upon. The most extreme form of non-resistance is to be found among those animals who become temporarily paralyzed or immobile when attacked. Among men the philosophy of non-resistance is sometimes called pacifism. Where the enemy is ruthless and incapable of a sense of moral obligation and social justice pacifism works wholly to the advantage of the stronger party, as the unprepared countries conquered by Hitler in 1940 had occasion to learn. Appeasement is an extreme form of non-resistance and is operative when the pacifist group adopts a policy of conceding the demands of the stronger and thus of legitimizing them. Like non-resistance proper, this control only serves to strengthen a ruthless and conscienceless enemy. . . . Non-cooperation operates as a control in cases in which resistance is limited to a failure to carry out the orders or requests of another party, as where one or more persons refuse or fail to pay taxes, give military service, obey health or defense regulations, or any other laws or administrative or moral requirements. Gandhi and his followers have used this method effectively in India. If the opposition is weak in its powers of enforcement of its rules or regulations it may be worn down by such passive or negative resistance and finally be demoralized. This was the case in connection with the Eighteenth Amendment to the United States Constitution, in which non-cooperation of a large body of the people and of the liquor interests finally led to a repeal of this amendment.

The boycott is closely allied to non-cooperation. It is refusal to buy from, employ, or use the products or services of an opposition group. It is most commonly exercised in economic relations, but it is also applied in political, religious, and other sectarian relationships. The embargo is partly complementary to the boycott and is a somewhat more extreme or active form of passive controls. It prohibits the furnishing of materials or of services to an opposition group, whereas the boycott prohibits the use of the materials or services of the opposing group. It usually requires more energetic supervision to enforce an embargo than a boycott, since the profit motive may be more active in connection with the former. The lockout is essentially an embargo, while a black list may be employed in connection with either of these controls.

The strike is the most active and the least passive of all of the negative controls, but there is a considerable range in the quality of the various types of the strike. The hunger strike, the sit-down strike, and the student strike may be essentially and predominantly methods of non-cooperation or even of the boycott. The buyers' strike is essentially a boycott to which the term strike has been applied. The general strike, planned by the syndicalists and attempted occasionally in recent times, partakes of both non-cooperation and the boycott, but it usually develops some elements of active violence in resistance. In fact, all strikes are very likely to manifest sooner or later some elements of retaliative violence no matter how passive the resistance may be in the initial stages. This is particularly true of the typical industrial strike. This type of strike may even begin in aggression on the part of the striking workers and it is certain to become aggressive when picketing is resorted to as a supplementary measure of control.

The Active Controls

The active control techniques are much more numerous than the passive. Strictly passive or negative controls have never had much acceptance by the larger portion of mankind. They have been most used in disorganized societies in which the machinery of justice had broken down and protective traditions had largely ceased to safeguard the masses. Thus Jesus, in the so-called Sermon on the Mount, advised his disciples not to put up resistance against the powerful who abused and exploited them, since it would be useless and would hinder their service to a larger and higher cause. Weak minorities are commonly most successful when they make little or no outward resistance but work vigorously for their causes underground. Eventually such minorities, like the Christians under the Roman Empire and the Jews under the Christian civilization of the middle ages and early modern times, may come off victorious. In such cases strong personal self-discipline and social solidarity counts for much in the way of success.

The active control techniques of course include the five types of historical controls discussed earlier in this chapter, as well as their numerous subdivisions. We shall therefore not repeat any analysis of these forms of control previously made but extend our account in the direction of a further analysis of some of the derivative forms of the active control techniques. Among the more important of these are intolerance, censorship, and repression. The first two of these are essentially negative in form and the third is more likely to be negative than positive. However, all are active at the same time that they are negative. Intolerance is the mildest of the three. It consists essentially of the attitude of preserving a closed mind.

If intolerance is involuntary and results from a traditional prejudice, such as one may be subject to as a result of his religious or
political home environment, it may approximate to a passive control. But if the intolerance results from a consciousness of a special
interest which the intolerant are seeking to defend it is of course
an active control. Intolerance not only results in the withholding
of cooperation but it may also lead to acts of sabotage of the opposing interests or points of view. A less reprehensible active manifestation is proselytism, by which the opposition are propagandized
in an effort to bring them into the fold of the intolerant. If the
control activities of the intolerant become actively coercive they may
add intimidation and even violence to interested propaganda and
other forms of fraud as means of control.

Censorship is frequently an extension of intolerance and is an
act of fraud which supplements propaganda in favor of the interest
which censors opposition propaganda. The dictators have always
supplemented their propaganda activities with a strong censorship
of counter propaganda. By such means they could the more easily
facilitate their own propaganda. They have also enforced their
censorships by means of fraud, intimidation, and violence, even to
the application of the death penalty against those who violated the
censorship. Censorship is a form of repression, but there are
other types of repression also. The most common of these are imprisonment, fines, discriminatory taxation, prohibitory legislation
of a sumptuary type or the exclusion of certain individuals, classes
or races from competitive opportunities, and the imposition of extra
service burdens of a military or civic character. These forms of
repression are chiefly legal, but repression is also exercised through
the mores, as where women are held to a higher moral standard than
men, or where men are compelled to assume more extensive economic
responsibility in family support than women. Ecclesiastical bodies
are particularly active in repressing freedom of thought and the
expression of unorthodox opinion, the latter being a form of censorship. Economic and political interests frequently rival the ecclesiastical interest groups in these types of repression.

The Fraudulent Active Controls

The active controls just discussed appeal perhaps more frequently to the support of force and intimidation than they do to
fraud in general and propaganda in particular. Rarely do they

enlist the aid of rational persuasion, since they do not ordinarily operate aboveboard. More definitely of a fraudulent character, but very subtly so, are the active controls known as manipulation, intrigue, deception, and confusion. All four of these subtle methods of fraud are closely interrelated and they largely overlap. Their most common instrument is emotional persuasion or propaganda, but upon occasion they may implement their processes with intimidation and even sometimes with a limited use of force.

Manipulation consists in applying stimuli to individual personalities or to a group of people in such a way as to cause them to respond according to a premeditated pattern. This is commonly done through flattery, praise, rewards, bribes, ridicule, commands, the use of name calling and the skilful employment of slogans and other propaganda techniques. Flattery is perhaps the most effective means of manipulating individuals, although ridicule is almost as powerful as a negative technique. The group is usually manipulated by means of propaganda, which includes, among other techniques, appeals to loyalty, patriotism, class interest, group or special interest, to tradition and custom, and employs such pseudo-rational appeals as slogans and name calling. Manipulation places before the person or group to be controlled a pattern of behavior and then proceeds to make this pattern attractive by attaching to it the values of interest, regularity, respectability, novelty, conformity, or whatever else is calculated to make an appeal. Husbands and wives manipulate each other; teachers, preachers, employers and other classes of leaders manipulate those who are in their charge; political machines and ecclesiastical hierarchies manipulate their adherents; and governments their subjects.

Intrigue is in large measure a form of manipulation, but it emphasizes more largely the techniques of fraudulent trading of favors and support and even such coercive measures as blackmail and other intimidating pressures, than it does direct appeals to choice. Here propaganda is much less active, and pressure—from self-interest or fear—stands out more prominently. The professional politician is especially given to intrigue and political trading. Royal courts and ecclesiastical hierarchies were and are reputed to be constantly under the influence of intriguing factions who work for selfish interest and profit. There is also much intrigue in higher business circles, but perhaps more still in competitive social circles, such as cliques, sets, and other exclusive groups.

Deception is of course a chief adjunct to all forms of manipulation and intrigue. Neither would be possible without a considerable element of deception, although the employment of deception is perhaps more obvious in manipulation than in intrigue. Those manipulated must nearly always be deceived, perhaps through flattery, possibly through the arousal of false hopes, or the overemphasis of obligations and the arousal of unnecessary fears. In intrigue the manipulators or controllers may frequently do work on a much more candid basis and an explicit understanding with one another, although they nearly always undertake to deceive and exploit a larger group of third persons, as is the case when a political machine intrigues to capture the government on the basis of false issues or promises in order to rule at the expense of the citizens and taxpayers. An effective method of exercising deception is through the creation of confusion. Confusion of facts, of values, of interests, of opinion, and in many other forms, renders the deception of individuals and masses relatively easy. Politicians who cannot make an honest appeal for support to the voters nearly always seek to confuse the issues and then to misrepresent the facts. Thus misrepresentation is a powerful adjunct to both confusion and deception.

The More Obvious Forms of Fraud

In our time we hear much of racketeering. It takes on many forms, the most actively publicized of which is that carried on by small predatory criminal groups exploiting individuals who operate more or less outside of the law. Thus powerful criminal rackets live parasitically off of the proceeds of illicit liquor and drug peddling, prostitution, gambling, and all manner of "skin games," such as counterfeiting, green goods and gold brick selling, harboring of stolen goods, etc. The more successful rackets of this sort are composed of three types of personnel: the criminally employed persons, who are the exploited; the police who are privy to both the exploited criminals and the criminal exploiters or racketeers, and thus participate in the racketeering; and the racketeers proper, who force upon the first group their "protection," which usually means that they act as the go-betweens with the police and themselves refrain from further persecution of the criminally employed as long as these pay over substantial assessments to the leading racketeers and the police. Not infrequently there is a fourth group involved in this type of racketeering, the members of the dominant political machine who control the police and who have to be paid "hush money" to prevent them from forcing the police to arrest the racketeers. Many particularly vulnerable legitimate business, such as laundries, dyeing and cleaning establishments, bakeries, and dairies, are exploited in a similar manner by professional racketeers who either spoil, destroy, or steal their products or services unless tribute is paid them. If the racketeers in turn bribe the police to inefficiency these legitimate businesses cannot hope for governmental protection.

While the forms of racketeering here described are among the most commonly recognized types of criminal control in our society, there are other less well known forms of racketeering which are probably even more inimical to social welfare. Among these may be mentioned political bosses and their machines, which mislead and exploit the people not only at the polls but also by corrupting their governments through fraud and graft; the dictatorial forms of government, which are huge national rackets built on essentially the same pattern as the private criminal rackets first described; financial rackets, by means of which the great banking and industrial interests exploit the investing and producing public and take from them most of their surplus incomes; various so-called benevolent rackets which collect money supposedly for philanthropic purposes but frequently for their own profit or prestige; the armament makers' preparedness racket, which is now pretty generally understood; the patrioteering rackets staged by business, political, and class interests who wish to exploit the masses of the people in the name of idealism. Even ecclesiastical hierarchies, operating in the name of religion, may sometimes partake more of the nature of racketeering groups operating for the control and exploitation of their loyal members than of the character of servants of morality and social welfare. Because such rackets as those here described are much more abstractly organized than those first mentioned and because they operate invisibly and for the most part behind the screen of professed benevolent ends, they are less well understood and the average citizen protects himself against them with difficulty. A wisely and beneficently controlled society takes active steps (1) to enlighten its citizens regarding these and many other forms of exploitive controls and (2) to organize them for purposes of riddance against such racketeering exploitation. We shall now pass over many forms of more obvious graft, corruption, and blackmail—for the description of which space is lacking—and proceed to describe some of the constructive control processes which aim at the rendering of just this type of service.

Education as the Basic Constructive Social Control

The controls we have just described are those we have inherited from the socially uncritical past. But mankind have gradually become conscious of their society and of its control problems. This growing social awareness has led to the desire to use social control methods for constructive ends, that is, for social improvement, instead of merely for individual advantage. This movement for social betterment came to a head in the eighteenth century and produced the revolutionary social philosophy of that "age of enlightenment," which protested against the ancient exploitive governmental and class systems still in operation. Then began those revolutions in the name of humanitarianism, typified by the American and the French revolutions. In the nineteenth century the new principle of social control for the common welfare had been so generally accepted that the advocates of the old exploitation were compelled to refit their arguments in conformity to it in order to hold on a little while longer to their exploitive practices. Thus the laissez faire philosophy, which began in the eighteenth century as a protest against excessive and unjust regimentation of individual interests and behavior, was transformed into a new instrument of exploitation. Its advocates now claimed that the best way to promote the common welfare was to leave the problems of social control to individual initiative, while at the same time they discounted the fact that people are very unequal in their powers to defend or promote their own interests. As a consequence, the laissez faire that had been advocated as a means of emancipation of the individual from collective tyranny, as in the assertion of the right of freedom of contract, now came to be a means to racketeering in the hands of unscrupulous persons who held sufficient power to compel the weak to accept their terms as to wages, conditions of labor, the distribution of wealth, and the like. The very term "freedom of contract," which had once been the symbol of emancipation, now became the badge of a new servitude. Society has found it necessary to protect the weak against the strong advocates of laissez faire by building up a system of benevolent and constructive governmental interference.

The revolutions of the eighteenth and nineteenth centuries resulted in the overthrow of kings and the rule of the nobility and clergy and placed, at least nominally, the control of governments in the hands of the people. As a consequence it became necessary for the people as a whole to develop methods of social control which would preserve and promote their own interests. In other words, they were face to face with the necessity of learning social self-control. This they could not do without knowledge or enlightenment. Genuine leaders of the masses understood this early. Condorcet in France and Thomas Jefferson in the United States developed plans for popular education. Jefferson's plan to educate the masses, extended by Horace Mann and others, gradually went into effect, at least partially, in the United States. It was later carried to Argentina by the great Sarmiento and thus was spread to South America. The chief shortcoming of our system of the education of the masses for social self-control lies in the fact that our public schools have continued to cling to such traditional subjects as ancient languages, mythology, sentimental literature, and military and diplomatic history instead of acquainting the future citizens of a democracy with knowledge as to how social, economic, and political life really operates. They are still largely left in ignorance of how governments, politics, and business are actually manipulated and how they should be operated in the interest of all the people instead of the racketeers, big and little, who may manage to control them. As a consequence, no people have yet learned how to govern themselves, but are still controlled by groups of self-appointed leaders who generally serve their own interests. The first problem of democracy is to remake the public schools in such a manner that they will serve the interests of democracy. Fascist and Nazi schools are organized to support the dominant ideologies in the countries where these philosophies operate. Even in our own country parochial schools are so constituted that they inculcate the principles and beliefs of the religions supporting those schools. The public schools of our democracy, however, are prevented by hostile powers from teaching the philosophy and the techniques of democracy. Yet this teaching could easily be accomplished without sacrificing the legitimate interests of impartial science and culture if the people would insist that their schools speak for themselves instead of for those opposed to a full development of democracy.

Lester F. Ward, the first great American sociologist, saw this fact clearly some seventy-five years ago and he stated it in his

theory of sociocracy. His *Dynamic Sociology* (1883) was a plea
for the two great essentials of democracy: (1) a social organization
which would promote investigation in science, including the social
sciences especially, and (2) the widespread diffusion of the results
of these investigations among the people in order that they might
order their private lives and control their social relations in keeping
with the facts and principles of science. These principles of Ward,
although never abandoned, have not had the wholehearted support
of sociologists, of educationists, and of the people themselves, which
they deserve. Until they become the watchwords of democracy,
democratic or popular social control will not be possible.

Legislation as a Second Step in Constructive Control

In a very simple society, where the machinery of social control
is not much developed, and each individual is his own controller,
knowledge alone may in a majority of cases be a sufficient control.
But in a highly complex modern society it is necessary to formulate
knowledge into rules for the guidance of the people as a whole.
Such objective rules are necessary as a means to a reasonable degree
of uniformity of conduct of men in society. These rules for the
guidance of human conduct in society began to be formulated fairly
early among men and subsequently they have taken on various
forms. In very early times they assumed the largely unconscious
forms of custom and tradition. Under these aspects they were
scarcely recognized as social rules. But as the need for greater uniformity of behavior became apparent under the influence of conflicting customs and traditions, compulsory uniformity was consciously and purposively achieved by means of revelation. In all
religions revelation appears to have been a conscious or an unconscious method of ironing out conflicts of custom and tradition as the
intermixture of cultures became more marked in ancient times. It
was a method of priestly law-making which was later copied by the
kings in the making of their civil codes. Hammurabi, for example,
was faced with the necessity of harmonizing the conflict of customs
which arose from the establishment of his empire, inclusive of various subject peoples. He solved this administrative problem by
having prepared about 2200 B.C. the first code which has survived
to our time. Many other codes followed, until all the ancient peoples possessed bodies of objective laws controlling individual and
collective behavior.

At first these codes were attributed to the gods in order to give to them greater prestige with the people. Hammurabi claimed that his code was revealed to him by the Babylonian gods Bel and Marduk. Later on the kings and emperors came to issue laws in their own names and by virtue of their royal authority, which they continued to trace back to divine sanction, until in very recent times the masses have refused to believe that the gods had anything to do with installing their oppressors in power. As the people became more intelligent and more powerful in social control, senates, councils, parliaments, congresses, and other legislative bodies were recognized as competent to make laws for the people. Finally, the people acquired the privilege of electing representatives to these legislative bodies charged with the obligation of legislating in their interest. Thus nominally at least the people in the more advanced countries acquired the power to govern themselves through their own elective legislative, executive, and judicial representatives. But this popular or democratic self-control through laws made and administered and adjudicated by their representatives has never been made completely effective, even in the most highly civilized countries. This fact is due (1) to failure of the people completely to inform themselves of the workings of their social system and of the techniques of effective democratic control, (2) to the inadequacy of their schools and other educational agencies to provide them with the necessary information, and (3) to the widespread use of fraudulent propaganda by the interests who seek to confuse the people as to their own needs and the methods by which they may be satisfied. Until the masses can correct these three adverse situations they cannot secure a rational social self control. More recently the dictatorships have arisen with the expressed purpose of preventing the achievement of democratic self-control by the masses, and to this end the dictators employ not only fraudulent propaganda and other forms of fraud, but also intimidation and force. If the people sleep much longer they will awake only to find themselves permanently bound.

Several attempts at giving the people more control over the legislative process have been developed in recent decades. Prominent among these are direct popular primaries, the initiative, the referendum, the recall, the short ballot, non-partisan elections, non-partisan publicity of candidates and issues, proportional and functional representation, legislative reference aids and non-partisan bill drafting. But such devices cannot of themselves give to the people wise popular self-control. Until the people can emasculate fraudulent propaganda and become sufficiently informed regarding their own problems they will continue to be at the mercy of exploiters, totalitarian or otherwise.

The Spirit of Social Reform

The eighteenth century enlightenment, already referred to, by teaching men to consider the common welfare initiated a spirit of social reform. This spirit flowered into a vast number of reform programs in the nineteenth century, many of which were realized in practice. Social reform in the interests of the masses could not become effective before the masses themselves gained some directive power. This is the reason why reform of the suffrage and of elections were regarded as basic to almost all other important social reforms. Enlightenment alone was not sufficient. Without suffrage and parliamentary participation the people could seek control in their own interest only through revolution. Thus political revolutions preceded electoral reforms and parliamentary participation in all countries. But once the people had gained through revolution the privilege of electing representatives to legislate and administer for them they gradually abandoned the method of control through revolution and turned increasingly to parliamentary procedures. There is not space here even to enumerate all of the reforms secured by the people since they achieved the power of participation in government. Nor can we list all of the reforms they have failed to achieve. But some of those accomplished stand out as great landmarks in civilization. They include the abolition of slavery, the improvement of conditions of labor for men, women, and children, the provision of economic security for the aged, the infirm, and the unemployed, a larger education of the masses, some improvement in political, economic, and social morality, vastly improved public health and sanitation, greater freedom of thought and expression, reform of penal practices and some reform in legal procedure. These reforms are not due exclusively or perhaps in all cases even primarily to the efforts of the masses of the people; but that most of them have been largely implemented by popular demands backed by popular power can scarcely be doubted.

The chief agencies of social control, as distinguished from the techniques of social control, have developed under the patronage of the masses. The enlightenment of the masses was both the result and the cause of the great growth of popular education in the last century and a half. The ability of the masses to read and their desire for knowledge and entertainment have made it possible to finance the chief agencies of symbolic or verbal controls which have grown so rapidly in recent times. Books and magazines and newspapers can now be published cheaply and in immense numbers. The telephone and the telegraph have been made relatively cheap means of communication. The lyceum and chautauqua first became possible as the fruit of extensive popular education, later to be supplemented by the radio. The movie has grown into an unparalleled instrument for the uniformization of the folkways and the mores, with the result that all the world may be made over after one pattern, and that not the best. As a result of all these agencies of control, public opinion has come to be the most powerful of all social controls, supplementing the power of kings and armies. Stemming as it does mainly from the radio and the periodical press, it is peculiarly subject to manipulation by propaganda. As a consequence, popular control has had to face a powerful obstacle in the form of a propagandized public opinion manufactured by these agencies of control which are not as yet dominated by the people themselves. Not only do special interests dominate the press and the radio and the movies in all countries, but in the dictatorships their control has been centralized in a racketeering political group professedly hostile to democratic control. As a consequence, these powerful agencies have been largely lost to the future cause of social reform. The next step in constructive democratic social control would seem to be for the people to get possession of the powerful public-opinion-making agencies. But here again we are face to face with the fact that such a control could not be truly effective unless the popular intelligence equalled the people's power.

Social Planning

Social reform measures mark the beginning of social planning. All transitory or piecemeal social reforms are short-time social plans. Therefore, an age of social reform, if it develops normally, should initiate a period of social planning. Social planning at its best looks forward to the reorganization of society over a long period of time and in such a manner as to include a wide range of social functions and adjustments. Planning may be for the whole of society or for some fundamental aspect of it. Economic planning has been the farthest advanced up to the present, since economic life is so largely basic to the other aspects of social control. Social planning is not wholly new, but it has attracted widespread and serious attention only recently. Only recently also has it been undertaken extensively.

The methods of social planning may be illustrated by a brief analysis of three examples undertaken by as many governments. Social planning by private business organizations antedates these three examples, but only governments have sufficient power to control all of the situations and resources that are necessary to render it adequately successful. It was the Russian Five-Year Plan which first attracted international attention early in the nineteen-thirties. Russia being industrially backward sought to become industrially self-sufficing by planning her total economy in such a manner as to achieve a higher degree of industrial efficiency. In this she largely succeeded in spite of many obstacles. The second example is that of the national planning of the Hitler regime in Germany. When Hitler came into power he already had a fairly well developed plan for the German people which he had sketched in *Mein Kampf*. This plan aimed first at making the German nation superior in a military way to all other countries. His plan also included various international alliances and ultimately a series of world conquests. This plan was subject to modification in process, but it was remarkably well developed, even in 1932. It is a curious fact that other countries, including England, France, and the United States, took little notice of this plan until it was well on the way to realization. When Mr. F. D. Roosevelt came to the presidency in 1933 he formulated a tentative and somewhat halting plan for social reconstruction in the United States, which he called the New Deal. . . .

The Future of Social Planning

The most significant thing about the growing interest in social planning is that so many people have become aware of the desirability of applying the principles of science to social control, and not only immediately and temporarily, but over a long period of time and with respect to a wide range of social adjustments. For two centuries or more far-seeing leaders have been applying science to economic production, commerce, and finance, and for a shorter time to medicine and public health and sanitation. More recently science has been applied to agriculture. Planning on a scientific basis has been applied to all of these interests, sometimes with re-markable results. But only recently have the masses of men been won over to the planning of human association and collective wel-fare on a large scale. Two strong motives have worked against such a trend. On the one hand, people have been afraid to entrust great powers to government, especially to the semi-corrupt and relatively inefficient governments that have been established in the more democratic states. The people remember the oppressions of the old governments which were dominant before they gained power. In many cases they would prefer to put up with inefficiency rather than risk governmental oppression and exploitation. In the second place, the powerful special interests oppose social planning through government because it threatens their opportunity to exploit the people. Failing to control government, they still hope to keep the government sufficiently weak that their exploitive schemes will not be seriously interfered with. Powerful business, ecclesiastical, and political interests and factions are especially likely to oppose scien-tific social planning on this score. Owing to such obstacles long time social planning by government might have been retarded yet many decades had it not been for the fact that the dictators, work-ing under the necessity of utilizing to the maximum extent every resource at their disposal, demonstrated to the rest of the world its effectiveness. Hitler especially has taught the more democratic coun-tries a lesson in this respect which they will probably never forget. England, under the immediate threat of invasion, changed over night from a policy of dawdling and appeasement to a rigorously planned and centralized economy. The United States followed at a distance and less efficiently under a less distinct threat of in-vasion. . . .

Two problems in social control confront democratic peoples in connection with the future of social planning. The first of these is whether it requires such concentration of power in government that it will necessarily lead to the totalitarian form of government. Many persons believe that such is the case. . . . The other problem is as to whether the masses of the people will ever sufficiently disci-pline and enlighten themselves as to participate intelligently in a planned society. Some say that they must first be reduced to the status of serfs or slaves before this is possible. These, however, are questions which cannot be answered from an a priori standpoint. Only the test of time will give a definite reply, and perhaps only the people themselves can provide the answer.

Chapter 25

LEADERSHIP

By Dr. J. F. Thaden
Michigan State College, East Lansing, Michigan

ELEMENTS OF LEADERSHIP

Leadership is one of a multiplicity of social processes. It is essential in any directing of desirable change. One may ask, have the phenomenal cultural and social changes during the past century and especially during recent decades, been due to proportionately more leaders than formerly? Have they been caused by a considerable increase in new types of leaders? Have the masses become more willing to follow their leaders? Has cultural accumulation been paralleled by a training of leaders, or of followers, for anticipated changes? These questions suggest possible cause and effect relationships between leadership and social change. It is the purpose of this chapter to indicate the part that leaders may play, either directly or indirectly, in changing culture and social institutions.

Social Change and Culture Change

Change is inevitable. Survival necessitates adjustment and this means change. It is frequently said that change is as certain as death and taxes. Within the memory of many now living there have been many changes in methods of earning a living, training the young, caring for the aged, the infirm, the unemployed, the antisocial; and in all other phases of life. These changes have been affected by mechanical and social inventions for which innovaters, thinkers, idealists, philosophers, scientists, organizers—leaders of one kind or another—are to some extent responsible. Fifty thousand patents a year, universal education, and democratic policies accelerate the changes.

In this chapter a sharp distinction between culture change and social change is not important. The two terms are commonly used interchangeably. In general it may be said that *social* change refers to modification in society, such as shifts in the age, sex, or marital composition of population, density and mobility. On the other hand *culture* change generally refers to such interaction patterns as competition, conflict, accommodation, and assimilation. Social change and culture change are to a considerable degree causally connected. Social change generally induces culture change, and equally often culture change impels social change. For example, the invention of the mechanical stoker and its use in steam engines on railroads has resulted in longer passenger trains, thus necessitating more "Red Caps" and encouraging the northward migration of negroes. On the other hand, the present world war is encouraging many technicians in munition factories in their discoveries and inventions of deadlier weapons.

Opportunities for Leaders

Uncertainties and insecurities call for leaders. The opportunity for leadership is apparent in all fields of human endeavor. Multitudes lament over the apparent dearth of contemporary leaders. Some of those lamenting might be the last to acknowledge one, or to follow him if he were recognized.

Expressions of need for leaders generally betray a desire for social change productive of greater social and economic security and happiness. The slow emergence of mankind from a monarchial environment to a somewhat democratic one, where many more leaders, and these of a socialized type, are required, partly explains the desires for new types of leaders. Dictators and commanders are out of place in the evolving social and democratic order where guides, interpreters, coordinators, synthesists and planners are in demand. The need of today in democratic countries, says Chapin, "is the development of leadership—not the leadership of the centralized few, but rather a diffused and spontaneous leadership among the masses of the people."[1] The editor of the official trade organ of the United States Chamber of Commerce, *Nation's Business,* says "If democracy is to endure, it must be protected against itself, and hope lies through enlightened and intelligent leadership of group unity."[2] Furthermore, he says "The need for group leadership is apparent. The opportunity for such leadership is as great as ever in the world's history. This amazing age with its many currents, invisible, likely at any moment to change the career of an individual, an industry, or a community, calls for leadership of the highest order."[3]

[1] F. Stuart Chapin, "Socialized Leadership," *Social Forces,* Vol. 3, 1924, p. 60.

[2] Merle Thorpe, *Organized Business Leadership,* Harper & Bros., 1931, p. XII.

[3] Thorpe, *Ibid.,* p. 29.

Numerous writers have decried the sparsity of leaders of national caliber in government and industry. Carey writes "The national leaders of the type of Washington, Jefferson, Hamilton, Franklin, Charles Sumner, John Marshall, and the Adamses have apparently passed from the politics to the universities. In the national arena, we now have too many Tom Heflins; in the State too many 'Pa' and 'Ma' Fergusons and Mrs. Florence Knapps, and in the city too many Bill Thompsons and Bossie Gillises and their less touted prototypes."[4]

Popular Concepts of Leadership

All groups have leaders and all leaders have followers. Leaders and followers are interdependent. One is a leader if he has a following regardless of how small or how informal the group may be. Concepts of leadership are many and varied.

In the mind of the populace a leader is commonly one who exercises power, such as a commander, a dictator, or an executive. This is to be expected inasmuch as mankind from the dawn of history has lived in a predominantly militaristic environment. Tribal warfare was once quite universal. Rulers reigned supreme. Most history texts give an impression that the world's work has been largely accomplished by military heroes. However, in this country particularly, the industrial revolution has tended to supplant the military-political type of leader.

A handful of industrialists control the economic existence of millions of families. Closely associated with those in the manufacturing and mechanical industries are the financiers and business men. With them leadership tends to be salesmanship and salesmanship is leadership. Annual conventions honor him who has secured the largest number of signatures on the dotted line. To be a successful business man is currently regarded by some as *ipso facto* evidence of leadership. Poets, essayists and philosophers, as men of prominence, have apparently given way to tycoons. Of the 3931 biographical sketches appearing for the first time in the 1928–29 edition of *Who's Who in America* business men were most numerous, comprising about one in five of the entire list as compared with one in six for educators, one in eight for clergymen, and one in twelve for lawyers.[5] Such statistical studies as have been made of the occu-

[4] Henry R. Carey, "But Not One Cent for Leadership," *Independent*, Vol. 120, 1928, p. 545.

[5] *Who's Who in America*, 1930–31 edition, pp. 24–5.

pation of *Who's Who* registrants in the earlier editions indicated a considerably smaller proportion of business men.

Hero-worshipping

We are strongly inclined to hero-worshipping. Emerson said "Every man is a hero and an oracle to somebody, and to that person, whatever he says has an enhanced value." From early childhood we have been conditioned by our parents, teachers, and preachers to emulate some member of the family tree, some national character, or some Divine. Of course those worshipped have more to gain than to lose by encouraging the attitude of hero-worshipping on the part of their followers. Hero-worship has aided those in power to preserve the status quo. Since a primary function of education, through the ages, both formal and informal, has been to secure conformity to the mores and emulation of a few leaders designated by the elders tended to entrench even more securely established customs and institutions. The daily paper, radio, and movie now tend to nullify efforts of our near relatives and school-room educators in circumscribing our acquisition of knowledge, so that additional heroes are worshipped yearly, and the new generation is conditioned to a continuous succession of heroes, and thus to change.

Definition of Leadership

It is necessary that the distinction between *authority* and leadership be clarified. A traffic officer, for example, may give you a red ticket, a judge a thirty-day sentence, a clergyman may pronounce you "man and wife," and a college president may confer upon you a degree—by virtue of the authority vested in the official positions they represent. "Authority" refers to the power attached to office and the submission or favors demanded of its subjects. An officer of the law represents authority, not leadership *per se*. So does a teacher, preacher, meat inspector or king in so far as his power depends on the influence attached to his position. All institutional leaders and officers of organizations are vested with authority which may take a multitude of forms, all involving an attitude of responsiveness.

By personal leadership is meant those physical, mental, social, and psychological traits that endear others to him and cause him to have an eager and voluntary following. Some of those traits may be innate, such as native capacity and stature, but most of them are acquired, such as altruism, conscientiousness, honesty, and versatility. Personal leadership assumes many forms. One normally acquires but a few of the multitude of traits that attract others to him. Some people, for example, are attracted by tactfulness while some are repulsed by it. Frankness may be the open sesame for such. Aggressiveness may be a winning trait for one and the "Waterloo" for another.

As human relationships increase in complexity the criteria of leadership also tends to become more complicated. We are reminded of this by Hooker when she says "The word *leader* has radically different meanings, all more or less vague, for the politician, the Y. M. C. A. county secretary, the superintendent of rural churches, and the director of university extension. Fully as great variety and uncertainty exist regarding the functions of leaders, the qualities essential or desirable in them, their motives and rewards, the conditions favorable to their development, and the technique of leadership. Everybody desires to be moving in this matter; but all show about as much uncertainty as the Bandar-log regarding the destination and the route."[6]

If the "special influence of one person over other persons" is leadership as Bogardus[7] sees it, then leadership is universal wherever two or more are gathered together. This influence may be temporary or transitory and operative in a single phase of interaction or in a mosaic of interactions.

Bernard characterizes leadership as the "capacity of presenting stimuli for collective response."[8] This may be done unconsciously or involuntarily. Lindbergh probably little dreamed that his solo flight across the Atlantic would have the response that it did. The rapidity of diffusion of cultures in modern time frequently forces one to be heralded as a leader before he himself has become aware of his contribution to existing culture.

Leaders are persons with a multiplicity of selves in the sense that a person "has as many selves as there are individuals who recognize him and carry an image of him in their minds."[9] Persons carrying

[6] Elizabeth R. Hooker, "Leaders in Village Communities," *Social Forces*, Vol. 6, 1928, p. 605.

[7] E. S. Bogardus, "World Leadership Types," *Sociology and Social Research*, Vol. 12, 1928, p. 574.

[8] L. L. Bernard, *Introduction to Social Psychology*, H. Holt and Co., 1926, p. 574.

[9] William James, *Psychology*, H. Holt and Company, 1924, p. 179.

mental images of Edison, Ford, Lindbergh, and Burbank are considerable in contrast with the number harboring the image of John Doe. A definition given by Tead is, "Leadership is the activity of influencing people to cooperate toward some goal which they come to find desirable."[10] This mutuality between the members of a group, both leaders and followers, is also stressed by Pigors when he emphasized "Leadership is a process of mutual stimulation which, by the successful interplay of relevant individual differences, controls human energy in the pursuit of a common cause."[11]

Regardless of how leadership may be defined the leader is limited in what he can do. Leadership is a group phenomenon and a product of group life. Even dictators, sometimes thought of as one type of leaders, must have followers. They are not at liberty to do as they please, for fear of being overthrown. There is no understanding of leadership apart from its group. Living is an associative process and leadership is an integral part of that process. Leadership does not exist independently of a group. Groups tend to change slowly when conditions are normal, consequently social change is generally slow.

Classification of Leaders

No hard and fast line can be drawn between different types of leaders, because each tends to overlap with one or more of the other types. A more satisfactory classification than most of them is a twofold one, namely: (1) direct or personal, and (2) indirect or impersonal. Direct leaders are readily identified. They work with people rather than with things. Teachers, preachers, band leaders, and cheer leaders are examples. Each secures attention, arouses enthusiasm, and inspires action in face-to-face association. Results of his leading are soon apparent.

Indirect leaders are not readily observed. They work primarily with things and ideas. Writers, playwrights, poets, painters, composers, sculptors, philosophers, inventors, are examples. Their handicraft may not become well known for many years after its inception or even after its completion.

As to which of the two types tends to induce the greater measure of social change is difficult to evaluate because the results of indirect leadership are usually slow in attaining fruition. For example,

[10] Ordway Tead, *The Art of Leadership*, McGraw-Hill Book Co., 1935, p. 20.
[11] Paul Pigors, *Leadership or Domination*, Houghton-Mifflin Co., 1935, p. 16.

mastering some of the compositions of Bach, Beethoven, Chopin, Mozart, Schubert, Wagner, and others, though written generations ago, is still considered basic in a musical career.

Traits of Leadership

No two men do a job of leading in the same way. No two persons possess the same qualities of leadership. Nor do any two persons have the same combination of physical, mental, social, and personality traits. Almost every popular writer on the topic of leadership has listed traits which to him seemed important. Burke, bringing some of them together, says, "Ellwood lists the following traits of leadership: a high degree of intelligence; large sympathy with one's group; an efficient social imagination; moral and physical courage; capacity for enthusiam; complete consecration to the cause he represents. Allport holds the following traits to be of prime importance: ascendance of manner and physique; high motility; social participation; drive. Bogardus lists the following evidences of a democratic leadership: increasing the opportunities for the development of other persons; promoting the welfare of groups as such; taking the side of injustice against special privilege; showing an at-one-ness with the humbler members of society; consulting with authorities, even opponents, before acting; using the discussion method of securing adjustments; showing the way and sacrificing self; rendering service without expectation of reward."[12] Cooley remarks that "If we ask what are the mental traits that distinguish a leader, the only answer seems to be that he must, in one way or another, be a great deal of a man, or at least appear to be. He must stand for some thing to which men incline, and so take his place by right as a focus of their thought."[13]

Other traits that leaders commonly possess to a greater or less extent are: native ability, education, communicability, friendliness, conscientiousness, broadmindedness, integrity, altruism, cooperativeness, health, confidence in self and in people, vision, perseverance, self-control, cheerfulness, trustworthiness, experience, and ability to plan or organize. Many other traits might be added. It cannot be said that any one trait is universally more important than another in fostering social change.

[12] Margaret M. Burke, "Leadership and Tennyson," *Journal of Applied Sociology*, Vol. 11, 1926–1927, p. 344.

[13] C. H. Cooley, *Human Nature and the Social Order*, Charles Scribner's Sons, 1902, p. 293.

An important characteristic, closely associated with native ability and cooperativeness is education, as will be noted later. In any discussion of leadership traits the element of sex should not be left out of consideration. There have been no women Presidents in United States, few women Governors, and these usually successors to their husbands upon death in office, few women senators, representatives, judges, presidents of colleges and universities, or inventors, and so on. Women had to be emancipated before they were at liberty to compete on an equality with men. Gradually women leaders are becoming more numerous in various fields of endeavor. Of the total number of registrants in *Who's Who in America* 7 per cent are women. Of the 72 in the Hall of Fame a tenth are women. A study of the records of the United States Patent Office reveals that women have already made material contributions to the sum total of creative achievements. ''For 19 years after the enactment of the patent law in 1790 not a single one of the 10,000 patents issued was granted to a woman.''[14] Now over 10 per cent of the patents granted annually by the United States Patent Office are granted to women.

One normally acquires positions of leadership through leading. Some acquire positions of leadership easily, readily, and at very early ages. Others find it a long and difficult road. Studies of the age of *Who's Who* registrants indicates that the median age is 60 years, and the likelihood of attaining eminence, in general increases with age, particularly with the men. Among the men all of the five-year age groups beyond ''Three-score years and ten,'' excepting the age group 95–99 are represented in larger relative numbers in *Who's Who* than are the age groups under 65, indicating that age and eminence are closely associated. Dr. William Osler's theories as to the comparative uselessness of men above 40, and the entire superfluity of the sexagenarian, are certainly nullified as regards the nation's eminent men and women.

One characteristic of leaders is the extent and variety of their organizational affiliation. For example, the biographical sketch pertaining to Nicholas Murray Butler in the 1940–41 edition of *Who's Who in America* lists, among many others, membership in the following: Am. Acad. Arts and Letters, 1911; Amer. Philos. Soc. (1901–); Am. Psychol. Assn; N.E.A; Am. Hist. Assn; N. Y. Hist.

[14] *Women's Contributions in the Field of Invention*, Bulletin of the Woman's Bureau, No. 28, U. S. Dept. of Labor, 1923, p. 11.

Soc. (1905–   ) ; Germanistic Soc; Am. Scandinavian Soc; Amer. Acad. in Rome (1905–   ) ; Univ. Settlement Soc; France-American Soc; N. Y. Chamber of Commerce; Am. Soc. Internat. Law (1906–   ) ; Amer. Hellenic Soc; Nat. Inst. Social Sciences (1937–   ) ; advisory bd. Lycee Francaise de New York (1939–   ). He holds or has held the presidency or vice-presidency, or some official position, in many of them.

Organizational membership averages higher among leaders than among laymen, and higher for practically every type of organization, especially in county, state, inter-state, regional, national, foreign, and international organizations. Laymen tend to restrict their affiliations to local groups while leaders tend to be identified with more far-flung organizations.

It is not possible to state that some traits are more influential than others in bringing about social change. A seemingly influential trait in producing change in one situation fails in another.

EXTENT OF LEADERSHIP

Biographical Registers

Some knowledge of the contribution to culture and to social change may be gleaned from a perusal of biographical registers. Such registers are numerous. The most widely used is *Who's Who in America*. It is published biennially. The 1940–41 or 21st edition contains 31,752 biographical sketches of contemporary "best known" men and women "in all lines of useful and reputable achievements." It tries to list those who have distinguished themselves in one or another of the various fields of human endeavor, and gives the facts about them that are of greatest interest—place of birth, date of birth, parentage, residence, education, occupation, marital status, children, organizational affiliation, writings, and so on.

Many countries have biographical registers of their eminent persons. Germany has her "Wer Ists?" France her "Qui Etes-Vou?" Italy her "Chi E?" Sweden her "Vem ar Det?" Norway her "Hvem er Hvem," and England has her "Who's Who." The idea in the modern sense may be said to have originated in England in 1849, the date of the appearance of the first "Who's Who" in London. This book was primarily a directory of the nobility and landed gentry of the British Isles and for about half a century it remained little more than a red book or a blue book of English aristocrats.

The last or 93rd edition (1941) gives some 35,000 brief biographical sketches of notable English men and women whose position or achievement make them of general interest.

In recent years numerous works have appeared containing biographies of noted people in specific fields of human activity, such as science, engineering, literature, music, drama, jurisprudence, writing, finance, medicine, agriculture. There are also biographical registers of eminent women, of eminent negroes, and of persons in the labor movement. Furthermore, there are now also a goodly number of such registers pertaining to the more eminent people in a specific region, state or city.

The implication in these paragraphs has been that notables and persons of eminence are leaders. Although this is not always true there is in general a fairly close association.

Statistical Studies of Men of Eminence

More quantitative studies have probably been made of eminent men and women listed in *Who's Who in America* than of all other biographical works combined. To determine the relative importance of heredity and environment in the production of eminence has been the stimulus that set many to work in this realm. The geographic origin and distribution of notables have been favorite fields of investigation, since they have been supposed to contain the answer to this perpetual and complex problem. Results of studies in this field reveal that the prominent persons engaged in urban occupations were generally born and raised in urban areas, while leaders in agriculture and allied fields were generally born and raised on farms.

That higher education is a preliminary to a successful career is one of the most common generalizations of social researchers. This attribute is becoming increasingly prevalent among persons in leadership positions. The editors of *Who's Who in America* occasionally do some analyzing of their own accumulated data themselves. They find that of the 29,389 persons furnishing educational statistics for the 1934–35 edition, 75 per cent were college graduates and 86 per cent had attended college. These figures are higher than they are in comparable studies, for example, only 77 per cent of those in the 1924–25 edition had attended college. About three-fourths of the college graduates have two or more degrees. Since the median age of *Who's Who* registrants is about 60 years it means that approximately one-half graduated from college previous to

1900, in an age when relatively few went to college. The tendency has been steadily growing in favor of higher education for leaders in all phases of American life.

A college graduate is nine or ten times as likely to attain national recognition as one who is not a graduate. There are other factors in the academic environment, besides the acquirement of facts and a habit of thinking, which stimulate one to achieve and to attain a position of leadership. Many alumni treasure more highly than the acquisition of knowledge the intimate and enduring friendships with classmates, house and roommates, and a few faculty members. Gauss says "The greatest thing I gained from my college life was learning to talk and deal with my fellow men, and the opportunity which I had of meeting fellows from all walks of life and all parts of the country in the friendly and intimate way which I could never have enjoyed otherwise."[15]

Scholarship and sociality need not be incompatible. In fact each tends to reenforce the other. College graduates with high scholastic standing and those who win Phi Beta Kappa honors, or the equivalent, attain sufficient achievement in after life to merit *Who's Who* recognition more often than the average college alumnus. Dexter concludes that a Phi Beta Kappa man's chances of success (getting into *Who's Who*) are nearly three times those of his classmates as a whole.[16] Jastrow comes to a similar conclusion from his study of an early edition of *Who's Who* and generalizes that not only does the college man "meet in a very decidedly greater degree than the non-collegian the requirements of a successful career in after life, but the high-grade college man meets these requirements very much more generally than does the average college man."[17] Lowell took the 4011 graduates of Harvard in the classes of 1861 to 1887 and found that the proportion of distinguished persons among those who had graduated in the first seventh of their classes was nearly twice as great as the proportion of distinguished persons among the other graduates.[18]

[15] Christian Gauss, *Through College on Nothing a Year,* Scribners, 1915, p. 168.

[16] E. G. Dexter, "High Grade Men in College and Out," *Popular Science Monthly,* Vol. 62, 1903, p. 432.

[17] J. Jastrow, "Distribution of Distinction in American Colleges," *Educational Review,* Vol. 31, 1906, p. 24 ff.

[18] A. L. Lowell, "College Rank and Distinction in Life," *Atlantic Monthly,* Vol. 92, 1903, p. 514.

Although there are some leaders in all occupations, the nation's "best known" persons, both men and women, are engaged predominantly in professional pursuits, both in absolute numbers and in relative numbers. The United States Census for 1930 shows 92 per cent of the men twenty years of age and over to be engaged in gainful occupations. Of those men 5 per cent are engaged in professional services as compared with 74 per cent of men in *Who's Who* in professional services. The same source shows 24 per cent of the women twenty years of age and over to be gainfully employed. Of those women 16 per cent are engaged in professional services as compared with 96 per cent of women in *Who's Who* in professional services.

The chances of a person who is engaged in professional service of attaining eminence, as evidenced by admission to *Who's Who,* is some twenty-six times greater than that of the average person. Among those in the professions many factors contribute to the attaining of national cognizance, among them higher education and writing. The physicists are not mere physicists, they are astrophysicists, biophysicists, and electrophysicists. The M.D.'s are not mere physicians they are aurists, dermatologists, gynecologists, laryngologists, neurologists, oculists, ophthalmologists, oral surgeons, orthopedists, otologists, pediatricians, roentgenologists, urologists, et cetera. Similar tendencies prevail in most of the other professions. Each is a highly educated, trained, and skilled expert or specialist.

Among *Who's Who* registrants educators, until recently, have predominated numerically. Somewhat over a decade ago the editors of *Who's Who in America* considered a reduction in the relative number of educators in subsequent editions justifiable although still holding to the belief that there were more persons of influence, of eminence, of leadership in the field of education than in any other field.[19] Consequently, educators of all kinds, representing about 22 per cent in the 1926–27 edition, comprised only about 16 per cent in the 1928–29 edition.

Writing, sharing our ideas and knowledge with others, makes for renown. It is largely through writings that we are privileged to share the choicest thoughts of the ages. It is quite certain that more people get into the public eye, and more quickly, through writings,

[19] Personal interview with one of the editors, December 27, 1928.

than by other channels. Plato said "Books are immortal sons deifying their sires," and Rufus Choate said, "A book is the only immortality." Channing regarded writings as the voices of the distant and the dead, making us heirs of the spiritual life of the ages. Henry Ward Beecher viewed a book as "the symbol and presage of immortality." One-third of the men and over one-half of the women in *Who's Who* have written one or more books. Leaders are impelled for one reason or another to enlarge their circle of followers through writing.

Valuable as biographical registers are, especially for statistical purposes, the reciprocal relationships between a leader and the social situation can also be gleaned from case studies in the form of biographies and autobiographies and life history documents.

Hall of Fame

Seventy-two persons, 7 women and 65 men, have so far been chosen for the Hall of Fame for Great Americans. They are assigned to one or another of 15 categories. Sixteen are classed as authors, editors; 5 as educators; 5 as preachers, theologians; 3 as philanthropists, reformers, home and social workers; 7 as scientists; one as engineer; 5 as inventors; one as explorer; 5 as soldiers, sailors; 4 as lawyers, judges; 15 as statesmen; and, 5 as artists. To date no physicians, surgeons nor business men have been honored in this respect. The Hall of Fame was created in 1900, and is administered by the Senate of New York University. Quinquennially the list of Great Americans lengthens as additional names are chosen by the approximately 100 electors throughout the country.

The men and women in the Hall of Fame—Emerson, Walt Whitman, Horace Mann, Frances and Emma Willard, Audubon, Agassiz, Eli Whitney, Elias Howe, Penn, William Morton and all the others made notable contributions to American civilization. William Morton was the first to give to the world a demonstration of the use of sulphuric ether as a practical surgical anesthetic in a major operation. The first steam-propelled warship was built from plans devised by Robert Fulton. Harriet Beecher Stowe's book "Uncle Tom's Cabin" became a powerful factor in the anti-slavery agitation. Joseph Henry was the first to demonstrate an electro-magnet wound with silk-covered wire, and he perfected the magnetic telegraph. These and the other "Great Americans" inspired many in making this a still healthier, happier, and more humane world.

ORIGIN OF LEADERSHIP

Biological Foundations

Such contribution as physical heredity or the biological organism may make to leadership rests largely upon the genes and the endocrine glands. The twenty-four pairs of chromosomes with which a human life starts contain hundreds of genes or factors which are determinants of physical and mental traits. The appearance of these traits seems to conform to uniformities first discovered by Gregor Mendel in 1865. For example, tall parents tend to produce tall children, and short parents tend to produce short children. Stature, manual dexterity and musical ability are a few of hundreds of traits that seem to conform to a law. Four generations of musicians, of ship-builders, of college presidents, and so on, are frequently cited as examples of the relationship between heredity and leadership. Although a larger percentage of superior offspring arise from distinguished parents than from the mass of mediocre parents, geniuses do not always produce geniuses, and sometimes superior offspring may come from inferior parents.[20] This is not incompatible with the laws of inheritance and would be readily understandable and explainable if we knew the whole history of a given person's heredity, and especially if we had complete anthropological and psychological data for his ancestors for several generations.

In analyzing the origins of leadership of any person it soon becomes apparent that physical environment, physical heredity, and social heritage are intricately interwoven. Leadership is partly grounded in the nervous system and the endocrine glands. These are not controlled directly by consciousness. The autonomic nervous system regulates the vital organs and processes: heartbeat, respiration, digestion, and basic neural activity, the normal functioning of which is usually necessary in the maintenance of socially approved personality traits. The endocrine glands—the thyroids, the parathyroids, the pituitaries, the adrenals—by the production of hormones—thyroxin, pituitrin, adrenalin, insulin—help to regulate energy, self-control, endurance, and personality balance. The abnormal functioning of any of these glands may contribute to nervousness, irritability, weakness, lethargy, and other traits of a

[20] H. S. Jennings, *The Biological Basis of Human Nature*, W. W. Norton and Company, Inc., 1930, pp. 247–8.

kind which hinder one in his accomplishments.[21] The malfunctioning of these glands can now be corrected in many instances by medical treatments.

The biological origins of leadership remain obscure, and soon after birth social heritage and biological nature become meshed. There is then a tendency to consider the cultural influence on behavior as biological. Even among primitives social heritage supplements the organic immeasurably. Mumford in his analysis of the beginning and genetic development of leadership among primitive peoples through the hunting, pastoral, and early agricultural stages finds among the prerequisites for eligibility to tribal leadership the following: physical strength, physical endurance, promptness of decision, superior ability in making motor coordinations, age plus activity, exceptional ability in control of food supply, warrior ability, oratorical ability, recognition as a medicine man or wizard, knowledge of the customs and traditions of the tribe. He further finds that what serve as factors of leadership depends upon size of the group, its stability, degree of complexity of group activity, definiteness of its organization, nature of its food resources, its sedentary or nomadic character and its relation to other groups.[22]

It was probably the observance of the interrelationships of the inborn traits and the acquired traits plus the social situation that prompted Cooley to say "It must be evident that we can look for no cut-and-dried theory of this life-imparting force (leadership or personal ascendancy), no algebraic formula for leadership. We know but little of the depths of human tendency; and those who know most are possibly the poets, whose knowledge is little available for precise uses."[23]

Biological man and cultural man are usually so thoroughly integrated that they can not be readily untangled. Social influences tend to stimulate the development of inherited aptitudes. As a rule children with musical ability are given more musical training than those with a deficiency of this talent. A child who shows a mechanical interest is encouraged by receiving appropriate presents at Christmas and when he has a birthday. The boy large for his age commands attention. Much is expected of him. He grows up and

[21] See Louis Berman, *The Personal Equation*, The Century Company, 1925, and *The Glands Regulating Personality*, The Macmillan Company, 1928.

[22] Eben Mumford, *Origins of Leadership*, University of Chicago Press, 1907.

[23] C. H. Cooley, *Human Nature and the Social Order*, Charles Scribners Sons, 1902, p. 285.

more is expected of him in one way or another than of the average man. He feels obligated to live up to those expectations. This reciprocal relationship probably accounts in large part for Gowin's findings, "It appears that the executives are taller and heavier than ordinary men."[24] The social situation and social heritage supplementing and reenforcing original nature tends to hasten rather than retard social change.

Social Heritage and the Social Situation

The anthropologists find no evidence of an increase in the mental capacity of the human race during historic time yet important changes in social heritage have occurred, even during the past century—sewing machine, steam railroad, cotton gin, telephone, telegraph, motion picture, typewriter, automobile, x-ray, plastics, radio, rayon, tractor, truck, school bus, mail delivery, lie detector, chain store, house trailer, electric refrigerator, airplane, photo-electric cell, and thousands of other inventions. A statement in the review of the findings by the President's Research Committee on Social Trends reads, "Most of the changes which are taking place today are in our social environment rather than in the natural environment and biological heritage. The fact that conditions in 1930 are different from those in 1920 or 1900 is explained by changes in culture, not in men or nature."[25] One clue to the growth in the United States, at least as far as material culture is concerned, is reflected in the number of patents granted, although not all mechanical inventions are patented. The number of patents granted by the United States Patent Office numbered 77,000 during the decade 1860–69 and had increased to 288,000 during the decade 1930–39.

The Cro-Magnon could not have invented any of the things on which those patents were granted because the elements necessary for the invention were lacking in his day. For example, he could not have invented the telegraph even if he had had a greater mental ability than modern man because wire, the electro-magnet, and the battery, cultural elements upon which the telegraph is dependent, were non-existent. In paleolithic times culture traits were few so that the possibility of new inventions by a combination of existing known culture traits, or by an addition to any of them, was meagre.

---

[24] E. B. Gowin, *The Executive and His Control of Men*, The Macmillan Company, 1921, p. 332.

[25] *Recent Social Trends*, McGraw-Hill Book Company, Inc., 1933, Vol. I, p. XXV.

As culture elements multiplied, the possibilities of putting together the new elements accelerated social change. In theory, the growth of culture conforms to the exponential curve like that for the growth of compound interest. Every invention from its inception to its ultimate satisfactory use undergoes many modifications, each of which may result in an application for a patent. The sulky plow, for example has had a total of 549 patents issued on it between 1855 and 1923, with the peak being attained between 1880 and 1884.[26] Ogburn states that 900 patents have already been granted on cotton-picking machines.[27] The electron tube makes possible the photo-electric cell or electric eye as it is popularly known and is now used in supplementing the human eye, ear and hand. Functions which this apparatus is capable of performing are said to run into the thousands.[28]

A society may encourage inventions or it may discourage them. History gives many examples where mechanical and social inventions were resisted by the masses, many of which subsequently proved themselves of inestimable value to mankind. The use of cast-iron plows was resisted because farmers feared detrimental effects from iron in contact with the soil. Tomatoes were thought to be poison 100 years ago. Louis Pasteur was threatened with expulsion from the medical profession for his contentions that germs cause disease. The nickname SPUD applied to potatoes had its origin in England where a society was formed in opposition to potato eating. They were called the Society to Prevent Unwholesome Diet. Taking the first letter from each word of this title gave the potato its lowly name. Slosson tells us that "When Coryate in the 17th century came back to England from his travels in Italy he brought back an outlandish implement known as a 'fork,' and roused much ridicule for using it for holding meat instead of his fingers. It was regarded as an insult to Providence that a man should be ashamed to touch wholesome food with his fingers."[29] Andreas Versalius, Professor of Anatomy at Padua University, was hounded to death by King Philip II of Spain for maintaining that there were an even number of ribs on both sides of the human body. Molinaeus in 1546 wrote a

[26] F. Stuart Chapin, *Cultural Change,* The Century Company, 1928, p. 359.

[27] William F. Ogburn, ''National Policy and Technology,'' in *Technological Trends and National Policy,* National Resources Committee, 1937, p. 7.

[28] See C. C. Furnas, *The Next Hundred Years,* The Williams & Wilkins Company, 1936.

[29] E. E. Slosson, *Chats on Science,* The Century Company, 1924, p. 46.

book dealing with interest in which he stated that it is necessary and useful that a certain practice of taking interest be retained and permitted, for which, among other causes, he was exiled and his book suppressed. A decade ago in scores of different American communities farmers forcibly opposed employees of the State and of the Federal Government to test their herds of cattle for tuberculosis in accordance with state laws.

The new and the foreign have always been feared. In almost every case there are both cultural and psychological factors present. Not the least of them is the tendency of groups to coerce their members to conformity, and thereby to retard social change.

The Group

A leader normally arises within a group of which he is a member. The group proclaims one of their members as their leader. This may be accomplished by means of a secret ballot, acclamation, seniority rating, or any other arrangement that the group may provide. His leadership is normally limited directly to those within that particular group. In this connection we are reminded by Bogardus that "The Pope is not accepted as a leader by Protestants, and Robert G. Ingersoll, by either Catholics or Protestants. Al Smith is not an enthusiastically cheered leader of the W.C.T.U., and Kirby Page is not worshipped by the R.O.T.C.."[30]

A man may be aggressive, self-confident and ambitious, and may attempt to create a following around some principle. Such an instigator is commonly termed a natural leader, but if he is not accepted by a group he has no leadership. Dr. Townsend seemingly found a large following in his proposal of government pensions of $200 monthly to sexagenarians. Millions have much to gain economically from the operation of such a plan and little or nothing to lose. Social and economic conditions were such—unemployment, frozen currency, exhaustion of savings, wheels of industry idling along—that millions of elderly persons were ready to follow any one regardless of his name or residence or occupation who advocated "Thirty dollars every Thursday," or some thing they thought as good or better. The times made Townsend. However, Townsend also influenced the time by hastening the day that states and organizations enacted old age pension legislation.

[30] E. S. Bogardus, "World Leadership Types," *Sociology and Social Research*, Vol. 12, 1927–28, p. 573.

Leadership has a tendency to beget leadership. Children of fathers in the professions tend to pursue professional careers. The son of a governor is more likely to be elected governor than is the average person. The son of a Secretary of Agriculture is more likely to be appointed to the President's cabinet than is the average person. Studies of leaders indicate that they come preponderantly from homes offering more opportunities than the average. Professor Visher, who has made a study of *Who's Who,* finds that "the business and professional man fathered seven and sixteen times, respectively, the number of notables that would be expected on the basis of the small proportion they made of the population. . . . Thus, although only one *unskilled* laborer in about 36,500 fathered a son or a daughter sufficiently noteworthy to win a place in *Who's Who,* one *skilled* laborer in 1,250 had that distinction, one farmer in 550, one business man in 62, and one professional man in 27."[31] Studies of distinguished persons in other countries indicate similar trends.[32]

The interrelationships between the leader and the group are built around some common interest, and as the Encyclopedia of Social Sciences states "The relation of leadership arises only when a group follows an individual from free choice and not under command or coercion and, secondly, not in response to blind drives but on positive and more or less rational grounds. . . . A representative leader is an individual who satisfies the expectation of the group by acting on its behalf. . . . Creative leadership emerges when a personality becomes the propulsive force for a value or complex of values or in certain circumstances for a systematic program, rallying about himself a group of men which on a small or vast scale creates a stronger pressure than could emanate from any individual."[33]

Inventors and Discoverers as Leaders

The present age is characterized by mechanization which is causing our mode of life to differ radically from that of the past and from that in less industrialized parts of the world. The modern

[31] Stephen S. Visher, "The Occupational Environment of Fathers of American Notables," *Who's Who in America,* 1926–27 Edition, p. 27. See also his *Geography of Notable Americans,* Published by the Author, 1928.

[32] See M. Albert Odin, *Genese des Grands Hommes,* pp. 546–7; and Havelock Ellis, *Study of British Genius,* Rev. Ed., 1926.

[33] Article on "Leadership" in the *Encyclopedia of Social Sciences,* The Macmillan Co.

American urbanite surrounds himself with tools and machines for personal use, such as the telephone, automobile, radio, toaster, cigarette lighter, percolator, refrigerator, gas or electric stove, lawn mower, alarm clock, fountain pen and typewriter. Inventions, whether mechanical or social, produce social changes. For example, the automobile did away with the livery stable, is creating new villages in suburban areas and killing off the small ones in predominantly rural areas, is causing special interest groups to supplant neighborhoods, is fostering installment buying, has weakened craft unionism and strengthened industrial unionism, and has encouraged the growth of state police systems.

Being worshippers of heroes we are prone to credit the man who received the patent on an invention as "the inventor" rather than to credit the inventors of the existing culture. That culture grows by means of inventions and discoveries and their diffusion is apparent to all. Few realize that most of our inventions were inevitable until we learn of the many things which were invented by two or more persons working independently—evidence of the influence of culture in determining particular inventions. Kroeber cites many multiple instances of the same invention. He says "The right to the monopoly of the telephone was long in litigation; the ultimate decision rested on an interval of hours between the recording of concurrent descriptions by Alexander Bell and Elisha Gray. . . . The discovery of oxygen is credited to both Priestley and Scheele. . . . For the invention of the steamboat, glory is claimed by their countrymen or partisans for Fulton, Jouffroy, Rumsey, Stevens, Symington and others; of the telegraph, for Steinheil and Morse; in photography Talbot was the rival of Daguerre and Niepce. Aluminum was first practically reduced by the processes of Hall, Herault, and Cowles. . . ."[34] It seems that if Wright or Langley had never been born others would have invented the airplane about the time that it was invented because the culture elements underlying such a machine had been perfected by that time. If Columbus had died in infancy some other navigator would have discovered the West Indies. If Dorothea Dix had been born some decades earlier or later it is quite unlikely that she would have gained renown for her work in the humane treatment of the insane. Existing culture may be said

[34] A. L. Kroeber, "The Superorganic," *American Anthropologist*, New Series, Vol. 19, 1917, No. 2, p. 200. See also Wm. F. Ogburn, *Social Change*, B. W. Huebsch, Inc., 1923, pp. 90–102.

to be the mother of invention. However, man is the medium through which these changes are brought about. Some men are better mediums for this than others.

Social Movements and Their Leaders

Inventions and discoveries invariably affect social institutions but institutional inertia causes social changes to be slow, and frequently results in social maladjustments. Reads a recent report, "The growing number of inventions and scientific discoveries has brought problems of morals, of education, of law, of leisure time, of unemployment, of speed, of uniformity, and of differentiation, and its continuance will create more such problems. Some institutions are not easily adjusted to inventions. The family has not yet adapted itself to the factory; the church is slow in adjusting to the city; the law was slow in adjusting to dangerous machinery; local governments are slow in adjusting to the transportation inventions; school curricula are slow in adjusting to the new occupations which machines create. . . . Unless there is a speeding up of social invention or a slowing down of mechanical invention, great maladjustments are certain to result."[35]

Radicals, agitators, muckrakers, crack-pots, social deviants of one kind or another, are often charged with inciting reform or social movements. They simply voice the sentiment of those suffering from some social maladjustment and of those who seek to lessen the hardships caused by unequal rates of culture change. For example, it takes decades for the masses to perceive that every step in the conquest of disease calls for a curtailment in the size of families if over-population is to be avoided. If birth control had paralleled death control so that population and natural resources kept somewhat in balance Francis Place, the Drysdales, and Margaret Sanger could not have agitated for a Neo-Malthusian movement. If the pronouncement that woman's place is in the home had remained unrecorded the white woman would probably have suffered less from seclusion and isolation, and Mary Wollstonecraft, Lucy Stone, and Madam de Stael could not have pleaded so vigorously for sex equality. National self-sufficiency has diminished with increasing trade and transportation between nations. This has created an appropriateness of uniformities in monetary exchange and methods of reckoning time.

[35] Report of the President's Research Committee on Social Trends, *Recent Social Trends,* Vol. I, McGraw-Hill Book Co., 1933, pp. XXVII, XXVIII.

Social movements are reactions of groups to maladjustments. Movements tend to traverse a cycle of change in the course of several decades or centuries. The Woman Suffrage movement may be said to have started with the publication of "Vindication of the Rights of Women," in 1792 by Mary Wollstonecraft and virtually culminated in the Nineteenth Amendment of the constitution in 1919. The assassination of President Garfield and the Civil Service Act of 1883 sounded the death knell in the Federal Government of a century-old Spoils System.

Some see three and others find four, five, six and seven steps or stages in the complete series of a social movement. Davis analyzes it as follows: "First of all, there arises a tangible need, and some individual or group begins to voice this need more or less publicly. Second, propaganda and agitation result. Third, there follows a growing consciousness of this need in a small or large group. Fourth, they organize. Fifth, concerted action and strong leadership develop and new converts are won. Sixth, if the movement is successful it becomes institutionalized—becomes the pattern of the majority, and group control sets in. Any one who does not conform to the new pattern code is disciplined. Seventh, eventually bureaucracy, inflexibility, and reaction become dominant."[36] Each step in the series passes over into the next by almost imperceptible changes so that any division of a movement into parts is quite arbitrary.

The early stages of a social movement frequently receive newspaper publicity because of the somewhat rebellious activities of the leaders to arouse the populace from its lethargic condition. In the more advanced stages increasingly conservative leaders tend to replace the more aggressive agitators and innovators. The executive or administrator in the later stages may become intolerant of change after a movement has become institutionalized. The tendency is for those in authority to support an existing institution. If it becomes too fossilized and too inflexible to allow modification with changing conditions, it tends to engender another reform movement.

Leadership in Social Planning

Increasing interdependence between groups and rapidly changing conditions makes a demand for social planning as never before.

[36] Jerome Davis, *Contemporary Social Movements,* The Century Company, 1930, pp. 8–9.

The philosophy and practice of laissez faire produced or accelerated slums, sweat shops, child labor, deforestation, exploitation of land, monopolies, unequal distribution of wealth, business depressions, unemployment, and other widely deplored developments. Attempts are being made to curb and counteract some of those conditions at present through social planning. Forty-seven State Planning Boards, all created since 1930, have made partial inventories of their social and natural resources. Some four hundred counties also have planning units, and over a thousand cities have planning commissions or committees. These and various Regional Planning Boards, and a National Planning Board—now the National Resources Committee—attempt to formulate practical, constructive programs for the future.

In some instances the state programs include consideration of land use, conservation of natural resources, flood control, integration of transportation facilities, regulation of public utilities, reorganization of local governmental units, the status of education, the development of public welfare agencies, and an alignment of these in such a manner as to promote the general welfare in the highest degree attainable. One of their objectives is to prevent the wastes arising from conflicting and clashing policies and to plan the wisest use of our resources.

A noteworthy development in 1938 was the adoption of a working agreement between representatives of land-grant colleges and the United States Department of Agriculture on a far-reaching program of land-use planning. Approximately 2200 counties organized local community and county committees during the year and carried forward some phase of land use planning. In about 450 counties, more intensive land use planning was developed. Significant contributions to local, county, and state agricultural adjustment are inevitable when most of the actual evaluation is done by the local farmers and homemakers themselves.

The high level of living in America is commented upon often. That it can be considerably higher is indicated by the following figures: According to the United States Bureau of the Census there were in 1930, 2,155,000 farms without automobiles, 5,390,000 farms without trucks, 4,150,000 farms without telephones, 3,295,000 farms without water piped into the house, and 5,450,000 farm homes without electricity. This situation can be changed rapidly under socialized, democratic leadership. The phenomenal change that can take place within a very few years under a cooperative planning program is seen in the field of electricity. In 1930 only 841,310 or 13.4 per cent of the farms reported their dwelling house lighted by electricity. Today approximately twice that number have electric current. In four years time, since the Rural Electrification Administration was set up, 688 REA cooperatives have been organized and some 180,000 miles of rural lines have been built to serve upward of 400,000 families.

Planning programs give consideration to technological developments. Recently an attempt was made by a governmental agency to study the kinds of new inventions which might affect living and working conditions in America in the next 10 to 25 years. It recommends that a series of studies be undertaken by planning boards on the following: "Mechanical cotton picker, air conditioning equipment, plastics, the photoelectric cell, artificial cotton, and woolenlike fibres made from cellulose, synthetic rubber, prefabricated houses, television, gasolene produced from coal, steep-flight aircraft planes, and tray agriculture."[37] An evaluation of many social changes, also, is sometimes undertaken by planning agencies, such as credit unions, Rochdale cooperatives, unicameral legislature, super-market retail stores, cold-storage locker plants, 4-H Club Work, Boy Scout and Girl Scout activities, indeterminate sentence of prisoners, parole system, citizenship days, group insurance, city manager plans, installment selling, tax exempt securities, old age assistance and benefits, public debt of 55 billion, universal language, world calendar, and discussion forums.

Planning is preventive and constructive and far less costly than the results of lack of planning. A national permanent all-over planning board can do much in hastening social adjustment to changing technological conditions, and minimizing possible social suffering and loss. Human adjustments for maximum security and contentment to ourselves and to our posterity in a dynamic social democratic order calls for many volunteer democratic leaders adept in the use of democratic procedures.

Training Leaders for Normal Social Change

Training of leaders and of laymen so that normal changes will be evolutionary rather than revolutionary induces a coordination of

[37] *Technological Trends and National Policy*, National Resources Committee, 1937, p. X.

all agencies which play a part in the conditioning of a person from earliest infancy. In the absence or ineffectiveness of such coordination an increasing number of organizations are impelled to conduct training courses of their own for the particular benefit of their leaders, both professional and lay leaders. Some activities of the Extension Service of the United States Department of Agriculture and of the Boy Scouts of America are examples.

The county agricultural agent, the home-demonstration agent, and the 4-H club leader long ago learned that the benefits of their training, experience and leadership efforts could be increased many fold through the use and training of local volunteer leaders. A report of the Cooperative Extension Work in Agriculture and Home Economics states that in 1938 a total of 586,000 volunteer local leaders were being trained, becoming invaluable assistants to the 6500 county extension agents. These agents held more than 100,000 leader-training meetings during the year with a total attendance of over two million men and women. Somewhat incidentally, it is interesting to note that the enrollment of 1,268,000 boys and girls in 4-H clubs in 1938 brought to approximately 7,500,000 the total number of young people who have received 4-H training since the work became nation-wide in 1914.

The thirtieth (1939) annual report of the Boy Scouts of America indicates that 1280 Scout executives work with and through 315,000 local volunteer leaders of whom over one-half have completed one or more leader-training courses, in offering Scouting to 1,042,000 boys. The registration of 1,390,000 boys and men with the Boy Scouts of America in 1939 brought to 8,999,000 the number who have been under the direct influence of Scout training as registered members since 1910. Both of these organizations, like many others, have leadership training manuals and increasing emphasis is given to the "group discussion" techniques as a method of training their leaders and members.

Group discussion, giving voluntary, frank and full consideration to an issue of mutual concern to the members of the group is stimulated by a growing number of leaders in various organizations. Discussion is part of a democratic way of life. It is a substitute for the use of browbeating, force or authority. Solutions reached through the channel of cooperative talking and thinking have the sanction of the members of the group and are therefore more likely to be accepted by the members than solutions presented to them either by experts, by a minority group, or by a dictator.

Group discussion emphasizes the importance of the individual. The discussion method assumes that every member of the group has some thing worth while to contribute. We tend to live up to expectations. A person comes to a true realization of his ideas only upon expressing them. Thus one of the purposes of discussion is to offer one opportunity to find out what he knows and thinks about an issue. The discussion group is an effective method for developing many latent abilities for leadership.

In most discussions the effectiveness is dependent to a considerable extent upon the leader whose functions include (1) to state clearly the problem under consideration; (2) to get everyone, if possible, to contribute; (3) to guide the discussion so that varying opinions and viewpoints are presented; (4) to see that all expressions are sympathetically considered; (5) to think with the group; (6) to make occasional, brief, impartial summaries; and (7) to summarize the discussions at the end of the meeting. The art of carrying out these functions effectively is acquired through study and experience.

One reason why the group discussion method is gradually supplementing other methods as a means of solving vital problems is that it tends to incite favorable action more readily. In this connection it is significant that a ''County Land Use Planning'' bulletin ends with this statement: ''Having farmers participate in planning means a lot of work, and some people are asking why the Department of Agriculture or the State Colleges, for instance, should not send technicians into a county, make the surveys, figure out scientifically what the county's plans ought to be and then just announce the results. The results are plain: In the first place, the 'hand-me-down' idea of doing things is not the way of a democracy; and in the second, this is simply not a job for technicians alone. It is one for the joint concern of farmers, technicians and program administrators. And the key to success in the entire task is to obtain the benefit of local support in participation in planning agricultural programs and goals.''[38] The same condition tends to prevail everywhere—we support programs that we have had a direct part in formulating, and we support leaders whom we helped to choose. We respect the group and its judgment in which the members mutually educate one another, as is inherent in the discussion circle.

[38] ''County Land Use Planning, County Planning Series No. 1,'' United States Department of Agriculture, 1940, p. 12.

Discussion groups are face-to-face groups and impart wholesome socializing influence upon their members.

It is apparent that if group discussion is to be effective there must be complete freedom of assembly, freedom of thought, freedom of speech, and freedom of press. Where grievances cannot be aired and where criticisms of existing conditions are not tolerated, normal social change, or rational social adjustment, are in jeopardy. Macaulay reminds us that "The liberty of discussion is the great safeguard of all other liberties." Various organizations, especially the American Civil Liberties Union, are continually engaged in the preservation of those liberties. Repression of the freedom of intercommunication is the seedbed of revolution and of abnormal social change. Leadership for democracy involves skills in promoting discussion.

SELECTED REFERENCES

Bogardus, Emory S., *Leaders and Leadership*, Appleton-Century, 1934.—Contains 23 chapters relating to the origins (heredity, social stimuli, and personality) of leadership, and some principles and theories of leadership. One appendix lists 100 world greatest leaders throughout history, and another the 100 persons receiving largest amount of space in the Fourteenth Edition of the Encyclopaedia Britannica (1929).

Busch, Henry M., *Leadership in Group Work*, Association Press, 1934.—Directs the attention of group workers, whether volunteer or professional, toward some of the basic issues underlying their activity. It combines a theoretical and practical approach. Gives practical suggestions for program making. The chief types of organizations utilized in group work are analyzed.

Fülop-Miller, Rene, *Leaders, Dreamers, and Rebels*, The Viking Press, 1935.— This translation from the German by Eden and Cedar Paul is an account of the great mass-movements of history and of the wish dreams that inspired them. Deals with situations in which history has presumably been made by vision in which dreams have operated formatively upon the life of human society.

Huntington, Ellsworth, and Whitney, Leon F., *The Builders of America*, William Morrow and Company, 1927.—Shows the differences between the birth rates, not only of the more and the less alleged competent classes, but, of different types of competent people and the dangers inherent in such differences.

Johnson, Robert U., *Your Hall of Fame*, New York University, 1935.—An account of the origin, establishment, and history of this Division of New York University from 1900 to 1935. Gives the manner of selection of names, consideration of candidates and brief biographical sketches of the 69 already honored for their unusual achievement or service.

Jones, Arthur J., *The Education of Youth for Leadership*, McGraw-Hill, 1938.— A simple but comprehensive treatment of the principles of leadership and of the leadership situation in United States, England and Russia. Suggests ways by means of which the school may organize its program more effectively for the selection and training of intelligent leaders.

Leigh, Robert D., *Group Leadership*, W. W. Norton and Company, 1936.—This book by the President of Bennington College is packed with practical advice for the chairman of discussion groups, mass meetings, conferences, and conventions, and for officers of organizations. The chapter on small group deliberation and the one on the conduct of large meetings are especially helpful. An appendix contains modern rules of procedure relative to the regular conduct of meetings.

Pigors, Paul, *Leadership and Domination*, Houghton Mifflin, 1935.—Contends that the leader is more useful than the boss, the commander, or the dictator. Shows how the leader orients his cause by the facts of the situation and by the needs of his followers and then tends to make himself unnecessary in that situation by setting up self-leadership in every follower. It gives a scholarly treatment of the meaning of domination and the functions of authority.

Tead, Ordway, *The Art of Leadership*, McGraw-Hill, 1935.—A lecturer in Personnel Administration gives a popular, commonsense account of the interdependence between leaders and followers, different types of leaders, necessary qualities, how leaders influence others, methods and manners of leading, training leaders, and the leader as conference chairman.

Whitehead, T. N., *Leadership in a Free Society*, Harvard University Press, 1936.—A study in human relations based on an analysis of present-day industrial civilization. The production, manufacture, distribution and consumption of commodities are inevitable. Socialized industrialists and business administrators can integrate these more effectively and satisfactory to all concerned by the use of more democratic policies.

CHAPTER 26

EVOLUTION OF CULTURES

BY DR. F. A. CONRAD

Professor of Sociology, University of Arizona, Tucson, Arizona

DYNAMIC CHARACTER OF SOCIETY

Previous chapters have indicated the multiple factors that condition and influence man's social behavior. Some of these forces such as fires, floods, drought, earthquakes, wars, invasions, depletion of mineral resources, and plagues often interrupt social relations with sudden and disastrous effects. No less important, however, are the cumulative changes that come by erosion and soil depletion, growth, and pressure of population, accumulation of wealth, migrations, invention, and diffusion of cultures. These, in the course of time, necessitate widespread and fundamental readjustments in society.

In a functional approach to culture, we must view society as an unending series of changing situations requiring adjustments in the behavior of groups and individuals. All culture traits or changes in culture merely represent attempted solutions of such social situations. It is important to keep in mind that social and cultural changes are closely interrelated with changes in the physical environment and in the biological heritages.

The development and use of farm machinery, for example, helped to solve the food problem of our growing industrial population. But the use of power machinery and large scale production created problems of soil depletion, erosion, and floods in areas that have been stripped of forests, grasses, and other vegetation. The attempt to deal with these natural forces is now requiring a program of soil conservation, reforestation, flood control, and, to some extent, the regulation of agriculture. Here, important changes in the physical environment brought about by new culture patterns have in turn created a new situation which must now be met by further changes in our culture.

Viewed in this way, culture is never static. Its forms are never fixed or absolute. It is as dynamic as the situations which groups seek to control, or to adjust. In other words, culture grows and accumulates with the experience of mankind. This accounts for the increasing complexity of the modern world. If the mythical Rip Van Winkle had slept until now, he would be completely disoriented. The physical landscape, the character and habits of the people and their culture have changed so that there would be little resemblance to his former world. He would speak the English language, of course, but his limited vocabulary would include no reference to our world of automobiles, tractors, airplanes, radios, movies, skyscrapers, subways, submarines, electricity, super-power, or even to our ideas of constitutional government. He would have to begin like a child and learn what the manners, morals, religion, laws, arts, science, and government of our present generation are. It is the purpose of this chapter to analyze the sources, nature, and implications of these cultural changes. First, let us look at the sources of cultural growth.

SOURCES OF CULTURAL GROWTH

There are two main sources to which the growth of a given culture can be traced, namely, invention and diffusion. In a general sense, all accumulations of culture depend on invention. In a specific sense, however, no group invents all its culture traits. Borrowing is invariably a source of growth as well as invention when specific cultures are considered. Let us examine these two sources in more detail.

Invention

Invention is the creation of any new trait or element in a culture. The essence of invention is the application of knowledge to the solution of problems in such a way that new forms of culture are created. These may be material or non-material although invention, in the popular mind, is more commonly associated with mechanical devices. New traits are also constantly being added by individuals who write a poem, a song, or a philosophical treatise. The creation of the Fascist Corporate State was, perhaps, a more significant invention for our time than most of our machines. Luther Burbank's potato was no less an invention than Edison's phonograph although he never secured a patent for it. The important thing in the growth of culture, as Dr. Linton points out, is "the creation of new active elements within the frame of a culture"[1] and not whether it is a material, patentable product.

[1] Ralph Linton, *The Study of Man*, Appleton-Century Company, 1936, p. 306.

Inventions are usually complex and involve the participation and cooperation of many individuals. Who invented the alphabet, the plow, or the automobile? The attempt to answer such questions confronts one with amazing difficulties. Even the simple stone hammer of the Neolithic period involved a remarkable combination of ideas concerning materials to be used, sizes and shapes for different uses as cutting or pounding, methods of grinding and polishing to secure a good cutting-edge, and a handle of the right size, shape, and strength to facilitate the use of the hammer. Such an invention was not conceived in the mind of any particular inventor; it was the product of the Stone Age involving the labor of countless persons.

The account of Edison's invention of the electric light may serve to illustrate how complex the process of invention is. Incidentally, it disproves the popular notion that the "wizard of electricity" was some sort of magician capable of pulling live rabbits out of an empty hat. The following statement is Edison's version of how his work began:

> In 1878 I went to see Professor Baker, at Philadelphia, and he showed me an arc lamp—the first I had seen. Then a little later I saw another—I think it was one of Brush's make and the whole outfit, engine, dynamos, and one or two lamps, was traveling around the country with a circus. At that time Wallace and Moses G. Farmer had succeeded in getting ten or fifteen lamps to burn together in a series, which was considered a very wonderful thing. . . . It was easy to see what the thing needed; it wanted to be subdivided. The light was too bright and too big. What we wished for was little lights and the distribution of them to people's houses in a manner similar to gas. Governor P. Lowry thought that perhaps I could succeed in solving the problem and he raised a little money and formed the Edison Electric Light Company. The way we worked was that I got a certain sum of money a week and employed a certain number of men and we went ahead to see what we could do.[2]

The work on this invention involved approximately 9,000 laboratory tests and experiments, a world-wide search for materials, and nearly two years of painstaking labor by Edison and a large staff of intimate associates and laboratory assistants. Under Edison's direction his assistants followed every conceivable clue to find the filament which finally gave the incandescent light to the world. Be-

[2] F. A. Jones, *Thomas Alva Edison*, T. Y. Crowell, 1924, p. 141.

fore it could be put into practical use, it became necessary to develop light and power plants and means of distributing, regulating, and measuring electric currents. This required the further invention of dynamos, motors, sockets, switches, cut-offs, plugs, fuses, meters, fixtures, bulbs, etc. Edison was credited with over 300 patents on the subject of electric lighting during the ten years following his original invention although it must be kept in mind that these inventions represent the combined labor of Edison and his staff.

The work of Edison's company marks the beginning of a great industry which now illuminates homes, highways, factories, mines, cities, and remote rural areas. Innumerable inventions and technical improvements have been made in the course of the development of this industry. These have indirectly necessitated a lot of general changes in other culture traits. With the introduction of electric lights, candles, oil and gas lamps were gradually discarded and, also, the habits and modes of life which were based upon them. Thus, the electric light was not added to our culture as a deposit is added to a bank account. The addition of this invention directly and indirectly involved many modifications in other parts of our culture.

We may note in summary: (1) that the invention of the electric light did not occur as an isolated fact in our culture scheme; (2) it involved a complex process of interaction between many individuals; (3) one invention led to another in endless succession—a continuous process; (4) it was not added mechanically to our culture but by a process of mutual adaptation. Many inventions are comparatively simple but this brief description of the electric light suggests how important inventions become dynamic and integral parts of an evolving society.

Factors Conditioning Invention

There are certain factors which generally facilitate or retard the process of invention. They are (a) group needs and social crises; (b) superior individuals; (c) the culture base; and (d) group attitudes.

The student can easily associate basic inventions with specific needs and problems. The incandescent light solved the problems of eye strain, danger, and inconvenience for millions of people who crowded into cities and factories following the Industrial Revolution. So, too, the steam engine, the cotton gin, the macadam road, the telephone, and the automobile came in answer to the needs of a new industrial era.

Group problems or crises occur when old culture patterns no longer satisfy group needs. This situation becomes the object of attention to alert individuals who seek a practical solution of the difficulty. In this sense, "necessity is the mother of invention." This may be stated as a general rule applicable in the evolution of the basic and universal patterns of culture. Certain exceptions to the rule should, however, be noted. Necessity is not the only possible stimulus to invention, nor is the utility of an invention its sole *raison d'etre*. Imaginative minds, artists, or mechanical genuises who, in their leisure moments, "play with ideas," "fix things," "get hunches," day dream, or "accidently stumble" upon something are not necessarily motivated by a consideration of group needs. The latest "song hit," Surrealist art, the humorous limerick or a poem may represent creations for the sheer love of creation. Utilitarian motives are, however, frequently present in such creations and artists, as a rule, are not unmindful of the demands and requirements of the commercial market.

Mental ability is also an important factor in invention because the idea of an invention must originate in the mind of some individual or in the mind of several individuals working independently as in the case of duplicate inventions. With the stimulus of group crises "superior individuals will furnish the inventors." But superior heredity does not, per se, lead to inventions. Inventions do not occur in a social vacuum. The mental processes of the inventor are conditioned by his social and cultural background and by the individuals with whom he interacts in a given social situation. What the inventor can do depends upon the kind of tools furnished to him by his social environment, as well as upon his innate ability. The general development of arts, sciences, skills, knowledge, material equipment, and social organization are thus necessary aids to invention. Ignoring the importance of this cultural factor in invention leads the student into the pitfalls of social theory. Hero worshippers frequently make naive assumptions concerning the roles of great men in determining the course of history. Such assumptions commonly ignore the slow and laborious accumulation of knowledge and the contributions of great numbers of unnamed persons without whose help the "great inventor" would not succeed in making his discoveries.

The culture base, or the sum total of culture traits at a given time, may be used to explain the differences in invention between one period and another and between one culture group and another. A rich and diversified culture furnishes the basis for many and diversified inventions. A poor culture base, such as one finds in primitive and backward societies, offers the inventor limited opportunities to invent. The many and diversified inventions of Edison could have occurred only in an advanced scientific and machine age. His library of approximately sixty thousand volumes "included every magazine and journal dealing with scientific research published during the past fifty years or more." His stockroom contained every substance used in science and everything necessary to scientific experimenting. The continuous search for new ideas and the checking of experiments with the findings of other scientists was a part of the laboratory routine of Edison and his associates. Obviously, if he had lived in the Colonial Period few, if any, of his inventions would have been possible. Had he lived among the early Apaches or Navajos of Arizona, he might have invented a rude violin or lover's flute but not a phonograph.

Dependence upon a common culture base explains the fact of duplicate inventions and the fact that, in periods like the Stone Age or the Machine Age, many closely related inventions occur in a cumulative sequence. Our policy of crediting inventions to the person who registers the first application for a patent or who makes the first public announcement of his discovery often obscures the fact that many individuals may be working on the same problems with the same scientific background and that their discoveries are relatively only a matter of time. It frequently happens that important inventions are announced simultaneously by persons who have been working independently upon the same problem. Professor Ogburn in his book *Social Change* lists 148 important inventions and discoveries made independently by two or more persons. For example, the invention of the telegraph in 1837 was made by two other persons besides Morse and by a previous inventor in 1831. In 1877 the phonograph was invented by Cros and possibly by Scott as well as by Edison. Such data[3] show the danger of attributing important discoveries and inventions to the genius of particular individuals. Professor Young aptly summarizes the principles involved as follows:

[3] W. F. Ogburn, *Social Change*, B. W. Huebsch, Inc., 1922, pp. 90–122.

It is apparent that inventions and discoveries do not depend so much upon one particular exceptional person as upon the nature of the culture out of which the new elements in invention arise. If there were no superior persons available to make inventions, the rate of invention would be retarded; but since advances in invention depend so much upon minor accretions to the total body of knowledge, it is indeed doubtful whether any one particular invention is essential at a given time. Yet society cannot afford to neglect those things which make the production of superior persons possible: sound biological stock and ample educational and other social opportunities. Both are essential. Great men alone do not make inventions, but neither can culture as a body of knowledge produce them. Both factors must operate together.[4]

Group attitudes are important in determining the number and kinds of inventions and in deciding whether particular inventions will be accepted as active elements in a given culture scheme. Much depends on whether groups encourage invention and give recognition to the inventor or whether they resist change and condemn and punish the innovator.

A basic change of attitudes, which is closely related to the transformation of modern culture, came with the introduction of science and the machine. Instead of the dependence upon superstition, magic, speculation, and dogma, science began a search for precise methods of controlling and manipulating natural forces for the benefit of mankind. The phenomenal rise of the physical sciences, mechanics, and engineering during the past two centuries gave us the ability to exploit mineral, metal, plant, and animal resources and placed us in a new relationship to the physical universe. Just as science helped us to understand these natural forces, the machine helped us to control and utilize them. The utilization of coal, iron, steam, and, later, oil and electricity marked the rise and development of the Machine-Power Age and the Capitalist Economy. The profitable use of the machine served as a great stimulus to research, experimentation, and invention. Patent rights, by giving the patentee a monopoly on a product, stimulated the invention of practical mechanical devices. In the course of time, the promotion of research and invention became a definite social urge. Although organized research is not more than thirty years old, there is an estimated number of 930 scientific and technical societies and 1,700

[4] From Young's *An Introductory Sociology*, copyright 1934, p. 38. Used by permission of American Book Company, publishers.

industrial laboratories now engaged in research in the United States.[5] Industries are devoting great sums to research as a business proposition. The Bell Telephone Laboratories, for example, with approximately 4,000 employees and an annual budget of $15,-000,000 maintains one of the best equipped laboratories in the world.[6] Just as corporations have found research necessary to compete, so the public has come to accept research as a means of promoting the national interest.

On the other hand, the work of scientists and inventors is not always approved and accepted by society. Hostility to social change may prevent inventions from becoming active elements in a culture scheme or greatly retard their acceptance. Resistance is of two types, psychological and socio-economic. Psychologically, ignorance, habit, fear, desire for status and security, and the tendency of groups to regard conformity to existing folkways and conventions as a virtue are factors favoring resistance to change. Socially, innovations disrupt the orderly procedure of group life, "disturb established relations, upset routines, and cause temporary confusion. Caviling criticism, ridicule, and disparagement, economic discrimination, social ostracism, and violence are used" against such innovators. On the economic side, vested interests are fearful of losses following disturbed market relations, of obsolescence of capital investments, and risks attending the introduction of new products. There are also complex labor and political problems attending basic social and technological changes.

The difficulty of changing established systems of thought is amply demonstrated in Andrew D. White's *A History of the Warfare of Science and Theology* (2 vols., 1896). Although Roger Bacon (1210–1292) made the early prophecy that "experimental science would enable men to move ships without rowers, carriages might be propelled at an incredible speed without animals to draw them, flying machines could be devised to navigate the air like birds, and bridges might be constructed without supports ingeniously to span rivers,"[7] five centuries elapsed before his vision of the machine age began to be realized. Bacon's interest in experimental

[5] National Research Council, *Scientific and Technical Societies of the U. S.*, Bul. 101, 1937. G. E. Pendray, "The Crucible of Change," *North American Review*, Vol. 247, No. 2, pp. 344 ff.

[6] D. Sleisinger and Mary Stephenson, "Research," *Encl. Soc. Sci.*, Vol. 13, p. 331.

[7] J. H. Robinson, *The New History*, Macmillan, 1912, p. 243.

science led to his imprisonment—a common fate of those who rejected the dogmas and authority of the medieval church and pioneered in various fields of science. Securing public acceptance of an invention involves many difficulties even in a scientific age. Power driven vehicles, for example, appeared in England as early as 1820. The opposition of horse breeders, stage coach proprietors, and railroads and the general indifference of the public, however, delayed their use until the end of the 19th century. In 1865 an act of Parliament was passed "requiring three drivers for each vehicle, one of whom must precede the carriage at a distance of 60 yards carrying a red flag by day and a red lantern by night. Speed was reduced to 4 miles per hour for the country and 2 miles an hour for the towns."[8] This doomed power vehicles in England until the repeal of the act in 1896.

In the United States the first automobiles also met with public disfavor. Clergymen denounced automobiles as "deleterious to morals and religion." Physicians predicted "the peril of brainless men driving brainless machines." A brain specialist, in 1901, pointed out the danger of increasing speeds beyond 20 miles per hour and declared that neither the brain nor the eye could keep pace with a machine traveling 80 miles an hour. One state passed a law requiring a man to advertise publicly, one week in advance, his intention to go on a road with an automobile.[9]

The following statement by Henry Ford shows some of the practical difficulties encountered by an inventor:

> My "gasoline buggy" was the first and for a long time the only automobile in Detroit. It was considered to be something of a nuisance, for it made a racket and it scared horses. Also it blocked traffic. For if I stopped my machine anywhere in town a crowd was around it before I could start up again. If I left it alone some inquisitive person always tried to run it. Finally, I had to carry a chain and chain it to a lamp post whenever I left it anywhere. And then there was trouble with the police. I do not know quite why, for my impression is that there were no speed limit laws in those days. Anyway, I had to get a special permit from the mayor and for a

[8] B. J. Stern, "Resistances to the Adoption of Technological Innovations," *Technological Trends and National Policy*, National Resources Committee, 1937, p. 43.

[9] David L. Cohn, *The Good Old Days*, New York: Simon & Schuster, 1940, p. 154.

time enjoyed the distinction of being the only licensed chauffeur in America.[10]

Definition and Nature of Diffusion

Invention is a slow, difficult process and ordinarily groups and societies invent comparatively few of the culture traits they actually use. The term diffusion is used to designate the process of borrowing culture traits from other groups or their transfer from one society to another. It denotes the spread of culture spacially and should not be confused with the transmission of culture from one generation to another by imitation or education. Thus an invention in one area may, if conditions are favorable, spread to adjacent areas until its use becomes universal. Christianity, for example, spread from Palestine to Europe and America and thence to other parts of the world. Likewise, the use of tobacco was adopted from American Indians by European explorers who carried it to Europe from whence it spread to every corner of the globe.

Diffusion may be planned or unplanned. Foreign missions, the spread of Fascism and Communism, campaigns of commercial advertising, trade missions to secure new markets and similar movements represent planned diffusion. On the other hand, the spread of important inventions like the alphabet, the calendar, the Roman arch, Gothic architecture, the plow, and the wheel were unplanned. Diffusion of particular traits may be both planned and unplanned. The early diffusion of tobacco was wholly unplanned, whereas the current slogan, "A cigarette in the mouth of every Chinaman," represents a planned effort of tobacco companies to spread the use of their products. The spread of present-day "isms," such as Fascism or Communism, represents both planned and unplanned diffusion.

Again, diffusion may be direct or indirect. In direct diffusion personal contact of individuals or groups is the medium by which culture elements are transferred. This is the case in migrations, colonization, trade relations, and foreign missions. Indirect diffusion occurs where the infiltration of goods and ideas is brought about without personal contact by means of the press, the radio, the importation of foreign goods, and other indirect methods.

Diffusion and invention are closely related. Neither must be conceived as a mechanical process by which new traits are merely

[10] From *My Life and Work*, by Henry Ford, copyright, 1922, by Doubleday, Doran and Company, Inc., p. 33.

added to the existing culture patterns. Such additions would in the course of time make every culture a mere collection of unrelated and conflicting elements. In reality, groups and cultures must possess a certain degree of unity if they are to survive or to function efficiently. The addition of new and divergent culture traits, whether they come by invention or diffusion, always involves the problem of fitting them into the existing culture patterns. This implies a process of mutual adaptation of old and new elements within the framework which unifies a culture. Thus the adaptation of a borrowed culture trait to the conditions of a new environment implies a degree of invention. Under the impact of Roman culture, Christianity, for example, underwent significant historical changes. When Catholic missionaries carried Christianity to the Indian tribes of the Southwest, it was adapted to the conditions of a primitive culture. The present forms and ceremonials of these primitive Christians of the Southwest are wholly unlike those of the primitive Christians of Jerusalem nineteen centuries ago. In other words, the Indians of the Southwest conceived Christianity through the medium of their own cultural backgrounds and invented the forms and ceremonials to express their idea. This, in brief, was the process through which historical Christianity became a vast accumulation of diversified forms in the various countries to which it was introduced. Likewise, we borrowed the use of corn and tobacco from the Indians, but cornflakes and cigarettes represent inventions added to what was originally borrowed.

Factors Determining Diffusion

Contact between groups does not necessarily imply that the diffusion of their respective cultures will follow. When Christians and Mohammedans meet they do not exchange their respective religions, although they may exchange Oriental rugs for Occidental drugs and medicines. What occurs in the contact of peoples representing different cultures is highly problematic and is subject to the particular set of circumstances affecting their relations. While no arbitrary rules can be laid down concerning the diffusion of particular culture traits, there are a number of general conditions which determine the process of diffusion.

Dr. Linton[11] points out that diffusion involves three steps: (a) the presentation of the new traits; (b) acceptance of the new traits

[11] Ralph Linton, *op. cit.*, p. 334.

by the receiving group, and (c) integration of such traits into the pre-existing culture patterns. Each of these steps depends upon multiple influences which have a bearing on the probability of diffusion and the rate at which it occurs.

(a) The presentation of new traits depends upon the opportunity for contacts between groups and the agencies for diffusion involved in such contacts. Trade, commerce, colonization, immigration, migration, travel, wars, conquests and slavery, missions, systems of communication, radios, movies, newspapers, etc., have played a variable historical role which requires detailed study. Only a few general considerations can be briefly suggested.

In the past direct personal contacts were the sole means of presenting new culture traits. Adventuresome individuals traveling abroad, explorers seeking new lands, traders seeking markets, mobile tribes and peoples seeking new homes, and soldiers on military expeditions were the important bearers of culture. The great trade routes of ancient civilization provided for the exchange of goods and ideas at the commercial crossroads where traders met. Folk migrations, conquests, and slavery redistributed population and cross-fertilized cultures. The influx of immigrants to the United States gave us a diversified culture, not found in areas with a homogeneous population. Missionaries, attempting to teach others a new way of life, have also been important conveyors of the arts, science, medicine, education, and religion.

With the invention and development of mechanical means of communication during the past century, indirect diffusion has become possible on a large scale. There is no present way of estimating the influence of the press, the telegraph, telephones, radios, and movies. They have, however, exposed peoples everywhere to the ideas and non-material values of present-day civilization.

The utilization of these agencies has an important bearing upon the historic roles which cultures themselves come to play. The early explorations and colonization by European countries and the later migration of approximately sixty million Europeans to the Americas and other lands served, for example, to establish European culture on a world-wide basis. Modern systems of transportation and communication have carried Western goods and ideas to the remotest frontiers. Likewise, wars and conquests have imposed European culture upon backward peoples. Millions of soldiers, traders, travelers, missionaries, and immigrants have furnished the direct personal contacts through which Western culture was offered to the rest of the world. The rise of modern systems of communication has, furthermore, broken down geographic isolation and has facilitated indirect diffusion on a world scale. Newspaper and radio reporters have penetrated every important world center, and international broadcasting has become a trait of contemporary culture.

It must be noted that the agents of Western culture have been much more active and numerous than those of any other contemporary culture. No comparable group of emissaries has pressed the cultures of Africa or the Orient upon Western nations. In other words, contact between divergent culture groups does not imply reciprocal cultural stimuli. Some cultures are more active and dynamic than others. Other things being equal, dynamic cultures generate the necessary enthusiasm to spread while others lag. Such was the case of Western civilization during the past century. A comparable case is found in the spread of Roman civilization throughout the Mediterranean world.

(b) Acceptance of new traits depends mainly upon group attitudes toward change and group conceptions of the value of the invading culture. Resistance to diffusion is much the same as previously stated with respect to invention except that diffusion, at times, encounters racial and nationalistic prejudices which are not involved in accepting inventions made within a group. Such a case is found in the Balkan Peninsula. Within an area not much larger than California, a score of hostile races and peoples have maintained their distinctive languages and customs for centuries—Magyars, Slavs, Croatians, Servians, Dalmatians, Slovenians, Roumanians, Bulgarians, Germans, Latins, Greeks, etc. Slavic hatred of the Magyars had its origin in conquests and oppressions which date back ten centuries. The slogan ''The Magyars are coming,'' used by Roumanian peasants in their resistance to Austrian invasion in 1940 indicates how deep-seated some of these traditional hatreds are. In a wider sense, the whole of Central and Southeastern Europe represents a mosaic of cultural groups which have successfully resisted assimilation by their neighbors. The recent American boycott of Japanese goods and the Japanese slogan ''Asia for Asiatics'' suggests the probable resistance to diffusion in other areas.

A certain amount of diffusion may be forced upon conquered peoples such as the ''modernization'' of Ethiopia by Italy, or, by the less obvious policies of peaceful penetration, setting up ''spheres of influence" and bringing small nations within the "orbit" of larger ones. The extension of German spheres of influence in Europe and the conquest of smaller states by Hitler will, no doubt, result in many cultural changes in the future. Conquests and oppression, however, invariably create hatreds and conflict which, in the end, operate as a barrier to free and voluntary borrowing.

Assuming the more typical case where the acceptance or rejection of alien culture traits is a matter of voluntary choice, what determines such a choice? Basically, acceptance of a new trait depends upon its value to the receiving group. This, however, involves the variable conceptions of values held by different groups which in turn are based upon their respective cultural heritages. Obviously, therefore, diffusion becomes a complex process in which there are many variable factors.

Ordinarily, culture traits whose practical utility is easily recognized are more easily diffused. The starving colonists immediately recognized the value of Indian corn, and the Indian recognized the superiority of the gun to his arrow. Guns, watches, matches, tools, toys, armaments, machines, cloth, and material goods are more readily accepted than ethical systems, religions, social and political ideologies. Americans accepted the cultivation of tobacco, potatoes, beans, and maize from the Indians but rejected their mode of rearing children because its utility was not apparent.

Once the diffusion of important traits has begun, it opens the way for the acceptance of many related elements. If the new elements gain prestige, diffusion may take place rapidly. The acceptance of machine production in the Orient was followed by an industrial revolution which, in a comparatively short time, industrialized Japan and, to a lesser extent, China. The acceptance of a basic trait like the automobile opened the way for the acceptance of oil, gasoline, paved roads, service stations, tools, garages, and other related elements. The superior value attached to such articles as automobiles and machines is easily transferred in the popular mind to other things of more doubtful value. Thus drugs, cosmetics, styles of clothing, refined foods, and cigarettes may also find ready acceptance, and diffusion becomes a cumulative movement in which goods of variable values are transferred rapidly from one culture to another. Such a movement occurred in the adoption of Western ideas by Japan and China. Once the resistance to change was broken down, Japan and China deliberately copied

Western science, education, industry, and military methods. It must not be assumed, however, that diffusion ordinarily proceeds so rapidly. There is a natural conservatism which generally favors adherence to the established behavior patterns and the choice of new patterns is subject to many variable conditions and influences.

(c) Lastly, borrowing depends upon how easily the new traits can be integrated into existing patterns. This depends, in general, upon the levels of the cultures involved and the compatibility of particular traits. Neighboring peoples with the same general folkways and institutions such as Canada and the United States can borrow more readily from each other than they can from the Eskimos or the Navajos. These primitives have little to offer us and what they have could not be easily adapted to our culture. Similarly, our form of representative government, machines, sky-scrapers, electric appliances, and railroads would have no practical value to primitive groups. As a rule the greater the difference in cultural levels, the less groups will borrow from each other, and backward cultures tend to profit more by borrowing from advanced cultures than vice versa.

In the case of borrowing between cultures on the same levels, there are many incompatible elements which cannot be accepted without disturbing or disrupting the existing culture patterns. Unless the value of new traits compensates for such disturbances, nothing is gained by borrowing. Thus, we accepted Japanese toys, silks, and table ware without difficulty, but to replace our alphabet by Japanese script would disrupt basic patterns in our culture. No possible advantage could compensate for the loss involved in such a change.

Relative Importance of Invention and Diffusion

Invention is the basis of all culture growth, but the growth of particular cultures occurs mostly by borrowing. Few groups invent much of their own culture. Dr. Linton estimates that "there is probably no culture extant today which owes more than 10 per cent of its total elements to inventions made by members of its own society."[12] It is easy, however, to attribute such borrowing to invention when the sources of culture are obscured by time. The average citizen, who takes his American culture for granted, would have a rude awakening if he should be deprived of what he has borrowed.

[12] *Ibid.*, p. 325.

Suppose, for example, that the prosperous dirt farmer in the Corn Belt should accidentally be denied the use of borrowed elements in his culture. How would he prosper? In the first place, without the rudiments of agriculture, the use of metals, tools, and domesticated animals borrowed from ancient Egypt, he would get a bad start. Without a calendar and the method of calculating time and the seasons, likewise borrowed from Egypt, he would have little idea of the proper time to plant and to harvest his crops. That would be of little concern, however, because without horses and a plow, also borrowed from Egypt, he couldn't till the soil. Without corn and cereals borrowed from primitive and ancient peoples, he really would have no crops to plant. He would have no cattle, hogs, and chickens to feed and no cows to milk. Even his dog would be missing, because he, too, was borrowed from the early ancients. He couldn't sit down to a warm breakfast, drink a cup of coffee or a glass of water, read his morning newspaper, calculate his bank account, or write to his friends about his predicament, because the use of fire, the knowledge of cooking, paper, pens, ink, glass, glazed pottery, numbers, writing, and the alphabet were borrowed mainly from Egypt. If he should decide to hunt for his dinner, he would have to get along as well as he could without a gun, a bow and arrow, a tomahawk, and a boomerang. In true aboriginal style he would, no doubt, resort to clubs and stones found at random. Perhaps, if he were not already disillusioned, he would decide to dress and, in the typical American fashion, go to town in his automobile. He would, however, have to discard his customary clothing; and his automobile would be without wheels or an engine, for a knowledge of metals, textiles, and the use of the wheel were also borrowed from ancient Egypt. Lastly, he couldn't sit down in his easy chair and smoke his pipe, because his furniture and tobacco were also borrowed. In other words, our dirt farmer, without these elements borrowed from ancient and primitive cultures, would not be a farmer at all. He would probably still be an aboriginal grubber and hunter searching for those rudiments of knowledge which marked the beginning of civilization.

Such a hypothetical case is, of course, misleading if it is taken too literally. Americans have a rich culture because they have borrowed freely and extensively. In turn, they have added much to what they have borrowed. This, as has been pointed out, is the usual process of culture growth. Although the origins of metal working can be traced to early Oriental civilization, it is obvious that the 500 varieties of steel products made into 100,000 grades, sizes, and shapes, and the 5,000 varieties of alloys now in use in the United States have not been added to our culture wholly by borrowing.[13] American inventors are also, no doubt, largely responsible for the 5,000 more or less intricate parts found in the farmer's Model T Ford automobile. Viewed critically, invention and diffusion are always interacting phases of the process of culture growth and the attempt to evaluate them separately is somewhat arbitrary.

Effect of Inventions and Diffusion

In the previous discussion it was pointed out how social changes necessitate changes in culture and how additions to culture stimulate further changes. By a process of continuous additions and modifications, cultures not only grow but their patterns constantly change. Thus, the patterns of 1940 are more complex and differ in important details from those of 1930 or even those of 1939.

The added traits have variable effects upon the total cultural pattern. Some are added as single traits which have little or no effect on other traits; others act as a complex which influences related patterns and causes a change in the whole cultural framework. A Chinese puzzle, for example, acts as a single, unrelated trait that may be added to our culture without causing further changes. Borrowing gunpowder from the Chinese, however, changed the methods of warfare and, in the course of time, became a factor in the decline of Feudalism. Additions of important traits such as the steam engine, the radio, the automobile, and the electric eye act as energizing elements which start changes in every direction.

The introduction of power and machinery marked one of the most significant changes in modern times. The mechanization of the home relieved the housewife of drudgery and gave her leisure for other things. Mechanization of agriculture revolutionized farming and released millions of farm workers, who have swelled the ranks of urban workers. Peace-time conscription, which broke down an American tradition of one hundred and fifty years' standing, can be traced to the mechanization of war in Europe. The daily contact of the city dweller with automobiles, trains, elevators, subways, radios, refrigerators, and hundreds of devices used in fac-

[13] W. F. Ogburn, *Machines and Tomorrow's World*, Public Affairs Pamphlet No. 25, 1938, p. 10.

tories, offices, and homes shows how his life has been geared to the machine age. What is not so obvious is that the building and utilization of power-machinery changes human relations and requires new forms of social and industrial organization.

The new technology, which produces more goods by more efficient methods, represents both material and non-material cultural changes. On the material side, it represents the increasing use of high-speed automatic machinery and improved processes of production resulting in new materials and new products such as plastics, synthetic rubber, or rayon. On the non-material side, it represents improved systems of organization and management of enterprises. Thus, job analysis and scientific management represent innovations quite as important as automatic machines. These changes are not, however, limited to operations within the factory itself. Changing markets require the analysis of market trends, changing consumers' demands, and the forecasting of the probable short and long-term demands for particular products. Without these new types of organization and methods of management, the new machines would have limited value.

The new technology has had important repercussions in other parts of our social system. Automatic machines and new industrial processes displace men and destroy old crafts. Communities have been confronted with problems of relief, technological unemployment, labor unrest, and insecurity of wage earners. The inability to meet these problems individually has brought about the abandonment of a policy of *laissez faire* by the government. Thus, social legislation attempting to maintain minimum standards of living and to give the industrial worker a measure of security has come, perhaps inevitably, as a result of the new technology. It will be noted here how social institutions are affected by changing technology, and that machines and the organization for their utilization are coordinate parts of the new technology.

We may now illustrate in more detail how the addition of an important material trait stimulates invention, how multiple inventions converge in a complex pattern, and how new social institutions and new social problems become an integral part of the development. For this purpose, let us review the effect of the gasoline motor and, specifically, the introduction of the automobile.

At the time of the first national automobile show in 1900, "horseless carriages were driven around a track, dodging barrels to prove that they could be steered.'' At that time there were only 8,000 cars registered in the United States, and it cost 30 cents per mile to own and operate a car. The models were without top, headlights, windshield, fenders, or bumpers; but they did run. A skeptical public still regarded the automobile as a luxury and expressed interest chiefly in its use for racing. ''From a few mechanics and bench hands who puttered away in barns making a handful of cars at the turn of the century, present-day automobile manufacturing makes possible, directly and indirectly, an annual employment of 6,380,000 people.''[14] The family car has replaced the family horse and buggy as a means of travel, and the truck has largely replaced the team and wagon in local transportation. Within a single generation, the automobile has changed the pattern of American life. How did this transformation come about?

Once the utility of the automobile became apparent, changes and improvements in the automobile began to appear rapidly. During the period from 1905 to 1930, over 9,000 automobile patents were granted by the Patent Office. Every succeeding year brought additions to the original patterns which improved the styles, speed, power, safety, durability, utility, economy, and performance of the automobile. Paralleling these developments, the idea of the motor car was extended in other directions; and we got trucks, busses, motor-coaches, ambulances, police and station wagons, fire trucks, tractors, and trailers. To accommodate the building and use of these, new industries sprang up and old ones expanded. Oil, rubber, tools, steel alloys, glass, paint, and other allied industries were vitally affected. Then a host of service agencies appeared—filling stations, garages, parking lots, sales rooms, credit, financing and insurance agencies, tourist courts, trailer camps, etc. A whole new highway system had to be created to accommodate a travel-minded public. Finally, a body of regulating agencies had to be established, such as traffic regulations and signals, traffic police, traffic courts, a system of licensing operators and registering cars, and of levying taxes to cover the public costs of such services.

The introduction of such a new transportation complex could not be made without directly or indirectly affecting other related parts of our culture. American folkways and institutions have undergone significant changes since 1900. These changes cannot

[14] Automobile Manufacturers Association, *Automobile Facts*, Vol. 2, No. 1, September, 1939.

be attributed to any single influence. It is obvious, however, that the automobile has had a significant influence upon the habits, modes of living, and social behavior of the present generation. Consolidated schools and libraries, suburban communities, national parks and recreation areas, hospitals for rural areas, declining villages, roadhouses, country clubs, and golf courses indicate changing patterns of life which depend on the automobile. The increasing mobility and redistribution of population, the disorganization of families and other primary groups, the increase of crime and delinquency, the toll of accidents on the highways, new moral hazards, problems of recreation, housing, and traffic congestion in the city indicate a few of the new social concerns connected with these changes. Obviously the mechanical problems of producing the means of efficient motor transportation have been largely solved, but the stability and equilibrium of contemporary society has been shaken by the impact of this change. "So numerous and far-reaching are these changes that the automobile may be called Radical Number One. The radicalism of the automobile has been, in its way, as basic as that of Lenin, the most famous radical of the past quarter century. Destroying the aristocracy and redistributing wealth, the revolution under Lenin's leadership altered the course of a government and social classes, yet the influence of the automobile has been spread over a far greater range."[15]

The introduction of an important non-material trait may likewise have revolutionary effects. The assumption that "greater revolutions come out of laboratories than are made by ideologies" is only partially true and does not warrant a materialistic interpretation of cultural evolution. Such a statement ignores the fact that a major revolution in the ideology of the Middle Ages was necessary before the modern laboratory could be established and that a scientific ideology is the basis of our present technology. Without the acceptance of scientific attitudes and methods, the world of machines would not have developed. Our research laboratories would have little significance to primitive people who believe in magic. During the days of Queen Elizabeth, the remarkable discoveries now coming out of General Electric's House of Magic would have been regarded as black magic. Under the law against witchcraft, the research staff of such a laboratory would have been convicted as "felons

15 From *Social Change* by William Fielding Ogburn, copyright 1922, by B. W. Huebsch, Inc., p. 4. By permission of The Viking Press, Inc., New York.

without benefit of clergy" and would have paid the extreme penalty for their supposed alliance with the Devil.[16] So definite were the fears concerning black magic that Roger Bacon created an uproar at Oxford University by proposing to perform a few simple experiments—an uproar among students and faculty because "it was believed that Satan was about to be let loose."[17] With such a theory the logical procedure was to do away with the magician—a procedure which unfortunately delayed the advance of science for centuries. Here it should be noted that ideas and beliefs are a necessary counterpart to material changes in culture. In the last analysis, a scientific viewpoint, laboratory methods, technology, and machines represent interacting phrases of contemporary culture. The growth of material and non-material traits must always be viewed as such an interdependent relationship.

RATES OF CULTURAL CHANGE

Acceleration of Invention and Diffusion

The acceleration of change is one of the obvious and striking facts of our time. The Cro-Magnon man required, perhaps, twenty thousand years to learn how to perfect and polish his stone implements. The cultural evolution of early peoples must be measured in terms of millenia because little change could be noted within the span of a single century. This was still true, for the most part, in the period of early American history. The life of the Western frontiersman in 1850 was much the same as that of the colonial settlers two centuries before. Today, however, the record of world-shaking events greets us on the front pages of our daily newspapers. Behind the headlines we read casually that coal and petroleum can be made out of grass, that synthetic silk made out of coal, water, and air is superior to pure silk, and that some mysterious formula called U-235 "will yield the energy of 30,000,000 pounds of TNT." New energy, new products, and new industries have transformed our material culture within a single generation.

An important index of the ratio of change is found in the records of the U. S. Patent Office. Less than 10,000 patents were issued during the first half-century of the Patent Office. More than

[16] J. W. Wickwar, *Witchcraft and the Black Art*, Herbert Jenkins, London, n.d., p. 170.

[17] A. D. White, *A History of Warfare of Science with Theology*, Appleton, 1896, Vol. 1, p. 389.

121 years elapsed between the first patent and the millionth patent issued in 1911. Only twenty-four years were required to reach the second millionth patent in 1935. The following table indicates the increasing rate of patents by decades.

PATENTS ISSUED BY U. S. PATENT OFFICE, 1790–1940

1790–1836	9,957	1871–1889	138,355	1911–1920	401,495
1836–1850	8,387	1881–1890	217,821	1921–1930	452,382
1851–1860	25,087	1891–1900	234,956	1931–1940	476,803
1861–1870	85,910	1901–1910	323,909		

(*Statistical Abstract of the U. S. Census*, 1939. Page 836. Figures for 1939–1940 are estimated.)

In comparison with our 2,000,000 patents, France had issued up to January 1, 1934, 871,532 patents; Great Britain, 797,153; Germany, 583,728; Italy, 273,598; Japan, 83,361; and the U.S.S.R., 63,992. What explains this phenomenal growth of inventions during the past century? First, our expanding culture base has made an increasing rate of inventions possible. The above data indicate an enormous growth of culture, which in turn has stimulated new inventions. A second reason lies in the competitive nature of our present industrial civilization. Ownership of important patents relates directly to the success or failure of competing groups. The urge to invent or to borrow important patents, by fair means or foul, has thus become an important phase of the struggle between industrial corporations and nations. This has been a significant factor in accelerating the rate of inventions. Without this incentive to profit by the utilization of our social heritage, it is doubtful if such an accelerated rate of change would have occurred.

Evolutionary and Revolutionary Changes

The rate and manner of introducing new elements into a culture has a significant bearing upon the stability of the social order. Gradual and orderly changes are usually called evolutionary, while sudden and abrupt changes are classified as revolutionary. The distinction is, however, relative when the whole process of cultural change is kept in mind.

Evolution comes about by the processes of invention and diffusion, as previously discussed. Ordinarily these require more time than is commonly assumed. Our present transportation system, for example, has a long history dating back to contributions of ancient inventors. Without the foundations in science, mathematics, chemistry, and physics, the locomotive and automobile could not have been built. The change from a wooden to a steel plow depended upon the cumulative knowledge of metal working and the discovery of the Bessemer process of making steel. This stimulated a rapid development in the structure, efficiency, and durability of the plow in succeeding decades. Upon closer examination, it will be found that important culture trails always involve a long series of minor inventions and discoveries which represent a cumulative growth. These accumulations, in the course of time, may change the characteristic patterns of culture without seriously disturbing the unity of the culture as a whole. Such changes are classified as evolutionary.

The term revolution is used in several ways. It may refer to sweeping and fundamental changes in the entire social order, such as the Reformation and the Industrial Revolution. Again, it may refer to radical changes in particular institutions and culture complexes such as a revolution in transportation, communication, or agriculture. Such changes are not necessarily violent or abrupt.

In the more common political use of the term, revolution implies " a violent change in government" or "an abrupt shift of the center of dominance."[18] The violence usually attending such a shift tends to divert public attention from the deeper phases of the revolutionary movement which precede and follow the actual overthrow of the government. Edwards estimates that it takes three generations to develop a real revolution.[19]

During this preliminary period, a gradual change in basic culture patterns is taking place. The attitudes and loyalties of the people toward old historic institutions and traditions also undergo a change. The failure or the unwillingness of the dominant class to recognize these facts turns an otherwise peaceable revolution into a violent and bloody one.

What is the significance of revolution as a means of cultural change? Obviously, it breaks up "the cake of custom" and releases new forces which may in time introduce important changes. Revolutions do not, however, make wholesale changes in culture.

[18] E. A. Ross, *Principles of Sociology*, Appleton Century, Third Edition, 1938, p. 649.

[19] L. P. Edwards, *The Natural History of Revolution*, University of Chicago Press, 1927, p. 16.

The arts, science, skills, tools, language, beliefs, values, folkways, and institutions which represent the cumulative growth of thousands of years are not basically changed by a sudden transfer of authority to a new ruling class. When people return to their homes and work after the period of violence has spent itself, they must rely upon the existing culture patterns. They cannot suddenly invent new culture traits or discard established thought and action patterns. "The reconstructed social order, in its essential features, is much like the old system which the revolution aimed to abolish. The new revolutionary principles are simply fitted into the old scheme of things."[20] We must thus view this "abrupt shift of the center of dominance" as an interesting but relatively insignificant event in the long-time perspective of cultural evolution.

Culture Lag

When the different parts of a given culture develop uniformly in relation to each other, culture maintains its unity and balance in the midst of change. Such unity, however, is rarely found. Related complexes change at variable rates, thus altering their relative position in the culture scheme. This tendency of some parts of a culture to lag behind other related parts in their development is called a culture lag.

Culture traits may be classified according to their rates of change as conservative and dynamic. Automobile manufacturers, for example, constantly use the inventions in technology to produce more saleable cars, but they depend upon the stability of our system of patents, property rights, law and judicial procedure to maintain the security of their enterprise. Such a lag normally appears between non-material and material changes in culture. Much confusion would arise if constitutions, courts, marriage, or forms of government should change as rapidly as the styles of our automobiles, clothes, and ornaments. Institutions become deeply rooted in the thought and habit systems of society and are, consequently, inclined to change more slowly than related material traits. In some respects the unequal rates of change bring about what are commonly adjudged to be inconsistencies among the traits of a culture. Tensions result.

It should be noted that such tensions within the framework of our culture become the basis of further change. Because of unequal

[20] *Ibid.*, p. 196.

rates of change society is confronted with new problems; crises arise which make old systems untenable. In the effort to meet these situations, old institutions are modified and new ones are created. Culture lags may thus be viewed as a part of the dynamics of cultural evolution.

OUTLINE SUMMARY

I. Society is dynamic, and social change is unending.
   A. Social changes require new adjustments.
   B. Culture represents such adjustments.
II. Two principal sources of cultural growth:
   A. Invention.
      1. Invention implies
         a. Creation of new elements in culture,
         b. A complex process of interaction,
         c. A continuous process rather than a single discovery,
         d. Mutual adaptation of new and old traits.
      2. Four factors condition the process of invention:
         a. Group needs and social crises,
         b. Superior individuals,
         c. The culture base,
         d. Group attitudes which may encourage or resist invention.
   B. Diffusion
      1. Diffusion is a process of borrowing or spreading geographically.
         a. It may be planned or unplanned, direct or indirect.
         b. It is a complex process involving many changes.
      2. There are three main steps in diffusion:
         a. Presentation of new traits which depends on group contacts;
         b. Acceptance of traits which involves problems of
            (1) Nationalistic and racial conflicts and prejudices,
            (2) Group habits and conception of relative values,

> (3) Acceptance or rejection usually on a utilitarian basis;
>
> c. Ability to integrate borrowed traits into the existing patterns. This depends on
>
>> (1) The degree of similarity or difference between cultures in general;
>>
>> (2) The compatibility or incompatibility of particular traits.

C. What is the relative importance of diffusion and invention?

D. Analysis of the effects of invention and diffusion show that

1. Traits may be added as single units with little effect.
2. Important traits involve complex changes:
   a. Invention of material traits like the automobile have important effects upon the material and institutional patterns of society.
   b. Important non-material inventions as the scientific method also change basic social patterns.
   c. The growth of material and non-material traits involves an interdependent relationship.

III. Rates of Cultural Change:

A. Acceleration of invention and diffusion is attributed to

1. Cumulative growth of the social heritage,
2. The competitive nature of industrial civilization.

B. Evolutionary and revolutionary changes:

1. Evolutionary changes imply gradual changes through the usual processes of invention and diffusion.
2. Revolutionary changes may imply
   a. Sweeping changes in the entire social order,
   b. Radical changes in particular institutions,
   c. A political shift in the center of dominance.

C. Culture Lag:

1. Culture lags involve differences in rates of change.
2. Lags which cause tensions and discontent are a stimulus to change.

REFERENCES

Beard, Charles A., *America in Midpassage*, The Macmillan Company, 1939.— This is the third volume of the series, The Rise of American Civilization. It represents a popular description and interpretation of the changes in the life and culture of the United States since the first World War.

Chapin, F. Stuart, *Cultural Change*, The Century Co., 1928.—This book traces the historical development of European culture and is valuable for its analysis of the invention of non-material as well as material culture traits.

Davis, Jerome, and Barnes, Harry Elmer, *Readings in Sociology*, D. C. Heath and Company, 1927.—This book contains much valuable material on culture. Book I stresses the historical evolution of society. Book II, part IV on ''Society and Its Cultural Heritage'' contains numerous articles on the nature and growth of culture.

Hart, Hornell, *The Technique of Social Progress*, Henry Holt and Company, 1931.—Chapters 3–4 give interesting indices and measurements of progress in the development of tools and technology.

Kaempffert, Waldemar B., *Modern Wonder Workers: A Popular History of American Inventions*, Blue Ribbon Books, 1924.—This book traces the development of important inventions. It stresses the role of the great man in invention and the difficulties famous inventors encountered in introducing their inventions.

Linton, Ralph, *The Study of Man*, D. Appleton-Century Company, 1936.—This book is excellent in its interpretation of anthropological material and in its comprehensive view of culture. Chapters 18–19 are good readings on invention and diffusion.

Lowie, Robert H., *Are We Civilized*, Harcourt, Brace and Company, 1929.—This book is valuable for its popular presentation of facts concerning the origins of Western culture and for its analysis of misconceptions concerning modern civilization.

Ogburn, William F., *Social Change*, B. W. Huebsch, Inc., 1922.—This book has chapters on the factors in social change and on the nature of culture lag.

Technological Trends and National Policy, National Resources Committee, U. S. Government Printing Office, 1937.—This is an excellent study of the social implications of new inventions. Part I, Sections III–IV presents an interesting analysis of the social effects of inventions and the resistances to innovations.

Winston, Sanford, *Culture and Human Behavior*, The Ronald Press Company, 1933.—This book gives a functional interpretation of culture. Chapters 5–7 are good readings on invention and diffusion.

INDEX OF NAMES

INDEX OF SUBJECTS